T.J.: A LIFE OF DR THOMAS JONES, CH

T.J. at his desk at the Cabinet Office.

T.J.

A Life of Dr Thomas Jones, CH

E.L. ELLIS

UNIVERSITY OF WALES PRESS
CARDIFF
1992

ISBN 0-7083-1138-5

A catalogue record for this book is available from the British Library.

Typeset by Afal, Cardiff
Printed and bound in Great Britain by Biddles Ltd., Guildford
Jacket design by Design Principle, Cardiff

TO PAMELA

PREFACE

ALTHOUGH he wrote three volumes of autobiography, and published four volumes of extracts from his diaries, liberally sprinkled with his correspondence, Thomas Jones is much less well known than he ought to be. This is partly of his own making: he demonstrated that, although it presumes a sense of personal importance, autobiography is not necessarily an exercise in vanity; and he was that most curious of oddities, a self-effacing diarist. Indeed, from choice and, for a time, professional necessity, he made anonymity almost a fetish during his lifetime. Even his commonplace name, *pace* Henry Fielding, seemed a convenient camouflage.

Yet he obviously hoped that full justice would be done to him by posterity. Why else would he so carefully collect during the course of his life nearly three hundred volumes of his papers? All evidence is valuable, but also of course is suspect; the wary biographer, like the historian, is an instinctive sceptic permanently on guard against artifice, even, perhaps especially, from the grave. However, it is fair to say that there is no sign at all that Thomas Jones's papers have been culled of any material that would show him in a poor, much less a shameful light. In fact, on the evidence available, the virtually unanimous opinion of his peers as well as an overwhelming body of documentary material, few men would appear to have so little cause to shuffle uneasily, even to fidget, under public scrutiny as Tom Jones.

Mercifully, the days of the exemplary life are long gone; indeed putative saints and heroes nowadays are likely to be drowned in a sea of scornful disbelief. On the whole these days it is easier and, it must be admitted, probably more immediately entertaining, to seek explanation of behaviour in the darker side of human nature. Whether that is always in all cases the best or sole guide to the rough approximation of truth that is the most a biographer can reasonably hope for, is another matter. In fact, although it goes against the grain of the times, there is a case, in the examination of personal character, for being sparing with supposition, holding cynicism at arm's length, and allowing the evidence, so far as possible, to speak for itself.

There is also no reason to suppose that the official and metropolitan dimensions are the only ones that matter. Tom Jones was on the threshold of middle age when he first went to work in Downing Street. His earlier years are not simply or solely a tiresome provincial apprenticeship to be dismissed as quickly as is decently possible. For although subsequently Tom Jones appeared to be authentically Whitehall on top, he remained stubbornly Rhymney underneath. That is the justification for the examination here at some length of the first half of his life.

During these years he was customarily called Tom or Thomas Jones; T.J., 'the affectionate initials', as Lord Macmillan of the Pilgrim Trust once called them, was an invention of civil servants which gradually achieved a general currency. There seems no good reason why a modern biography should not follow the historical precedent: 'T.J.' therefore does not appear in this story until early in 1917.

It is a story very well worth telling: the life of one of the most remarkable men in Britain in this century; the 14-year-old Welsh clerk who later became the trusted adviser of four very different Prime Ministers, privy to the most confidential business of the state between 1916 and the outbreak of war in 1939. He was one who also took important political initiatives himself, with considerable success in the Anglo-Irish negotiation of 1921, less so between 1919 and 1926 when his repeated attempts to promote a humane response to the cruel logic of the coalfield largely failed. In fact, there is hardly a public event of consequence during the inter-war years in which he was not involved, directly or otherwise, and about which he did not publish later a well-informed account innocent of vainglory. He was one of the most honest, trustworthy public chroniclers in a notably dishonest political age.

Such public attention as there has been, has hitherto been concentrated almost exclusively on Thomas Jones's official life. The reality is, however, that the aggregate of his creative achievements as a private citizen was at least as important as the sum of his success as the servant of the government. He was a leading figure in the world of education for half a century; he did more to mitigate the social ravages of mass unemployment in Britain through his work in the voluntary agencies and by independent initiatives than any other individual; and he inspired several remarkably successful attempts to give music and the arts generally a much wider popular appeal. All these activities, perhaps naturally, were pursued with special vigour and to particular effect in Wales, which was the focus of his strongest loyalty.

The time, therefore, is ripe for a full-scale study of Thomas Jones, CH.

CONTENTS

LIST OF ILLUSTRATIONS

ACKNOWLEDGEMENTS

I have many obligations to acknowledge. I am grateful to the following institutions and individual owners of the copyright of papers who have given me permission to quote from collections in their possession: University of Reading Library for the Viscount (Waldorf) and Viscountess (Nancy) Astor MSS, University College of North Wales Library for the letters of Silyn Roberts and Annie Ffoulkes. The Hon. Mrs Anne Stacey for the Bridgeman MSS. The BBC Written Archive Centre at Caversham. Mr E.J. Bickersteth for the Burgon Bickersteth MSS. The Syndics of the University Library, Cambridge, for the Earl Baldwin of Bewdley MSS. Cabinet papers, Crown copyright, in the custody of the Public Record Office. The Bodleian Library for the papers of Lionel Curtis, the 1st Lord Sankey, H.A.L. Fisher and Sir Alfred Zimmern. The Master, Fellows and Scholars of Churchill College, Cambridge, for the Hankey MSS. Lady Drusilla Scott for the Lord Lindsay of Keele MSS. The Clerk of the Records, House of Lords, for the papers of the 1st Earl Lloyd George. Lord Lothian for the 11th Marquess of Lothian (Philip Kerr) MSS. Mr Alexander Murray for the Gilbert Murray MSS. Copyright material from the Ramsay MacDonald papers is reproduced by permission of the executrix of the late Malcolm MacDonald. Illustration no.8 is reproduced by permission of the National Library of Wales; all the other photographs are in the possession of Thomas Jones's family.

Part of the cost of my research was defrayed by generous grants from the Sir David Hughes Parry Fund of the University College of Wales. I derived great benefit from the recollections of T.J. written for me by Mr David Astor, Mr Aneurin Davies, Mrs Ruth Evans, Mr Walter Oakshott, Professor Ian Parrott, Mrs Marlene Yeo and the late Mr A.J. Sylvester. I am indebted to the staff of the National Library of Wales, in particular to Mr Gwyn Jenkins, whose patient assistance on so many occasions was invaluable. Mr Richard Brinkley and the staff of the Hugh Owen Library were unfailingly helpful. I have received valuable assistance from Dr John Davidson, Mr Andrew Gregson, Dr Bill Jones, Mr J. Graham Jones, Mr Hywel Roberts and Dr Sian R. Williams. I benefited greatly from the encouragement and advice of Mr W.S. Jones, Professor Ieuan Gwynedd Jones and, to an exceptional degree, Professor J. Gwynn

Williams, who read my transcript either in part or in its entirety. My two typists, Miss Linda James and Miss Gill Parry, coped heroically with a difficult manuscript. This book would certainly not have been completed without the devoted assistance and support I received from Mrs Pamela Ellis.

Finally, I wish to thank Eirene, Baroness White, and her brother, the late Mr Tristan Jones, who invited me to write a life of their father and provided me for several years with a subject of absorbing interest.

ABBREVIATIONS

ABCA	Army Bureau of Current Affairs.
Autobiography	*The Autobiography of Sir Patrick Hastings* (1948).
Bodl.	Bodleian Library, Oxford.
BIAE	British Institute of Adult Education.
CCR	Committee of Civil Research.
CEMA	Council for the Encouragement of Music and the Arts.
CUL	Cambridge University Library.
DNB	*Dictionary of National Biography.*
HLRO	House of Lords Record Office.
J. Cards. Ant. Soc.	*Journal of the Cardiganshire Antiquarian Society.*
NCCS	National Council of Social Service.
NLW	National Library of Wales.
NLWJ	*National Library of Wales Journal.*
Parl Deb	*Hansard's Parliamentary Debates.*
PRO	Public Record Office.
PT	Pilgrim Trust.
RM	*Rhymney Memories* (Newtown, 1970).
THSC	*Transactions of the Honourable Society of Cymmrodorion.*
Two Lovers	*Two Lovers: Letters from ETL to TJ* (Newtown, 1940, privately printed).
UAB	Unemployment Assistance Board.
WD	*Thomas Jones: Whitehall Diary* (ed. K. Middlemas, Oxford, 1969, 1971).
Webb Letters	*The Letters of Sidney and Beatrice Webb* (ed. N. Mackenzie, 1978).
WHR	*Welsh History Review.*
WO	*The Welsh Outlook* (Newtown).

BIBLIOGRAPHICAL NOTE

Full details of the printed sources (place of publication is London unless otherwise stated) and unpublished theses cited are given in the footnotes. The book is based on the 295 bound volumes and 26 boxes of papers and notebooks in the Thomas Jones archive at the National Library of Wales, the several volumes of autobiography cum diary that he published, and his extensive writings in the quality press and elsewhere.

The following manuscript collections have also been consulted:

Alexandra Hall Papers. 'Life at Alexandra Hall at the End of the Nineteenth Century', at the University College of Wales Library, Aberystwyth.

David Astor letters in private possession.

2nd Viscount (Waldorf) and Viscountess (Nancy) Astor MSS at Reading University Library.

Bangor MSS. The letters of Annie Ffoulkes and R. Silyn Roberts at the University College of North Wales Library, Bangor.

1st Viscount Bridgeman MSS at the Shropshire Record Office.

BBC Archive at Caversham Park, Reading.

Burgon Bickersteth MSS at Churchill College, Cambridge.

1st Earl Baldwin of Bewdley MSS at Cambridge University Library.

Cabinet Papers at the Public Record Office.

Coleg Harlech MSS.

Lionel Curtis MSS at the Bodleian Library, Oxford.

1st Lord Davies of Llandinam MSS at the National Library of Wales.

G.M.Ll. Davies MSS at the National Library of Wales.

Gwilym Davies MSS at the National Library of Wales.

J. Glyn Davies MSS at the National Library of Wales.

Sir O.M. Edwards MSS at the National Library of Wales.

H.A.L. Fisher MSS at the Bodleian Library.

1st Lord Hankey MSS at Churchill College, Cambridge.

T. Mervyn Jones MSS at the National Library of Wales.

Tristan Jones MSS in private possession.

A. Bonar Law Papers at the House of Lords Record Office.

1st Lord Lindsay of Keele MSS at Keele University Library.

1st Earl Lloyd George of Dwyfor Papers at the House of Lords Record Office.

11th Marquess of Lothian (Philip Kerr) MSS at the Scottish Record
    Office, Edinburgh.
J.R. MacDonald MSS at the Public Record Office.
M. McKenzie letters in private possession.
Sir James Morton of Darvel MSS at the Scottish Record Office.
Gilbert Murray MSS at the Bodleian Library.
National Council of Social Service Papers at the National Council
R   of Voluntary Organisations at Bedford Square, London.
Sir Horace Plunkett Papers at the Plunkett Foundation, Oxford.
1st Lord Sankey MSS at the Bodleian Library.
Sir Ben Bowen Thomas MSS at the National Library of Wales.
David Thomas (Bangor) MSS at the National Library of Wales.
Baroness (Eirene) White letters in private possession.
Sir Alfred Zimmern MSS at the Bodleian Library.

CHAPTER ONE

RHYMNEY

DURING the century and a half before 1900 the face of south Wales was changed dramatically. An industrialism based on iron, coal and, to a lesser extent, tin and copper had transformed the landscape of much of Glamorgan and Monmouthshire and of limited portions of the counties of Brecon and Carmarthen. Small villages that had remained largely unchanged for centuries became ugly, bustling towns full of mean dwellings thrown up in haste by impatient entrepreneurs in congested confusion on the narrow floors of formerly remote valleys. South Wales had vast reserves of high grade coal, and the close proximity of iron ore deposits and outcrops of limestone in some of the valleys provided a cluster of raw materials ideal, at least for a time, for the development of large-scale ironworks. The men of enterprise who provided the capital and the creative drive for these undertakings were usually, initially at least, English ironmasters and London or Bristol businessmen like the dynamic Richard Crawshay, or less famously, William Forman, who apparently was engagingly known in the City as 'Billy Ready Money'.[1]

Whatever unsightly havoc rapid industrialization wreaked on the natural beauty of the countryside in south Wales, it created work. The lure of more stable employment and better wages drew many thousands of migrants from the peripheral areas of rural Wales to the magnetic south. Sometimes the newcomers were pushed rather than pulled. Some, for example, were impelled by the collapse of lead mining in Cardiganshire, many more, later on, by the further decline of agricultural economies already operating on narrow margins.[2] They flooded into a raw, dynamic industrial society that, in the second half of the nineteenth century, despite occasional setbacks and some changes that were to lead in the long term

[1] M. Atkinson and C. Baber, *The Growth and Decline of the South Wales Iron Industry 1760–1880* (Cardiff, 1987), pp.1–16. H Carter, *The Towns of Wales* (Cardiff, 1965), pp.69–75. E.E. Edwards, *Echoes of Rhymney* (Newport, 1974), pp.17–29.

[2] Brinley Thomas, 'The Migration of Labour into the Glamorganshire Coalfield, 1861–1911', in *Industrial South Wales 1750–1940* (ed. W.E. Minchinton, Cardiff, 1969), pp.44–5. K.O. Morgan, *Rebirth of a Nation. Wales 1880–1980* (Oxford and Cardiff, 1967), pp.5–6.

to serious vulnerabilities, could justly be called a boom economy: one which, with due allowance for differences of scale, as has often been asserted, bore comparison in some respects with the United States of America at that time.[3]

In the last decade of the century south Wales continued to prosper, and indeed now began powerfully to draw in immigrants from the wider hinterland of England, particularly the West Country. Hitherto, apart from the crossing into south Wales in the 1840s of some thousands of Irish who were driven from their homes by general poverty and the cruel spur of the Famine, immigration had been overwhelmingly 'short distance movement' within the Principality. The industrial counties had accordingly remained Welsh. Now, however, great swarms of English people and some Scots moved in and significantly altered the national character of the population of much of south Wales.[4]

There were some important changes too in the economy and the location of some industries. The south Wales iron companies had taken their opportunities well in earlier years. They had specialized in cheap rolled products like rails and prospered exceedingly during the great age of railway construction.[5] They had also adapted reasonably quickly to the technological advance from iron to steel. But from the 1860s onwards the iron ore deposits in some of the valleys began to peter out, or were found to be less suitable for the more sophisticated methods of steel-making. Moreover, inland locations, not easily accessible, made the importation of foreign ores prohibitively dear, and some of the initial low-cost leases of mineral rights had to be renegotiated less advantageously. Eventually, one by one, in sorry succession, the valley iron-works closed down or moved to sites on or near the coast.[6] It was to some extent true that, in consequence, the south Wales coal industry freed 'itself from the leading strings of the iron trade', prospered, and built up an enormously profitable export trade.[7] But it was at the expense of an increasing dependence on international

---

[3] W.E. Minchinton, op.cit., Introduction, pp.xxviii–xxxi. K.O. Morgan, op.cit., pp.59–72. A.E. Zimmern, *My Impressions of Wales* (1921), p.29, who first noted the analogy, wrote: 'There are three Wales. There is Welsh Wales; there is industrial, or, as I sometimes think of it, American Wales; and there is upperclass or English Wales'.

[4] T.M. Hodges, 'The Peopling of the Hinterland and Port of Cardiff'. in W.E. Minchinton, op.cit., pp.3–18. K.O. Morgan, op.cit., pp.5–7. A Gray–Jones, *A History of Ebbw Vale* (Risca, 1970), p.149.

[5] F. Crouzet, *The Victorian Economy*, (1982) p.234.

[6] Ibid., pp.238–9. E.E. Edwards, op.cit., p.28.

[7] Brinley Thomas, loc.cit., p.41.

economic forces which remained benign until 1914 but subsequently turned disastrously hostile.[8]

The Rhymney valley in Monmouthshire and the one-time village
of Rhymney itself exemplify many of the social and economic
changes that affected industrial south Wales in the nineteenth
century. In and around Rhymney there were enormous stocks of
coal, substantial deposits of iron-ore and limestone, and ample
water supplies. The industrial history of the area began around the
turn of the century in 1800 when a small group of venturers, most
of whom came from Bristol, built a furnace for making pig-iron.
From this small beginning, despite a subsequent chequered history
marked by complicated company amalgamations and bitter
quarrels over leases as well as the swings of fortune in an unstable,
primitive capitalist economy, iron-making in Rhymney gradually
prospered and grew in scale. So too did coal-mining: the Rhymney
railway was opened in 1858 and ten years later carried nearly
700,000 tons of coal to Cardiff for export.[9]

By the 1860s the Rhymney Iron Company, formed in 1837, was a
huge concern comprising a dozen smelting and rolling mills and
over seventy puddling furnaces spread out over more than a
hundred acres. In 1875 the labour force was more than five
thousand strong. The Company specialized in railway products; its
rails were exported world-wide and were used extensively in the
construction of railways in Germany, the USA and China.[10] There
was a massive influx of people into the area; between 1861 and
1891 the population of the Rhymney valley increased fivefold from
eight to over forty thousand. 'The empty valley', wrote one local
commentator later on, 'was turned into a long trough full of
human beings bustling and jostling each other for food and
drink'.[11]

The whole district was gradually stricken with the ugly blight that
helter-skelter industrialization brought in its wake. The town of
Rhymney itself was perhaps 'the least attractive spot' of all in the
area; most of the houses had been built by the Iron Company with
scant regard for amenity and none at all for beauty. A damp climate
did not help. 'Rain was the rule', wrote the same observer, without
too much exaggeration. The Rhymney river was no consolation, it

[8] Crouzet, op.cit., pp.263–71.

[9] J.H. Clark, *History of Monmouthshire* (Usk, 1869), pp.293–4. E.E. Edwards,
op.cit., pp.16–28. Minchinton, op.cit., Introduction, p.xix.

[10] E.E. Edwards, op.cit., pp.26–7.

[11] T.M. Hodges, loc.cit., p.11. The commentator is Thomas Jones, the subject
of this book, in *Rhymney Memories* (Newtown, 1970. Hereafter cited as *RM*), p.5.

was an eyesore. 'To call it a river is to flatter it. It was and is a thin trickle of water turned into the colour of rust by limonite and by the off-scourings of the brewery'.[12] In 1887 an admittedly less than sympathetic account in the *South Wales Daily News* asserted bleakly that in Rhymney everything had

> either a half-finished or a half-ruined appearance . . . everywhere vegetation is stunted or altogether destroyed, whilst the landscape is composed in varying proportions of railway lines, huge chimneys, grotesque looking furnaces and slag heaps.[13]

Among the crowds of migrants to this unlovely place some years before was David Benjamin Jones, a teenage boy who hailed from Llangeitho, a small village in the remote uplands of Cardiganshire, which has a certain fame because of its important place in the history of Welsh Methodism. His father, also Benjamin (but known locally as Bennie Gwynfil, which was the name of the cottage in which he lived), was a builder of small dwellings who doubled up 'in season' as the peripatetic groom of a stallion hired out to stud. Those who hired Bennie to build got exactly what they paid for. It was said in the village that he could build with either hand: 'with the right if he were well paid, with his left' if not. It is not clear why his son David Benjamin left home at so tender an age; it may have been the pull of adventure, but more probably it was the Hobson's choice of economic necessity. At any rate, the youngster had made his way south-eastwards to Merthyr, to Tredegar, and finally to Rhymney where he got a humble job in a large shop owned by the Rhymney Iron Company. In no time David Benjamin had become D.B. to almost everybody and he began to do well in the service of the Company.[14]

A more senior employee of the Company at this time was the storekeeper, Enoch Jones. He had been born in Rhymney, the son of parents who had been drawn there from a small hamlet in Carmarthenshire by the prospect of better opportunities. They had settled in Twyncarno, Upper Rhymney, the dominantly Welsh part of the town. The great tide of English immigrants into south Wales came in the late nineteenth century, but of course there had been trickles of incomers long before and among them was Job Cook, a West Country master-collier from Clutton in Somerset, who had moved with his wife and large family to the Rhymney valley in the 1830s. One of his daughters, Harriet, later went into domestic

[12] Ibid., pp.2, 155, 160.
[13] *South Wales Daily News*, 23 September, 1887.
[14] Obituary in the *Monmouth Guardian*, 3 October, 1919. RM, p.35.

service in Rhymney where she met and married Enoch Jones. Enoch was a staunch member, eventually a deacon, of Ebenezer Calvinistic Methodist Chapel that he had helped to build.[15] Enoch and Harriet Jones had eight children, including a daughter, Mary Ann, sometimes called Polly, who grew up to work as a straw-hat and bonnet maker who used a particularly serviceable straw that could be refashioned on wooden blocks to suit changing styles and limited pockets. In due course Mary Ann met David Benjamin Jones, who was no scholar but whose passion for her broke through the constraints of his limited command of the English language, as the one surviving love letter he wrote to her makes plain:

> I am sure you are tired already of reading such folly [he wrote touchingly] but you must think at all times that one that wrights [sic] is always faithful and true . . . I see the week very long. I shall trust and hope that on Sunday before dinner I shall received [sic] your sweetly kiss and arms around my neck.

In December 1869, when he was twenty-five years old, Mary Ann and D.B. were married. Enoch Jones helpfully vacated 100 High Street, the small terraced house he owned in the centre of town, and his daughter and new son-in-law moved in. The following year, on 27 September 1870, Mary Ann gave birth to a son, the first of the nine children she was to bear. It was in these relatively humble circumstances that Thomas Jones, future Companion of Honour, trusted agent and confidant of certainly three, possibly four, Prime Ministers, one of the greatest Welshmen of recent times, was born.[16]

However, despite the contrast between these early beginnings and the glittering sequel, it should be said that, by the standards of life in Rhymney at least, the circumstances of Thomas Jones's birth and upbringing were not all that humble.[17] His grandfather, Enoch Jones, was a man of some consequence in Rhymney: he was the chief deacon and secretary of a large Nonconformist chapel, a house owner and, ultimately, the chief storekeeper of the Company. Thomas Jones's father, D.B., had been promoted to the status of

[15] Obituary in unidentifiable south Wales newspaper, 2 April 1893. Sian R. Williams, 'Rhai agweddau cymdeithasol ar hanes yr iaith Gymraeg yn ardal ddiwydiannol Sir Fynwy yn y bedwaredd ganrif ar bymtheg' [Some social aspects of the history of the Welsh language in the industrial districts of Monmouthshire in the nineteenth century]. Unpublished Ph.D. thesis (University of Wales, 1985), pp.88, 140, 335. *RM*, pp.32–3.

[16] Ibid., pp.35–7.

[17] No.100 was evidently above the Plimsoll line. The front door and window frames were 'grained a golden brown with a comb and then varnished, a sure sign of respectability'. Ibid., p.59.

grocer's assistant, and in time was to move up into the ranks of the
Welsh *petit-bourgeoisie* when he became the manager of the
Company shops and farm at a salary of £250 per annum.[18]

The Company, in one or other of its many forms, utterly
dominated Rhymney. Apart from the iron-works and coal-mines, on
which directly or indirectly the livelihood of almost all residents of
the town depended, the Company had built a church, a school, and
a large brewery. And central to the life of the community was the
so-called Lawn Company shop and its four outlying branches.
These, run in harness with the farm and the brewery, had been
built up over thirty years by Andrew Buchan, a canny Scot who had
most effectively managed these assorted businesses. The Lawn Shop
itself was a large emporium, a Victorian version of a supermarket,
that answered nearly all the normal family needs of Rhymney
people: provisions, ironmongery, clothing, furniture, and a myriad
of items of haberdashery were on offer. 'Even the last requirements
– a shroud and a coffin – were to be had'.[19] It was a substantial
undertaking that employed a large staff; unmarried shop assistants
lived in a house that adjoined the commercial premises and near by
there were stables for the many ponies used in the business. The
shop was a minor miracle of organization; its stone floors,
notwithstanding constant traffic, were kept scrupulously clean;
despite considerable economies of scale, prices were not lower than
elsewhere but the quality of goods was almost certainly better.[20]

It was here that D.B., Thomas Jones's father, made his way up in
the world. God-fearing, immensely strong physically, versatile
(there was no job in the shop that was beyond him), D.B. was
permanently at war with indolence, debt and dishonesty. At the
time of his marriage he was paid 32 shillings a week and there was
the additional perquisite (crucially valuable to the father of a
steadily growing family) of being allowed to buy all goods at the
shop at cost price.[21] For ordinary customers, however, there was a
darker side to the operation of the Company shop. There was some
weak competition in Rhymney but the Lawn Shop had quasi-
monopoly power, which apparently was exercised with moderate
benevolence. However, for years the prohibitions of the Truck Acts
were blithely ignored or cunningly circumvented by the Company.

[18] Enoch Jones's obituary, 1893, and *Monmouth Guardian*, 3 October 1919.
[19] 'The Rhymney Iron Company II: The Shop', *South Wales Daily News*, 27
September 1887, E.E. Edwards, op.cit., pp.33–7.
[20] *RM*, pp.110–111.
[21] *South Wales Daily News*, 27 September, 1887. E.E. Edwards, op.cit., pp.33–6.
RM, pp.107–18.

It was no doubt convenient to shop in one place, take goods in lieu of money, and bridge the long interval between pay days by being able to run up a bill that could be paid off slowly in small amounts. But these arrangements did not encourage prudent domestic management, much less thrift, and they bound the customer hand and foot to the shop and, as a worker, left him vulnerable, incapable of any effective protest against the Company's industrial policies.

There was no doubt something to be said on either side, although the balance was scarcely even. It is perhaps curious that D.B. and, later on, his son, both men of high principle, never questioned the morality of the system. Others, however, did protest. In January 1878, for example, *Tarian y Gweithiwr (The Worker's Shield)* complained bitterly of the terrible deeds of oppression perpetrated by the employers at Rhymney against those workers who refused to sell themselves 'as slaves to the Company' and accept 'their bread and cheese' from the Lawn Shop under a truck arrangement. About a hundred of the protestors had been forced 'to leave their country and their homes' as a consequence. Evidently, the Company would not hesitate to use an iron fist if necessary. However, in 1886 the Company was charged with violations of the Truck Act, and although 1,800 out of 2,000 workmen signed a petition in favour of the retention of the system, the case was lost and truck at Rhymney came to an end.[22]

This did not alter the fact that Rhymney was a company town lock, stock and barrel.[23] But however overwhelmingly dominant the Company's authority was in social as well as industrial matters in the town, external economic forces were less easily controlled, In 1875 the Company was operating flat out. 'At night the sky was lit with a crimson glow from the blazing furnaces and during the daytime the town was enveloped with clouds of smoke from ten 195 feet chimneys'. Three years later an advanced Bessemer steel-making process was introduced.[24] But in fact the best years were over and in the next decade one difficulty after another cropped up: local ores proved to be less suitable for sophisticated steel-making, and although for a time the hope was that the large

[22] The advantages and disadvantages of truck from the workers' point of view are analysed in E.W. Evans, *The Miners of South Wales* (Cardiff, 1961), pp.73–85.

[23] Even the passage of time in Rhymney was punctuated if not regulated by the Company. 'The domestic and working lives of every family were interlocked within an iron-framework and ordered by the Company's hooter which blew daily, without hesitation or variability', seven times a day. *RM*, pp.158–9.

[24] E.E. Edwards, op.cit., p.27.

existing capital investment in plant would make it still worthwhile
to import dearer ores, eventually a run of adverse balance sheets
destroyed that possibility. In 1887, a group of disgruntled
shareholders publicly stated that they were 'greatly dissatisfied and
alarmed at the disastrous state of affairs revealed in last year's
accounts'.[25] It was however market forces not managerial
incompetence, as the irate shareholders alleged, that had brought
about this situation. The logic of the balance sheet could not much
longer be gainsaid and in 1890 the Company abandoned steel-
making and concentrated its attention on coal-mining. Rhymney's
long painful industrial decline had begun.[26]

Rhymney had a rumbustious reputation. In 1861, for example, it
was said to be 'a tough township' where customary urban
amusements were few. Some of the rougher elements enjoyed bouts
of bare-fist fighting, continued bloodily up to the point of
surrender, that prompted heavy side-stake gambling, in the
backyards of public houses. Sometimes in the surrounding country
there was clandestine cock and terrier fighting.[27] There was
however another, very different Rhymney, one centred on the
Church, the chapels and the Sunday schools, which was self-
consciously respectable and hostile to 'drink' and its attendant
social evils. Here the popular form of entertainment was a 'Penny
Reading' of the classics combined with a variety of musical items
and recitations incorporating ingenious competitive elements. This
was the world of Enoch and D.B. Jones and his son, Thomas.

Many years later in 1938 Thomas Jones published *Rhymney
Memories,* an autobiographical volume, a delightful evocation of his
upbringing in the town.[28] Thomas Jones was the eldest of nine
children (not all of whom survived) in the family.[29] Indeed he was
much put out by the appearance of the 'recurring babies' in the
household, and confessed later that he felt 'quite a Malthusian
towards his mother for thoughtlessly giving him so many little
brothers and sisters'.[30] In fact, the family was a close-knit, generally
happy unit in which grandfather Enoch Jones, who lived nearby,

[25] 'The Rhymney Iron Company I: What the balance sheet shows', *South Wales
Daily News,* 23 September 1887.

[26] E.E. Edwards, op.cit., p.28. Crouzet, op.cit., p.288.

[27] E.E. Edwards, op.cit., p.72.

[28] *RM, passim.*

[29] He himself survived an attack of scarlet fever when he was four, a
providential escape that presumably safeguarded him from danger during a scarlet
fever epidemic in Rhymney and nearby Tredegar and Ebbw Vale in 1882 when
nearly four hundred died. Ibid., pp.1, 39. A. Gray-Jones, op.cit., p.109.

[30] *RM,* p.69.

exerted a benign but firm authority. Enoch was a man of parts; chief deacon of the large Brynhyfryd Calvinistic Methodist chapel, he was substantially more than the first among equals in the group of elders there. He was in almost every respect the natural leader, the spokesman, guide and inevitable peacemaker in disputes, a man with a feeling for words who, on occasion, could rise to real eloquence. He carried himself well. 'There was', wrote his grandson proudly, 'something aristocratic in his bearing which made him appear superior to his surroundings'. But this evident distinction of manner did not lead to hauteur, much less arrogance. On the contrary, 'he was tender and compassionate', his was a leadership by example, of gentle persuasion, not blunt command. *Toujours Chevaleresque* might have been his motto had he moved in knightly circles'. And Enoch Jones was no narrow-minded Puritan ascetic; he took snuff, smoked a churchwarden pipe, and enjoyed an occasional glass of beer. Tom Jones loved his grand-father with that special feeling which, when reciprocated, as it was here, sometimes makes that particular blood relationship uniquely close and heartwarming. Once a month young Tom went to his grandfather's house in Penuel Row where Enoch, with an artist's pride, cut his hair. It was to Penuel Row too that Tom Jones escaped when he wanted to be able to read in peace away from the wailing racket of his young brothers and sisters at home.[31]

Of course, like most small boys, Tom Jones spent many happy hours out of doors with his friends, bowling his iron hoop, playing marbles, cricket and a primitive version of football. There were no motor cars to interrupt the games or endanger life or limb, but the children sometimes had to dodge smartly out of the way of a local young man showing off riding a penny-farthing bicycle up and down the street. Behind 100 High Street ran a small stream laced with coal dust on which paper boats were sailed and in which small boys found dozens of ways to get happily dirty and wet. Tom Jones was as mischievous as the next boy: he banged door knockers and ran away to the fury of householders. One night he played truant from a chapel meeting to watch open-mouthed a travelling conjuror perform his magical tricks. Nemesis, however, caught up with him swiftly: on the way home he was chased by a dog, tripped on a tram-line, and five stitches were needed to close the gash on his forehead. It is not clear whether this painful injury was

[31] Enoch could also dig his heels in. He agreed under protest (muttering darkly about graven images) to be photographed, but refused absolutely to take out an insurance policy because it would show a 'lack of faith in Providence'. *RM*, pp.137–8, 140–4.

considered sufficient punishment for truancy or even if his absence came to light. Sometimes even guiltlessness was no defence; Tom Jones was soundly thrashed for helping himself to biscuits from a barrel in the Company shop that, in his innocence, he imagined his father owned.[32]

D.B. Jones had a quick, hot temper and was not easily restrained from verbal violence when roused. Not that he ever used bad language; 'dank it all' was his very mild limit, but minor transgressions roused him to fury and even when his temper subsided he was rarely prepared to apologize. Little escaped his eagle eye and he pounced swiftly on slovenliness of any kind. Unfortunately, he could not communicate easily and thus could never be a companion to his children. But despite his occasional outbursts he was infinitely kind to his family and worked without stint for their material advantage. D.B. was devoid of cupidity, never mean-spirited, and was a generous host to the many visitors to his home. He had an absolute faith in the Bible and wrote out verses which he learned by heart and used, along with other aphorisms he came across elsewhere, to raise his spirits when downcast. D.B. had no politics, read little other than the *Grocer* and the *Ironmonger,* mandatory reading for senior staff in the Company shop, and he usually nodded off to sleep over a long book. Despite that, he had the habitual Welsh regard for education and later on generously allowed his eldest son to save a portion of his wages to help to pay his way through the college he aspired to attend.[33]

Apart from a small Roman Catholic school for the Irish immigrants, there were three elementary schools in Rhymney: one a Church foundation (erected, inevitably, by the Iron Company in 1858), and an Upper and a Lower Rhymney British Society School, built and maintained with difficulty by Nonconformists until 1870 when all three became Board Schools under Forster's Education Act. The financial worries of the Nonconformists were eased by the Act but for years the School Boards were riven by bitter wrangles over religious instruction in the schools. The early School Boards included a disproportionate number of Anglicans because the Church's concentrated vote was more effective than the more numerous Nonconformist electors who dissipated their strength among candidates from the different sects. This was a cause of strong local resentment.[34]

Tom Jones went to the Upper Rhymney School that had been

[32] Ibid., pp.52–4, 60, 69.
[33] *Monmouth Guardian*, 3 October 1919. *RM*, pp.115–16.
[34] E.E. Edwards, op.cit., pp.68–9. *RM*, p.50.

built in 1848 by a combined effort of Methodists and Independents. There were usually about three hundred pupils but numbers fluctuated considerably; a strike in the locality could lead to a disrupting influx of boys temporarily out of work in the pits and not much interested in school or the three Rs. When Tom Jones, aged six, joined the school, the headmaster was George Berry Kovachich, a Wesleyan lay preacher despite the unlikely name, who ran the school with the aid of his wife, two pupil teachers, who were more hindrance than help, and assorted teaching candidates and monitors. Kovachich was a large, formidable man, poorly qualified but strong on organization and discipline, who fought a guerrilla war with the school authorities over resources and repairs. Kovachich was no teacher and Tom Jones warmed much more to his successor as headmaster, Daniel Thomas, called by the children *Mishtir Bach* ('Little Master', where *Bach* incorporates an element of affection as well as an indication of size). *Mishtir Bach* was an engaging character, a devoted follower of Mr Gladstone and an ardent Rechabite. He introduced more music and singing into the school. Much of the teaching was mechanically repetitive, a spelling class meant copying on a slate words written on the blackboard, history was a collection of names and dates, and geography meant lists of rivers, capes and capital cities. *Mishtir Bach* had a fondness for Byron and Scott and hundreds of their lines were learned by heart which sometimes excited imaginations and perhaps enriched vocabularies.[35]

A permanent headache for headmasters of the Rhymney schools was the limited range of Welsh surnames. Christian names, at least for boys, were less of a problem because devout parents found in the Bible a rich choice of names like Obadiah, Zachariah or Zephaniah with which they often adorned their children's humdrum surnames. D.B. had wanted to add Benjamin to his son's name but his wife's alternative suggestion of Nicholas had cancelled that out; in the end the baby was christened simply Thomas Jones at Brynhyfryd Chapel. But there were eight boys called Tom Jones on the register at Upper Rhymney School, and as the fifth place was for the moment vacant the new boy became 'Tom Jones Five' and remained so ever after to many of his contemporaries.[36]

[35] Ibid., pp.43–52. E.E. Edwards, op.cit., p.69. When he was in his eighties, Thomas Jones could still recite at length from Scott's 'The Lady of the Lake' and Byron's 'The Prisoner of Chillon'.

[36] *RM*, p.42. North Wales got around the national difficulty about surnames in the same way. Sir Henry Jones's brother was called 'William Jones One . . . by the schoolmaster to distinguish him from William Jones Two'. *Old Memories. The Autobiography of Sir Henry Jones* (ed. Thomas Jones, 1922), p.30.

He had been brought up in a Welsh-speaking home but from this time onward, as the children one by one went to school, the family turned to English; Welsh was reserved for Sunday School and the chapel and was not taught in the schools at this time. Along with many others, Kovachich believed that the Welsh language hindered pupils from properly mastering English. Far more important, however, was the hostility towards the Welsh language of the Board of Education Code of 1862 which prohibited the teaching of Welsh in state-aided schools, a ban rigorously enforced by HM Inspectorate of Schools until the late 1880s.[37] However, despite this long-term sapping, Rhymney remained for some time an important Welsh-speaking enclave in Monmouthshire. Welsh remained the language of the Iron Works until its closure in 1890, thereby retaining what has been called a 'survival value': that is, to live and work in Rhymney some knowledge of Welsh was necessary, and many English and Irish immigrants knew enough at least to get by. Tom Jones's West Country grandmother, Harriet Cook, learnt to speak and read Welsh as did his mother, also English-born.[38]

Tom Jones was to develop a fine command of the English language; his many published works are written with grace and an enviable style, and on set occasions he was an equally fluent speaker. His mastery of Welsh was much less certain. In later life he claimed that he had 'never had a lesson' in the language, that the early restriction of his family's Welsh to the chapel, his long years of residence outside Wales and the resultant lack of daily practice much reduced his fluency in the language. He also maintained, citing Albert Schweitzer, that it is not possible to be able to think with equal ease in more than one language.[39]

The actual position is apparently not so straightforwardly conclusive. The most advanced modern research suggests that in terms of ease of use, all bilinguals have a 'preferred' and a 'second' language for every discrete area of experience.

And . . . ease of use is determined not only by the level of language proficiency of an individual in the two languages but also by social and psychological factors, since these can impede, or enhance, his facility in either language in specific situations.

[37] A. Gray–Jones, op.cit., p.149. *RM*, pp.51–2.

[38] Sian R. Williams, op.cit., pp.88–91 (citing D.T. Williams, *My People's Ways* (Bridgend, 1978), p.76, for the quotation). In Rhymney a Jewish pawnbroker and an English couple who ran a chemist shop learnt Welsh as a matter of course. *RM*, pp.52, 147, 156.

[39] *A Diary With Letters. 1931–1950* (Oxford, 1954), p.367. *RM*, p.52.

Moreover, the preferred language may not be the same one for all areas of experience; that is, a bilingual may have two preferred languages at any given time. This would seem to dispose of Schweitzer's discouraging conclusion, although it appears that there are no discrete areas of experience where a speaker 'is equally at ease in both languages, i.e. equilingual'.[40]

According to the model on which this argument is based Tom Jones, despite a lack of formal schooling in Welsh, was not far from being a 'balanced bilingual' for a time, certainly until he gave up preaching regularly in Welsh, and perhaps until he went to live permanently in London. Thereafter his oral command of Welsh was gradually reduced by the overwhelmingly English environment in which he lived and worked. He recovered some degree of his former fluency when he returned to live for a time in Wales during and after the Second World War and once again had more or less daily need of spoken Welsh. But for a good deal of his adult life he was a shade uncomfortably aware that his Welsh, picked up as a young child at home and later improved by extensive reading, was stiff, 'bookish', as he conceded defensively, lacking in ease and facility.[41]

As Tom Jones moved on from Rhymney Upper School it was Latin declensions and the mysteries of algebra, not Welsh mutations, that absorbed his attention. In 1881, D.B. had a step up in the world when he became an assistant manager in the Company shop. In consequence of his new status, the family moved from the old home in High Street to a larger house in The Terrace, where the Company's managerial staff lived in strict hierarchical order in residences where the standards exactly matched the commercial or industrial rank of the occupants. The Terrace was flanked at each end by two large, detached walled-in houses, one occupied by the chief colliery manager, the other by D.B.'s boss, the manager of the Company shop. Next in line inwards were the houses (carefully scaled down in size and amenity) of the deputy senior staff. The row was completed by houses half as big as those, in one of which D.B. and his family now came to live. They had not, however, joined a social community despite the prestigious seclusion shared by the inhabitants of The Terrace, which was semi-detached from the rest

---

[40] This interesting and persuasive theory is set out (p.327, for the words quoted) in C.J. Dodson, 'Second Language Acquisition and Bilingual Development. A Theoretical Framework', *Journal of Multicultural Development* VI, No.5 (1985), pp.325–46. Professor Dodson, a leading authority, is Director of the Centre for Bilingual and Language Education at the University College of Wales, Aberystwyth.

[41] *RM*, p.52.

of the town. There was no shortage of ordinary friendliness or neighbourly help if required, but quite apart from the constraints of differing seniorities, D.B. and his family were Nonconformists and most of the others, certainly the ranking families, were Church. That created a social divide beyond bridging.[42]

Another consequence of D.B.'s promotion was that his son was sent as a day-boy to the school endowed in the eighteenth century by Edward Lewis, a local squire, at Pengam a few miles away down the valley. Tom Jones had not managed to win a scholarship but the fees for day-boys were less than £2 per annum, a sum which D.B. could now well afford. Over the years the Lewis School has justly enjoyed a first-rate reputation.[43] Initially a free elementary establishment, it had become a secondary school in 1875 and the value of the original bequest had been much enhanced by industrial developments. In time the school was to become the pride of the valley and the district around but it was not quite that in 1881 when Tom Jones first went there. A school is rarely very much better than its headmaster, and David Evans, a classicist who had come up the hard way via the Borough Road Training College, the Theological College at Bala and the soul-destroying examination system of London University at that time, for all his other virtues, was not the man for the job. His interests lay in the history and concerns of the Methodist Church, in which he was active; he was notably short of patience and, perhaps in consequence, harsh in his punishments.[44]

Needless to say, many of his pupils were far from angelic. Some of the boarders were determined idlers who paid hard-up day-boys to write out their laborious impositions for them. The day-boys were, if anything, worse. 'We were for the most part', Tom Jones candidly admitted later, 'a rough and uncouth lot of loons and dolts' given to mindless vandalism on the train to and from school. But violence did not always win. Tom Jones once got into a fight with another boy (the only recorded instance of his involvement in physical violence during his eighty-five years) and part way through burst out laughing at the solemn absurdity of it all and in that way

---

[42] Ibid., pp.79–80. The Works police sergeant occupied one of the houses 'which was provided with a prisoner's cell at the rear of the dwelling'. E.E. Edwards, op.cit., p.33.

[43] A. Wright, *The History of Lewis' School, Pengam* (Newtown, 1929), p.83. In September 1905, Lloyd George, no stranger to encouragement by hyperbole, offered the hope (pp.113–15) that Pengam might 'become the Eton or Winchester of Wales', the first, perhaps, of a number of 'picked schools' open to the talents, educating the 'ideal Welshman'.

[44] Ibid., pp.85–91, 171–2.

brought it to an end. He was no more successful at cricket or other games and simply could not learn to swim.[45]

However, one thing that he could do was to respond wholeheartedly to the stimulus of an exceptionally gifted teacher. Roger W. Jones, the second master at Pengam at that time, was very different from the headmaster. The assistant master, then in his early thirties, had presence and a natural authority: in his classes a caning was a rarity. He insisted on the importance of good manners and was quick to praise and encourage effort; he did not spoon-feed, he excited interest, awakened curiosity and had the first-rate teacher's ability implicitly to persuade that the work in hand is infinitely worthwhile. In that way he opened many doors and gave his pupils the will and the confidence to enter them.[46] He certainly had a profound and lasting effect upon Tom Jones. Years later, in 1917, when he stood in some doubt at one of the several crossroads in his career, it was to Roger Jones that he turned for advice. The response was a model of clarity, eloquent testimony to the pride the old teacher felt in the success of perhaps his brightest pupil.[47] That admiration and regard was requited in full. 'He, more than anyone', said Tom Jones, 'planted in me a love of books'.[48]

That love quickly blossomed into a consuming passion: Tom Jones read almost everything he could lay his hands on. Other than the Bible, some hymn books, a copy of *Pilgrim's Progress* and one or two popular editions of volumes on religious subjects, there were no books at home. But at Pengam school there was a cupboard in the common room which was full of books. There were marvellous tales of heroic adventure and derring-do by such as Samuel White Baker, a big-game hunter, who built a Balkan railway, served as a major-general in the Ottoman army and explored the upper reaches of the Nile. And there was the published travelogue, improved apparently with touches of pure invention, by the intrepid James Bruce who survived shipwreck, crossed burning deserts and penetrated deep into Abyssinia in the eighteenth

---

[45] *RM*, pp.74–6. A former headmaster had been hard put to cope with 'half a dozen devil-may-cares as boarders who were up to all sorts of mad tricks'. Wright, op.cit., p.169.

[46] Roger Jones, a Welsh Mr Chips (his wife, who died in 1904, whose intercessions were always 'exerted on the side of mercy' to the boarders, would also seem to fit the analogy), taught at Pengam for forty-four years. He was headmaster from 1886 to 1919, when it was publicly stated that much of the credit for the school's reputation 'was undoubtedly due to him'. Ibid., pp.87–94. *RM*, pp.74–5.

[47] Thomas Jones MSS. [Hereinafter TJ]. Class X, Vol.4. No. 1.

[48] TJ, Class Z (Diary 1924), p.133.

century, returned safely home and then, ironically, had a simple fall
from which he died.[49]

Roger Jones, of course, suggested more demanding reading. He
put the boy on to Macaulay's *Essays,* and with a new taste for history
Tom Jones discovered the works of the Pinnocks, father and son,
prolific authors of immensely successful textbooks. William
Pinnock, senior, made a great deal of money (much of it lost in
rash speculation) from his popular abridgement of Goldsmith's
celebrated *History of England* which Tom Jones read and re-read
with delight.[50]

He was by now a modestly discriminating book-worm. There was
more room at The Terrace compared with the house in High Street
but the problem remained of peace to read in a noisy household
full of small children. His grandfather's house in Penuel Row
became a regular haven, where to his delight he came across a
forgotten cache of illustrated volumes devoted to the voyages of
discovery of the Cabots, Frobisher, Hudson and others. There were
other quiet bolt holes. On weekdays he could read happily in a pew
at Brynhyfryd chapel; once, impatient to finish reading *Far From the
Madding Crowd,* he went off by train to the quiet of the countryside.
He began to buy books: he thumbed through any available
catalogue. He haunted the village book shop and, a rare treat,
Dobbins Shop in Cardiff.[51]

His boyhood was a carefree and happy time. In the summer
there were holidays: in Swansea in rather dingy lodgings, in the
Rhondda at a public house kept by relatives, where he got a new
slant on the sleazy side of life. But most happily remembered were
the days at Alltddu, a farm near Tregaron in Cardiganshire, a mile
or two from the village his father had left to go to Rhymney long
before. Years later Tom Jones recalled his days on the upland farm
and the frugal, ordered life close to nature of the rural community
from whom he received much kindness. He did not recognize in
them the forebears of the Cardiganshire people so savagely
pilloried later by Caradoc Evans.[52]

Much to his dismay, Tom Jones's days at Pengam school soon
came to an end, even though he had done well there. He had
passed the Cambridge Local examination at fourteen, placed

---

[49] *RM*, pp.77–8. M. Brander, *The Perfect Victorian Hero: Samuel White Baker*
(Edinburgh, 1982). Bruce is noticed in *DNB. The Oxford Book of Literary Anecdotes*
(ed. J. Sutherland, Oxford, 1975), p.103, for Bruce's alleged embroidery of the
truth.

[50] *RM*, pp.77–8.

[51] Ibid., pp.79–81.

[52] Ibid., pp.89–94.

second on the school list, and began to think of going on to one or other of the public schools at Llandovery and Brecon, even to dream of going up to a university. But Enoch Jones, his grandfather, the undisputed arbiter in family matters, had decided it was high time that his grandson came down from the clouds and went to work. This might seem to be a puzzling decision by one who had himself been given a better education than was customary at that time. And as chief deacon and connoisseur of sermons, Enoch was in constant touch with things of the mind, the spirit and the imagination. On the other hand, enough was perhaps enough. Tom was becoming unhealthily reclusive and obsessed with books and extravagant flights of the imagination. It may well have seemed to a sober-minded Calvinist deacon a form of unacceptable self-indulgence, an escape into a make-believe land that was no proper preparation for life in the harsh, immediate world of industrial Rhymney where his grandson's future obviously lay. As Enoch said, it was high time that Tom entered 'the university of life'.[53]

There was, of course, no disputing Enoch Jones's decision, and not much difficulty about a job. Tom Jones too, like his father, grandfather and most of the people in Rhymney, would go to work for the Company. He had in the past helped out in the shop on busy Saturday mornings; he had also had a holiday job as timekeeper of the hay harvesters on the Company farm. This short apprenticeship was an introduction to the full-time work he now began at the age of fourteen as a timekeeper in the main Iron Works. In terms of the working day, full-time was an appropriate description. It ran from 5.45 a.m. to 6.45 p.m., for which he was paid 9 shillings a week, reduced sharply from an initially suggested 12 shillings by the Chief Cashier, the Company's resident expert in value for money.

However, there were compensations despite the long office day. Certainly there were hectic, even frantic, moments at the start and ending of stints. In between times, however, there were slack periods and Tom Jones was in luck. He was caught reading surreptitiously from a threepenny booklet concealed in a ledger, but John Rees Williams, the office manager, did not punish him, he encouraged him to read openly when he had the chance, and, indeed, provided him with books to do so, among them *Self-Help* and Samuel Smiles's other primers for the ambitious young.[54] In

[53] *RM*, p.95.

[54] Ibid., pp.95–8. Williams also encouraged him to learn shorthand. In due course Tom Jones was to regret his halfhearted response to that particular piece of advice.

fact, the interruption in Tom Jones's regular education was to be more apparent than real. One way and another, he found opportunities at least to keep up and extend his reading. He drew up a plan of study and sent it to Roger Jones who was full of encouragement and helpful advice. Opportunities for study at home had also improved; his mother, who was always supportive in many practical ways, let him have a small room which he made his own. There, in happy solitude, he read far into the night. But there was another side to things as well. Enoch Jones was almost certainly right in the judgement he had come to about his much-loved grandson. Tom Jones himself, writing much later with customary candour of this time, admitted that single-minded ambition had made him self-centred. 'No doubt', he wrote, 'I was a horrid little prig'.[55] The daily routine of work was an effective antidote to this sort of conceit; and even more so when, about a year later, he was promoted by a move to the Mill Office at the Works. Here there were few slack periods but the operation, concerned with the paper-work of despatching the products of the Iron Works and the hiring, firing and paying of steel workers, was much more interesting. Tom Jones was brought into daily contact with all sorts of shapes and sizes of men and women, some highly skilled, others with little more than great physical strength to offer. There was a good deal of absenteeism prompted by drudgery, discouragingly low pay or the attractions of daytime drinking in the Rock Inn or the Bute Arms, notorious hostelries in a raffish part of Rhymney then called Sodom and Gomorrah. There was a constant parade of human oddity, utterly fascinating to an impressionable young man.

> I knew every man and woman [he wrote later] . . . the steel mills provided a sample of the sorts and conditions which compose mankind. The rollers and the roughers, the heaters and the hookers-in, the wheelers and picklers of the time-books were also [reflecting the polyglot nature of the population] John Jones, Bill Smith, or Pat Murphy. There were scroungers and scrimshankers among them, no doubt, but that did not make them less interesting.

Enoch Jones had been right. There was much to be said for 'the university of life' as a corrective. 'My bent for books was balanced by a bent for people', concluded his grandson.[56] Some of those who worked alongside him were equally interesting. Robert Thomas, his immediate senior in the office, was a tiny man with a great fighting heart, a fine natural orator and a fearless controversialist. Sooner or

55 Ibid., p.97.
56 Ibid., pp.99–101, 104–5.

later, so open and formidable a nonconformist critic of the local establishment was almost certain to be punished for his boldness. When the opportunity occurred, Robert Thomas was duly dismissed from his job.[57] There were also interesting fellow-workers in the Mill Office nearer Tom Jones's age. With one he carried on a running debate at work on the case for and against dis-establishment of the Church in Wales. With another, Henry Lewis, who had a remarkable head for figures and ended up as an accountant in South Africa, he argued in public the case of Creation versus Evolution. The two young men were well matched in their evangelical earnestness: they took regular early morning walks together reading aloud passages from monumentally long Victorian poems of high moral purpose that were well-regarded in their day but are now almost wholly forgotten.[58]

Not all of Tom Jones's reading was quite so self-consciously didactic. Now in his late teens he was 'a voracious reader', feeding on a weekly diet provided by the volumes of Cassell's National Library. In this way Shakespeare, Pepys, Samuel Johnson, indeed pretty well all of 'what was worthwhile in the whole realm of English Literature', as well as translations of many foreign classics came within his ken.[59] A focus was given to his ambition by his decision to sit the examination for a junior clerkship in the Civil Service, a purpose suggested to him by James Evans, a boy he had known at the Lewis School, Pengam. Tom Jones sat the preliminary examination in book-keeping, arithmetic and similar subjects successfully in Cardiff in 1887, but the more demanding open competition that was to follow was postponed for some time by a parliament aghast at the rising costs of government. James Evans sat out the delay, passed the restored examinations, and went on eventually to a distinguished career in the Civil Service.[60] Tom

[57] Ibid., p.99.
[58] Ibid., pp.102–3. Robert Pollock's *The Course of Time* (Edinburgh, 1869) is said 'faintly' to recall Milton; Philip James Bailey, extravagantly admired by Tennyson and tremendously popular for a time, was the 'father of the so-called Spasmodic School of Poetry'. *Everyman's Dictionary of Literary Biography* (ed. D.C. Browning, 1958), pp.30, 54). Margaret Drabble's opinion of *Festus*, 'unreadable' *The Oxford Companion to English Literature* (Oxford, 1985, p.59), tersely expresses the modern view. The two young men in Rhymney also recited Wordsworth, Shelley and Keats, whose reputations have stood the test of time rather better.
[59] *RM*, pp.147–8.
[60] Ibid., pp.98–9. James Evans, as a family photograph shows, sported a dandy's boater and blazer on an outing. Tom Jones wore a sober three-piece suit and a cloth cap.

Jones's attention meantime had turned in a very different direction.

From his earliest childhood days religion had been a pervasive influence in Tom Jones's life, the Calvinist faith dominated the daily existence of the whole extended Jones family, their home was a natural extension of the chapel, around which the family's life revolved. The Calvinistic Methodists were numerically the strongest of the new Nonconformists in Wales although not in Monmouthshire. Nevertheless, they were the first to build a chapel in Rhymney. It was called Ebenezer and was subsequently enlarged several times, but by 1860 the influx of immigrants from rural Wales made a substantially bigger chapel necessary. Enoch Jones, assisted by three colleagues, was deputed to arrange for the building of a chapel in Lower Rhymney at a cost of nearly £2,000, a large outlay that reflected a serene confidence in Providence. The chapel, which was called Brynhyfryd, was a simple rectangular block which bluntly asserted that an architectural plainness just short of outright ugliness was itself a moral virtue.[61]

Tom Jones spent many hours during the formative years of his life in Brynhyfryd chapel. He would attend three times on Sunday, and on Monday and Thursday evenings at additional meetings. Quite apart from the spiritual guidance provided, the chapel made an important contribution to his general education. Yet again he struck lucky in the classroom. His Sunday School teacher, John Davies (*Ossian Gwent* in bardic terms), was a poet of modest distinction, a gentle being who helped his class with books and tried always to offer honest answers to puzzling biblical questions. This informal instruction in the Sunday School classes was buttressed by the probing method of catechism in the children's meetings of the chapel. In these ways an extensive knowledge of the scriptures was built up, and, in stages, children were brought to some awareness of the great questions of human existence. There was too the regular discipline of scripture examinations, where published results acted as a spur to serious application. Tom Jones had an aptitude for this sort of test; he was placed seventh in the county examination when he was fourteen, and in 1890, aged twenty, he shared the gold medal, the laureate award to candidates who headed the national list in the denomination's examinations. This was a triumph, as he said, 'which gave my father and mother more pleasure than anything else I ever did'.[62]

[61] E.T. Davies, *Religion in the Industrial Revolution in South Wales* (Cardiff, 1965), p.90. E.E. Edwards, op.cit., pp.57–62.
[62] *RM*, pp.125–8.

It should not be thought that Tom Jones at this stage was always serious and solemn: the behaviour of a lifetime argues otherwise. Impishness, humour and an engaging sense of fun are inherent not cultivated personality traits and Tom Jones had already shown he possessed them in full measure. And he was as healthily interested in the opposite sex as anyone else of his age. When Roger Jones advised him to avoid the perils of calf-love, Tom Jones 'gave no heed'.[63] Moreover, his chapel's prescriptive code was not all that severely restrictive, sometimes it prompted finely balanced compromises, even the odd quirk. For example, Tom Jones was allowed to go to see Wombwell's menagerie of wild beasts when it made its annual visit to Rhymney because animals were, after all, innocent creatures of God. Sanger's Circus, however, with its suspect clowns and scantily clad acrobats, was beyond the pale. His father, D.B., would not drink beer, but decided that a glass of cider was just about acceptable.[64]

Curiously, the attitude of the chapels in Rhymney to the question of drink at that time was a mutedly cautious one that did not insist on total abstinence. This was apparently a matter more of economic necessity than of ethics. The Iron Company's brewery was a large concern that provided work for many Rhymney people, and most of the public houses in the town were Company owned and, on the whole, well run. But drink was a subject on which Tom Jones felt very strongly. He had seen at close hand the destructive social effects of excessive drinking very early in his life. As a young timekeeper at the Works he was all too aware of the problems of drunken absenteeism and the outbreaks of rowdy violence that were a regular feature of the delayed pay-days when the balance of wages accumulated under the truck system was distributed and, all too often, haplessly frittered away.[65] It should not be forgotten that Rhymney at this time, in common with other towns that had sprung up pell-mell in the same way, was in some respects a wild, semi-lawless, mixed community, a 'frontier society', as it has been called, with barely adequate means of social control.[66]

Moreover, Tom Jones's family had painful, personal experience of this sort of brutish violence and of the seductive pull the raffish world exerted on the feckless. Enoch Jones had a charming son who could not resist the bottle and died in his early thirties. Enoch also had a ne'er-do-well brother, who was eventually mugged,

[63] Ibid., pp.97–8.
[64] Ibid., pp.55, 138.
[65] Ibid., pp.138–9.
[66] I.G. Jones, *Explorations and Explanations. Essays in the Social History of Victorian Wales* (Llandysul, 1981), p.233.

robbed and murdered when he was drunk. An Irishman was sent to trial but was acquitted of the murder and, for a time, the Irish community in Rhymney had to be protected from the threat of riotous assault.[67]

There were, therefore, strong personal reasons why Tom Jones was so hostile to drink, and later experience with his own brother, who was susceptible in the same way, strengthened his conviction. Moreover, quite apart from this harrowing aggregation of family experience and his awareness of the social evils of drink, his religious beliefs provided an even more important reason for uncompromising teetotalism. It is clear that whatever shuffling evasions were made by the local chapels, Tom Jones himself made no concession to the economic interests of the Rhymney Brewery. On this question he was sternly unbending. No doubt the gruelling, mind-numbing monotony of much of the work in the industrial world offered a variety of plausible explanations or justifications for anodyne drinking. But in Tom Jones's opinion explanation was not justification; he believed, as did Welsh Nonconformists generally, that drunkenness was moral backsliding, delinquency not forgivable weakness or illness. A solemn declaration in his denomination's journal of 1870 expressed his attitude exactly: 'Upon social grounds alone the drinking habits of our country should be combatted with earnestly; but how much more so upon religious grounds'. There was no room for equivocation: the drunkard would 'not inherit the Kingdom of God'. Although subsequently Tom Jones was not to be quite so invulnerable to doubt on the main essentials of his religious faith, and to become rather less cocksure in his moral judgements generally, he retained to the end of his days 'a prejudice against alcohol'. As he mellowed later in life he did accept a glass of wine occasionally, but repeated efforts on his part to be rather more tolerant of other peoples' tastes never quite overcame his disapproval.[68]

This concern with moral values was something that deeply interested him during his late teenage years. 'One went daily to the office, did one's work properly and without exhaustion and all the time the mind dwelt in an inner world of thought and speculation', he wrote later. Increasingly his reading turned to works on

[67] *RM*, pp.143–4.

[68] *The Treasury* 7 (1870), p.119, quoted in W.R. Lambert, 'Some Working Class Attitudes Towards Organised Religion in Nineteenth Century Wales', *Llafur* II (No.1), Spring 1976, p.11. *RM*, pp.133–4. Tom Jones's crusade against drink began early. He held office in a children's lodge of Rhymney Rechabites.

theology. He read everything available in the public library. He had been promoted again at work, this time to a clerkship in the Cashier's Office, an important step-up that meant a better wage and more money for books. He bought the biblical commentaries in Welsh published annually by the Calvinistic Methodist Bookroom at Caernarfon. He sent to Edinburgh for handbooks written by learned Scottish divines, and wrestled even with the formidable writings of heavyweight German theologians in translation. He conceded later that this had given him a mere smattering not a proper mastery of these great matters. But at the time it was profoundly satisfying and provided him with an explanation of human existence, 'from everlasting to everlasting', as he put it, that was for him, then at least, convincing and comforting.[69]

Tom Jones was not as yet, in almost any respect, a political animal. His one recorded foray into politics was his debate with a young Anglican colleague at the Mill Office on the rights and wrongs of Church disestablishment. His father, D.B., had 'no politics', nor had grandfather Enoch. The chapel, apart from its set hostility to the power and status of the Church, was largely apolitical, and sermons were concerned with cosmic matters not the mundane problems of daily existence. Those tribulations, however much they derived from the social, political or economic structure of society, were to be surmounted, withstood or, if need be, endured; heaven was to be found in Heaven not in some contrived earthly paradise. Predestination seemed to imply restraint if not political indifference.[70]

Welsh Calvinistic Methodist Church polity, however, suggested a different message. It laid emphasis on individual dignity, on full lay participation in the affairs of the chapel, and on a leadership sanctioned by democratic election not designated by hierarchic authority. In the long run this was to have a considerable, if probably immeasurable, influence on the growth of democratic sentiment in Wales, as Calvinist church government in its other forms allegedly did elsewhere. Thomas Jones's assertion in 1938 that these doctrines of individual worth and lay participation substantially countered the fatalist resignation inherent in Calvinist dogma was no doubt right. Whether it was quite so consequentially true, as he maintained, that Calvinism 'held the seed of Liberalism and wherever the seed fell freedom sprouted', is perhaps more open to argument. Without question, however, in the short run chapel membership offered satisfying opportunities for self-

[69] Ibid., pp.148–9.
[70] E.T. Davies, op.cit., p.61.

expression not so readily available elsewhere to ordinary people. The chapel too was closely associated with a wide range of cultural activities, choral singing, penny readings, debates and the like. There were also less high-minded, equally popular activities such as outings, tea-parties and soirées. In fact, the chapel provided a whole way of life, social as well as religious, almost a self-contained existence. Tom Jones was energetically involved in all these pursuits. Small wonder therefore that, referring to this time, he wrote, 'I felt and knew myself to be a Methodist much more actively and intensely than I felt myself to be a Welshman'.[71] More prosaically, despite his youth, Tom Jones began to take some part in the running of Brynhyfryd chapel. Enoch Jones was not only chief deacon but also secretary of the chapel (which did not have a resident minister) for over thirty years. He had charge of the building account and was not unduly perturbed by the large debt outstanding. D.B., on the other hand, more ledger-conscious, was constantly anxious to pay it off and was notably generous in his contributions for that purpose. Tom Jones gave assistance as required to his grandfather in chapel business and acted as secretary to several fund-raising groups.[72]

It was hardly surprising therefore that the Brynhyfryd deacons should encourage him to think of entering the ministry, especially as he was obviously convinced that the pulpit was his 'manifest destiny'. There had been no instant blinding revelation about his Christian commitment. 'I had never known any memorable experience that could be dignified with the name of conversion', he wrote later. It was, in a phrase with which he would be familiar later in another context, a case of the inevitability of gradualness. In 1890, the year of his gold medal triumph in the scripture examination, the Monthly Meeting, the Methodist district body, readily accepted him as a candidate for the ministry.[73]

There was no real question about where he would go for his further education and training. The choice would seem, at first sight, to lie between one or other of the two Methodist seminaries at Trefeca or, more probably, Bala which, under the inspirational leadership for over half a century of the majestic Dr Lewis Edwards, had become a miniature Welsh version of Geneva. But Tom Jones looked elsewhere. Not, of course, to St David's College, Lampeter, the Church foundation, which despite the support it

[71] *RM*, pp.120, 135–8. Dancing, however, was 'tabooed' in Welsh Methodist circles. 'Step-dancing with clappers, for drinks, was confined in Rhymney to the public houses'.

[72] Ibid., pp.140–2, 150.

[73] *RM*, p.150.

received from the University of Oxford 'was not quite respectable' in Nonconformist eyes. There was, of course, near at hand, less than an hour away by train, the recently-established university college at Cardiff. In fact, it was to the other, more senior college at Aberystwyth that he decided to go. Fees there were slightly lower, and lodgings were a couple of shillings cheaper, 4/- as opposed to 6/- a week, not a negligible consideration to one who intended to work his way through college with the help of paid preaching engagements. There was, of course, its inaccessibility, the best part of a day's travel away, but this was all of secondary importance. The 'decisive attraction' at Aberystwyth for Tom Jones was the magnetic power of the name and reputation of its principal, Thomas Charles Edwards, famous preacher, master-teacher, charismatic son of Lewis Edwards of Bala. Thomas Jones was not the first or last gifted young Welshman to be affected in this way by that compelling influence.[74]

It is clear that the notion of their eldest son going off to college had been fully accepted by D.B. Jones and his wife for some time. For some years they had allowed 'weekly driblets' of Tom's wages to be set aside for the purpose, an encouragement all of a piece with the love and concern that Tom Jones had always received from his parents. D.B.'s 'overflowing kindness to all', especially his children, was proverbial.[75] Mary Ann, English ancestry notwithstanding, was almost the very model of the Welsh 'Mam', ceaselessly caring, self-sacrificing to the point of unwisdom, especially where her sons were concerned. Her 'persistent unflagging devotion to "her boys"' was sometimes pushed so far as to be painful, in the opinion of one not unsympathetic observer. 'Her watchful housewifery' was evident all over the home.[76] She had had no education to speak of and had no intellectual pretension; she could not distinguish between fact and fiction in literature and took every word of the few novels she read as gospel truth. But she had stamina, D.B., intrigued by the title, once bought a copy of Henry Fielding's *Tom Jones,* but soon dozed off when he tried to read it. Mary Ann, on the other hand, plodded her way determinedly through to the last page. Beyond question, Mary Ann was a 'wonderful mother'.[77]

It was therefore a considerable wrench having to leave such a hearth and home. Tom was given a heartwarming send-off by the chapel on the evening of 9 July 1890, when his Sunday-school class

[74] Thomas Jones, *Leeks and Daffodils* (Newtown, 1942), pp.1, 6.
[75] *RM*, p.116. T.J. Class X Vol.3, No.84.
[76] Eirene to Thomas Jones, 13 January, 1903. T.J., Class X, Vol.7, No.1.
[77] *RM*, pp.42–3. T.J., Class X, Vol.7, No.1.

presented him with a hymn-book, and their teacher, the poet
Ossian Gwent, offered some verses in farewell.[78] Tom felt regret too
about leaving Rhymney where, with only very rare absences, he had
spent his first twenty years. The town was as ugly as ever. 'Tips,
tunnels, tramroads, dumps of old brick and stone, and an
indescribable litter of scrap iron abutted on the dwelling houses'.
Even The Terrace, for all its genteel pretension, was hemmed in at
the front and rear by railway lines in regular industrial use. At the
age of twenty, as Tom Jones recollected later, he was so habituated
to unlovely surroundings that he had no aesthetic feeling for the
environment, although he did appreciate man-made things of
beauty 'made, sub-rosa', by craftsmen in the Works. And cheap
local supplies of coal meant that houses were at least warm and
comfortable, no matter how persistently bleak the weather
outside.[79]

Moreover, the people of Rhymney also knew how to create and
sustain social warmth in the community at large. In addition to the
obvious class distinctions, the population of the town was divided
into those who went to the Anglican Church, those who went to
Nonconformist chapels, and 'those who went nowhere but
remained outside, "in the World"'. Even so, in a mining town death
was rarely far away and brought the community together, not least
by the elaborate funeral rituals. There was also a natural
cheerfulness, a sort of communal defiance of hardship; there was
the cherishing of personal idiosyncrasy, the pride in the often
brilliant amateur talents in different fields of so many people.
There was a strong, unifying sense of locality evident, for example,
in the performances and competitive triumphs of the Rhymney
choirs that were drawn from the whole town.[80] It would, of course,
be sentimental to suggest that there were not, as in so many similar
small intimate communities, personal jealousies, family vendettas,
and a fair amount of malicious gossip. There was too the fondness
for nicknames which were often amusingly harmless, but which
sometimes focused on mental or physical frailties in a cruel
enduring way.[81] But these falls from grace should not obscure the
fact that, for most of the time, the harsh rigour of industrial life in

[78] *Penillion i Mr. Thomas Jones* (Verses for Mr. Thomas Jones), 9 July, 1890.
Tristan Jones MSS.

[79] *RM*, pp.71, 156, 160.

[80] Ibid., pp.131, 137.

[81] 'Johnnie Fresh Air' perhaps as an actual example of the innocuous; 'Evan
Bolgi' (literally, 'large bellied dog', i.e. 'glutton') as a less kind instance. Ibid.,
p.41.

Rhymney was offset in many ways by a pervading warm humanity in the general community.

From 1890 onwards Thomas Jones returned to Rhymney regularly for some years, although more rarely later on. But no matter how far afield socially and intellectually his career was to take him, the links with home and family retained an unbreakable tensile strength. 'Whithersoever I went', he wrote in retrospect years later of his kin, 'I could never go beyond their love and pride and help, neither folly or frailty' could sunder the 'ties forged on the warm hearth within the family circle'.[82]

Tom Jones was twenty years of age when he left home. Short and slight in build, he had a wiry strength and a great inner store of energy; his gait was quick, urgent, as if he were impatient with time spent on mere movement. He lacked physical presence, but his face and head were interesting: thin brown hair, parted at the side, topped a broad brow above a long challenging nose. One trained observer, a professor in the Glasgow School of Art, told him that his nose was his 'only feature'. *Pace* the professor, this was not entirely true. Tom Jones's eyes would not go unnoticed by most people. They could twinkle engagingly in teasing fun, flash alarmingly in temper and appear disconcertingly appraising to some of those upon whom his gaze settled.[83]

At this time he was full of earnest endeavour, much given to thoughtful speculation about the eternal verities, the very model of the young Welsh Nonconformist. Time and different circumstances were to bring about changes, but it is fair to say that, throughout his long subsequent life, he never forgot whence he had come.

---

[82] *Leeks and Daffodils*, p.10.

[83] Ibid., pp.5–6. Joyce Grenfell, who became an honorary niece to Thomas Jones later, noticed that 'his eyes went up in the corners when he was amused': *Joyce Grenfell Requests the Pleasure* (1977), p.159.

CHAPTER TWO

ABERYSTWYTH

IT MIGHT seem odd that the Brynhyfryd congregation should meet
to wish Godspeed to Tom Jones in July rather than perhaps in
September nearer the start of term at Aberystwyth. The fact was,
however, that he left Rhymney immediately after the official
farewell to spend the best part of three months in seclusion at a
cottage in the tiny hamlet of Bwlch in the foothills of the Black
Mountains. There, in blissful solitude, he hoped to get through
a great deal of hard work on the standard text-books in Latin,
Greek, mathematics, and the other subjects he intended to offer
for matriculation in the University of London. It did not quite work
out as he planned. He was immediately taken up by the local
Methodist minister, a doughty individualist with very strong
opinions, who decided that the young man had far too narrow a
theological outlook that must be broadened by a course of im-
proving literature; works such as the Anglican Charles Kingsley's
Two Years Ago, the early feminist Olive Schreiner's *Story of an African
Farm,* and rather surprisingly, the novels of the perhaps heterodox
George Eliot. Given the run of an extensive library, Tom Jones's
fine plans for disciplined preparatory work soon went by the board.
The summer passed agreeably but the text-books remained
unopened for most of the time.[1]

In late September 1890, accompanied by a large corded trunk,
Tom Jones set out north-westwards by train for Aberystwyth. The
journey of rather more than a hundred miles took the best part of
seven hours. It followed a zig-zag route with lengthy stops at four
railway junctions, too isolated and single-purposed to attract
settlement, monuments to the fact that Wales, to this day, is divided
as much as united by its communication systems.[2] This was a
journey that he was to make several times annually for five years. It
was no trip for the impatient.

Aberystwyth was very different from Rhymney. It knew little or
nothing of industrialism. Once the site of an ancient hillfort
settlement, it had grown around its medieval castle, a strong-point

---

[1] *Leeks and Daffodils,* pp.3–5.
[2] H. Carter, *The Towns of Wales* (Cardiff, 1965), pp.73, 92–3.

in the Norman grip on Wales. For centuries it was simply a little market town. In the nineteenth century there was some small-scale shipbuilding, a declining export trade in lead ore mined in the hinterland, a handful of small iron foundries, and a rather torpid fishing industry. The coming of the railway in 1864 reduced its importance as a port but opened up the possibility of greater development as a seaside resort. Aberystwyth had achieved some status as a minor watering-place attracting the gentry of the area in Georgian times, but now it aspired to be a much more popular holiday resort. In anticipation of this, several large hotels were built and, in 1865, a grand pier, a minor wonder of the age in this part of the world.[3] In recent decades the population had been growing steadily and in the census of 1871 was nearly 7,000.[4] It was a time of great optimism: it seemed that Aberystwyth, too, at long last, was to be transformed and brought to vigorous commercial life by the irresistible power of Victorian enterprise. It was publicly proclaimed that the town would soon become 'the Brighton of Wales'.[5]

Just before, however, there had been a disconcerting hiccup. The railway had been brought to Aberystwyth through the enterprise of the remarkable David Davies of Llandinam, a country carpenter in the early stages of a career that ultimately made him a millionaire industrial tycoon, and his partner the less well-known but scarcely less interesting Thomas Savin, a former draper from Oswestry.[6] Savin had tremendous driving energy and a limitless ambition. Perhaps cannily, David Davies had dissolved their partnership and turned his attention to south Wales. Savin, however, continued with his grandiose plans for a string of hotels on the mid-Wales coast linked, in the first instance, by his own railways to the great centres of population. Savin's imagination far outran common prudence and his schemes were probably founded on too many doubtful propositions to succeed. He was caught, hopelessly over-stretched, by the Stock Exchange panic in 1866; with bank rate at 10 per cent Savin was forced into bankruptcy and his unfinished Castle hotel at Aberystwyth came on the market at a knock-down price.

Savin's ill wind, however, did blow some general good elsewhere. His building was snapped up in 1867 for a fraction of its cost by an

[3] W.J Lewis, *Born on a Perilous Rock: Aberystwyth Past and Present* (Aberystwyth, 1980), *passim*.

[4] E.A. Benjamin, *Footprints in the Sand of Time. Aberystwyth 1800–1880* (Dyfed County Council, 1985), pp.2–3.

[5] The Aberystwyth *Guide* (1874), p.v.

[6] Ivor Thomas, *Top Sawyer* (1938), pp.40–70. R. Christianson and R.W. Miller, *The Cambrian Railways* (Newton Abbot, 1967), I, 14–71.

unofficial committee set up to establish a university for Wales. But
the committee too, like Savin, was beset by money troubles. It got
no financial help from the government, the Anglicized Welsh
aristocracy and gentry were coldly indifferent, and there were few
rich private benefactors prepared to help other than David Davies,
who was now to teach his family how to spend money
philanthropically as well as how, phenomenally, to make it. For a
variety of reasons, mainly financial, it was not until October 1872
that the promoters of the university venture, with considerable
remaining hesitation, felt able to open their grandiloquently styled
University College of Wales.

It began in very low key with a Principal and two professors, the
lowest possible representation of one each for Arts and Science,
twenty-six ill-prepared students, a small endowment, a large debt,
and no regular source of income other than public subscription. It
really was the most forlorn of hopes, not least also because there
was no supporting network of secondary schools in Wales to
provide adequately prepared students. Carried away by their
patriotic fervour, the promoters had put the cart before the horse.
For years the College struggled on, living precariously from hand to
mouth, rescued on more than one occasion by the interventions of
David Davies. There seemed no end to the College's tribulations:
governments, Liberal as well as Conservative, steadily refused
applications for a grant; a commission of enquiry into higher
education in 1880, bowing to Welsh parochialisms, recommended
the founding of officially funded university colleges at Cardiff and
Bangor, which seemed to leave Aberystwyth stranded without
purpose. Finally, in 1885, a disastrous fire gutted half the College
building. It seemed like the end of a brave adventure.

In fact, things in future were to be quite otherwise. On the
occasion of the opening in 1872 a local newspaper had claimed
that 'a *bona fide* national college belonging to the country
irrespective of creed, religious or political, has been established'.[7]
However doubtful that had seemed to many at that time, during its
early difficult years the College had touched a sympathetic chord in
the hearts of the Welsh people, and its continuing heroic struggle
against the odds, the elements, and its occasionally malevolent
critics, seemed to many to symbolize in educational terms the
struggle for national regeneration which was proceeding at that
time in politics and in other areas. Principal Thomas Charles
Edwards, who had led the fight for survival, was quite certain that
the great wave of sympathy for the College that swept through the

---

[7] *Cambrian News*, 11 October 1872.

Principality after the great fire had guaranteed its future. 'Wales', he wrote, 'will never now let it die'.[8]

And so it proved. The government bowed to a sustained popular clamour and Aberystwyth was given a grant on the same terms as the colleges at Cardiff and Bangor, and a year or two later a charter in which it retained its original proud title maintaining its claim to be the senior university college enshrining its national rather than regional significance. In 1889, a Welsh intermediate education bill was passed that, within a decade, produced ninety or so secondary schools from which, at long last, the Welsh colleges could recruit students who had been much better prepared for advanced work.[9]

The College to which Tom Jones came in 1890, therefore, had a short but romantic past and even a touch of glamour. Several of his predecessors, untutored young men of parts, had come to Aberystwyth and gone on to achieve great distinction in a very short time at Oxford, the Bar, and in Parliament. Among them were Owen M. Edwards, Oxford don and later the cultural spokesman for Wales, Samuel T. Evans, a future Solicitor-General, and Thomas Edward Ellis, Liberal Chief Whip on the verge of greater things when he died at the age of forty. These and others scarcely less gifted had helped to build up an attractive reputation for the College which, in turn, seemed to evoke in its students a quite exceptional commitment and loyalty. But no one had done as much as Principal Thomas Charles Edwards, the foremost preacher of his day in Wales, scholar and master teacher, a figure renowned throughout the Principality, revered by his students who, in private, called him 'The Prince'. The College owed its very survival in large part to him. It now seemed in 1890 on the threshold of much greater things.

Meanwhile, however, it had several serious shortcomings and could scarcely be said to be able, as yet, to live up to its ambitious title. With so many inadequately trained entrants, inevitably much of the work was remedial, more appropriate to a school than a university college. There was then no University of Wales to award degrees so students sat London University examinations from matriculation upwards. There were other limitations, too, of which Tom Jones was made aware.

He settled in quickly; he found excellent lodgings at 13 New Street, near to the College, which he shared with another first-year

---

[8] Letter to the Mayor of Aberystwyth. Ibid., 31 July 1885.
[9] This account of the College is drawn from my centenary history, *The University College of Wales, Aberystwyth. 1872–1972* (Cardiff, 1972), pp.1–94.

student, a quiet young man named Williams, later the headmaster of a secondary school. The landlady, Mary Williams, a spinster, knew her business. 'I like this house very well', Tom Jones reported home on 4 October, 'everything is carried on very systematically'. He had just enjoyed the substantial 'dinner of the week', and although he knew he would not be as well fed there as at home, he was confident he would 'be able to manage'. He was already in the thick of things at College. 'I have plenty to do as you may imagine. In fact, a little too much. I get up at 6.30 and work 'til eleven'. He was disconcerted by his teachers who were nothing like his old mentor Roger Jones. 'The professors', he wrote, 'are rather queer men. They do not take very great pains with anybody'. At least he drew one useful conclusion: 'I believe the success of the student depends almost entirely on his home work'. It was not all academic slog, he had joined the College Mission Society, whose members went to 'the work-house, the hospital and the low lodging houses' in the town on Sunday afternoons and evenings 'to speak and teach'.[10]

The academic community at Aberystwyth that Tom Jones entered in 1890 was a small, closely-knit society comprising a teaching staff barely twenty strong and just over two hundred students, about a quarter of whom were women. From the outset staff and students had been accustomed to live and work closely together. The original intention had been to make the College entirely residential, on something like the Oxford model, in Savin's hotel *manqué* with some of its many rooms converted into student study bedrooms and accommodation for members of staff. For a time after 1874 this had been done on a small scale with very great success, but the great fire of 1885 brought it to an end.

Elsewhere, however, the tradition of close co-operation continued to mutual advantage. Staff and students entered together on a whole range of social cum intellectual activities: debates, 'dramatics', concerts, specialist societies, College dances and athletic clubs. The College *Magazine* was for some time a joint venture. There is very little evidence that suggests that students were inhibited by the participation of their teachers. Quite the contrary in fact. Of course it was not all sweetness and light. Given the *mores* of Victorian society, the fact that many students were very young when they first came up, that many of them were female and that the College stood *in loco parentis* to them, it is not surprising that social regulations governing relations between men and women students were strict and the authorities were concerned

[10] T.J., Class X, Vol.I, Nos. 25 and 27.

with chaperonage to the point of obsession. At that time women lived in small makeshift halls under the eternally watchful eye of Miss E.A. Carpenter, the so-called Lady Principal. Conversation between men and women outside College was forbidden, and within the walls was allowed only on certain carefully prescribed conditions. This was a situation made to measure for inventive, high-spirited young students. All sorts of contrivances were developed to circumvent restrictions. Just before Tom Jones arrived at Aberystwyth an ornamental inner roof was built over a wide open corridor space inside the College to create an indoor balconied quadrangle. From this time onwards the 'Quad', as it was called, became the great focus of student life. It was perhaps natural that the student body in a small college in a remote location, dependent as they were substantially on their own resources, should develop an intricate social life. And out of it came a tremendous camaraderie which became a distinguishing feature of the College. It was in this social setting that Thomas Jones lived as a student at Aberystwyth, and it has a particular additional importance because it was here that he first met the woman who later on was to become his wife.

Thereafter the College loomed large in their lives. Aberystwyth got a grip on Tom Jones's loyalty that was never subsequently broken. It was not that he viewed the College through rose-coloured spectacles. He was never less than candid about it; he did not love its several warts and made no attempt to pretend that they did not exist. His first snap judgement on the teaching staff, as has been seen, was less than flattering.[11] Just over fifty years later Tom Jones published his recollections of his student days at Aberystwyth.[12] The judgements that he offers there are the result of his experience at Aberystwyth supplemented by a mature reflection on a lifetime's interest in educational practices in many places. Teaching at the College in the 1890s was a curate's egg of the very good and the very bad. There was little that was good that could be said about the system in general: it was based on formal lectures that encouraged voluminous note-taking buttressed by much desperate learning by rote. He conceded in fairness that his teachers were the victims of an alien tyranny, tied as they were to 'the external emetical examinations of London University', that placed a heavy premium on knowledge rather than intelligence.[13] Some of the instruction on the science side was hilarious. The large

[11] See p.32, above.
[12] 'College Memories', in *Leeks and Daffodils*, pp.1–88.
[13] Ibid., pp.18–19.

Chemistry class, when not hastily scribbling dictated definitions or formulae worked out at lightning speed on the blackboard into their fat notebooks, sat mesmerized by the demonic energy of their professor, a gifted scientist but no teacher, who insisted on doing everything himself. The Chemistry apparatus, such as it was, could be examined by the eye at a discreet distance by students but it was not to be handled, much less used. The Physics professor, on the other hand, was himself dubiously wary of his instruments, or perhaps simply accident prone: many of his demonstrations moved his audiences to laughter like a haplessly unsuccessful conjuror whose tricks go repeatedly and predictably amiss.[14]

There was, of course, another side to things; indeed, there were some outstandingly gifted teachers on the staff. There was C.H. Herford, for example, professor of English, one of the most considerable scholars of his day in his field, who had the capacity to inspire large classes. And there was the remarkable Hermann Ethé, a refugee from the illiberalism of Bismarck's Germany, master of umpteen languages, an orientalist of European reputation, whose astonishing scholarly range and robust personality compelled attention and admiration.[15] There was even a teacher with gifts close to genius. This was the Principal T.C. Edwards, who taught Greek; Tom Jones called him 'the great expositor' within whom 'the fire burned'; he loved to encourage his students into adventurous speculation about moral and religious questions, and on one occasion in full emotional flow on the death of Socrates moved his listeners deeply. He did not spend his time communicating information, he ignited imaginations.[16]

But it was through his experiences outside rather than inside the classroom that Aberystwyth established its hold on Tom Jones's affection. Some years later, in 1916, he argued that students were 'as much educated by each other and their environment as by their professors'.[17] Although it has a certain Victorian Gothic charm, Savin's building did not engage Tom Jones's affections. Built on rock with an apron of sea-front terracing, the College by the Sea, as it was popularly known, had no green surrounding land. But there was the town's Promenade, half a mile long in those days, which became an unofficial annex to the College, a handy Victorian campus free of cost, shared with the town to which it belonged. At

[14] Ibid., pp.21–3.
[15] For Ethé see *The College by the Sea*, ed. I. Morgan (Aberystwyth, 1928), pp.97–8.
[16] *Leeks and Daffodils*, pp.30, 38–9.
[17] 'A Memorandum on Aberystwyth. July 1919'. *A Theme with Variations* (Newtown, 1933), p.75.

the far end stood the various houses that were used at that time as hostels for women students which added to the attraction of the Promenade. Thomas Jones's account of its place in the scheme of things is almost lyrical.

> Up and down the broad pavement in twos and threes we walked and talked *ad midnightum* under the stars to the sound of the sea as it rolled the pebbles and battered the breakwaters. We argued, above the belt and below, we argued in triangles and circles, we boxed the compass, we begged the question, we made the worse appear the better reason. We discussed religion, politics, economics, nationalism, women . . . all the subjects in which we were passionately interested.

And, of course, there were the women students, outnumbered four to one in 1890, reduced to two to one in 1895 as more and more women were attracted to the College's new Normal training department for teachers. 'We fell in love and fell out of it', and circumvented the Mrs Grundy-like prohibitions of College regulations with 'furtive meetings and a silent kiss'.[18] College rugby and football matches regularly drew large attendances of women students who knew little or nothing of the games themselves. 'Such rare games of tennis as I played', wrote Tom Jones, who throughout his life had no interest at all in popular sports of any kind, 'were really opportunities for conversation with women students'. The importance of the Promenade and the roofed quadrangle inside the College in the scheme of co-education at Aberystwyth, in Tom Jones's opinion, could not be exaggerated. It was this marvellous intellectual intimacy, this corporate social existence in a small college in a small town, enlived by a powerful *esprit de corps* known as the 'Aber Spirit', that made up 'the best education that Aberystwyth provided, unplanned, unexamined, spontaneous, free'.[19]

Also central to student life was the Literary and Debating Society ('Lit and Deb' in student terms). 'It is the Sovereign of College Societies', stated the *Magazine* of 1892. 'To ignore it is nothing short of high treason against that most exciting of all tribunals – the College conscience'. Lit and Deb was the best index of 'the general health and intellectual robustness of College life', and

[18] *Leeks and Daffodils*, p.40. 'Nearly every girl in Hall went to the College football match', wrote the future Lady Stamp in February 1899. 'They only went (most of them) for the sake of talking to the fellows. They are allowed to on the football, hockey and tennis grounds'. See the manuscript account, 'Life at Aberystwyth and Alexandra Hall at the end of the nineteenth century', in the Hugh Owen Library, Aberystwyth.

[19] *Leeks and Daffodils*, pp.40–1, 49.

'brilliancy of performance' there raised a student on 'to a platform
of eminence and recognition'.[20] There were especially gifted
speakers at that time as always in that assembly; J.H. Edwards, for
example, a future Liberal MP, who could 'talk like a leading
article'. Tom Jones was no Rupert of debate; throughout his life he
disliked having to speak off the cuff, and freely confessed that he
sometimes made the mistake when addressing the house at
Aberystwyth of being 'heavily humorous' to no good effect.[21]
Nevertheless, he was active in debates, had some occasional
triumphs, and his interventions give some indication of his general
opinion on public affairs at that time. In a debate on land
nationalization in November 1892 he seconded the motion in
favour and 'waxed eloquent over the present misery and
wretchedness of the country'. Two years later he spoke in favour of
women's suffrage. In that session Tom Jones had been elected Vice-
President of Lit and Deb, the senior student post as the President
was invariably a member of staff, often the Principal himself. Jones
was by now a man of standing in student affairs. In October 1894
he stood as the Labour candidate in the annual mock parliamentary election. His set-piece speech (he was a first-rate platform
performer when properly prepared) was described as 'the best of
the four'. He argued in favour of women's suffrage, a national
minimum wage, an eight-hour working day, the nationalization of
land and an extension of municipal enterprise. In a constituency
usually overwhelmingly Liberal he was narrowly beaten into second
place.[22]

He was also an active committee member of the Celtic, the
College society devoted to the discussion and promotion of matters
of special Welsh concern. At one meeting he opened for the
affirmative in a debate on the question whether it was desirable
that the Welsh should retain and develop their separate nationality.
Not surprisingly in that assembly, he won hands down.[23]

He lived a very full, busy student life, all the more hectic because
he was away usually over the weekends on preaching engagements.
After all, his main purpose in coming to Aberystwyth had been
to begin his preparation for the Calvinistic Methodist ministry,
to which in 1890 he had dedicated his life, a commitment he

---

[20] *The UCW Magazine*, XIV, 2 & 3.
[21] *Leeks and Daffodils*, p.53.
[22] *The UCW Magazine*, XIV, 63, XVI, 308, XII, 35–7, 290.
[23] Ibid., XIII, 126, XV, 72. In a general debate in 1891 on the need for a Welsh
University he had taken a very vigorous patriotic line. Ibid., XIV, 29. T.J., Class X,
Vol.1, No.49.

reaffirmed publicly in 1892 with undiminished earnestness.[24] At a rather less elevated level the preaching engagements were an economic necessity. The few pounds he earned in this way made all the difference to his ability to pay his way through College. Many of the Welsh people of this time were connoisseurs of pulpit performance. C.H. Herford, the Professor of English at Aberystwyth, had been struck by 'the extraordinary religiosity' of the people. He was convinced that it was possible for a Welshman to listen a whole day long to the word of God.[25] That was almost literally true on the days when the *Cyrddau Mawr* (the Great Meetings) were held. Large congregations often drawn from a wide area would assemble to hear six or eight sermons on the same day by some of the great preachers who were household names in Welsh society. Most of them had a physical presence, a remarkable skill in the use of language, a great range of voice and gesture and an extraordinary power to move, uplift, transport, sometimes to chasten, even terrify, those who listened to them. Each of the really great preachers had a well-known individual style.

Tom Jones never achieved that sort of national renown in the pulpit. However, the number of invitations to preach that he received when he was a student increased year by year. He preached thirty-seven times in 1890 (which brought in £11.3.2d after the deduction of expenses), on sixty-nine occasions in each of the next two years (with a net margin of almost £27 annually) an in 1893 he delivered one hundred and five sermons for which he received in all the sum of £62.1.0d.[26] Most of those engagements were in small towns and villages around Aberystwyth to which he travelled in the cheapest way possible, more often than not on foot. When a minister expected at Brynhyfryd chapel in Rhymney had to withdraw earlier that year, Enoch Jones hurriedly summoned his grandson home to preach to his own people. Tom was evidently showing some promise. 'It seems', wrote his father, D.B., in September 1891, reporting the death of a well-known minister, the Revd D.C. Davies, 'that the Lord is making his part to cut down the Great Pillar of the *Corph* [the Welsh Calvinistic Methodist denomination], and if the Building is to keep up' he added in

[24] In a debate on 'Popular Culture in Wales', 16 March, 1892, *The UCW Magazine*, XIV, 235–6.

[25] 'But for all that', he added, maintaining a proper balance, 'the public houses are pretty well filled'. 'A German Philologist in Wales'. Ibid., XIII, 4.

[26] The importance of this source of income is apparent at a time when his average weekly lodging bill in 1890 was 8/3d. *Leeks and Daffodils*, pp.16, 60. A year later it had gone up by 6d. T.J., Class X, Vol.J, No.31. The preaching weekends also meant good Sunday dinners and other filling meals.

exhortation, 'some must gain strength to be put in their places'.[27]

In fact, Tom Jones did begin to make something of a name for himself in a modest way. He began to be invited to chapels further afield in Cardiff and Liverpool, and even, in 1893, to take part in some of the great preaching festivals. He had had one particularly unnerving experience on his way up the ladder. Principal Edwards once asked Tom Jones to deputize for him at short notice at Llanidloes. The visit of a great nationally-known figure such as the Principal would arouse a tremendous expectation in a very large congregation, and there would be an obvious disappointment, that could humiliate, when it was announced that a mere student was to preach in his place. Could any apprentice on the stage, however promising, effectively substitute for Henry Irving? However, it was no small compliment to be asked to fill such a gap.[28]

Principal Edwards was, of course, a distinguished theologian whose sermons were concerned, at an elevated level, with the fundamental questions of Christian doctrine.[29] The popular style of preaching at this time in Welsh chapels, however, was strongly evangelical in spirit and often highly emotional in presentation. 'To listen to a preacher's *hwyl*', wrote Alfred Zimmern not too fancifully a year or two later, 'is to hear the echo of the muezzin from the minaret'.[30] Tom Jones's pulpit style was different from both these models. He avoided intricacies of high doctrine and shunned extravagant fervour or hell-fire language. 'I chose happy comforting texts, verses full of blessing, pressed down and running over', he said. It began to be noticed, however, and some took marked exception to it, that his sermons were much more ethical than formally doctrinal in content, and that he had rather too much to say on current social and economic questions for the comfort of many deacons who were not accustomed to having recent industrial history presented to them through the prism of the New Testament.[31] It took some time for Tom Jones to realize it, but the fact was that the course of his life was beginning to veer in a new direction.

It would, of course, have been very odd indeed if his time at the College at Aberystwyth had not altered, at least to some extent, Tom Jones's view of the world. It was not his attendance at the formal lectures and classes that wrought the change. He was, after all, in the first two years, working at a relatively elementary level on

27   Ibid., Nos.40, 42, 43.
28   *Leeks and Daffodils*, pp.27–8, 60.
29   Thomas Jones, 'The First Principal', *A Theme with Variations*, p.132.
30   Op.cit., p.19.
31   *Leeks and Daffodils*, pp.27, 61–2.

the subjects he needed for matriculation, and those courses were
primarily concerned with the humdrum requirements of examination syllabuses, not the great profundities of life. But he was not
one to be confined to prescribed texts or recommended lists of
commentaries. He was, as he wrote later, 'a bus not a tramcar', free
to travel in directions of his own choosing not set simply to run on
predetermined lines. During 'ravenous reading' far and wide he
came upon Giusseppe Mazzini's *The Duties of Man* and Madame
E.A. Venturi's *Life* of the Italian patriot. Tom Jones was captivated;
he became an immediate disciple. 'These books gripped me as no
others before or since', he wrote fifty years later.[32] By that time, of
course, older and wiser, certainly less immediately impressionable,
Tom Jones was rather more eclectic in his judgement and had
come to see that Mazzini's teaching had its limitations, that there
were other thinkers whose understanding suggested truths about
the problems of humanity that he had not perceived.

Even so, Mazzini remained a powerful influence on Thomas
Jones throughout his life, and in the shorter term exerted an
overwhelmingly compelling effect. Earlier Jones had been attracted
by the nationalist writings of the Irishman Thomas Davis, as were
many other patriotic young Welshmen at that time. But Mazzini's
democratic nationalism stirred him more strongly, all the more so
as it led on naturally to a much wider vision of international
harmony in which all humanity had its place. But persuasive as
these general political principles were, Mazzini appealed to Tom
Jones above all because of the moral grandeur of his teaching with
its abnegation of self-interest, its insistence that obligations ranked
at least equally with rights, that life was a mission, the fulfilment of
duty its supreme imperative. 'Mazzini', Tom Jones wrote in 1905,
'ranks with St. Francis of Assisi . . . his heart always beats in response
to the call of the afflicted and the distressed'; he was 'the most
virtuous . . . of men'.[33] This, of course, was outright hero worship,
of which Tom Jones was not unaware. But, he wrote in November
1895, at least Mazzini had 'not feet of clay'.[34]

There were other powerful influences at work on him at this
time. There was a great ferment of ideas in these years and
Aberystwyth, for all its geographical isolation, was not *ultima Thule*
intellectually. Earlier he had been interested in some of the ideas of
F.D. Maurice and Charles Kingsley, and more recently he was

[32] Ibid., pp.50–1, 72–3.
[33] Article on Mazzini in the *Glasgow Herald*, 22 June, 1905. See also Tom
Jones's Introduction pp.vii–ix to his edition of *The Duties of Man* (Everyman
Library, Vol.224, 1907).
[34] To his sister, Liz. T.J., Class X, Vol.1, No.59.

attracted by the Christian Social Union and the social gospel of
Canon Barnett and Toynbee Hall. Jones had been moved by
General Charles Booth's horrifying disclosures of the degradation
of the great army of the poor in London, intellectually stimulated
by the *Fabian Essays,* and he was paying increasing attention to Keir
Hardie and the emerging challenge of the labour interest in public
affairs.[35] Tom Jones had not yet quite decided that the Methodist
ministry was not for him, but his former declared purpose was now
undergoing some re-examination.

So too were his political convictions, if such they may be called,
as they had not hitherto been very clearly defined. There had been
no place for political discussion during the years of his upbringing
at home in Rhymney. Neither his father nor his grandfather was a
political animal and sermons at Brynhyfryd chapel were devoid of
political content.[36] All the same, there were Nonconformists in
Wales who, with little conscious effort and a minimum of reflection
on their part, nonetheless had become Liberal by a process of
osmosis from their religious beliefs and associations. 'The Liberal
creed and the individualism of the prevailing Protestant theology
were in fundamental accord', Tom Jones wrote.[37] This appeared to
be the route by which he had become a Liberal, an allegiance he
formally declared at Aberystwyth in 1890.[38] These were the years
when Welsh Liberals were much more assertive than they had ever
been before. Inspired by a new cultural and political consciousness,
aware of their increased numbers and greater leverage inside the
Liberal party, under the leadership of Tom Ellis and Lloyd George,
they were much more disposed than formerly to demand the
redress of Welsh grievances. Some of them were determined that
they would no longer be treated like tame poodles, contemptuously disregarded by the party leadership at Westminster.
They were prepared, if necessary, to take an aggressive independent nationalist line.[39] It is clear from Tom Jones's activity in the
College Celtic Society, of which eventually he became secretary, and
the tone of his speeches in debates, that he fully supported this

[35] *Leeks and Daffodils,* p.78. T.J., Class X, Vol.1, No.59.
[36] 'I never remember hearing a political sermon at Brynhyfryd', *RM,* p.153.
[37] *Leeks and Daffodils,* pp.69–70.
[38] Ibid., p.28. The Principal suggested he should regularly read the Tory
Western Mail to keep his Liberal convictions under challenge.
[39] In September, 1889, for example, the North Wales Liberal Federation
solemnly warned Gladstone that continued tergiversation over the disestablishment of the Church in Wales would put Welsh Liberal loyalty under the greatest
strain. See *Lloyd George. Family Letters, 1885–1936* (ed. K.O. Morgan, Cardiff and
London, 1973, p.23, editor's note).

Welsh Liberal belligerence. By the later 1890s, however, the offensive at Westminster, after having achieved some successes, for a variety of reasons such as the disunity between the Liberals of north and south Wales and some skilful manoeuvring by Stuart Rendel, Gladstone's agent in Wales, had petered out.[40] By that time Tom Jones's political loyalties lay elsewhere.

It will be remembered that he had joined the Mission Society almost as soon as he had arrived at the College. Since then he had become more and more interested in problems of poverty and social deprivation. He and his friends ran a manuscript magazine to propagate their ideas within the student community and met regularly in private to discuss social problems. Several of them worked energetically as volunteer helpers during vacations in the mission halls of the slums of big cities run by the Forward Movement of the Presbyterian church. Tom Jones gave a public address on Mazzini, who became thereafter their patron saint. This 'set' of 'young people in a hurry', as Tom Jones called them, consisted of a tightly-knit group, about twenty strong, of men and women students in roughly equal numbers.[41] So far as they were able to do so within the constraints of the severe regulations governing the conduct of men and women students, they lived in close association, freely sharing money and such goods as they possessed, linked by affection and a common purpose. Some of the women brought an exceptional energy and a splendid selflessness to their mission activity. It is clear that Thomas Jones was the moving spirit and unofficial leader of the group. They called themselves 'Squatters', or, more usually, 'the Settlers', because eventually, after a long and serious debate, they decided ambitiously to set up a mission settlement of their own. Aberystwyth had no slum district of any size and few, if any, instances of the sort of miserably degrading destitution that was all too common among those who lived in big cities. The enthusiasm, idealism and eager self-sacrifice of the group insisted on a much more demanding challenge for their campaign than Aberystwyth could provide. The larger industrial towns in south Wales were obvious possibilities, and after an extensive reconnaissance by members of the group, Tom Jones sought the advice of S.G. Hobson, the Fabian and socialist, and J.S. Mackenzie, Professor of Philosophy at University College, Cardiff. Eventually it became clear that the Splott and East

[40] K.O. Morgan, *Rebirth of a Nation. Wales 1880–1980*, pp.26–45. Wyn Jones, *Thomas Edward Ellis 1859–1899* (Cardiff, 1986), pp.15–73. John Grigg, *The Young Lloyd George* (1973), pp.99–202.

[41] *A Theme with Variations*, p.134. T.J., Class X, Vol.2, Nos.6, 13.

Moors districts of Cardiff offered the best opportunities for the sort of relief work they had in mind. 'Henceforth Cardiff is the hub of the universe', Tom Jones wrote after the group had voted unanimously in favour of that city.

> In the Welsh metropolis there was a combination of spiritual deadness, civic apathy and social wreckage which it would be hard to parallel outside the largest cities. Here was a town given over to commercialism in the grossest form . . . Thitherward must all squatters bend their energies. We must learn to cherish for Cardiff that [feeling] which the Jew has for Jerusalem, which Mazzini had for Rome.

There followed a high-toned two-line invocation above his signature as *rapporteur:*

> On to the bound of the waste
> On to the Kingdom of God.[42]

There is no question that those young people were utterly sincere and thoroughly in earnest. At that same meeting, which they called the Settlers' first Annual Conference, they 'solemnly undertook to beg, borrow or steal about £45', a very substantial sum in those days, to finance nine months training in social work for the Misses Daniel and Millard, who intended to dedicate their lives to that cause.[43] Indeed, a year before, Tom Jones himself had indicated that he was seriously considering a similar outright commitment.

> I do not now propose becoming a pastor in the usual way [he told his sister, Liz] but am bent on living in closer contact with the people and in working not merely for the *soul's salvation,* as it is called, but for their *life's salvation,* in all its phases . . . I think a band of fellows can be got to club together to live without the comforts of home and slave themselves day and night for the common good.[44]

Their idealism was not in doubt, but there were serious practical difficulties in the Cardiff scheme, as J.S. Mackenzie had pointed out. 'The question', he said soberly, was 'chiefly ways and means', and he could not see how the group planned to finance the venture. S.G. Hobson had drawn attention to other daunting hindrances. Cardiff was 'intellectually dead . . . utterly destitute of

[42] T.J. Class X Vol. 2, No.7. See also Nos. 8–13.
[43] Ibid., Nos. 6 and 7.
[44] T.J., Class X, Vol.1, No.59.

real vitality and idealism'. Its desperate social problems had been 'absolutely ignored by conformist and nonconformist Philistines who flounder helplessly in those methods of charity dear to the heart of Samuel Smiles'. The large Irish populations would be suspicious, if not hostile, and there would be little useful help from dissenting pastors who would forever be nosing for heterodoxy. 'Cant', he observed contemptuously, 'plays a large part in Cardiff nonconformity'. Nevertheless, such people would have to be reconciled. Hobson urged a bold approach, 'timid touting' was useless, and despite the long list of discouragements, Hobson insisted that Cardiff was 'a splendid field for work'.[45]

The Aberystwyth 'Settlers' did have plans of a sort. Several members of the group managed to get teaching posts in the secondary schools that were springing up around Cardiff as elsewhere in Wales at this time. They hoped also to enlist the support of students at University College, Cardiff, and although for the moment Bangor was 'unknown country' to them, they were confident that they would 'find kindred spirits' in the north Wales college who would be prepared to assist. Meanwhile, every member of the group must 'preach his Squatter gospel freely' in all places, and each one of them, it was agreed, should aim to become 'a sort of encyclopaedia in that particular branch of . . . good works' to which he or she had been assigned. Tom Jones's designated specialism was the problem of unemployment; others variously were assigned to municipal socialism, temperance, the poor law system, education and, not surprisingly considering the balance of the group, women's rights.[46] But it was clear that, for the moment at least, for all the noble intention it remained a dream, even perhaps a chimera.

Despite this temporary disappointment, Tom Jones had shown a natural aptitude for organizing and a capacity for working with, indeed giving a lead to, all sorts of people with differing qualities and varying temperaments. He had displayed, on a much more modest scale of course, the same combination of talents that explained Canon Barnett's success as the leader of co-operative social efforts in the East End of London.[47] Tom Jones had not succeeded on this occasion, but time and time again later on he was to operate successfully in much the same way at the centre of a web of people committed to the promotion of some good cause or other.

[45] Letters to Thomas Jones, T.J., Class X, Vol.2, Nos.10 and 11.
[46] Ibid., No.13. *Leeks and Daffodils*, pp.80–4.
[47] Henrietta Barnett, *Canon Barnett. His Life, Work and Friends* (1919), I, p.182.

Given his preoccupation with social and economic problems at this time, it was highly likely that, along with many others, he would become dissatisfied with the Liberal party's neglect of 'bread and butter' issues, and the refusal of Gladstone and most of the hierarchy of leaders seriously to attend directly by legislation to the problems of poverty. 'Political Liberalism', Jones wrote in his account of these years, 'had done fine work in opening all problems in heaven and earth to discussion', and in making most of the running in franchise reform, but 'confronted with economic inequality and chronic distress', Liberalism had no effective prescription to offer.[48] Accordingly, he was being drawn more and more to the different political priorities asserted by Keir Hardie and other spokesmen for the Labour interest. In 1894, Tom Jones was among those, considered 'reckless enthusiasts' at that time, who tramped the valleys of south Wales advocating 'direct labour representation' in Parliament and a break with old Liberal loyalties that had become meaningless.[49] And at College in the same year, as has been seen, he stood as the Labour candidate in the annual trial of political strength.[50]

In the light of all these activities it is not surprising that at the end of his time at Aberystwyth, Tom Jones should be recognized as one of the 'big-wigs', as they were called, the leaders and spokes-men for the student community.[51] What, however, is remarkable is that as early as 1891, during his first year at the college, he should be singled out by the Principal for an important and peculiarly delicate commission. T.C. Edwards was being strongly pressed by leading Calvinistic Methodists to take over the headship of their theological college at Bala in succession to his late father. The Principal was torn between the opportunity thus presented of turning Bala into a great theological centre open to all the denominations and his deep loyalty to Aberystwyth which he had largely created and now embodied. Sorely troubled by the decision, Edwards consulted several of the leading figures in Welsh life. Typically, he also sought the opinion of his students at Aberystwyth, a remarkable, indeed possibly unique, request by the head of a college and an illustration of how genuinely close-knit this small academic community was at that time. And significantly it was to Thomas Jones, then aged twenty, that the Principal turned.[52]

[48] *Welsh Broth* (1950), p.42.
[49] *A Theme with Variations*, p.1.
[50] See p.36, above.
[51] T.J., Class X, Vol.1, No.58.
[52] *T.C. Edwards Letters*, ed. T.I. Ellis (Aberystwyth, 1952), p.289.

Curiously enough, two years before, when the move to Bala had first been proposed Thomas Jones had written anonymously as 'a true and loyal young Methodist', to Principal Edwards imploring him to accept such an invitation, if it were made, as the only way of resolving the 'severe and trying crisis' with which the denomination was faced. Even with due allowance for the Principal's exalted status in religious circles, it is couched in astonishingly obsequious terms. Indeed, it is the one letter that Thomas Jones ever wrote that has an unmistakable touch of unctuousness.[53]

His letter to the Principal in 1891, however, was very different. It illustrates how far Tom Jones had come in a very short time from the perhaps naïve gaucherie of 1889.

> You asked me for a few lines on the bearing of the future of Theology in Wales and your going to Bala from a student's standpoint.
>
> I have spoken to many of the students and have jotted down the result. It is evident that the finger of Theology beckons you unmistakably to Bala and we are reluctantly constrained to admit that it should be obeyed, *provided you have good hopes of a competent successor here.*

Some weeks later, however, a general meeting of students voted unanimously to ask the Principal to remain. 'The Bala College', they stated, 'is an important institution, but it is not a national one' as is Aberystwyth. Principal Edwards, nonetheless, did go to Bala, although with rather a heavy heart as his valedictory address to the students makes clear.[54]

His successor as Principal was very different from the magnetic, occasionally explosive T.C. Edwards. T.F. Roberts, an old Aberystwyth student who had gone on to a brilliant career at Oxford, was thirty years old, earnest, unusually grave in manner with no great sense of humour, and with no shred of his predecessor's charismatic attraction. He was, however, patently sincere, utterly devoted to the College, unfailingly helpful to his students and a superb teacher of Greek philosophy. He, too, had a high opinion of Thomas Jones, whom he once described as 'a model student'.[55] This appraisal was certainly not based on his prowess in

[53] Ibid., p.274. The original (NLW T.C. Edwards MS No. 5175) is clearly in Thomas Jones's hand, though not signed.

[54] College Notes, *UCW Magazine*, XIII, 213, 285–7. Tom Jones's letter home (12 June 1891, T.J., Class X, Vol.1, No.38) indicates how he too felt the pull of divided loyalties over the decision.

[55] David Williams, *Thomas Francis Roberts 1860–1919* (A Centenary Lecture), (Cardiff, 1961). E.L. Ellis, op.cit., pp.100–1. *Leeks and Daffodils*, pp.30, 88.

examinations where Tom Jones's record was undistinguished to say the least. In June 1892, he managed to matriculate, not without difficulty, being placed in division II of the second class. It is evident that he had found the matriculation course irksome, unexciting intellectually. Indeed, it appears that at one time these disgruntlements and his subsequent mediocre examination performance had led him to consider a career in journalism.[56] He sought the advice of T.F. Roberts and, characteristically, received a long reply that set out the academic options in considerable detail.

The Principal acknowledged that matriculation work had been something of a dull grind, pointed out that Tom Jones could now turn to 'more congenial work' much better suited to his 'tastes and aptitudes'. There were, in practice, two courses open to him, although the question of finance was no doubt crucial. Tom Jones had hoped to answer the problem of money by working for a Dr Daniel Williams scholarship, then worth £40 per annum, tenable at the University of Glasgow. Dr Williams was a Welshman, a Presbyterian minister with a taste for polemics who survived in the dangerous waters of politico-religious controversy in London in the late seventeenth century, married in succession two rich heiresses, and left £50,000 which, under a complicated will, was used to endow a famous library in London, a boarding school for girls in Wales, and scholarships at Glasgow University for aspiring candidates for the Nonconformist ministry. Many gifted Welshmen had taken advantage of the Glasgow endowment. After matriculating, Tom Jones had initially intended working for the BA degree of London University, as did most of the students at Aberystwyth at that time. There was one difficulty about this scheme, of which he already had an uncomfortable inkling. London University examinations had to be passed in one fell swoop: failure in one subject could not subsequently be recouped separately; one slip meant disaster all along the line. Tom Jones was already aware of his vulnerability in one compulsory subject, mathematics, and in any case he disliked the London syllabus which a year before he had denounced in a public debate as 'hollow and empty'.[57]

Principal Roberts, with a marvellous academic record at St John's College behind him, would, perhaps naturally, have preferred Tom Jones to set his sights on Oxford and, if successful in an attempt to get an Exhibition in either Hebrew or Modern History, to go up directly from Aberystwyth. 'I should hardly recommend going to Glasgow as one avenue to Oxford', he wrote,

---

[56] E.H. [Jones] to Tom Jones, 14 September 1892. T.J., Class X, Vol.1, No.48.
[57] *UCW Magazine*, XIV, 29.

1. T.J.'s grandfather, Enoch Jones.

2. 100 High Street, Rhymney, T.J.'s birthplace.

3. The Lawn Company Shop, Rhymney, derelict in 1937.

4. College days at Aberystwyth. Principal T.F. Roberts is seated in the centre with T.J. immediately behind him.

5. T.J. in his early thirties.

7. Eirene, Tristan and Elphin, T.J.'s children.

6. Eirene (Rene) Jones, née Lloyd, T.J.'s wife.

'because it cuts up your course too much. It is well to preserve simplicity and directness'. However, he conceded that there was many a slip between cup and lip, even for the most gifted; and so whatever the choice, Oxford or Glasgow, he thought Tom Jones would be well advised, while preparing for whichever university he finally chose, also to continue his work for the London BA degree, which would be a sensible form of insurance. Moreover, there was no reason, in the Principal's judgement, why the London course could not be fashioned by an imaginative choice of essay subjects into 'an instrument of the best culture'.[58]

Tom Jones took the Principal's advice, at least in part, rather to the surprise of one of his 'inner circle' of student friends. 'I do not know what to say about your decision to pursue the London course', commented E.H. Jones, adding apparently crushingly, 'I hope that at the end of the pursuit it will be the London examiners who will have to give up and not you'.[59] As it turned out, E.H. Jones was a more accurate judge of the matter than Principal Roberts. For the plain fact was that Tom Jones simply could not get through his London intermediate mathematics papers, and repeated failure made it clear that, therefore, he would not graduate under the London scheme this side of doomsday. To some extent he had brought this upon himself.

The truth was [he admitted subsequently] that

> I was far too absorbed in and distracted by preaching, college societies, ravenous reading outside the prescribed subjects, denominational politics, affairs in Rhymney, women students, letters innumerable.

On any long or larger view of education and life, who would say his priorities were wrong? But the immediate difficulty remained. At the time Tom Jones blamed an 'inborn incapacity'; he was convinced that mathematics was, and always would be, for him 'an impenetrable mystery'. Successive failures destroyed his confidence completely, the whole thing became 'a nightmare'. He was reduced to the point where he could not even remember basic trigonometrical formulae except by the desperate mnemonic of their translation into singable jingles worked out for him by his friend, the musical R.R. Williams. This abject failure haunted Tom Jones

[58] 5 August 1892. T.J., Class X, Vol.1, No.47.
[59] 14 September 1892. Ibid., No.48. This acid comment was not unkindness; it was the reaction of a well-disposed candid friend, who in the same letter tried to persuade Tom Jones to join him in his lodgings.
[60] *Leeks and Daffodils*, p.50.

for years. Later in life he drew comfort from A.N. Whitehead's admission that the fundamental ideas of mathematics, as often as not, were badly presented to beginners, to the persistent confusion of many of them thereafter.[61] There was some truth in this explanation so far as he was concerned. Aberystwyth's mathematics teachers in the early years were clever men who simply could not teach. The first, the splendidly named Horatio Nelson Grimley, 12th Wrangler at Cambridge in 1865, was dismissed for incompetence in the classroom in 1878.[62] And his successor, R.W. Genese, professor of mathematics in Tom Jones's time, was a slave-driver with no patience with dullards, whose teaching featured swift juggling on the blackboard with symbols that were erased 'before you can whistle'.[63] Genese robbed Tom Jones of his customary sense of proportion so far as teachers in that discipline were concerned. In 1895, he found it quite remarkable that William Jack, Professor of Mathematics at Glasgow, was 'a most reasonable and intelligent gentleman', because it was such 'an unusual thing in teachers of that subject'. Nearly fifty years later the jaundice, if anything, had increased: 'The proportion of mathematicians who are not normal human beings', Jones wrote in 1942, 'is high'.[64]

There was no escape for him from the tyranny of the hated subject because it was a compulsory requirement also in examinations for the Daniel Williams scholarships. He and his friend R.R. Williams went up to London to take their papers. Williams succeeded and went on to Glasgow, Tom Jones came a miserable cropper, as he did again in the following year. Early in 1895 therefore his career appeared to be in ruins. He had now come to believe that Oxford was academically as well as financially quite beyond him. In the midst of an overwhelming gloom he thought of returning home with his tail between his legs to Rhymney and whatever job he could get from the Iron Company. That course would have been the ultimate humiliation for Tom Jones and his family in a society that, for all its praiseworthy democratic interest in, and support for, widespread educational opportunity, had a very narrow notion of its meaning and purpose. If education did not end in the entitlement to add the graduate's magical letters to a name what, local opinion would ask, did it

[61] Ibid., pp.32–3.

[62] E.L. Ellis, op.cit., pp.36–54. David Williams, op.cit., p.14.

[63] See T.R. Dawes, later a distinguished headmaster, on Genese in *The College by the Sea*, p.82. *Leeks and Daffodils*, p.83. Genese's assistant was more amiable but no better as a teacher.

[64] Thomas Jones to his sister, 17 November 1895. T.J., Class X, Vol.1, No.59. *Leeks and Daffodils*, p.34.

mean? Anything less meant the indelible brand of failure. To have moved from Aberystwyth to a theological college would have been construed, no doubt absurdly, as a face-saving subterfuge. It never seems to have been considered, now the University of Wales had come into existence, that Tom Jones could have stayed put and worked for the new Welsh degree.

As yet, of course, that scheme was barely under way and was not without some initial confusions. 'There is a rumour', reported the College *Magazine* with heavy humour, 'that the University of Wales intends to grant a few degrees to those who can understand the syllabus'. One fierce critic, a distinguished former Aberystwyth student, asserted that the new Welsh graduates, when they appeared, like Samson's foxes, would go forth and spread universal destruction.[65] It is unlikely that Tom Jones was much influenced by this alarmist nonsense; indeed, a year or two before he had argued vehemently in favour of the establishment of a University of Wales.[66] But he had already spent five years at Aberystwyth, and with his record of examination failures there felt that he was 'a disgrace to the black cap and gown', the so-called College 'academicals', that he had bought for a pound in the days of high optimism in October 1890.[67] It was time he moved on to a fresh start elsewhere. Not, however, to the Theological college at Bala, because it was now by no means certain that he would end up as a pastor, at least not in the ordinary sense.

The place for him was obviously the University of Glasgow. There were several strong reasons for that choice, one of them personal. It was a relatively ancient university foundation with a very considerable reputation; Adam Smith had occupied a chair there; James Watt, the famous inventor, had at one time been the University's instrument maker. The Principal in 1895 was John Caird, once, according to Thomas Jones, 'the greatest pulpit force' in Scotland, who was considered by Dean Stanley to have preached 'the greatest single sermon of the century'.[68] William Thomson, the future Lord Kelvin, a giant among scientists, was professor of Natural Philosophy, and there were many other distinguished scholars on the staff, including G.G. Ramsay, the classicist, Richard Lodge, the historian, the young Gilbert Murray, and, of special attraction, the Welshman Henry Jones, reputedly the best teacher in Scotland, whose high-toned eloquence had fired Thomas Jones's

[65] *UCW Magazine*, XVIII, 32, 171.
[66] Ibid., XIV, 29.
[67] *Leeks and Daffodils*, p.88.
[68] T.J., Class X, Vol.1, No.59. Dean Stanley's opinion is in the *DNB*.

imagination when he had heard him speak some years before in a
village chapel in north Wales. Furthermore, Glasgow was a great
industrial city, 'a social laboratory containing a million samples' of
humanity, many of them living immured in squalor in great swathes
of slum tenements that afforded open-ended opportunities to a
young man who was now at least as much concerned about the
improvement of people's secular lives as the salvation of their souls
in the hereafter. Moreover, on a less elevated plane, there was the
practical but, in his case, crucially important fact that in the
Glasgow degree scheme failure in mathematics was not the
impassable barrier to further progress that it was at London
University. As for money, Glasgow was almost an ideal choice. The
poor scholar getting an education by existing on the shortest of
short commons had been the staple student at this Scottish
university for centuries.

It is clear that, despite the disappointment caused by the
examination failures at Aberystwyth, his family's confidence in his
natural abilities remained unshaken. And there was no question
either of their willingness to continue to make sacrifices in order to
support him, so far as possible, at college. Tom Jones's mother,
especially, had an absolute belief in her eldest son; and no word of
cavil ever came from her husband about the levy their son's
education made on the family's income. The same unwavering
support came from the two unmarried daughters, Liz and Har',
who remained at home.[69] The family's senior counsellor, Enoch
Jones, Tom's much-loved grandfather, was, however, no longer
there to give his advice. Enoch Jones had died, aged sixty-six, two
years before. He had continued to work for the Iron Company to
the end. Technically, he died of bronchitis, but Tom Jones was
convinced that his grandfather's health had been broken by the
grief and worry of a series of domestic tragedies, the murder of his
brother and the early death of his drink-ridden son some years
before.[70] Rhymney had turned out *en masse* on 24 July 1893 to
honour a man who was regarded with great respect and affection
on both sides of the industrial fence. It was one of the largest
funerals ever witnessed in Rhymney. One of the most powerful
formative influences in Tom Jones's upbringing had passed from
the scene.[71]

[69] See Eirene White's account of the family's response in her Epilogue to *RM*,
p.164.

[70] See pp.21–2, above.

[71] *RM*, p.142, and *passim*. Obituary notice in 1893. Enoch's wife, Harriet,
survived him, but does not ever seem to have played a very large part in her
grandson's life.

The family remained a warm close-knit unit, but not without its share of internal strains. This organic oneness was under particular stress during the middle months of 1895 because Tom Jones was a puzzle to the family at this time, and there is a suggestion that his sisters particularly were thoroughly put out by his behaviour in one respect. He broke, rather abruptly, with his Rhymney sweetheart (an old-fashioned word for a relationship conducted in an old-fashioned way) Charlotte Griffiths, who was usually called Lal. The attachment had existed since his early days at college; they were not formally engaged, but there was evidently an understanding of sorts. According to the oral history of the family, Tom Jones's sisters were annoyed at what they regarded as his insensitivity.[72] In the circumstances, some such outcome, although by no means inevitable, was highly likely. During his five years at Aberystwyth, despite the embarrassing question mark raised by mathematics, Tom Jones had developed a great deal intellectually, was much more experienced socially, and had become altogether a more substantial, indeed impressive, personality.[73] Charlotte Griffiths was certainly intelligent, but she remained in Rhymney, living a life inevitably humdrum by comparison. Distance, long months of separation, diverging interests and disparate accomplishments weakened the relationship beyond redemption. The break-up thus appears as a simple response to ineluctable facts. It is an altogether reasonable explanation, and it is the one put forward with a discreet, well-phrased brevity in Tom Jones's published account of the episode.[74]

There was, in fact, rather more to it, although that is not to gainsay the truth of his narrative so far as it goes. His decision to call off the semi-engagement cannot be taken in simple isolation as a cool-headed, sensible recognition of unfortunate circumstances. The situation was much more complex. The fact is that in the

---

[72] Recollections of Eirene White and her cousin Miss Mary McKenzie.

[73] 'When I was in Aber', said R.E. Davies, a contemporary, in 1900, 'Tom Jones was the student of all for whom I had the greatest respect. I still feel him to be one of the finest men I have ever known'. T.J., Class X, Vol.6, No.17.

[74] *Leeks and Daffodils*, pp.87–8. Lal evidently did not feel ill-requited, much less scorned. She was a person of considerable dignity, 'an extremely handsome woman . . . and a strong personality', as Thomas Jones's niece, Miss Mary McKenzie, who knew her, testified. Lal, who lived with her brother, Caleb, who had a small business in Newport, was severely crippled in middle age by rheumatism. Even acute physical pain of that sort could not overcome her spirit. 'She was', says Miss McKenzie, 'a happy person in spite of her infirmity'. She certainly was not soured in any way by the ending of her relationship with Thomas Jones. A year or two later she was on perfectly friendly terms with him and his new wife.

months before he went to Glasgow in October 1895, Tom Jones was
mentally in turmoil, beset by doubt and difficulty about a number
of things central to his life that previously had seemed beyond
question. It was a tangled knot, a concatenation of problems of the
heart and head. It is not surprising that his family were puzzled by
his behaviour at this time, all the more so because, for a variety of
reasons, it was impossible for him to open his mind and heart to
them. Indeed, for some time that would have been difficult with
the most understanding of listeners because Tom Jones himself was
unclear where precisely he stood on some of the issues that
disturbed him. One or two of these perplexities continued to
concern him for a considerable time. However, within a couple of
months of going up to Glasgow, he had come to some decisions
which he relayed home in a long letter to his sister, Liz, in whom, of
all his family, he was most disposed to confide.

He confessed that the breach with Charlotte had caused him
great anguish which he believed would 'hover . . . like a black
cloud' over him for the rest of his life. It had not been a simple
matter of growing incompatibility; there had 'been two great causes
at work producing the breach'. They are worth setting out in his
own words substantially in full

> 1. I have felt recently as never before my obligations to Mamma. As
> you know Dada's health is very precarious. Such men as he are taken
> suddenly. You know too that we are as a family totally unprovided for,
> so that if something happened to him, I should probably have to break
> off college instantly and return to work for Mamma and the others. I
> shall never marry while Mamma lives – so I feel now. True, I ought to
> have seen this long ago, but I did not.

> 2. You know that my views as to the purpose of life and method of
> living have changed very greatly since I commenced to read the Life
> and Writing of Mazzini and some works on Christian Socialism. I do
> not now propose becoming a pastor in the usual way, but am bent on
> living in closer contact with the people . . . You see I cannot look
> forward to any secured salary in such work. Possibly I may have to earn
> my living in some (so-called) secular occupation. At any rate, the
> responsibilities of marriage under such circumstances are too great to
> my mind to justify the step.

He had persuaded himself that he had a commitment to a
celibate life of social service to the underprivileged that his
Aberystwyth Settler friends, for various understandable reasons,
probably would not feel to the same degree. He had gone through

agonies of soul-searching before he reached this lonely state of spiritual exaltation.

> I need not say [he told Liz] how great a grief it has been to me, how great waves of anguish sweep over me. But I have not doubted the wisdom of that step. 'Twas better now than again.[75]

It was not, therefore, that Tom Jones and Charlotte had simply grown apart. A change of his vocational purpose, and, above all, an overwhelming sense of obligation to his family and the need to repay them for their unstinted support, now extended for a further period, accounts for his break with Charlotte.

Later in life, Tom Jones described this promise not to marry as honest but quixotic.[76] There is perhaps something in the idea that when he first went up to Glasgow in October 1895, after all this wearing introspection, he was less than his usual self. There is hardly a hint in the record of his life at this time of his customary impishness, his self-deprecating sense of fun. It seemed all sober, even sombre, high-seriousness; indeed, judged by the long-term pattern of his life, not without an uncharacteristic tendency to take himself rather too seriously.

It should be said, however, that he had not unburdened himself entirely in his letter to his sister. Some things remained unresolved to trouble him. In particular, he was obliged for a year or two longer to wrestle with his conscience over some of his religious beliefs. Meanwhile, he had to buckle down to student life and serious study at Glasgow, where at least he had been given another chance.

---

[75] 17 November 1895. T.J., Class X, Vol.1, No.59.
[76] *Welsh Broth*, p.60.

CHAPTER THREE

GLASGOW · I

GLASGOW brought a renewed zest into Tom Jones's life. The city itself had grown phenomenally during the nineteenth century. In less than a hundred years the population had increased tenfold to over three quarters of a million in 1895. It was then the second city of the British Empire, a great bustling port crammed with ships and shipbuilding, a thriving industrial centre of coal and steel, tobacco manufacturing and large textile, printing and dyeing works and warehouses.[1] The Irish had come over in force, particularly from the 1840s onwards when they were brought across from Belfast at fourpence to sixpence a head. By 1881 they made up nearly a fifth of the population of the city.[2] Glasgow was a great monument to Victorian enterprise and self-confidence. It had many fine buildings, even a splendour of sorts. Its characteristic feature, the three or four-storey tenement, had a certain architectural dignity, at least originally before the blight of urban shabbiness set in on a large scale. But rapid growth and great numbers of people had also brought serious social problems, especially of chronic over-crowding, worse than anywhere else in the United Kingdom, in the closely built working class districts. Here in the four-storey tenements and sordid wynds large families lived in one or two rooms sharing a wholly inadequate number of water taps and lavatories with the crowd of others who lived on the same staircase in an appalling communal squalor.[3] A brutally crude capitalist system, which still retained a powerful dynamic, produced great wealth, but at a considerable cost in poor social conditions, unemployment and abysmally low wages for much of the labour force. Women in particular suffered harshly in the industries in which they were employed from the effects of cut-throat competition and the employers' resort to sweated labour. 'Slavery is

[1] D. Daiches, *Glasgow* (1977), p.179. J.K. McDowall, *The People's History of Glasgow* (Glasgow, 1970), p.109. J.B.S. Gilfillan and H.A. Moisely, 'Industrial and Commercial Developments to 1914', in R. Miller and J. Tivy (ed.), *The Glasgow Region* (Glasgow, 1958), p.187.

[2] J. Tivy, 'Population Distribution and Change', ibid., p.260. D. Daiches, op.cit., p.137.

[3] Ibid., pp.135–6. W. Smart, *Second Thoughts of an Economist* (1916), p.xiii.

a thriving institution here', Tom Jones wrote in his first letter home in November 1895. 'The more one looks about the more one feels the crying need of consecration to social reform'.[4]

It should be said that Glasgow had not lacked municipal leadership or civic pride. Indeed, the Town Council had been busily active since the middle of the century and had taken over the supply of water, gas and electricity and had begun rehousing schemes and a variety of other municipal enterprises.[5] Great pride was legitimately taken in the city's transport system. In July 1894 the new horse-drawn tramcars, owned and operated by the corporation, began to carry passengers, over six million of them in the first few weeks. Within four years there were nearly 40 miles of tramways, which were electrified in 1902 and further extended before 1914. This extensive system was a remarkable model of cheapness and efficiency.[6]

But civic energy notwithstanding, Glasgow's social problems were too many and too great to be easily solved. In time Tom Jones was to make a contribution to alleviating at least some of those truly dreadful conditions, but for the moment the University absorbed most of his attention. The first month had been especially hectic. 'I have been rushed off my feet', he reported home breathlessly.[7] Happily, there had been no trouble about lodgings. He was more than glad to join R.R. Williams, his old Aberystwyth student friend, the musically gifted apprentice minister, who had come up to Glasgow a year before on a Daniel Williams scholarship.[8] Their lodgings, at 57 Clarendon St., Partick, in West Glasgow, were depressingly 'gloomy' and cramped, much less spacious than the 'digs' they had shared in Aberystwyth. Some of the space in their living room was pre-empted by the landlady's massive wardrobe which was forbidden territory to them. During the winter they huddled over wisps of smoke from a pile of coal dust that passed for a fire. They slept in a shared bed in a large cupboard that opened out from the living room. The food was in keeping: a cooked joint on Sundays, and a daily serving of cold mutton for the rest of the week. It was at least cheap, averaging 10/- a week for lodgings and part board, without benefit of laundry. Unfortunately, they felt cold for much of the time, more or less permanently hungry and usually

[4] T.J., Class X, Vol. I, No.59.

[5] *Welsh Broth*, p.40. The Glasgow Improvement Trust and the Glasgow Workmens Dwellings Company were also waging heroic private campaigns against housing squalor. Daiches, op.cit, p.157. Smart, op.cit., pp.xxxvi–xxxvii.

[6] Daiches, op.cit., pp.150–1.

[7] T.J., Class X, Vol.I, No.51.

[8] See above, p.48.

short of energy. The truth was that they were cutting things too fine and simply not eating enough.

They did not blame their landlady. Mrs Paterson was a hard-working, elderly widow who rose each day before 5 a.m. to see her sons off to work. Tom Jones, at first at least, thought she was 'a most perfect landlady', who mercifully had little to say and kept herself to herself. 'Her only weakness', he said, 'which is a national one, is that she cannot see the point of my jokes'.[9] Nor had he managed to make much of the Scots generally as yet. 'The Scottish character is an unexplored region to me. As yet I have discovered only its most obvious features – caution and reserve'. He was glad of R.R. Williams's company.

> Even though [as he said] I know we are very different in many ways. My whole heart rebels instinctively against some views which he unconsciously entertains . . . He has certain hereditary, traditional tendencies to eject from his nature . . . just as, in other directions, [I] have to do the same.

These differences of temperament, upbringing and belief, apparently, led 'often' to sharp debates on social problems. Williams was a staunch, old-style Liberal, Tom Jones's approach was increasingly Fabian and collectivist, even, in the language of the day, socialist. But they were sensitive men, well accustomed to the cut and thrust of undergraduate debate, bound by a mutual respect and affection and a shared sense of humour. Once, for example, they accepted together a challenge to see who could best attract a crowd on Glasgow Green. Tom Jones, masquerading as a Polish refugee, harangued listeners with an impassioned oration in Welsh and broken English. R.R. Williams, who had a superb voice, sang a moving Welsh air, supposedly a lament for their Polish homeland: they could well have taken a substantial collection. Not surprisingly, as Tom Jones concluded, 'we work without discord'. They continued at Mrs Paterson's for that session, and then moved to live together elsewhere. Their friendship lasted a lifetime.[10]

Despite the other deficiencies of their lodgings, they were at least fairly near to the site of Gilmorehill, to which the University had moved in 1870. Founded in 1451, it was the fourth most ancient foundation in the British Isles, preceded only by Oxford, Cambridge, and St Andrews. For centuries it had flourished on a

---

[9] T.J., Class X, Vol.1, No.59, *Welsh Broth*, pp.8–12.

[10] T.J., Class X, Vol.1, No.59. One other potential source of trouble was their differing bio-rhythms. 'He [R.R.] is better at night time than I, but in the morning I am more alert'. The Glasgow Green episode is in *Welsh Broth*, p.78.

site in the High Street near to the cathedral as befitted a creation of the church. In the course of time the need for space had prompted 'hand to mouth' alterations that destroyed much of the beauty of the old building. The surrounding areas too had declined into a degrading malodorous squalor; evening classes in law, for example, had had to be abandoned because of the level of violence in the area and aggressive soliciting by swarms of prostitutes. Eventually, the old site was sold to the City Union Railway Company, which built a goods station on the land.[11] The new rectangular University building at Gilmorehill was erected on a commanding site by Sir George Gilbert Scott, whose vision is generally thought not to have come up to the full range of his opportunity. Tom Jones, for one, thought the building less than inspired, its fussy detail a distraction from the dignity of the whole.[12]

At Aberystwyth in 1890 there had been barely two hundred students all told. At Glasgow in 1895 there were nearly 1,900, of whom women (first admitted in 1892) numbered 246. Students wore scarlet gowns. They could on occasion be boisterously rowdy; in 1896, for example, there was a great 'students' disturbance' in Sauchiehall St.[13] Most of the undergraduates were of modest means and perhaps all the more purposeful for being so. According to Tom Jones, they fell into two categories.

> A large mediocre majority who want a general education with a pass degree at the end of it; and a very small and able minority, who read wide and deep for the honours degree.[14]

Years later, writing in 1950, Thomas Jones with an absurd excess of modesty claimed that there was a third category, 'where I belonged: the modest student trying to do his best'.[15] In fact, he was, or at any rate soon became, an undoubted high flier.

Academic standards at Glasgow were high. The Arts faculty in particular was dominated at this time by a number of distinguished scholars, all of whom took their teaching duties seriously, and were extremely exacting in their requirements from students. Gilbert Murray, the young professor of Greek, appointed from Oxford not long before, had been moved to 'awe and admiration' by some of his colleagues. He liked the general atmosphere of the University, which was full of vigour and public spirit. He found that he had to

[11] D. Daiches, op.cit., p.155. McDowall, op.cit., pp.8–9.

[12] J. Miller, op.cit., p.302, *Welsh Broth*, p.9.

[13] Ibid., p.10. D. Daiches, op.cit., p.177. Introduction (p.vi) by J.B.S. Gilfillan in McDowall, op.cit.

[14] Introduction (p.xxxii) to W. Smart's *Second Thoughts of an Economist* (1916).

[15] *Welsh Broth*, p.14.

work extremely hard with 'interesting pupils' who had been brought up 'to expect good lectures – audible and intelligible at least, and, if possible, interesting'.[16] Tom Jones was taken aback at first by the amount of 'home work', as he called it, that was required. Essays were written regularly, and those of the more promising students were read and criticized by the professor himself. Much preparation for other work was also necessary, for 'all the classes are conducted on the *viva voce* plan'. One could be called upon at random to stand up before a large class and translate from English into Latin; woe betide the ill-prepared or haplessly hesitant! G.G. Ramsey was merciless and devastatingly witty in his public punishments of backsliders. Moreover, 'if one is caught unprepared the negligence is entered down against the student at the end of term'. Few people needed to be bitten more than once. 'It makes me nervous', Tom Jones admitted of this hectoring technique, 'but it will pay'.[17]

A.C. Bradley, professor of English Literature, who turned his training in philosophy to the unravelling of the intricacies of language and thought in poetry, made a different appeal. A very powerful one to Tom Jones, uplifting rather than unsettling. 'To sit under Bradley . . . was to be ever in the presence of transparent truth and honour'.[18] He was a supreme teacher whose subtle use of language in the analysis of character in literature could be enthralling: 'We felt . . . our minds being quietly remade'. Moreover, Bradley was interesting for another more personal reason: he too, as a young man, like Tom Jones, had been deeply influenced by Mazzini.[19] A chair in History at Glasgow had been established in 1893, and the first occupant was Richard Lodge, an authority on Richelieu and author of the much-thumbed volume, *The Close of the Middle Ages*. Lodge was a lively and vigorous lecturer, eloquent and compendiously knowledgeable. He was sufficiently impressed to invite Tom Jones to read for honours in History, but he had already committed himself to Philosophy and Economics.[20]

[16] Gilbert Murray, *An Unfinished Autobiography* (1960), pp.93–8. For an alternative, highly critical view of the quality of students and teaching at Glasgow at this time, see R.H. Tawney, 'Kenneth Leys, 1876–1950' (*The Oxford Magazine*, 9 November 1950), pp.104–10. 'Pray for me, as I begin on Monday at 10', Leys, then an assistant in History at Glasgow, wrote in 1906, 'to a crowded room of very raw men and women, some rude and nearly all quite indifferent to the subject'.

[17] T.J., Class X, Vol.1, No.59. Thomas Jones's Introduction (pp.xxxii–xxxiii) to W. Smart op.cit., *Welsh Broth*, pp.15–16.

[18] T.J., Class X, Vol.1, No.59.

[19] See below, p.121.

[20] *Welsh Broth*, p.26.

Henry Jones, Professor of Philosophy, who occupied the chair once held by Adam Smith, was a remarkable man by any standards. His influence on the life of Tom Jones was so important that some fuller consideration of him is called for. Henry Jones was born in an upland village in Denbighshire in 1852, the son of a poor shoemaker. He left school before he was thirteen and was at first apprenticed to his father. Thereafter, his education was an heroic struggle against overwhelming difficulties which, ultimately, he won triumphantly in almost fairytale fashion. The combination of first-rate ability and dauntless determination took him via scholarships to Bangor Normal College, and after a brilliantly successful interlude as a schoolteacher, when his local reputation almost trebled the school roll, to Glasgow University on a Daniel Williams Scholarship. Once there, his talent blossomed under the influence, especially, of the distinguished philosopher Edward Caird, the future Master of Balliol. Henry Jones was awarded a first class in Philosophy, and collected a number of valuable prize scholarships, one of which gave him four years in Germany, which was then the chief fount of philosophical enquiry in the world. After a short period at the college in Aberystwyth where he was unhappily caught between Aberystwyth's desperate struggle to exist and the emerging threat of a new college at Bangor, Henry Jones was appointed to professorships at Bangor, St Andrews and, ultimately, in 1894, to Caird's prestigious chair at Glasgow.[21]

Henry Jones was to achieve a considerable reputation as a philosopher, although he never quite fulfilled his early promise, not least because of the diffusion of his interest and energies in an astonishing range of other activities, most of them of great public worth especially in relation to Wales. He was quite unable to heed Edward Caird's plea that he should 'resist the pressure . . . on him to be useful in all directions'.[22] Henry Jones's greatest talent undoubtedly was his ability as a teacher. He too, in common with most of his colleagues at Glasgow at that time, 'worked his classes very hard', and although sympathetic to those who were sick or otherwise unfortunate he 'was merciless to mere slackness'.[23] He

[21] Thomas Jones, 'Sir Henry Jones, C.H.', in *A Theme With Variations*, pp.85–91. E.L. Ellis, *The University College of Wales, Aberystwyth. 1872–1972* (Cardiff, 1972), pp.75–6, for the Aberystwyth episode.

[22] R.B. Haldane, no mean judge of a philosopher, said that Jones 'could not be a great philosopher plus all the other things he was. Had he concentrated on philosophy he would have made a great name'. T.J., Class Z, Diary (1923), p.61. Caird's comment is cited in Thomas Jones, 'Sir Henry Jones C.H.', loc.cit.

[23] H.J.W. Hetherington, *The Life and Letters of Sir Henry Jones* (1924), p.77.

insisted on high standards and forced his students to examine vast demanding questions. The first essay he set for Thomas Jones in his first year Moral Philosophy class, for example, required him to determine the relationship of Metaphysics and Ethics. This class met five days a week at 8 a.m.; some of those present had left home before six o'clock. The class numbered 160–190 who invariably listened with 'perfect attention'; often there was singing as the class assembled. Promptly at 8 a.m. Henry Jones would appear; after a short prayer the roll was called and the lecture would begin. Henry Jones, who paced up and down the rostrum, made the lecture room 'a place of inquiry', though there was no shortage of fun and playfulness either. He did not purvey certitudes, he believed that there was 'no thinking where there was no doubt'.[24] He was scrupulously fair in his treatment of philosophers, Bentham, Mill and Herbert Spencer for example, with whom he did not agree. Meantime, as Tom Jones said, he induced 'you to work your own mind, such as it is, to the utmost'. Tom Jones was soon assigned a more mundane duty.

> Before many weeks had gone by, I was charged by him with the task of arresting his eloquence by dangling his watch to catch his eye five minutes before the lecture was due to stop.

Only thus could the hour-long weekday 'quest for truth, goodness and beauty' be temporarily halted. Afterwards some of the students would be taken to the professor's home for breakfast. At the end of it all students left 'braced' to continue their studies.[25] Subsequently, Tom Jones went on to read for honours under Henry Jones. These classes were small, ten or a dozen students at most, and the professor's effect was in consequence all the greater; students participated fully and were amply practised in philosophical reasoning.[26] A year or two later, in 1900, Thomas Jones described the influence Henry Jones had exerted on him. The professor used to say that he himself had been 'born in Wales, and born again in Edward Caird's class'. Tom Jones would not go quite that far:

> I would hardly put it so strong in my case, but would say that Henry Jones completed [in his philosophy classes] the work which Mazzini commenced . . . I owe a lot to Henry Jones. He helped me to

[24] Ibid., pp.73–5.
[25] Thomas Jones, 'Sir Henry Jones', *Y Cymmrodor*, Vol.XXXII, p.175.
[26] H.J.W. Hetherington, op.cit., p.80.

rationalize my own vague natural instincts and the passionate ideals which I had imbibed from Mazzini.

Henry Jones's philosophical position was

> Hegelianism as represented by Caird, F.H. Bradley, Bosanquet . . . though H.J. is no slavish follower of any of these. It is the sworn foe of Herbert Spencer, Leslie Stephen, Sidgwick . . . and of materialists and institutionalists and Utilitarians of all sorts. Balfour, Romanes and the High Churchmen who proclaim the impotence of Reason and take refuge in Faith as a religious Sense exalted on high beyond the reach of secular criticism H.J. is never weary of denouncing. He is a most inspiring teacher and often in his class one feels thrilled with visions of the spiritual meaning of the world. You will see [he told his future wife] how these regulating ideas of his teaching harmonise and enrich my Squatter [i.e. Settlement] aspirations.[27]

This powerful intellectual and spiritual mentorship was no transient thing. It continued long afterwards and was buttressed by their increasingly close friendship over subsequent years. 'I feel', wrote Tom Jones in 1911, 'that in you [I] have one who never fails . . . in the crucial decisions of life. I can only promise to try to be loyal to the inspiration of the old moral [philosophy] classroom'.[28]

Equally influential, although in much less an intellectual way, was William Smart, Professor of Political Economy. Although much more than merely respectable as a scholar, Smart was not in the same intellectual class as Bradley, Ramsey, Gilbert Murray and Adamson, the aggressively clever Professor of Logic at Glasgow. Smart was not an original thinker, but he was an excellent expositor, on paper as well as orally in the classroom. Unlike many economists, as Tom Jones commented years later approvingly, 'he did not think in equations and then convert his algebraical thoughts into tortuous and turgid prose'. Indeed, 'he never wrote a paragraph' that was 'not intelligible to an educated layman'. This clarity was essential, particularly for Thomas Jones who was prone to doze off in the classroom in the afternoon, because Smart's class met at 'the sleepy hour of 2 pm'. Smart, who had had an early career in his father's engineering business, was glad to escape into academic life in which he revelled. 'I thank God every day that it has fallen to me to be an economist', he once wrote. And in 1910,

[27] T.J., Class X, Vol.6, No.6. He was, however, not being brainwashed. His work in Theology earlier had given him 'some ballast wherewith to withstand the sweeping tide of [Henry Jones's] eloquence'. Ibid., No.22.

[28] 18 December 1911. T.J., Class U, Vol.1, No.5.

when he was asked to stand for Parliament, he insisted that he loved his professional life just as it was: 'I would not, in fact, change it to be Prime Minister and Andrew Carnegie rolled into one'.

Tom Jones read for honours in Economics, or Political Economy as it was then more sensibly called. Smart's teaching was in the tradition of Adam Smith and John Stuart Mill, intermingling scientific methods, practical aims, and social ideals. The teaching in the pass class leaned heavily on T.H. Marshall's *Economics of Industry,* with the theory of value as its spinal column. In the honours class there was some specialization in finance and taxation, but a considerable emphasis too on contemporary socio-economic problems, local and national. Smart and his students occupied no ivory tower. It was impossible to have the city out of one's mind in the Economics classroom in Glasgow.

> The clang of the hammers on the Clyde mingled with the professor's voice as you sat on the benches. Through the windows you saw the smoking chimneys of factory and foundry.

There was no escape into the abstractions of pure theory where industrial reality was so noisily at hand.[29]

Tom Jones had the strongest possible reason to be grateful to Smart, a debt he fully acknowledged. He had however become aware, and could not forbear observing, that the professor's early enthusiasm for the teaching of John Ruskin, 'whom he thought a preacher of righteousness', had 'paled somewhat with advancing years and increasing possessions'.

Smart had the utmost confidence in his pupil. 'He has thrown me into I don't know how many pools believing I could swim', Tom Jones wrote in 1900. No simple believer in market forces, Smart was a persuasive exponent of enlightened capitalism. However, after five years' exposure to his teaching, Jones could write, 'I don't think he has seriously shaken my Fabian faith'. A very strong rapport gradually developed between pupil and teacher, and Smart, in so many kindly ways, continued as the 'generous patron' whose countenance was eventually to open up professional opportunities to his protégé that altered the course of his life.[30]

At Glasgow, as at Aberystwyth previously, Tom Jones was busily active outside as well as inside the classroom. So much so indeed, that among his intimates he was affectionately nicknamed

----

[29] This account is drawn largely from Thomas Jones's affectionate biographical notice in his preface to Smart's *Second Thoughts of an Economist.*.

[30] T.J., Class X, Vol.6, No.6.

'perpetual motion'.[31] He was, of course, twenty-five years old when he went to Glasgow and not lacking in confidence or political purpose. During his first term in 1895, according to *University Jottings,* he was said to have 'highly distinguished' himself in the debate at the Dialectic Society, the University's premier student society modelled in form and tone, like the Oxford Union, on the House of Commons.[32]

In those first weeks, too, he had attended a meeting of the Christian Socialist League at the Gordon Hall to hear Ronald Burrows, who was then Gilbert Murray's assistant in Classics, speak on 'Why Christians must be Socialists'. Tom Jones was inspired by the address and 'was burning to speak' in the ensuing discussion, but thought it wiser, 'as a fresher', to stay silent. After the meeting, however, he did join the League which was open to all 'who desired the ethics of Christ applied to economic, political and social problems'. A year later Jones was on the committee of the League, and gave an address on 'Community Life and Social Problems'.[33]

Within weeks of arriving in Glasgow in 1895, he had joined the Partick branch of the Independent Labour Party. His signed Declaration of Adherence stated that he believed

The interests of Labour are paramount to and must take precedence of all other interests, and that the advancement of these interests must be sought by political and constitutional action.[34]

Even more boldly in that first session, quite independently he proposed the formation of a University branch of the Fabian Society, of which he was elected secretary. 'It has proved', he wrote five years later, 'the focus of a good deal of earnest reading and discussion, and has probably exercised some influence on the average student'.[35] In the following session, Sidney Webb, who was the first Honorary President of the branch, came up to speak and was followed a month later by Tom Jones, re-elected secretary, who gave an address on 'The Revolt of Religion'.[36] He was bursting with

[31] R.H. Tawney in the *Manchester Guardian,* 18 March 1952.

[32] T.J., Class X, Vol.1, No.72. In the following session he and R.R. Williams were elected to the Dialectic Society's committee. Ibid., No.61.

[33] T.J. Class X, Vol. 1, No.59 and ibid., Vol.2, No.14.

[34] 13 December 1895. T.J., Class X, Vol.2, No.1. In December 1895 he paid fivepence, and in February 1896 ninepence in branch dues..

[35] 11 February 1900. T.J., Class X, Vol.6, No.6. R.R. Williams, following a different route, was elected to the committee of the University Liberal Club a year or two later.

[36] Ibid., Vol.2, No.15.

energy and ideas that could not be contained within the University Fabian Society. 'I have mixed up a good deal in all sorts of working class organisations in the city, and got some experience not obtainable in Aberystwyth', he wrote in 1900. Particularly valuable in this respect was his work for the Scottish Co-operative for Women's Trades that had its head-quarters in Glasgow. This involved the detailed investigation of conditions in 'the badly paid trades, preparing bills to remedy the more obvious iniquities', and some missionary lecturing on behalf of the Co-operative.[37]

But his major contribution on the social front during these years was his work at the University Settlement. This had been established in 1889 on the initiative of Henry Drummond of the Free Church College and Professor Smart after the latter had visited Canon Barnett at Toynbee Hall in Whitechapel. There was certainly room and need for such a venture: Glasgow's social problems were, if anything, worse than those of the East End of London. In 1892 the Glasgow Settlement moved to new quarters in Possil Road in a slum area close to the old site of the University. In 1896 R.R. Williams and Tom Jones, after dutifully completing a session in their dingy lodgings, went to live in the Settlement. The residents were nearly all students 'making for the ministry', in Tom Jones's phrase, members of the Established Church or evangelical Free Churchmen. Residents paid their own way: Tom Jones's expenses in fact went up to 14/- a week, but at least he and Williams had better rooms and a more filling diet than in their lodgings. Around them lay a mass of misery and squalor in the slum tenements. Tom Jones was allotted a six-storey staircase which had forty-four families, each one living in the confines of one room. Conditions were heartbreaking: 'one would need the hide of a rhinoceros', he wrote, 'to be indifferent to the misery around us'. It is impossible to determine how much the ministrations of the student settlers did to mitigate the miseries of the living conditions the tenement population had to endure. The Workmen's Club (of which Tom Jones was President in 1897–8) attached to the Settlement was open six nights a week from 7 to 10 p.m. It at least offered a refuge from overcrowded homes; there were occasional lectures, musical evenings, and of course a Burns Night.[38] Many people doubtless were indifferent to the overtures. Even so, the Settlement was infinitely worthwhile: it indicated concern, offered

[37]   Ibid., Vol.6, No.6.
[38]   Ibid., Vol.2, No.22. In 1884, according to John Bright, 100,000 people in Glasgow lived in one-roomed homes.

help of a sort and kindled and nourished hope, at least for some people.[39]

Tom Jones put his back into his work at the Settlement. It is clear, for example, that during the three years he lived there he put more time and energy into his social welfare and mission work than he did into his political activities, multifarious as they were.[40] It is also evident that the material welfare of the poor came higher on his list of priorities as a settler than their conversion to a formal religious commitment. Most of the student settlers did not agree with him, although some three or four of them shared his views. Crucially, the Warden, William Boyd, took the orthodox view. Eventually, these 'differences in "ideals" of what a Settlement should be', as he described the disagreement, led Tom Jones and the other dissidents to leave the Settlement in the spring of 1899. There was no acrimony: those who 'differed from the Warden' had done so 'in a friendly way'. Indeed, even after his departure, Tom Jones returned regularly 'to talk to the Bible class'.[41] In 1899 he succeeded R.R. Williams as President of the University Christian Association. The 'predominant tone' of the Association was strongly evangelical, but the new President used his influence 'to widen the scope' of the topics discussed and several meetings, as he said, were 'devoted to social problems, Settlements, and so forth'. But despite his manful efforts over three years at the Possil Road Settlement, it could hardly be said that his achievement there had quite lived up to the high hopes that he had cherished for his social mission work. Moreover, the unity of the old 'Squatter band' that he had led at Aberystwyth had been broken up by the disruptive effects of separation, the pull of careers and in some cases the overriding demands of marriage.[42] But Thomas Jones's connection with Settlement work was by no means over. Other times and other places were to give him many more opportunities for service in welfare work of that kind, although he was never again to be so closely involved personally at the immediate point of need. And of course he was never able to achieve that complete abnegation of self in a life of service that, perhaps extravagantly, he had aspired to originally.

[39] Thomas Jones in *Second Thoughts of an Economist*, pp.xx–xxxix. *Welsh Broth*, pp.12–13.

[40] T.J., Class X, Vol.6, No.6.

[41] Ibid. It is not entirely clear where R.R. Williams stood in this particular dispute. 'R.R., and I are just as ever, tho' differing widely in our views', Tom Jones wrote in general terms in the same letter.

[42] Ibid.

It is hardly surprising that this incessant round of politics and welfare work on top of long hours of study should exact a physical toll. Towards the end of the session in May 1898 he felt utterly jaded. It was evident to a friendly deacon, with whom he stayed during a weekend preaching engagement at Seacombe in the Wirral, that the young man was thoroughly run down. A bracing voyage of convalescence on a tramp steamer, dirt cheap at five shillings a day plus a few pounds for miscellaneous expenses, was suggested and quickly arranged. It was to be an exhilarating experience, one of the best holidays he ever had. On 12 May, accompanied by a friend, Lewis Miles of Aberdare, he set sail from Barry as a passenger in the small tramp steamer the *Isle of Anglesey* bound for Genoa. The trip began discouragingly, he was repeatedly seasick. But there were compensations. The captain, a forty-year-old Aberystwyth man named Jones, who had gone to sea at the age of twelve, was a character.

> He knows a number of Welsh 'Penillion' of the tap-room type [Tom Jones reported home] but will pass into 'O Fryniau Caersalem' or 'Gad im deimlo' as smoothly as his ship glides through a calm sea. He swears, like all captains, but [saving grace] not more than is necessary and then only for emphasis.

The first mate, Mr Edwards, was also an Aberystwyth man.

> He weighs [said Tom Jones] anything you like after twenty stone and makes a difference in the ship's ballast . . . he has been thirty years on the rolling deep and [so he claimed] shipwrecked four times.

Tom Jones saw little of the crew in the forecastle. 'The fear of fleas has kept me out of it so far', he said rather prissily. As they sailed southwards at 200 miles or so a day out of touch with land and news of the great world, three questions exercised his interest. How was Mr Gladstone, who was ailing? 'How goes the [Spanish-American] war?', and what was happening in the great coal strike in south Wales? – in particular what effect had it had on the Rhymney Iron Company? He needed as much distraction as possible for he continued to be seasick every day. So much, he concluded, for the Mediterranean's reputation as a gentle and lovely sea. 'Hang the Mediterranean! What care I what the poets have sung'.[43] But it was all to be more than thoroughly worthwhile,

---

[43] Ibid., Vol.1, No.66. There is some additional detail in *Welsh Broth*, pp.50–1.

for at last they reached Genoa, birthplace of his hero Mazzini. The local boatmen, however, were less than admirable.

> The Genovese can give points to the Jews in the matter of bargaining [he wrote]. As the Engineer says, let them know you're an Englishman [or even a Welshman masquerading as, or passing for one, apparently], and on goes half-a-crown.[44]

He was not to be put off. Indeed, he was so exhilarated by Genoa that for the one and only time in his life he forgot his hatred of drink long enough to become pleasantly tipsy on wine in the company of Captain Jones and the Chief Engineer, whose inclinations on going ashore ran to 'wine shops' rather than an uplifting tour of the cathedral and the *palazzi* of the city.

> I remained quite clear-headed and able to contemplate my legs objectively [Tom Jones wrote fifty years later of 'this unique experience'], but I had some difficulty in planting one foot in front of the other firmly on the pavement, each leg was inflated and as uncontrollable as a balloon.

The next day, he set off alone to visit Mazzini's birthplace and pay homage at his dignified, unadorned grave. What followed was rather less than solemn. *Welsh Broth* includes an hilarious account of Tom Jones's subsequent attempt to get the inscription on a tablet in memory of Mazzini at the University translated. The pidgin English of the only available cicerone could make nothing of the inscription. Ultimately, in desperation, he made do with the help of a passing professor who knew no English but offered his services in Latin, of which Tom Jones then had a rather uncertain grasp. Still, in spite of the touches of farce, he felt he had 'learned a great deal' about Mazzini by communing even thus imperfectly with the shade of his hero.[45]

Five days later the *Isle of Anglesey* left Genoa for Chanak in Turkey. The cargo of coal had been off-loaded and the ship set off for the eastern Mediterranean to take on a return freight. Tom Jones's seasickness was now less troublesome as the ship passed through the Straits of Messina, skirted Cape Matapan and threaded its way around the clusters of Greek islands in the Aegean. At any

---

[44] T.J., Class X, Vol.1, No.67.

[45] *Welsh Broth*, pp.51–2. T.J., Class X, Vol.1, Nos.67, 68. The 'pilgrimage', as he called it, induced him to be more charitable towards Roman Catholics. 'They ought not to be lumped together as all and equally frauds and humbugs. Surely they deserve our helpful pity rather than our proud contempt'.

rate, he now spent the time lazing in the sun on the upper deck reading the novels of Thackeray and Meredith, and later, nudged by a touch of conscience, the Acts of the Apostles. He spent a pleasant day ashore at Chanak, but, disappointingly, although he got ashore at Constantinople the next day for an hour or two, he was denied a sight of St Sophia and the other Byzantine glories of that ancient city by nervous officials driven to wariness in their dealings with foreigners by the horrific massacre of Armenians that had taken place in the streets of Constantinople a short time before. The *Isle of Anglesey* went through the Black Sea to drop anchor in the Taganrog Roads, where over four hectic days a cargo of Russian wheat, delivered by wretchedly ill-paid coolie-style labour, was taken on board. Ships such as the *Isle of Anglesey* had to wait upon the often unpredictable convenience of their customers and a long delay at Malta seemed likely, so Tom Jones and his friend Miles got a passage home via Gibraltar and Rotterdam in the SS *Craigmore*, which was laden with timber.[46]

He returned home early in July refreshed and reinvigorated and was soon as busy as ever. He resumed his political activity immediately. Late in August 1898 he asked to be allowed to hold a socialist meeting in the schoolroom of a large Methodist chapel in Porth. In support of his application he argued, not altogether convincingly, that if the request were refused they would perhaps be driven to hold the meeting in a public house. This was tartly dismissed. 'I don't see any necessity for going to a public house', the chapel elder wrote in reply, 'as you say, any association with the drink traffic does not seem consistent in a Society which has the welfare of humanity as its aim!'. There was also the difficulty, as the spokesman pointed out, that 'we have diverse opinions in our Church re politics, hence the difficulty to open the door to hold such meetings!'. For his part, the elder thought that religious buildings were 'for worship' not politics, even if 'many' of those who would attend the meeting derived their political views from the New Testament. Despite this unpromising response, Tom Jones persisted with the application. It was brought formally before the chapel members early in September and flatly rejected, even though the elders, as they said, were sorry to have to refuse such an old friend.[47] It did one's reputation very little good in those days, even in south Wales, to be known as a socialist. Still less so for an aspiring Nonconformist pastor, as Tom Jones still was nominally.

---

[46] Tom Jones's detailed log of the voyage is in Class Y, Vol.1, No.3.

[47] John and Charles Morgan to T.J., 30 August and 12 September 1898. T.J., Class X, Vol.2, Nos.24 and 26.

Those were the days of the 'furtive beginnings, the despised infancy', in Tom Jones's words, of the Labour movement which was forced to hold its meetings wherever it could. One important inaugural regional meeting was held in a coffee house in Caerphilly, others took place in obscure church or co-operative halls. On occasion, there was nothing for it but to meet out of doors. The first meeting of the Rhymney Socialist Society was held in a cricket field at twilight.[48]

Despite the risk of becoming a marked man, at least in respectable religious circles, Tom Jones played a prominent part in these political activities. In the 1890s he took the initiative in arranging tours of 'the slumbering valleys of south Wales' by the propaganda vans of Robert Blatchford's *Clarion*.[49] Even more boldly, in the late 1890s he shared platforms, indoors and out, in south Wales with the redoubtable Tom Mann, secretary of the ILP and a vigorous exponent of an aggressive labourism even if he had not yet become a syndicalist and a crypto-Marxist.[50]

However daring this activity and these associations were in the circumstances of that time for a man so placed, Tom Jones was never at any time a believer in class war. The turn of the century, the years of the birth and youth of the Labour movement, were for him 'a thrilling time of splendid hopes'. He looked forward to the day, which he fervently believed was not too far distant, when poverty was eliminated, ugliness in the world and war had become things of the past. In 1896 he seems to have considered joining sometime in the future one or other of the small socialist communes then in existence in different parts of England. He was sent an account of a 'Free Communist and Cooperative Colony' at Forest Hall, Newcastle. This venture in land colonization, based on market gardening and grain growing, involved twenty-four men, women and children. It scarcely accorded with Tom Jones's interests or previous experience. He also enquired about a small socialist commune of four men and two women established at Clay Pit Lane, Leeds. This was not dedicated to any definite ideal; residents went out to teach or work at their trades during the daytime, a woman came in daily to cook and clean. Weekly costs to the residents averaged 12/-, there were no formal rules, matters of common concern were settled at informal meetings. 'We find our life cheaper, pleasanter and more satisfactory generally than when

[48] *Welsh Broth*, pp.29–31.
[49] T.J. Class Y, Vol.3, No.4.
[50] *Welsh Broth*, pp.35–6.

we lived in isolated homes', reported Mary Laslet, who replied to Tom Jones's letter.[51]

But this sort of closed or semi-detached society, devoid of specific purpose or a commitment to social service, had no attraction for Tom Jones. His sights were on the wider British world and the real prospects of effecting striking social improvements on a nation-wide scale. 'We were the light bringers', he wrote of this time, 'music makers, dreamers of dreams, movers and shakers, prophesying to the old with Messianic fervour the message of a new world coming'.[52] It was not a revolutionary world, certainly not a bloody one in any way, that he presaged. Writing in 1951 of those years he claimed that he stood then no further to the left politically than was indicated by his membership of the Fabian Society. And he was not thereby applying a gloss to hide an immoderacy as a young man that in ultra-respectable old age he had come to regret. It is possible to identify in some considerable detail the political views Tom Jones held at that time. His papers include a long article entitled 'What is Socialism?' that was published in the *Scottish Guardian* on 23 June 1899. The piece was written by 'a Glasgow Fabian', and there is no doubt that this was Thomas Jones for the proof copy carries amendments in his hand and the internal evidence of the language and the arguments of the article support this conclusion overwhelmingly. It is worthwhile quoting at some length.

The introductory paragraphs are unexceptional enough and include passages that were common form in the socialist gospel of the day. He agrees with those socialists whose analysis of British society confirmed Matthew Arnold's description of it: 'an upper class materialised, a middle class vulgarised, a lower class brutalised'. Jones asserts that the problems of society are 'mainly economic in origin', and the current industrial system fosters 'the degradation of labour, the exaltation of idleness'. There is 'the waste of competition, of unemployment, of commercial crises', and an 'absence of any lofty ideal for the individual and for the State'. Only the emancipation of land and industrial capital from individual and class ownership and their transference to 'the community for the general benefit' will bring about a fair and just society.

The remainder of the article is rather more interesting. Socialism, he claims, to disarm objection, has grown out of 'its early crudities'. There are of course some socialists who misguidedly

---

[51] T.J., Class X, Vol.2, Nos.16, 17 and 18.
[52] *Welsh Broth*, p.33.

cling to those old hyperboles but he makes his position clear with some half dozen or so 'disclaimers'.

1) Socialism does not involve a revolution, sudden and sanguinary ... It is the application to industry of the principles of democracy ...

2) Socialism does not aim at reducing all men to 'a dead level of equality'.

Socialists are thus [and here surely is the fruit of the teaching of his mentor, Henry Jones]

the truest individualists. They oppose the sacrifice of the individual to the special development of a class ...

4) Socialism is not incompatible with private property; it is only the property used as capital, and that only when it is harmful to the welfare of the community, that it objects to [an echo perhaps here and below of William Smart's teaching].

5) Socialists disclaim the economics of Karl Marx, as they do many of the doctrines of Adam Smith. It was not always so, and echoes of exploded heresies linger in certain quarters. But a socialist who knows his business plants himself on the theory of rent and the theory of value as expounded by standard economists like Jevons and Marshall.

6) Socialism is not bound up exclusively with one political party, although there is one party, the I.L.P., exclusively bound up with it ... [that is] Socialism as the gradual process outlined above.

He adds an addendum of his own.

7) Socialism is an economic theory of social reconstruction, but it is not unrelated to ethics and religion. Many of its most earnest adherents are so because they think socialism postulates a profoundly moral conception of civic life and industry.

He insisted that 'a system which is economically unjust cannot be ethically right'. He was prepared to assert the 'affinity of socialism and Christianity'; indeed, his purpose in life was 'the realisation of the Kingdom of God on earth'.[53]

There was in all this not the slightest sight or sound of the

<hr />

[53] T.J., Class X, Vol.2, No.30. As he wrote more succinctly in *Welsh Broth* (p.31): 'We were striving to bring the economic and religious factors into a right relationship'.

tumbrils, but not much appreciation either of the tremendous resistant power of the established political and economic order. It is Utopian Socialism *par excellence*. Five years later Tom Jones was to define his ideal of British trade unionism in similar high-toned ethical terms that rose well above the level of mere wage bargaining.[54]

His life at this time remained incessantly, almost frantically, busy. In addition to his political activity in Glasgow and south Wales as a member of the Fabian Society and the ILP, there was also his social mission work that continued although he no longer lived in the University Settlement. He remained active in the Christian Socialist League, and it will be remembered that in 1899 he succeeded to the presidency of the University Christian Association. Moreover, there were chapel services to attend, usually with R.R. Williams, and famous Scottish preachers to be heard and appraised in the accustomed way of the Welsh connoisseur. And of course he still fulfilled preaching engagements himself as occasion arose. It is, however, to be noticed that his attendance at chapel in Glasgow was not now so regular as formerly, and that less and less of his preaching was done in Welsh chapels for reasons (which will appear) that had nothing to do with the fact that for much of the year he lived far away from Wales. His religious faith in fact was under considerable strain at this time, although it was nowhere near breaking point.

Meantime, he continued, with great advantage, to widen the range of his experience. On the recommendation of Professor Smart, who thought him 'a finished and polished writer', Jones was invited to review books on economics for the *Glasgow Herald*. Also by invitation, he joined the 'Forty Club', which had a membership of young doctors, lawyers, accountants and journalists, together with three university students, who met every fortnight to discuss matters of public interest.[55] In a modest way he was making a name for himself in influential circles in Glasgow. In the autumn of 1899 he was invited to lecture on economic subjects to a class of thirty-five young men in their twenties and thirties at the Athenaeum, a 'sort of polytechnic', as Jones described it. It had grown out of the Glasgow commercial college and had transferred to new premises dignified by a handsome frontage in Buchanan Street in 1888.[56] Here, once a week, Tom Jones lectured to young men studying for professional qualifications in banking and accountancy. Even more

[54] See below, pp.104–5.
[55] T.J., Class X, Vol.1, No.76; Vol.6, No.6.
[56] Ibid. For the Athenaeum, see McDowall, op.cit., p.59.

encouragingly, at the same time he had also begun to do some teaching at the University itself. By now, William Smart had developed a golden opinion of his pupil.

Mr. Jones [the professor wrote in June 1900] is the most promising student I ever had; and in constant intercourse with him I see the promise fulfilling itself . . . He has an infinite capacity and love of work [and a] neat, methodical, business-like way of doing his work . . . He is a man of high ideals . . . but I have never known his sympathies warp his judgments.[57]

In March the year before, Smart had invited Tom Jones to act as his private assistant at a stipend of fifty pounds a year. He was required to set and mark essays and examination papers for students reading for the MA degree in Economics together with 'any other work incidental to the class'. Smart also wanted Jones to do some lecturing for him 'if permitted by the Court'.[58] This was a golden opportunity that Tom Jones naturally accepted with enthusiasm. There was, however, one embarrassing snag. Although in all other respects he was a paragon of academic virtue, he had not yet managed to take his degree and thereby was, as he ruefully admitted, 'disbarred' by the University Court from lecturing to Smart's students. Once again the stumbling block was his implacable enemy mathematics.[59] Latin had caused some difficulty, but had been eventually overcome. Mathematics formidably remained, but at least now in stark isolation. Finally, with the aid of some expert private coaching, at long last in 1900, the examiners in mathematics were persuaded to agree that they were satisfied. This meant that he could now take his degree. The delay occasioned by mathematics aside, it was a glorious triumph. He came first in Moral Philosophy in a class of 140, and first in Economics out of 70 candidates. In History he was placed third (out of 40) and was ranked eighth in an English class of 125. On the basis of this fine all-around demonstration of quality, he was awarded a Clark scholarship at Glasgow worth £50, and, twice as valuable financially, a Bertrand Russell studentship tenable for a term at the London School of Economics.[60]

[57] T.J., Class X, Vol.1, No.76.

[58] Ibid., Class W, Vol.17, No.212.

[59] Gilbert Murray (op.cit., p.85) too had had problems with mathematics. 'It was a joy to think that I should never, as far as man could foresee, have to face another examination in that subject', he wrote after scraping through in the general entrance examination at Oxford in the 1880s.

[60] T.J., Class X, Vol.6, No.6. *Welsh Broth*, p.55

Tom Jones accordingly spent the early summer weeks from May 1900 onwards most profitably at the LSE. Beatrice Webb, perfectionist and waspish critic, considered the School, then five years old, 'extremely imperfect: its reputation better than its performance'.[61] There were in fact some outstanding scholars and teachers there at that time, some of them vigorous exponents of ideas radically different from those Tom Jones had come to accept. W.A.S. Hewins, the Director of the LSE, for example, considered by most contemporary political economists to be reactionary, was shortly to emerge as an uncompromising imperialist and a leading supporter of Joseph Chamberlain's campaign for tariff reform. Tom Jones, along with his mentor Smart, was and remained an ardent free trader. Edwin Cannan, not yet a professor but the effective head of the Economics department, was an especially severe critic of the classical economists. His actual delivery of lectures was poor, but he had a compensating mordant wit, and would have appealed to Tom Jones because he too had a strong dislike of the mathematical approach to economics and believed, as did William Smart, that economic truth could and should be expressed in language intelligible to the layman. Tom Jones also sat at the feet of Graham Wallas, one of the Fabian Essayists of 1889, a pioneer thinker in political psychology, an excellent teacher much concerned with what he considered to be the unrealized dangers to the delicate fabric of democracy then emerging in Britain. Tom Jones, whose intellectual curiosity was never less than avid all his life, was immensely stimulated by these classes he attended during the weeks of his studentship in London.[62]

But in terms of personal interest and experience, far and away the greatest boon was that during these weeks in London he stayed at 10 Aldelphi Terrace, where George Bernard Shaw and his new wife, Charlotte, had an upstairs flat. In this way Tom Jones came to meet and know one of the great characters and fascinating personalities (in the old, not the present-day trivial sense) of modern times.[63] Subsequently, they remained in intermittent contact on a friendly and mutually appreciative footing. In April of the following year, Tom Jones rounded off his career as a student at Glasgow when he took a First in the Honours School of Economics

[61] 20 February 1900. *The Diary of Beatrice Webb*, Vol. II, 1892–1905, ed. N. and J. MacKenzie (1986), p.171.

[62] *Welsh Broth*, p.56.

[63] In 1893, not surprisingly, Shaw had not yet come up to Beatrice Webb's demanding standards: 'he is not yet a personality', she wrote on 17 September 1893 (*Diary*, II, p.37), 'he is merely a pleasant though somewhat incongruous group of qualities'.

and Philosophy. It had been a long haul of almost ten years' duration since he had left Rhymney for Aberystwyth. Of course his vulnerability in mathematics accounted for much of the delay, but a good deal, too, was a matter of his own choice, as he freely admitted. 'I have allowed other things to bulk too largely and postpone my graduation', he wrote in February 1900 on the eve of another almost despairing, but mercifully this time successful, assault on mathematics.[64]

Although his apprenticeship had been an unduly long one, made possible by the willing sacrifice of his family, it had all been very worthwhile. Ultimately, as those at home, despite repeated disappointment, had believed all along, he had distinguished himself academically and done them proud. Some of the family, however, were rather less certain of some other developments in the life of their son and brother at this time. To their surprise, indeed consternation, he had told them that he had fallen in love and was thinking of marriage. Moreover, it was now clear that he would not become a Methodist pastor. Indeed, one or two of the family even wondered if his religious faith itself was quite as rock solid as it had been formerly.

[64] T.J., Class X, Vol.6, No.6.

CHAPTER FOUR

MARRIAGE

THE LOVE affair that prompted such dismay among the family in Rhymney had developed with a startling, indeed irresistible, speed during 1901. Its origins, however, lay some years back when Tom Jones was a student at Aberystwyth. The establishment in October 1892 of a Day Training Department for elementary school teachers drew a number of English women students to the Welsh college. Among them was Eirene Theodora Lloyd, a Liverpool girl who celebrated her seventeenth birthday on 7 December 1892, a few weeks after her arrival. Her father, Dr R.J. Lloyd, knew Aberystwyth well. He had been shortlisted for the chair of English there in 1886 and had acted as *locum tenens* for a term until C.H. Herford, the successful applicant, was able to take up the appointment in 1887. Moreover, in 1891 R.J. Lloyd had unsuccessfully applied for the Principalship at Aberystwyth.[1]

As the surname suggests, the Lloyds hailed originally from Wales. The family had been tenant farmers at Maesgwyn, Chirk, since the thirteenth century. Originally members of the Established Church, in the eighteenth century the Lloyds became followers of John Wesley, who once preached a sermon in the large kitchen at Maesgwyn House and stayed overnight there. The Lloyds continued to farm at Maesgwyn until the 1930s, but during the nineteenth century one of the family, R.J. Lloyd's father, Richard, moved to Liverpool where he followed others of the family into the semi-private business of port-gauging. In 1855 he became the official Port-Gauger for Liverpool.[2] As a young man, Richard Lloyd had been vigorously active in the Methodist church in Chirk. In

---

[1] Professor E. Arber of Birmingham, one of his referees, loftily informed the benighted Welsh College Council that the appointment of R.J. Lloyd, an English scholar of distinction, would be the best possible safeguard against 'the formation of a Welsh and English "Pigeon English" [*sic*] at Aberystwyth'.

[2] An ancient office conferred by Quarter Sessions, the gauger's duty was to check the quantities in casks of imported wines, spirits and oils. His certification was conclusive between buyer and seller. This account of the arcane mysteries of this trade is drawn from a copy of Richard Lloyd's manuscript 'History of the Port Gauging business in relation to the firm of Richard Lloyd and Brothers' in the Tristan Jones MSS.

Liverpool he soon became a leading figure in the Free Methodist church; indeed, in 1896 the movement's journal asserted that during the earlier difficult times Richard Lloyd had been 'the life and soul of the Liverpool Churches' and 'for years [had] carried the burden'. He had been particularly concerned with chapel building and was chiefly responsible for the construction of the splendid Free Methodist chapel in Grove Street, Liverpool. In addition to these sterling moral qualities, Richard Lloyd was a notably benign patriarch; 'such a dear old man', as his great-granddaughter fondly recalled.[3]

His only son, Richard John, was an even more interesting man, but rather less agreeable in personality and manner. At the age of twenty, R.J. Lloyd passed the Indian Civil Service examinations and was about to take up an appointment in Bengal when a partner in his father's firm died. Apparently at his mother's request, he gave up the Indian post and joined the family firm as a junior partner. The heavy demands of a full-time career in business did not exhaust his remarkable energy. After his day's work was done, he worked long and late on academic subjects. In the circumstances his success in London University examinations was astonishing. In 1875 he took a bachelor's degree with first class honours in Philosophy. Ten years later he was placed fifth in the list of successful candidates for the London MA degree in Classics, and a year later added an MA in English, French and Anglo-Saxon. In 1890 he became the first successful candidate since 1885 for the D.Lit. degree in English. Thus formally qualified, R.J. Lloyd developed into a scholar of formidable quality whose precision of mind and range of knowledge won the respect and even admiration of leading German professors of Philology and Phonetics, subjects in which he became an authority. He developed exceptional powers of distinguishing and describing speech sounds and his published research in Phonetics was thought to have opened up 'new horizons' by one leading European authority. R.J. Lloyd was no narrow specialist. Indeed, he was a genuine polymath. His early interest had been in mathematics and physical science. He mastered modern languages with ease and was a pioneer in the promotion of Esperanto. For some years he travelled to teach Latin and Greek at the Methodist College in Manchester, and was an energetic promoter of speech schools for the mentally deficient.

[3] 'A Short History of the Lloyd Family', and 'Brief History of Methodism in Chirk ' in Jubilee Celebration Programme (1875–1925) of the United Methodist Church, Chirk Green. 'The Free Methodist Movement in Liverpool' in *The Calendar* (December 1896), pp.366–7.

He, too, like his father, was a pillar of the Methodist church, serving as treasurer of the Grove Street chapel for some years.[4]

It is evident therefore that Eirene Lloyd had a middle-class family background, a domestic comfort provided by bourgeois prosperity, a home where the importance of intellectual improvement was axiomatic, and a Christian upbringing, devoutly Methodist, in which a commitment to public service in support of worthy causes was taken almost for granted. There was another, less eligible side to this family scene, as will appear. But it is hardly surprising that Eirene Lloyd was a serious-minded young lady who was determined to succeed academically and who quite quickly began to think of devoting her life to Christian missionary work overseas.[5] At a meeting of the College Christian Union in February 1896 she was moved by 'a passionate desire' to get up and pray that all present should be 'led to face the foreign question'. She was held back only by her youth and the knowledge that 'some folk do not care for women praying in a place of worship'. Unfortunately, when the president, Dr Snape, asked her to pray, she was seized by an almost uncontrollable 'fit of nervous trembling' that prevented her from saying all she was longing to utter. More generally, she regretted that the burden of thirty-five classes each week and the need to answer her father's expectations of examination success meant that she barely had time to read her Bible. 'I hate to think' she wrote earnestly, 'I am doing so little for God – very little beyond trying to live right myself'.[6] Mercifully, there was a lighter side to her life as a student. She spoke in meetings of 'Lit and Deb', was amusingly critical of certain pettifogging rules at the women's hostel, and participated in a St David's Day presentation of a classical drama.[7]

It was highly likely that Eirene Lloyd would be drawn to take a strong interest in the plan to establish a student settlement in Cardiff proposed at this time by Thomas Jones and his 'Squatter' friends. She was certainly a member of the group by 1895. Along with many other students, 'some scores' as she wrote later, she regarded him with an awed respect just short of outright worship. This did not last long. The respect remained undiminished, but his

    [4] 'People Talked About'. *The Porcupine* (1898) *The Methodist Monthly* (October 1906) XV, No.10, p.305. R.J. Lloyd's references for the Principalship at Aberystwyth in 1891. Thomas Jones's memoir of R.J. Lloyd (1906).

    [5] T.J., Class X, Vol.6, No.4. It was perhaps natural that she should be asked to write the account in the College *Magazine* (XVIII, pp.338–4) of the visit of two well-known missionaries working in China.

    [6] T.J., Class X, Vol.6, No.1.

    [7] *UCW Magazine*, XVIII, 138, 231, 281, Ibid., XIX, 109.

natural warmth and easy approachability quickly dispelled the
distancing awe. She soon began to think of him as a 'splendid big
brother' in whom she could confide without 'fear of ridicule or
violation of trust'. And the relationship remained on that
cheerfully friendly, mutually trusting level for some time.[8]

The story of its transformation into secret betrothal and,
ultimately, a marvellously happy marriage, is a complicated one. It
has to be pieced together from a variety of sources. Happily, a large
number of Eirene's letters to her future husband remain.
Unfortunately, most of his letters to her at this time are missing, or
rather, and exasperatingly, were destroyed by Thomas Jones
himself. It is a curious affair, not easily understood or, from the
perhaps narrow point of view of a biographer, lightly forgiven. Tom
Jones's explanation of the matter is certainly the least convincing
piece of would-be persuasion he ever wrote. In 1940 he brought
together a very substantial selection of his wife's letters to him in
the days of their courtship and early marriage. Ten copies of the
correspondence were printed for private circulation to his two
surviving children, to his niece, and to several close family friends.
At the same time, his own letters to his wife were destroyed. It is
true that in those dark post-Dunkirk days the call was for as much
old paper for pulping for the war effort as possible. In the
dedication of the book to his two children Tom Jones claimed that
he responded in part to this patriotic appeal. 'I have com-
promised', he wrote, 'and on the principle of fifty-fifty have
preserved your mother's letters and sent my own to be pulped'.[9] It
is a palpably weak, even absurd argument that conveniently ignores
the fact that he carefully safeguarded nearly 300 volumes of his
papers, including a great deal of material of much less interest than
his letters to Eirene. And his succeeding assertion that his letters
were 'only equal to hers in number and devotion', is demonstrably
false. In fact, a few of his letters to Eirene at this time have survived,
and their quality is obvious.[10] Eirene herself was never in doubt. 'My
Tom', she wrote early in 1902 'I can't answer all these splendid
letters now, one, two, three, four of them – each more exquisitely
beautiful than the last'. And, more generally, a year or two later:
'You will kill me . . . with the Celtic poetry of your letters. Did I ever

---

[8] T.J., Class X, Vol.6, Nos.3, 4 and 34. Later on, describing her feelings for
him in the early 1890s she talks of her 'reverence', and indeed says he was 'nearly
worshipped' by some students who saw him as a 'Prophet and High Priest . . . a
Herald of a Better Day'.

[9] *Two Lovers: Letters from E.T.L. to T.J.* (1940, Welsh Outlook Press, Newtown,
1940. Cited hereafter as *Two Lovers*).

[10] See T.J., Class X, Vol. 7, No.3, for example.

write such letters? . . . No, No, No, . . . you monopolise all the beautiful utterances'.[11]

There is something here which evades explanation. It may have been simply a matter of avoiding personal embarrassment, a natural disinclination to reveal his private, innermost thoughts and family secrets during his lifetime. It is also apparent that there was some further hesitation in 1940, for as one of the favoured recipients has testified, 'He actually kept [the ten copies] for ten years after their printing before giving them to anyone'.[12] Given this sort of continuing reservation, there was certainly a case for not printing any of the letters, even perhaps for destroying them. But once he had decided to print an edition, one restricted to the sympathetically trustworthy, there was no case at all for excluding his marvellously interesting contribution to the romantic story. He is left to suggest lamely to his children that they could 'catch glimpses' of their father at the age of thirty from the 'partial pages' that he allowed to remain. And he completes the case against himself by recalling that he had been severely handicapped in writing *Rhymney Memories*, the account of his boyhood, by the fact that only one of his father's letters had survived, and none of those of his mother.[13]

It was perhaps inevitable that, when Tom Jones went off to Glasgow and immediately began a hectic existence in and out of the classroom, his relations with his Aberystwyth student friends should be rather less close and continuous. Indeed, so far as Eirene Lloyd was concerned, after 1897 contact between them even by letter ceased for two years. At Aberystwyth, Eirene was evidently highly regarded by the authorities, for in 1896, her last year there, she was put in charge of Brighton House, one of the buildings pressed into hostel service until the large purpose-built Alexandra Hall was completed.[14] Later that year Eirene left Aberystwyth to take up a teaching appointment in Blaenau Ffestiniog, where the Headmistress was Miss Annie Dobell, a former Aberystwyth student and one time Squatter and a woman of some future distinction. Eirene stayed there for two years; it was not altogether a happy experience, 'more or less a period of stagnation', as she described it later. She was so busy teaching and preparing lessons that private reading 'went to the winds. I hardly read three books whilst I was

[11] *Two Lovers*, pp.225, 311, 315.
[12] Mrs. Dora Herbert Jones in an interview on a Harlech Television programme, 1969.
[13] Dedication to *Two Lovers*.
[14] T.J., Class X, Vol.6, No.1.

there'. Equally frustrating she found no scope for social work, although in that bleak locality it could scarcely have been due to an absence of need in the community. It was perhaps a matter of language. 'The district is very Welsh (too much so I think)', she wrote, 'for they will hardly tolerate an English speech in a public meeting and always call out 'Cymraeg' [Welsh]'. It was not that she was unpopular. 'I was well-liked I know', she said, *'as far as they could go with me'*, and she loved the children, who returned her affection. In fact, she picked up a fair amount of Welsh during the time she was there. But she achieved no real mastery of the language; at any rate, 'not enough to talk fluently or enjoy a completely Welsh meeting'. And certainly not enough to make possible the trusting intimacy upon which effective social work is based.[15]

Nonetheless, she still yearned for an opportunity to do some social work, if only on a part-time basis. She had abandoned her ambition to become a Christian missionary overseas because she was now less sure of her ability to be quite so selfless. She hoped now to get a job in a big city and devote her spare time to settlement work. The letter in which she recounted these plans was written in May 1899 from Aberystwyth, where she was attending the annual reunion of the Old Students' Association. Formed in 1892 on the initiative of Tom Ellis, a distinguished alumnus whose meteoric rise in Liberal politics was to be ended tragically by his early death, the OSA, as it was popularly known, quickly became and remained until modern times 'the most durable single support to the College' outside official funding.[16] From the outset, the Association accepted the raising of money for College purposes as one of its chief obligations. Curiously, in the light of his strong commitment to Aberystwyth, Tom Jones did not join the OSA until 1900, when Eirene prompted him to become a life member. She, however, was vigorously active from the start; in 1897 she was sufficiently prominent to be elected to the Association's main committee.[17] Eirene tried to use the OSA to drum up a wider support for settlement work. She wrote two articles in the College *Magazine* and spoke up strongly in favour of the idea at the OSA reunion in 1900. Indeed, she feared that she had given the impression that she was 'trying to run the show'. At one time there had been a suggestion, that owed something to Tom Ellis, that the Aberystwyth OSA should take up settlement work in London. But

[15] Ibid., No.4.
[16] E.L. Ellis, *The University College of Wales, Aberystwyth 1872–1972* (Cardiff, 1972).
[17] *UCW Magazine*, XVII, 264; XIX, 358.

that appeared to have died with Ellis.[18] The slum areas of Cardiff, the target singled out by Tom Jones and the Squatters a year or two before, remained the most likely possibility. But very few of the old Squatter group lived within easy distance of Cardiff, and it seemed obvious that students of the university college in that city provided the most likely source of recruitment for settlement work there. In June 1899 Tom Jones wrote an article entitled 'University Settlements and Social Problems' for the Cardiff College magazine.[19] He pointed to the 'ennobling influence' of Toynbee Hall, the 'mother of Settlements', and less famously, the work of the Student Settlement at Glasgow, of which of course he had personal experience. He called on Welsh students to play their part 'and pay their debt to their less favoured fellows by sharing the goods of the higher life'. The need for such work in Cardiff was over-whelming.

> One has but to recall [he wrote] the ignorance and bitterness revealed on all sides during the recent [1898] coal strike to be convinced of this. Settlements can do something to help forward the moralization of industry in our midst. They can bring ethical ideals to bear on the struggle of capital and labour.

But there was no gainsaying, as he revealed in a letter to Eirene a year later, it was 'uphill work'; there was little that they could do at a distance other than maintain interest at Aberystwyth and elsewhere. They certainly ought not to be forward in meddling in the practical steps taken in Cardiff, particularly as a lead there was now being given by some members of the staff at the University College, notably Professors J.S. Mackenzie, S.J. Chapman and Ronald Burrows, formerly of Glasgow, whose address in 1895 Tom Jones had found so moving.[20]

Eirene never did have the opportunity to do any serious settlement work. Other influences now pushed her back into full-time academic work. In November 1897 she had taken the BA degree of London University with second class honours in Classics. She now fell victim to the remorseless tyranny of her father's expectations. She had left Blaenau Ffestiniog because he had wanted her to go to Newnham College, Cambridge, and after some early resistance to the idea, she gave way and began to work for a

---

[18] T.J., Class X, Vol.6, Nos.8 and 23.
[19] Vol. XI, No.5.
[20] T.J., Class X, Vol. 7, No.22. *Leeks and Daffodils*, pp.85–6. For Burrows, see p.63, above.

scholarship to enable her to do so.[21] R.J. Lloyd evidently had a chip on his shoulder.

> I think he feels deeply [Eirene wrote] the lack a purely London man has in educational circles, and so would wish me at least of his children to take advantage of what *he* couldn't get. I seem to be the only one likely to carry out his aims . . . I had very little *personal* desire to take up this Cambridge plan myself at first. I just felt that, as father had climbed so high himself, he would be disappointed if some of us did not follow in his steps (to a certain extent) at any rate, and I am contemplating Cambridge more from a desire to please him than from any great personal longing to take a Cambridge Tripos course.[22]

It would be foolish and churlish to suggest that Eirene did not gain a great deal from her time in residence at Newnham, as her father had hoped. But the cost to her of this proxy attempt to compensate for her father's disappointment was severe. For some time she had suffered from back trouble (stemming originally it seemed from a slight curvature of her spine) and this painful ailment got steadily worse during her Cambridge years. And certainly she found the less than bracing Cambridge climate a sore trial to her health.[23] But even more important, the attempt to please her father ended in what she regarded as an academic disaster. She had fully expected a second class in the first part of the Classical Tripos, as indeed her examination results of the year before, 'a kind of sessional' as she described it in Aberystwyth terms, had suggested. In the event she got a Class III (2) result. She was utterly demoralized. She had never ever before had 'a third in any exam' of any importance', and while she could point to the fact that ill-health had hampered her work since March, that she had had no luck in the examinations and performed badly even in the papers in which she had expected to shine, it was all no more than the coldest of cold comforts to her. Perhaps it really was 'misfortune rather than desert' that governed her placing, but, inescapably, it was 'a day of humiliation', all the more cruelly disheartening because there had been no word from her father. 'He hasn't written to me', she wrote forlornly, 'so I don't know yet what he thinks of it'. There was little doubt that he would be bitterly disappointed.

[21] She was also continuing her work for the bachelor's degree of the University of Wales at the same time. She won a scholarship of £50 *per annum* for three years.

[22] T.J., Class X, Vol.6, No.4.

[23] *Two Lovers*, p.88. 'Robert Hall used to say' she wrote in December 1900, 'the flat land of Cambridge made his brain feel flat – and oh! how well I understand what he meant'. T.J., Class X, Vol.6, No.18.

You remember his words about a Second being perhaps a fallen First [she wrote], but a Third being to all intents and purposes a Third for ever, whether a fallen Second or not. But I don't see how he can be riled. He knows how seedy I've been all along . . . so if he's reasonable, he'll be willing to count it a bad accident rather than a real downfall.[24]

Hell evidently hath no fury like a father whose daughter was branded with the mark of a Third, if only for an interim period. Eirene had come to expect very little from her father. When she was nine years of age, her mother had left home, been divorced and had subsequently remarried. R.J. Lloyd, too, had remarried, and in Eirene's eyes his new wife was always and ever the cold-hearted stepmother of classic legend.

I lost my mother under circumstances of terrible sadness [she told Tom Jones her future husband in 1900] and the loss of her has never gone out of my life. For with her I lost my father too, if ever I had him before. Since then I have had as it were only the shell of a father – a little outward affection but rarely expanding to anything deeper, an absent-minded interest in my undertakings, an occasional scrap of advice. His wife comes between us at every point; he has not the faintest knowledge of how I could love him, or could have loved him (for with nothing to feed on love grows weak and sick at heart). Yet I have always lived hitherto in the hope of pleasing him by my actions.[25]

In that respect Part I of the Cambridge venture had been a failure. There was however one area where, perhaps surprisingly, Eirene had earlier come to her own decision without reference to her father, and did not seem in the least perturbed by the knowledge that in so doing she would be flying in the face of her family's powerfully entrenched religious beliefs.

It is not clear exactly what led her to question her former piety; certainly her crisis of belief had nothing to do with Charles Darwin and the challenge of science. At any rate, in 1899 when she was again in touch with Tom Jones she immediately confessed that she had been 'undergoing a metamorphosis' during the previous two years:

I am utterly at a loss to say when and where it will end and into what I shall be landed when my present turbid ideas on religious matters have at last crystallized out. Briefly, I am in a complete mist as regards Christianity. The only essentially *religious* beliefs that cling to me are

[24] T.J., Class X, Vol.6, No.6.
[25] Ibid., No.17. In 1902 the second Mrs. Lloyd was 'a most refined and brutal housekeeper', in her stepdaughter's opinion. Ibid., No.77.

the firm conviction of my own natural reason (not from outside inspiration or revelation) that there must a God of *some* kind (whether he is a personal God is another question or just a mere ruler of the Universe), and that there must be a future state *better* than the present one.

This utility version of Deism was essential as

Otherwise Life would be an absolute and unfathomable enigma to me. I have a kind of ethical creed also, very strong and very practical, formulated from *within*. At present that is all that guides my actions (and mayhap will always be so).

Of course I am not mentally happy in these unsettled circumstances. Yet to try to force myself back into the old state of happy acceptance of traditional beliefs would be useless. The days of implicit faith seem to have gone for me.

She had kept these rivening doubts to herself. She could 'join hands' with the Christian Union in any matter of practical Christianity, such as the Hague Resolution in favour of International Peace, 'but on the theoretical side, I infinitely prefer to keep silence'. She acknowledged that she was thus forced into a position where she was 'false' to herself. 'I am afraid you can't help me, can you? I only wish you could', she concluded in some desperation.[26]

It seems inconceivable that Tom Jones did not respond to this *cri de coeur* immediately. It is possible, of course, that he did respond and that the reply was among the letters to Eirene that he destroyed in 1940.[27] In fact, for reasons that are not apparent, they were out of touch for some months at this time.[28] However, a few weeks later he responded at great length in a letter inscribed 'To be taken in small doses'.[29] Eirene was not alone in her tribulations; he too had been sorely troubled by problems of faith and conscience.

What of one's own personal religion? [he asked]. What of Christ and Christianity, and Welsh Methodism and the village chapels of Wales with their evangelical creed? Have I given up preaching? Am I likely to? What of the Atonement and Prayer and the Holy Spirit?

You have changed you tell me. Your positive standing ground has narrowed. The sea of doubt has encroached more and more and left

26 Ibid., No.4.
27 His letters to Eirene (Class X, Vol.7) begin in 1903.
28 'Across the months I greet you', runs her friendly postcard to him, 23 December 1898. T.J., Class X, Vol.6, No.5.
29 Ibid., No.6.

you with little beyond the pin-point of solid foundation. My story is not dissimilar, though I would not put it quite that way. I would say that my old beliefs have been transmuted rather than destroyed. They have been stripped of a great many irrational excrescences which cling to them in Wales. – While not minimising the contribution of the Jews to human progress, I have increased my appreciation of what we owe to Greece and Rome.

Not surprisingly, he found he could not express the course of his spiritual evolution over the last four years with any accuracy in précis. Broadly, his beliefs accorded with those of Principal Edward Caird expressed in his Gifford Lectures at St Andrews University in 1890–2, published the following year as *The Evolution of Religion.*

'In many ways', Tom Jones said, 'I think his Christian Idealism sums up my present situation, though even on so basic a doctrine as the Incarnation I am unsettled'. That statement immediately prompted a cautionary note. 'Don't build too much on this sentence. I don't think I am Unitarian, and certainly don't think Ethical Societies have the whole truth'.

These thoughts would have seemed to the brethren in Wales a strange set of beliefs to be held by a Calvinistic minister. Tom Jones was fully aware of the difficulty and had taken evasive action to ensure at least a breathing space. He still ranked simply as a 'preacher' in the denomination, as he had not yet passed the Synodical Examination and been ordained. 'At the ordination', he said, 'one has to subscribe publicly to the Confession of Faith. I therefore will remain meanwhile a *pregethwr* [preacher]'. But diplomatic delay did not answer day-to-day problems. The strongly evangelical tone of the Christian Union in Glasgow prompted 'practical difficulties': happily, most of his colleagues at the University Settlement were 'Broad'. But the family in Rhymney deeply regretted his reluctance to be ordained and did not 'altogether understand the matters as they appear'. In most chapels in Wales he was 'beset with the problems of religious conformity'. Luckily, as he put it, he had been able to spend the best part of each summer vacation out of Wales; but on occasion there was nothing for it, preaching engagements in some Welsh chapels, 'where the air is more stifling', simply had to be cancelled. There were fewer problems in churches in England, where he was free usually to go his own way. In his sermons there he insisted on the ethical aspects of social and industrial questions and the duty of the Church to give a lead. 'A most inadequate gospel taken alone', as he conceded, 'but one which the people surely need, and the only one which just now I can preach with any *hwyl*'.

Half a dozen years and wider experience had wrought surprising changes in the religious outlooks of Tom Jones and Eirene Lloyd. Their traditional Christian pieties had given way to less orthodox beliefs less certainly held.[30] During 1901 their personal relationship too was to change with an explosive suddenness. At the time neither of them was entirely fancy-free. Eirene had had an unsatisfactory, long-standing relationship with a man called Gordon, who remains something of a mystery. His surname is not known, and there is no mention of his occupation, where he lived, or even where Eirene met this elusive shadow. What is certain however is that the liaison (there is no suggestion it was illicit in any way) lasted several years, that Eirene at least contemplated marriage with a man for whom at one time she felt a 'passionate attachment'. It appears that her feelings were simply not requited and in time atrophied.

> Love . . . can't feed on itself all the time [she said], and if nourishment from without never comes, it seems to me almost inevitable that it will . . . at length slip quietly out of existence and with hardly a death pang, so colourless will it have become. This is what happened to me.

Gordon may well have been her first love, and for all her apparent philosophical acceptance later of its failure, at the time she spoke of the ending in classically romantic high tragic terms: she insisted that she could never ever love another as she had loved Gordon. In fact, within a month he was well on his way into limbo. In a lighter vein, she repeatedly had had to fend off Professor Genese at Aberystwyth, her father's old schoolfellow, masquerading, as she said, as a 'giddy young kipper', who simulated an interest in settlement work in order to catch her attention.[31] And in Cambridge she was pursued with some persistence by R.E. Davies, a contemporary at Aberystwyth. Not the least of the strengths of the Aberystwyth Old Students' Association was the supporting network of Societies established wherever groups of old students were to be found. There was one in London, a very active one in Oxford, one even in Berlin in 1897, and of course a strong branch in Cambridge, where Eirene and R.E. Davies often met socially.[32] He was assiduously attentive and evidently felt deeply about Eirene. When eventually she was forced into some plain speaking in order

---

[30] In September 1900 she said she was still drifting uncertainly in religious matters, but thought she was on the way to a 'serenity of spirit'. Ibid., No.15.

[31] T.J., Class X, Vol.6, No.21. Ironically, Genese was the mathematician whose teaching methods at Aberystwyth had left Tom Jones hopelessly bemused.

[32] *Two Lovers*, pp.71–132.

to make him understand the 'hopelessness' of his suit, he was terribly hurt and, for a time, rather bitter. Eirene did her best to make amends, evidently successfully for he accepted his new status of good friend. It was perhaps a little easier for him to do so when he was told that his successful rival was Tom Jones, a man for whom, as has been noticed, he had the utmost respect. When Eirene left Cambridge, R.E., as she called him, behaved handsomely and gave her 'a beautiful 2 volume edition of Burns as a parting gift'.[33]

Tom Jones too had to extricate himself from a romantic entanglement. Indeed, he had always had a more than passing interest in the opposite sex. He had enjoyed rather more than his fair share of light-hearted dalliance with women students at Aberystwyth; indeed, he cites that as one of the reasons for his repeated examination failures. He also admitted later that the women in the social improvement group centred around him there were 'more important' in his life than the men. Glasgow had not changed him; there too as many of his friends were women as men. On a sunny day in Sauchiehall Street, when women shoppers looked their best, he and a visiting Welsh friend gaily awarded them marks and classes for good looks as they passed by.[34] Rather more seriously, in 1901 when his relationship with Eirene at last became overtly romantic, Tom Jones, in some obvious embarrassment, had to make difficult explanations to a girl called Amy, with whom he had had an attachment for some time. It was not entirely a bolt from the blue for Amy and her family. It seems clear that, some short time before, perhaps skilfully to prepare the way, he had told them that he had lost his emotional bearings and was utterly confused. In late August 1901, not surprisingly feeling 'harrassed and uneasy', he went down to Rothesay, where Amy lived, to confess that he was now committed to Eirene. Once again, astonishingly, as with Charlotte Griffiths in 1895, he was let off lightly and, what perhaps is significant, without the merest hint of recrimination on her part. Indeed, her behaviour was almost unbelievably noble. 'My one aim', she wrote to him, 'will be to help you in the only way I can . . . by being brave and rejoicing in your happiness'.[35]

Amy, as Eirene said, may well have had 'something of the grand resolution of the Puritan and ascetic' in her make-up, but one

[33] Ibid., pp.19, 65, 79, 127. R.E. Davies later became Professor of Theology at Knox College, Dunedin in New Zealand.

[34] *Leeks and Daffodils*, p.50. *Welsh Broth*, pp.2, 77.

[35] *Two Lovers*, pp.35–45. Eirene's letter citing these words was in fact dated 3 September, not, as in the printed version, 3 October, 1901.

suspects that the episode (and the earlier one with Charlotte Griffiths) says a good deal too about Tom Jones. He would certainly have been kind, considerate, and indeed gentle towards Charlotte and Amy. And he certainly had a remarkable gift of sympathetic understanding, and always seemed able and willing to find time to listen to his friends and intimates. These things are incontrovertible. There is a mountain of evidence from virtually all and sundry who knew him that he was a positive paragon of these virtues. It does not follow however that one so blessed would necessarily prompt an intense passion and a physical yearning in those with whom he had a loving relationship. It is a shade unusual, if not odd, that neither Charlotte nor Amy felt a whiff of jealousy or anger about the way she had been treated, and each of them seems to accept her fate with an immediate calm equanimity. It suggests that, in both cases, what Charlotte and Amy felt for Tom Jones, and what he prompted in them, was affection, regard and admiration, rather than any consuming desire to keep his love at any cost.

Perhaps of course it was simply that in these two instances the personal chemistry was wrong. For Eirene's feeling for him, at least judging by her letters, was exactly that of overwhelming passion, though not, as he made clear later on, of physical desire.[36] Because only Eirene's letters remain, it is not possible to say precisely why their relationship changed so dramatically in the summer of 1901. But what is clear is that the decisive initiative came from Tom Jones, and that it was made in mid-July. It is worth while briefly charting the course of change. In February 1896 Eirene's letter is addressed to 'Dear Mr. Jones', who, just over a year later, became 'Dear Big Brother Tom'. There then followed the two year period when they were out of touch. When contact was resumed at the end of December 1899, the tone was warmly friendly on both sides, but no more than that. Indeed, his long letter of 11 February 1900, when he gave a general account of his life at Glasgow and described his perplexities over religion, ends thus: 'What else is there? Am I engaged? No. Likely to be? No'. And he added that he had written in that fashion at that length because they could be 'helpful to one another. What did Browning say about lending our minds out?'.[37]

However, from that point onwards, the relationship became very much closer and certainly more intimate in tone. Indeed, in February 1900 he had invited her to stay for a time during the vacation at his parents' home in Rhymney. She would have been delighted to have been able to accept, but she could barely make

[36] See below, p.116.
[37] T.J., Class X, Vol.6, Nos.1, 3, 5 and 6.

ends meet at Cambridge. She had been forced to supplement her scholarship by borrowing from her father and it was expected that this would be repaid at some time, so she kept her indebtedness to 'Twenty pounds a term of borrowed money'. She simply could not afford 'to travel about much on a princely income of – nothing'.[38] Later that year they began to reveal more of their innermost thoughts and feelings towards each other. He wrote of the need he felt to suppress 'the fires' that burned within him, a broad hint of his capacity at least for smouldering deep feeling. And that was in response to her 'sacred and tender unveiling' of her outer and inner selves. A few days later he received a letter from her full of gloomy introspection about the unhappy fate that left her capacity to love and be loved unfulfilled, 'a cruel hunger which never had and most likely never will have an opportunity of being appeased'.[39] Here, surely, was an opportunity crying out to be taken. But it was missed. Their relationship continued for some time on a rather prosaic level where she borrowed small sums of money to eke out her scholarship.[40] However, his moral support was becoming more and more important. 'How thoughtful and kind you have been to me these past months', she wrote in June 1901. 'Not one in a thousand would have gone to so much trouble'.[41]

His long hesitation in coming to the point is not a mystery. Tom Jones was caught painfully on the horns of a real dilemma. He knew that he had come to love Eirene intensely; and he knew, too, that, once declared, that emotion would probably sweep all before it. There was of course his attachment to Amy, but as events showed, an honourable release from that could be obtained. Much more serious was the solemn promise that he had made to his sisters in 1895 that he would never marry so long as their mother was still alive. That had been given in good faith and accepted by his sisters as binding. If the promise were now to be broken, it would be seen by some of the family as an unforgivable disloyalty. Small wonder, therefore, that he hesitated for so long to cause pain to those he loved so well, and to whom he owed so much. The emotional confusion he had instanced to Amy at this time was thus real enough. However, he had at last made up his mind, the decision triggered apparently by Eirene asking for his photo-

[38] Ibid., No.9.
[39] Ibid., Nos.13 and 15.
[40] Ibid., Nos.18, 20, 27, and 29. In between examinations at Cambridge and others forthcoming for the London MA degree, she was so pushed for money that she applied for some 'London matric. bulldozing: i.e. paid marking'.
[41] Ibid., No.28.

graph. In July 1901 he wrote to her declaring his love in unrestrained lyrical terms. 'The great love you have poured on me', Eirene wrote, 'was overawing and it is still'. She was overwhelmed 'to have had the one man whose goodness I almost worshipped . . . tell me that I am dearer to him than any woman in the world'. Once released, he continued to write with a violent ardour. A day or two later he tore up unsent some 'pages of wild passionate stuff'. It was perhaps the exceptional poetic vehemence of his language with a wholesale resort to hyperbole in his letters to Eirene at this time that persuaded him forty years later to keep them unseen by any other eyes.[42]

This ardour had another consequence. Initially, for family reasons, they had intended to keep their love affair secret for a time, and wait three or four years before marrying. These politic intentions went by the board in days, although they still kept quiet about their marital plans.[43] And in those first heady days, in order to be together, they were prepared even to ignore the proprieties. Eirene, who was already in Scotland staying with relations, was persuaded apparently to stay for a day or so at Tom Jones's flat at 11 Westminster Gardens in Glasgow, more or less unchaperoned, at least by current standards. Tom's mother, who had been staying at the flat, had gone home.

> It would be such a glorious opportunity for us to pour out the hundred and thousand things we have still to say to each other and which *can't get said* for months and months unless said now. [Eirene wrote] . . . yes . . . I think I'll stay.

In fact, it was not quite so daring or unconventional as this suggests.

> Personally [she added] of course I should politely wish 'the proprieties' to go and hang themselves but at the same time, while not caring a button myself about such externals, I'd rather it wasn't blazed abroad at 11 W. Gdns., when only the master and his brother [Enoch] and his housekeeper were there. It isn't strictly correct, Tom sweetheart, despite your seemingly conclusive reasoning. Miss C doesn't constitute a chaperone in the same way as Mrs. Jones does, particularly since she does not take meals or sit with you . . . As a

[42] Ibid., No.39. *Two Lovers*, pp.13–20.

[43] Eirene's mother, Mrs Holloway, who was let into the secret, asked in an interesting letter to her 'dear son-in-law in future' what had changed their minds so quickly. Tom Jones, in rueful expectation of difficulty, pencilled in the margin 'What?'; that is to say. 'What indeed changed our minds?'. The answer is impatient ardour. T.J., Class X, Vol.6, No.34.

tribute to Mrs. Grundy's feelings, I should like a due reticence observed by you, me, and all of us about my doings that particular week . . . *In any case,* I will stay 2 or 3 days, unless the unforeseen happens.[44]

They were to demonstrate a much greater unconventionality when they were married at the end of 1902. But they had to endure several months of great anxiety before that occurred. It was to be a useful preparation for the inevitable stresses and strains of marriage that lay ahead. Eirene was to demonstrate the truth of her mother's opinion that while she was 'happy-natured . . . gay and lively', with a fondness for 'music and dancing and prettyness', she also had a 'blessedly elastic nature which simply defies knocks and blows and bounces up quite serenely after and in the midst of overwhelming troubles'.[45] Eirene needed all her emotional resilience during these months. In the first place, she and Tom were far apart for most of the time. And it was evident that breaking the news of their intention to marry some time in the not too distant future would provoke an emotional storm of crisis proportions within the family circle at Rhymney. That was a situation that would have to be handled by Tom alone at first, and it would test even his renowned delicate tactfulness. Meantime, at Cambridge Eirene faced the daunting task of recouping in Part II of the Classical Tripos the disaster of her result in Part I. As if that were not enough, her general health remained poor, and there were very few days when she was not troubled by severe back pain. She claimed, in February 1902, that she had endured these agonies *'constantly'* for the last six or seven years.[46] There was perhaps an understandable touch of exaggeration here; and there is a suspicion that the pain was, in part at least, psychosomatic in origin, though not any the less painful for that. It was certainly not true, as she maintained, that she was incapacitated or even seriously hampered every day during that time. If that were so, her stoicism would have been truly heroic. For on occasion during the two years when she lived in Blaenau Ffestiniog, she bicycled, in a day, from there, up hill and down dale, on rough roads more than sixty miles to Aberystwyth.[47] It could well be that her general malaise was the result of intermittent back pain coupled with a nagging worry of the need she felt to provide an academic sop, in the form of a

[44] *Two Lovers*, p.6., It appears probable (p.24) that she did stay for a day or two.
[45] T.J., Class X, Vol.6, No.34. She scarcely needed to tell her future son-in-law that Eirene at this time, as her photographs show, was pretty and attractively petite.
[46] *Two Lovers*, p.152.
[47] Ibid., p.241.

good Tripos result, to the Cerberus that her father had become to her.[48]

There was now however an even more powerful influence in her life; that of her future husband Tom, who was increasingly coming to agree with her mother that Eirene had spent 'far too many years of her life grinding away at books' at the cost of 'ill health and crookedness of body'.[49] She was ill again during Michaelmas Term, and Tom suggested several times that she should simply give up the Tripos. After some delay, she eventually agreed to leave Cambridge at least for the time being, and take an extended period of rest and holiday in France, with the option of returning to sit the Tripos examination in 1902 remaining open. The Newnham authorities were generously prepared to allow her to keep a fair proportion of her scholarship money for the purpose, and this supplemented by forty-four pounds that she had in hand from her father (who was not an ogre where money was concerned) would suffice to give her 'a happy and beautiful rest time'. It was, she said, 'almost like a fairy tale' to her.[50]

Eirene was concerned too about Tom's health, or at any rate about his unwillingness to take proper exercise. 'I *wish* you played footer or something, you'd get such a lot of good in such a short time', she wrote in October. 'Do you think you could join the Great Western Swimming Club and have regular lessons? Why not? You mightn't get on very fast or be able to do many strokes at first but . . . it's the *exercise* you want not skill in the arts so much'. She suggested too that perhaps instead of walking he should ride a bicycle. This really was the most forlorn of forlorn hopes. Tom Jones firmly believed that taking exercise was 'a dreary occupation'; he attended a gymnastics class in Glasgow two or three times but soon retired to 'a couch instead'.[51] Eirene had hoped that he might have been encouraged to take up one or other of these activities by the presence in Glasgow of his friend Richard Jones, who was staying with him at 11 Westminster Gardens at this time. Tom and Dick Jones had first met in 1885 at the Park Hall, Cardiff, where they were sitting Cambridge Board examinations. They became firm friends and continued so until Dick Jones, who was to have an important influence on the course of Tom's career, died in 1947. Richard Jones was born in Merthyr in 1870; at the age of thirteen

[48] 'Cerberus (by which I hereby irreverently designate Dr. R.J.L. for the minute)', as she wrote in December 1901. Ibid., p.90.

[49] T.J., Class X, Vol.6, No.34.

[50] *Two Lovers*, pp.89–92. In January 1902 she left for Paris where she stayed for five months.

[51] Ibid., p.78. *Welsh Broth*, p.59.

he started work in a solicitor's office in the town. But a few years later his grandmother put up £20 to send him to the Calvinistic Methodist college at Trefeca. He was ordained and served for several years as pastor to a chapel in Wiston, near Haverfordwest in Pembrokeshire.[52]

The college at Trefeca had aroused Dick Jones's intellectual curiosity but had not satisfied it. For years he hankered after the rigorous training in philosophy that he believed was obtainable only at a university. He paid private visits to Oxford to savour its atmosphere, and indeed was sorely tempted to accept 'secret offers from deacons' who were prepared to finance his going into residence there on condition that subsequently he would become their minister. He rejected these offers and worked privately for an external degree from the Royal Irish University. It was to say the least uphill work. But this was also a situation made to measure for his friend Tom's initiative and good will. In 1900 things were going very much Tom Jones's way: he had at last completed his degree, won two scholarships, and been invited by his professor to do some teaching at Glasgow.

> When I heard Smart's proposals to me [he wrote to Eirene in December 1900] I thought of Dick at once, of course, and sent him a proposal of board and lodge and sundries gratis for a session in Glasgow so that he might read under Adamson and [Henry] Jones . . . and realise a little of his old hopes. I knew he would view the offer in the proper spirit of comradeship, and also that he would see he was helping me to justify the holding of *two* scholarships. If he can pay back in five years or fifty well and good. If not, so be it. We'll praise the Lord just the same.

In December 1900 Dick and Tom Jones met in Rhymney to discuss the proposal further. The Wiston congregation was reluctant to let their popular pastor go, and two maiden ladies, with whom he lodged, had to be propitiated with his promise to visit them during vacations. Tom Jones would not be put off. In his opinion, Dick had 'stuff in him'. It was a time for 'Spurs and Boots'.[53] In the autumn of 1901 as agreed, therefore, Dick Jones, having mean-time completed his BA degree, moved in with Tom Jones at the flat in Glasgow and began his work in philosophy, presumably

---

[52] This account of Richard Jones is drawn from 'A Village Boy Remembers', the unpublished memoirs of his son T. Mervyn Jones (Chairman of the Wales Gas Board 1948–70) at the National Library of Wales. See also, T. Mervyn Jones, *Going Public* (Cowbridge, 1987), pp.13–43.

[53] T.J., Class X, Vol.6, No.22.

unofficially for a session, under Henry Jones for the Irish MA degree.[54]

The presence of his close friend, in whom he confided, was doubtless a considerable support to Tom Jones at this time. For the problem of his family's reaction to the prospect of his future marriage weighed heavily upon him during these months. He had decided to broach the matter during the Christmas vacation in December 1901. Eirene confessed that she felt 'dreadfully nervous' at the prospect.[55] It was certain that the atmosphere at Rhymney at Christmas this time would be very different from that of a year before when there had been happiness, much warmth and some laughter. One day his father, D.B., had come home from the Lawn Shop complaining that though times were certainly good commercially, 'people were brazen' and forgot the bad days that would certainly recur. Moreover, there was 'no satisfying them'. They all demanded 'legs of mutton', and as he said plaintively, 'a sheep has only four in good times and bad alike'. Tom, pushed to keep a straight face, suggested that D.B. should abolish the credit system to ease the difficulties, but his father insisted that he was 'no Gladstone and could not work revolutions'. At that time, too, Tom Jones had thoroughly enjoyed an evening he had spent at Pengam with Roger Jones, his old teacher, 'a rare cultured spirit', who talked until the small hours of R.L. Stevenson and Meredith, Wesley and the Methodist Fathers, and the silver question in America.[56]

As he had feared, Christmas 1901 in the family home at Rhymney was an unhappy time. Tom made his explanations honestly and as gently as possible. But his mother was deeply hurt that he had not confided in her earlier, and his two sisters Liz and Har were stonily unforthcoming. Deeply troubled, he returned to Glasgow and wrote at length to his sisters, who did not reply. Tom and Eirene had agreed that she would not write to Rhymney at least until he had explained matters. In February, however, when there was still no response, Eirene, in despair, wrote a long letter to Liz and Har, which, on reflection, she did not post. It is a remarkable document that perhaps ought to have been sent. Written from the heart, it is impressively persuasive, completely devoid of any narrow possessiveness, and shows Eirene at her best.

[54] There were lighter moments. Richard Jones was the Welsh visitor who helped Tom Jones to classify lady shoppers for their attractiveness.

[55] T.J., Class X, Vol.6, No.46.

[56] Ibid., No.22. Tom said then that he wished he could take his mother and father away from all worries back with him to Glasgow.

My dearest Liz and Har,

> . . . I have been longing to write and beseech you to try and look at
> matters in a different light . . . Tom . . . loves you both so dearly that I
> could not bear to think that a barrier was slowly rising between you . . .
> which, if suffered to grow, might in time become insurmountable . . . I
> know that mere words will be powerless to express to you one tenth of
> the intense and yearning desire in my heart to see matters set straight
> between the man I love and the sisters for whom he cherishes an
> affection so deep and true . . . I wd do anything, short of denying my
> love for Tom, to see things straight between us.

She went on to say that she understood that they felt that Tom
had 'broken faith' by not keeping the promise he had made to
them not to marry as long as his mother was alive. She said that
when first she heard of this promise in the days when she and Tom
were no more than good friends, she thought it was quixotic and,
indeed, unnecessary. Given the right sort of wife, Tom could help
his mother and sisters 'quite as well married as unmarried'. It had
been a mistake for Tom to offer such a pledge, and for Liz and Har
to have accepted it. It could not be gainsaid that men did often
change after marriage, but not always for the worse, and certainly
not a man 'naturally full of generous impulse and devotion to
duty'. Was it likely, she asked, 'that Tom would ever choose as his
wife a woman whose desires and whose conceptions of duty stood
quite opposed to his own?' She pledged that when they were
married, their first concern would '*always* be the welfare' of Tom's
mother. As for the charge that he had not consulted his sisters
beforehand, 'who', she asked, 'could possibly consult anyone else
about falling in love? . . . it is a thing which comes without
foreknowledge'.[57]

There is no evidence that this letter was ever posted on to Liz
and Har, but doubtless the sentiments and arguments contained in
it were put forward again and again, in one form or another.
Eventually, to some effect. Tom's mother was the first to come
round. In March, after he had been home to plead yet again, she
went up to Glasgow to spend Easter with him, and it was soon
apparent that she was prepared to meet Tom and Eirene 'more
than halfway'; she had come to accept the fact that her much-loved
son had at last found in Eirene his 'life's happiness'. Tom was
convinced that the reconciliation was complete when his mother
herself suggested that he should make a flying visit to Paris to see

---

[57] *Two Lovers*, pp.182–3, 185–90.

Eirene as soon as possible.[58] But the key figures in this family disagreement were the two sisters Liz and Har. His eldest son apart, it is evident that the real strength of will and character in D.B.'s children was to be found in his daughters, particularly Liz, the eldest, who could be formidable when roused, not unlike her brother Tom, whom at that time she resembled physically as well as to some extent temperamentally. As her family photographs show, she had a determined jaw, commanding eyes and a direct gaze that betokened a strength of will. Har at this time worked with her father in the Lawn Shop, Liz remained at home. Yet it was Liz who intervened, put up 'a splendid fight' as Tom Jones described it, to put a stop to a popular long-standing practice at the Company Shop.

> In the old days [Tom said] there was beer *ad lib* given for odd jobs and for 'obliging' the Shop in various ways. All this has been changed. There is no beer and there is no 'obliging'.

Not surprisingly, as he admitted, this caused 'a lot of trouble at the Shop', but Liz was not one to be deterred from what she considered her moral duty by difficulties of that kind. Drink was a demon: there was therefore no more to be said.[59]

It seems that Liz and Har (their tandem response appears to have continued unchanged) also made up their differences with Tom during March. Liz wrote to Eirene early in that month, more now in sorrow than in anger. But it did no more than suggest to Eirene, who was determinedly optimistic, that perhaps 'the horizon was growing brighter for all of them'.[60] She was in fact right. A month later things had improved to the point where Har accompanied Tom, at his invitation, on an Easter visit to the Old Students' reunion at Aberystwyth. Two months later it appeared that all had been forgiven; Tom, on holiday early in June, was addressing his letter home to 'Everybody' at the Terrace, and writing naturally without any constraint about Eirene. The one and only serious rift that ever occurred in the family lute was, happily, more or less closed again.[61]

The long months of worry, however, exacted their toll. During the time she spent in France, Eirene discovered that although the

[58] Ibid., pp.183, 217, 220–1. D.B., immersed in the Lawn Shop and his business worries, seems to have played little or no part in this episode.

[59] T.J., Class X, Vol.6. No.22.

[60] Ibid., No.71. Eirene replied with a letter (ibid., No.81) that reiterated the sentiments expressed in the unsent letter of February. Ibid., Vol.1, No.85.

[61] *Two Lovers*, pp.191, 222, 241.

Parisian climate was much more agreeable than that of Cambridge, it did nothing to ease her back pain. Eventually, pushed by Tom, she agreed to see a doctor who prescribed treatment, principally massage, which was expensive and not especially beneficial. She had to borrow again from her father, receive some help from Tom and took on some paid coaching at sweated labour rates. Meanwhile, she attended classes in French language, literature and politics at the Sorbonne. The strain was considerable; she had neither the will nor the opportunity to keep up her reading for the Cambridge Tripos. That, clearly, would have to go by the board.[62] Late in May Tom came over and they enjoyed a short cruise together on a French ship in the western Mediterranean.[63] By now it was clear that Eirene would not only give up her Cambridge ambitions, she would also abandon her alternative plan to stay in France for two or three years. After their holiday they returned together to Britain.

Despite the holiday, Tom was still nervously on edge. In August, he was ruffled by an untoward word of criticism of Eirene by Har; a vestige, at least, of 'the Terrace problems' obviously remained. At the start of term in October he was sufficiently overwrought to consult Professor Stockman, a medical specialist, who told him he had made himself 'ill with worry', adding perhaps unwisely that his 'mind would be affected' unless he had perfect quiet for some time. Throughout his life Tom Jones had a tendency towards hypochondria. He was driven now to write what was probably the only hysterical sentence he ever wrote in his life. 'I am trying to stop worrying myself', he wrote to the family at Rhymney, 'for I foresee that I shall end in the asylum if I don't stop'.[64] He had discussed the matter with Professor Smart and it had been agreed that he would give up his flat at Westminster Gardens and move out to live in a cottage at Balmore, Torrance of Campsie, five miles out of the city. Despite the family rapprochement earlier, it is evident that it was the problems caused by his intention to marry that had prompted this further bout of debilitating worry. In his letter home, he reiterated his intention after he was married to continue making his full contribution 'to the common fund we have all shared through and through'. His concern for his family would continue undiminished. His brother Enoch had been living with him at the flat for some time, and more recently his brother Alf had

[62] 'Paris'. *Two Lovers*, pp.135–263.

[63] T.J., Class X, Vol.1, No.83. He discovered that 'smoke sickness' caused by cheap Algerian cigarettes at 20 for 3d was worse than seasickness.

[64] *Two Lovers*, pp.264–9. T.J. Class X, Vol. 1, No.87.

joined them there. Tom had found work for his two brothers, who were to be joined later by their other brother Willie. Tom suggested that if Enoch and Alf went into lodgings, they could at least join him in the cottage at Balmore at weekends. As to his marriage, that would depend on Eirene's response to the treatment she was receiving in Liverpool, but it would be as soon as possible, in January or the following Easter at the latest.

In fact, it occurred sooner, and the decision to go ahead at an earlier date was taken within days of this letter to Rhymney. Their friends Dick Jones and R.R. Williams were 'chortling' happily at the way the period of their unofficial betrothal (they could not be bothered with the solemnity of an official engagement) had dropped from three or four years to months, 'and *now* to weeks', as Eirene said. 'They simply would not believe that it was *circumstances* rather than ourselves which ordained an early marriage'.[65] The case for an early wedding was, in fact, overwhelming. Eirene found that living in her father's house in Grove Street, Liverpool, again was less than congenial. There was what she regarded (not altogether fairly, perhaps) as the constant baleful presence of her stepmother. Eva, Eirene's older sister, had rebelled years before and gone on the stage before settling down in marriage. Lily, her younger sister, was very dear to Eirene but was in no position to do anything but do as she was told at home. Eirene was close to her brother, Frank, who was kind and sympathetic but quite unable to stand up to his father in any way. Not that Dr Lloyd himself was a domestic bully; he was a quiet man, rather deaf, inclined to be abstracted and often absent-minded in small matters. Tom Jones, who had an exceptional gift for getting on easy terms with an infinite variety of people, confessed that he was nonplussed by his father-in-law, who had no small talk or any disposition it seemed to ease the flow of ordinary conversation.[66]

But Dr Lloyd did have a temper, and during this difficult period he and Eirene on one occasion had a shouting match in which there was some thumping of the table. Eirene's position was obviously difficult: Cambridge had been given up, the French plan had petered out. Meanwhile, she had no teaching job in prospect and was undergoing medical treatment for her back under the direction of a cheerfully insouciant specialist who prescribed a course of ten-minute pummelling exercises that Eirene found painful, exhausting, and not very effective. The doctor had one

[65] *Two Lovers*, pp.273, 295.
[66] Tom Jones's account of Dr R.J. Lloyd's death in the Tristan Jones MSS.

saving grace at least; he said that Eirene was not an invalid and there was no reason at all why she should not get married.[67]

Tom's position was less difficult. He seems to have recovered quickly from his melancholy in October. At any rate, he resumed his teaching duties at the University in the normal way when the new term opened, and indeed took on an additional advanced class at the Athenaeum. He had by now of course adorned his degree with first class honours. In every way he was coming up to William Smart's expectations. The professor was a generous man; in 1901 he raised his assistant's stipend from £50 to £250, and advised him 'not to rush off and get married at this sudden and vast accession of income'.[68] That, in fact, is what Tom did, fairly quickly if not exactly at the rush. There was one final flurry of difficulty over the actual arrangements for the wedding. It was not a matter of petty detail. Neither of them was sufficiently settled in religious conviction to warrant 'going through the church marriage service in an ordinary way with its invocations and expressions of belief'. To do so, they felt, would be 'acting a public lie'. Eirene declared that she retained no more than 'two fragments of a credo . . . a belief that there *is* a Supreme Mind which breathes through all things [and that] there must be a life after death'. Beyond that, she said, 'I can't say I *believe* anything except self-proven moral truths'. If anything, Tom's opinions were even less orthodox: he wanted their act of marriage to be 'free from everything of a religious nature (in the accepted sense of the word *religious* as applied to the marriage service)'. Indeed, eventually Eirene had to persuade him that his insistence on an outright Bohemian unconventionality was 'practically impossible', not least because he failed to grasp 'the woman's point of view'. It would invite a 'social ostracism' that would cut her off from those she might otherwise help. 'How, I ask you, *how* could a woman possibly help other women who would not speak to her, who counted their morality immeasurably above hers?'. Some compromise, she insisted sensibly, with the support of William Smart, was necessary.

There were other questions that caused difficulty. Were they to be married in Rhymney or Liverpool, in church or out? 'What we honestly should *prefer* of all would be marriage in the open air in the country or else in the house where we were going to begin our married life', she told her father. And preferably too in the presence only of their two fathers with Dick Jones to officiate.[69]

[67] *Two Lovers*, pp.267, 269, 282.
[68] Ibid., p.272, *Welsh Broth*, p.60.
[69] *Two Lovers*, pp.273–88.

Curiously, the two families, despite their strong Methodisms, did not react angrily. Dr Lloyd, in particular, responded with calm sense. And indeed with some generosity, amongst other things cancelling Eirene's outstanding debts to him. In this complicated situation she behaved with a consistent good sense; in one instance, of all things, gently rebuking Tom (citing verses from Romans XII with their call for charity to transgressors) for his vindictiveness towards her father.[70] Finally, all was settled: principle and practicality were brought to terms. The marriage took place on 31 December 1902 in the vestry of the United Methodist Free Church in Grove Street, Liverpool, in the presence of Dr R.J. Lloyd and Tom's father, D.B., representing the two families. The form of service, which was not in any way wanting in dignity or solemnity, had been chosen by Tom and Eirene together. 'It was a medley of noble thoughts on love and duty interwoven from the Bible and the writings of Mazzini and Ruskin'. It had been hoped that Tom's 'best friend', the Reverend Richard Jones, would officiate. R.R. Williams had to act as a last minute substitute. Dick Jones was held up by one of his congregation inconveniently 'dying at the wrong time'. But he travelled up overnight to Liverpool and arrived in time at least to be present.[71]

Eirene had once written from Paris: 'I want to make you a good wife, a useful and sensible manager as well as a loving and understanding companion, Tom'.[72] Over the next thirty-two years, she was to be all that, and much much more.

[70] Ibid., p.281.

[71] Ibid., pp.299–301. *Welsh Broth*, pp.60–1. Dick Jones, too, was 'at loggerheads' with official Methodist doctrine on certain points. T.J., Class X, Vol.6, No.41.

[72] *Two Lovers*, p.224.

CHAPTER FIVE

GLASGOW · II

TOM AND Eirene were no more conventional about a honeymoon than they had been over the form of their marriage service. There was a wedding breakfast of sorts, at 6 p.m. in Dr Lloyd's house, to which Dick Jones and R.R. Williams were invited. There were no formalities; indeed Dr. Lloyd was due to leave the house soon after seven o'clock for another engagement that evening. The bride and bridegroom took a tramcar to the station and caught a train for Glasgow. Only Dick Jones apparently was there to see them off.[1] They returned to the sparsely furnished cottage at Balmore, which they now called Anwylfan (the beloved place), a cherished name they were to carry with them to other houses in which they lived.

But their happiness was short-lived; two weeks later, Tom's mother died suddenly at the age of fifty-four. She had been unwell, confined first to the house then to her bedroom, for a fortnight or so. Frail and assailed by an 'awful feeling of weakness', she had struggled to write a letter full of family news to Tom and Eirene. It ended with a farewell that was surely sadly presentient: 'Goodbye and God bless you . . . Your loving mother'.[2]

Tom, who had loved her dearly in an especially protective way, was deeply grieved. His mother had embodied the Rhymney hearth and home and been utterly, sometimes absurdly, unsparing in her care and concern for her family, especially for her sons, and particularly perhaps for her eldest son Tom, of whom she was inordinately proud. It was all the more bitterly ironic that the differences that had so unhappily divided the family a short time before had turned on the assumption that D.B., whose work in the past at least had been so demandingly physical, assuredly would be outlived by his wife. Tom and Eirene (or Rene, as most people called her) could at least console themselves that before she died his mother had come to approve warmly of their marriage.[3]

---

[1] *Two Lovers*, p.298. *Welsh Broth*, p.61. T. Mervyn Jones, 'A Village Boy Remembers', unpublished memoirs held at the National Library of Wales, p.10.

[2] T.J., Class X, Vol. 1, No.90.

[3] *Two Lovers*, pp.303–4.

Inevitably, that, too, had its stresses and strains, especially in the early months of their mutual adjustment. Indeed, in this respect, their marriage was entirely normal: within weeks of their wedding, they had a painful disagreement, the prelude to a period 'alternately supremely blissful and wretchedly miserable'. But they derived much enjoyment from the careful joint selection of the décor and furnishing of their home. They were agreed that there 'is a morality of things', as well as of people and ideas, and were content to wait until items of beauty and quality could be discovered and afforded.[4] Rene, whose experience in the kitchen was slight, soon learned to cook. But she never did become, as she had once modestly hoped to be, the 'junior partner in the firm of Thos. Jones and Co., bookwriters'. They had at one time planned jointly to write a book on 'The Welsh Collier'. It was never finished. The one piece of research they did was to write to Tom's aunt Harriet (his mother's sister), whose grandfather, Job Cook, it will be remembered, had worked in the mines in the Rhymney valley fifty years before.

> Regarding colliers wages and etc. [Aunt Harriet wrote in reply], they earned about 15/- or 16/- a week, but the Hitcher [who linked the tramcars carrying the coal] at the bottom of the pit about 19/- . . . some used to get 20/- if they had a good piece of work. Granny says that grandfather [a master-collier who possibly subcontracted] used to earn £5 in four weeks, but it was hard work. As to hours they come and go when they liked. As for women and girls, they went down the pits and worked as men earning about 7/- . . . some [women] used to drive the horses on top of the pits and others tipping the trams, and others unloading and loading . . . Granny remembers her Brother Reuben and his wife working at Blaina in a level . . . they had no horse at all, they would fill the tram and push it out themselves.[5]

Working conditions underground had improved since those early days of course, but Tom Jones was in no doubt about how hard a collier's life was still at the turn of the century. Family lore aside, he had been brought up in Rhymney and knew all too well the toll in life and limb that coal mining exacted. He could therefore, with justification, discount the necessity for a ritual expression of affinity with them in the preface of his speech to the

---

[4] Ibid., pp.304–6. *Welsh Broth*, pp.61–5. They began their married life, as Tom said at its end, 'with a dowry of £50 and about £10 which I had got saved – ample for unbounded happiness'. Tristan Jones MSS.

[5] T.J., Class X, Vol.7, No.4. *Two Lovers*, p.11. Harriet James to Tom Jones [1901]. Tristan Jones MSS.

miners of the Rhymney valley at Bargoed on Federation Day, 13 June 1904. This was a great gala occasion in centres all over the coalfield with huge processions headed by brass bands. The one at Bargoed was smaller than those of Dowlais, Pontypridd and elsewhere; even so, there were 'about 2,000' men present. Tom Jones had been invited to speak by Tom Richards, general secretary of the South Wales Miners' Federation, formed six years before, who was shortly to be elected to Parliament as a Lib-Lab member, a hybrid definition linking the past and the future to ensure success in the present.[6]

This was not a particularly buoyant time in the history of *The Fed*, as the south Wales union was called. There was an economic recession and membership of the union had dropped in each year since 1900.[7] But Tom Jones made no concession to current difficulties or to the susceptibilities of his listeners. His speech was bold and challenging, laced with an occasional tart home truth, and devoid of any trace of flattery of his audience. He had been introduced as an economist, but, typically, preferred to speak on 'The Social Aspects of Trade Unionism'.[8] His address was closely argued, a sustained exhortation (not entirely free of some sermonizing) of his large audience to raise their sights above the ruck of mere wage-bargaining to the task of creating a much better, happier, more civilized society in the mining valleys. The speech, with its emphasis on duties rather than rights, owed much to the influence of Mazzini. He made no reference to the miners' strike of 1898 or to the current bitter dispute between Lord Penrhyn and the quarrymen of north Wales. Their aim, he told the miners, should be the educating of public opinion; their ultimate purpose, good citizenship. 'I wish to plead', he said, 'for the widening of the social outlook of trade unionists and for a deeper sense of their civic responsibility'. Education was the key: before them 'lay a stupendous task . . . of elevating the whole tone of their society. Every mining village should have a well equipped social institute and a library'. They had to hand the

[6] Tom Richards, 'one of nature's gentlemen', who preferred peaceful settlement to militant confrontation (*Leeks and Daffodils*, p.184), was exactly the sort of trade union leader of whom Tom Jones strongly approved, then and subsequently. There is a report of the Bargoed meeting in the *South Wales Daily News* (14 June 1904).

[7] R. Page Arnot, *The South Wales Miners* (1967), p.70.

[8] Printed in *A Theme With Variations*, pp.1–25. As an indication of how little known he was at this time, even in south Wales, it is to be noticed that a newspaper account identifies him simply as 'the son of Mr. D.B. Jones of Rhymney'.

means of collective self-help. 'Do not wait for Carnegie or the government'. The choice was theirs: they could either 'provide an elevating or a degrading environment'.

Immediately after his address he was brought face to face with what he regarded as a degrading spectacle. *En route* to the traditional lavish meal for speakers and union officers upstairs in the local public house, the official party had to push their way through the bar. It was crammed with dust-streaked, grimy-faced colliers, whose shift had just finished, slaking great thirsts and perhaps replacing loss of fluid by gulping down pints of beer in quick succession. It was a scene guaranteed to repel Tom Jones, who could be prissily fastidious and was of course inveterately hostile to drink in all its manifestations. The undisciplined guzzling of 'these slaves of appetite', as he called them, was so different from the sober, thoughtful demeanour of the colliers in the large audience. 'I was haunted by what I had just seen', he wrote, 'and with my distance from, not my identity with, these men'. No sympathy, precious little understanding, so it would seem. At thirty-four, Tom Jones was still occasionally a bit of a prig. But his account of this episode was written in 1950. He freely admitted that his revulsion in 1904 had been 'utterly un-worthy of a Christian and a comrade', and he conceded that gradually later he came to see that he, too, had his sensual appetites and, accordingly, became rather more tolerant and compassionate about the shortcomings of others. Here, as in almost all of his writings, he displays a remarkable candour, with no disposition whatsoever to hide his warts or cover up follies or misjudgements.[9]

This was his first professional contact with the miners' union. It was the first of many. The coal industry and its problems loomed large in the subsequent course of his career. So, too, did the even more deep-seated problems of Ireland, whence he had come to speak to the miners. In 1904 he had been chosen in open competition out of thirty-three candidates by the Barrington Trustees in Ireland as their lecturer in political economy. It was a plum appointment for a junior lecturer, an invaluable supplement to the £250 he received from Professor Smart. At his interview in Dublin he was asked to speak last out of four candidates before an audience of a hundred or so Trustees on the fiercely controversial question of free trade versus protection. His three rivals committed themselves passionately on one side or the other, thereby inevitably alienating many of the Trustees. Tom Jones was, in fact, an ardent

[9] *Welsh Broth*, pp.36–8.

free-trader, but cannily recognizing that this was a situation where
enemies were more easily made than friends, he avoided
advocacy and took refuge in a teacher's objective exposition of both
sides of the argument. He was appointed. It was not the last
time that Irishmen were to be impressed with his capacity to
offer a disinterested opinion on questions that roused great
passion.

The Barrington lecturer received the handsome fee of two
hundred guineas for delivering fifty lectures in small towns and
villages all over an Ireland that was not yet partitioned if scarcely
united. He had to make his own arrangements about venues,
lecture halls, publicity beforehand and press reports after meetings.
He had to be especially careful to keep a proper balance between
Catholics and Protestants as chairmen of meetings. He relied upon
his 'methodical wife' Rene to deal with the straightforward detailed
arrangements. But Ireland was a minefield for a speaker who had
not done his homework on local, provincial and national
conditions beforehand. Tom Jones left nothing to chance. He
mastered a mountain of Irish statistics, read Blue Books and local
newspapers innumerable, and consulted every available helpful
authority on the affairs of Ireland, especially its agriculture, which
was of fundamental importance, and its history in its several
uncompromising subjective forms, from which there was no escape,
least of all for a public lecturer. But he was careful, too, to observe
the injunction in 1890 of Sir Thomas Raleigh, the Oxford
lawyer, to those who would understand the Irish Question, to see
the country for themselves unencumbered by partisan company or
commentary. He spoke on topics such as Emigration and
Agriculture, the Protection of Industry, Democracy, and those
subjects in which he was particularly interested, Education and
Unemployment.

The lectures were delivered to audiences of between fifty and
three hundred people during the Christmas vacation and in the
spring and autumn weeks. Sometimes Rene accompanied him.
Usually he would establish himself in a small seaside town for a
month and from there go off to villages over a radius of twenty or
thirty miles to give short courses of three or four weekly lectures. In
all, he visited fifty or so places scattered all over Ireland. He came
to know the different localities and met a host of people of all ages
at every social level, Catholic and Protestant, informed and
otherwise. With the best will in the world, of course, he, too, had
his preconceptions and indeed prejudices about Ireland. He had
spent a short holiday in Dublin in 1885 and encountered some

instances of Irish whimsicality. He had been brought up in the Gladstonian Home Rule tradition, and in the 1890s at Aberystwyth, it will be remembered, he had supported the assertive nationalism of the Welsh Liberals at that time. Not surprisingly, he had an instinctive sympathy with the Irish, who were struggling to be free of an English establishment dominance that often did not even attempt to hide its contempt for them. He had also, however, 'in full measure the antipathy of a Welsh Calvinistic Methodist to Roman Catholicism', even if it did not prevent his establishing excellent personal relations with parish priests and several Roman dignitaries, including one Archbishop, whom he met during his lecture tours.

In 1904, the Irish countryside through which he moved was relatively peaceful. It appeared that land purchase, turning the tenant with government assistance into a small scale peasant proprietor, the policy known as 'killing Home Rule by kindness', was succeeding. It seemed reasonable to believe, as, not surprisingly for a professional economist, Tom Jones did at that time, that the removal of the worst economic grievances would sap the power of Irish Nationalist separatism. He was wrong. The hiatus in murderous violence was to be very short. The Irish Question was not a matter merely of economics, to be solved by a belated grudging reversal of the flow of tribute from Ireland. Tom Jones was to play an important, arguably a crucially important, part in a more desperate, infinitely more complicated attempt to answer the problems of Ireland some years later. The knowledge, in particular the feeling for Ireland and Irishmen, that he gained as a Barrington lecturer at this time was to be of inestimable value.[10]

If for the moment the Irish were less troublesome to British governments, the champions of women's rights in the United Kingdom presented a rapidly mounting challenge. Tom and Rene Jones had been strong supporters of women's suffrage ever since their student days. In the early days of their marriage they were energetically active in the movement in Glasgow. Tom continued to lecture far and wide on behalf of the Scottish Council for Women's Trades. For some years he was chairman of the Council committee that sought to improve the conditions of employment of women and children. In her annual report in January 1904, Margaret Irwin, the secretary, referred to the great voluntary contribution Jones had made to the work of the Council, and in particular to 'his wholehearted enthusiasm in the

[10] Ibid., pp.81–108.

cause of reform' over several years. Rene, too, was a member of this society.[11]

They were also active together in the Glasgow and West of Scotland Association for Women's Suffrage.[12] Here, naturally enough, Rene took the lead. She spoke several times in public debates, sometimes in militant terms, although she did not go so far as Colonel Denny, shipbuilder and the sitting Tory MP for Kilmarnock, a fellow member of the Glasgow Association who, as early as October 1905, asserted bluntly that what was 'wanted was a species of shillelagh. Arguments were of no use' against such obtuse opponents.[13] Women suffragists had high hopes that the return of a Liberal government in 1906 would lead to their getting the vote, but three bills for that purpose were talked out of the House by opponents and lost. The Women's Social and Political Union (WSPU), founded in 1903 by Mrs Emmeline Pankhurst, Mrs Pethick-Lawrence and others, decided upon more direct methods, including a campaign of civil disobedience and, ultimately, in 1913, a resort to arson. There is no evidence that Tom and Eirene Jones endorsed such action. But they were in touch with the Women's Social and Political Union for a time. Mrs Pankhurst stayed with them in Glasgow when, as Tom Jones wrote, she was *persona non grata* in respectable circles.[14] Early in 1907, Rene wrote to the secretary of the WSPU, Mrs Edith How Martyn, who had been her contemporary at the University College in Aberystwyth in the 1890s.

> I am glad to hear that you are so interested in our work [Mrs Martyn wrote in reply]. I take it you are a member of our Glasgow branch. I write to reassure you that we are going to give the Government every chance before striking another blow, but just when that time should be I think can be left to those of us who are on the spot and prepared to face the music.[15]

The leadership of the WSPU was authoritarian, as perhaps Mrs Martyn's final sentence suggests. Rene was not the sort to take kindly to that sort of patronizing guidance. Probably, too, she and

[11] T.J., Class W, Vol.10, No.150. Ibid., Class X, Vol.2, No.82. See also Tom Jones's article, 'Women's employment', in No.98 of *Organised Help* (journal of the Glasgow Charity Organization Society, October 1909), in which he asserts that the arguments in support of Labour Exchanges for men 'apply with equal force in the case of women workers ... The best charity is to provide work and training'.

[12] Perhaps ironically in a society that strove for equality of the sexes, the subscription for men was 2/6d, for women 1/6d.

[13] T.J., Class X, Vol.2, Nos.82. 93, 96, 98 and 101.

[14] *Welsh Broth*, p.34.

[15] T.J., Class X, Vol.2, No.89.

her husband were put off by the increasing violence of the tactics of the WSPU. At any rate, although they met again later socially, there is no evidence in their papers of any subsequent political contact with Mrs Pankhurst and her associates.

Nevertheless, Rene had a continuing strong commitment to the cause and she could expound the case for women's suffrage and the tactics that ought to be followed with admirable clarity. The franchise came first, it was 'the essential thing' in which all other rights for women were subsumed. 'It is my opinion', she wrote in 1908, 'that the ultimate and only logical democratic ideal is manhood and womenhood suffrage, and the parliamentary representation of women by women as well as by men'. If necessary, however, she was prepared to accept something on account. That is, votes for 'qualified women', those who possessed a property qualification. It was absurd to wait for outright victory. 'Since when', she asked, 'has human nature learnt to prefer no bread to half a loaf?'. It was difficult to see how society could 'do without women's counsel' in the making of laws, but it was not necessary to make a case on grounds of sex. 'Women need the vote on exactly the same political and economic grounds as men need it . . . Women have citizen duties to perform as important as those of men'. It had been proved time and time again that 'the only way to make people fit for responsibility is to give it to them'. And it should not be forgotten that 'people denied the privilege of citizenship are apt, quite naturally, to forget its duties'. Much needed to be done. The struggle for women's economic freedom was 'still in its infancy'.[16]

These arguments, which are much more sensibly direct than the Byzantine tortuousness by which Beatrice Webb, in 1906, came belatedly to the same conclusion, were deployed apparently at a meeting in 1908 of the East Kilbride Liberal Association, of which Rene was a member.[17] The chief obstruction to women's suffrage then was a Liberal government that was divided on the question and unwilling to act. Rene looked to history for guidance: every extension of the franchise in the past had been gained by 'forcing the Government, never by an act of voluntary justice on the part of those in power'. She had her own ingenious prescription to offer. It broke no law; and it had its possibilities.

What would please me very much would be to see a great strike of various women's political organizations at the next general election,

[16] T.J., Class X, Vol.2, No.92 and 96.
[17] *Our Partnership*, by Beatrice Webb (ed. B. Drake and M.I. Cole, 1947), pp.360–3.

and an absolute refusal on their side to do a stroke more work for their party until a government women's suffrage bill was definitely promised. We can no more send the modern woman back to the home than we can stop the sun in its course.

It was time for action.

Women have been patient, too patient for the last six years, and the result of this policy has been contemptuous tolerance on the part of the powers that be.[18]

Her suggestion of course was ignored. It took another ten years and perhaps the turmoil of total war before the continuing injustice of women was even partially redressed.

There had been an attempt to tackle the problem of pauperism rather sooner. During the last three decades of the nineteenth century there was a growing concern in Britain about poverty in all its manifestations. The statistical evidence of social investigations, buttressed by common observation, made it plain that a disconcertingly large proportion of the people lived in conditions of squalor and poverty, and indeed destitution. The public conscience was powerfully aroused. Experience had shown that Samuel Smiles's doctrine of self-help as a means of improvement was an irrelevant absurdity for the overwhelming mass of people. Organized charity had obvious limitations. Industrial and commercial depression had disturbed complacency and added to the growing doubt that economic advance would produce an all-embracing prosperity that would substantially eliminate poverty. There was, of course, another side to the debate. There were those who maintained that the broad principles on which the Poor Law settlement of 1834 had been based still retained their validity. Poverty, they insisted, whatever tender consciences might say, stemmed from feckless idleness and moral depravity. Deterrence not indulgence was still what was needed; the old system had been undermined by lax administration and rising costs, its national uniformity destroyed by local extravagances. The old guard had lost the argument by 1900, but their criticisms helped to create in official circles 'an uneasy feeling', as Beatrice Webb called it, that in recent years the old Poor Law system had somehow gone steadily amiss. At any rate, in December 1905, on the eve of resignation, perhaps to forestall his Liberal opponents, A.J. Balfour, the Prime

---

[18] 'Women's Suffrage', notes in Rene's hand for a speech at the East Kilbride Liberal Association, October 1908. T.J., Class X, Vol.2, No.96.

Minister, announced the appointment of a Royal Commission on the Poor Law.[19]

Included among the twenty Commissioners appointed to sit on this grand inquest of the nation on poverty was Professor William Smart of Glasgow University. In 1904 Smart, President of its Economic Science section, had addressed a British Association meeting in Cambridge where he met Balfour who, evidently impressed, appointed him as one of the two political economists on the Commission. Smart was greatly pleased with the honour. He rearranged the work of his department (inevitably this meant more responsibility and some personal difficulty, as will appear, for his assistant, Thomas Jones), leased a flat in London and journeyed to and fro, usually overnight, between Glasgow and London. 'He did the work of two men', Tom Jones wrote later, 'and shortened his life'.[20] Smart was made Chairman of the Documents Committee which examined Blue Books and virtually any publication that had relevance to the Commission's broad terms of reference. Beatrice Webb was a member of the Commission and of the Documents Committee. As Chairman, Smart coped as best he could with her restless energy and determined assertiveness. According to Thomas Jones, Smart was 'scared of her'.[21] The professor's name flits in and out of her detailed Diary account of the work of the Commission; her accompanying comments on him vary sharply as he either supported or opposed her proposals. At one time she thought he might be persuaded to agree with her that the old poor law 'should be swept away', and that, disarmingly, he could be drafted in to put forward proposals which, if made by her, would arouse automatic opposition. Subsequently, Smart disappointed her by abstaining on a 'crucial question'. Finally, she lost all patience with him. He was dismissed with contumely. Not only was Smart a glutton at the dinner table, he was 'a dull fellow without intellectual purpose – and with precious little intelligence with all the less attractive qualities of the Scotchman'.[22]

Lord George Hamilton, Chairman of the Commission, had a very different opinion of Smart's abilities. In 1916, at Tom Jones's request, he wrote an account of Smart's 'invaluable' contribution as a Commissioner. His work on the Drafting Committee, which filtered a host of amendments into the main body of the Report,

---

[19] *Our Partnership*, p.317. M. Bruce, *The Coming of the Welfare State* (1961), pp.154–200.

[20] 'Biographical Sketch' (pp.xlii–xliii) in William Smart, *Second Thoughts of an Economist* (1916).

[21] *Welsh Broth*, p.72.

[22] *Our Partnership*, pp.381, 390–1, 397, 410, 416.

was of extraordinary quality: his fairness in the examination of witnesses was exemplary, and his summary of social and industrial developments in Britain since 1834 (Beatrice Webb called it 'longwinded') was 'masterly'. Hamilton thought that Smart was 'able, simple and unaffected'.[23]

Given the composition of the Commission and the strength of settled conviction with which some members approached their task, it was highly unlikely that there would be sufficient agreement finally to produce a unanimous report. 'You and Sidney', H.G. Wells, no mean practitioner himself of that disruptive art, wrote to Beatrice Webb in 1909, 'have the knack of estranging people'. Certainly she seemed to go out of her way during the course of the inquiry to produce disagreement.[24] And there were some other members scarcely less unwilling to compromise. Ultimately, two reports were published. The Majority Report (signed by fifteen of the Commissioners) called for substantial reform of the Poor Law but not its abolition. Mrs Webb and her four supporters demanded in the Minority Report (which ran to almost a thousand pages) the breakup of the system and the reallocation of the variety of services it performed to different specialist government agencies.[25]

It was natural that Smart should recruit Tom Jones's services as a special investigator in Scotland for the Royal Commission. He was excellently equipped for the post. 'If ever they put the right man in the right place, they did it then', wrote Mrs Richard Barrington, wife of the leading Barrington Trustee, who had seen Tom Jones professionally at work in Ireland.[26] In one area of enquiry Jones was already well versed: he wrote a special report on those industries which employed women paupers.[27] The whole range of his work as an investigator, as his mentor Henry Jones pointed out with pride, was marked by the thoroughness of his research, the clarity and fair-mindedness of his presentation and the excellence of the literary style of his reports.[28]

The Liberal government did not act on either of the two Poor Law reports, nor on the substantial measure of agreement between them on certain questions, other than perhaps the introduction of

[23] 'Biographical Sketch' (pp.xliii–xlviii), in William Smart op.cit. *Our Partnership*, p.416.
[24] *The Letters of Sidney and Beatrice Webb* (ed. N. Mackenzie, Cambridge, 1978), II, 325. *The Diary of Beatrice Webb, 1905–24* (ed. N. and J. Mackenzie, 1984), III, 9.
[25] Bruce, op.cit., pp.202–8. 'We will break up, once and for all that nasty old Poor Law', Beatrice boasted to Beveridge, in 1908 *Webb Letters*, II, 319.
[26] T.J., Class Z (Diary 1899–1919), pp.1–2.
[27] T.J., Class X, Vol.2, No.72.
[28] Ibid., Vol. 3, No.31.

Labour Exchanges. Ministerial attention was absorbed by Lloyd George's proposals for old age pensions and an extensive insurance scheme, to which the Webbs in fact were opposed. Beatrice noted that during 1909 they had been 'quite strangely dropped' by the Liberal ministers.[29] But the Webbs had no intention of giving up and accepting their defeat. 'We shall do all we can to stir things up all over the country', Sidney Webb declared in a letter to Tom Jones. 'I shall presently be writing to the local Fabian Societies, inciting them to take part in the agitation'. The Webbs had welcomed Tom Jones's appointment as an investigator in Scotland.[30] They now set up a National Committee for the Promotion of the Break Up of the Poor Law. 'A cumbrous and equivocal title', as Beatrice admitted.[31] There was to be a Scottish campaign and in September 1909 Sidney Webb sought Tom Jones's assistance in recruiting a president and treasurer 'of repute', and, especially, an efficient honorary secretary for the organization in Scotland.[32]

This request put Tom Jones in rather a difficult position. Smart, his professional superior and generous patron, who had recruited him for the Poor Law Commission work, had differed from the Webbs and signed the Majority Report. Tom Jones gave some limited assistance, but apparently this did not quite answer Webb's expectation. 'Your intervention has evidently been most helpful', Webb wrote on 10 September 1909, 'but what we want is a *name* and an *office*'.[33] There is no evidence that Jones gave any further assistance (indeed he left Glasgow shortly afterwards to take up a post in Ireland) to the Webbs' campaign, which was a failure and conceded by them later on to have been a mistake.

Webb had clearly taken it for granted that Tom Jones agreed entirely with the Minority Report. This was certainly not the case. He wrote a series of five articles under the general title 'Pauperism and Poverty', that were published on succeeding Saturdays in February–March 1909 in the *Glasgow Herald*, which expressed considerable reservation about the tactics of the Webbs and some dissent from their conclusions. He conceded that the Minority Report, 'proceeding from one mind' (Beatrice and Sidney, quite reasonably, being considered intellectually one), was more organic in structure than that of the Majority, which was the work of several hands of 'unequal skill'. Undeniably the Minority Report exerted a

---

[29] *Our Partnership*, pp.423, 428–9.
[30] T.J., Class W, Vol.20, No.27.
[31] *Our Partnership*, p.422.
[32] T.J., Class P, Vol.1, No.4. Ibid., Class W, Vol.20, No.28.
[33] Ibid., No.29.

powerful cumulative effect on the reader. The Webbs, with their
fertility of suggestion and power of generalization, were undoubtedly 'the true successors' to Edwin Chadwick. But it remained
to be seen whether 'Mrs. Webb's deliberate partiality' would be
entirely effective.

> Many would not be able to resist the impression that in their
> enthusiasm for a symmetrical mechanism, the Minority have failed to
> take account of some characteristics of the average sensual man,
> pauper and official alike.

Jones went on to point to the considerable agreement there was
between the Majority and Minority Commissioners, and regretted
that the Minority had not been content to express their dissent on
particular points instead of seeking to demolish the system entirely.
He thought that the Minority lost sight of the fact that it was the
family (which would be dispersed) that needed to be rebuilt rather
than the individual. He believed, too, that a Registrar of Public
Assistance proposed by the Minority, a 'Napoleonic official' who
would exert 'the chilling influence of the pure bureaucrat', would
accumulate too much unrestrained power. And the proposed
'dispersals' of functions to government departments already heavily
burdened would also place too much power in the hands of a
'tyrannical bureaucracy'. The nourishing influence of the public
spirit of local authorities ought not lightly to be discarded.
Finally, he said that he did not believe that the Charity Organization Society was, as its critics and enemies maintained, a mere
'pad or pillow devised by the employing classes to break the fall of
victims damaged and sacrificed in the race for wealth'. On
the contrary, it represented a great moral force. 'The humanitarian spirit', he said, 'was never stronger or more eager to serve'
than at present. It ought not to be ignored. For the rest of his life
Tom Jones was to cling tenaciously to this belief in the value of
public-spirited voluntary effort. It was to be a source of particular
inspiration to him during the difficult years between the two world
wars.[34]

It was already apparent that Tom and Rene Jones could not
hope, even in a modest way, to operate together in tandem in the
manner of the Webbs all along the line in those public matters in
which they were interested. Quite apart from anything else,
although her health was incontestably much better since their
marriage, Rene still suffered occasionally from back pain and an

[34] *Glasgow Herald*, 27 February, 6, 13, 20 and 27 March 1909.

enervating lassitude.[35] 'I wish for your sake, darling, my store of energy were not so fractional', she wrote to Tom in 1904. She hoped that he did not think that she had become a mere 'unpractical housekeeper and pudding concocter'. She insisted that she had not lost her 'taste for the old things, the classics, the poetry, the music', but fully to satisfy Tom's 'craving' for 'a wife in the study', they would 'need to have no meals at all except compressed tablets'.[36] But she was certainly not housebound. She accompanied him to Ireland on his Barrington lecture tour in 1904, and enjoyed a holiday in Dresden with their friend Marianne Rheinhold in February 1906. 'I hope you are coming home', Tom wrote forlornly on the 17th, 'I have had about enough of this splendid desolation'.[37] But inevitably a good deal of her time was taken up in running the home. And the presence there of her brothers-in-law was sometimes rather a trial. Tom had brought them to Glasgow with the best of intentions. He found work for them and they lived in the cottage at Balmore. The arrangement, as he wrote with some understatement some years later, 'was not entirely successful'.[38]

Willie and Alf were very different from their elder brother Tom. They were temperamentally so unlike him that, with the best will in the world, it must have been difficult for them to fit easily into Tom's high-toned and, in some respects, rather sober ménage. On the other hand, Willie could be exasperatingly unreliable. 'I am sorry this affair of Willie has come to worry you', Rene wrote to Tom in 1904, 'I would have kept back the letter but feared the consequences if Willie were late, say, the next two or three mornings. He is a problem: why doesn't he say he's too out of sorts to get up to his work if that is the case? There's nothing to be ashamed of in it'.[39] Willie was evidently disposed to malinger now and again. He must have sorely tried the patience of Tom, for whom time was 'life's greatest gift', never to be squandered.[40] Alf was a jaunty extrovert, full of impossible schemes, but at least he did not take himself too seriously. 'Dear People', he wrote home in March 1906 from the S.S. *Sardinia* en route for Canada, 'You all know that I am a good one at building castles, and I hope you also

[35] In March 1904 she went for treatment to 'Phillips Hydropathic' at Dunblane, Perthshire. *Two Lovers*, pp.306–10.

[36] T.J., Class X, Vol.7, No.4.

[37] *Two Lovers*, pp.307–9, 318–20. T.J., Class X, Vol.7, No.16. She was also on holiday in Switzerland on New Year's Eve 1906.

[38] *Welsh Broth*, p.64.

[39] *Two Lovers*, p.308.

[40] *The Native Never Returns*, p.186.

know they fall occasionally'. The letter is signed 'Alf. The favourite
and best looking on the boat. That is the compliment I have had
paid me over and over again'.[41] Enoch, the third of the brothers,
four years older than Alf, had his lighthearted moments, as family
photographs indicate, but he was less volatile than Alf and seems to
have fitted in at Balmore more successfully and for a longer period.
Ultimately, however, two of the brothers left Glasgow and returned
to south Wales.[42]

Family matters continued to be important, at either end of the
span of life. In August 1906, Rene's father, Dr R.J. Lloyd, died
in curious, indeed thoroughly mysterious circumstances. Accompanied by Lilian, the daughter of his second marriage, he had gone
to Geneva to attend a congress of Esperantists. During a walk
together along the banks of a tributary of the Rhône, Dr Lloyd
(after having written a long letter to his wife) suddenly disappeared
up a slope into some bushes. He did not return. There were reports
that he had been seen the next day, looking dishevelled and
distracted, at several places in the district around. Tom and Rene
hurried out to Switzerland. Rewards were offered, a large-scale
search was organized. To no avail. A fortnight later Dr Lloyd's body
was found floating down the river Rhône twenty miles away. He was
buried in a village cemetery in the shadow of the Jura mountains
with a simple epitaph: 'He laboured for the advancement of
knowledge'. Tom Jones believed his father-in-law had 'paid the
penalty of a life of excessive mental concentration'. It was a tragic
end to a life that for years seemed to have had a strong undertow of
unhappiness.[43]

In 1905 Tom and Rene left Balmore to live in a substantial new
house that they rented in East Kilbride, some nine miles to the
south-east of Glasgow. They took the name Anwylfan with them to
their new home. During 1907 Rene began, increasingly, to bring up
the question of children. Before their marriage they had agreed to
remain childless. Rene's reasons were threefold: 'first, a disgust with
the physical side of marriage'. As she pointed out, Tom himself had
knocked down that objection. He had been, unfailingly, a 'kind and
gentle' husband, who had nonetheless insisted all along 'on the
divinity of the body . . . and the rightness of physical love'. Her
second objection stemmed from 'a fear for the religious upbringing
of children to whom I had no religion to give'. That fear had
subsided. 'I should be content, with you, to give them our *practical*

---

[41] T.J., Class X, Vol.3, No.25.
[42] *Two Lovers*, p.280.
[43] *Welsh Broth*, pp.74–5. There is much fuller detail in Tom Jones's (4pp.)
account of his father-in-law's life in the Tristan Jones MSS.

creed to go on. The religion of humanity'. Finally, she had believed formerly that children engrossed interest and attention to an extent that precluded all hope of service to the community. That idea too had been laughed out of court.[44]

Tom's objection to parenthood remained. He feared that children would deflect him from his academic work, his political activity and his powerful desire to do a 'citizen's best' in social matters before he died. These reasons were buttressed by an unreal fear that his health was poor, or at least unreliable, and that they did not have financial security as his academic position depended precariously on Smart's continuing good health. Rene maintained that Tom had been 'shirking the issue' for some time, taking refuge in cloudy talk of eugenics, the birthrate and avant-garde ideas derived from H.G. Wells, George Bernard Shaw and others. She meant to force a decision. Her husband was keeping up a 'bogey' because he was frightened of 'carrying out the ends of marriage'. Tom, who was away at this time, wrote back in some agitation to say that, reluctantly, he was persuaded to agree. Rene would have none of it.

> I will not *accept* children from you if you only 'yield', nor even if you 'acquiesce'. Unless I succeed in making you actually wish for them, we remain in *statu quo* . . . If I cannot persuade you that child-rearing is the first and highest duty we owe to the State . . . then not even a dozen children could make me a happy citizen. So let there be no talk of 'yielding' to my wish. I won't have that sort of co-operation at any price. That's final and definite and you needn't refer to it again.[45]

Rene won this argument. Two years later in November 1909 Tom wrote of 'the state of anxiety' in their household. 'We are expecting our first born this evening', he told his friend David Thomas, a schoolmaster in north Wales. 'The doctor has just come'. Happily, he was able to add a postscript: 'Later. A little girl came. May she be as good a citizen as her mother'. That hope was to be amply fulfilled.[46]

[44] T.J., Class X, Vol.7, No.3. *Two Lovers*, pp.320–2.
[45] Ibid., pp.322–7.
[46] 8 November 1909, NLW David Thomas (Bangor) MSS. This child, named after her mother, grew up to be, as Eirene White, an MP, a Minister of State in a Labour government, chairman of the Fabian Society and the NEC of the Labour Party, later Deputy Speaker of the House of Lords, and by her membership of innumerable voluntary and other bodies to continue her father's example of a lifetime's public service. 'I am immensely proud of her, with her mother's sterling qualities and more than a dash, a whole dose, of my initiative', Tom Jones wrote in 1948. Lochhead letters, White MSS.

This letter was written from Belfast, where a few months earlier Tom Jones had been appointed to a chair in Economics. Thereby he had achieved the permanent academic appointment and the reasonable financial security which went with it that he had hankered after since his marriage. It was not that he was unduly worried about money; as Rene had pointed out to him in their debate about parenthood, it was 'a side of life that never bothered you'. And it played little or no part in his relationship with Smart. 'I think I owe you £30-12-8d', the professor had written to him in 1908. 'I thank God it was never the cash nexus between you and me'.[47] But Tom Jones naturally wanted a permanent position and it was this, together with the opportunity it offered of returning to Wales, that had prompted him to apply for a lectureship in Economics at University College, Cardiff, in September 1905. There were, however, some difficulties about the post. The salary offered was only £200 and he already had an income of about £250, made up of his stipend from Smart, £80–100 from the Barrington lectures and £10–20 in fees for reviewing books for the *Glasgow Herald*. He set out the difficulty of his position in the draft of a long letter to J.S. Mackenzie, Professor of Philosophy at Cardiff, to whom he had turned some years before for advice over the establishment of a student settlement in Cardiff.[48] Jones said that he was prepared to accept £200 initially (although £250 would, of course, be much better) provided that it was raised to £300 at the end of the session, 'if all went well'. The new house at East Kilbride was a steady drain on their finances, they had no reserve of any kind, and he and his wife were 'still liable to our respective families for about £300'. He was nonetheless eager to come to Cardiff.

> Aberystwyth would be better for health reasons but the economic life is much richer in and around Cardiff. I believe in the reconciling influence of the study of Economics (broadly conceived) upon employers and employed . . . [There is] abundant need of such a study in Wales. I think I can win the confidence of some of the Labour leaders without pandering.

Mackenzie had written to say that there was a formidable rival for the post, H. Stanley Jevons, 'a son of the great Jevons'. As Mackenzie said, 'Jevons is a great name, and this one appears to be not unworthy to bear it'. Nevertheless, Tom Jones was appointed to the lectureship, although there was one final difficulty to be

[47] *Two Lovers*, p.322. T.J., Class W, Vol.17, No.215.
[48] See above, pp.41–2.

overcome. The Cardiff authorities wanted him to take up the appointment in October, or at Christmas time at the latest. This placed him in an awkward position. Smart, it will be remembered, had taken what amounted virtually to a year's leave of absence, and was naturally depending on Tom Jones to run the department at Glasgow during his absence. In the end, his obligations to Smart outweighed everything else.

> I have resigned the Cardiff post [he wrote to a Glasgow friend James Morton], mainly in order to take over nearly all the work here next winter to allow Dr. Smart to give undiminished attention to the Royal Commission and live in London while it is going on . . . It has been a very upsetting business.[49]

This was the first but not the last time that Tom Jones's academic ambitions went astray in Cardiff.

Henry Jones had not wanted his protégé to leave Glasgow but with some reluctance had advised him to apply for the Cardiff post. 'If you are not in Glasgow, Wales should have you . . . South Wales, where you can do so much for the workers'.[50] Almost a year later, Henry Jones tried another tack. In May 1906 he wrote to John Rowland, who was then Lloyd George's private secretary, recommending Tom Jones's appointment as a paid Commissioner to work in Wales on behalf of the Poor Law Commission. Strictly speaking, this appointment was not the concern of Lloyd George, but by 1906 the Liberal government would be likely to heed any recommendation that he made to appointments in Wales. Henry Jones described his candidate as 'supremely qualified by his economic attainments and knowledge of Welsh Wales . . . an advanced Liberal in politics and well known to the Glasgow Labour members and most popular'.[51] Nothing came of this. Lloyd George, at this stage, knew nothing of Tom Jones. And in the light of their less than amicable personal relations later, it is ironic that John Rowland was asked to intercede on Tom Jones's behalf.[52]

Henry Jones was not discouraged. When, in 1907, a Welsh Department of the Board of Education was being established, it was

[49] T.J., Class X, Vol.6, Nos.11, 22, 23, 24 and 38. Morton MSS. GD326/81/1.

[50] T.J., Class U, Vol.1, No.2. Henry Jones's reference in support of Tom Jones was glowing. It was difficult, he wrote, to do justice to him 'without seeming to exaggerate. He was not only the best student of his time in the University of Glasgow [in Economics and Moral Philosophy], but, in my opinion, the best student I have ever had among my pupils'. Ibid., Class X, Vol.3, No.28.

[51] NLW MSS. 21787 D, f.56.

[52] See below, pp.147–8.

first suggested that Henry Jones himself should be made its Permanent Secretary. But he was unwilling to leave Glasgow and refused. Instead, he suggested Tom Jones's name and pressed for his appointment forcefully.

> I struck as hard as I can [he told Tom Jones]. I think you have the devotion, the enthusiasm, the tact, the resolve, the practical wisdom, and the enterprise which the situation demands, and you are not to think of blenching before its difficulties. You can be frank – I know you can be nothing else; but you can also be fearless . . . God bless you my lad, and your dear wife, and make you a great and growing power for good.[53]

But Henry Jones failed here, too. The appointment went to Alfred T. Davies, a Liverpool solicitor, a Liberal who had strongly supported Lloyd George's campaign against Balfour's Education Act in 1902.[54]

In the mean time, while all these alternative possibilities were in train, Tom Jones was hard at work establishing and enhancing his academic standing. His quality as a teacher was recognized. If not inspiring in quite the manner of Henry Jones, he was certainly much more than thoroughly competent in all he did in the classroom. 'I have been recommending your Seminar to people in Glasgow', wrote his friend Kenneth Leys, an Oxford don, in 1909. 'It's on the best German lines, Sir!'.[55] Tom Jones was also recognized by the editor of the *Economic Journal* as the best reviewer of a certain class of books in Economics. He continued to make a special study, based on local conditions in Glasgow, of industrial relations, of the problem of unemployment and the allied disease of chronic underemployment. In 1908 he fulfilled a promise made some time before to Ramsay Macdonald 'to do something for the *Socialist Review*', the recently established journal of the Independent Labour Party. His article, 'Unemployment, Boy Labour, and continued Education', was a useful and interesting piece of work which examined in some detail the social and industrial history of men under forty years of age. Jones concluded that the fate of many of them was decided before they had reached the age of twenty, when, inadequately educated, they were pitchforked into dead-end jobs, from which they were dismissed when they reached

[53] T.J., Class U, Vol.1, No.1. See also Gareth Jones, *Controls and Conflicts in Welsh Secondary Education* (Cardiff, 1987), pp.14–15, 39.
[54] K.O. Morgan, *Rebirth of a Nation. Wales 1880–1980* (Oxford and Cardiff, 1967), p.112.
[55] T.J., Class W, Vol.12, No.199.

manhood and demanded a man's wage. There was here, in this 'thoughtless drifting', an 'enormous waste of youthful life power'. He argued powerfully for the introduction, by law, of a system of continuation schools that apprentices would attend on part-time day release from work until the age of eighteen. 'It will be objected', he said, 'that we are interfering with the law of demand and supply of labour. We are, but in the wisest way . . . As usual, Germany had set the example as to what should be done'.[56]

As one of his referees, H.B. Lees Smith, Professor of Economics at Bristol and a future Labour cabinet minister, wrote in 1909, Tom Jones was 'one of the few economists who combine a deep knowledge of the subject with great powers of popular exposition'. He used those powers to awaken the interest of Glasgow business and professional men in the relatively new subject of Economics, and in 1905 he suggested that descriptive economics at least could be usefully taught in schools.[57] He also brought out an edition of some of the works of his old hero, Joseph Mazzini, to which he wrote an introduction.

This was a venture that dated back to 1898 when Tom Jones was a student. He wrote to the publisher J.M. Dent suggesting the inclusion of a new edition of Mazzini's works in their Temple Classics series. Dent turned down the proposal on commercial grounds but said that he would 'risk it' if Jones could indeed persuade the distinguished philosopher A.C. Bradley to write an introduction, as he had suggested. The negotiations meandered along rather purposelessly for years. Even more discouragingly, Bradley eventually declined to write an introduction, but flatteringly suggested that Tom Jones, who had been 'thinking about [the] subject continuously for a long time', would do it rather better himself. There then followed a comic exchange with Dent.

> Are you going to give the public your services, or what shall I pay you? [the publisher asked on 19 August 1905]. I think I ought to pay some nominal fee . . . or if you like we will leave it this way, that if I gain I am to pay you £10 (ten pounds) [lest there be any doubt!] for the work, or if I lose I pay you nothing, or something of that sort.

Dent did not know that Tom Jones had ancestral connections with Cardiganshire and had lived among Scotsmen for years.

---

[56] T.J., Class X, Vol.3, No.33. 7 October 1908. Macdonald Papers, PRO 30–69–1152, f.162. *The Socialist Review*, II (January 1909), 857–70.

[57] T.J., Class X, Vol.3, Nos.33 and 37. Ibid., Class Y, Vol.3, No.3. Lees Smith had been runner-up for the Barrington Lectureship in 1904.

I am an impecunious Assistant not a professor [he replied]. And it would be bad economics to go unpaid. I am willing to accept £10 if you gain . . . If you lose, I shall be content with £5 for my work.

After six weeks' careful deliberation, Dent replied agreeing to those terms, adding a rider of protest

against the ethics that a publisher may lose to any extent, but the author must be paid. [All labour should be paid for] It should be the law of the Medes and Persians, and ought to be the ethical principle upon which all governments should build. But alas, human life does not work in that way. [Please] proceed with the work at once.

Despite the lordly condescension, Dent continued to haggle about costs and cut an unexpected corner or two. Finally, helped by the good offices of Ernest Rhys, who was general editor of the series, *The Duties of Man and other Essays* by Joseph Mazzini, with an Introduction by Thomas Jones, was published in 1907 as volume 224 in Dent's Everyman Library.[58] Despite the long premeditation and Tom Jones's abiding interest in Mazzini, his Introduction is not among the best of his writings. Certainly it has many graceful passages, and there are several instances of his sharp eye for colourful illustrative detail but his hero-worship is all too evident.

But social and political philosophy continued to retain his interest. If anything, he had been more attracted to that side of his undergraduate work than to economics. Indeed, it could be said that he became a professional economist by default as much as by choice. In 1899, with no other offer in sight, he had accepted Smart's proposal, become his assistant, and, for good or ill, a student and teacher of economics. But there is some evidence that Henry Jones still hoped that his best pupil could be reclaimed for philosophy. In 1909 the professor talked in confidence of the possibility of the establishment of a lectureship in Social Philosophy in three years' time. Tom Jones was worried by this; exactly why is not clear. Rene, never short of robust common sense, told him to put the matter out of his mind. If, however, the post were established in the future, and Tom were to be appointed, it would have to be on his own terms, not those of Henry Jones.

If you were bound down in lecturing to ideals that were not your own you'd be miserable under the restraint and do bad work, neither your own ideal nor his.[59]

58 The extensive correspondence is in T.J., Class Y, Vol.1, Nos.4–27.
59 *Two Lovers*, p.312.

Nothing came of this scheme, and nothing subsequently occurred to ruffle his relations with Henry Jones in the slightest degree. That friendship remained rock-like. Indeed, most of the friendships that Tom Jones made in Glasgow were remarkably durable and rewarding. There were, for example, the brothers Norman and Kenneth Leys, his student colleagues at the Possil Road Settlement. Norman Leys, a doctor, intrepid champion of the rights of native African peoples and uncompromising critic of British imperialist exploitation, became later the stern voice of principle in Tom Jones's official ear. Kenneth Leys, rescued by Smart and Tom Jones from being miscast as an accountant, became a History don at Glasgow and subsequently, for thirty years, at University College, Oxford; he was an unfailing source of sage advice.[60] An even more interesting man in some ways was James Morton, industrial chemist and dynamic entrepreneur, who remained one of Tom Jones's devoted friends for the rest of his life. They met when Morton gave a lecture on his hero William Morris to the Glasgow XL Club, of which Tom Jones was a member. Their friendship was cemented by a mutual interest in the crafts and in public affairs.[61] And there were the Lochheads, Jack and his sister, Lizzie, who spent a lifetime in Settlement work in the Glasgow slums, with whom he was on the best of terms for over fifty years.[62] Of his Glasgow friends, the choicest spirit of all was perhaps R.H. Tawney. Tom Jones first met him at Toynbee Hall in 1905. 'I divined his exceptional quality at once', Jones said, 'and easily persuaded Smart to add him to our overtaxed staff'. But although they were colleagues at Glasgow for only two years, they retained thereafter an immense respect for each other's qualities.[63]

At this time Tawney's membership of the Fabian Society and the ILP was rather more 'passive' than that of Tom Jones.[64] Indeed, during 1909 it was proposed that Jones should stand for Parliament as a Labour candidate in Merioneth where a by-election was pending. The invitation to consider standing came from the Revd Robert Silyn Roberts, poet, Methodist minister at Tanygrisiau, near Blaenau Ffestiniog, and the founder of a small but lively ILP

---

[60] *Welsh Broth*, pp.47–9. R.H. Tawney, 'Kenneth Leys, 1876–1950', loc.cit., pp.104–10.

[61] Jocelyn Morton, *Three Generations of a Family Textile Firm* (1971), pp.203–5.

[62] Lochhead letters (1938–1954), White MSS.

[63] *Welsh Broth*, p.70. *Manchester Guardian*, 18 March 1952.

[64] *R.H. Tawney's Commonplace Book*, ed. J.M. Winter and D.M. Joslin (Cambridge 1972), Introduction, pp.xviii–xix.

branch among the quarrymen in that district.[65] The two men had
met at Fabian Society summer schools that were held at Llanbedr, a
few miles from Harlech, during those years. Early in March Tom
Jones consulted Alderman William Sanders, 'the organiser of the
Fabian Society', as he called him, 'about possibilities in Merioneth-
shire'. A fortnight earlier, in a long letter to Silyn Roberts, Tom
Jones, without prejudice to any decision about standing, had
defined his general attitude on a number of points. 'I have never
seriously thought of a political career though it has once or twice
been offered to me', he wrote. He doubted whether he had 'the
powers which would make for parliamentary success', but he
believed he could be useful in promoting 'democratic education,
and in mediating between the Liberal and Labour positions. Work
of this sort is urgently needed and it attracts me'. On the other
hand, he believed that 'any "Lib-Lab" arrangement is unstable and
unsatisfactory to both parties'. If he stood,

> it would be as a Labour candidate (assuming that the Labour party
> would approve of me). I could not agree of course to all that is said
> and proposed by every Labour member but, generally, I would be in
> agreement with Ramsay MacDonald, Snowden, Percy Alden, Chiozza
> Money and members of that type, who are Fabian in attitude.

Tom Jones was, of course, an ardent Free Trader, and he was
concerned that his candidature might split the vote and let in a
tariff reformer, which 'would be a grave danger to the country'.
    There were other difficulties too.

> It would be impossible to put me forward as a Methodist, for although
> I have never removed my name from the Diary, my views are no longer
> those of the "Cyffes Ffydd" [The Methodist Confession of Faith, the
> litmus test of denominational orthodoxy]. *You* will not of course rush
> to the conclusion that I am therefore irreligious or a rank secularist.
> "Cairdian" would hit me off as well or as badly as any other label!

There was another 'but minor' difficulty.

> My Welsh was never very efficient and it has now lain long out of active
> use. I should find it very difficult *at first* to discuss social questions in
> Welsh. I could only hope to improve quickly with practice. Of course I
> can read and understand Welsh perfectly, and talk it colloquially.

[65] Bangor MS 19519. David Thomas, *Silyn 1871–1930* (Liverpool, 1956),
pp.74–6.

There was, too, the question of finance; he had 'absolutely no money' to spend on electioneering. 'Mrs. Jones's illness [presumably recurrent back pain] and insurance premiums' absorbed any surplus of his income. He would not lightly hazard his university post: 'the demand for teachers of Economics is limited'. His caution was understandable.

> Are you strong enough in Merionethshire to hope to return a Labour candidate? I see the present member was returned unopposed . . . What is the numerical strength of the I.L.P.? What is the position and attitude of the Quarrymen's Union, the leaders and the rank and file? How do the quarrymen compare numerically with the tenant farmers and the "middleclass"? . . . Are any of the ministers and deacons, Bala students sympathetic at all? . . . would any of them appear on a platform with me?[66]

To pose these questions was almost enough to answer them. The ILP in the county was very weak, the Quarrymen's Union, while sympathetic to Labour, for a variety of local reasons, steadily refused for some years to affiliate to the Labour party. Some months later, when Silyn Roberts himself was asked to stand, he replied that if he were to do so, he would 'appear in his true colours as a Progressive Socialist'. But, as he conceded, 'I can scarcely hope that political thought in Merioneth is advanced enough at present to elect such a candidate'.[67]

Not surprisingly, therefore, Tom Jones ultimately decided not to stand. But for a time he was active in ILP and Labour politics in the area. He addressed a small group of 'the Comrades' in Caernarfon in April, and gave some help to his friend David Thomas in the revision and publication of his book *Y Werin a'i Theyrnas* (The People and its Kingdom), an exposition of socialist principles in the Welsh language.[68] In May 1909 Jones was retailing to Silyn Roberts with great enthusiasm a plan to issue a number of booklets which he proposed to call the Little Boy Blue Books. He thought that his address to the miners at Bargoed, 'as I am frequently asked

---

[66] Bangor MSS 19521 and 19527. R.H. Tawney welcomed the possibility of Jones standing in Merioneth and thought that, if he were elected, he would succeed in the House of Commons. 'I think it would like you, even if you didn't like it'. T.J., Class W, Vol.18, No.25.

[67] R. Merfyn Jones, *The North Wales Quarrymen 1874–1922* (Cardiff, 1982), pp.317–21. C. Parry, 'The Independent Labour Party and Gwynedd Politics, 1900–20', *WHR*, IV, 49–52. Bangor MS 17217. A later attempt to run a 'Lib–Lab' candidate was also dropped.

[68] Bangor MS 19524. NLW David Thomas (Bangor) MSS.

for it', could be No. 1 in the series, followed by 'Coal and Colliers', a talk that he had given in Penrhiwceiber. He suggested that in due course, with assistance from others, they could publish several more booklets, 'some English and some Welsh, with, as a rule, the needs of Wales especially in view and not necessarily socialist'. Subjects which occurred to him were, in order, inevitably first, Mazzini, followed by Marx, Robert Owen, William Morris and perhaps a Welsh 'Song Book for Demonstrations'.[69]

Moreover, on Labour Day, 1 May 1909, he shared the platform with Philip Snowden in the Pavilion at Caernarfon when they addressed the North Wales Quarrymen's Festival meeting, Snowden, of course, in English, Tom Jones in Welsh. He had been 'extremely nervous', as he said, about speaking to a large audience in Welsh. As it was, his blending of 'the careful speech of the classroom lecture, often breaking into natural eloquence', with a touch of 'the old pulpit oratory', as the local newspaper put it, was admirably suited to his earnest audience. In cold print, the address does not live up to this eulogy, but the reporter was T. Gwynn Jones, future distinguished man of letters, whose judgement of style and language in Welsh is not to be lightly set aside. Tom Jones's address was entitled *Y Mudiad Llafur Yng Nghymru* (The Labour Movement in Wales). In a wide-ranging address, that traced the history of the co-operative and trade union movements in Britain, he insisted again that the worker was also a citizen and that the problems of Wales were those of the world at large. There was a need not only for Labour party branches in Wales, but also for a Welsh Labour party. The ILP was its advance guard. As for current talk of war in Europe, what was wanted was a war on poverty. The common people did not want to fight; they should join the army of labour which, along with its brothers in France, Germany and other countries, was prepared, if necessary, to resort to a general strike to stop a war.[70]

When war actually came in 1914, Tom Jones, in common with most European socialists, had changed his mind quite considerably

----

[69] Bangor MS 19518. For various reasons, not least his move to Belfast, the plan was not pursued.

[70] Bangor MS 19524. The *North Wales Observer and Express*, 7 May 1909. For T. Gwynn Jones's authorship, see David Jenkins, *T. Gwynn Jones: Cofiant* (Denbigh, 1973), t.200. In his address (printed in *A Theme with Variations*, pp.26–46) Tom Jones argued strongly that the Quarrymen's Union, in association with the University College at Bangor, should establish extension course classes dealing with contemporary as well as historical subjects. This proposal was acted upon soon afterwards.

on that question.[71] But by then his life had changed in many other ways too. In 1908, at long last, what he believed to be his precarious position in the Economics department at Glasgow had been improved by his appointment to an independent lectureship created for him by the University Court.[72] He was then thirty-eight years old and naturally aspired to a chair in Economics. In the following year, four opportunities opened up for him. The first one ended quickly in disappointment. In March 1909, Sir Charles Eliot invited Tom Jones to apply for a chair in Economics which the University of Sheffield proposed to establish. He did apply but was not successful. It appears that the authorities, no doubt hard pressed for money, asked candidates to state the lowest salary that they would be prepared to accept if appointed. G.I.H. Lloyd, a member of the staff at Sheffield who was a candidate, described it as 'an absurd dutch auction', adding wryly that it was perhaps 'appropriate in the appointment of an economist'. Tom Jones's irreducible minimum salary is not known. The fact that he had not, as yet, published a substantial book in the field seems to have told against him, not unreasonably. He might perhaps have derived some consolation from the warning given him by Lees Smith, one of his referees, that Curtis, a friend of his who taught history at Sheffield, 'had little liberty of speech and was pulled up sharply once or twice'. Lees Smith said that the University was strongly supported by the Conservatives and he believed 'therefore that any labour sentiment had better be kept in the background'. He was prepared to concede that professors might perhaps enjoy rather more freedom. Whatever the truth of this, 'the Yorkshire idiots', as Kenneth Leys called them, did not appoint Tom Jones.[73]

Also in 1909, Sir Robert Falconer, acting on behalf of the Governors of the University of Toronto in Canada, invited Jones to apply for an associate professorship in Political Science. The stipend immediately on offer was on a scale of £500-600, but once the man appointed had demonstrated his worth, the post would be transformed into a full professorship with a salary rising to £740. Moreover, 'in a young country, undisturbed as yet by many of the problems of the older lands, but soon to be face to face with them', Falconer wrote persuasively, 'there is a large opportunity for a strong man in such a chair'. Jones again consulted Kenneth Leys. He pointed out that acceptance would mean staying in Canada for at least four or five years, and that, as he said, would be 'a sad gap

---

[71] 'War and the Labour Movement', ibid., pp.61–7.
[72] T.J., Class X, Vol.3, No.38.
[73] Ibid., Nos.28, 32 and 39. Ibid., Class W, Vol.12, No.199.

for me, a strange gap'. It would not altogether mean a move to outer darkness: '*I believe*', he said, effortless Oxford superiority breaking in, 'Toronto University is quite a good place'. But on balance he advised Tom Jones not to go, 'I think your future at home quite certain'. From Germany Marianne Rheinhold sent an impassioned plea: 'I've just been looking up Toronto on the map – no, no, no! Don't go there. I should feel as if you might just as well be on another planet'. And R.H. Tawney weighed in on the same side. Ultimately, Tom Jones decided against Toronto, and, other reasons apart, his sense of continuing obligation to his father and sisters had an important bearing on the decision.[74]

The third possibility was an intriguing one. It was that he should apply for the Principalship of Ruskin College, Oxford, which had been established in 1899 by two American philanthropists who believed that the growing importance of the Labour movement in America and Britain required that its leaders should be equipped educationally for their much greater responsibilities. 'We wish to instruct the young men who one day may control the English speaking peoples', said Walter Vrooman, one of the founders, 'to teach them how to control things'.[75] It was a residential college for working men, in Oxford but not connected with the University in any way. Indeed, according to one early student, it 'was run on Yankee lines at first and in blatant defiance of the Varsity'.[76] The assumption was that students would return to their former jobs when their studies at the College were completed. According to Vrooman, the College would 'have no 'ism to teach'. It was to be of 'no party' and have 'no creed'. Within a few years, all these matters were furiously in dispute.[77]

There were several causes of the difficulties that came to a head in dramatic fashion in March 1909 when the Principal, Dennis Hird, was dismissed, a majority of the students went on strike in protest, and, eventually, a breakaway Central Labour College was established, first in Oxford subsequently in London. It is clear that there were disruptive personal antagonisms among the small staff, and some failure of understanding between middle-class tutors (two of whom were very inexperienced in work of this kind) and politically militant, class-conscious worker students. But there was also the much more important issue of a head-on collision between

[74] Ibid., Class P, Vol.1, Nos.1 and 2; Class W, Vol.12, No.199, Vol.16, No.204, and Vol.18, No.25. Class Z (Diary 1899–1916), p.5.
[75] H. Pollins, *The History of Ruskin College* (Oxford, 1984), p.10.
[76] T.J., Class X, Vol.2, No.71.
[77] H. Pollins, op.cit., p.10.

two different concepts of the nature and purpose of workers' education. A conflict between those who believed in the virtues of a liberal tradition of teaching that at least aspired to be objective, and those, not all of whom were confirmed Marxists, who insisted that that concept was bogus, a wilful deception.[78]

It is evident therefore that to become Principal of Ruskin College in 1909 was to accept an invitation to take charge of a hornets' nest. Tom Jones was not immediately deterred. He sought the advice of Tawney, Kenneth Leys and T.I. Mardy Jones, a former Ruskin College student and future ill-fated Labour MP. Tawney admitted that Ruskin's immediate future was uncertain. On the other hand, it might in time 'do great things' and become 'a model and pioneer to other colleges'. He advised Jones to insist on certain terms, a free hand, full backing from the executive committee, and liberty to lecture in the University if he so desired, before taking matters any further.[79] Mardy Jones, who was the chief exponent of the Ruskin establishment's case in south Wales, where the student critics were especially active, argued strongly that Tom Jones should apply and that he would be successful if he did so. Moreover, he was confident, 'if you can come matters will soon be right'.[80]

Leys, who was in Germany and apparently unaware of the crisis in the College, replied at very great length. He said that Tom Jones would be a 'Godsend' to the Ruskin authorities: 'From their point of view you are the very man'. Jones should 'banish' immediately any apprehension he had of being out of place or out of his depth in the University town. 'You needn't be afraid of Oxford . . . You'd be far and away *the* man in any common-room that I'd take off my hat to!' The real problem, however, was: 'What is the College going to be worth?'. Was it really going to be 'a serious and weighty thing?'. Leys had his doubts. He felt that his friend would 'be wasted there'.[81]

In the event, Tom Jones looked elsewhere. It is possible that with his vision, drive and rare ability to enlist aid in all sorts of unlikely places, he might have achieved an exceptional status for Ruskin and, given his powerful interest in that direction, used it to very great effect in strengthening the adult education movement in Britain. There were however some obvious limitations to the post,

[78] Ibid., pp.17–23. R. Lewis, 'The South Wales Miners and the Ruskin College Strike of 1909', *Llafur*, II (1976), 57–73. T.J., Class X, Vol.2, No.71.

[79] Ibid., Class W, Vol. 18, No.25.

[80] Ibid., Class X, Vol.2, No.71.

[81] Ibid., Class W, Vol.12, No.199. Tom Jones himself felt that it would have been a mistake to have gone to Ruskin before he had become 'a full-blown professor'. Bangor MS 19525.

and Mardy Jones's optimism to the contrary, there was to be a lengthy bitter aftermath to the recent imbroglio.[82]

The post to which he was appointed ultimately was the one that he had least expected to get: a chair in Economics at the Queen's University in Belfast. This was a new foundation, centred on the existing Queen's College in the city but now given an independent power to confer degrees. It was the outcome of the belated British attempt to remedy some of the grievances of Ireland and, to that end, was to be a non-sectarian institution. For five years it would be governed by a Senate nominated by the Crown, and professors would be appointed by a statutory commission. Tom Jones had applied for the chair with little expectation of success. With him on a short list of three was W.R. Scott (who was eventually to succeed Smart in the chair at Glasgow), who had just completed a monumental three-volumed history of British joint stock companies. Tom Jones, despite the urgings of Kenneth Leys and Tawney, had not yet published anything as substantial as a book. Tawney had been keen for him to get the Belfast chair; Leys would have preferred Sheffield, because it would have kept Jones in closer touch and, for what it was worth, he thought 'the Northern Irish . . . more pigheaded even than Yorkshiremen'. On the other hand, Leys thought that Jones, despite his pessimism, might very well be appointed to Belfast. He should not fear Scott's competition. 'You are much superior. He's a nice man; but quite armchair; you can do both'. This was possibly a telling point which was emphasized by Smart in his reference in support of Tom Jones.

> It is pleasant to write a testimonial in which I have nothing to keep back, and [an echo of Henry Jones] where the only difficulty is in speaking in terms which will not suggest exaggeration. Mr. Jones was the most promising student I ever had . . . he has already become a power in the social life in the city.[83]

Relaxed and with nothing to lose, Tom Jones was perfectly at ease. 'It was a delightful interview', he reported exultantly to Rene, 'I never really dreamt for a moment I'd get it'. But he had. Smart was both sad and delighted, and characteristically generous: '*Le Roi est mort; vive le roi*. That is to say, the Department must go on although it has lost its chief ornament'.[84]

[82] See W.W. Craik, *The Central Labour College 1909–29* (1964).

[83] *Welsh Broth*, pp.115–17. T.J., Class W, Vol.12, No.199; Vol.18, No.25. Ibid., Class Z (Diary 1899–1916), p.10.

[84] Ibid., No.43. Ibid., Class W, Vol.17, No.219.

CHAPTER SIX

THE NATIVE RETURNS

HIS APPOINTMENT to a chair in Belfast had improved Tom Jones's financial position quite substantially. Previously his income had been about £400 a year. His professional salary was now £700. In July 1909 Tom was busy house hunting in Belfast. He eventually managed to rent a house in St John's Avenue, to which, inevitably, they transferred the name Anwylfan yet again. The property had been unoccupied for a year and had accumulated 'twelve months' dust on the paint work'. With the help of Lizzie, an energetic Irish charwoman, Rene worked hard cleaning house and staining floors to make their new home comfortable.[1] Tom meantime had dashed over to Rhymney to attend the wedding of his sister Har to Matthew McKenzie, a Cardiff accountant.

Rene had no faith that Tom, who had no dress sense at all and throughout his life cared nothing about clothes, would be properly turned out for the occasion. She called on her sister-in-law Liz to help. Tom had unearthed his frock coat which had been in 'hiding for seven years' since their wedding day. At a pinch his old silk hat would do, but he would need a new waistcoat and gloves. He had a green silk tie which would pass muster, 'if someone sees that he puts it on straight'.[2] Liz evidently did take charge, for in the wedding photographs Tom appears impeccably well dressed.

In his autobiographical volume *Welsh Broth,* Tom Jones claimed that he 'enjoyed every hour' of his short stay of barely twelve months in Belfast.[3] There is perhaps a touch of diplomatic forgetfulness in this comment written forty years after the event, for his introduction to the Queen's University was not entirely easy. Not surprisingly, the business of organising a new department of Economics in a recently established university, that had been erected on an existing institution, was not without its difficulties. He was surprised at the outset to find that there was no honours school in Economics for Arts students. That was soon remedied, but he was taken aback to discover also that the Queen's University

[1] T.J., Class X, Vol.3, Nos.47 and 48. Bangor MS. 19525.
[2] T.J., Class X, Vol.3, No.48.
[3] *Welsh Broth*, p.117.

Commissioners expected him to double up as professor of Commerce as well as Economics. There was, according to his Irish friend A.E. Dobbs, Fellow of King's College, Cambridge, something of a tradition in Irish higher education of attaching several subjects to one chair. There were other complications. There was the difficult job of co-ordinating the work in Commerce in his department with that done at the Technical Institute in order to avoid a wasteful duplication. Eventually, after several months of time-consuming effort, which involved visits to Birmingham and Manchester to study departments of Commerce there, a Faculty of Commerce was established jointly with the Technical Institute. This had been of some particular importance because town-gown relations in Belfast in 1909 were strained, and in order to conciliate business opinion, which wanted to see some tangible sign of an academic return for its support of the new University, it was decided to proceed as rapidly as possible in developing the Faculty of Commerce, although Tom Jones had counselled caution.[4]

However, in other respects, he was just the man to build up good relations with the municipal community. He had the good sense to eschew politics and religion, that permanently baited double trap for the unwary in Ireland, and concentrated on economics and education. He had never been an armchair economist and had no great interest in, or aptitude for, the higher flights of economic theory. He preferred to operate on the margin where academic knowledge bordered on the real world of industry. In addition to the usual stint of formal lectures, he conducted tutorials in international trade, and, typically, persuaded Belfast business men to address the class on subjects, the Stock Exchange and the Irish linen industry, for example, in which they had expert knowledge. And continuing his practice in Glasgow, he lectured extensively (seventeen times in all in that first demanding session) to business, literary and other societies in the city of Belfast. His addresses were usually on subjects of social concern: pauperism and poverty, and the need for the medical inspection of schoolchildren. In April 1910 he accepted an invitation from the Viceroy, Lord Aberdeen, to speak in Dublin to the Women's National Health Association of Ireland on the same topics. He stayed at Dublin Castle and, among others, met George Russell (A.E.), the poet and painter, and re-newed his acquaintance with Horace Plunkett, who had laboured

[4] T.J., Class Z (Diary 1899–1916), p.15–18. Tom Jones to James Morton, 22 April 1910. Morton MSS GD326/82/1. *Welsh Broth*, p.117. A Dean of the Faculty of Commerce later commented that Tom Jones had shown 'exceptional tact . . . without suppressing his own opinion', a performance 'which would do credit to an experienced diplomat'. T.J., Class X, Vol.4, No.17.

so hard to bring new economic life to the Irish countryside, a man for whom Tom Jones had the greatest admiration.[5]

Of course, he did not restrict his extra-mural activities to the business world in Belfast. It was an industrial city of shipyards, linen, tobacco and many other manufactures as well as a variety of engineering works. He visited mills and factories and maintained his intense interest in working conditions, industrial relations and the causes and consequences of unemployment. More especially, he was at work in the field of adult education, which was then and subsequently perhaps the greatest single interest in his life.[6] At first sight, Northern Ireland was unpromising ground. A.E. Dobbs, who hailed from Carrickfergus and was an authority on the adult education movement, had warned him that until the Gaelic League some years before had prompted an interest in literary and historical subjects, there existed 'no form of education which could possibly appeal to the great mass of the Irish people'. Within months of his arrival, Tom Jones was forced to agree.

> I thoroughly agree with you about the urgent need of . . . W.E.A. [The Workers' Educational Association] work [he wrote to James Morton, who had commercial interests in Ireland], and I am doing my utmost in this benighted place . . . to push the idea.

Luckily, he was not alone. For the moment Rene could not help. 'I miss my Secretary and ADC this session', he told Morton, 'but there is no dragging her from the absorbing attention of the cherub', their baby daughter Eirene. However, on the day Tom Jones was appointed Professor of Economics, the chair of History had gone to F.M. Powicke, the distinguished scholar who in due course was to occupy the Regius chair of Modern History at Oxford. Together Tom Jones and Powicke canvassed the support of local trade unions, the Co-operative Society, the University, and private individuals and succeeded in raising enough money to 'provide a special man for the job', a tutor to organize extra-mural work. Jones also started a Poor Law Reform Association in Belfast. He gave an inaugural address on the Majority and Minority Reports to this avowedly non-political society, which was devoted to the study of the Irish problem in the light of the work of the Poor Law Commission.[7]

Ulster and the demands of a new university department did not absorb all of Tom Jones's energies. Indeed, nothing could ever

[5] Morton MSS GD326/82/1. *Welsh Broth*, pp.117–22. T.J., Class X, Vol.6, No.41. Ibid., Class Y, Vol.3, Nos.8 and 9.

[6] E.L. Ellis, 'Dr. Thomas Jones C.H. and Education' *THSC* (1982), pp.86–109.

[7] T.J., Class Z, (Diary 1899–1916), pp.15–18. T. Jones to Morton, 22 April 1910. Morton MSS GD326/82/1. *Welsh Broth*, p.120.

confine or constrict his interest in adult education. From Belfast he maintained a long-range contact with the movement in Wales. When he came over for his sister's wedding, he interrupted the visit to lecture to the WEA in Merthyr. Moreover, he already considered the whole of Wales his bailiwick. It will be remembered that in his speech to the quarrymen at Caernarfon in 1909, he had urged the establishment of adult education classes in that area. The Quarrymen's Union had promptly invited him to deliver a series of lectures in the district later that year. But his appointment to the chair in Belfast soon afterwards had made that impossible, and the Union had accordingly turned to the University College at Bangor for assistance. J.F. Rees, a young lecturer at Bangor, later principal of University College, Cardiff, conducted a course on industrial history for a class of twenty-five quarrymen at Blaenau Ffestiniog. In the spring of 1910, on the eve of a meeting at Aberystwyth summoned to consider establishing extra-mural classes under the auspices of the University College of Wales, Tom Jones arranged for J.F. Rees to give a proselytizing account of his pioneer work to some of those who would play a part in deciding matters the next day, when, in fact, the College formally agreed to begin extra-mural work. 'The hand of Tom Jones', wrote David Thomas, his colleague in WEA work at this time, 'is to be seen everywhere impelling the movement forward'.[8]

He was equally energetic, though rather less successful, in seeking to maintain the momentum of Fabian Society activity in Wales. The metropolitan Fabians had arranged to hold their usual Summer School at Llanbedr in Merioneth in August 1910. It was to be conducted by Sidney and Beatrice Webb, who hoped generally to inspire young university Fabians to promote their campaign in support of the Minority Report of the Poor Law Commission.[9] Tom Jones and David Thomas, however, sought additionally to arrange a subordinate conference of young Welshmen to discuss social, economic and educational problems on a special 'Welsh day'. In addition to a discussion of the relation of the Minority Poor Law Report to Wales, Tom Jones said that he was 'anxious to ventilate W.E.A. ideas', and make plans for the following winter.[10] A Welsh conference did take place, but no more than a handful of Fabians from the Principality attended. It did little to promote Fabian

   [8] David Thomas, *Silyn* (Liverpool, 1956), pp.68–71. E. L. Ellis, *The University College of Wales Aberystwyth, 1872–1972* (Cardiff, 1972), pp.169–70. B.B. Thomas, 'R.D. Roberts and Adult Education', *Harlech Studies* (ed. B.B. Thomas, Cardiff, 1938), pp.32–4.

   [9] *Webb Letters*, II, 345–6.

   [10] NLW David Thomas (Bangor) MSS.

strength in Wales; indeed, if anything, it had the reverse effect. There appeared to be little common ground between most of the Welsh Fabians and the cosmopolitan bigwigs from London who had little interest in provincial concerns. It seemed, too, to the Welsh members that the ILP was likely to be a more effective agency for the promotion of their ideas in Wales.[11]

But it is doubtful if Tom Jones himself was alienated to the same extent, or for that matter in any respect at all. He had a wider experience than most of his Welsh colleagues, and he had been on reasonably close terms with the Webbs for fifteen years or so. Moreover, it is clear that in the last year he had moved closer to the Webbs in his understanding of the causes of poverty, and become less critical than formerly of the conclusions of their Minority Poor Law Report. It was not that he had succumbed to their personal influence or to high pressure missionary teaching at the Fabian Summer School. Months before, he had written an article and delivered a public lecture in which he had expressed his substantial agreement with their views. And it was not that he had now left Glasgow and was thus free of William Smart's influence. He had never hesitated to disagree with Smart on intellectual issues when so minded, even in his student days. It is possible that his experience of poverty in the new setting of Belfast, which had its own versions of crippling hardship, had sharpened his perception. Moreover, his original objections had been more to Mrs Webb's methods than to her arguments. What is clear is that the occasionally hysterical objections to the 'full-blown wickedness of the Minority Report', as some critics described it, had driven him to recognize its merits more fully. He now appreciated its heartening optimism; in particular, 'the compelling power of a new gospel to thousands of young men and women eager for a constructive organic campaign against squalid poverty in our cities'. He now had no hesitation: the nation should opt for the Minority Report which struck at 'the sources and roots of pauperism'. The Majority Report's preoccupation with mere symptoms did not go far enough. This change of mind was a matter of honest intellectual conviction. The Webbs' Poor Law Campaign had at any rate made one enthusiastic convert.[12]

[11] C. Parry, *The Radical Tradition in Welsh Politics* (Hull, 1970), pp.36–9.

[12] Thomas Jones, 'Pauperism: Fact and Theories'. *The International Journal of Ethics* (January 1910), pp.1–14, and 'Pauperism and Poverty', An Address to the Statistical and Social Survey Society of Ireland, 18 February 1910. T.J., Class Y, Vo.5, No.22. In his address, anticipating the National Health Service of 1948, he called for 'a State medical service [to] be established and the cost thereof defrayed out of money voted by Parliament'.

Tom Jones continued as an active Fabian for many more years even though the Society officially made very little effort to extend its influence in Wales. But he also supported the campaign waged by David Thomas to establish a separate Welsh Independent Labour Party. In his speech in Welsh at Caernarfon in 1909 Jones had argued strongly in support of that proposal. It was true, he said, that Wales's problems were much the same as those of England and the world in general. But Wales was not England writ small. The Welsh had their own traditions and their own ideas on how matters could best be arranged to suit their own particular needs. It was necessary for them to examine the relationship of socialism and nationalism and to understand the effect the adoption of a Labour standpoint would have on the national spirit. It was important to maintain Wales's separate national identity, and for that purpose to contain, to control and beneficially to transmute powerful English influences which, if allowed to flood in without proper regulation, would engulf Welsh nationhood, thereby making the world a poorer place.[13] These sentiments earned warm applause on the platform at Caernarfon. It was an altogether different matter to put them into effect. During Tom Jones's absence in Ireland, most of the work of organising support for a Welsh ILP devolved on the indefatigable David Thomas, who was used to ploughing a lonely political furrow. He had some limited success and indeed managed to arrange a conference at Carmarthen in support of the idea in August 1911. But the matter got no further. The national leadership was hostile and Keir Hardie himself declared his opposition.[14]

Tom Jones was not present at Carmarthen. He had been unable to attend because he was engaged elsewhere: not as one might expect in Ireland, but a mere sixty miles or so away in Newtown in mid-Wales.[15] During the late summer of 1910 Tom and Rene and their baby spent a holiday with Dick Jones and his wife, Violet, at Llandinam in Montgomeryshire. Richard Jones had accepted a call to the Calvinistic Methodist chapel there in 1908.[16] During the holiday Dick Jones introduced his friends to 'the coal magnates', as Tom Jones first described them; that is, Margaret, Gwendoline and David Davies, the millionaire grandchildren of David Davies of

[13] *A Theme with Variations*, pp.33–4.

[14] C. Parry, op.cit., pp.40–3. K.O. Morgan, 'The New Liberalism and the Challenge of Labour; The Welsh Experience 1885–1929', *WHR*, VI, 303–4.

[15] On 25 July he wrote to Thomas to explain his absence. NLW David Thomas (Bangor) MSS.

[16] T. Jones to J. Morton, Tues [Aug.?] 1910. Morton MSS GD326/82/1. T. Mervyn Jones, *Going Public*, p.20.

Llandinam, builder of docks and railways, coal magnate, and mainstay of the University College of Wales at Aberystwyth in its early years of struggle.[17] The three grandchildren had inherited in full the philanthropic inclinations of their grandfather. Their meeting Tom Jones at this time seems, in retrospect, almost providential. So began friendships and associations that were to be of immense social benefit to Wales and the Welsh people.

David Davies MP and his two sisters had already decided to offer the sum of £125,000 as the basis of a public appeal for money to finance a national campaign to eradicate tuberculosis in Wales as a suitable memorial to the late King Edward VII. It seemed an appropriate choice because some years before, when it had been suggested that this particular disease could be brought under control, the King had tersely asked: 'If preventable, why not prevented?'[18] On 30 September 1910 David Davies wrote inviting Tom Jones to return to Wales to serve as the full-time paid secretary of the proposed new foundation.

> This movement [he wrote] is really a chance of doing something for Wales, something really practical. I am sorry for your Irish friends, but if your heart is in Wales don't hesitate to take on the job *at once.*[19]

This was an offer Tom Jones could not and would not refuse. 'I see in it', he told David Thomas, 'a unique opportunity', a chance, as he wrote slightly later, to assist in 'the solution of some of the pressing social problems in Wales'.[20] He had, of course, always hoped and indeed expected one day to return to work and live in Wales. But that aside, the alacrity with which he accepted David Davies's offer suggested that he and his wife were not all that enamoured with their life in Belfast. That is not to say that they did not sincerely regret taking leave of several warm friends but Tom Jones seems to have felt no particular regret at relinquishing his chair. He had never delighted, much less gloried, in being an economist, as had William Smart, who, according to his own account, had done so every day of his professional life.

There was no doubt that tuberculosis, or consumption as it was then more usually called, was, as Tom Jones said, 'a terrible scourge' throughout the western world. Most of the advanced

---

[17] See above pp.29–30. Morton MSS GD326/82/1. *Welsh Broth*, p.123.

[18] David Davies, 'A Great National Effort; The Welsh Crusade against Conumption', *Wales* (January 1912), II, 11.

[19] T.J., Class R, Vol.1, No.1.

[20] Ibid., Class H, Vol.2, No.2, 11 October 1910. NLW David Thomas (Bangor) MSS.

industrial countries were setting up anti-tuberculosis associations around the turn of the century.[21] There was no doubt either that Wales was especially affected by the ravages of this particular disease. 'Wales', said the Memorial's public appeal leaflet, 'is the blackest spot on the T.B. map of England and Wales'. Seven out of the fifteen counties with the worst mortality rate of tuberculosis were in Wales; the death rate in Cardiganshire was nearly double the national average.[22] Tom Jones threw himself into this new work with characteristic energy. The Memorial Association opened temporary offices at Newtown; the Secretary, his wife and child moved into a house in Llandrindod Wells, twenty-five miles away, which inevitably they called Anwylfan. The Memorial Association sought the assistance of a small group of six medical experts, including Sir William Osler and Dr Christopher Addison. This advisory committee recommended that, instead of the originally envisaged tripartite division (education, dispensaries and sanitoria), the campaign should be organized into five main sections: education, machinery of detection, treatment, after-care, and research.[23] As it turned out, not all of the recommended methods of attack were developed by the Memorial Association to the same extent, with some unfortunate consequences. Indeed, one modern commentator, with the benefit of hindsight, goes so far as to question whether the existence of the Memorial Association 'was in the best interests of the people of Wales'. At the time, it seemed overwhelmingly otherwise. In accord with the thinking of the time, the Association concentrated on institutional treatment; it took over existing sanatoria and adapted old mansions and other suitable buildings in different parts of Wales.[24]

Tom Jones of course had no medical training, but his version of the policy he believed the Memorial Association ought properly to follow is not without its interest. His emphasis was on the broad social rather than clinical aspects. *En route* to take up his post in October, he wrote from the train exhorting his friend David Thomas to join him as his bilingual private secretary. 'There is great work to be done', he wrote persuasively, 'I want to have around me men and women who themselves care for the cause'.

[21] 11 October 1910. NLW David Thomas (Bangor) MSS. Linda Bryder, 'The King Edward VII Memorial Association and its Policy towards Tuberculosis, 1910–48', *WHR*, XIII (December 1986), 194–5.

[22] 'The Ravages of Consumption'. T.J., Class H, Vol.1, No.2.

[23] 'A Crusade against Consumption'. 4 November 1910. Ibid. *Welsh Broth*, pp.126–7.

[24] Linda Bryder, loc.cit., *passim*, and especially p.194. See also, Glyn R. Jones, 'The King Edward VII Welsh National Memorial Association 1912–48'. *Wales and Medicine* (ed. J. Cule, Llandysul, 1975), pp.31–4.

And he went on in some detail to describe the range and scale of the cause he had in mind. There was the obvious purpose of preventing, even (reflecting a rather misplaced current general confidence) perhaps abolishing tuberculosis. But Tom Jones's aims went far beyond even that large ambition.

We shall be in a specially favourable position to quicken the whole nation to a sense of social ills through the press and platform.

He believed that an exceptional opportunity now presented itself:

We shall be bound presently to run up against housing problems, milk supply, infantile mortality and physical education.

And anticipating the language of a later age, a domino effect, this time working to the advantage of the angels, would come into play:

We ought to be able to influence public opinion and get the authorities to use the powers they already possess and obtain others on the lines of the [Poor Law] Minority Report.[25]

David Thomas responded to this imaginative blueprint for social action. He was prepared to join the crusade; he was interviewed by David Davies who, to Tom Jones's regret, turned him down because Thomas had no formal administrative experience and did not know shorthand and office routine.[26] It is odd that David Davies, whose patience with impedimenta to executive efficiency was not great, did not push Tom Jones to drive a car. It is possible of course that he did do so, and that Jones, whose lack of physical co-ordination made him hopeless at games, failed to master the motor car. As Secretary, he travelled all over Wales to meetings and exhibitions. He was chauffeur-driven everywhere but this journeying was not as luxurious as it appeared for he travelled in, of all things, an open car, which seemed ill-adapted to meet the vagaries of Welsh weather.[27]

A horse-drawn caravan was also trundled around Wales as part of the paraphernalia of the advertising campaign in the early days of the Memorial Association. Exhibitions lasting a week or more were held in most of the centres visited. Tom Jones usually opened the proceedings with a general discourse on the aims of the Association and an appeal for money and support. On subsequent days a team

[25] 11 October 1910. NLW David Thomas (Bangor) MSS.
[26] Tom Jones's letters, 28 September, 11, 13 and 17 October. Ibid.
[27] *Welsh Broth*, p.134.

of speakers, most of them medical men, addressed audiences in Welsh and English. There were photographs, lantern lectures, cookery classes, 'showing how to live cheaply but well', and many exhortatory pamphlets on offer.[28] This educational work was the Memorial Association's major contribution to preventive medicine, and so far as it went, was considered subsequently to have been generally successful. The Association had its defects, particularly its relative neglect of after-care work. And for many years official government policy refused to concede that there was any significant correlation between the incidence and spread of tuberculosis and social and environmental factors such as poverty and bad housing, or that malnutrition was often a predisposing agent in the onset of the disease.[29] It took many years therefore for officialdom, in this area at least, to catch up with ideas that Tom Jones was advancing in 1910.

In the following year, he went on a mission of enquiry to Germany, where, it was thought, the fight against tuberculosis was being more effectively waged. It took some time for the work of the Memorial foundation to get fully into its stride and, in fact, before that had occurred, Tom Jones had moved on to another job. However, his work for the Memorial Association had brought about the most important introduction of his life, so far as his professional career was concerned: his first meeting with David Lloyd George, Chancellor of the Exchequer. Tom Jones had gone well prepared. Accompanied by David Davies, who was Chairman and Treasurer of the Association he had founded, Jones had gone to Downing Street to ask for the Chancellor's support in obtaining a Royal Charter for the Memorial foundation. As it happened, they were probably pushing at an open door. Lloyd George's father had died of tuberculosis, and the Chancellor had been impressed by the sanatoria he had seen on his visit to Germany in 1908.[30] Even so, Tom Jones had come fully briefed by David James, the poet Defynnog, secretary of the Welsh Language Society of that time, who had provided him with heartrending details of the 'Victims of Consumption in Wales', nine young poets of promise cut off in their early years by the disease. 'There are many more', James wrote, 'if I had time and opportunity to hunt for them'.[31] Tom Jones made good use of this material; in his appeal he made great

[28] 'The National Crusade against Tuberculosis', Merthyr 10 February 1911. T.J., Class H, Vol.1, No.6.

[29] Linda Bryder, loc.cit.

[30] *Lloyd George's Ambulance Wagon: The Memoirs of W.J. Braithwaite 1911–12*, ed. Sir H. Bunbury (1957), p.71.

[31] T.J., Class H, Vol.1, No.5.

play with the piteous condition into which young men of talent, and by remorseless infection whole families, in Wales were thrust by the onset of tuberculosis. He moved the Chancellor by reciting Welsh verse written by a poet who had been driven to black despair by the relentless grip of the illness. Lloyd George, who often came to important decisions by inspired impulse, immediately responded. He promised to make some financial provision for sanatoria in the National Insurance Bill upon which he was then working.[32] Indeed, according to W.J. Braithwaite, the Civil Servant who did most of the detailed groundwork for the Insurance Bill, who was irritated by what he regarded as a troublesome distraction, 'the difficulty in the early stages was to prevent L.G. spending all his money on building sanatoria which might not be wanted'. In the event, the National Insurance Act provided £1,500,000 for sanatoria for the benefit of the whole population, not merely those who were insured.[33]

David Davies and Tom Jones had brought off a considerable coup. It could well have been that, given his apparently strong interest in the subject, Lloyd George would, in any case, have turned his attention to it sooner or later. On the other hand, in the press of the violently controversial issues of these years, the matter might easily have been overlooked. As it was, there was immediate action, and the clauses relating to tuberculosis proved to be among the most valuable and least contentious provisions of the great Insurance Act. In this instance the Chairman and Secretary of the Memorial Association had worked in perfect harmony. It was not always so.

David Davies was a remarkable man, in many ways the embodiment of the Manichaean principle of equal light and dark. He was educated at Merchiston school, Edinburgh, and King's College, Cambridge, where he read history. He had inherited many of the personal qualities of his unlettered grandfather who had amassed enormous wealth which, along with his two sisters, David Davies inherited when he was a very young man. In 1906 he was returned unopposed as, nominally, the Liberal MP for Montgomeryshire. He was in fact a political maverick: he insisted on absolute freedom from party constraints, local or national. At Cambridge he had been brainwashed in favour of protective tariffs by one of his tutors and he adhered unabashed to that policy during the great con-

[32] *Welsh Broth*, pp.131–2. M. Bruce, *The Coming of the Welfare State* (1961), pp.214–15. B.B. Gilbert, *The Evolution of National Insurance in Gt. Britain* (1966), p.449.

[33] *Lloyd George's Ambulance Wagon . . . the Memoirs of W.J. Braithwaite 1911–12*, ed. Sir H. Bunbury (1957), p.105. Bruce, op.cit., pp.214–15.

troversy of 1906, when the Liberal belief in free trade was being reasserted with all its old gospel fervour. At that time, too, David Davies (or D.D., as he was almost universally known) was opposed to Home Rule for Ireland. He reserved the right to change his mind, as in fact he did in time on both these questions. He had courage, a creative mind, great energy and a strongly developed sense of the obligations of wealth. 'No one in the history of the Principality had excelled Lord Davies' record for benefactions to Welsh institutions and organisations', an admiring associate wrote much later.[34] He was, or at least could be, immensely kind and a good friend. No man, it is said, is a hero to his valet. David Davies was so, at least to his long-serving chauffeur, Chapman, a sceptical knowing Londoner, who used to call D.D. 'Double Diamond', and thirty years after the event, said simply of his employer, 'My life ended when he died'.[35]

There was another, less attractive side to D.D. He could be overbearing, even vindictive; he did not take kindly to criticism and quickly resorted to bludgeoning tactics when opposed. Despite his vision in some things, he could be astonishingly obtuse and seemed to have persuaded himself that stubborn wilfulness would finally move even the biggest mountains of opposition. He was a warm, intensely human personality with great virtues and matching faults. As Tom Jones said, he 'took some managing'.[36]

Early in November 1911, D.D. was reported to be 'angry' with Tom Jones because he 'did not agree' with the Chairman's proposed response to a government refusal of a request for additional money for the Association. Predictably, D.D. wanted to mount a frontal attack: Tom Jones, supported by a senior colleague, was prepared to concede the matter so as not to hazard other possible gains.[37] But this was a very small storm in a teacup. Most of the time the two men were on excellent terms. D.D. affectionately nicknamed the Secretary 'Microbe', not inappropriately in the circumstances. And to all his senior staff at the Memorial Association and on the family estate, D.D. was 'the Chief', a title that was thought to strike the right balance between proper respect and friendly intimacy. Despite the difficulties occasionally created

[34] 'Some Notes on the Career of Lord Davies'. NLW Gwilym Davies MSS I/3 f34.

[35] Personal interview with Mr Chapman (then a spry ninety-five-year-old; D.D. called him 'Chap') at his home in Llandinam.

[36] *Welsh Broth.* p.135. D.D. was a whole-hog believer in temperance. Accordingly, with a touch of not untypical seigneurial authoritarianism, as Chapman said, 'he shut up the pub' in Llandinam village.

[37] T.J., Class Z (Diary 1899–1916), pp.21–2.

by David Davies's temperamental frailties, there is no question that
the Memorial Association would not have been established on a
firm foundation without his restless drive and determination, quite
apart from the crucial importance of his princely financial support.
The Association broke new ground. At that time it was the only
body which had executive and administrative authority for the
whole of Wales and Monmouthshire in the area of its activity.[38]

It was, however, becoming apparent during 1911 that the
Association's position was likely to be profoundly affected, perhaps
to the point of its supersession, by Lloyd George's Insurance Bill
proposals. That is, assuming that the bill could ever be enacted in
the face of the opposition of powerful vested interests,the drumfire
hostility of the Northcliffe press and much malevolent playing on
the ignorance of the general public by its political opponents.
Ultimately, of course, the bill was passed. It is doubtful whether any
contemporary politician other than Lloyd George could have
piloted through so contentious a measure.[39] Initially, it had been
intended that the scheme would be administered by one body of
Insurance Commissioners for the whole of the United Kingdom.
But the Irish Nationalist party, which had powerful additional
leverage after the general election of 1910, insisted on a separate
administration for Ireland. Once that had been conceded, similar
demands for Scotland and Wales could be not refused, despite
Braithwaite's centralist and, as it appeared subsequently, misguided
objections.[40] It is probable that the fact that David Davies's
Memorial Association was already in being on a national scale, gave
the Welsh claim a sufficient substance to prevent its being
summarily thrust aside with the insistence in Whitehall that Wales
was simply a slightly quirky extension of England. Doubtless the fact
that Lloyd George was at the Exchequer was also important. At any
rate, the Act setting up the Welsh Insurance Commission instructed
it 'to have regard' to the activities of the Memorial Association. In
the course of many meetings an apparently satisfactory relationship
between the Commission and the Association was worked out,
although time alone would tell how effective that would be.[41]

[38] Sir Percy E. Watkins, *A Welshman Remembers* (Cardiff, 1944), p.111.

[39] Braithwaite, op.cit., provides a fascinating picture of the incredibly
complicated processes of the bill, with its many compromises and improvisations
en route from drafting to completion. It is also clear that Dr Christopher Addison's
assistance on certain points was of crucial importance. K.O. and Jane Morgan,
Portrait of a Progressive: the Political Career of Christopher, Viscount Addison (Oxford,
1980), pp.10–23.

[40] Braithwaite, op.cit., pp.30–1.

[41] Tom Jones's account of the Memorial Association in T.J., Class H, Vol.1,
No.80, adds some detail to the description in *Welsh Broth*, pp.133–7.

In these circumstances, it was natural that the officers of the
Memorial Association were concerned that the Welsh Insurance
Commission should include at least one member who was sympathetic towards the foundation. Tom Jones was under considerable
pressure from another quarter to apply for an Insurance
Commissionership. Professor Henry Jones saw the Commission as a
marvellous opportunity for Tom Jones to serve Wales. He pressed
him strongly to apply, and Henry Jones himself, who was staying
overnight with Lloyd George in Downing Street on 6 December,
did his utmost in person to persuade the Chancellor of Tom Jones's
merits. 'I don't believe there is any man in Wales who would work
the Act better than you', Henry Jones wrote to his protégé, 'and I
told him so'. It was at least encouraging that Lloyd George had said
that he had the 'highest esteem ' for Tom Jones. 'You will *arrive*
somehow, perhaps now', Henry Jones concluded.[42] Tom Jones did
apply. He said he had returned to Wales in 1910 in order 'to help
forward the solution of some of the pressing social problems'. He
had not in any way regretted his decision to return, but the
Insurance Bill 'alters the outlook of the Memorial campaign', and
the emphasis would now inevitably 'shift to the Government
scheme', which he would like to help 'become the beneficent
power' that the Chancellor 'desired it to be'. Jones's application
drew attention to the extensive work on the Poor Law he had
carried out, and he laid claim to possessing 'some sympathetic
insight into social problems'. As Secretary of the Memorial Association, he had worked well with its Executive, although its members
held 'diverse views' about social progress. Finally, he suggested that
Lloyd George would want at least one Welsh Commissioner who
would 'not easily become a bureaucrat'.[43]

The application, however, did not succeed. At least he was not
made a Commissioner; instead, he was appointed Secretary to the
Commission. 'You must feel a pang of disappointment', a friend
wrote in commiseration. Professor William Smart, on the other
hand, was prepared to think 'more highly' of Lloyd George than
formerly for having the sense to appoint Tom Jones, who thereby
had been given a great opportunity. So much so, that Smart said he
was prepared to 'pardon' his former assistant 'for giving up
Economics, the only profession . . . worth living for'.[44]

[42] T.J., Class U, Vol.1, Nos.3 and 4.

[43] 4 December 1911. Ibid., Class H, Vol.2, No.1.

[44] Ibid., Class X, Vol.3, Nos.71 and 72. There are pen portraits of the
Commissioners (except, curiously, Miss Douglas-Pennant, the one woman
Commissioner) in *Wales*, II, 33–4.

Tom Jones had been concerned that his leaving the Association after only a year 'looked liked desertion', but he was persuaded otherwise, not least by its Chairman, David Davies. At the end of December D.D. wrote:

> I am very glad for two reasons, and also very sad for two other reasons. First, it is a great lift for you, and therefore a matter for personal congratulation. Now I know you don't care a rap for that, so I won't enlarge. (2) [*sic*] Your appointment will give a great lift to the Memorial and we can now regard the Commission as a sympathetic body – as I know you will soon make your influence felt there – and you will never lose your affection and interest in your first love.
>
> Now for the other side. We shall find it very difficult to replace you on the Memorial . . . Lastly, I am afraid this new appointment will mean that we shall see much less of you in future, which is a great blow to myself. During the last twelve months we have been thrown together so much . . . that you are now quite an old friend, and it makes me sad, that's all.

Quite the handsomest of benedictions.[45]

The Welsh Insurance Commission faced enormous problems at the outset. A great administrative scheme had to be organized in detail. 'For, surely', as Smart wrote, 'never was a more undigested mass thrown to the lions than this to the Commissioners'. Moreover, at the turn of the year, 'the medical storm', whipped up by the very many doctors who bitterly opposed the Insurance scheme, seemed to be getting worse. The 'utmost tact and diplomacy' would be needed to conciliate them, while at the same time it was important 'not to upset the Friendly Societies', with whom the doctors were at loggerheads. However, Dan L. Thomas, who wrote thus from London and who was himself a disappointed candidate for a Commissionership, was at least confident enough to add in his letter to Tom Jones, 'I have not the least doubt you will be able to do it'.[46]

Part I of the Insurance Act provided that nearly all male and female workers between sixteen and seventy years of age, who earned less than £160 a year, were to be insured against ill health by joint contributions from themselves and their employers, to which the State added an additional sum. Medical and sanatorium benefits were to be administered by newly created Insurance Committees in each county and county borough. Other benefits were administered through such friendly societies and trade unions

[45] Ibid., Class P, Vol.1, No.2.
[46] Ibid., Class X, Vol.3, Nos.71 and 72. B.B. Gilbert, op.cit., pp.375–403.

as became self-governing 'Approved Societies'. The unemployment provisions in Part II of the Act were to an extent experimental; they represented, as Winston Churchill had said in 1908, part of 'the Untrodden Field of Politics', territory the Liberals 'must enter'. Some two and a quarter million workers in selected industries were organized into a contributory scheme of insurance against unemployment.[47]

The Welsh National Insurance Commission and its senior officers thus had to establish and maintain effective relationships with a great range of people, professions, public bodies and interest groups in Wales: the army of those insured, the doctors, nursing associations, medical officers of health, public health committees, trade unions, friendly societies, insurance committees, and, not least, the Welsh National Memorial Association and the network of institutions it had established in the fight against tuberculosis.[48] Thomas Jones does not say so directly in his autobiographical account, but there is at least a suspicion that he found much of his work as Secretary of the Commission less satisfying that he had hoped or perhaps expected. Even his slightly fuller manuscript account, unusually for one who regularly recorded so much at great length, breaks off abruptly without any attempt to recount the broad sweep of the Commission's work. The reader is simply referred to the short account given by Sir Percy Watkins, who became Tom Jones's deputy and successor. Indeed, Jones cites the appointment to the Commission staff of Watkins and several promising younger men who went on to distinguished careers in the public service, as one of his most important contributions to the work of the Commission. He seems to have had little opportunity for the sort of creative social initiatives to which he had looked forward on his return to Wales.[49]

The fact was that whatever fond notions he had entertained to the contrary, and despite his earlier comment to Lloyd George, as Secretary to the Commission Jones inevitably had become a bureaucrat, though evidently an effective one. In the autumn of 1912 L.G. Brock, Assistant Secretary to the English Insurance Commission, had been seconded to Cardiff for some weeks to report on the organization of the Welsh office. His report included several sharp criticisms. Some of the subordinate staff at Cardiff, he said, 'write English as if it were a foreign language'. This was no doubt the case. On the other hand, he conceded that much was

[47] Ibid., pp.251, 283–8, 398–8. Braithwaite, op.cit., pp.19–20.
[48] Sir Percy Watkins, op.cit., pp.108–113.
[49] *Welsh Broth*, pp.135–9. T.J., Class H, Vol.1, No.80.

owed to the enthusiasm of the staff. But the general efficiency of the office was low, 'hardly anyone appears to have a clearly defined province'; there was some empire building by one of the Commissioners, and, in general, a 'needless duplication because of the lack of the systematic exchange of information' between the Welsh and English Commissioners. On the face of it, this indictment would seem to reflect heavily on the competence of the Secretary. Yet, according to Brock, this was not so. Indeed, his report specifically refers to the 'cordial assistance' he had received from Tom Jones and the Chief Inspector, James Evans. And in further correspondence about his visit to Cardiff, Brock plainly indicates his high regard for Tom Jones in both personal and professional terms.[50]

The recruitment of staff for the Welsh Insurance Commission had been an unpleasant business in some respects. Public men (and women, Mrs Lloyd George, for example) were badgered shamelessly to exert their influence on behalf of candidates. 'The applicants are legion', Haydn Jones MP wrote ruefully to Tom Jones, 'I hope there will be an examination for other appointments'. There was a strong whiff of jobbery about. 'I am told', one determined aspirant for an inspectorship wrote, 'Mr. John Rowland [a Commissioner] is the man to work re appointments . . . Of course they state that the Commissioners are not to be approached, but it seems that, after all, is the only way to success'. Thus the voice of cunning experience in some public appointments in Wales.[51] Tom Jones had tried hard to get his friend David Thomas appointed as one of the full-time lecturers whose brief was to explain the Insurance Act at public meetings up and down the country. Once again, however, for technical reasons, he was unable to bring it off.[52]

There was one other reason why Tom Jones was not entirely happy at the Welsh Insurance Commission. He simply could not get on with John Rowland, who was one of the four Commissioners. This was one instance where the fraternal amity that was customary between old students of the College at Aberystwyth did not work. Rowland (who in the fullness of time became Sir John) was a Cardiganshire man, a former schoolmaster in Cardiff, who became private secretary to Lloyd George at the Board of Trade, and continued in that capacity when he moved to the Exchequer.

[50] Ibid., Vol.2, Nos.31, 32 and 33.

[51] Ibid., Nos.9, 10 and 15. The first of these letters suggests that Tom Jones, in private at least, admitted there was some truth in the charge of jobbery. Ibid., Class A, Vol.1, No.2 for Mrs Lloyd George's intervention.

[52] 3 and 30 January 1912. NLW David Thomas (Bangor) MSS.

Rowland had played some part in the framing of the Insurance Bill.[53] He was close to Lloyd George, who used him as a set of eyes and ears in Welsh affairs. Some observers seemed to believe that Rowland and Tom Jones were direct rivals for a Welsh Insurance Commissionership.[54] Rowland was successful, but it did not seem to have prompted him to magnanimity towards his defeated rival. He and Tom Jones cordially disliked and distrusted each other from the start. Rowland was physically unprepossessing: short, stocky and grossly overweight, he looked for all the world, perhaps unfairly, a bully and a boss. He was able, energetic, ardently patriotic, pugnacious and shrewd; a naturally dominating personality who was all too apt to domineer. It should be said that many people other than Tom Jones subscribed to this opinion of Rowland. Dr Meredith Richards, a fellow Commissioner, thought his appointment was a disaster for Wales. Another Commissioner, the Hon. Violet Douglas-Pennant, the statutory woman, had no good word to say for him. L.G. Brock of the English Commission accused Rowland of monopolizing authority and treating a deputy unjustly. W.J. Burdon Evans, David Davies's major-domo and therefore not unused to coping with awkward temperament, said bluntly after meeting Rowland, 'I really could not work under that man. Constant friction or worse would be inevitable'.[55]

No doubt virtue was not all on one side. Rowland certainly brought out something like the worst in Tom Jones, who was made to feel uncomfortable if indeed not unnerved by him. 'I felt surrounded by an invisible web', Jones wrote many years later in an account that came as near to outright malice as anything he ever wrote about an individual. Rowland was as assiduous, persistent and guileful as Jones, though much less subtle and certainly less scrupulous in his dealings. In this situation Jones's customary patience and good temper wore thin. He and Rowland were enemies and there was little point in trying to disguise the fact: the Secretary and the Commissioner were locked in a permanent vendetta. It had the unfortunate ripple effect of dividing and confusing the subordinate staff.[56] Nor did it stop there. The bitter hostility between the two men was an open secret among the professional and literate classes in the Cardiff area and to some

[53] Braithwaite, op.cit., p.150.

[54] Dan L. Thomas, for example. T.J., Class X, Vol.3, No.72.

[55] Sir Thomas Hughes, long-suffering Chairman of the Welsh Commission, also ultimately wrote Rowland off. Ibid., Class H, Vol.2, Nos.24 and 33 and Vol.4, No.12. Ibid., Class W, Vol.17, No.16. Ibid., Vol.1, No.60.

[56] *Welsh Broth*, pp.136–9. By 1918 Rowland's supporters and clients had become 'the J.R. clan'. Bangor MS 17218.

extent throughout Wales. When, in February 1914, J. Hugh Edwards MP, for reasons that will be examined in due course, published a savage lampoon on Tom Jones, the most malignant part of the attack is made in words put into the mouth of John Rowland, whose relish for this 'opportunity' is made clear. The episode is, of course, an invention, a strained contrivance. But what is not in doubt, indeed is taken as common knowledge, is the abiding enmity between the two men.

> That is Tom Jones, or 'Professor' Tom Jones, as he likes to be called [Rowland is made to say]. He is the most self-contented man in Wales, and I sometimes think he must be a lineal descendant of the Pharisee who used to thank God that he is not as other men are.[57]

It is scarcely surprising therefore that Tom Jones felt a certain relief two years later when he left that unhappy situation at the Welsh Insurance Commission, for good as it turned out.[58]

The Welsh Insurance Commission offices were in Cardiff, and naturally Tom Jones and his family had had to move to that district when he was appointed to the Secretaryship. They decided to live in Barry, ten miles from Cardiff but linked to it by a good railway service. Barry was a town of some thirty-five thousand inhabitants that had grown phenomenally quickly as a result of the decision to develop it as a port, an alternative, eventually a rival, to Cardiff, for the export of coal from the south Wales valleys. It had some of the cosmopolitan features of a large port, and some of the raffishness too. On the other hand, in recent years it had begun to be developed as a seaside resort and was soon ambitiously to claim to be the 'new Brighton'. There was much ugly housing thrown up hastily by speculative builders. But there were also some very attractive residential areas, 'Swelldom' in local parlance, which attracted professional people, many of them, like Tom Jones, prepared to commute daily by train to Cardiff.[59] Their house in Barry overlooked the British Channel. It had a large attic called the Crow's Nest, which Tom used as an office cum study. The house of course bore the name that was now traditional: Anwylfan.

During the last year or so Tom Jones had been much less active in politics than formerly. At first this was simply the result of the pressure of work in his new job as Secretary of the Memorial Association in the first year of its existence. 'I cannot take any

[57] 'The S.F.S.G.' *Wales* (February 1914), V, 239. Jones, said the author, 'seems to have a dread of John Rowland'.

[58] *Welsh Broth*, p.137.

[59] *Barry – The Centenary Book*, ed. Donald Moore (Barry, 1984), p.279.

engagements' at present, he wrote to David Thomas in November 1911 by way of apology for his inability to continue to work on behalf of the ILP. Indeed, he had had to cancel several engagements, and was unlikely to be able to help politically in any way for some time.[60] Just over a year later, he had moved on to his new job in the Insurance Commission that had to operate on ground that was entirely uncharted. 'An administrator', said Jones, 'is a person who knows the rules which govern the institution whose servant he is'.[61] The Secretary of the new Welsh Insurance Commission had a mountain of rules and regulations that he had to master and, on occasion, to discover or establish. There was at first little time for extra-mural activities of any kind. And of greater importance in the longer run was the fact that, now he was a fully-fledged Civil Servant, the sort of overt, ideologically committed political activity in which he had engaged since his student days was no longer possible. Tom Jones's days as a political activist were over.

It is of course possible that he would have subsided into political quietism anyway as, perhaps, in common with many others, his young man's optimism was worn down by time and circumstance. But given the strength of his political convictions hitherto, that would be a lengthy process. As it was, he had had a considerable practical experience in the last twenty years of the social and economic problems that bedevilled British society. The time he had spent unravelling the intricacies of the Poor Law, on Settlement work in slum land in Glasgow, in combatting disease in the length and breadth of Wales, together with his understanding as a professional economist of the seeming intractability of the problem of unemployment, had made him sceptical of glib answers. 'I knew too much of the causes of poverty', he wrote of Edwardian Britain, 'to imagine that it would be easy to abolish them'.[62] 'Poverty' is used here of course as an omnibus term encompassing every sort of social, economic, educational and cultural inequity that, in his opinion, blemished British society. His awareness of the obstacles in the way of redress did not drive him to look for extreme political remedies. 'Compromise', he wrote of his attitude at this time, 'is the essence of any British Utopia'.[63]

His moderate opinions were already under attack from some critics within the Labour movement. The editor of *Justice*, journal of the Marxist Social Democratic Federation, always eager in pursuit of what he regarded as political or economic heresy, asked his

[60] 26 October 1911, NLW David Thomas (Bangor) MSS.
[61] *Welsh Broth*, p.138.
[62] Ibid., p.38.
[63] Ibid., p.33.

readers for information about J.H. Jones MA, described as a lecturer at Liverpool University, whose lectures in south Wales on economic subjects had aroused suspicion.

> I think the name should be Mr. Tom Jones, M.A., who is assistant to Professor Smart [one of the Glasgow faithful wrote to the editor the next week]. I know that he is a lecturer in Wales on . . . the subject of economics . . . He is a member of the Fabian Society and attaches himself in an adjustable way to the I.L.P. [but] . . . is not likely to do better than to mix middle-class views with a few socialist ideas.

Tom Jones intervened in the correspondence to point out that J.H. Jones did indeed exist: he taught at Liverpool, and often lectured without payment on 'The Right to Work' and other subjects in south Wales, where his powers of expounding economic problems were widely appreciated. Tom Jones got short shrift. The editor of *Justice* pointed out, scornfully, that Jones had said nothing of 'the character', that is, the ideological purity, of J.H. Jones's teaching and his letter was therefore valueless.[64]

This hostility was reciprocated. 'The S.D.F. are impossible to deal with', Tom Jones complained to James Morton. They were wilful and simply would not listen to reason: they had 'tried to wreck Tawney's scheme of working-class education' at Ruskin College, and he himself had been 'attacked all over in their paper *Justice*'.[65] Tom Jones does not appear ever to have made any formal study of Marxism other than to have become familiar, as an economist, with the Marxian theory of value. The nearest Henry Jones's Philosophy class got to the subject was to study Hegel. But in the eighteen-nineties, when Tom Jones was converted to socialism, the Marxism of that time dismissed moral and ethical arguments, the *sine qua non* of his commitment, as utopian irrelevances.[66] Jones's political views had not changed since the eighteen-nineties. In common with many other members of the ILP, he believed in evolutionary reformism and social engineering on the Fabian model. 'To raise the squalid level of the poorest, to elicit their starved energies and aspirations . . . this was what in our coolest moments we envisaged, hoped for, worked for', as he described it. He would not be bound, as he believed Marxists were, 'by a narrow economic doctrine', and he rejected completely class war as the dynamic of change to a socialist society. That was, as Alfred Zimmern said, 'militarism

---

[64] *Justice*, 23, 30 January and 6 February 1909.
[65] Morton MSS GD 326/81/1.
[66] D. Howell, *British Workers and the Independent Labour Party 1888–1906* (Manchester, 1983), p.359.

under another name'. Jones believed also that although trade unionism was a necessary defensive shield for the working class in a capitalist world, it could not bring about a socialist society.[67]

But above all, Tom Jones pinned his hopes for social improvement on popular education. Years later, in a public speech in 1941, he conceded that many of his political opinions and expectations in the years just before 1914 had been absurdly naïve. For example, his conviction that the Labour Party would prove to be an immense improvement on the Liberals; that trade unionists were, or could be persuaded to be, wholehearted idealists, and that international socialist solidarity would prevent war.[68] It could also be said that his easy assumption at that time that the parliamentary system in Britain was, and always would be, politically neutral falls into the same category of unsophisticated innocence. With customary honesty, he did admit some years later that he had underestimated the difficulties besetting democratic politics in Britain.[69] He had been brought up on 'the pure milk of the democratic gospel' to believe in 'the equality of man before the ballot box', and the realization of the common good 'in and through a common will'. In time he was to see that many of his assumptions were false: the vote was not 'free, independent or rational'; nor was the voting booth a place 'from which heat and passion were excluded', and the *mores* of society all too often created 'tariff rings of mental prejudice'.[70]

On the other hand, he had been clear from the beginning that liberation from these crippling constraints lay in education. The obvious place to start was in the schools.

> Let me think of education as gardening and by and by we may give the children in our streets the same chance as we give flowers, with results as beautiful.[71]

But his chief concern lay elsewhere; his attention was concentrated on adult and university education. Two problems, at opposite ends of the political process, especially engaged his attention. Firstly,

[67] *Welsh Broth*, pp.22–44. See also an account of his speech to Welsh miners at Penrhiwceiber in the *Western Mail* (31 December 1908). Zimmern's comment is in T.J., Class C, Vol.19, No.6.

[68] 'Adult Education after Thirty Years', *Leeks and Daffodils*, p.141.

[69] Given the exclusion of women before 1918, perhaps 'quasi-democratic' would be the most that could be said.

[70] 'Dilemma of Democracy', *The Welsh Outlook*, XIX, 174–8. See also my article, 'Dr. Thomas Jones, C.H. and Education', *THSC* (1982), pp.86–109.

[71] Thomas Jones, *The Medical Inspection of Schoolchildren* (Dublin, 1910), pp.9–10.

how best could the leaders of British society be educated for their responsibilities? The supreme problem of a democracy was to discover and train the best and wisest leaders, because, as he insisted, 'to no form of government is leadership so vital'.[72] The education of the governing élite was a matter for universities, institutions with which he was to be much concerned during the next few years. But of more immediate concern was the question at the other extremity: how could the British people *en masse* be sufficiently well educated to enable them to exercise the duties of citizenship effectively? Perhaps mistakenly, he did not believe this could be done in the schools. He thought that good citizenship rested on an understanding of subjects such as civics, ethics and economics which meant little to schoolchildren until they had had 'personal confrontations with life and labour'. Moreover, the formal schooling of the overwhelming number of children ended at the elementary stage. State secondary schools were miscalled 'intermediate'. For most of the children who went on to it, so-called intermediate education marked the terminal stage of their formal teaching, not a springboard to higher things.[73]

He was clear, therefore, that British democracy must look for its long term nourishment, perhaps even its survival, to the various forms of adult education, in particular, to a vigorous expansion of the WEA, 'the educational expression of democracy'.[74] And if his Civil Service status ruled out political party activism, he was not debarred from taking a lively part in adult education. Happily, there already existed a strong WEA tradition in Barry, where he now lived. Indeed, the first class every organized by the WEA in Wales had been established there in 1906. Tom Jones ran a class in Barry in 1913 and soon became treasurer of the Welsh district of the WEA.[75]

At that time Tom and Rene Jones had a very agreeable social life. Foremost among their friends were Silyn Roberts and his wife, Mary. For some time Roberts, a Calvinistic Methodist minister and poet, had been uneasily aware, as he said, that he had been 'drifting' away doctrinally from his brethren. His standing within the denomination was low; 'my socialism', he told Tom Jones, 'has ruined me in that respect'. He had been urged to go into politics,

---

[72] 'Adult Education after Thirty Years', loc.cit., p.152.
[73] 'Dilemmas of Democracy', loc.cit., pp.174–8. 'The Educational Outlook in Wales'. Ibid., I, 152.
[74] 'Adult Education after Thirty Years', loc.cit., p.145.
[75] David Thomas, op.cit., p.110. *Leeks and Daffodils*, pp.145–6. Sir Percy Watkins, *Adult Education among the Unemployed in South Wales* (1935), pp.2–5.

but he could not stomach 'the shams and hypocrisies of Parliamentary life'. He sought Tom Jones's assistance for a job in the King Edward VII Memorial Association and subsequently at the Welsh Insurance Commission. He was given a temporary post for some months as an agent in Canada soliciting contributions for the Memorial Association. Ultimately, in 1912 he became Secretary of the Appointments Board for Wales, an agency designed to bring together employers and graduates seeking placement. Silyn Roberts too worked in Cardiff and lived in Barry. From this time onwards he remained one of Tom Jones's closest friends and a most valued associate in a number of activities.[76] An equally interesting member of the coterie was Edgar Jones, a Montgomeryshire man, an old Aberystwyth student who was headmaster of the Barry Intermediate School from 1899 until 1934. He was a dynamic, charismatic character who became and long remained the very model of the Welsh grammar school head. Indeed to many, with some exaggeration, he seemed to be the 'Thomas Arnold of Wales'.[77] Also in the group were Annie Ffoulkes, one-time student at Aberystwyth, who taught French at Edgar Jones's school, Olive Morgan, who taught Welsh, and R. Williams Parry, a Welsh poet of real distinction, who joined the staff in 1915. And close at hand in Cardiff were W.J. Williams, a future Inspector of Education in Wales, and Percy Watkins, Tom Jones's deputy at the Insurance Commission, an industrious, self-educated, equable man, never in the way and never out of it, who soon became his trusted aide and devoted follower, but nevertheless retained an independent mind.[78]

During 1913 Rene and Tom had a much longed-for addition to their family: on 3 January a son, who was named Tristan Lloyd, was born at Anwylfan.These years at Barry were a happy period in the social life of the family. Their domestic circumstances were comfortable and they had a large circle of interesting friends. Religion, or at least the formal observance of it, did not now play so large a part in their life. Indeed, when they had lived in East Kilbride in Scotland, for a time at least, Eirene had given up chapel-going. Eventually, she began to attend services again, despite some residual qualms, partly on general moral grounds but partly because she had come to see that the public often put a false construction on absence from church.

[76] T.J., Class H, Vol.2, Nos.19, 20 and 26. Bangor MS 17218. David Thomas, op.cit., pp.104–9. *Welsh Broth*, pp.146–9. 'I loved that man', Tom Jones said of the gifted poet and inspired teacher when he died in 1930.

[77] *Barry: The Centenary Book*, pp.422–3.

[78] David Thomas, op.cit., pp.109–10. Sir Percy Watkins, *A Welshman Remembers*, *passim*. *Welsh Broth*, pp.137–8.

You will remember [she wrote to Tom in 1919] how, when I stood for the School Board at East Kilbride, certain of the electors said they would have supported me but they understood I was against the Church and they did not care for their children to be under the control of such a one . . . You cannot help the people as you might if you alienate their sympathies on this one big side of their lives.[79]

It is not clear whether Tom also gave up chapel-going for a time at East Kilbride. On the whole, it seems unlikely, for in September 1908 he attended the annual conference of the Welsh Calvinistic Methodist church at Colwyn Bay, and gave an address on the relation of Christianity and Socialism. It is noticeable, however, that much of his speech was defensive in tone, and he confessed that ten years' experience in Glasgow had made him much less certain of his conclusions on this question. Christianity was 'a very chameleon of a word'; Jesus had prescribed no 'political or economic programme', and the Gospels gave no 'definite guidance as to the methods of social reform'. This was a rather different conclusion from the one he had so confidently advanced in his early days in the pulpit when, to the sharp annoyance of many elders, he had had no difficulty in construing the New Testament in political terms. His retreat, however, was not total: Christianity and Socialism did have an 'affinity' of ideals, even if their methods differed. Socialists tried to change the environment to the advantage of man who was seen as a victim: Christianity sought to change man himself, who was inescapably a sinner.

I am absolutely convinced in my own mind [he said in conclusion] of the tremendous power of adverse circumstances to check man's capacity for a full rich life . . . Riches may be a danger, but poverty is a disaster.[80]

He had evidently given up preaching, at least regularly, by this time, although as late as June 1913 his name remained formally on the Monmouthshire Presbytery's list of preachers.[81] But in those years when he lived in Barry, Tom Jones's major social concern was his work for the WEA, Albert Mansbridge's ingenious formula for bringing university standards of scholarship to the service of

[79] *Two Lovers*, pp.349–50.

[80] T.J., Class Y, Vol.3, No.4.

[81] The Revd Evan Armstrong wrote in very friendly terms (T.J., Class Z, Diary 1899–1916, pp.26–7) to ask if he wished to keep his name on the list. The letter implied that he had not been active in the pulpit for some time.

workers' education.[82] It was wearing work. Mansbridge certainly felt the strain. After seven years of unremitting effort to establish the WEA his nervous system was near to collapse. 'The first to take positive action' to help him, he said, was Tom Jones, who arranged in 1910 for Mansbridge, his wife and son to go on a voyage of convalescence to the Mediterranean in a small tramp steamer, with the same beneficial results that Tom Jones had derived from his trip in the SS *Isle of Anglesey* in 1898.[83] The toll exacted of Mansbridge by his pioneering work was exceptional. But those who worked in local WEA classes also faced great difficulties. As Tom Jones conceded sadly some thirty years later, 'the passion of the multitude' was for sport, entertainment and gambling, 'not for Plato or Shakespeare', or any other form of bookish study. The discouraging fact was that, while the WEA had successfully mobilized many university teachers for the cause of popular adult education (including R.H. Tawney, perhaps 'the greatest adult education tutor of all time'), the working-class response was decidedly lukewarm.[84] And quite apart from the dispiriting effect of widespread indifference, the WEA also had to face the challenge of an aggressive competitor for the attention of the working classes.

This was simply the extension on a national scale of the war of ideas that had disrupted Ruskin College in 1909. Subsequently, the breakaway Central Labour College movement, which was Marxist in inspiration, kept up a monthly barrage of criticism in its journal *Plebs*. The WEA was alleged to be a bourgeois front organization, a conspiracy subsidized by capitalists to dupe and mislead the workers. As G.D.H. Cole ruefully conceded some years later: 'Much mud had been thrown, and some had stuck'. Cole had also argued that, in England at least, the WEA had been 'three parts asleep', was unsure of itself, and had relapsed into hapless Micawberism.[85] At least this could not be said of the WEA in south Wales. Tom Jones and his associates certainly were not short of energy and were at least clear about their objectives. They refused to accept that class war in society was inevitable, much less desirable. The WEA,

[82] A. Mansbridge, *An Adventure in Working Class Education: being the story of the W.E.A. 1903–15* (1920), *passim*. M. Stocks, *The W.E.A.* (1953), pp.22, 80.

[83] A. Mansbridge, *The Trodden Road: an Autobiography*, p.105. Some years later Mansbridge established 'the Seafarers Education Service, with its College of the Sea'.

[84] *Leeks and Daffodils*, pp.150–1. D. Lleufer Thomas, 'University Tutorial Classes for Working People', *THSC*, 1915, pp.78–82. M. Stocks, op.cit., p.39 for the comment on Tawney.

[85] G.D.H. Cole, *The Place of the W.E.A. in Working Class Education* (1924), pp.6–7. W.W. Craik, *The Central Labour College 1909–29* (1964), pp.92–111.

with its commitment to what they claimed were objective teaching standards innocent of political motivation, was the best antidote to popular ignorance and class misunderstanding. They stood for ameliorative reform and social cohesion which, given reasonable goodwill on all sides,they thought attainable.

> The vast majority of working men [wrote Professor R.M. Burrows of Cardiff, formerly of Glasgow, an associate of Tom Jones, who specifially endorsed these opinions], whatever their political and industrial views, have the national characteristics of moderation and good sense . . . They look forward to a regenerated nation, not the triumph of a particular class, even though it be their own . . . It is mad to acquiesce in the inevitableness of a class war.[86]

Burrows was probably right in terms simply of numbers, and would certainly have been so a few years before. But south Wales, at least, had changed dramatically in recent years. Although the Labour party was still relatively weak, the foundations of Liberal supremacy were being steadily undermined. On the industrial front, the changes were already spectacularly evident. The coal industry, now dominated by industrial combines, was beginning to feel the effects of sharper competition and, increasingly, to be made aware of the difficult geology of the coalfield. The chapel did not bring employers and working-class leaders together in the same way as formerly. Capital and labour were now arrayed apparently in permanent confrontation. In the intensely class-conscious, industrially militant setting of south Wales at that time the aspirations of Tom Jones and company looked rather forlorn, their fine ideals mere daydreams.[87]

And to make a difficult situation for the WEA worse, the challenge of the Labour College Marxists was especially strong in south Wales at this time. This is not surprising as most of those who had led the Ruskin College strike in 1909 came from south Wales, where the chief strength of the breakaway movement lay.[88] Led by Noah Ablett, a gifted ideologue with a remarkable charismatic appeal, these young men proselytized on behalf of what they called

[86] 'Evolution or Revolution', *The Welsh Outlook* (1914), I, 28.

[87] K.O. Morgan, *Wales*, op.cit., pp.62–9, 137–48. See also, his article, 'The New Liberalism and the Challenge of Labour', *WHR*, VI, 288–312. R. Page Arnot, op.cit., pp.165–9.

[88] This guerilla warfare in adult education is exhaustively examined in R. Lewis, 'Leaders and Teachers: the origin and development of the workers' educational movement in South Wales, 1906–1940' (unpublished University of Wales Ph.D. thesis, 1980).

independent working-class education with great energy and the gospel fervour of utter conviction.[89] Sometimes, too, the local education authorities in south Wales were less than helpful, and looked askance at those active in the WEA as interlopers encroaching on local government preserves. As Percy Watkins ruefully admitted, the WEA's progress in south Wales at this time was painfully slow.[90]

There were, of course, more direct methods available, and other, perhaps more amenable, audiences that could be addressed by those in Wales who were socially concerned. The founding of *The Welsh Outlook* is a classic illustration of Tom Jones's creative instinct at work.[91] He and his friends had come to the conclusion sometime before that the weekly and monthly press in Wales was too partisan in attitude, too parochial in outlook, and too much concerned with theological and literary subjects to provide effective comment on the great social and political changes that had occurred or were impending. People were bewildered by rapid change and conflicting or uncertain moral standards. There ought to be a proper debate in Wales, and enlightened opinion should take the initiative. 'Where there is no vision the people perish' (Proverbs 29:18), was the precept inscribed on the cover of the first number and all subsequent copies of *The Welsh Outlook*.

It was a co-operative venture, but there is no question that Thomas Jones was the key man: he was the leader, the most widely experienced and the most creative of the group centred on the Barry and Cardiff area. And of crucial importance, he was the link with David Davies of Llandinam, who was to provide the necessary financial backing. D.D.'s first notion was to establish a weekly newspaper 'with no soap or froth in it'. Alternatively, Tom Jones had thought of 'a Welsh "Punch"', a curiously oblique approach (surely an aberration) to the audience they had in mind. On further consideration, it was clear that a weekly newspaper was beyond their resources of time and David Davies's limited willingness to provide money.[92] Eventually, in October 1913, it was decided to establish a monthly journal devoted to the promotion of 'national social progress'. The whole scheme rested on the

[89] D. Egan, 'Noah Ablett 1883–1935'. *WHR*, IV, No.3, 19–30.

[90] *Adult Education Among the Unemployed of South Wales*, pp.2–3. T.J., Class D, Vol.3, No.3.

[91] For fuller detail, see Gwyn Jenkins, 'The Welsh Outlook 1914–33', *NLW Journal*, XXXIV (Winter 1986), 463–92, and, much more briefly, Trevor L. Williams, 'Thomas Jones and the Welsh Outlook', *Anglo-Welsh Review* (No.64, 1979), pp.38–46.

[92] Bangor MS 19527. Silyn Roberts was briefly considered as a possible editor.

conviction, despite their discouraging WEA experience, that 'latent' in the Welsh people was a 'desire for education and a sympathy with unselfish endeavour', which properly guided would lead to social action of splendid quality.[93] The group of people involved in founding the *Outlook*, as it was usually called, had a considerable range of practical experience. Some of them were allocated special responsibilities: Silyn Roberts for literature and drama, Edgar Jones for education, and the Revd Richard Jones of Llandinam for religion and philosophy, for example. Tom Jones took over social and industrial questions, but over and above that he was, in fact, though not in name, editor of the journal during the first three years of its existence. He was assisted editorially by Ralph Wright, a WEA lecturer who was paid a small stipend; Frank Murrell, a Barry neighbour who was a director of a Cardiff printing firm, took charge of technical production, and W.J. Burdon Evans, David Davies's business secretary, became chairman of the Board. But Tom Jones was the mainspring and moving spirit. In a sense he was simply reverting to type. James Morton wrote to say that he and his wife were delighted that Tom had 'turned Prophet again' and was no longer content to be 'just a prim Secretary'.[94] Morton knew his man: Tom Jones could never have remained for long merely a bureaucrat, not even a highly placed one.

Not everyone welcomed the new journal or its editor. J.H. Edwards MP launched a scurrilous attack. Too ponderous and short of wit to be effective satire, it descended rapidly to crude abuse. Tom Jones and Silyn Roberts were accused of self-seeking opportunism in deserting the pulpit for lucrative secular positions obtained by cunning jobbery; and of currying favour with a millionaire who financed a journal for the benefit of their 'little gang', or as John Rowland fictively described it, 'The Society for Self Glorification'.[95] Edwards had conveniently forgotten that two years before in the same journal he had warmly endorsed the 'chorus of approval' in Wales for those appointed to the Insurance Commission. All of them, including Thomas Jones, who was mentioned specifically, were said to be admirably qualified patriots who had already rendered 'brilliant service' to Wales.[96] The fact was that Edwards was infuriated that his own journal *Wales*, which was already hard pressed to survive in its oligopolist position, would

[93] G. Jenkins and Trevor L. Williams, loc.cit. *The Welsh Outlook* (Cardiff, January 1914), I, No.1 (Foreword) *Welsh Broth*, pp.142–6.
[94] 10 January 1914, Morton MSS G.D. 326/82/1.
[95] *Wales*, V, 237–41.
[96] Ibid., II, 33–4.

now face serious, probably crippling competition. His chagrin at the fact that his new rivals had the financial support of David Davies was perfectly understandable. His foreboding was justified: *Wales* ceased publication in August 1914. It is difficult to say how far this was prompted by the outbreak of war rather than the competition of *The Welsh Outlook*.

It had never been expected that the *Outlook* would be a commercial success, although it was hoped that it might just pay its way. David Davies was prepared, if necessary, to underwrite a small deficit. It sold an average of three thousand copies in the first nine months of its existence; David Davies's subsidy amounted to nearly £900 per annum down to 1917.[97] Without that support, the *Outlook* could never have survived in the difficult conditions of wartime. When war broke out in August 1914, the world changed for ever. Things were never to be the same again. Not in Europe or for the people of Britain. And although he was not called upon to fight, Tom Jones's course in life too was to be drastically altered by the unforeseen exigencies of total war.

---

[97] 'The Welsh Outlook' [1914] in NLW O.M. Edwards MSS Trevor L. Williams, loc.cit., pp.39–41. T.J., Class H, Vol.4, No.27.

CHAPTER SEVEN

THE GREAT WAR

THE OUTBREAK of war in 1914, or at any rate British involvement in
the conflict, took Tom Jones, along with many, perhaps most, of his
compatriots, completely by surprise. His editorial comments in the
August edition of *The Welsh Outlook* were entirely devoted to fairly
humdrum matters of purely Welsh concern, Europe was not even
mentioned. Of course, as he wrote in a special 'War Number' a
month later, the air had been 'thick with rumours' when they were
going to press, but Britons, after several years of recurring crises,
had 'become used to scares'. Indeed, fittingly in high holiday
season, as he thought, he had planned to produce 'a light summer
number' in August and again in September, offering his readers 'a
rest' from grave and disturbing matters of state. However, despite
being caught unawares, his response to the war was unequivocal,
cool-headed, even, in some respects, remarkably prophetic. He was
certainly no vainglorious jingo: he was quite clear that British
intervention 'was necessary', indeed inevitable, once Sir Edward
Grey, who had done 'all that was possible' to preserve peace, had
failed. In all probability Britain ultimately would have supported
France in a straightforward defence of British national and
imperial interests. As it was, the German violation of Belgian
neutrality, in flagrant breach of solemn undertakings, made it a just
war in defence of a high moral principle. He maintained that the
central issue of peace or war was so clear-cut that it was not
surprising that opinion in Britain was virtually unanimous and
wholehearted in support of the government's action.

But Jones was also aware that the situation could not be
dismissed thus simply. Virtue was not all on one side. France and
Britain, the two 'most democratic' of the larger European powers,
were fairly respectable champions of freedom and justice, but their
ally Russia (whose precipitate mobilization bore some share of
blame for the war) was scarcely the ideal partner in a moral
crusade. 'Let us remember', insisted the editor of the *Outlook*,
'tyranny in Russia has been greater than anything the German
knows of'; moreover, 'an all powerful Russia might be as great a
menace to European civilisation as an all powerful Germany'.

Recalling the Duke of Wellington's dictum that the 'next most terrible thing to a great defeat was a great victory', and indeed that, in certain circumstances, victory was 'more to be dreaded' than defeat, Jones hoped that Germany would not be 'utterly crushed'. The best outcome of the war would be that, of its own volition, Germany would get rid of the Hohenzollerns, become a republic and join Britain and France in establishing better machinery for the maintenance of peace and the regulation of international affairs. But first, the German worship of militarism must be extirpated. No doubt, under the strain of mounting losses of men, some would succumb to a blind hatred of the enemy. This should be constrained as far as humanly possible. But Jones went further. At the outset and in anticipation of any such fall from grace, he registered a 'protest against all manifestations of that ignorant and malicious spirit that can despise a whole nation'. Not all Germans were Junkers: Germany's immense contribution to music, art, science and philosophy could not be expunged. Under the caption 'Lest We Forget', the war issue of the *Outlook* in September 1914 included the grouped portraits of Beethoven, Goethe, Kant and Johann Sebastian Bach. 'Let us remember that', he concluded, 'it will save us from much that is cheap and foolish'. It would not in the least weaken the conviction that the British were 'bound to fight the war', and it would certainly be fought 'to the end with all the strength we have got'.[1]

Not all his predictions came true. He went along with the current popular assumption that the war would be over in a matter of months. And, grotesquely as no doubt it appeared later, he could write at this time of the war as 'a deserved experience', a needful catharsis to purge the nations of their dangerous addiction to secret diplomacy and competitive armaments, the prime causes of the conflict. This complacent doctrine was perhaps just barely tenable given his expectation that the loss of life would be measured in some thousands not, as it proved, hideously, in millions. Years later, he wrote that for mankind the Great War was a 'Station on the Cross', a tortured passage 'along *Via Dolorosa*'.[2] Nevertheless, during the war years he never wavered in his conviction that Germany must be defeated. By October 1914 sombrely he had come to see that the war might last bloodily for years. If that were so, the terrible price must be paid, for it was 'a life and death struggle – a fight for freedom'.[3]

[1] *The Welsh Outlook* [hereinafter *WO*], I, 335–41, 375–7, 388.
[2] Ibid., I, 376. 'Retrospect', December 1933. T.J., Class Y, No.3, No.18.
[3] *WO*, I, pp.415–17.

He had, in fact, seen something of the by-products of war at closer hand. Many Belgian families had fled before the advancing Germans; there were terrifying stories, not all true, of brutal atrocities. The heroic resistance of the Belgian people whose country was being destroyed around them evoked a great wave of sympathy in Britain. Many Belgian refugees crossed the Channel. This was a situation to which the Misses Gwendoline and Margaret Davies of Llandinam, David Davies's sisters, instinctively responded. They commissioned Tom Jones, together with Burdon Evans, D.D.'s business manager, and Dr Fabrice Polderman, a Belgian academic at University College, Cardiff, to go over to the continent to rescue a number of Belgian artists, painters, poets, sculptors and musicians and a few politicians who were marooned on holiday near Ostend when the war broke out.[4]

> You will remember [Burdon Evans wrote to Tom Jones years later] we went to Belgium towards the end of September 1914, and were there a couple of weeks I think. We visited Ostend, Zeebruge, Knocke, Bruges, Ghent, Nieuport, Heyst and La Zoute. We brought back 91 refugees of the better class, and these were placed mostly at Aberystwyth and Barry.

The Misses Davies and their stepmother 'bore the whole cost until the party was distributed . . . I cannot tell you what the total cost was for the whole period but it ran into hundreds of pounds'.[5]

Tom Jones and the Davies family had not restricted their concern to this artistic élite. Indeed, initially they had gone up to London to bring a group of humble artisans and tradesmen back to Wales but had been blocked by Roman Catholics who had tried to restrict the number of Catholic refugees going to Protestant homes.[6] Nor did Burdon Evans and Tom Jones see themselves as daring Pimpernels, although they and their refugees had left Belgium on the last but one boat to get away before the Germans arrived. Burdon Evans added with some amusement that one letter of thanks he had received 'piled it on so thick that I almost felt that we each deserved the VC or at least the DSO for courage and devotion to duty under fire!!!'.[7] However, although their response to the needs of the refugees was genuinely humanitarian, Tom Jones and the Misses Davies were certainly also anxious to enlist the impressive artistic talents and skills of some of the Belgians for their

---

[4] On this episode see M. Vincentelli, 'The Davies Family and Belgian Refugee Artists and Musicians in Wales.' *NLWJ* XXII, 226–33, and *Welsh Broth*, pp.149–54.

[5] T.J., Class Z (Diary, 1933), pp.89–90.

[6] M. Vincentelli, loc.cit., p.226.

[7] T.J., Class Z (Diary, 1933), p.30. *Welsh Broth*, p.152.

schemes of cultural developments in Wales, in particular those which they hoped to establish under the aegis of the University College at Aberystwyth.

In the meantime, Tom Jones acted as secretary of a committee to look after the Belgian refugees who settled in Wales. As editor of *The Welsh Outlook,* he regularly included news and comment about Belgium's continuing ordeal and her cultural achievements.[8] Some of the refugees were exceptionally gifted: for example, George Minse, a sculptor of international repute, Emile Verhaeren, said to be 'the most imposing poet of the French tongue since Victor Hugo', Emile Claus, a gifted painter of Flemish landscapes, and Emile Vandervelde, leading socialist and persuasive orator.[9] Tom Jones's home Anwylfan in Park Road, Barry, became the administrative clearing house for the refugee cause in Wales.

Anwylfan was a large spacious detached house with an extensive garden at the rear; Romilly and Porthkerry parks were near by. Indeed, in material terms these years at Barry were the most comfortable of Tom Jones's life. He was never himself much interested in money, but this was one time in his life when circumstance had struck a most agreeable balance, solely and efficiently managed by his wife Rene, between his income and expenditure. They were able to afford a good deal of domestic help. Lizzie had been with them since their days in Scotland, they also employed a Flemish refugee and there was Maggie Davies from Blaenau Ffestiniog, carefully chosen by Mrs Silyn Roberts, who was recruited partly in the hope (vain as it turned out) that her domestic presence would help the children Eirene and Tristan to achieve an easy fluency in the Welsh language. There was also an occasional gardener to see to the surrounds and tend a large kitchen garden.

From this comfortable ménage Tom Jones was as active as ever in his many public activities. Soon after he moved to Barry he had become a leading member of the committee of the local Brotherhood Social Club that had rapidly grown from eighty to over three hundred members, making the club's existing premises at 18 Broad Street hopelessly overcrowded. The Brotherhood Club was part of a national movement: it was a non-sectarian attempt to promote Christian fellowship, temperance and a commitment among working men to social service. Religious meetings and educational classes were held, there were recreational and bathing

    [8] Ibid., p.149. *WO,* I, II and III, *passim.*
    [9] *Welsh Broth,* p.152, M. Vincentelli, loc.cit., p.230, 'Emile Verhaeren'. *WO,* I, 423.

facilities, and refreshments were available.[10] The committee hoped to move to larger premises by converting the semi-derelict Temperance Hotel nearby at a cost of about £3,000. Tom Jones appealed for help to David Davies, whose industrial connection with Barry was so strong. 'There are several of us now residing in Barry', he wrote to D.D. in May 1913, 'prepared to give a good deal of our time to the project'. The club membership, he said, consisted of 'the pick of the workmen' of the town who should be helped to withstand the temptations of drink. The correspondence continued for some time. Tom Jones also tried to attract the interest of the Misses Davies, on this occasion unsuccessfully. Finally, much later in the year, David Davies, while not ruling out a sizeable contribution, laid down conditions which the local committee apparently could not meet.[11]

Tom Jones's interest in education was unabated. In October 1914 his Barry WEA class, adapting to the times, waived its original syllabus in favour of considering the 'Balance of Power in Europe in Modern Times'. Jones had delivered an important address on 'The Present Position of Education in Wales' to the Merthyr Teachers' Society in March 1914 in which he vigorously attacked complacency among educational leaders, denounced over-large classes in schools and the neglect of music and aesthetics in education. 'Beauty', he asserted, 'was ignored in our national life'.[12] Much of his energy at this time was absorbed by the controversy, labyrinthine in its complexity, over the establishment of a medical school in Cardiff. This ill-tempered mêlée was to continue for years. At this time there were four main protagonists: the authorities at University College, Cardiff; Sir William James Thomas, a wealthy coalowner whose philanthropy made the undertaking possible but who could be prickly and disconcertingly obstinate about people and procedures; the Exchequer, concerned as always about the burden falling on public funds and, at this time, with Lloyd George as Chancellor, lynx-eyed about Welsh affairs; and, finally, some of the leaders of the other constituent colleges in Wales who asserted that the Medical School was a national institution which should be part of the federal University of Wales in its own right and not simply become an extension of the College in Cardiff. The affair aroused very strong feelings. The Cardiff authorities were aggrieved because, as they pointed out in a formal Council resolution in July

[10] 'The Barry Brotherhood Social Club'. T.J., Class X, Vol.2, No.76. WO, I, 184.
[11] T.J., Class X, Vol.2, Nos.74–8; Class W, Vol.6, Nos.136–9.
[12] WO, I, 443. The Pioneer (Merthyr), 21 March 1914. See also the highly flattering references in the leader column 'A Welsh Idealist'.

1914, the School was to be based on the Physiology department (that had provided pre-medical training ever since 1893) established and maintained at the cost of great 'sacrifices' by the College from its slender resources since that time. All the participants in the argument were armed with formidable batteries of high principle, technical or legal objection, strong prejudice and, in some cases, downright vested interest. It was not going to be settled quickly.[13]

Tom Jones's position was quite clear. He worked closely with David Davies, who was then Vice-President of the Aberystwyth College, and Lord Kenyon, the President of University College, Bangor.[14] They were determined that the Medical School should not fall entirely under the control of the Cardiff college. Jones, their agent on the spot in 1914, thought that the Cardiff authorities were impossibly 'difficult' to deal with.[15] Luckily, from their point of view, Sir William James Thomas was not a man to be rushed, and, even more decisively, early in 1915, the Treasury announced that control of the Medical School and its funds would not be determined until the whole structure of the University of Wales had been reviewed. Tom Jones and some of his associates promptly submitted a memorandum to the Cardiff college Council pleading that no proposals should be put forward by Cardiff for the time being; and when in due course a scheme was formulated, that it should ensure that the medical school was 'an organic part of the University of Wales', that the arrangements should produce 'as little essential change' as possible in the position of other constituents of the University, while retaining for the Cardiff college 'the maximum degree of initiative and autonomy'. It is evident that this situation called for a Solon if not a Solomon. No equivalent of either was in sight in Wales in 1915, and the dispute rumbled along unresolved for some time.[16]

This disagreement was merely one of a number of serious problems with which university education in Wales was faced at this time. Chickens were coming home to roost. Wales was paying the price for hapless concessions to the parochial wilfulness in the past that had insisted on three weak colleges rather than one central

[13] *Welsh Broth,* pp.154–5. T.J., Class J, Vol.15, No.103.

[14] Ibid., No.103 in which Jones called on D.D. and Kenyon 'to take hold of the situation' to prevent it from being 'badly bungled'.

[15] Ibid., No.101.

[16] Ibid., No.107. See also Nos.87, 101–6. *WO,* II, 255. Even the Treasury mandarins, usually so cocksure in the all-embracing wisdom of their judgements, confessed that 'an ideal organisation' was beyond their power of invention. D. Emrys Evans, *The University of Wales* (Cardiff, 1953), pp.67–8.

university. It was evident long before 1914 that the three constituent colleges were inadequately endowed and badly underfunded, that resources were wasted in needless duplications, and that the machinery of the University was both weak and cumbersome. The Advisory Committee of the Treasury on University Grants had reported to that effect in February 1914.[17] It was plain that Sir William McCormick, chairman of the Advisory Committee, favoured a considerable strengthening of the powers of the University at the expense of the colleges, particularly over finance. Lord Kenyon was thoroughly alarmed. 'I see many difficulties', he wrote to Tom Jones, who shared his fears, 'the two chief being the jealousy that will be created and the log-rolling' to become a member of any body set up to 'divide the spoil'. Was there any way, Kenyon asked despairingly, of strengthening the University without causing a disruptive friction? 'Will you put your brain to work?', he asked Jones.[18]

During the three years when he was editor of *The Welsh Outlook* Tom Jones devoted more space to education, especially at the university level, than to almost any other topic. He did not pretend that he had any immediate answer to the constitutional conundrum posed by Kenyon, but Jones did examine the serious structural inadequacies of Welsh higher education, and commissioned several articles on the same subject by others. His own observations are either in the editor's leading articles (styled 'Notes of the Month') or in unsigned contributions which from internal evidence – ideas, argument and language – are almost certainly his.[19] For example, in April and May 1914 he published a two-part article entitled 'The Educational Outlook in Wales'. It appeared with a broadside against familiar targets: cramming and an examination system that stifled free inquiry and starved the imagination of children; a putative university education that degenerated into 'vocational schooling', where students 'in nine cases out of ten' had 'not heard of metaphysics', were indifferent to the glories of Greece and heedless of anything without obvious 'marketable value', anything not formally part of their degree course. 'Cannot Sir Henry Jones be called in?', he asked.

If he were . . . instead of information potted, tinned, and labelled, the

[17] Ibid., pp.60–7.
[18] T.J. Class J, Vol.15, No.87.
[19] *WO*, I, II and III, *passim*. See especially, I, 152–4, 196–205; II, 123–4, 166–7, 254–5; III, 97, 140, and very probably, the skittish 'An Examination Paper for University Commissions', pp.143–4.

sound and light and heat of a world could blaze and thunder through the classrooms and the wonder and wild delight of creation burst upon the eyes and ears of . . . these scribbling students with their spectacled noses buried in their note books.[20]

Thereafter, passion part spent, the article set out the various suggestions that had been made for university reform. One proposal was to put the University into the hands of an elective representative council with 'a Superman', designated 'a working head', as its chief executive officer. Tom Jones, who always put a premium on action and believed that his countrymen had a congenital fondness for self-indulgent rhetoric, dismissed this out of hand. 'The persistent faith in huge amorphous National councils amazes me', he said. Supposedly designed to promote democratic freedom, this suggestion would simply end in 'bureaucratic despotism'. Nor would it do to strengthen the existing University Court and Council. That would threaten the 'substantial independence' of the colleges, intensifying friction, and concentrate 'the present diffused rivalry by converting the University Court and Council into an arena of strife'. The third proposal was to recognize that the federal university had failed and turn the colleges into universities, each perhaps with a particular bias: Cardiff in technology, Aberystwyth and Bangor, singly or together, in the humanities. There were, of course, other suggestions and variations on these three main proposals. There was certainly no agreed consensus. The existing federal system, which was not devoid of virtue, was 'delicately adjusted' and should not be disturbed until there had been the fullest inquiry and the fullest discussion. In his opinion, this called for a departmental inquiry or, preferably, a royal commission.[21]

The university and college authorities in Wales, however, could not agree on what ought to be done. Principal T.F. Roberts of Aberystwyth and some others, ostrich-like, insisted that the existing University was 'a very great success'. Principal Reichel of Bangor wanted to postpone action until after the war; on the other hand, Principal E.H. Griffiths of Cardiff, rarely the most restrained of commentators, said that he would 'rather see the University smashed than that the same condition of things should be allowed to continue'. Thus divided and wary of outside interference, the authorities agreed reluctantly, at government suggestion, to a University conference in the hope of resolving their many

---

[20] *WO*, I, 154.
[21] Ibid., I, 220–3.

dilemmas.[22] Tom Jones thought that this was an absurd irrelevance; the situation was 'ripe' for a Royal Commission; the issues, he said, were too great to be answered by 'lawyers puzzling over the clauses of a charter'.[23] In fact, the conference ended in stalemate. Finally, the government stepped in: there would be no increased grants for higher education in Wales unless the University and colleges asked for the appointment of a Royal Commission, and agreed beforehand to accept whatever decision the government arrived at on the basis of the Commission's findings. Tom Jones had had advance notice of this decision, of which he thoroughly approved, from Sir Henry Jones.[24]

Indeed, at this time he was kept fully briefed about the hopes and fears for the future of most of the university leaders in Wales; or, at any rate, those who spoke for the Bangor and Aberystwyth Colleges. He was not in the confidence of the Cardiff leaders whom he strongly suspected of separatist ambitions.[25] Nobody doubted that Lloyd George would exert a powerful, probably paramount influence over the selection of the Commission. Sir John Williams, former royal physician, the venerable President at Aberystwyth, anxiously probing, had discovered, as he told Tom Jones, that the Chancellor was highly critical of the performance of the Welsh colleges, and was determined that the Commission would be made up of 'independently-minded men of stature, not solely or even chiefly drawn from Wales'.[26] The key nomination, of course, was that of the chairman. Many names were bruited about: Sir William McCormick, Lord Bryce and several others. Henry Jones, an influential insider, eventually settled on another. 'What of Haldane?', he asked Reichel, 'he believes in education, has a large intellect, somewhat loosely packed [and] . . . more generous ideas of education than almost anyone we could get'. In the event, Haldane was appointed, and Henry Jones, with some reluctance, agreed to be a member of the Commission. 'I was reluctant, my dear laddie', he told Tom Jones. 'It is not the sort of work I like'. But the appointment of Haldane, who might take the chance to set up 'a model', had persuaded him.[27] As Lloyd George had predicted, the Commission was made up of people of standing:

[22] T.J., Class J, Vol.1, Nos.29, 46. Ibid., Class U, Vol.3, No.6. *WO*, III, 296. D. Emrys Evans, op.cit., pp.67–9.

[23] *WO*, II, 167.

[24] T.J., Class U, Vol.I, No.10.

[25] E.L. Ellis, *The University College of Wales, Aberystwyth 1872–1972* (Cardiff, 1972), pp.178–9.

[26] T.J., Class J, Vol.II, No.1 (in Welsh).

[27] T.J., Class U, Vol.I, No.11; Vol.III, Nos.27 and 29.

Henry Jones and Sir Owen M. Edwards, who were Welsh, W.N. Bruce, who was partly so by association, together with a distinguished group of Englishmen (Sir William Osler, of Oxford, the physicist W.H. Bragg, W.H. Hadow, an authority on music, A.D. Hall, an agricultural expert) and Miss Emily Penrose of Somerville College, Oxford.

It has been necessary to consider the problems of education in Wales in some detail because, at that time in particular, Tom Jones's life was to a large extent taken up with these matters. He was to be one of the more interesting of those who gave evidence to the Royal Commission, and, as will appear, it seemed quite likely that he would be elected to the headship of one or other of the Welsh university colleges, and thereby achieve his heart's desire. His strong personal preference was for the principalship of his old college at Aberystwyth. As he saw it, there were sound reasons for this, quite apart from the powerful pull of sentiment. There was, of course, much to be said for Cardiff. Looking ahead, Jones was convinced that the 'truce to industrial warfare' would 'vanish' with the end of the war when the nation would be plunged again into bitter 'economic and political conflict', nowhere more dangerously so than in south Wales, the storm centre of class hostility. 'Nothing', he wrote in July 1916, 'is more urgent than the attempt to moralize our economic relationships and to reshape society on a more cooperative basis'. In the never-ending campaign for social justice and amity the University should 'stand for the public good against all class and sentimental interests'. It should be 'a great reconciling force', militant, not comfortably passive, in its assertion of the overriding priority of the common weal. Such opinions, so strongly held, would seem to indicate that Cardiff, the commercial capital of industrial south Wales, was the ideal base.[28]

But persuasive as this was, Tom Jones believed that other considerations tipped the balance in favour of Aberystwyth. He thought that the 'College by the Sea' had some unique virtues. Its province (especially in the recruitment of students) was the whole of Wales to an extent not matched by Cardiff and Bangor, whose catchment areas, at that time, were much more localized. Moreover, he said, it was 'possible to have a far intenser college life' at Aberystwyth than at the sister colleges. This intimate corporate experience with its emphasis on 'social intercourse' was 'a priceless factor in any fine system of education'. And the presence nearby of the National Library of Wales gave opportunities for advanced scholarship unparalleled elsewhere in Wales. Taken together, these

28 *A Theme with Variations*, p.84.

considerations meant that Aberystwyth could be developed 'gradually into a great centre of humanist education'. He proposed that there should be an open 'avowal of the training of character and personality' as the primary purpose, to which 'examination success' (which of course had its place) would be subordinate; tutorial and seminar teaching should be the staple of instruction, and there ought to be hall and refectory accommodation for all, for students are 'as much educated by each other and by their environment as by their professors'. Here was a blueprint for a modest Welsh version of Oxbridge, to which he added a great hall cum theatre and a college picture gallery.

Aberystwyth also had other academic advantages. After the war, which had shown the crucial importance of technology, there would be a demand for a great extension of the teaching of applied science. This was natural and proper, but there were dangers. 'The secularization of science had been the curse of Germany and we must beware of imitating her'. There was a real danger that at Cardiff the emphasis might become unduly commercial and technological. 'We must try at Aberystwyth', he wrote, 'to think things together, the arts and the sciences, and to subordinate the two great disciplines to the spiritual enrichment of the people'. The three Welsh colleges should foster particularly the specialisms for which they were best fitted. Aberystwyth should aim for 'a quality and range unsurpassed' in the United Kingdom in Agriculture, Celtic Studies, Music and Art. And he pointed to the proposal, currently being considered, to introduce a multi-disciplined degree scheme in Social Sciences, 'essential to any centre of humanist culture', which would capitalize on what he asserted was the Aberystwyth college's long tradition of special concern for public service. If this suggestion had been implemented, as he urged, Aberystwyth would have anticipated the establishment of the much admired PPE honours school at Oxford. Tom Jones's memorandum was a cry from the heart for excellence; a plea, as he was to make explicit later, for at least 'one uncommon college in Wales. . . . We might then', he said, 'have a few more uncommon Welshmen'.[29]

But there was one other crucial factor in Aberystwyth's favour. Tom Jones, for all his visionary idealism, was also strongly practical. He knew very well that without adequate financial backing these schemes were idle daydreams. Conditional promises of more government money sometime in the future had been made to the

[29] 'The University College of Wales, Aberystwyth', ibid., pp.68–84. Leeks and Daffodils, pp.202–3.

Welsh colleges, but there was no chance of public funds for the sort of qualitative changes he envisaged for Aberystwyth. Jones however knew that there was the real possibility that a very large sum of money would be donated to the College for some of the proposals he had put forward. The peroration of his memorandum ended in an invocation to a spiritual mission with the words: 'You can help Aberystwyth to work out this fine destiny as no one else known to me'.[30] These words were addressed to the Misses Davies of Llandinam. Since they had first met in 1910, the friendship between Tom Jones and the two ladies had become steadily closer and it was to continue, unsullied by any sort of serious rift or pique on either side, to the grave. It rested on their common belief in the cultural importance of music, art and the higher crafts, their concern for the alleviation of social distress and their commitment to the interests of Wales and the Welsh people. And above all, it was based on complete trust and the absolute belief the sisters had in the sincerity of Tom Jones's idealism, and the knowledge that his advice, increasingly sought, was utterly disinterested.

Gwen and Margaret (or Daisy, as she was alternatively called) Davies were very wealthy spinsters (they had, apparently, had their suitors in their time) who were exacting in their standards, straitlaced, reserved and shy, sometimes painfully so. Despite their material advantages, their domestic circumstances were not altogether easy: their mother died when they were very young, their much-loved father Edward (who later married his former wife's sister in Canada, thus circumventing the prohibition of British law), a kind and studious man, suffered a very severe mental breakdown and died relatively early in life. The stepmother, Elizabeth, who lived on into her eighties, was a woman of ability, active in public affairs, a dominating (but not unkind) personality. The household also included Miss Jane Blaker, a formidable governess-companion, socially practised but in personal terms forbidding. The no doubt well-intentioned protective effect on the sisters of these 'two dragonesses' (as one who saw the household at first hand has called them) was, perhaps inevitably, inhibiting.[31] Tom Jones, instinctively kind, naturally sympathetic, prepared to listen patiently to those who had a serious purpose, was a welcome relief to the sisters, a shrewd, experienced counsellor whose sure touch in personal matters melted their

---

[30] *A Theme with Variations*, p.84.
[31] Eirene White, *The Ladies of Gregynog* (Cardiff, 1985), pp.11–17. The usually irrepressible Joyce Grenfell (op.cit., p.160), on a visit some years later, thought the atmosphere in the household 'cool, correct and daunting'.

reserve. In time, the relationship was underpinned by warm affection. From this time onwards the alliance between Gwen and Daisy Davies's wealth and Tom Jones's remarkable eye for a workable scheme often succeeded in giving practical effect to the generous ideals to which they aspired.

Tom Jones also had some power of persuasion where David Davies was concerned; but with so assertive, indeed headstrong, a character as D.D., this was inevitably much weaker and of an entirely different order. David Davies was not short of ideas of his own, some of them boldly imaginative. Tom Jones's role where D.D. was concerned was cautionary rather than inspirational, although on occasion he could cajole 'The Chief', as he continued to call him, into altering his decisions slightly. During the three years when Tom Jones edited *The Welsh Outlook* his relations with D.D. were generally amicable although occasionally of course their opinions differed and this sometimes prompted a passing irritation. Accustomed to issuing orders, D.D. had no experience of, or patience with, detailed administration; as Jones wrote some years later, 'twelve months at a desk or in a coal tip in his youth' would have been a valuable apprenticeship for D.D.[32] Certainly it is doubtful if he ever fully realised the very heavy demand that his editorship of the *Outlook* made on Tom Jones's reserves of energy. It was an exhausting labour of love undertaken usually at weekends after the normal round of the week's work at the Insurance Commission. He had useful editorial assistance for a short time in 1915 from W.J. Williams, a Newport teacher, but that ended when he joined the school inspectorate. Williams, who had first-hand knowledge of Jones's 'magnificent work' at the *Outlook,* resented 'the carping spirit' of some of David Davies's critical comments which he thought showed 'no understanding of the difficulties of running a thing like this by the voluntary energies of a few men – more especially, one man'.[33]

Tom Jones had been open-eyed about difficulties from the start. 'We are being told on all sides', he wrote in February 1914, 'that we shall fail'.[34] And of course the wholly unexpected outbreak of the war had compounded difficulties. It was as well that the editor was not thin-skinned. Comments, even from the thoroughly

[32] *Welsh Broth*, p.135..

[33] T.J., Class HH, Vol.2, No.38. There is much interesting detail on Williams and editorial difficulties at the time in Gwyn Jenkins' 'The Welsh Outlook, 1914–73', loc.cit., pp.470–3.

[34] *WO*, I, 46.

well-disposed, must sometimes have ruffled the most equable of editors: Professor H.J.W. Hetherington of Cardiff, for example, who succeeded Tom Jones as editor for a short time, despite his academic status, thought that under his predecessor the *Outlook* had shown an undue 'bias in favour of education questions; there were, after all, 'other things in the world'. H. Idris Bell, a distinguished correspondent, qualified general praise with the complaint that there were rather too many contributors who were 'not worthy' and insufficient attention was paid to Welsh literature and to what was 'going on inside Wales'. Professor H.J. Fleure of Aberystwyth, the distinguished geographer, one of Tom Jones's closest allies at that college, 'felt a little sad' about the *Outlook's* '"cultural nonconformist" tone at times. It seems', he said, 'to suggest those *fin de siècle* chapels that ran to Browning Societies and such'. A few 'pungent cartoons' would help to enliven it.[35]

There was, of course, no perfect answer to these problems of style and content. But at any rate during the last months of Tom Jones's editorship the *Outlook* had one or two lively moments. The November edition of the journal included an article, 'Lord Rhondda's Religion', written with a pen dipped in gall by *Beati Pauperes*, the editor in the thinnest of disguises. In an after-dinner speech on receiving the freedom of the city of Cardiff, the millionaire coal-owner Lord Rhondda had admitted that he was an unashamed hedonist, interested largely in his own concerns, who might well do something for Wales one day so long as, at the same time, he could also help himself. His speech was at least engagingly free from hypocrisy. Nonetheless, Tom Jones was provoked and caution went to the wind. The article in the *Outlook* ('hot stuff with a vengeance' and, arguably, 'libellous', as David Davies in some alarm called it) attacked with impassioned scorn the values Lord Rhondda embodied. 'The civilisation of Wales did not begin with the Taff Vale railway' (which carried the coal for export upon which Lord Rhondda's fortune depended). 'It would be nearer the truth to say that it ended and that we relapsed into barbarism, brutality and squalor', where ruthless American-style capitalist money-grabbing prevailed and success and public esteem were measured by sordid commercial 'Cardiff standards'. Jones believed that, 'much as he loves money', Rhondda would gladly change places with Lloyd George. 'But wealth cannot give you genius, eloquence, political sagacity, charm. Mr. Lloyd George is a

[35] T.J., Class H, Vol.4, Nos.32 and 35; Class W, Vol.7, No.16.

8. The Welsh National Insurance Commission, 1912–16. T.J. (Secretary) is standing and John Rowland is seated next to Miss Douglas-Pennant.

9. Belgian refugees, including Verhaeren, Vandervelde and Claus, with T.J. and Rene at Anwylfan, Barry, 1914.

16. The Cabinet Secretariat with Sir Maurice Hankey. *Back row:* Col. Lancelot Storr, Paymaster Rowe (Admiralty), Col. Leslie Wilson, Cpt. Burgis. *Front row:* T.J., Col. Dally Jones, Sir Maurice Hankey, Cyril (later Lord) Longhurst, Cpt. (later Sir) Clement Jones.

11. T.J. with Lloyd George and Sir Robert Horne on international business at Cannes, January 1922.

12. 'Gair bach' (Just a word), Lloyd George and T.J. at the National Eisteddfod of Wales.

13. Carefree at St Moritz.

14. T.J. (first left) and friends enjoying themselves at Cairo, February 1927.

15. A latter-day Don Quixote: T.J. outside the Prado, Madrid, March 1936.

Welshman, Lord Rhondda is an American'. And, thus, evidently beyond redemption.[36]

David Davies thought that Rhondda had 'asked for it', and therefore, perfectly 'fairly . . . got it in the neck'. But D.D. was somewhat aggrieved: he did not object to the attack on avaricious captains of industry, for Jones had carefully said there were unnamed 'honourable exceptions' of whom David Davies, who had a magnificent record of philanthropy, was obviously one. But 'I think you ought to have let me see it before you put it in', D.D. complained, 'or one of these fine days I should find myself in court – Not that I mind that so long as I have taken the risk on my own responsibility'. He thought it probable that, as a result of Jones's article, 'the *Western Mail* and Rhondda press' would now attack the Welsh National Memorial and 'other projects in which we are interested'.[37]

With little choice in the matter, Tom Jones began to send on sensitive copy to be vetted by the journal's paymaster. Perhaps surprisingly, D.D. did not object to an article, 'Unrest in the Coalfield', written by Edgar Chappell, an ardent socialist and member of the ILP, which appeared in the December *Outlook*, despite the fact that it asserted that the miners' grievances were genuine and that some coal owners were virulent class warriors whose stupidity in the past made the hope of industrial reconciliation in south Wales after the war bleakly unreal.[38] Chappell's article was in general written in restrained language, and D.D. could scarcely gainsay most of what he had to say.[39] But it alerted him and thoroughly ruffled his capitalist susceptibilities.

[36] *WO*, III, 341–3. T.J., Class H, Vol.4, No.15. This, like many another effective lampoon, was not entirely fair to Rhondda, who is considered in a more balanced, though not uncritical way, in *The Dictionary of Welsh Biography*. Years later, drafting a speech for Stanley Baldwin, Tom Jones, perhaps remembering Rhondda wrote, 'You cannot graft materialism onto a Celt. If you do, you make a terrible compound'. T.J., Class A, Vol.7, No.48.

[37] Ibid., Class H, Vol.4, No.15. D.D. was also concerned about the reaction of Lloyd George (who had his own mutually useful relationship with Rhondda). At this time (see p.179–81 below) Davies and Jones were deeply involved in the campaign which brought Lloyd George to the premiership.

[38] *WO*, III, 379–82.

[39] Writing to Tom Jones on 15 December about a meeting of the Haldane Commission on Welsh education, Sir Henry Jones said: 'We had the coal owners yesterday, not on education, but on the manufacture of raw humanity into money making machinery. The Philistinism of it all made me sick . . . Tom! The *unconscious* attitude of these coal owners was appalling . . . I almost despair'. T.J., Class U, Vol.1, No.18. Tom Jones replied (Class P, Vol.1, No.21) that he was not in the least surprised and Sir Henry would see why south Wales was 'such a centre of extreme agitation'.

Chappell's second article was never published. D.D. returned the galley proof, which Jones had sent on to him, with a fusillade of outraged rejoinders in the margins alongside what he considered Chappell's worst calumnies.[40] D.D. readily agreed ('true', appears in the margin) that Lord Rhondda, arch-enemy of the men, was filled with 'lust for industrial power'. Elsewhere, D.D. went up and down the scale of denunciation. The notion that employers wished to destroy 'the Federation', the miners' union, was 'folly'; the Marxist assertion that shareholders' additional dividends were filched from wages was 'absolute twaddle'. D.D.'s fury overcame the proprieties: it was 'balls' to say that owners could always make up the financial 'leeway' caused by a strike; it was 'absolute balls' to assert that owners could oppose the men with impunity at any time.[41]

The galley proof was returned with a long letter, a combination of threat and reproof, to the hapless editor.

> I am very disappointed that you should allow such poisonous stuff to be printed [he told Jones]. If the *Outlook* is to become the medium for socialistic propaganda, then the only thing to do is "to shut it up" . . . I am not going to become a party to the dissemination of an idea of which I most emphatically disapprove and repudiate.

D.D. went on to lay it down that the benighted Chappell was not to be allowed to write again on the subject; he must confine himself to housing and other topics of which he was less ignorant. D.D.'s spleen even upset his spelling: no doubt Lord Rhondda's activities were 'unscrupuleous [*sic*] and wicked', but they would not be put right by handing over 'the control to a hair-brained [*sic*] and ambitious crowd of young socialists'. After several more paragraphs D.D. gradually calmed down: state ownership of the mines could not succeed, oil fuel posed an ominous threat to coal in the future, 'mutual trust' and the 'joint efforts' of owners and men, which Tom Jones should be advocating, were 'indispensable to the success of the industry'. But at least he ended on a friendly seasonal note: 'Best wishes for Xmas and the New Year to you all – *holl teulu* [all the family]. D.D.'[42]

[40] The episode is examined from a slightly different angle by Trevor L. Williams, 'Thomas Jones and the Welsh Outlook', loc.cit., pp.38–46.

[41] T.J., Class H, Vol.4, No.23. D.D.'s grandfather, of course, was a brilliantly successful venture capitalist: his father, Edward, however, was believed by the family to have been driven to an early grave by worry over the cost of the construction of the Barry Dock. Eirene White, op.cit., p.13.

[42] Ibid., No.21. Tom Jones was still 'My dear Microbe'.

There is no evidence that Tom Jones made a stand against this imperious intervention. It may be, as has been suggested, that he knew that D.D. would always be D.D.: headstrong, tactless, volatile, but well intentioned, even possibly generous-minded in the ultimate, if not too openly opposed. So why, therefore, hazard the *Outlook's* existence?[43] The fact is that, by this time, Tom Jones's view of the industrial scene lay somewhere between those of Chappell and D.D. He shared Chappell's opinion that bitter industrial conflict would reappear after the war, but he did not concede that all hope of reconciling capital and labour was gone.[44] It is impossible to say how he would have reacted to further bullying intrusions by D.D., except that he would probably have tried patient persuasion rather than a dramatic resignation in the first instance. Much later on in life, in different circumstances, he had no hesitation in opposing D.D. publicly when he behaved badly. For the moment that heroic gesture was unnecessary anyway, for at this juncture, for reasons unconnected with this particular contretemps, Tom Jones gave up the editorship of the *Outlook*.

All things considered, his tenure had been reasonably successful. He had had no previous experience in journalism, he operated unpaid on a part-time basis with irregular assistance, and inevitably on occasion he had to accept contributions of doubtful quality. His *Outlook* was sometimes dull, even in some respects, despite its initial high-toned pretensions, shallow and mundane. He was prepared to admit that there had been a scandalous neglect of science in its pages, but he refused to concede that the attention he had devoted to music and art was misguided.[45] Despite all the errors of commission and omission, during the first three years of its existence *The Welsh Outlook* had avoided parish pump attitudes, had offered space to contrary opinions, and had made itself a window opening from Wales on to the wider world outside. It had at least proved to be rather better than any similar English-language journal published previously in Wales.[46]

Tom Jones's outside activities were so varied and of such interest that there is the danger that his professional life at the Welsh Insurance Commission at this time will be overlooked, particularly as he was so unforthcoming about it. Relatively well-paid and secure as it was, it was scarcely the ideal post for him. There was no great call for his particular creative talents in a place where the mastery

[43] Trevor L. Williams, loc.cit., p.41.
[44] *A Theme with Variations*, p.84.
[45] 'Note re Welsh Outlook'. T.J., Class H, Vol.4, No.74. *Welsh Broth*, p.144.
[46] *The New Statesman* (27 January 1914), reported in *WO*, I, 338, said it was 'much superior'.

of technical detail and administrative competence were the supreme virtues. To Percy Watkins, his deputy, who seemed to have been born in a committee room with a manual of Civil Service procedure in his fist, Insurance Commission work was an absorbing delight. But for once in his life, Tom Jones was bored with his job. Indeed, it was worse than that. He had outside interests galore, many interesting friends, and the immense compensation of an exceptionally happy home. But his daily life at the Insurance Commission was not only humdrum, all too often it seemed to be an endless round of personal enmities, clashing ambitions, and devious manoeuvring: a thoroughly depressing experience. There was one upsetting episode after another. In April 1914, for example, alerted by a Home Office friend, T. Huws Davies, he hurried up to London to kill off an ill-intentioned rumour that he had prompted an embarrassing parliamentary question about the Welsh Insurance Commission. 'You must take steps', Huws Davies wrote, 'to put down the infernal intriguing that is going on around you'.[47] In 1916 there was an ill-tempered dispute among the Commissioners, ostensibly over the inability of an official to speak Welsh, but in fact the outcome of a bitter long-running struggle for influence in Whitehall and Cardiff.[48] At the centre of it all lay the persistent hostility between John Rowland and Tom Jones. Rowland was as formidable as ever, 'dangerously smooth' as one opponent said, at office in-fighting. He was expert at enlisting the support of any disgruntled assistant of those to whom he was opposed. And he was all the more dangerous because he had clandestine links with Mrs Lloyd George and other influential people. By 1917 'one Commissioner after another . . . had broken with him'. Even the good-natured Chairman was finally outraged by his 'back-stair work and log-rolling'.[49] No doubt those who complained were not entirely innocent either. Regardless of the balance of blame, the fact was that the atmosphere at the Commission was often thoroughly unpleasant. Luckily for Tom Jones, deliverance was at hand.

He had first seen and heard Lloyd George in the early 1890s, when the young Liberal MP came to Aberystwyth to speak on temperance.[50] They first met, of course, in 1911 when Jones and David Davies went to Downing Street on behalf of the King Edward Memorial Association. Subsequently, briefed in detail by Sir Henry

    [47] T.J., Class H, Vol.2, Nos.48, 49 and 50.
    [48] Ibid., No.57.
    [49] Ibid., Nos.73, 77, 138 and 145; Class P, Vol.1, No.60.
    [50] 'Lloyd George: Some Personal Memories'. NLW TJ Misc. Box (un-calendared). There is no College record of the meeting.

Jones about Tom Jones's virtues, Lloyd George, who knew a useful man when he saw one, began to call on his services for various purposes in Wales. Tom Jones acted as the link between Lloyd George and 'some young men who count in Wales', the poet T. Gwynn Jones and others. Lloyd George invited Tom Jones to spend the weekend at his home in Cricieth, and by 1915 it was public knowledge that they were on the best of terms.[51]

Tom Jones succumbed very quickly to Lloyd George's personal magic. It was a fascination that he never ever quite shook off. At this time, he was filled with admiration for the astonishing range of the Chancellor's talents, and the hope he embodied of a significant improvement in the life of the common people. Moreover, after 1914, Lloyd George seemed to him to be the one national leader who understood the unprecedented demands made by total war, and had the capacity to rouse the British people to an effective response. The defeat of Germany was, for Tom Jones and David Davies, as for Lloyd George, the overriding immediate necessity. The editorial pages of *The Welsh Outlook* expressed that determination steadfastly, despite the mounting cost and savagery of the war. More and more explicitly, even stridently, the *Outlook* demanded that Lloyd George should be given a commission to direct the war. 'A great leader is more than ever necessary', Tom Jones wrote in June 1916. 'Events, so far in this war, point to one man – Lloyd George – the Man of Destiny'.[52]

By this time, Jones and D.D. were occasional members of Lloyd George's entourage. At the end of April, when there was yet one more shift in the continuing dispute between Asquith and Lloyd George, D.D. and Jones were up in London to assist. 'I spent Monday night and most of Tuesday with the Chief in town', Jones told Burdon Evans. 'He saw L.G. and we saw Dr. Addison, but I think Asquith's speech on Tuesday for the moment seems to have put the extinguisher on the rebels'.[53] At this time Tom Jones's status was a modest one, and 'the Chief', D.D. (who in turn at this time deferred to Lloyd George by name as *his* 'Chief'), was only one of a number of agents at work on Lloyd George's behalf.[54] In

[51] T.J., Class W, Vol.12, No.14; Vol.3, No.23; Class A, Vol.1, No.3; Class Z (Diary 1899–1916), pp.32–3. D. Jenkins, *Thomas Gwynn Jones: Cofiant*, (Denbigh, 1973), pp.231–2, 329.

[52] *WO*, III, 180.

[53] T.J., Class W, Vol.6, No.142. Jones thought that D.D. underestimated the difficulty of 'beating the party machine' and L.G.'s weakness 'by being bracketed with Northcliffe and company'. In July, when Lloyd George went to the War Office, D.D. became his parliamentary secretary.

[54] T.J., Class H, Vol.4, No.15.

August, aware that Lloyd George was 'very anxious' that Jones should become an MP, David Davies suggested that he should consider standing for South Glamorgan at the next election because he would be able to do far more for his country as a member of the Commons than he could as a Civil Servant. Jones had already made it plain that he had no political ambitions, but he did discuss the proposal with his wife. It may be that his recent first-hand experience of high politics had whetted his appetite for more; perhaps the wearisome bickering at the Insurance Commission had driven him to consider other possibilities. His wife Rene was unimpressed. She pointed out crisply that a political career was dangerously uncertain for a man without a private income, who, handicapped by a late start, might find it difficult to rise quickly above the 'time-marking rut' to which back-benchers were usually condemned. Moreover, it was a life 'frequently charged with peculiar excitement; you are excitable enough already don't you think?'.[55]

Jones stayed put. But not for long. At the end of November 1916, he was hastily summoned to London to join D.D. in his flat at St James's Court. Lloyd George temporarily occupied the flat next door: 'to secure more privacy', as Tom Jones wrote blandly years later.[56] Initially, he had gone up for only a few days, and, the last man in the world to stand on his dignity, had made himself useful acting as a discreet doorkeeper, making the tea and even some sort of supper for D.D. and others who were in and out of the flat during these days of prolonged crisis. But he was also engaged in much more important matters. At Lloyd George's request, Jones, together with Tawney, Alfred Zimmern of the Foreign Office, and two others wrote a long memorandum outlining a policy for winning the war. It was a high-toned document that demanded a great deal, perhaps too much. It called on any reconstructed government that might emerge from the current crisis to give the nation a much stronger lead to enable it to live up to the genuinely lofty ideals which it had entered the war to defend. It demanded an immediate policy of 'thorough', obstructive social prejudices and class interests must be swept aside; the nation, which was ready for sacrifices, must be held to the same obedience to duty as the soldier at the front; promotion in the army and in the public services should be by merit; incompetents, no matter how highly placed,

[55] Ibid., Class P, Vol.1, Nos.11 and 12; Class X, Vol.III, No.80.

[56] *Welsh Broth*, p.161. Jones writes that he was summoned 'out of the blue'. However, he told Joseph Davies (*The Prime Minister's Secretariat* (Newport, 1951), p.9), with whom he travelled up to London, that he had been 'in continuous touch' with Lloyd George and D.D. 'all last week'.

should be ruthlessly dismissed; there must be equality of treatment for all; certain important industries should be brought under government control and the liability to national service raised to sixty.[57] This was almost exactly the policy that Jones, month in month out, had been advocating in *The Welsh Outlook*.

There is no room here for an examination of the controversy surrounding the events that made Lloyd George Prime Minister. Tom Jones's opinion, expressed in 1951 after many years' mature reflection on the events in which he played an interesting if minor part, was that Lloyd George 'was determined to get the direction of the war into his own hands', and that he was 'for retaining Asquith as Prime Minister', although probably not for long. Jones cites approvingly the judgement of Churchill (the other political genius of twentieth-century British history who had been similarly circumstanced) on Lloyd George in 1916: 'He coveted the place; perhaps the place was his'.[58] On 7 December Lloyd George became Prime Minister. Two days later, breakfasting alone with him, Tom Jones, as he said in fun, offered the Premier 'some good advice on how to succeed'.[59] The next day, again alone together, Lloyd George offered Jones some sound advice in return. They had discussed the future of D.D., then Lloyd George's parliamentary secretary, who had ambitions of his own.

> He always imagined himself as filling some job where some hustling of laggards is required [Tom Jones wrote to his wife] and no doubt he'd be good at that . . . he also fancies himself as something of a strategist. He may be, I can't judge . . . He would like to be Secretary of the new War Council, but there is already a something Hankey [*sic*] who has had long experience of such work . . . Zimmern tells me he is a very able chap. Anyhow, I can't see D.D. as an ideal Secretary.

Lloyd George, the brilliant outsider who had mastered the British political system from the inside, offered the opinion that 'close and constant access to two or three chief ministers gives a man far more power than much more conspicuous posts . . . the "influence" is at work all the time'. It was advice that Jones heeded: his career subsequently bore out the substantial truth of the Prime Minister's dictum. It was not yet clear exactly what position Tom

---

[57] T.J., Class C, Vol.3, No.1. The document has several marginal amendments in Jones's hand, most of them laying an even stronger emphasis on the citizen's duty, which do not appear in the printed version in *The Whitehall Diary, 1916/1925*, ed. K. Middlemas (Oxford, 1969) [hereafter *WD*], I, 3–5.

[58] Thomas Jones, *Lloyd George* (Oxford, 1951), pp.84–6.

[59] *Welsh Broth*, pp.161–2.

Jones should be given; several possibilities had been mentioned. For the moment, as he told his wife, he had agreed to Lloyd George's request that he should stay up 'for a few months', in the role, as he told his father in a hasty note, of 'an unobtrusive helper of the Prime Minister'.[60]

In 1916 Thomas Jones was forty-six years of age, his character largely formed, his personality substantially developed. It had been a long apprenticeship for the more remarkable public career that lay ahead of him, which is much more widely known. For these reasons, the first half of his life has been examined at length.

It is clear that in 1916 Tom Jones was not 'a disguised Bolshevik' conjured up by Lloyd George from the depths of a Welsh coal-mine, as Sir Ernest Swinton, a Civil Service colleague, confessed later that, half-seriously at any rate, he believed him to be at first.[61] However, Jones certainly looked and perhaps sounded like an outsider in the higher reaches of Whitehall at that time. Utterly uninterested in clothes, he cherished a superannuated bowler hat until David Davies insisted that he should buy a new one. Years later, Warren Fisher, head of the Civil Service, in despair, threw one of Jones's more disreputable hats overboard from the deck of the *Mauretania*.[62] His speech which, to the end of his life, was entirely without affectation, had a soft lilting music of its own, the English of an educated Welshman; he thought the attempt to obliterate a provincial accent misguided, an absurd artifice. In 1916 he was still slim in build, as urgent in movement as ever. One who met him in Whitehall then for the first time warmed to his friendliness, his natural manner, and 'flexible, subtle and quick mind'. This observer also took note of Jones's 'steel blue-grey eyes which suggested', he thought, 'a degree of hardness in his nature'.[63]

The young man who had left Rhymney in 1890 had changed considerably. He was now highly educated and widely experienced. His former earnest Calvinism had been transmuted into a mild agnosticism; his youthful political optimism had been tempered by experience but not wholly surrendered. Perceiving that freedom meant more than simply emancipation, he became a Fabian socialist, a collectivist who retained his belief in liberal values. Subsequently, no longer a party activist, he remained strongly critical of

---

[60] T.J., Class X, Vol.7, No.32. The note to his father is in the Tristan Jones MSS.

[61] The suspicion was taken sufficiently seriously for Special Branch officers for a time to keep an eye on visitors to his flat. *A Diary with Letters* (Oxford, 1954), Introduction, p.xviii.

[62] *WD*, I, 15. *Western Mail*, 27 September, 1950.

[63] 'Notes on Thomas Jones', provided privately by the late A.J. Sylvester, later Lloyd George's secretary.

current British capitalism, but utterly rejected Marxism and the class war. Moreover, first-hand experience of slumdom, urban and industrial, had convinced him that social necessity could not wait for the millenium; pressing need made him a beaver for immediate, even if only partial, improvement. Although his faith in religion and politics had weakened and waned, he retained an absolute belief in the power of popular education. It was to him, beyond questioning, a moralizing agency, perhaps a surrogate for his lost religion: it would transform and uplift society, it alone could make democracy secure. He called himself at this time a Welsh nationalist, which he thought entirely compatible with a patriotic loyalty to Britain. He wanted devolution for Wales, but was opposed to separatism. Born in Rhymney in Monmouthshire half-way between England and Wales, he was not then, or at any time in his life, a Welsh David casting about for a stone to hurl at the English Goliath.

Instinctively agreeable towards most of the people he met, Tom Jones was curtly dismissive of time-wasters, and he could be severe, even savage on paper, with those whose sense of public responsibility he thought remiss. His own social patience had limitations: he could not understand, still less condone a liking for drink, and he was a heretic so far as the national worship of rugby football was concerned. But his sense of humour was not absent for long; even the occasional dreary committee meeting at the Welsh Insurance Commission could not stifle his sense of fun.[64] In 1916 Tom Jones had a wide, interesting, influential acquaintance and many friends, some of them deeply devoted to him. He was too forthright, perhaps too able and successful, not to have made some enemies, a few of them for life. But he also had a secure and happy home, the love and support of his wife and three children.[65]

In 1914, a Welsh newspaper had described Jones as 'probably the most brilliant of the young Welshmen' of the day.[66] His talents were now to be put to a more demanding test in a less familiar setting.

[64] Sir Percy Watkins, op.cit., pp.107–8.

[65] A second son, named Elphin (derived from *The Mabinogion*, a book of Welsh folk legends), had been born on 22 January 1916 at Anwylfan.

[66] 'A Welsh Idealist', *The Pioneer* (Merthyr), 21 March 1914.

CHAPTER EIGHT

WHITEHALL · I

TOM JONES'S career in London was almost over before it had properly begun. The day after he had agreed to stay up to help the Prime Minister, it was announced that Lord Rhondda had been made President of the Local Government Board. Jones and D.D. were bitterly disappointed; this was not for them a Welsh vendetta simply transferred to London. They wanted Lloyd George to lead a united crusading nation in arms, and they were convinced that the presence in the new government of a notoriously combative industrial tycoon like Rhondda would alienate the labour movement, which was already distrustful. D.D. talked of resigning his parliamentary seat and disappearing to 'Egypt, Salonika, any place'. Tom Jones was in despair; he thought he had better return home to his family, a mood that persisted all day. D.D. worked off steam playing his pianola and 'yelling his heart out': Tom Jones 'went to Westminster Cathedral to meditate'. It was all the more infuriating because earlier Lloyd George had asked his opinion about the post and for once Jones did not have a name to put forward.[1]

In fact, Tom Jones and D.D. were wrong about Rhondda's usefulness in the conditions of total war. Some months later he was made Food Controller in the desperate circumstances of 1917. He was a great success. All his life Rhondda had pursued the glittering prizes: he had had no great success earlier in the House of Commons, but then turned his attention to industry and amassed an enormous fortune. It was one of the ironies of the time that Rhondda, the quintessential acquisitive individualist, should be successful director of food rationing, one of the great co-operative, quasi-socialist ventures of the war.[2]

Jones and D.D. had been no more successful in their earlier attempt to persuade Lloyd George over a much more important appointment: the nomination of a labour representative in the

[1] *WD*, I, 12–14.
[2] 'I don't care to make more money', Rhondda said in December 1917. 'my motive has been to make any damned thing I take up a success.' Bodl. Fisher MSS, Box 8a Diary.

small cabinet that the Prime Minister intended to set up to direct the war more effectively. Jones and D.D. argued strongly in favour of J.H. Thomas, leader of the railwaymen, who, in their opinion, was (with the exception of Robert Smillie, the miners' president) 'the most forceful man in the Labour movement'. The original suggestion came from Tom Jones, who thought that J.H. Thomas would be an infinitely better choice than the other possibility, Arthur Henderson, chairman of the Labour party, who had been a member of Asquith's government. Lloyd George was not 'enthusiastic' about Thomas, whose devious cunning almost matched his own. However, Tom Jones was instructed to sound Thomas out, which he did to apparent satisfaction. But in the end, Henderson was invited to join the cabinet, and J.H. Thomas was offered the new Ministry of Labour that it was proposed to establish, an offer which he declined.[3] Tom Jones's assertion that Henderson was as inferior to Thomas as Bonar Law was to Lloyd George was scarcely borne out subsequently. There was, however, something to be said for his preference for Thomas at the time. Jones believed that the willing support of labour was vital for the existence of the new government and the efficient waging of the war. J.H. Thomas had already been a powerful influence (as Lloyd George was later to acknowledge in his *War Memoirs*) in securing the agreement of the Labour party, by a narrow margin, to support Lloyd George's government. Moreover, labour was far more important in the country than it was in Parliament, and in national terms trade union influence was more significant than that of any of the parliamentary leaders. In that sense, J.H. Thomas was a key figure.

It is evident that Tom Jones was not in the least inhibited by his political inexperience from offering suggestions to the Prime Minister. Jones believed that clever political manoeuvring simply would not suffice. The nation's morale had to be dramatically improved and this was best done by 'forcing the pace' and bringing in 'new blood', if need be from outside. One of his imaginative suggestions, initially prompted by Sir Henry Jones, was to recruit H.A.L. Fisher, the distinguished historian, Vice-Chancellor of Sheffield University, as President of the Board of Education, a crucial office in any effective mobilization of the nation's human resources. On this occasion, Jones's suggestion, passed on via Addison, was accepted. Fisher was summoned to London and offered the post. He was taken aback and did not accept

[3] *WD* I, 5–13. Joseph Davies, *The Prime Minister's Secretariat* (Newport, 1951), pp.8–26, gives a full account of Jones's negotiation with Thomas.

immediately. This time Jones was ready with dismissive comments on alternative candidates: one was simply not suitable, another was 'a friend of the WEA', but not exactly right. Henry Hadow, the music authority, was 'too purely intellectual' and 'not a good democrat'; Michael Sadleir was 'too viewy and wordy'. Eventually, to Jones's relief, Fisher accepted and was duly appointed.[4]

Jones's energy during these hectic days seemed inexhaustible. He spent a great deal of time with Tawney, Mallon, J.L. Hammond, Zimmern, the politician Christopher Addison, several senior Civil Servants, and, of course, D.D., endlessly discussing, sounding opinions, exploring one possibility after another, including the structure of the proposed Ministry of Labour. Some in this highbrow circle wanted to make Jones the Prime Minister's private secretary 'to keep the charlatans away'. 'If I *could* do that', Jones wrote, 'I would be his door porter'. He clearly did believe that he had a duty in that direction, as he explained to his wife.[5] From the outset, Tom Jones was as open-eyed about Lloyd George's frailties as he was appreciative of his unique qualities. The new Prime Minister had no regard for traditional forms or other people's convenience. Sir Maurice Hankey, Secretary of the Committee of Imperial Defence, was summoned one night almost at midnight and asked 'to organise what was virtually a new system of government'. He immediately began to recruit additional staff for a new secretariat to serve the reconstructed cabinet, which was in effect a small committee of ministers largely unencumbered with departmental responsibilities. Hankey claimed later that Lloyd George had given him *'carte blanche'* over the choice of personnel.[6] This was not entirely true. Indeed, Hankey had to fight hard to fend off what he regarded as undesirable aspirants to a place on the secretariat, some of them powerfully sponsored. To Hankey's fury, for example, Alfred Milner, a member of the new cabinet, suggested that his protégé, the Tory politician Arthur Steel-Maitland, should be made head of the civil side of the secretariat, 'as an equal colleague of Hankey'. Stung to the quick, Hankey listed for Lloyd George's benefit Steel-Maitland's overwhelming disqualifications for the post: 'the fact is no-one seems to want him'. He was not liked in the House of Commons, which was 'a very fair barometer as a rule'. Above all, Steel-Maitland was tactless

[4] WD I, 10–12. H.A.L. Fisher, *An Unfinished Autobiography*, (Oxford, 1940), pp.89–92.

[5] WD, I, 13–15. Another suggestion was that Jones should ask for an Under Secretaryship in Education or at the Local Government Board.

[6] 'Hankey's Address to the Secretariat'. 10 November 1918. T.J., Class B, Vol.1, No.9. Lord Hankey, *The Supreme Command 1914–1918* (1961, II, 589).

and, as Hankey said, 'a tactless man in my office is grit in the machine'.[7] Hankey was thoroughly put out by these attempts, as he thought, to usurp his authority.

He had been filled with suspicion two days before when Lloyd George seemed 'very anxious to foist on me a Welshman called Tom Jones'. Hankey scarcely relished the prospect of the presence at his elbow of the Prime Minister's countryman and, perhaps, his spy. In general, Hankey did not care much for the Welsh; they were deficient, in his opinion, 'in honesty and good faith', and too prone to make 'success the only criterion'.[8] Moreover, apparently this particular Welshman was especially objectionable: he was reported (predictably, as some would say, by another Welshman) to be 'a peace-monger and syndicalist'.[9] This malevolent nonsense perhaps explains the early interest taken in Tom Jones by Special Branch policemen. However, when he interviewed Jones it proved much better than Hankey had feared:

> I rather liked the man, despite rather a sly face like Ll.G's and I think I could use him on the industrial side. Anyway he had ideas, and as a result of our interview I caught on to a scheme of organisation of the office into two groups – machinery and ideas – which may fit in with these people.[10]

'So began', Hankey concluded in rather less patronising terms, 'a long, valued and intimate friendship'; a comment which is very largely but not entirely true.

It was agreed that Tom Jones was to join the secretariat on secondment as an assistant secretary, but as there was still some delay he hoped to make a flying visit to Cardiff where the Insurance Commission Office had been disrupted by a 'regular storm' over his replacement.[11] The obvious answer was to promote Jones's deputy, Percy Watkins, to be acting secretary of the Commission, a course ultimately taken after a long bitter wrangle. Commissioner John Rowland, who had himself expected to be called up to

[7] HLRO Lloyd George Papers, F/38/2/1, and F/23/1/2. Under protest Hankey was persuaded to accept L.S. Amery, another of Milners protégés, in a subordinate post.

[8] Churchill College, Cambridge. Hankey Diary, Vol.2, 1/3. f28.

[9] S. Roskill, *Hankey: Man of Secrets* (1970), I, 339. The informant was J.T. Davies, Lloyd George's private secretary. No doubt alerted by Hankey's questions, Tom Jones had a 'plain talk' with J.T. Davies and it was soon apparent that the mischief had been concocted by his old enemy John Rowland in Cardiff. T.J. Class Z (Diary 1899–1916), p.69.

[10] S. Roskill, op.cit., I, 339 and *Supreme Command*, II, 589–90.

[11] T.J., Class P, Vol.1, No.23.

London by L.G., was beside himself with rage at the success of his hated rival. He had written 'violently protesting' at Lloyd George's 'forgetfulness of his old supporter', and had even stooped to the crudest sort of character assassination.[12] Meantime, in Cardiff, Rowland vented his spleen on Percy Watkins, proxy target for the absent Jones, and succeeded for some time in holding up the promotion of the acting secretary. Meanwhile it was agreed the Welsh Commission could occasionally consult Jones. Characteristically, most of this work was fitted in during lunchtime meetings. He was more and more certain that the Insurance Commission had misused his talents. 'I hope', he wrote to Percy Watkins in November 1918, 'that I shall never have to return to Insurance work'.[13]

It might seem that much of Jones's work at the Cabinet Office in hastily adapted premises at 2 Whitehall Gardens was not all that different from his duties at the Insurance Commission, at least in outward form. As Hankey wrote, the secretariat was 'principally concerned with machinery': the minuting of Cabinet discussions and decisions and the transmission of executive instructions to the various arms of government.[14] But this was an entirely different, fascinating world: Jones now had privileged daily sight of the leaders of the nation grappling with the problems of total war, taking decisions that profoundly affected the lives of millions and the fate of empires. As he told his wife a year later, it was an utterly 'enthralling' experience. However, it was not the secretarial side of his work that most interested Jones. Indeed, at their first meeting he had told Hankey that he 'didn't want to touch office machinery, but rather to act as a fluid person moving about among people who mattered and keeping the P.M. on the right path so far as possible'.[15]

Lloyd George had no illusions about the difficulties he faced. Never at any time short of belief in himself, he realized nonetheless that he needed all the help he could get, and quickly added to his personal staff a number of able men ('illuminati' in H.W. Massingham's less than friendly description) whose chief function was to furnish ideas. They were housed in temporary buildings set up in the rear of Downing Street; the unit, which had no official connection with the Cabinet secretariat, was soon popularly called

[12] p.178, above.

[13] T.J., Class J, Vol.12, No.2. T.J., Class X, Vol.7, No.56.

[14] Described in detail by Hankey in *Supreme Command, II*, 582-91, and S. Roskill, op.cit., I, 334–71. See also, J.F. Naylor, *A Man and an Institution: Sir Maurice Hankey, the Cabinet Secretariat and the Custody of Cabinet Secrecy* (Cambridge, 1983).

[15] *WD*, I, pp.15, 40.

'the garden suburb'.[16] Tom Jones was closely involved in the appointment of its principal secretary. Jones had elicited glowing references in favour of Professor W.G.S. Adams, then working under Addison, from Sir Henry Jones and A.L. Smith of Balliol, who said that Adams, who had no peer in Oxford, combined 'thinking power with practicality' and grasped the Labour point of view 'with sympathy but not uncritically'. Thereafter, despite maladroitness by David Davies, who upset Addison, Tom Jones 'fought for Adams' tooth and nail, ultimately successfully.[17]

Adams was joined by Philip Kerr, the future Lord Lothian, and David Davies, MP. Each of them was responsible for keeping the Prime Minister in close touch with a clutch of government departments, D.D. concentrating on the military side. Jones welcomed the introduction of this supporting brains trust enthusiastically and began to work closely with the three men. He had been immediately impressed with Philip Kerr, who became a lifelong friend.[18] Hankey, ever watchful against encroachment, had some reservations about the garden suburb. Tom Jones's willing capacity to co-operate with Adams and company was therefore a useful means of easing relations between the secretariat and the garden suburb.[19] Some months later, Hankey listed various un-official groups which exercised important influence on affairs at this time. There was some overlapping of membership. One, 'which I associated with Tom Jones', Hankey wrote, 'meets more or less weekly. It comprises, beside Tom Jones, Professor Adams, Vaughan Nash [formerly Asquith's private secretary], Philip Kerr and [Waldorf] Astor intermittently'. It was in close touch with H.A.L. Fisher, Minister of Education. Hankey did not altogether approve of this group; he believed that it exercised 'a good deal more influence than one would expect from its composition', and perhaps worse, it was 'rather socialistic in character'.[20]

Tom Jones's agreeable manner made him readily acceptable to most of his colleagues in the secretariat. Two of them, Lancelot

[16] *The Nation* (24 February 1917), cited in J. Turner.

[17] T.J., Class W, Vol.1, Nos.18 and 20; Class X, Vol.7, No.51.

[18] 'The Prime Minister's Secretariat'. HLRO Lloyd George Papers F/74/2/1 and 3. *WD*, I, 18–22. Waldorf Astor, who had replaced D.D. as Lloyd George's parliamentary secretary, was added soon afterwards. Joseph Davies was responsible for statistical work.

[19] Hankey, curiously, missed a chance to eliminate a possibly troublesome development for he did not realise that Adams, as he told the Machinery of Government Committee in March 1918, had 'thought throughout that the Cabinet secretariat and the P.M.'s secretariat should be one'. HLRO Lloyd George Papers F/74/10/4.

[20] S. Roskill, op.cit., I, 353–4, 422–3.

Storr and Clement Jones, were especially friendly. Tom Jones however found the politician Leo Amery uncongenial and avoided him so far as possible, and was put off by another colleague G.M. Young, the historian, who was determinedly 'super Oxonian . . . a bit *difficile* as yet . . . very much the Fellow of All Souls'.[21] At first Jones was concerned that his capacity to assist was hampered by unfamiliarity with Whitehall ways and his lack of knowledge of the 'right people to go to'. This was soon remedied. He was invited to join a small group of senior Civil Servants, known as 'The Family', who in turn hosted weekly dinner parties at which they exchanged information and discussed matters of common interest. 'I have found my knowledge of these men most helpful', Jones told his wife.[22] His social gifts made him welcome elsewhere too. He first met Waldorf Astor, the American-born millionaire, some years before through their work in the campaign against tuberculosis. They immediately struck up a warm friendship. Jones became a frequent and welcome visitor to the Astor home at 4 St James's Square, and occasionally to their country house Cliveden in Buckinghamshire. He was fascinated by the effervescent Nancy Astor, whose 'pervasive personality' was too much even for his considerable powers of description.[23]

Despite the heavy, often open-ended demands of his work at the Cabinet Office, Jones maintained his interest in the general traffic of social and political ideas. For this purpose he joined the Romney Street Group (RSG), founded in the spring of 1917 by Joseph Thorp, the dramatic critic of *Punch*, which met weekly or fortnightly in Romney Street at lunch time for 'omelet [*sic*] and talk', as the founder said.[24] The chief value of the Group, according to Thorp, was 'the play of each temperament and view upon the others'. During the first two years more than thirty people were intermittently present at meetings. In addition to Tawney, J.L. Hammond, Kerr, Zimmern and Mallon, there were some of the Civil Servants who also belonged to 'The Family'. Walter Elliot MP, the rising young Tory politician, was a member, as were the economists H.D. Henderson and Henry Clay. G.D.H. Cole often came up (or perhaps down) from Oxford, and Sir Horace Plunkett,

[21] *WD*, I, 20–2. A.J. Sylvester ('Notes on Thomas Jones'), who was then Hankey's private secretary, states that Jones 'was liked by the whole staff'.

[22] *WD*, I, 17, 20, 36 and 37. The group included J.J. Mallon, Arthur Salter, E.M.H. Lloyd, Frank Wise and others, men who had shared sympathies, including the conviction that wealth ought to be conscripted.

[23] *Welsh Broth*, pp.127–8. *WD*, I, 21.

[24] T.J., Class C, Vol.19, No.24. J. Thorp, *Friends and Adventures* (1931), p.145, for an apparent forerunner, the Agenda Club launched in 1910.

the promoter of co-operative agriculture in Ireland, attended as often as possible. Arnold Toynbee first appeared in March 1918 and Elie Halévy, the great French historian, was 'always especially welcome' during his annual visits to London.[25]

It was an exceptionally distinguished group and there was much sharp cut and thrust in their debates. The membership, as Thorp said, consisted of people who were 'entirely progressive . . . but entirely free from extremism'; they were all strongly interested in the prospect of social betterment, though not necessarily by socialist means. Indeed, when Mallon (who was made moderator) proposed that the Group should 'work out a revised pro-gramme . . . of socialism', Tawney replied that they should avoid 'the definite implication of socialism' and concentrate on defining their understanding of the word 'reconstruction', the shorthand term for post-war hopes of social, political and economic improve-ment. Nevertheless, at the next meeting of 20 April 1917, Alfred Zimmern delivered a paper on socialism, which, it was unanimously agreed, was 'brilliant'; it is an excellent illustration of the high quality of contributions to discussion at RSG meetings. Zimmern was not a socialist, although he had at times 'been as near to it as Agrippa was to Christianity'. He went on to make a sweeping attack on the fundamental assumptions of socialism. There were some interesting asides: 'Socialist perorations', he said, 'had done as much harm as the cursing clauses in the Athanasian Creed'; 'the Webbs' ideal of a universal card index could only be realised in Prussia or in Hell'. But most of the discussions at the RSG were not on questions of theory. As Tawney said: 'our object is to find out, not abstract plans, but what suits us; that is the British way'. Members were chiefly interested in practical reforms not ideological purity. At subsequent meetings at this time papers were delivered on reparations (Henry Clay), industrial combines (Thorp), democratic reform (Tawney and Arthur Greenwood), production for profit (John Hilton), and guild socialism (G.D.H. Cole, naturally).[26]

All this was meat and drink to Tom Jones. He and Thorp 'were almost invariably present'. In fact, he remained a leading member of the Group for the next twenty-five years and often took the chair at meetings. It is an index of his interest that in March 1920 a friend seeking to dissuade him from applying to replace Sir Robert Morant in a senior Civil Service post suggested that one of the most

[25] There is a full list in *R.S.G. 1917–19* (privately printed booklet), in the McKenzie MSS. T.J., Class C, Vol.19 and No.2; Class Z (Diary 1918), p.68.

[26] T.J., Class C, Vol.19, Nos.9–21.

powerful reasons against his doing so was, 'You could not call
your soul your own – no more Thorp!'. That is, active RSG
membership.[27]

In these ways, in addition to work at the Cabinet Office Tom
Jones very soon became a familiar figure in the world of Whitehall
and its associated clubs and salons. In Rhymney, it will be
remembered, his name was so commonplace that he had to be
designated 'Tom Jones Five'. Now in a society where English
surnames, sometimes hyphenated, overwhelmingly predominated,
the plain Welsh character of his name made him stand out. No one
now thought him a quaint rustic, still less some sort of wild
revolutionary. He was now fully recognized as an immensely
shrewd, widely experienced adviser of those in power, a man
blessed with an equable temperament and an exceptional gift for
making and keeping friends. He was accepted, respected, and,
indeed, often the object of much affection. Very soon he became,
to an increasingly numerous acquaintance, not Tom Jones but
'T.J.': 'such is the desire to conserve energy in Whitehall', he wrote
modestly later, that he was left 'clinging to [his] identity by two
eyelashes so to speak'.[28]

Hankey very quickly came to value T.J. 'He was one of the
juniors when he joined me, but within three months I had
promoted him', Hankey said years later. 'I delegated to him the
position of head of the civil branch of the secretariat', he wrote
early in 1918.[29] T.J. thus became the principal assistant secretary,
directly responsible for serving four main Cabinet commitees:
Home Affairs, Housing, the Irish, and the National Emergency
Committee. These committees were concerned with twenty-five
areas of government business, including finance, labour relations,
agriculture, education, health insurance, police, shipping and
railways, mines, imports and exports, economic policy, and the Irish
Question. During Hankey's long absences abroad after 1918, T.J.
took his place.[30]

There is no doubt that Hankey, whose organizational skill
amounted almost to genius, really was, as T.J. called him, 'the
prince of secretaries'.[31] Hankey had seemingly inexhaustible energy
and was something of a slave-driver where his staff was concerned.
This in no way troubled T.J., who also was remarkably energetic and

---

[27] T.J., Class Z (Diary, 1920), p.20.

[28] *RM*, p.42.

[29] *The Observer* (16 October 1955). T.J., Class X, Vol.4, No.14.

[30] 'Cabinet Secretariat Distribution of Duties: Head of Home Affairs (Mr. T.
Jones)'. T.J., Class B, Vol.1, No.11.

[31] *A Diary With Letters*, Introduction, p.xviii.

temperamentally disposed to an absolute commitment to any obligation he assumed. Hankey soon realized that he had nothing to fear from T.J. whose ambitions, if any, lay in other directions, and whose instincts were loyal. Moreover, their interests were different: Hankey's chief concerns, apart from the machinery of government, were naval and military matters and imperial and foreign policy. T.J., as he freely confessed, knew nothing of military strategy, and his attention was concentrated on domestic questions, particularly labour relations. Hankey and Jones thus complemented each other and made a superb team. The division of labour between them was obvious and mutually satisfying. They were, however, temperamentally very different. Hankey, for all his brilliant talents, was remarkably self-regarding and humourless, as frequent entries in his diary make plain.[32] T.J., though sometimes guilty of mock modesty, was not prone to that sort of vanity and he had a great sense of fun.

Politically, Hankey was a mildly liberal conservative. T.J.'s inclinations all his life were consistently, if moderately, to the left. Not surprisingly, given very different origins and experience, their social instincts differed considerably. T.J.'s sympathies were with the disadvantaged: Hankey was genuinely outraged by the Webbs' insistence that, in order to make society more equitable, there should be positive discrimination in favour of the rights of labour.[33] These differences did not seriously affect their partnership, but they explain a certain reserve that was always present and seem fully to justify the considered opinion of A.J. Sylvester:

> Hankey and Tom were entirely different in most respects. If Hankey had measured up Tom, Tom had measured up Hankey. They always worked well together, but Hankey held Tom at a distance and was aloof: that was his nature.[34]

There was no sign of this sort of reserve in T.J.'s relations with Lloyd George at this time. There was certainly never a trace of social constraint between them. 'Our common background . . . made intimate relations with Lloyd George easy', T.J. said later. Of course there was rather more to it than that. Jones had a good eye for measuring just how far he could go in persuasion of the Prime Minister. There is only one recorded occasion when, apparently, he

[32] S. Roskill, op.cit., I, 564, for example.

[33] Ibid., I, 481. Jones said that Hankey 'conserved his nervous energy by political objectivity and indifference to measures other than those bearing on national defence'. *A Diary with Letters*, Introduction, p.xviii.

[34] 'Notes on Thomas Jones'.

overstepped the mark and was ordered out of the room. Typically, this arose over his persistent protests against unjust Establishment treatment of a relatively unknown officer in the women's services, not some matter of high policy.[35] T.J. knew only too well how thoughtless and utterly exasperating the Prime Minister could be in the treatment of his staff: 'You hate and love him by turns', as Kerr put it to T.J., who did not disagree. These frailties were simply the reverse side of Lloyd George's genius: in these matters, as in his sometimes ruthless use of people, especially his chosen agents, as T.J. said, 'the P.M. could not be changed'. It did not matter: Lloyd George was unique, head and shoulders above the other ministers, and currently indispensable.[36]

As T.J. well knew, the Prime Minister was 'a hard realist', who cared little for friendship and was sparing in his trust.[37] Tom Jones could be classed as a friend, and was certainly a trusted agent, at least in certain areas of business. Above all, he was supremely useful to the Prime Minister. 'He is very quick at seeing what advice is good and measuring it up by the quarter from which it comes', wrote a Tory critic in reluctant admiration of Lloyd George at this time. 'He knows pretty well the qualifications which his advisers possess to be regarded as authorities on the various subjects [and] he never misses the chance of appropriating any useful bit of information presented to him'.[38] Lloyd George admitted that, at best, he only half-read letters.[39] Tom Jones wrote and received letters constantly from people in many different parts of the country in several walks of life. He moved freely in political and governmental circles; he was in close touch with intellectual opinion; he was an excellent sounding board for likely Welsh reactions; but, above all, he knew the world of labour, of industry and the trade unions, and was on good terms personally with many of the leaders of working-class organizations. Tom Jones was Lloyd George's most useful, most trusted industrial scout whose political and social partialities he knew, whose discretion was a byword, and whose opinions, though not of course always right, were never less than honest. Small wonder, therefore, that Lloyd George made such extensive use of him.

In February 1917 Lloyd George reconstituted the so-called

[35] *A Diary With Letters,* Introd., pp.xxix–xxx.

[36] *WD,* I, 26–7, 40.

[37] *A Diary With Letters,* Introd., p.xxx.

[38] The Tory politician Willie Bridgeman in February 1918. Bridgeman Diary, I, f 279.

[39] Nor did he 'read memoranda' or 'abide by the Agenda' at Cabinet meetings. *WD,* I, 105, 124.

Reconstruction Committee, concerned with post-war plans, under the chairmanship in practice of Edwin Montagu, his Liberal colleague. J.H. Thomas was a member, as was the redoubtable Beatrice Webb. Tom Jones had some success in nominating personnel (Vaughan Nash as secretary, and J.A. Dale 'a first rate Civil Servant', as his assistant) for the committee, and had argued strongly for the inclusion of someone, presumably other than trade union leaders, who knew 'the Labour world', preferably his friend J.J. Mallon. In fact, to his surprise apparently, T.J. himself was appointed to the committee. At the first meeting Lloyd George spoke briefly but inspiringly of 'the need of painting a new picture of Britain with fewer grey colours in it', and of the importance of working out ready schemes for the post-war situation.[40]

T.J. was immediately bombarded with letters from Beatrice Webb, who 'began devouring reports'; she fired off a memorandum which asserted that as the committee's functions were purely 'deliberative', it would achieve nothing. She wrote to T.J. accusing Edwin Montagu of seeking to engross all power into his own hands thus stifling the committee's initiative. Beatrice suggested small private meetings of the 'keen' members as the only way of making things 'happen'. She invited T.J. (and his wife, who was up in London) to lunch, when, doubtless, the pressure was kept up.[41] Eventually, Mrs Webb came to the conclusion that the committee was a waste of time and had better be 'scrapped'. As she said, 'it was clear the machinery had grit in it from the start'; and this time, the Webbs had concluded that T.J. was 'too busy with the war cabinet to do more than hold a watching brief for the P.M.' on the committee.[42] In fact, in private, T.J. had been consistently pressing Lloyd George to act in ways of which Beatrice Webb would approve: standing up to obstructive interests, for example, and taking action to stabilize wages and prices.[43] Early in 1917 *The Welsh Outlook* published a superbly written call to the government and the nation for 'a new direction and spirit' in policy which would make victory a 'symbol of the social aspirations of the mass of Englishmen'. It was written by R.H. Tawney under the pen-name 'A Soldier'. The thrust of the argument was entirely in keeping with T.J.'s attempted persuasions of the Prime Minister. The article created quite a stir

[40] Ibid., I, 21–6. According to T.J., Lloyd George had described it as 'a committee at large to advise about everything'. *Beatrice Webb Diaries 1912–24*, ed. M. Cole, pp.81–2.

[41] Ibid., I, 24, 34. T.J., Class P, Vol.1, Nos.31, 32, 42 and 43; Class W, Vol.20, Nos.30–6.

[42] *Beatrice Webb Diaries, 1912–24*, p.85.

[43] *WD*, I, 24–6.

and there was a rush to publish it more widely. T.J. had played a large part in the whole exercise, and made sure that Lloyd George's attention was drawn to Tawney's assault on the government's reluctance to disturb 'carrion crow' vested interests that battened on the community while men died in their thousands on the Somme and elsewhere.[44]

It did not have the effect T.J. hoped for. Beatrice Webb had also been right: the Reconstruction Committee was wound up in September and its responsibilities, perhaps not unwisely, transferred to a minister, Christopher Addison. It is clear that some of his friends, who were disillusioned with Lloyd George and his government, were concerned that T.J. might be bespattered by the moral decay by which he was allegedly surrounded. According to Tawney's bitter comment, T.J. was 'the only white man in that den of thieves'; George M.Ll. Davies, a Welsh friend, furiously denounced Lloyd George for selling out 'in order to be great' [*Y mae o wedi'n gwerthu ni i fod yn fawr*]. Davies appealed to T.J. to return to socialism. 'I wonder how you, a dreamer of a better world, can fail to see the rationale of it and to join in this the greatest adventure of all'. Even James Morton, the calmest of men, wondered uneasily if T.J. had got what he really wanted.[45] Soon afterwards, Nancy Astor joined in; she accused Lloyd George of cynically using her husband and Philip Kerr 'as virtuous window dressers' while in the background he worked through moral delinquents like William Sutherland and Lord Northcliffe. T.J.'s reply was that Lloyd George was the only possible man, 'the load upon him was overwhelming', the war must come first, but when it was over, it might be possible, 'to get him again at the head of the moral and progressive forces'.[46]

One of T.J.'s friends had already departed in disgust. David Davies was too impatient, and perhaps too naïve politically, to swallow Lloyd George's equivocations.[47] Indeed, D.D.'s appointment to the garden suburb had been an oddity in some ways. Although he occasionally had what he called 'brain waves' (the

---

[44] 'Democracy or Defeat', *WO*, IV, 8–13. T.J., Class H, Vol.4, Nos.39 and 42. T.J. persuaded David Davies, with the help of J.H. Thomas, to distribute two thousand free copies of Tawney's article at the TUC. T.J., Class Z (Diary 1899-1916), p.75.

[45] T.J., Class W, Vol.3, Nos.133, 173 and 197. Morton MSS GD326/8/1.

[46] *WD*, I, 40. Waldorf Astor earlier had pleaded with Lloyd George not 'to lose touch with the advanced advocates of Liberty and Democracy'. HLRO Lloyd George Papers F/83/1/6.

[47] D.D., typically, had been 'furious' that that King had shilly-shallied over inviting Lloyd George to form a government. *WD* I, 7.

campaign against tuberculosis was one, and there were to be others), D.D.'s chief talent was for entrepreneurial bustle rather than disciplined thinking. He had first been surprised and then increasingly outraged by Lloyd George's devious behaviour. D.D., never daunted by the odds, no matter how hopeless, decided to become the Prime Minister's conscience: whenever he thought Lloyd George erred, D.D. sent in a memorandum of protest. T.J. begged him to lay aside his pen for a month. Mercifully, soon afterwards, D.D. accompanied Milner on a fact-finding mission to Russia, then in the preliminary throes of revolution. On his return (a useful memorandum on this occasion correctly predicted the fall of the Czar) D.D. was 'very unsettled': one minute he fancied accompanying the mission bound for Washington, the next he said he would like to be military attaché to Venizelos, the Greek Prime Minister. Meanwhile, he had tried in vain to buy the *Westminster Gazette,* partly because, as T.J. said, 'a man with a paper in his pocket has a big leverage', particularly with the Prime Minister who 'humours such people'. Sooner or later, D.D. was bound to go too far in ruffling Lloyd George. The Prime Minister, who discovered that he needed all his cunning in dealing with an entrenched military hierarchy in which he had little confidence, was utterly exasperated by D.D.'s reiterated insistence that, as 'the nearest way between two points was a straight line', the Prime Minister could simply dismiss recalcitrant generals and publicly expose 'the War Office's stupidity'. In April they had a semi-public row in which Lloyd George finally told D.D. to 'go to Hell!'. In June 1917, he was, in effect, dismissed.[48]

The rupture did not adversely affect relations between T.J. and D.D. Although they now saw each other much less frequently, D.D.'s withdrawal put an end to what was inevitably for Jones a thoroughly embarrassing situation in which his two powerful patrons were at loggerheads. D.D. now threw his energies into building up a newspaper empire (in which T.J. acted in part as his agent) and into a campaign to establish a purposeful, but non-separatist, Welsh national 'pledgebound' political party, a scheme which ended quickly in fiasco.[49] T.J. clearly had learned how to pick his way discreetly through the most dangerous personal minefields. He had done so in this instance without compromising his integrity in any way in the eyes of either of his two powerful friends.

Although Tom Jones had given up the editorship of *The Welsh*

[48] T.J., Class X, Vol.7, Nos.48, 61 and 62. *WD,* I, 14, 31 and 39.
[49] Ibid, I, 26. T.J., Class P, Vol.1, Nos.50, 58, 75, 76; and Class C, Vol. 19, No.14.

Outlook when he went up to London, he still retained an important
influence in the determination of its affairs until its demise in
1933.[50] Busy as he was in London, Jones still found time from long
range to counsel and encourage his successors as editor. His friend
Professor Hetherington took over for some months, but then, with
regret, as he thought it 'an amusing job', had to give it up because
of the pressure of academic work. T.J. then cajoled two other rather
reluctant friends, Edgar Jones and Silyn Roberts, to run the *Outlook*
for some months, in an uneasy partnership marred by petty
jealousies.[51] When the *Outlook's* financial troubles worsened Jones
suggested economies which were adopted. But now that he was
editor emeritus, some different permanent arrangement was
necessary. At that point David Davies, now 'freelancing', as T.J. said,
in politics and public affairs, intervened in his usual masterful style.
T.J. had suggested that David Davies should take on the editorship
himself, but that was turned down. D.D. produced a six-page
proprietal fiat which set out the editorial policy he demanded.
There was, in fact, very little in this set of commandments to which
Tom Jones would object, but he was less happy about D.D.'s
apparent determination to reduce the literary and artistic emphasis
in the *Outlook*. T.J.'s 'Note re. *Welsh Outlook*' put forward at this time
is not written with his usual persuasive power. He said the *Outlook*
should be educative and propagandist, it should redress its previous
neglect of scientific subjects and make the cause of 'Welsh
autonomy the King Charles' Head' of its editorial policy. This
seems a mere token contribution. D.D., for the present at least, had
taken over more or less completely: he brought in a competent
business manager and installed a new editor. This was, of all
people, the formerly benighted Edgar Chappell,[52] who, ironically,
was now to give full vent to David Davies's pet nostrums: the
October *Outlook*, for example, was a special 'Serbian number' that
included a violent attack by D.D. on British military strategy.[53] T.J.
decided to wait for this latest enthusiasm of the moment to blow
itself out. Meantime, he and his closest allies would lie handily low.

> About the *Outlook* [T.J. wrote to Percy Watkins, his aide on the spot in
> Cardiff] . . . my view is that you should not go on the Board but should
> retain a quite unofficial connection. So that [as a civil servant] you

[50] Gwyn Jenkins, loc.cit.

[51] T.J., Class H, Vol.4, No.53. The extent of T.J.'s continued involvement is
indicated by the correspondence in ibid., Nos.32–67, and in Bangor MS 172218.

[52] See p.175–6 above.

[53] *WO*, IV, 329–70. The editor confidently insisted that Serbia was a subject
that would 'appeal irresistibly to Welshmen'.

might truly deny any responsibility for the policy of the paper. It is certain to become more political under D.D.'s direct guidance. This ought not to debar you from keeping in close touch with those who will be on the Board. It is quite clear to me from any experience up here, that highly placed civil servants do keep in very close touch with those who direct public opinion. Of course it is done with infinite discretion, but it is done . . . you should prevail on Hetherington to serve in order to have a foothold.[54]

The tactical withdrawal did not last long; Chappell soon departed. His successors at the *Outlook* for some years regularly referred to T.J. for advice or assistance.[55] Jones's relations with D.D. were again entirely unaffected by this episode. They continued to work closely together on a number of schemes in which they were interested, and T.J. did not hesitate to comment in the most forthright way on D.D.'s wilder notions.[56]

But Jones's chief concern at this time, apart from his Whitehall work, was, as always, education. In March 1917 he appeared on behalf of the University College of Wales, Aberystwyth, before the Haldane Commission on the Welsh University. His evidence related to the proposal to establish a new faculty of public administration and social studies at Aberystwyth.[57] Under cross-examination T.J. expounded his now familiar creed: as well as nourishing the human mind and spirit in general, the university ought to be 'a great fellowship of reconciliation', interpreting the classes to one another and promoting harmony and a strong sense of social obligation. This 'missionary' purpose was especially necessary in south Wales, for employers just as much as for workmen. He was indifferent whether economics was called a science or not: the vital thing was that it should never be divorced from ethics. He was not worried about a variety or clash of opinions: 'Let the teachers go free always, I say'.

T.J. suggested that the proposed new faculty (which would offer a coherent scheme – no mere 'smattering' of subjects – in law, history, philosophy, politics, economics and public administration) would provide a first-rate training for public service, particularly in local government. The range of government activity generally was

[54] T.J., Class H, Vol.4, Nos.52–76.

[55] Gwyn Jenkins, loc.cit., pp.476-80.

[56] *WD* I, 40-1, T.J., Class P, Vol.1, Nos.50 and 70, for particularly withering comments. D.D. was not affronted, he invited T.J. to stay with him over Christmas.

[57] 'You're the godfather of the new department', a friend wrote, 'you should see that it is properly dowered and given a good start'. T.J., Class W, Vol.18, No.178.

steadily increasing and the importance of the municipal service was certain to become very much greater in the future. It was high time that local government officers, social workers and the like were adequately educated. At the Welsh Insurance Commission he had seen in a limited way how valuable this sort of training could be for public officials. Local authorities in Wales were notoriously reluctant to lose their power of patronage in appointments, but they should at least be more open to the influence of educationists and prepared to recognize the envisaged degree course as a qualification for municipal employment. The degree would be equally valuable for administrators in central government, even though, traditionally, the Civil Service had been completely open-minded about the particular disciplines studied by candidates at its examinations.[58]

T.J. hoped that, in due time, he himself would be able to play an important part in the implementation of this scheme if it were endorsed. He had as yet not taken root in London. It was by no means certain that the Cabinet secretariat would be anything more than a temporary expedient to meet the exceptional needs of war. Nor was it at all clear how long Lloyd George, with whose fate T.J.'s fortunes were now apparently linked, would continue as Prime Minister. Jones assumed that, sooner or later (and it was not an unwelcome prospect), he would return to work in Wales. He certainly did not want to go back to the Insurance Commission: he had his eye on a post in Welsh higher education, possibly the principalship of the one of the university colleges.

For reasons which have already been established, Jones's strong preference was for Aberystwyth. But in 1917 E.H. Griffiths, Principal of University College, Cardiff, resigned, and T.J. was pressed by his friends to apply for the post. Sir Henry Jones, in particular, was 'full of it', and Lloyd George, too, said he was 'all for it'. David Davies had been persuaded that Cardiff, where T.J. would be well placed to influence labour relations, was the more 'important arena'. From the outset T.J. had a feeling in his 'bones' that he would not succeed. Perhaps the wish was father to the thought. Of course he had lived in the Cardiff area for six years and had some inkling of the size and strength of the likely opposition to his appointment. He had ruffled a number of people during his years at the Insurance Commission. Over the next three months

---

[58] *Minutes of Evidence, March-June 1917, Final Report of the (Haldane) Royal Commission on University Education in Wales.* (Cmd. 8991), pp.44–52. Fleure had proposed (T.J., Class W, Vol.7, No.15) that the degreee should be entitled 'Bachelor of Civil Science. Social Science seems doubtful, Sociology has a bad name, Administration a worse one.'

Jones's correspondence was filled with letters from his friends, Watkins, Hetherington and Edgar Jones at the front in Cardiff, Sir Henry Jones, agent at large, whose campaign was more aggressive than persuasive,[59] A.L. Smith of Balliol, and others, retailing the course of the struggle for opinion and, crucially, for votes. His opponents, some of whom could legitimately be called enemies, were at least as active. The 'Black Hand' of John Rowland, implacable as ever, was busily at work.[60] As usual T.J. did his homework properly; he consulted his old schoolmaster Roger Jones of Pengam, who suggested that the 'real' difficulty was not T.J.'s 'socialist' tendencies, but doubt about his 'religious beliefs'. Sir Henry Jones was outraged: 'if your life is not sufficient proof of your faith', he wrote defiantly to T.J., 'nothing would induce me to make a verbal profession of it'. Jones, with a better eye to practicality, had to concede that it was 'a serious drawback' in practice. He admitted that he now had no 'religion in any ordinary or acceptable sense of the word. I have little or none of the theological creed left. All my faith is summed up in saying that the world for me is spiritual'.[61]

There was another great difficulty, too. T.J.'s thoughts and ambitions hitherto had been concentrated almost entirely on the future of his own college at Aberystwyth. His ambitious plans for its development depended upon the financial support of the Misses Davies of Llandinam. In December 1916 it was announced that they had donated £100,000 (called the Gregynog Gift) to Aberystwyth on condition that it was used to carry out the proposals that T.J. had set out in his Memorandum on the College in July.[62] Gwen and Daisy Davies were utterly dismayed by the prospective loss of T.J. to Cardiff. At a weekend consultation at Llandinam at the end of December 1917 they told him that he was 'a broken reed and prophesied the collapse of the Aberystwyth programme'. He had to

[59] T.J. said that Henry Jones had been talking to many people and 'challenging them', as he put it, 'to drive me out of Wales as they drove him'. T.J., Class P, Vol.1, No.57.

[60] Bangor MS 17218. In January and February 1918 there was a 'big agitation in the Cardiff press' against his election; dock interests, wary of any strengthening of labour power, were 'very much alarmed'. The newspapers owned by Lord Rhondda were markedly hostile. T.J. to James Morton, 6 February 1918. Morton MSS GD326, 83/1.

[61] T.J., Class X, Vol.4, No.1; Class P, Vol.1, No.57. WD, I, 37–8. The comment of Lord Pontypridd, one of the potentates on the Cardiff College Council, on this was, 'why isn't the fool religious?'.

[62] Mary Rathbone, a leading member of the College Council, profoundly regretted that Bangor had no 'beggar equal to Mr. Thomas Jones'. T.J., Class W, Vol.16, No.28.

agree that it would be 'in serious danger' if he went to Cardiff, as the Aberystwyth principal, T.F. Roberts, and the influential registrar, J.H. Davies, cared nothing for 'beautiful buildings and the development of art and music'.[63] In some desperation, Jones suggested that perhaps the ladies could establish a national fund for the University earmarking the 'bulk' of the money for Aberystwyth; even if he were at Cardiff, he could act as chairman of the fund and administer it along agreed lines. The Misses Davies dismissed this forlorn and unworkable suggestion out of hand: 'Cardiff' they said crisply, 'has plenty of money, Aberystwyth has none'.[64] This flat refusal and a letter soon afterwards from Hetherington detailing bitter in-fighting among the Cardiff people seem briefly to have unnerved T.J. He confessed to his wife that he was 'very conscious of his shortcomings', especially his dislike of committee work and relative academic inferiority. His only clear competitive advantage over other candidates was his knowledge and 'passionate desire' to answer the needs of Wales. Rene replied with her usual blunt commonsense. If Cardiff could find a more 'suitable' man, Tom could stay 'happily' where he was. 'Your belief in your own incapacity', she added tartly, 'obliges the rest of us, absurdly, to spend time denying [it]'.[65]

T.J.'s referees included, among others, Tawney, Sidney Webb, Sir Robert Morant and Hankey, all of whom wrote in glowing terms. It was not enough. On 8 February the Cardiff Council decided to ask Principal Griffiths to stay on for another year. T.J.'s enemies had mustered 25 votes against 10 for him. Several of the 'Church and Tory elements' and all the Cardiff City councillors voted against him. The medical men, with one exception, were reported to have been 'strong' against him, denouncing him as a 'socialist' who had favoured the clause in the 1911 Insurance Act which gave 'workmen power to appoint their own doctors'. One opponent suggested that Jones had been personally 'responsible for the clause'.[66]

T.J. was almost elated: 'I feel as if a big load had rolled off my back today, a real release', he told Rene the next day. 'I am

[63] 'It is curious', T.J. added, 'how many enthusiastic students of poetry and fine literature are quite indifferent to the monstrous ugliness of our streets and public buildings and homes'. Even Henry Jones failed that test. Writing to H.J. Fleure about College developments in 1919, T.J. plaintively said: 'is art and craft always to be put last?' T.J., Class W, Vol.7, No.5.

[64] T.J. Class P Vol.1, No.70.

[65] T.J., Class X, Vol.4, Nos.9 and 20; ibid., Vol.7, Nos.75 and 78.

[66] T.J., Class W, Vol.10, No.169; ibid., Vol.7, No.84. It is evident from this letter that T.J. had been openly critical of the medical profession during his years at the Insurance Commission

absolved from further loyalty to Cardiff and my mind has all day been reverting to the Aber[ystwyth] programme'.[67] Hankey too had been relieved that Jones had not gone to Cardiff. A little earlier, Lord Haldane, chairman of the Royal Commission, perhaps with an eye to a probable increase in power at the centre, had suggested that T.J. should become the secretary of the reformed University of Wales.[68] Beatrice and Sidney Webb had suggested yet another possibility. They were 'determined' to drum up as many candidates as possible for the next election and asked T.J. to stand 'as a Labour candidate for a university constituency', a proposal that he tactfully fended off.[69]

As he told James Morton, T.J. had decided that, now he was going to 'settle down' in London for 'another spell', he was determined to find a way of 'bringing Rene and the children within hail'. Hitherto in London T.J. had endured almost a gypsy-like domestic life. D.D. had put him up for a time, later he had lodged at the Tawneys' chaotic though warmly welcoming house. In December 1917, partly to reduce wearisome travelling time, he persuaded J.W. Roberts, a civil service friend, to share a flat which was more convenient for the Cabinet Office. There were other advantages: 'The porters will wash up, do beds, set evening fire and clean a bit for one shilling a day. Coal ninepence a scuttle'. J.W. Roberts would be 'no strain' to live with; he was 'not talkative . . . not too intellectual', so T.J. would 'not be worried with dialectics at night'.[70]

For all the apparent glamour of his Whitehall post, the move to London had been expensive and his family was feeling the pinch. T.J.'s salary was still paid by the Welsh Insurance Commission and this was subsequently supplemented by various special bonuses from the Treasury which, in certain circumstances, brought his income up to £1,200.[71] This increase in money wages did not cover the very considerable addition to his expenses. He joined the Authors' Club (he continued his long-standing membership of the National Liberal Club); naturally, on occasion he had to return the hospitality of his friends Adams, D.D. and others, and take his turn as host to 'the Family'. He dashed home to Barry for hurried visits

[67] Ibid., Vol.4, No.42.
[68] Ibid., Vol.7, No.73, 80 and 81. Hankey said that T.J. could do much more for Wales if he remained at Whitehall at the centre of affairs.
[69] T.J., Class Z (Diary, 1918), p.14. In January, the Webbs told T.J. that they believed that Labour was not yet intellectually up to taking office; their immediate task was 'to rope in all the intellectual assistance possible'. WD, I, 45-6.
[70] Morton MSS GD 326/83/1. T.J., Class X, Vol.7, Nos.71 and 73.
[71] T.J., Class Z (Diary, 1918), pp.111–12.

whenever possible; these trips too were expensive although, because of the relentless demands of his work, not as frequent as might be supposed. Rene was the most understanding and supportive of wives but occasionally even she registered a protest. 'Parted presence is better in the abstract than in the actual', she wrote in February 1918. 'If you were at the Front one could bear the inevitable, but there is nothing inevitable about our present separation . . . the children have a right to be with you, if it can any way be managed. One thing is certain: we shall never again saddle ourselves with a house that is too costly for ourselves'. Naturally, it took some time to arrange the removal, and Rene occasionally was impatient at their continued separation. 'I quite thought you would endeavour to come home for Easter to see the children', she wrote on 10 March 1918. 'It will be two months then since they saw you . . . quite long enough in my opinion'. She pointed out that it was cheaper for T.J. to go home than for the family to come up to London; 'And we are desperately short of money all the time, so it is a consideration'. For the moment evidently Rene had reached the end of her tether. A few days earlier she had given T.J.'s explanations short shrift: 'Dear Wriggler, As usual you "make the worse appear the better course" by asserting that, if I have to leave you with short commons in letters, *you never complain*. You do worse. You begin to send wires asking if we are all dead'. She said that Tom did not seem to realize that his letters were the only interest she had at this time. As always, finally, where he was concerned, she softened: 'I forgive you and there's an end on't'.[72] Over the next year or so, Rene's love and understanding were to be irreplaceable supports to T.J. at a time of great strain, great hope and, ultimately, great disappointment.

T.J.'s opportunities of getting home more often were reduced still further by the great German onslaught on the Western Front later in March 1918. Russia was effectively out of the war, American power was not as yet decisively deployed. This was, in Lloyd George's opinion, the most serious crisis he had to face as Premier. However, by the narrowest of margins, the German attack was stemmed and military victory ultimately assured. Thoughts turned to the future and a new, or at any rate better world, at home and abroad. The Franchise Act, which became law in June 1918, at long last made Britain more or less a genuine democracy. But one of its less authentically popular features was the concession of a parliamentary seat to the University of Wales. T.J., having secured Lloyd

---

[72] T.J., Class X, Vol.7, Nos.81, 86 and 88. In July 1918 their house in Barry was put on the market.

George's endorsement, led a group of people who immediately tried to persuade Sir Henry Jones to stand. 'Their main purpose', Henry Jones told Sidney Webb, who had tried vainly to enlist him as a Labour candidate, was 'precisely that of breaking down the isolation of the universities and making [them] . . . open to the working classes'. For many reasons, but chiefly because he could not bear to give up his academic work, which gave to his 'life such value as it had', Henry Jones ultimately refused to stand.[73] As a consequence, it was suggested that T.J. should be the candidate. H.J. Fleure told him that it was a thought that had immediately occurred to him, as it was 'work [T.J.] could do so well of championing the labour cause in a "Brain and Hand" way'. Shortly afterwards, however, Fleure wrote to say that, although no doubt T.J. would very rapidly become 'the Vice-President of the Board of Education' if he did become the University's MP, it was unfair to ask him to make the financial sacrifice. More to the point, Fleure reminded Jones that T.F. Roberts, principal of the Aberystwyth College, was 'very poorly indeed'.[74]

During 1918 and 1919, while T.J. was involved for much of the time in political and industrial matters of the utmost importance, his private thoughts and ambitions were centred on University affairs in Wales, especially his hopes for the Aberystwyth college. The Haldane Commission Report, which was published early in 1918, was less radical than had been expected: the Commissioners recommended the continuance of the national federal University structure. There was some increase of power at the centre, but by and large the Commission succeeded in striking a balance between the University and the colleges, whose substantial autonomy in practice was not seriously infringed. T.J. had been opposed to 'an over-centralised University', because, among other disadvantages, he feared that that would place it firmly 'under the thumb of the Board of Education'. He had also played a significant part in the crucially important decisions made about University finance. He and Henry Jones had been the first to propose what was to be a main financial buttress in the future: the application of the proceeds of a penny rate from the Welsh local authorities to the support of the University. And Jones had also helped to prompt

[73] T.J., Class U, Vol.1, Nos.45 and 48. The John Rowland 'clan' in Wales declared war on Sir Henry's candidature as soon as it was bruited. Bangor MS 17218.

[74] T.J., Class J, Vol.14, No.134; Class W, Vol.7, No.24. In September T.J. was hard at work persuading J. Herbert Lewis, the MP for Flintshire, to stand for the University seat, which he agreed ultimately to do, because he did not want 'a lot of mediocre candidates'. T.J., Class V, Vol.1, No.30.

Lloyd George's decisive intervention which killed off any possibility that the Cardiff college would be able to pre-empt for itself the rate contributions of Glamorgan and Monmouthshire, far and away the wealthiest Welsh counties.[75]

During this time T.J. acted as the unofficial agent at large in London of the University of Wales and, more particularly, of the Aberystwyth college. He was of course ideally placed to do so. On occasion he had Lloyd George's ear; he was in constant friendly touch with H.A.L. Fisher at the Board of Education; and he was clearly recognized as the honest broker who alone was capable of persuading the wealthy Davies ladies of Llandinam, and perhaps their wayward brother David, to apply their beneficence not only to their own favourite projects but also to other urgent College and University needs. His work for Aberystwyth at this time was remarkable. 'I am determined to strive to gather in Aber' half a dozen of the richest personalities we can persuade to settle there', he told Percy Watkins in November 1918.[76]

Indeed, more than a year earlier, T.J. had tried to persuade R.H. Tawney to go to Aberystwyth as the head of the projected school of social science. Tawney turned this down because he 'felt Aber' was too far away'.[77] In November 1918, T.J. brought off a magnificent academic coup. At the end of 'the war to end all wars', David Davies, who since his dismissal by Lloyd George had become a fanatical champion of the idea of a League of Nations, had had another of his 'brainwaves'. He decided to establish a Woodrow Wilson professorship of International Politics devoted to the study of 'the project of the League of Nations' and problems of international relations. D.D.'s original intention was that the Wilson chair would go to Oxford and there would be another established at Strasbourg in honour of Sir Edward Grey. T.J. was 'summoned' to consider the idea. 'I fought with all my might for putting the former at Aber', he said, 'and was well backed by Miss [Gwen] Davies, and ultimately succeeded'. T.J. immediately 'sounded' his friend Alfred Zimmern, then at the Foreign Office, who agreed to allow his name to be considered. H.A.L. Fisher thought it a

[75] T.J., Class J, Vol.16, No.7; Class W, Vol.16, No.20; Class P, Vol.1, Nos.9 and 51; Class U, Vol.1, No.45. E.L. Ellis, *The University College of Wales, Aberystwyth 1872–1972* (Cardiff, 1972), pp.192–200. T.J. also did his utmost to persuade Lloyd George to direct the Treasury to accept the principle of pound for pound grants to match private benefactions. T.J., Class J, Vol.16, No.7; Class V, Vol.1, No.24.

[76] T.J., Class J, Vol.12, No.2.

[77] Typically, T.J. then suggested that efforts should be made to get Tawney a post at Cardiff, with which he could combine 'inspirational' work for the WEA. Ibid., Vol.14, Nos.125 and 126.

'brilliant nomination', for Zimmern was one of the outstanding 'political intellects of our time'.[78]

The Wilson Chair of International Politics was the first of its kind to be established anywhere in the world. It enabled Aberystwyth to pioneer a new academic discipline that was to become increasingly important in a world that was soon to be capable of self-destruction. Zimmern was at first outstandingly successful academically at Aberystwyth.[79] He immediately began 'head-hunting' for other talented recruits; he asked T.J. if a niche could be found for Dover Wilson, the Shakespearian scholar, and a chair in Spanish for their friend Salvador de Madariaga.[80] T.J. could not do anything about those two suggestions, but he did succeed in bringing the inspirational Walford Davies, then organist at the Temple in London, a music teacher of genius, to Wales and Aberystwyth. T.J. had to manoeuvre carefully to mask the jealousies of the colleges, win the agreement of the Royal Commission, satisfy the demanding requirements of the Misses Davies, who were deeply interested in music, and, not least, persuade Walford Davies to give up an established position in the London musical world in order to lead a crusade to induce the Welsh people to look beyond their traditional concentration on choral music. Walford Davies became the University Director of Music for Wales and accepted a chair (endowed by the Misses Davies) at Aberystwyth. He quickly demonstrated a possibly unique capacity to move large audiences to new enthusiasms for music.[81]

Concurrently, T.J. sought a man of similar inspirational capacity, the 'right "Walford Davies"', as he said, to induce his countrymen to take a larger interest in Art. It was not only the 'primary' concern of the Misses Davies, who, ominously, were complaining that their Gift was being frittered away on purposes of which they did not always approve, but T.J. himself had always deplored the fact that 'beauty' reached the Welsh through 'the ear but not through the eye'. To his lasting regret, T.J. failed in this quest.[82] But

[78] *The Times*, December 1918. T.J., Class J, Vol.12, Nos.2, 14 and 19. When D.D. proposed Zimmern's appointment at the Aberystwyth College Council later there were some whispers: 'Is he German?'. A lady member who asked T.J. about Zimmern's nationality was 'very much relieved' to be told that Zimmern had 'been to Winchester'.

[79] Numbered among his successors were C.K. Webster and E.H. Carr.

[80] T.J., Class W, Vol.20, Nos.209–27.

[81] E.L. Ellis, op.cit., pp.184–5. T.J., Class V, Vol.1, No.53. 'Every soul present felt that here was The Man', as Percy Watkins described the reaction of a vast Welsh audience to Walford Davies.

[82] T.J., Class J, Vol.3, No.73; Nos.185 and 211; T.J., Class W, Vol.18, No.211; Vol.7, No.27. *Leeks and Daffodils*, p.195.

he did a great deal to persuade some especially gifted scholars at Aberystwyth to remain on the staff. He persuaded the Misses Davies to endow a chair for H.J. Fleure, the distinguished anthropologist and geographer, and one in Welsh Literature for T. Gwynn Jones, the leading man in the field.[83]

Of course T.J. and his friends had always hoped that he too could be brought to Aberystwyth to lead the campaign to raise the whole quality of Welsh higher education. It was suggested that he should become Director of Social Studies at the College, a proposal which he rejected because, as he said, it was 'too restricted a position' to enable him to carry out 'the schemes' he had in mind.[84] Soon afterwards, Sir Henry Jones, whose impatient eagerness to get T.J. to Aberystwyth ran away with his sense of decency, proposed that David Davies and his sisters should provide a pension to enable the ailing principal, T.F. Roberts, to retire. D.D., who was not the most sensitive of men, rather tactlessly investigated the possibilities. Mercifully, nothing came of this crass proposal. T.F. Roberts was respected, indeed much loved; cavalier treatment of him of that kind would have provoked a storm of resentment. As usual, Rene offered sensible advice: she did not think her husband should become dependent on the Davies family. On 5 August 1919, however, T.F. Roberts died. The way to the coveted principalship was honourably clear.[85]

It was quickly apparent that there were three serious candidates, all of them former students of the College: J.E. Lloyd, doyen of Welsh historians, T.J., and J.H. Davies, well connected in the upper reaches of influential Welsh society, who in effect had been acting principal during Roberts's long illness. The election attracted enormous interest; it was the *cause célèbre* of Welsh public life in the post-war years. There was a great deal of devious manoeuvring in private; Machiavelli would not have felt out of place in Wales at that time. Despite his undoubted scholarship, J.E. Lloyd was largely ignored. T.J. came in for some very rough treatment in public, particularly from his enemies in Cardiff, the Welsh 'Gomorrah' in Henry Jones's contemptuous description. There was a concerted campaign of vicious innuendo in the Welsh press which implied that T.J. was the hireling of David Davies, a domineering plutocrat who intended to annex the people's College to his private empire.[86]

---

[83] E.L. Ellis, op.cit., pp.182–202. T.J., Class W, vol.7, Nos.42-48.

[84] T.J., Class U, Vol.8, No.78. *WD* I, 70.

[85] T.J. Class U Vol.1, No.77. NLW Llandinam MSS Class D Box 2/1. E.L. Ellis, op.cit., pp.187–9. Shortly before, T.J. had done his best, unavailingly, to persuade Lloyd George to recommend Roberts for a knighthood.

[86] *The Western Mail* (12 September 1919), for example.

T.J.'s friends saw in all this the fine hand of his ruthless old enemy John Rowland. Hankey wrote to Christopher Addison, the Minister of Health, to say that the Prime Minister was 'annoyed' and wished him to send for Rowland and warn him that the confirmation of his appointment as a Welsh Commissioner of Insurance depended, as Lloyd George put it, on 'Rowland's minding his own business'.[87]

T.J.'s referees included Lloyd George and Sir William McCormick, chairman of the Treasury Committee on University Grants, and his application was supported by seventeen letters of recommendation from Haldane, H.A.L. Fisher, Sidney Webb, Tawney, Lord Esher and the Master of Balliol among others. It was undeniably an impressive array, awesome almost, surely over-whelming in its power to convince. In fact, it was as futile in its purpose as so many of the apparently irresistible preliminary bombardments on the Western Front. The well-organized opposition on the College Council simply regrouped and used their unimpaired defensive strength to win the day. J.H. Davies received twenty-three votes, T.J. sixteen. Of course he behaved well in public, but privately he was bitterly disappointed and deeply wounded.

> Many dreams have been shipwrecked by the decision [he wrote in despair to his old friend James Morton], dreams which if they had materialized would have made an immense difference to the coming generations of Welsh students. You spoke of my 'prophetic qualities'. Like other prophets, major and minor, I have been sacrificed by the old who are in power to the loss of the Young. The *best* men were with me, but there were not enough of them. The religious (= chapel-going) prejudices had been stirred up and socialism etc. etc. But I must not complain, but be thankful for an 'appy 'ome and a wife who is like the shadow of a great rock in a weary land, and children full of delightful unconsciousness of how their future has been at the crossroads.[88]

Jones's friends were outraged by the decision which many of them, with understandable but not wholly justified certainty, ascribed to the dominance at Aberystwyth of a 'parish pump' mentality.[89] D.D. went off in a fury, his sister Margaret anxiously hoped that T.J. would not be utterly soured and 'turn Irish'.

[87] T.J., Class Z (Diary, 1919), pp.86–7. Addison said that Rowland was 'fully capable' of operating in that way.

[88] Morton MSS GD 326/81/1.

[89] It was certainly true, for example, that T.J.'s part in bringing in the gifted but unwisely brash Zimmern was not universally popular, and Walford Davies's phenomenal success aroused jealousy among some colleagues, 'the spiteful little musical gnats', as Fleure called them. T.J., Class W, Vol.10, No.195.

It might seem curious to the metropolitan mind that T.J. should be so willing, indeed eager, to give up a position of prestige and influence at the hub of imperial affairs to go to what, in London terms, seemed a position of limited influence in an unfashionable backwater. On the other hand, Zimmern, cosmopolitan in background and outlook, understood very well: 'I have no doubts as to the wisdom . . . on your part', he told T.J. in September 1919; 'shaping the future is more important than trying to knock the misshapen present into something not utterly calamitous'.[90] This, expressed in rather less bombastic terms, was exactly T.J.'s purpose. He had a belief that verged on the spiritual in the uplifting power of education. Moreover it is to be remembered that in 1918 public opinion in Britain was, for a time at least, propitious for a great and rapid advance in educational provision as never before, or perhaps since.[91] And quite apart from the powerful pull of sentiment where his old college was concerned, T.J. had imaginative plans, made feasible by the promise of larger government grants and, more particularly, the financial support of the Davies family of Llandinam, to transform the quality of university education available at Aberystwyth in new buildings of aesthetic appeal on a splendid new hill site overlooking Cardigan Bay.[92]

Now, however, the dream had been shattered. The one position that he had so long yearned for had been closed to him, almost certainly for ever. His friends did their best to console him. 'It seems clear', Hetherington wrote, comfortingly, 'that Providence intends you for the larger stage'.[93] It is remarkable that T.J. had been able to devote so much time and energy to his educational interests and ambitions in 1918 and 1919, because his life at the

---

[90] T.J., Class W, Vol.20, No.218. There was also T.J.'s wholehearted commitment to the interests of Wales. In January 1918 he turned down Hankey's offer of virtually the permanent Deputy Secretaryship after the war. 'I know how attractive London is', T.J. wrote, 'to many of our ablest Welshmen and how essential it is, therefore, that some of us should stay at home and face the issues'. WD I, 46.

[91] 'Speak on education in [Birmingham] Town Hall. Hall filled. Audience enthusiastic.', is a typical entry in H.A.L. Fisher's Diary. (Bodl. Fisher MSS. Box 8a, 31 January 1918) at this time.

[92] S.K. Greenslade, the gifted architect of the National Library of Wales, was at work on the plans.

[93] T.J., Class W, Vol.9, No.179. Lord Esher, one of T.J.'s referees, in a letter to Rene at this time said, prophetically, that T.J. should enlist the support of a millionaire, take over the running of the Garton educational foundation at perhaps £1,000 a year, 'and then make it the centre for all propaganda for the new world. He is cut out to be St. Francis of Assisi or Ignatius Loyola . . . Tell him to cheer up'. WD, I, 95.

Cabinet Office was one long record of hectic activity. Indeed, although after the war the secretariat's work was naturally reduced in some respects, T.J.'s duties, if anything, became even more onerous. During Hankey's long absence in Paris from October 1918 onwards, T.J. acted as his 'simply splendid deputy'.[94] There is some evidence, however, that Jones could not quite come up to Hankey's almost faultless organizational skill in managing the Cabinet Office.[95]

But T.J.'s real value lay in his work outside rather than inside the Cabinet Room and Office. After the war this became even more important. It is evident that T.J., at the time and subsequently, regretted that in the Coupon Election campaign Lloyd George, 'to secure a temporary advantage . . . played upon the baser passions of the electorate'. T.J. had hoped that after the war Lloyd George would become again, as before 1914, the democratic spearhead for social change.[96] H.A.L. Fisher was probably right that Lloyd George's 'chief strength' at the time was that the Tories could 'not do without him'. But that proved a temporary advantage, quickly reversed by the return in the election of a majority 'far too big to be wholesome', as T.J. described it, consisting overwhelmingly of Tories, whose interest in social reform was minimal.[97] Jones's prescription, which he urged upon Lloyd George with some force, was for the Prime Minister to use his exceptional authority to order government departments to formulate 'an advanced social programme'; in effect, by offering bold creative leadership to appeal to the people, who were 'expecting a big and rapid improvement' in conditions, over the heads of his supposed supporters in the Commons. T.J. asserted that the widespread unrest in the country and the 'prevailing distrust' of trade unionists were dangerous only to the extent that they derived from 'genuine grievances'.[98]

In 1916 T.J. had predicted that there would be serious industrial trouble after the war. It erupted in February 1919. From then on, for some time, apart from a clandestine network of spies who operated on a different level, T.J. was Lloyd George's most important source of reliable information on the labour front and

[94] Hankey to T.J. 19 January 1919. *WD*, I, 72.

[95] S.S. Wilson, *The Cabinet Office to 1945*, (HMSO 1975), pp.39–40, gently suggests that T.J.'s relative lack of experience explains the falling away of absolute managerial efficiency.

[96] T. Jones, *Lloyd George* (Oxford, 1951), p.163. *WD*, I. 73–75.

[97] Bodl. Fisher MSS, Box 8a, Diary. *WD*, I, 82.

[98] Ibid, I, 63–76.

his chief agent in confidential dealings with the trade union leaders and, indeed, others who were involved in the disputes. When the Prime Minister consulted the Webbs (who, in fact, first proposed the political balance of personnel that was later said to be a piece of Lloyd George's trickery) over the composition of the Commission on the coal industry, of which Mr. Justice Sankey was chairman, he told the Webbs to 'see Tom Jones about it . . . he has the matter in hand'.[99] T.J. had already sent on a report to the Prime Minister on possible members of the Commission in which two of the three men under consideration were 'damned' for their extreme bias in favour of employers.[100]

But T.J. was no simple-minded advocate of paying Danegeld to buy off trade union demands. He clearly would have supported forceful methods to overcome a threatened electricians' strike in February. And he advised Lloyd George to refuse the demanded 'big advances' for the better-paid miners and railwaymen until the wages of those lower down the scale had been improved.[101] However, T.J. had been strongly in favour of justice for the mass of miners all his life. And, social equity apart, he knew the extent of their power and the uncompromising determination of some of their leaders. He had always hoped to be able to play some constructive part in this sort of situation which was so fraught with danger for the whole of society. 'Tom Jones refused to let me send in his name for a CBE [Hankey wrote in his diary in May 1918] because the Welsh miners would say: "Here's Tom Jones, whom we thought such a good democrat, being bought like all the rest". I told him I respected him for it'.[102]

T.J. clearly did have the confidence of many labour leaders, political and industrial, at this time, as the following account of his activity in March 1919 indicates:

March 14 1919

The Prime minister

I've had some conversation with Smillie, Webb and Tawney separately as to the way that the Coal Commission is going. I enclose a statement of the position as it appears to Sidney Webb . . . The witnesses for the coal owners were described to me by Tawney, as extraordinarily

   [99] *The Diary of Beatrice Webb* (Mackenzie edition) III, 332–9.
   [100] 'Secret. The Prime Minister', HLRO Lloyd George Papers. F/23/4/17.
   [101] *WD*, I, 74–5.
   [102] S. Roskill, op.cit., I, 554. T.J., of course, also had social objections to accepting an honour.

incompetent, not to say stupid . . . The miners' representatives are absolutely clear that the question of Hours and Wages cannot be dissociated from the question of National Ownership; and Smillie and Hodges believe that unless the principle of Ownership [nationalisation in popular terms] is conceded . . . there will be a strike and I am convinced that they are not bluffing in this view but hold it quite sincerely . . . I am to lunch with [Sir Arthur] Duckham on Monday and possibly [Sir Thomas] Royden [employers' representatives] in order to avoid a bitter conflict with the men. It is most desirable that Duckham and Royden (who are the most likely to do so) should go some distance towards admitting the principles of National Ownership. Your hands would be greatly strengthened by some such breach in the unity of the Employers.

Tom Jones

In a postscript, T.J. said that the evidence already put forward of the 'unimagined magnitude' of coal owners' profits and 'the waste and extravagance' of the current individual ownership of the mines had made 'an immense impression, hostile to the status quo' not only on the 'public' but also on the 'rank and file of the miners', who were convinced that the testimony of official witnesses had proved the case for nationalization overwhelmingly.[103] Three days later Jones, after a consultation with Haldane (who had also sounded labour opinion), put forward their joint proposals for the consideration of the Prime Minister, who was, of course, at this time in Paris negotiating peace terms. They suggested that Lloyd George should concede a reduction in miners' hours and a substantial increase (a variable cost of living payment and a permanent 15 per cent addition) in wages, and, the vital consideration, which alone would enable Smillie, the miners' president, 'to hold back the men', to 'accept the principle' of nationalization. Jones added that his meeting with Duckham and Royden had persuaded him that they might 'split from the employers' and at least be willing to recognize the principle of nationalization.[104] T.J. had also strongly urged the Prime Minister to return immediately to London in order to exert his influence on the Commission so that its interim report averted the imminent strike.

Lloyd George's reply is a fine illustration of his persuasive power, but it also shows how much less effective this was on paper than

[103] HLRO Lloyd George Papers F/23/4/34.
[104] 17 March 1919. Ibid., F/34/4/37. T.J. thought it possible that Mr Justice Sankey might 'move in the same direction'. Sankey's anguished account of his chairmanship, 'like sitting on a barrel of gunpowder', is in Bodl. Sankey MSS English History e 273 (Diary, 1919).

when he was able to present a case in person. The Prime Minister said he could not return to London: the peace discussions had reached a 'critical' stage; he, Clemenceau and President Wilson were engaged in private conferences that must succeed in order to prevent a total collapse of the alliance. As for the industrial situation at home, he agreed that the Commission's work had shown up the coal owners' 'disgraceful neglect of their social duty' which was arousing 'the conscience' of the nation as never before. However, it would be 'folly' for the miners to 'appeal to force' when they were 'winning by reason'. A strike would mean families without fuel, withholding food from 'starving women and children', and hundreds and thousands out of work. Such a challenge would force any government, however reluctantly, to be 'ruthless', and the ensuing conflict would either put 'Bolshevism and Spartacism' in control, or leave a fear-inspired 'reaction . . . triumphant'. Ominous as all this was, he said, 'if I have to choose between letting things go smash in England or smash here, I feel that my first duty must be to the Peace Conference'.[105]

Lloyd George's vivid language (apart from the suggestion of imminent diplomatic catastrophe in Paris) did not overstate the potentially disastrous possibility of the situation. But the accompanying panegyric on Smillie's 'heroic' resistance to the 'wild men' in accepting the Commission and the suggestion that he could, apparently single-handedly, prevent a strike and thus become 'the first great statesman' labour in Britain had produced, was absurdly exaggerated, the sort of extravagant persuasive gambit that Lloyd George in person might have been able to use effectively but which on paper at long range sounded hollow.

As it was, T.J., acting as Lloyd George's proxy, passed on the letter to Mr Justice Sankey, who read it to the Commission at the next meeting. Jones reiterated the conviction that the strike, which could lead to 'civil war', must be avoided. And then, apparently, on his own initiative, he tried hard, but in vain, to persuade Sankey to commit himself to nationalization immediately. Sankey said that he needed another six or eight weeks to come to a proper decision; an immediate declaration 'would be regarded by the public as a flighty judgement reached in a fortnight and . . . therefore discounted'. In the interim report he would go no further than to say that the 'present system stood condemned and must not be continued'.

Tom Jones continued his contact with Sidney Webb, 'the stage

---

[105] HLRO Lloyd George Papers F/34/4/37.

manager' of the miners' cause on the Commission,[106] and then 'saw Smillie, Herbert Smith [vice-president] and Frank Hodges [secretary of the miners] together', to whom he put forward, as 'earnestly' as he could, Lloyd George's arguments and Sankey's plea for more time. Later T.J. continued to work on Sir Arthur Duckham and discussed the situation with Bonar Law, who was 'clear' that if nationalization were to be 'faced', Lloyd George must return 'to deal' with the cabinet and the Commons. Law did not think a strike would be such a bad thing, the State could 'outlast' the strikers, and 'he doubted whether the present Conservative House would swallow nationalisation'. T.J., thus driven back to the nub of his concern, replied that 'a strike would smash for a long, long time our hopes of cooperating in building up a better social order'.[107]

Tom Jones was fighting a dogged but losing battle in general and in this particular. Lloyd George did not return and declare the government's immediate acceptance of nationalization: the statement made in the Commons by Bonar Law, deputizing for the Prime Minister, accepted most of the miners' claims on working conditions but was ambiguous (a mixture of implied hope and verbal imprecision affording escape) on nationalization. In the event, the danger of an immediate miners' strike passed away, the political climate and the public mood changed (helped on its way by a rise in coal prices), and the Sankey Commissioners eventually published four separate reports, which produced endless bitter controversy rather than a workable conclusive agreement.[108]

Perhaps Lloyd George was simply bowing to immediate political necessity, and T.J. was naïve (as recently it has been suggested that Sankey was)[109] in recommending nationalization. In the longer term, however, Lloyd George was severely weakened politically by the decisions he took at this time. The distrust of the industrial Left turned to implacable hostility; the so-called 'Man of the People' of the past was now seen as the agent of working-class betrayal. T.J., in fact, did not really believe that nationalization was the best hope for

---

[106] The coal-owners' opinion, cited in B. Supple *The History of the British Coal Industry* (Oxford, 1987), IV, 131.

[107] HLRO Lloyd George Papers F/23/4/38. T.J. added that he had discovered that, privately, Bonar Law was not 'frightened by nationalisation' and, interestingly, that Stanley Baldwin said it 'was inevitable'.

[108] Supple, op.cit., IV, 132–40. Sankey recommended nationalization not for its economic benefits, but, like T.J., because it would dispel 'distrust' and promote 'harmony' in industrial relations. Duckham, too, took a line of his own that was much more sympathetic to the miners than that of the other capitalist members of the Commission.

[109] Ibid., IV, 136.

the future, in the mines or elsewhere in British industry. He continued to denounce the 'studied apathy' of most of the coalowners, but, as he told Lloyd George in April, 'some of us are working out schemes of *socialisation* as distinct from *nationalisation*' with 'representatives of the miners, consumers', and a few sympathetic coalowners, of whom 'our friend D.D.' was one.[110] On 23 July T.J. sent to Lloyd George a long newspaper account of the favourable 'attitude towards socialisation' of German trade unions, citing the Carl Zeiss works in Jena as a model.

> This [said T.J. in his covering letter] is the most successful example known to me of a genuine attempt to socialise a firm of competitive manufacturers, and it is full of instruction for this country just now. It has been tested in war and in peace over many years.

Nothing came of this, or other not dissimilar schemes at that time. As Tom Jones said years later of Lloyd George: 'If he had grown up in the Rhondda Valley he might have taken more kindly to trade unions. He never liked them'.[111]

The chance of a post-war accommodation between government and the trade unions, perhaps never more than a slim possibility at that time, was killed off during 1919. It became evident too that the more general hope that T.J. and others had nurtured for so long of a Reconstruction that would produce more social justice and, supposedly, a greater harmony among classes was becoming increasingly forlorn. The onset of serious economic depression, the inhibiting power of a steadily more confident Tory parliamentary majority, and Lloyd George's perhaps natural unwillingness to put his political trust in the conjectural good will of the new untried democracy defeated the progressive cause.

Meantime, T.J. soldiered on, his personal fortunes flourishing. Rene and the children had joined him in London at a house in Upper Norwood. In May, Hankey vainly asked again whether he would accept an honour, 'no one has deserved' one more. During the year T.J. was centrally involved in the threatened railway strike, in which Lloyd George was confronted by J.H. Thomas, a Celtic meeting of Greek with Greek. Unfortunately there is no detailed account in T.J.'s papers, but the opinion of Lancelot Storr, even allowing for the strong bias of a friend in the secretariat, in October 1919, is revealing:

[110] *WD*, 84, 89.
[111] HRLO Lloyd George Papers F/24/1/3. 'David Lloyd George', T.J.'s radio obituary notice broadcast on 26 March 1945.

My own conviction (which must be shared by every generous man "in the know") is that *you* really settled the recent railway strike. Consequently you deserve an earldom and at least £25,000. But you, as the most modest man of my acquaintance, would refuse.[112]

But there were also misfortunes. In September T.J.'s father, D.B., 'a helpless invalid' often 'thoughtless in the trouble he was giving' in the last two years, died. But neither Liz, who had tended him, nor T.J. wished to 'judge' him when his 'powers were failing'. D.B. had many admirable qualities. 'I owe him a lot', said T.J.[113] A few weeks later came the crushing personal disappointment at Aberystwyth, although there had been other academic offers. T.J. had curtly rejected a shamefaced overture, the outcome of collective second thoughts, from University College, Cardiff, and in December he turned down what amounted to the offer of the principalship of the new university college at Swansea, chiefly, as he said, because of 'the dearth of money to run a College properly', but also because he had decided to 'settle down' in London.[114]

During 1920, the hostility between the government and the trade unions became even more marked, but T.J.'s ideas on industrial policy were largely disregarded, except when Lloyd George veered tactically and called for radical suggestions for a speech. Jones could do little more than protest that there were 'other ways of averting discontent' then calling out the military, and make sardonic comments on the social attitudes of some of the ministers. During a discussion in February on the danger of revolutionary upheaval, 'Bonar Law so often referred to the stockbrokers as a loyal and fighting class [said T.J., that] one felt that potential battalions of stockbrokers were to be found in every town'.[115]

To add to his discomfort, in the late summer of 1920 T.J. had an acute attack of neuritis. Hankey urged him to take several weeks' leave. There was serious trouble in the coal industry but, as Hankey

---

[112] *WD* I, 85, 94. 'My congratulations', wrote his exacting friend Norman Leys at this time, 'on helping to drag Lloyd George back from complete surrender to the interests of wealth'. T.J., Class W, Vol.12, No.227. G. Blaxlund, *J.H. Thomas: A Life for Unity* (1964), pp.118–38, gives a fairly full account but does not mention T.J.

[113] T.J., Class X, Vol.7, No.99; Class P, Vol.1, No.81. *WD* I, 94.

[114] T.J., Class J, Vol.16, No.102, 105, 111. He did help the new Principal Frank Sibly with advice and assistance in staff recruitment and persuaded Lloyd George to present the College with its Charter.

[115] *WD* I, 98–105. A year earlier when there was a railway dispute, T.J. wondered (p.75) whether Curzon and Sir Walter Long, who had a good deal to say about working conditions, had 'ever been in a Tube'.

(quoting Eric Geddes) said, a miners' strike is 'a creeping paralysis, unlike a railway which is more of a stroke', so T.J. would not be wanted for several weeks, not until the 'acute stage' in the coal dispute had arrived, 'when negotiations to end the strike' began. T.J. went off to Harrogate to take 'a drastic cure'.[116]

> When I think of you with nothing to do for three weeks but put poisonous salts in your tummy and evolve schemes of local lift, my imagination fails [H.J.W. Hetherington wrote]. The least that can happen, I suppose, is the coercion of the local millionaires into funding a working mens' university there. The devils will get off cheap if that's all you do with them.[117]

The short period of rest enabled T.J. to recover quite quickly. This was just as well. In April 1918 he had been made secretary of the cabinet committee on an Irish home rule bill, a post for which he was even better equipped in some ways than for his work in industrial relations. On 20 April Jones told Hankey that he thought that the government's Irish policy, which included the imposition of military conscription, was 'a mad one'. From then on he became steadily more involved in 'the Irish business', about which, as he told Bonar Law, he 'felt intensely'; Jones said he was appalled by 'the ghastly things that were being done' in Ireland by the British. During 1920, when his advice on industrial matters was largely ignored, he began to take initiatives of his own over Ireland, encouraged by Esher who said that it was high time T.J. tried 'to switch the little P.M. off Boulogne and on to Ireland'. Shortly afterwards Lloyd George, his attention distracted by serious problems at home and abroad, said that he was 'still a Gladstonian Home Ruler',[118] and Bonar Law contemptuously dismissed the Irish as 'an inferior race' for whom coercion was the only answer. These two policies were already out of date. During 1921, his health recovered, his moral concern aroused, T.J. was to play a perhaps crucially important part in the ominously dangerous 'Irish business'.[119]

---

[116] Ibid., I, 122.

[117] T.J., Class W, Vol.9, No.192.

[118] But not then, or at any time, as T.J. pointed out later (*Lloyd George*, p.187), 'as Gladstone was, a crusader for Home Rule'.

[119] *WD* I, 61, 96. Ibid., III, 23–49. T.J., Class W, Vol.6, No.11.

CHAPTER NINE

WHITEHALL · II

IT IS not clear what part, if any, Tom Jones played in the settlement of the miners' strike in October–November 1920. It is, however, clear that Hankey had assumed that T.J. would be fully engaged in the later stages of the negotiation.[1] But for once, his papers for these three months are sparse and, such as they are, relate almost entirely to Irish affairs. However, as an indication of his consuming interest in industrial relations, it is to be noted that, even when on sick leave from the Cabinet Office, T.J. arranged for a detailed report of continuing negotiations with the miners' executive and an assessment of the possibility of an electricians' strike to be sent on to him before he left for medical treatment at Harrogate.[2] This mining dispute, the so-called 'datum line' strike, aroused serious alarm in government circles because there was a real danger that the miners would be reinforced by the railwaymen, who, for once, had ignored J.H. Thomas's advice, and voted to come out on strike on 24 October. Lloyd George, convinced for the moment that finesse would not divide and out-manoeuvre the two trade unions, acted swiftly: he reopened negotiations with the miners and made concessions including a wage increase which ended the strike and produced at least temporary industrial peace.[3] There is no direct documentary evidence to support the contention that T.J. would have endorsed Lloyd George's fire brigade intervention. It may however certainly be inferred. Jones was in favour of more generous treatment of the miners; he had a very great fear (too great as it turned out shortly afterwards) of the potential disruptive power of the Triple Industrial Alliance of miners, railwaymen and transport workers. And J.H. Thomas's inability to influence events at that time would persuade T.J. that a dangerous militancy was rampant that should be carefully headed off rather than resisted head-on.[4]

[1] Above, p.218.

[2] T.J., Class Z (Diary, 1920), pp.107–10.

[3] B. Supple, *The History of the British Coal Industry* (Oxford, 1987), IV, 148–53. A. Blaxlund, *J.H. Thomas: A Life for Unity* (1964), pp.147–9. The rail strike was postponed.

[4] *WD*, I, 139, and T.J., Class W, Vol.14, No.52, for T.J.'s wary attitude to the

The miners' victory however was more apparent than real. The settlement was a temporary arrangement that was to be replaced on 31 March 1921 by a permanent wage agreement currently under negotiation. More ominously, the government had already announced its intention to decontrol the industry from 31 August of that year. In fact, the miners were being forced more and more on to the defensive: the refusal to implement the majority Sankey Commission proposals had stifled their hope of nationalization; they could not deflect the government from its determination to rid itself of direct responsibility for the industry, and indeed the recently improved wages structure depended to a great extent on market forces, particularly export prices, which for the moment were mercifully benign. The miners were determined to fight for a national wages agreement and argued that for this purpose profits and wages should be pooled, the prosperous districts coming to the assistance of the poorer areas.

The morale of the mine-owners had risen steadily since the difficult days of the Sankey Commission. Nationalization had been shelved and the partial linking of wages with market forces was a victory of sorts for their version of economic realism. They were determined to resist any pooling of profits and insisted that wages should be governed by the varying capacity of the districts to pay. The government, which by the November agreement had guaranteed prices, became steadily more alarmed at the turn of the year as the coal export trade moved from incipient recession rapidly towards collapse and the Exchequer faced a large and probably increasing drain on its funds. In January 1921 the Cabinet hastily decided to advance the date of decontrol of the industry to 31 March.

The severity of the economic recession had taken everybody by surprise and had upset almost all calculations about the future of the industry. In the circumstances, riven by incompatible aims and some unreal ambitions, the industry could scarcely avoid serious trouble. In March the employers broke off their negotiations with the miners and posted district wage rates involving reductions of over 40 per cent in some areas, not least in traditionally militant south Wales, which was especially hard hit by the drastic decline in the coal export trade.[5] The miners were naturally outraged and many people, particularly other trade unionists, were shocked at the savagery of the cuts; even MacNamara, the Minister of Labour,

---

[5] B. Supple., op.cit., IV, 153–61. M.W. Kirby, *The British Coal Mining Industry 1870–1947* (1977), pp.49–59.

thought that 'a drop from 80/- to 44/-' was 'a bit thick'.[6] Here, surely, was a situation where the vaunted power of the Triple Alliance would be brought to bear by supporting strike action. All the signs were that this would be so; on 4 April J.H. Thomas, cheerfully blasphemous as usual, told Lloyd George that 'Jesus Christ couldn't prevent the railwaymen coming in'.[7] Shortly afterwards the railwaymen and transport workers did announce their intention to strike on 12 April.

If anything, this simply made the government even more determined to defeat the so-called strike, which technically was a lockout. Lloyd George, in particular, whatever he might say or do in public for political reasons, insisted in cabinet discussions on an uncompromising resistance to what he called the challenge of 'the direct actionists'. Austen Chamberlain and some members of the government were deeply concerned that adequate military force should be available to maintain order. Lloyd George however was more immediately concerned to break up the unity of the Triple Alliance. 'Everything depends', he said, on the influence brought to bear on the railwaymen and transport workers. 'When can you detach them best?', he asked Sir Robert Horne. The Prime Minister believed that the attitude of the railwaymen would be 'decisive', and he was confident, after seeing him, that J.H. Thomas, an ambitious opportunist who wanted some day to be Prime Minister, had no love for Hodges, the miners' secretary, and had no intention of being 'a commissary for Bevin', the transport workers' leader. 'I have complete confidence in Thomas's selfishness', Lloyd George said cynically.[8]

Tom Jones, although he conceded that a full-scale strike by the Triple Alliance would be 'a very great disaster', was for once openly critical of the Prime Minister's handling of the situation. He accused Lloyd George of bad faith in his treatment of the miners. At the time of the 'datum' strike settlement, T.J. told Hankey later, the Prime Minister had repeatedly urged the miners to produce more coal and said that the government was prepared to run 'the risk of a fall in prices'. The miners responded with an increase in output but when prices fell, 'the government ran away from that bargain', and hurriedly brought forward the date of decontrol so that it would not coincide with the projected return of the railways

[6] WD I, 134. Hankey, too, who usually had no great sympathy with trade unionists, thought (ibid., I, 137) that the 'very big drop in wages' should have been avoided.

[7] Bodl. Fisher MSS Box 8a Diary. Lloyd George, replying in kind, said Christ 'would have allowed himself to be crucified'.

[8] WD I, 133–6.

to private ownership.[9] T.J. was clearly out of step with his master at this time. Although he would not say so openly, Lloyd George was determined 'sooner or later . . . to [bring] wages down'. In public, said the Prime Minister, 'our line is to be moderate and conciliatory', but in private he resorted to wily manoeuvre. He refused to be drawn 'into a morass', pushed on 'from point to point', by allowing a full-dress debate in the Commons. He tried to focus public discussion on the controversial proposal of a coal subsidy (which he rejected) that deflected attention away from the question of owners' profits; he would not resume control of the industry as it prompted inefficiency, and he dismissed a wages pool as a foolish attempt to defy geology and economic reality, and perhaps as a back-door means of 'getting nationalisation'. Moreover, as he told T.J., Lloyd George was in no hurry to reopen negotiations: 'I think we had better have the strike. Let them kick their heels for a week or a fortnight'. This was an opportunity not to be missed. 'I believe you can prick the bubble', the Prime Minister told the Cabinet later that day. 'These men have always had the idea they can strangle the community'.

T.J.'s opinions differed on almost every one of these issues. He believed that the employers ought never to have put forward 'such a big cut in wages', and that whatever reduction was inescapably necessary should have been made gradually to coincide with a staged decontrol of the industry. This was the opinion of Montagu who, prompted by T.J., unsuccessfully suggested a wages pool; Montagu was seconded by Churchill, who in this industrial episode was a consistent advocate of conciliation. Luckily for the government, said T.J., the miners alienated public opinion by withdrawing the safety men and flooding some mines and demanding preferential treatment in the form of a subsidy. 'The P.M.', Jones said, 'fastened on this and rode off' out of difficulty taking public opinion in his wake. T.J.'s notes of Cabinet discussions on all these questions are very full, and he clearly disliked the tenor of most of the discussion. During a conference of ministers on 7 April, he recorded:

> Montagu passed me a note: 'I can't help wondering what is going on in your well-stocked brain. Have you anything to contribute?
>
> T.J.: 'Sorry, no, except nothing provocative should be said until the Triple Alliance moves; P.M. should see J.H.T. etc. at once'.
>
> Montagu: 'I hope you'll see to both those points'.

[9] T.J., Class W, Vol.14, No.52. *WD*, I, 137.

Time and again Jones tried to get the suggestion of a wages pool back on the agenda. He urged J.H. Thomas to get the matter reopened, and suggested to Seebohm Rowntree, the expert on social deprivation, that he should independently propose a compromise including at least a 'temporary pool', involving a small reduction in wages, a contribution from employers and some subsidy from the government. T.J. tried desperately during a ministerial discussion to get Lloyd George to offer some form of wages pool as an inducement to the other members of the Triple Alliance to exert pressure on the miners. The Prime Minister curtly refused.[10] However, when negotiations with the miners were resumed, Lloyd George's proposals for a settlement did incorporate some vestige of the suggestions T.J. had repeatedly urged: a temporary government subsidy for the unprofitable districts to cushion a gradual reduction in wages, and a weak attempt at a symbolic recognition of the principle of national wage bargaining. These terms were rejected by the miners, who defeated Hodges, their secretary, when he seemed momentarily to imply some willingness to compromise.[11]

It appeared, therefore, that the scene was set for a dramatic trial of strength between the government and the unions, with the employers, who had been unhelpful throughout, carefully playing possum. In the event, it was an embarrassing fiasco. Tom Jones believed that the miners were poorly led throughout the dispute; they had a strong case but forfeited much public support by their clumsy tactics.[12] They now exasperated their supposed allies by a wilful refusal to admit that the other two unions had any right to be consulted until they had actually come out on strike. The fact was that the miners' executive regarded their nominal allies as useful auxiliaries, not as equal partners. An attempt earlier by Williams and Bevin of the Transport Workers to establish proper machinery for conjoint action had been ignored.[13] As for J.H. Thomas, he freely admitted that he was for peace all along and claimed later, somewhat disingenuously, that he believed that a full-scale strike by the Triple Alliance could usefully be threatened but in practice never used, except at the price of national disaster.[14] The fact was that the supposed identity of interest of the three unions was largely an illusion. The miners were blackleg-proof, the transport

[10] Ibid., I, 132–53.
[11] M.W. Kirby, op.cit., pp.60–2.
[12] WD, I, 151–3.
[13] A. Bullock, The Life and Times of Ernest Bevin (1960), I, 167–77.
[14] J.H. Thomas, My Story (1937), pp.62–3.

workers were dangerously vulnerable in that respect. The traditional wariness of the NUR was not, as Lloyd George had implied, prompted by J.H. Thomas's personal ambition. Railwaymen were always reluctant to hazard their pension rights, and, in fact, an adroit union willingness to compromise at the right time had served the material interests of the members well in the past. Lloyd George had been right: the Triple Alliance relied heavily on bluff, lacked proper organization and even the semblance of a unified command. On Black Friday, railwaymen and transport workers called off their strike; the miners, heroically courageous and uniquely durable, fought on alone to an inevitable defeat some months later.

From the government's point of view the coal crisis had proved to be more apparent than real. But there was never the slightest doubt that the crisis in Ireland to which the government was forced to turn its full attention immediately afterwards, was as dangerously real as it was ominously apparent. It is evident that although Lloyd George and T.J. had differed sharply over the tactics and to some event the aims of industrial policy during the recent dispute, it had no effect on their personal relations. Whatever his private misgivings, T.J. was a Civil Servant whose duty it was to carry out the instructions of his political masters. As for Lloyd George, he was always eager to hear the widest possible range of opinion and intelligence, no matter how unpalatable some of it might be. Over Ireland, although they differed at the outset, Lloyd George and T.J. eventually came to agree on essentials. Between July and December 1921, working together as principal and trusted agent, they demonstrated a dexterity and indeed a finesse in negotiation that have rarely if ever been equalled in modern British experience. The difficulties they faced were formidable: they were called on to solve a conundrum that had baffled British statesmen for centuries, and the time available to them was alarmingly short.

At least T.J. was unusually well equipped for the task. He knew Ireland well; the country and its people, north and south, had engaged his affections and his interest years before. The Barrington lecture programmes had prompted a serious study of Irish history and society and leisurely annual perambulations of the countryside with unrivalled opportunities to meet local people in relaxed circumstances. And of course he had lived for almost a year in Belfast, 'the Black North', and had become closely involved in its industrial as well as its academic life. He thus had an intimate knowledge of the hard reality of Irish life: 'poverty', he wrote in 1904, 'is still the bottom fact in Ireland'. He was especially saddened by the long painful haemorrhaging of a society which 'was rearing boys and girls to the age of 18 or 20 and then exporting them as a gift to America'.[15]

Tom Jones believed that the curse of Ireland was that England had 'so seldom sent thither her best'. The élite had gone to India and elsewhere in the world while 'the vultures descended upon Ireland'.[16] The result was oppression and misgovernment and a burning Irish sense of wrong. Gladstone had tried but failed to make amends; and the rejection of his home rule bill in 1886 was 'a major disaster, one of England's greatest blunders'.[17] T.J. therefore had a strong sympathy with Irish nationalist aspirations. On the other hand, he was repelled by all forms of religious bigotry, distrusted political fundamentalism, and was utterly opposed to the men of violence.

In the late spring of 1921 Ireland was being torn apart by violence. A war of unrelenting savagery had been waged since 1919 between the forces of the British state, particularly after 1920 by the specially recruited 'Black and Tans', and the guerilla fighters of the Irish Republican Army (IRA), the military wing of Sinn Fein, the republican nationalist party. It was a grim competition in murderous violence. As T.J. recorded in the Cabinet minutes: 'If the military burned a cottage then the Sinn Feiners burned two, then the military four and so on'.[18] From the outset, Jones had argued that this policy was mistaken. It was not that he objected on moral grounds to the use of force. It might well be, ultimately, the only resort left to the government and would have to be applied without restraint. Even then, however, T.J. believed it would not succeed; 'repression', he wrote to Lloyd George in July 1920, 'however drastic will still leave the Irish problem unsolved'. Moreover, it was certain, in T.J.'s opinion, when applied with the utmost rigour, to alienate opinion abroad and 'lead to violent opposition' in certain quarters at home. Before this desperate and, as he argued, futile throw was made, the Prime Minister should try to 'conclude a pact with the leaders of Sinn Fein' and the Roman Catholic hierarchy by offering 'Dominion Home Rule' for the South of Ireland and 'self determination for Ulster', which, if accepted within a certain time limit, would constitute 'a final settlement'. In the mean time, the government should do nothing

[15] 'Economic Aspects of Irish Life'. T.J., Class C, Vol.3, No.8. *Welsh Broth,* pp.100–1.
[16] 'The Irish Revolution', June 1924. *WO,* XI, 161. T.J., Class H, Vol.5, No.4 for his authorship.
[17] *Welsh Broth,* pp.100–1.
[18] *WD,* III, 72.

to strengthen 'one of the most deeply rooted beliefs in the South . . . that Ulster has the government by the throat', and that Lloyd George would obey 'the dictation of Ulster'.[19]

To outward view it would appear that this advice was simply ignored by Lloyd George. The policy of 'Thorough', war to the death against the IRA, continued unabated. 'The ghastly tale of horror from Ireland continues', T.J. wrote in 1921. '. . . There is no change in the policy of the Government and there is to be no "sign of weakness"'. Undeterred, Jones put up to Lloyd George a paper written by his Oxford friends Kenneth Leys and A.D. Lindsay, which suggested calling in 'the Dominion Premiers as arbiters of the sort of Dominion status which might be conceded to Ireland'.[20] Soon afterwards T.J. met Jan Smuts of South Africa, who at this time was exerting an increasingly important influence on government policy where Ireland was concerned. 'I shook hands with Smuts and told him to hold on to this Irish business until he had put it through and I am sure he had got the psychology of the leaders right. He said "We will not let go now"'.[21] This rather over-confidently discounted a mountain of difficulty that lay ahead, but it mirrored some change of mind, at least on Lloyd George's part.

As usual the Prime Minister was mulling over other possible options. As far back as the autumn of 1918 Lloyd George had pointed out to some of his ministers that they would have 'to negotiate some day with the men who *do* represent Ireland'.[22] Two years later he asked his colleagues; 'do we want peace or not? Are we to stamp out the very embers of rebellion or is the policy a double one to crush murder and to make peace with the moderates?'[23] The difficulty was that there did not appear to be a moderate body of opinion of any weight with whom he could negotiate. 'Who is in control?', Lloyd George asked a deputation of Irish business men sometime before. 'Who can say: Give us this: let us cry quits'. The Prime Minister was afraid that the answer was 'No one'. Lloyd George did not altogether abandon his hopes of moderate Irish opinion, but he was being forced to concede that the power of Sinn Fein was formidable and could not be ignored. 'You are dealing with a fanatical group make no mistake', he said. A settlement would not be easy, it would take time, 'and there may be awkward steps'.[24]

[19] Ibid., III, 31–2. T.J.'s proposal is a remarkable instance of prevision.
[20] Ibid., III, 71.
[21] Ibid., III, 85.
[22] Bodl. Fisher MSS. Box 8a Diary. 15 Oct. 1918.
[23] *WD*, III, 46.
[24] Ibid., III, 34, 46.

There had already been some encouraging signs that the Irish were seeking some sort of accommodation. In January de Valera, one of the leaders of Sinn Fein, had asked for a secret meeting with Lloyd George who, with some hesitation, was inclined to agree to meet him: 'After all', said the Prime Minister, 'we have said repeatedly that we would see anyone who would deliver the goods'. This was more easily said than done; there was very strong resistance by some senior members of the Cabinet to having any truck with Sinn Fein. Bonar Law who, as T.J. noted with regret, 'had greatly influenced the Prime Minister throughout', was 'one of the most persistent opponents of conciliation'. Law insisted that 'coercion was the only policy', it would achieve all that was currently possible, 'quiet for about ten years'. A.J. Balfour, whose every comment on the Irish seemed to indicate distaste or contempt, wanted 'no further concessions made, for if made they'll only strengthen the Republicans'.[25] And Sir Henry Wilson, Chief of the Imperial General Staff, the Cabinet's chief military adviser, was, as Lloyd George said, 'scarcely sane on the question'. Wilson 'longed to crowd into Ireland every single soldier [he had] got on whom [he] could lay hands'.[26]

It is hardly surprising that Lloyd George should hesitate to commit himself. He continued to be full of doubts: he feared that Ireland was 'not ripe for conciliation', he did not want to be rushed into an abortive negotiation; he was looking, he said, not for the first, but for 'the best opportunity'. Dominion Home Rule was vague, a mere 'phrase'; if conceded, it would simply open the way to further unacceptable Irish demands.[27] But Lloyd George also knew that time was short; he was forced to admit in a Cabinet discussion that at best the military situation in Ireland was one of stalemate. 'If we do not do something within the next two or three months', he said, 'we may be beaten there in the coming winter'.[28] Other members of the Cabinet, the Liberals Addison, Fisher, Montagu, and Churchill, were also anxious in varying degrees for some constructive initiative.

It will be remembered that in 1920 the government carried through a Government of Ireland Act which provided for a home rule parliament in Dublin for most of Ireland, and one in Belfast for six counties of the historic province of Ulster. There was to be a Council of Ireland linking the two that, it was hoped, would give

[25] Ibid., III, 49, 53, 65.
[26] *The Wilson Letters 1918–1922* (Army Records Soc., 1985) p.250.
[27] *WD*, III, 65–8.
[28] T.J., Class Z (Diary, 1921), p.131.

some semblance of unity. After a long-drawn-out debate, the
Cabinet decided in April 1921 to go ahead with elections in the
north and the south despite the disturbed state of both parts of the
country. The Unionists gained control of the Belfast parliament;
Sinn Fein won every constituency except four seats in Dublin,
boycotted the southern parliament, and used the election as a
device for electing a new Dail, their self-constituted assembly. North
and south refused to recognize the Council of Ireland.

Although the murderous war continued in Ireland, Lloyd
George maintained contact by correspondence with de Valera, who
seemed however to be demanding outright independence for an
Ireland that would include Ulster, to which he was prepared to
concede no more than 'autonomy in local affairs'.[29] A peaceful
settlement seemed a very forlorn hope. Even T.J. confessed that he
was driven 'so near [to] despair' at this time that he thought that
'any sort of . . . practicable suggestion' was worth considering. T.J.'s
admission was made in a letter to A.D. Lindsay of Balliol who at this
time had forwarded his proposal that the Dominion premiers
might be called in to assist in settling the Irish question. Lindsay
also offered to act as 'a go-between' between some of his Sinn Fein
friends, who trusted him despite his imperialist opinions, and Lloyd
George. T.J. passed on the letter to the Prime Minister. Soon
afterwards Lindsay and Kenneth Leys went over to Dublin where
they had talks with a variety of people in Sir Horace Plunkett's
house. Jones pleaded with them to do all they could to persuade
Sinn Fein to negotiate.

> If you and K.L.[eys] have any influence with Sinn Fein in Dublin [he
> wrote to Lindsay], now is the moment to use it with all possible
> earnestness if you can. If we miss this chance we shall be plunged into
> all sorts of fresh horrors and darkness.[30]

Jan Smuts, too, was conscious of the urgency of the situation. On
14 June he suggested to Lloyd George that the King, who was going
over to open the Belfast parliament on 23 June, should 'foreshadow
the grant of Dominion status to Ireland' in his Speech as the
prelude to informal negotiations with the Irish leaders. The King's
Speech in fact did not include those words, but in simple language
it made a moving appeal for peace and amity, which evoked some
favourable response in southern Ireland. Soon afterwards Smuts

---

[29] De Valera's reply to Lloyd George, 17 May 1921. Bodl. Curtis MSS. Box 89
Diary.
[30] 19 and 27 May 1921. Lindsay MSS. (Keele Univ. Library). HLRO Lloyd
George Papers F/25/2/8.

went over to Dublin for exploratory talks with the Sinn Fein leaders. Finally, the Cabinet agreed to invite de Valera to come to London for talks.[31]

The Irish leader did not respond immediately. History, it was often said, was 'for Englishmen to remember and Irishmen to forget'. Eamon de Valera, the America-born son of a Spanish father and Irish mother, whose foreign pedigree alone had saved him from execution at the time of the Easter Rising, forgot nothing. He prefaced almost any discussion of the Irish question with a long harangue on British iniquities in Ireland. De Valera suspected that Lloyd George's invitation was mere trickery and that his acceptance would imply 'assent to the partition of Ireland'. T.J. was fully briefed about de Valera's attitude at this time by reports from his friend George M.Ll. Davies, the Christian pacifist, who had gone over to Dublin privately and in a number of meetings did his utmost to persuade the Irish leader of Lloyd George's sincerity.[32] It was some days, during which a truce to military operations was agreed, before de Valera consented to meet Lloyd George in London and it is evident that T.J. was not particularly impressed with the Irish leader:

> Those who met Mr de Valera in London [Jones said in an account written soon afterwards] found a tall, pale, be-spectacled, plainly dressed man, quiet and dignified in manner with a mind which revolved within a limited circle of logical abstractions ... He had been thrown up during the Easter rebellion into a position of leadership by moral strength rather than intellectual leadership. In public he was treated with marked deference by his colleagues.[33]

The Prime Minister and de Valera had four long meetings but, not surprisingly, failed to agree. Lloyd George, the past master of persuasion, could make nothing of de Valera. 'It is like trying to pick up mercury with a fork', said the Prime Minister. 'Why doesn't he use a spoon?', de Valera is alleged to have laconically retorted.[34]

T.J. was present at all these discussions as secretary of the British side. Hankey had sensed that Lloyd George 'did not want an Anglo-Saxon to run the show' and suggested that Jones should take his place. And at the first meeting Lloyd George went out of his way,

---

[31] *WD*, III, 74–85.

[32] NLW G.M.Ll. Davies MSS. 481. HLRO Lloyd George Papers F/25/2/14 and 15. *WD*, III, 87–8.

[33] 'The Irish Peace: The Story of the Negotiations', *Western Mail*, 12 December 1921.

[34] F. Packenham, *Peace by Ordeal* (1962), p.74

according to T.J., to welcome de Valera cordially 'as a brother Celt'.[35] It made no difference then or later in these talks, the two sides were poles apart. Lloyd George offered the Irish Dominion status subject to certain conditions dealing with defence, trade and debt. In reply, de Valera rejected the proposal and offered instead a 'treaty of free association' between an independent Ireland and the British Empire, but he did formally renounce any intention to use force against Ulster.

Lloyd George had eventually come round to an acceptance of the idea of Dominion status that T.J. and Smuts and some others had been advocating for some time. It may well be of course that Lloyd George had been working towards that all along and had been reluctant to declare his position plainly until the logic of the situation had worn down the resistance of his more stubborn cabinet colleagues. He had carefully chosen Balfour to assist in the negotiations precisely because, as Hankey said, he was, 'the most irreconcilable man in the cabinet'. In the event, de Valera preferred to meet Lloyd George alone. T.J. had spent much time in discussion with de Valera's colleagues Robert Burton and Art O'Brien, the Irish 'ambassador'.T.J. set out to persuade them to trust Lloyd George, that he was 'the one man' who could bring the British to accept an agreement that would satisfy Sinn Fein. Typically, in yet another letter reporting his activity, T.J. exhorted Bonar Law to use his influence to persuade Sir James Craig, the leader of Ulster, to be 'patient and conciliatory'.[36]

This was the burden of T.J.'s advice to everybody on Ireland over the next two months. Of course, he was not without allies, Alfred Cope, the Assistant Under-Secretary for Ireland in Dublin, who worked closely with T.J., sent over reports all of which counselled restraint. 'The great thing now, and the only thing now, is patience', Cope wrote from Dublin on 15 August.[37] Professor W.G.S. Adams, formerly of the garden suburb, who had returned to academic life, suggested after a visit to Belfast that it was high time that Ulster moderated its intransigence 'as a duty to the Empire, if not to themselves'.[38] This, too, was an opinion with which T.J. agreed. It was clear then, and increasingly so later, that while Jones accepted completely that Ulster could and should not be coerced by the British Government, he was severely critical of its blank refusal to make any concession. Field Marshal Sir Henry Wilson, for

---

[35] *WD*, III, 87, 89.
[36] Ibid., III, 87, 90–1, 248.
[37] Ibid., III, 99.
[38] HLRO. Adams to T.J., 29 August 1921. Lloyd George Papers F/25/2/7.

example, although he did not speak for all Ulstermen, reflected a powerful body of Belfast opinion when he wrote (to General Rawlinson) in mid-July: 'I simply cannot write what I think about inviting Valera [*sic*] over. In your own cockney language, "There ain't no bloody words for it"'.[39]

But for the moment the attitude of Sinn Fein and the South was the crucial one. In addition to his official contacts T.J. was also in touch again with George M.Ll. Davies, who continued to labour wholeheartedly for a peace settlement. Davies, who had suffered severely in prison during the war for his pacifist beliefs, was a Nonconformist minister, a leading member of the Fellowship of Reconciliation, who was in touch with a remarkably wide range of opinion. He was in friendly contact with the Archbishop of Canterbury, Lord Salisbury, Hamar Greenwood, the Chief Secretary for Ireland, and Arthur Henderson of the Labour party. Davies was also in touch with Erskine Childers and his American-born wife, leading members of an extremist wing of Sinn Fein. T.J. received useful confidential information from this source. He also used Davies to transmit warnings to Sinn Fein of the dangers of its 'unreasonable' attitude. It is clear that Jones's position was an uncomfortable one. Not everyone in government circles took kindly to his attitude to the Irish difficulties or to his apparently freelance activity. 'I think he is having a difficult time [because of] his Irish sympathies', George Davies's female emissary reported. 'Directly I telephoned and asked for Mr. Jones', she said, 'I was asked rather severely which I wished to speak to, the Secretariat of the Cabinet or Mr. Jones'. Faced with this evidence of suspicion, she concluded that it would not 'be fair to involve T.J.' in a clandestine negotiation with Childers.[40]

There obviously was a great deal of pent-up exasperation in Whitehall with Sinn Fein at this time. 'My real belief is that Sinn Fein is mad. No other hypothesis fits the facts', H.A.L. Fisher, one of the Cabinet ministers most sympathetic to Ireland, wrote to T.J. in September 1921.[41] For weeks de Valera had cleverly sparred by long distance correspondence with Lloyd George over their differences. At one time, in disgust, the Prime Minister called for plans for a full-scale renewal of the military campaign to extirpate rebellion in Ireland. British public opinion too was rapidly wearying of these 'epistolary subtleties', as T.J. called them. Cope

[39] *Wilson Letters 1918–1922*, p.282.
[40] NLW G.M.Ll. Davies MSS 481, especially Edith Ellis to Davies, 10 August 1921, and Mrs Childers' letter, 12 Sept. 1921.
[41] *WD*, III, 106.

and T.J. continued to counsel patience. Cope insisted from Dublin that the British military mind in the guerrilla war must be resisted if only because 'the Irish people had an almost oriental capacity for endurance'.[42] T.J. continued to spell out to Art O'Brien in London that the Irish demand for 'absolute separation' and their refusal to accept allegiance to the Crown were completely unacceptable to the British Government: Dominion status was the only realistic hope, all else was 'illusory'. At the same time T.J. told Lloyd George that, according to O'Brien, Irish tergiversation was simply a tactical move designed to 'educate the British public as to what Sinn Fein stood for'.[43] When Austen Chamberlain, whom T.J. thought 'much too nervous to be left to handle Ireland' in Lloyd George's absence, instructed T.J. to pass on a discouraging bluntly-worded message to the Irish, Jones on his own initiative 'toned [it] down'. In late September T.J. and Cope worked hard on successive drafts of Lloyd George's final invitation to the Irish to come to London to negotiate to make it acceptable to the Sinn Fein leaders. On the last day of September de Valera agreed to send delegates 'to explore every possibility of settlement by personal discussion'. At last Lloyd George and T.J. had secured the open-ended discussion without prior conditions for which they had striven for so long.[44]

For reasons concerning which to this day it is not possible to be certain, de Valera decided not to go to London himself. Although he had not succumbed in July to Lloyd George's persuasive charm, he may well have preferred to keep his distance the second time around. Lloyd George, who had an unrivalled experience of this sort of bargaining, thought that de Valera 'was an unskilful negotiator' in face-to-face meetings.[45] On the other hand he had been cunningly adroit in long-range parleying and there was much to be said for the unhurried consideration of proposals in calm home surroundings. It was a crucial decision that made some sort of peaceful settlement a possibility, although a most unlikely one. On current form, only the most reckless of gamblers would have put a penny on a successful outcome.

The leader of the Irish delegation, Arthur Griffith, chief founder of Sinn Fein, was a remarkable man: short, powerfully built, he was composed, sparing with words, difficult to fathom, not easily disconcerted. The British negotiators soon learned to respect

    [42] T.J., Class Z (Diary, 1921), p.209.
    [43] WD, III, 95–7.
    [44] Ibid., III, 96-7, 106–12. T.J. in The Western Mail 13 December 1921 and T.J. (1 July 1921) in NLW G.M.Ll. Davies MSS 1391.
    [45] WD, III, 110.

his capacity, to recognize his integrity and his moral courage. Griffith was a moderate man who hated bloodshed, a constitutionalist who longed for a peaceful, united, independent Ireland. Michael Collins, the second in command, was the daring romantic hero of Irish legend: tall, handsome, flamboyant and dynamic, he had an awesome reputation as a guerrilla fighter. 'Where was Michael Collins during the Great War?' T.J. once asked Bonar Law. 'He would have been worth a dozen brass hats'.[46] Nor were the three other Irish delegates men of straw: Gavan Duffy, cultured and well-educated, had abandoned a lucrative London law practice to represent Roger Casement in 1916; E.J. Duggan, 'transparently honest and fair', as T.J. described him, had also made great personal sacrifices for the Irish cause. Robert Barton, the delegation's economic adviser, was an Oxford-educated Irish Protestant country gentleman, a former British Army officer who changed sides with a late convert's customary exceptional zeal.[47]

The British delegation was formidable: it included four front-rank politicians of great experience, two of whom by common consent, then or later, were men of genius. Lord Birkenhead, the Lord Chancellor, fierce former opponent of Irish nationalism, provided support for Lloyd George that was crucial; Austen Chamberlain probably sacrificed his chance of the premiership in the same cause. Churchill stifled his imperial instincts and later on made an important contribution. Lloyd George, of course, dominated the British side of the negotiation. 'Throughout the Irish negotiation', Tom Jones wrote immediately afterwards, 'he was magnificent. All his great qualities at their best'.[48]

He needed to be so. In the shadows around the negotiation was a large, critical Tory majority in the Commons, on which ultimately Lloyd George depended, that included some die-hards who remained irreconcilably hostile to Irish nationalism. Their intransigence was more than matched by the profoundly suspicious Protestant Ulstermen, who apparently did not intend or, even more discouragingly, did not in the last resort need to make any helpful contribution. And it was soon evident that Irish claims were as incompatible as ever with the British proposals for a settlement. The Irish demanded in effect the recognition of Ireland, including Ulster, as an independent republic, not part of, but 'externally associated' with, the British Commonwealth, a relationship which at best involved only a limited acceptance of the Crown as the head of

[46] F. Packenham, op.cit., pp.110–12. *WD*, III, 55.
[47] F. Packenham, op.cit., pp.112–13. *Western Mail*, 13 December 1921.
[48] *WD*, III, 187.

that association. The British position was unchanged: they were prepared to concede Dominion status, which implied full membership of the British Commonwealth and allegiance to the Crown; and they insisted on such naval and other facilities in Ireland as were deemed necessary for British and imperial security. Between the first session on 10 October and the final dramatic meeting on 6 December the two sides were locked in argument of a near-theological intricacy.

T.J., principal secretary of the British delegation, was constantly involved, on occasion to decisive effect, particularly in the private discussions that he had with Arthur Griffith on Lloyd George's behalf. Mutual trust was the key requirement. The Irish, in Lloyd George's words, were 'drenched in suspicion', and Tom Jones's most immediate purpose was to persuade Griffith and company of Lloyd George's sincerity. Given his reputation for cunning manoeuvre and his responsibility for the policy of reprisals, that was no easy task. On the other hand, T.J. was able to deploy some powerful arguments. Lloyd George, a Welsh radical man of the people, was not an orthodox representative of the British establishment, he did not share its prejudices. The Prime Minister had an exceptional political authority in Britain, but it was precarious; he might well be overthrown and replaced by a reactionary Tory government hostile to all Irish hopes. The current negotiation represented by far the best, perhaps the only real, opportunity that Ireland would ever have in the foreseeable future for the achievement of most, if not all, of its ambitions.

T.J.'s own sincerity was scarcely in doubt. His sympathy for Irish wrongs had been common knowledge for years; even Erskine Childers, who was secretary of the Irish delegation, a fanatical Sinn Fein republican, had personal knowledge of T.J.'s untiring efforts to bring about an acceptable settlement. Jones too, like Lloyd George, was an outsider, a one-time Welsh nationalist, a late-comer to Whitehall after an education and an extensive professional and social experience in Wales, Scotland and Ireland. The sound of his voice was a constant reminder of his different and, from the Irish point of view, so much less objectionable origins. It is scarcely likely that Colonel Sir Maurice Hankey could have had the same reassuring effect. But for all his natural friendliness towards the Irish, T.J. was not an ingratiating wheedler: he did not flatter, nor did he ever hint that he himself thought Britain should go beyond Dominion status or weaken in its insistence on allegiance to the Crown or the other safeguards demanded. And at all times he vigorously disputed the stubborn Irish contention that Ulster was a problem contrived by the British that would disappear if north and south were left to negotiate without interference from London. T.J. was, therefore, the patient, sympathetic, cogent voice of sensible compromise. He was a go-between fully trusted by one side and increasingly so by the other, even if the messages he brought were not always palatable. 'Without his ceaseless efforts behind the scenes', wrote one who had first-hand knowledge of much of the inner action, 'the conference would have failed'.[49]

The Irish were wary of setting out their views plainly in writing because of 'their fear of being caught', as Duggan admitted to T.J., who replied that this sort of defensive trench warfare of words stultified all progress. T.J. suggested instead that 'a joint document' should be drafted by one man from each side. And additionally he asked Arthur Griffith to write 'a private letter of assurance' to Lloyd George, which would clarify the cloudy language of a document the Irish had submitted on their attitude to such questions as allegiance to the Crown and imperial defence.[50] Not content with that, T.J. himself wrote a draft of the 'letter of assurance' for Griffith's consideration.[51] This was not the last time that Tom Jones, as he admitted later, 'helped to draft some of Arthur Griffith's replies'. He was not in the least worried about its propriety; he believed it was his 'his job to keep the negotiations from breaking down'.[52] Griffith did subsequently provide Lloyd George with 'a letter of assurance', which the Prime Minister used to good effect to defeat an attack on the proposed settlement by die-hard Tories in the Commons.

It also helped in 'clearing the decks for a fight on Ulster', or rather, in the first instance, an attempt to persuade Ulster to come into some arrangement that would modify partition sufficiently to go some way towards satisfying the Irish. But at a meeting with Lloyd George, Sir James Craig, as the Prime Minister told T.J., would 'not budge an inch'. Lloyd George was utterly 'depressed' and for some time did not respond to Jones's attempt to raise his spirits. However there then followed a classic demonstration of Lloyd George and his surrogate T.J. in action.

> There is just one other possible way out [said Lloyd George]. I want you to find out from Griffith and Collins if they will support me on it; namely, that the 26 Counties should take their own Dominion

---

[49] (Sir) Geoffrey Shakespeare, Lloyd George's Private Secretary at this time, *Let Candles be Brought In* (1949), p.84.

[50] *WD*, III, 150.

[51] T.J., Class Z (Diary, 1921), p.358.

[52] T.J., 19 March 1924. *WD*, III, 227.

Parliament and have a Boundary Commission, that Ulster should have
her present powers plus representation in the Imperial Parliament plus
the burdens of taxation which we bear. I might be able to put that
through if Sinn Fein will take it. Find out.

This was the opening gambit of a move that had important
consequences. The next day Jones spent an hour and a half with
Griffith and Collins in which he described again Lloyd George's
difficulties with Craig and stressed how 'all important' it was to
keep 'the P.M. at the helm'. With the ground thus well prepared,
T.J. 'threw out the suggestion of the Southern Parliament plus
Boundary Commission as my own'. Collins disliked the idea;
however, Griffith was 'not alarmed at the proposal'. T.J., gentle but
persistent exponent of political reality, pointed out that the
alternative was 'Chaos, Crown Colony Government, Civil War'. On
9 November Jones saw Griffith again about the proposal and
elicited 'a pledge', that the Irish would 'not turn [L.G.] down on
it', nor 'make his position impossible', nor 'queer his pitch'. As T.J.
said, 'that was enough for me'.[53] Three days later, tête-à-tête with
Griffith, T.J. suggested that if Sinn Fein 'co-operated' on the
proposal Ulster might be brought in 'before many months had
passed'. Lloyd George himself later that day discussed the question
in detail with Griffith, who gave an assurance that while Lloyd
George 'was fighting the Ulster crowd', the Irish 'would not help
them by repudiating him'. The next day T.J. set out this agreement,
if such it can be called, in a short memorandum which he showed
to Griffith, who apparently accepted it. Lloyd George later used this
to telling effect. It is possible to argue that Griffith had been
trapped aforethought by Lloyd George's devious cunning and
Jones's disarming friendliness.[54] The Prime Minister would
certainly take full, even ruthless, advantage of any tactical error an
opponent might make.
    It should however be remembered that Lloyd George was really
in earnest in his desire for a settlement but he was dangerously
exposed politically at that time. He needed to be sure that the Irish,
by word at least, would not make the task of negotiating with Ulster
utterly impossible. And the surety was also necessary to encourage
Austen Chamberlain, in the speech of his life, and Birkenhead, by
private persuasion of party chiefs, to rout the die-hards at the Tory
Conference on 17 November. As for T.J., there is no question that

[53] Ibid., III, 154-7.
[54] Ibid., III, 164. F. Packenham, op.cit., pp.174–82, examines the episode in
very great detail.

the balance of his sympathies lay with the south; he was, for example, bitterly critical of the provocative activity in Ulster of Field Marshal Sir Henry Wilson, whom T.J. fervently wished had 'gone for a voyage around the world' at that time.[55] Initially at any rate, Lloyd George and T.J. saw the eliciting of the assurance from Griffith as the prerequisite of a genuine attempt to persuade Ulster to co-operate, not as some skilfully veiled ploy which ultimately could be used to defeat the hope of a united, or at least unpartitioned, Ireland.

Jones was unflagging in his efforts for understanding, and yet again on 22 November he used his discretion to soften an angry near-ultimatum from Lloyd George to Griffith into a firm but not threatening warning. Had he spoken as bluntly as instructed, the negotiation could well have come to an abrupt end there and then. At that meeting with Griffith T.J., in his 'most conciliatory manner', suggested useful modifications of the Irish statement of their position in order to keep the negotiation alive. When he reported back to Lloyd George he 'spoke as quietly and smoothingly' as he could, putting the most favourable construction on Griffith's attitude.[56] The negotiation was to come very close to breakdown more than once before it was concluded. The British submitted 'final' proposals for a treaty which the Irish negotiators took over to Dublin on 2 December to discuss with de Valera and the other Irish leaders. After a confused debate it was decided to reject the British offer and submit counter proposals which returned broadly to the position de Valera had held in July. It was agreed that any other draft agreement that was reached would be referred back to Dublin for consideration. The Irish proposals were totally unacceptable to the British: deadlock seemed to have been reached yet again.

Tom Jones was to make one last important contribution to the making of the treaty. Late at night on 4 December he had an emotional meeting with Griffith. It is evident from T.J.'s account that he and Griffith had established a remarkable rapport. Griffith, who had come to trust Jones, frankly revealed the differences among the Irish leaders and seemed to suggest that he and Collins, with some concessions from Lloyd George, whom they now believed to be sincere in his desire for peace, could carry the negotiation through successfully. At that meeting T.J. tried hard but in vain to arrange a meeting between Collins and Lloyd George: indefatigable to the last, T.J. returned early the next morning to

[55] T.J. to Hankey. PRO CAB 63/34.
[56] *WD*, III, 170–3

make a last appeal, which finally succeeded. Lloyd George saw
Collins later that morning and made some impression on him.

T.J. played only a subordinate part in the last dramatic stage.
This was dominated by Lloyd George. In one of his later reports to
him T.J. had written that Griffith had said:

> Will Mr. Lloyd George help us to get peace? He wants peace. He has
> difficulties. We too have difficulties . . . this is our first attempt at secret
> diplomacy.[57]

The Prime Minister had decided the time had come to break
through those difficulties. In his sternest manner Lloyd George
demanded a final Irish answer on Ulster and when the Irish
continued to prevaricate, Lloyd George produced the scrap of
paper, which now in his hands seemed to be a solemn affidavit, to
which Griffith had assented when T.J. had shown it to him on 13
November. Griffith, punctiliously honourable, conceded the case
and gave up the argument and the possibility of breaking off the
negotiation over the question of Ulster. In effect it meant that he
accepted a Boundary Commission to revise the Ulster border and
surrendered the immediate hope of a united Ireland.[58]

Thereafter, Lloyd George, in a charged atmosphere that he
himself had brilliantly contrived, gave the diplomatic performance
of his life. As Churchill said, 'Lloyd George was at his best when
trying to persuade ten or a dozen people'.[59] This time the persuasion
was heavily laced with menace: the Irish were given the final choice:
Dominion status, including complete fiscal autonomy and peace, or
refusal and war within three days. Moreover, he insisted that the grim
choice had to be made immediately. There was no time for reference
to Dublin; he himself was constrained by a promise to let Craig in
Ulster know the outcome one way or another, a destroyer was at
Holyhead ready for sea to take his messenger over to Belfast. After
much agonizing argument, the five Irish negotiators, who seemed
too tired or too bemused to challenge the absurdity of Lloyd
George's peremptory refusal of further time, agreed with varying
degrees of reluctance to sign the treaty.[60]

---

[57] HLRO Lloyd George Papers F/25/2/51.

[58] F. Packenham, op.cit., pp.236–7. In some respects too much has been made
of this dramatic moment. Griffith and Collins understood Irish political reality:
one of T.J.'s most important duties was to persuade them to admit the constricting
effect of political reality in Britain and Ulster.

[59] *Life with L.G: The Diary of A.J. Sylvester, 1931–45* (Ed. C. Cross, 1975), p.92.

[60] Collins admitted to Lloyd George (Bodl. Fisher MSS Box 8a, Diary, 6
December 1921) that 'they would never have signed without the coercion'.

'How was it done?', T.J. wrote soon afterwards. The simplest
answer, he said, was 'Mr. Lloyd George'.[61] Was it witchcraft? Others
had thought the Prime Minister capable of something like it.

'A deputation?' asked one trade unionist a year before. 'No', came the
reply. 'Better write to Lloyd George. A letter after all cannot be
mesmerized'.[62]

But T.J. knew better. Lloyd George had not really hypnotized and
deluded the Irish. He had used all his energy, tenacity, unique
persuasive power, patience, 'intuitive swiftness and unfailing temper
day and night in superlative measure' to bring the negotiators to
face reality. The Irish had demanded a republic and a united
Ireland. Political circumstances in Britain and Ulster at that time
made these unobtainable ambitions. The Irish were conceded
Dominion status for the south and a Boundary Commission which
Lloyd George, Smuts and Tom Jones honestly believed would, in
time, reinforced by 'the pull of economic and peaceful forces',
bring about a united Ireland.[63]

It was not a complete, much less an ideal solution. It was
certainly the best that could be obtained in the circumstances of
the time. It was the most determined and, for all its shortcomings,
the most successful attempt ever made to reconcile Britain and
Ireland. It is doubtful if anyone other than Lloyd George could
have succeeded even to that partial extent. And it is not too much
to say that it was also doubtful if even Lloyd George could have
done so without the shrewd patient assistance of T.J., 'who had
been all along the P.M.'s good genius', as Esher said. Others said
much the same. 'Next to the Prime Minister', Sir Robert Horne,
Chancellor of the Exchequer, wrote of the British team in a letter of
congratulation to T.J., 'you have done more to bring about this
settlement than anyone else'.[64]

Not surprisingly, at the end of it all T.J. was near exhaustion: the
'endless meetings and secret interviews by day and by midnight' in
recent weeks, as he told Hankey, had been his 'most frantic time'
during his five years at the secretariat.[65] Jones's staying power and
dogged devotion to public duty seem even more remarkable when
it is realized that throughout 1921 his wife had been ill. She was

[61] *Western Mail*, 13 December 1921.
[62] Lady Megan Lloyd George speaking, perhaps apocryphally, of her father.
(Broadcast talk, 4 June 1956, published in *The Listener*, p.6.)
[63] *Western Mail*, 13 December 1921.
[64] T.J., Class W, Vol.6, No.14. *WD*, III, 185.
[65] Ibid., III, 184.

afflicted, yet again, with a severe bout of rheumatism that drove her
for two months in the summer to Brighton and in the autumn, in
some desperation, to Aix-les-Bains for a month for treatment.
Meantime, the children had to be packed off to Mundesley on the
east coast out of harm's way. As if Rene's illness were not enough
misfortune for the family, T.J. and wife were also concerned at this
time with the general health of their son Tristan, who had
glandular fever, 'a sort of false mumps' as T.J. described it. Tristan
was sent to a small boarding school near the coast in the
hope that a change of air would bring about some improvement.
T.J.'s home at 7 Hampstead Hill Gardens, which they had bought
soon after Rene and the children had joined him in London, was
thus a bleak and lonely place to return to at night for over three
months in the early stages of 'the Irish business'. And when
later, as Jones said, it demanded 'every ounce of [his]
energy', he also had the nagging worry of Rene's continuing frail
health.[66]

Nor did the delight, even perhaps a natural euphoria, at the
signing of the Irish treaty last for very long. Esher thought, not
unfairly, that 'Lloyd George had outstripped Chatham by his Irish
achievement'.[67] But almost immediately there were ominous signs
of trouble in Southern Ireland that eventually erupted into a
tragic civil war in which Michael Collins, exponent of political
assassination, suffered the fate he had dealt out to so many others.
In a different way the Irish treaty, as Churchill said, was also 'fatal'
to Lloyd George. Within a year he had 'been driven from power',
and unforgiving Tory die-hard hostility over his Irish settlement was a major cause of his downfall.[68] Of course there were
several other reasons and there were many people whose views on
Ireland and in politics generally were diametrically opposed to die-
hard Toryism who were also bitterly resentful of Lloyd George.
Many high-toned 'progressive' intellectuals, for example, had been
driven by disappointed expectations to absurdly exaggerated
denunciations of Lloyd George and his government. 'I hope you
are as well as a man can be living so near to the centre of iniquity',
J.L. Hammond wrote to T.J. in the late summer of 1920. In
Hammond's opinion Lloyd George's government was the worst
'since Castlereagh'; George Unwin insisted that it was the worst
'since Thomas Cromwell'. Even Sir Henry Jones, who had clung for

[66] T.J. Class V Vol.1, No.108; Class W Vol.20, No.183: Class D Vol.10, No.23.
Morton MSS. GD 326/84/1.

[67] To T.J., 7 December 1921. T.J., Class W, Vol.6, No.14.

[68] W.S. Churchill, *The Aftermath: A Sequel to the World Crisis* (1929), p.307.

so long to the lifebuoy consolation that Lloyd George was at least sound at bottom, was driven to open criticism.[69]

During 1921–2 the frailty of Lloyd George's position became more and more evident. He had been brought to the premiership by the exceptional circumstances of total war; he had been kept there after 1918 by the widespread belief that although the guns were now silent, the national and international crises remained. But most of his support was pecularily evanescent: a huge novice electorate, unreliable over-mighty press barons, and, of increasing significance, a hybrid parliamentary majority in which most of the larger fraction, the Tories, were never much more than his conditional interim supporters. Within the limits imposed on him, he had tried to fulfil the expectations he had aroused at home and abroad. He had not succeeded. It was doubly unfortunate in Britain because a drastic reform of its economic structure was already overdue, and Lloyd George, the adroit pragmatist exceptionally receptive to a variety of opinions, was perhaps better equipped to lead it than any other prime minister of the twentieth century. His opportunity, such as it was, was quickly gone. The onset of economic depression brought mass unemployment and severe reduction in government expenditure, and strengthened the existing propensity in capitalist circles to look back to pre-war economic arrangements rather than to some new dispensation more in keeping with future needs.

Lloyd George's political position was gradually undermined. The Asquithian Liberals remained steadily hostile, the political and industrial wings of the labour movement increasingly distrusted him. Some of his National Liberal colleagues in the Cabinet were forced out of the government. Addison, who was scurvily treated, indeed sacrificed, by Lloyd George, was left with little option but to resign in July 1921. In March 1922 Edwin Montagu, who for the best part of a year had been cold-shouldered by the Prime Minister, resigned as Secretary for India. H.A.L. Fisher, thoroughly upset by reductions in expenditure on education, was gloomily talking to T.J. of returning to academic life, accepting an ambassadorship, or returning to the back benches as the 'unofficial member for Education'. T.J. did his best to put some life into Fisher, whose protests in the Cabinet against retrenchment and the swing to the right in government policy he thought much 'too anaemic'. Lloyd George, too, said that Fisher had become hopelessly ineffective; indeed, in June 1922, the Prime Minister complained bitterly to T.J.

[69] T.J., Class W, Vol.9, No.112. H.J.W. Hetherington, op.cit., p.126.

that he got 'no help from [his] Liberal colleagues'.[70] This blanket
indictment obviously also included Churchill, his designated
'second in command' of the National Liberal party, who in his own
highly individual way was drifting back towards the Tories at this
time.[71]

The rank and file National Liberals, mainly nonentities short of
talent, deficient in organization and electorally vulnerable, were of
less and less account, almost contemptuously ignored by Lloyd
George during 1922.[72] But the vital consideration for the Prime
Minister was his relationship with the Tories. That had been
substantially weakened by the retirement, prompted by serious
illness, in March 1921 of Bonar Law, who since 1916 had formed so
perfect a partnership with the Prime Minister, blending with him
'like soda to a brandy', a description Lloyd George thought
'exactly' right.[73] In the flush of coalition success just after the war
the emergence of 'a central party' comprising most of the Tories
and the Lloyd George Liberals under the Prime Minister seemed at
least possible.[74] It remained for some time a distracting mirage. In
fact, Tory opinion, encouraged by the party central office, was
becoming steadily more critical of Lloyd George.[75] Austen
Chamberlain, the new leader, was strongly committed to the
coalition, but he had nothing like the influence that Bonar Law
had wielded within the party.

Tom Jones had observed these events with growing alarm, not
least the changes in economic policy. In May 1921 he sent Tawney's
new book, *The Acquisitive Society*, to Horne, the Chancellor of the
Exchequer, in the perhaps ironic hope of saving his 'economic
soul' and guiding him in a more socially responsible direction. T.J.
was decidedly unhappy over the 'personnel' of the Geddes
economy committee, and in December 1921 Jones grimly warned
the Secretary of the National Council of Social Service that he
would have more than 'ample scope' for all his energies when the
economy committee's report appeared. T.J. was irritated by the
irresponsible levity of ministers who carelessly missed meetings

[70] K.O. and J. Morgan, *Portrait of a Progressive: The Political Career of Christopher,
Viscount Addison* (Oxford 1980), pp.131–48. J.H. Thomas, op.cit., p.217. T.J., Class
Z (Diary, 1922), pp.7, 9, 57. *WD*, I, 192.

[71] T. Wilson (ed.), *The Political Diaries of C.P. Scott, 1911-28* (1970), pp.416,
427.

[72] K.O. Morgan, 'Lloyd George's Stage Army: The Coalition Liberals,
1918–22', in *Lloyd George: Twelve Essays* (ed, A.J.P. Taylor, 1971), pp.235–51.

[73] *Sylvester Diary 1931–45*, p.229. *WD*, I, 152.

[74] Fisher (Diary, 21 February 1919) thought it 'probable'.

[75] D.D. Cuthbert, 'Lloyd George and the Conservative Central Office
1912–22', in *Lloyd George: Twelve Essays*, pp.167–87.

concerned with unemployment. He sent a telegram to Lloyd George urging a special initiative to help those out of work, particularly in black spots such as the East End of London. In the summer of 1922 Jones joined a 'private committee', set up by J.J. Astor, which included Henry Clay, Rowntree, Walter Layton, A.L. Bowley and others, to consider ways of reducing unemployment and mitigating its social effects.[76]

T.J. was fighting a series of losing battles. So, too, was Lloyd George. During 1922 the Prime Minister's record was one of almost unbroken failure. He had failed in January at the Cannes Conference to settle the question of German reparations, and his diplomacy was no more successful soon afterwards at Genoa, when his thunder was stolen by the Rapallo Agreement between the pariahs Russia and Germany. T.J., standing in for Hankey who was in Washington, had accompanied Lloyd George to Cannes, where he was much relieved to find that, despite his ignorance of French and Italian, he had 'pulled through well' as British secretary at an international conference. At Cannes Jones was badgered by an Italian socialist journalist, one Benito Mussolini, who wanted to interview Lloyd George. T.J. refused to arrange an interview but was persuaded to dine with Mussolini and some other Italians. It was 'a very flat affair'. *Il Duce* of the future was curiously wary and largely silent. T.J. did his best to draw him out with talk of Mazzini and the *Risorgimento*, the one Italian topic of which he knew something, but Mussolini was not to be drawn.[77]

In domestic affairs, too, Lloyd George was dogged by failure. He had just possibly missed a chance to strengthen his position with a snap general election soon after the Irish agreement, although given the temper of the Tory party even that was not likely. At any rate, Bonar Law concluded when he returned to Britain after convalescence abroad in February 1922 that Tory opinion had turned so strongly against the coalition that, as he warned Lloyd George, things could not continue unchanged.[78] Tory opinion was inflamed still further by the assassination of Field Marshal Sir Henry Wilson, outspoken champion of Ulster, in central London in June, and ever-increasing signs that Ireland, north and south, would be plunged into bloody anarchy by Irish republican activity. In midsummer, high-minded Tories were outraged by the Prime Minister's Birthday Honours list, and at the end of July a vigorous subalterns' protest by Tory junior ministers against the continuance

[76] *WD*, I, 158, 166, 172–3. T.J., Class C, Vol.11, Nos.1 and 5; Vol.12, 1, 6, and 10.
[77] *WD*, I, 189–90.
[78] R. Blake, *The Unknown Prime Minister: The Life and Times of Andrew Bonar Law 1858–1923* (1955), pp.428–9.

of the coalition was clumsily headed off by the party high command only with great difficulty.[79]

T.J. early on had come to the conclusion that Lloyd George's prime ministerial days were probably numbered. Jones had argued that he should not risk an election in January, and by February had half accepted that Lloyd George ought to resign. A month later T.J. agreed gloomily with Edward Grigg, Lloyd George's private secretary, that the Prime Minister, 'seemed to be losing his punch and grip'.[80] However, T.J. argued that Lloyd George, who specifically asked his opinion, should 'refuse to stand in a white sheet' and admit error in the Commons' debate on Honours. Indeed, with some spirit (surely wrongly applied in this instance), T.J. counselled the Prime Minister not to agree to the suggested introduction of an advisory committee on Honours. In July, Jones told Lloyd George he had come to the conclusion that there was 'a distinct danger of his outstaying his welcome'. The Prime Minister should 'go out of office with dignity', at least for a short time. T.J. could not see that there was any 'sort of positive programme' on which he could fight an election at that time.[81] Lloyd George was hardly the man to surrender power meekly, or in any way if he could possibly avoid it. He would stay until forced out. Jones of course would remain by his side. As T.J. sternly told Grigg who was wavering in August: 'it was up to both of us to stand by the P.M., it was both a privilege and a duty'.[82]

Quite apart from his strong personal loyalty, T.J. had also clung throughout 1922 to the hope that Lloyd George would be able to stay in office at least long enough to see the Irish agreement through Parliament. Ireland had continued to be a source of grave concern to the British Cabinet. T.J. persuaded himself, after an encouraging first meeting in January between Craig and Michael Collins, that there was a real immediate possibility of a united Ireland by agreement. Given the power of inherited hatreds and apparently institutionalized intransigence, T.J.'s optimism seems like the triumph of hope over experience and circumstance. Subsequently, he fell back on the presumed unifying effect over a longer term of economic forces. Meantime, there was a serious danger that events in Ireland would eliminate all future prospects of peace, and even destroy the limited improvement in relations

[79] Ibid., pp.440–4.
[80] T.J. to Lloyd George, Cannes, 6 Jan. 1922. HLRO. Lloyd George Papers F/26/1/1. WD, I, 197.
[81] Ibid., I, 203–5. Earlier in the year T.J. had refused an invitation from the retiring member to replace him as the Coalition Liberal at Denbigh.
[82] Ibid., I, 206.

that Lloyd George had already achieved.[83] As T.J. admitted to Churchill in June, he now 'felt far less biased in favour of the South' than he had been before the agreement had been made. But T.J. believed that it was essential that the British Cabinet should be 'absolutely fair as between North and South'. In particular that, at almost any cost, Britain should not allow itself to become embroiled in the troubled affairs of the Irish Free State (as southern Ireland was now called) and thereby play into the hands of de Valera and the IRA. Nor should the Cabinet permit the paramilitary extremists in Ulster to usurp the British government's responsibility for internal order and the defence of the border of the province.[84] Churchill, 'descendant of the Duke of Marlborough', as T.J. wryly referred to him, was more concerned than Jones about British imperial interests and the dangerous temper of Tory opinion. At one stage Churchill seemed not entirely to trust T.J. with confidential information on Irish matters,but it is significant that, immediately afterwards, he 'bade' T.J. 'keep as close' as he could to the Irish negotiators then in London and do his utmost to persuade them to co-operate.[85]

Against the odds in 1922, 'the Irish business' did not quite reach the point of total disaster. In August, when Arthur Griffith died, Tom Jones represented Lloyd George at the funeral in Dublin. This was especially appropriate because all along T.J. had been the exemplar of British good faith in dealings with the Irish and the consistent advocate in Cabinet circles subsequently of the belief that Griffith and those Irishmen who agreed with him could and would carry out their part of the bargain.

T.J.'s qualities were also publicly recognized in 1922 in happier circumstances. In June Glasgow University, of which he had such fond memories, conferred an honorary LL.D. upon him. In October Lloyd George and Hankey tried to persuade Jones to allow his name to be put forward for a Companionship of Honour, a major dignity that had no association with social flummery. T.J. said 'it would be a mistake'; he told Lloyd George that he was perfectly happy simply with 'his appreciation'.[86] Some months earlier, however, T.J. had prompted Lloyd George to recommend Sir Henry Jones, who was dying of cancer, for a CH.[87] It is typical of T.J.'s

[83] Ibid., III, 194–6.

[84] Ibid., III, 194–5, 198–210. 'Why should all your great efforts be wrecked by the die-hards of North and South', Jones wrote in a secret note of advice to Lloyd George on 29 May 1922. T.J. Class Z (Diary, 1922), p.45.

[85] *WD*, III, 197.

[86] T.J., Class P, Vol.1, Nos.143 and 145.

[87] T.J., Class U, Vol.1, No.131.

practical concern for his old friend and his family that, shortly afterwards, he arranged for Sir Henry's autobiography, 'Old Memories', to be published in *The Welsh Outlook,* as a discreet way of tapping David Davies's pocket for a useful sum of money for Sir Henry's widow, who was in some need.

At this time T.J. was closely involved in several activities of the Davies family. After some long discussions with T.J. in March 1920 Gwen and Margaret Davies had bought Gregynog Hall, a country house in Montgomeryshire. The purchase provided 'a glorious opportunity', Gwen exulted to T.J. 'I love the sun and beautiful things and I want others to share them too'. Over the next few years Gwen and Margaret Davies, relying heavily on T.J.'s guidance and only to a lesser extent on the assistance of Walford Davies, made Gregynog a remarkable centre of cultural activity of high quality. It naturally took a year of two before '*our* show, the home of disinterested endeavour', as Gwen described it to T.J., was fully established. But even in 1921–2, in the middle of his other pre-occupations, T.J. was eagerly at work on the Gregynog scheme.[88] And in 1923, he played a major part in establishing the Gregynog Press, which ultimately achieved a fine reputation for artistic quality.

In 1922 Jones also acted as adviser and trusted go-between in the joint attempt in September by Lloyd George and David Davies, who for the moment had papered over their differences, to gain a controlling interest in *The Times.* Lloyd George, conscious of his ebbing fortunes, was looking to the future and seeking control of an alternative source of political influence. If the bid succeeded, he would become managing director and editor within six months of leaving office. David Davies had now discovered the ultimate mission of his life: the League of Nations and international disarmament. He believed that the resurrected power of *The Times,* committed to those high idealistic purposes, would have an 'immeasurable' effect on world opinion, perhaps save millions of lives, and lead to 'the general uplifting of the nations'.[89] T.J. consulted Esher, who suggested that the chief aim should be 'to restore the Editorship to what it was in Delane's day'; the manager should be subordinate. 'The *Matin* is run on these lines,' he said, 'and is a gold mine as well as a power in France'.[90]

---

[88] T.J., Class R, Vol.2, Nos.24–59. One of his recommendations went badly astray. In October 1921, he suggested that George M.Ll. Davies should be recruited to help. The interview did not go well: 'He is willing to come', Gwen Davies reported tartly to T.J., 'providing we accept his principles of reconciliation, which it seems amount to handing over our shares wholesale to the miners'.

[89] T.J., Class P, Vol.1, No.134 (copy).

[90] T.J., Class W, Vol.6, No.22.

The consortium, however, had ludicrously underestimated the asking price. In a desperate attempt to raise additional capital, David Davies called in Tom Jones, who tried to persuade Gwen and Margaret Davies to make substantial contributions. At first T.J. thought he had succeeded, but he was mistaken. Gwen said that she and her sister were in 'full sympathy' with their brother's great ideals, but they were not prepared to accept 'a constant drain' on their resources that would 'cripple' their own artistic and educational benefactions. As she told T.J. sometime before, Gwen did not regard Gregynog just as 'a fascinating plaything'.[91]

Two weeks before, T.J. had been summoned to join Lloyd George at his new country cottage at Churt. The Prime Minister said he wanted 'to talk politics'.[92] Unfortunately, there is no record of this consultation. It hardly mattered anyway. Within weeks Lloyd George had been swept from office and Jones's future became very uncertain. At Churt, T.J. had no useful advice to offer on 'this Greek business' as he called it, the danger that Britain would be drawn into the conflict between Greece and Turkey. The Prime Minister's handling of the 'Chanak Affair' added to Tory distrust of him. The decision in mid-October by Lloyd George and Chamberlain to hold an election immediately, apparently a pre-emptive strike to forestall a hostile Tory party conference in November, led to the Carlton Club meeting on 19 October, Chamberlain's defeat, and, in effect, the immediate end of the coalition government. 'So, Lloyd George's sun has set for a time', Esher wrote to T.J. 'A pretty good glow he leaves above the horizon'.[93]

Esher and Tom Jones shared the general assumption that Lloyd George's removal from office would be temporary. In fact he never did hold office again; the remainder of his political life was a long unsuccessful struggle to recover commanding political power. But to the end of his days he remained a figure of great consequence, and certainly he continued to count for a great deal in T.J.'s life. They remained in touch and met frequently with their accustomed easy intimacy to discuss many matters of common interest. Whenever Lloyd George called for his assistance, Jones was usually prepared to drop whatever he was doing in order to help. Tom Jones's considered conclusion later was, simply, that 'Lloyd

[91] T.J., Class R, Vol.2, Nos.53 and 63. *WD*, I, 280–9.

[92] T.J., Class P, Vol.1, No.135.

[93] T.J., Class W, Vol.6, No.23. T.J., concerned that ratification of the Irish Treaty should not go astray because of the proposed dissolution, wrote on 17 October pleading with Lloyd George to take steps to avoid that possibility. 'If we fail them now', he said *(WD,* III, 216), 'all your work would be undone in a night – such is their psychology'.

George's gifts amounted to genius'.[94] At his best, he was the nonpareil, and T.J. sought at all times to get Lloyd George to rise to the
height of his political greatness. He always deplored Lloyd George's
'tendency to correlate God and the Devil', his resort on occasion to
'low artifice', and his susceptibility to plausible humbugs.[95] But
Jones understood that it was not simply a matter of Lloyd George's
personal frailties. The high hopes of 1918 were defeated also by the
character of the post-war world, which was 'debased, disjointed and
disillusioned', marked by 'a readjustment at lower levels'.[96]

On the other hand, T.J. did not appear to be disturbed by Lloyd
George's sexual adventures. At any rate, in all the many references
to him in Jones's papers there is barely a hint of comment of any
kind. It is difficult to believe that Jones was simply unaware of them.
It suggests perhaps that his celebrated discretion was never relaxed,
that he was on guard everywhere outside the safety of private
conversation with his wife.[97]

The fall of Lloyd George placed the Cabinet secretariat in
immediate jeopardy. It had many enemies, open and secret: it had
occasioned much jealousy in some senior Civil Servants, and it was
tainted with outright guilt by its association with Lloyd George and
his quasi-presidential style of government in the mind of many Tory
politicians. T.J. thought that he himself might be marked down for
removal by the die-hards, as he told Hankey, because of his close
association with L.G., 'whose nominee I was when I joined the
secretariat'. Jones was an established Civil Servant, so he would not
be simply dismissed. But, gloomily, he thought it possible that he
might be 'sent to the Mint or the Record Office out of the way'.[98]

The secretariat had been fiercely attacked in the Commons
earlier in June. Tom Jones heard the debate: he thought that much
of the 'obloquy' aimed at the secretariat was unfair. The critics
confused the secretariat with Lloyd George's personal staff
including the garden suburb, whose activity in international
matters on his behalf was bitterly resented in Foreign Office circles.
Luckily, Lloyd George, seizing on a weak point, was able to wipe the
floor with the critics.[99] But Hankey and T.J. knew that the attack

---

[94] *A Diary With Letters*, Introduction, p.xxix.

[95] T.J., Class W, Vol.20, No.237. *DNB* on Lloyd George.

[96] 'Retrospect' (December 1933), *WO*, XX, 315–16.

[97] It is of interest that Walford Davies (T.J., Class W, Vol.20, No.237) was
deeply distressed by what he considered T.J.'s unduly sophisticated tolerance of
the marital behaviour of their friend Alfred Zimmern, who left Aberystwyth under
a cloud in 1921. T.J.'s attitude (ibid., Vol.18, Nos.239–43) was that Zimmern's
personal affairs were no concern of the College authorities.

[98] T.J., Class P, Vol.1, No.142. *WD*, I, 212.

[99] Ibid., I, 202.

would be renewed and that retrenchment was inevitable. 'Some of us had better look out for jobs elsewhere', Jones, half-jokingly, said a few weeks later. It had occurred to some Civil Service mandarins in July that T.J. would be an ideal replacement for Selby-Bigge, Permanent Secretary at the Board of Education, who was thought to be on the verge of retirement. Jones showed some interest, but said that his overriding concern at that time was 'to stand by' Lloyd George, to whom he owed so much and who had allowed him to speak his mind so freely. Lloyd George insisted that T.J. was much 'more valuable' at the Cabinet Office: his labour 'sympathies' were well known and provided a valuable alternative 'standpoint'; moreover, Jones had the 'full confidence' of all the Tory ministers.[100]

This was to be of crucial importance to T.J. personally later in October when a much more formidable assault on the secretariat was mounted by the Press, the Tory back-bench, Sir Warren Fisher, Permanent Secretary at the Treasury, and several ministers including, ominously, the Prime Minister Bonar Law. The critics asserted that the secretariat was improperly intrusive, inordinately expensive and largely, if not entirely, unnecessary.[101] Hankey had been prepared for a 'drastic reduction', and was ready with a plan to cut costs by more than a half and to relinquish some responsibilities to the Foreign Office. But Hankey was determined to resist Warren Fisher's long premeditated plan, now put cunningly into play, to bring the secretariat under direct Treasury control. Fisher and Hankey fought an interesting duel distinguished by some clever footwork. At one point Fisher disarmingly suggested that Hankey should add the Clerkship of the Privy Council, 'practically a sinecure', as Hankey admitted, to the other offices he already held. This was an offer Hankey would not refuse, he had had his eye on the Clerkship for some time.[102] To some of his colleagues at the secretariat, however, the offer of the Clerkship looked like a sweetener if not quite a bribe. Unwisely, Hankey retailed the news to them 'with a smile'. T.J., thunderstruck, 'relapsed into a painful silence', and eventually left the room without a word: he obviously believed that Hankey was concerned only with his own fate.[103] This was less than fair. Certainly Hankey never for a moment forgot his own interest; he had decided earlier, for example, that he would

[100] T.J., Class Z (Diary, 1922), pp.99–100. *WD*, I, 204.
[101] *The Times* (27 October 1922), for example, claimed that the secretariat had been used for the 'subversion' of hallowed constitutional usages. The *Evening News* said that it was 'a green baytree-like growth of the war', and published details of the salary of Hankey (£3,000) and T.J. (£1,500).
[102] S. Roskill, *Hankey: Man of Secrets* (1970), II, 310–13.
[103] *WD*, I, 219.

ask for a peerage if the secretariat were scrapped; and his detailed account of his fight on its behalf is strongly laced with self-conceit.[104]

But in addition to his vigorous defence of the good name of the secretariat and a successful resistance to its incorporation under direct Treasury control, Hankey did what he could to secure the careers of most of his colleagues, and he was particularly active on behalf of T.J., who, he knew, was keen to stay with him at the secretariat.[105] The position remained in doubt for some days, so Hankey, who rarely failed to have an alternative plan in reserve, suggested to Warren Fisher that T.J. should be appointed Permanent Secretary of the Welsh Department of the Board of Education, with which he could combine the Welsh chief inspectorship that was then vacant. Hankey advocated the joint appointment (which he suggested should involve an increase in salary of £300) with considerable vigour.

> You know as well, if not better,than I do [he wrote to Fisher] the invaluable character of the services which T.J. has rendered to the State in various fields of activity during the last few years. Had he been a seeker after this world's goods he could no doubt have very readily obtained adequate pecuniary recompense from the late Administration. He possesses unique qualifications for this post.

Warren Fisher's reply was not less generous: 'My dear Hankey, I share to the full your regard for T.J. as you know; I will gladly see if anything is possible along the lines you suggest'. In the event, this expedient was not necessary.[106]

The ultimate arbiter of Jones's fate was of course the new Prime Minister. When Hankey had first discussed possible changes in the secretariat with Bonar Law he had emphasized that he was 'particularly anxious to keep Tom Jones'. Bonar Law replied that he too 'was very anxious' to keep T.J. and would 'save him' if at all possible. 'Personally', said the Prime Minister, 'I like Tom Jones better than any of them'. The element of doubt about his ability to retain T.J. almost certainly indicates no more than the strength of party pressure for economy and Bonar Law's habitual pessimism.

    [104] Diary account in S. Roskill, op.cit., II, 305–29.

    [105] Ibid., II, 307–8. T.J. said (Class P, Vol.1, No.148) that Warren Fisher, as head of the Civil Service, should and 'could have done more' to protect those of them who were established civil servants.

    [106] T.J., Class Z (Diary, 1922), pp.157 to 163. A few days later Jones discussed the matter directly with Fisher, who said that 'no Minister' had ever spoken to him about T.J. 'except on the friendliest terms'. Eventually, it was arranged that, if it became necessary, T.J. would be appointed to the Welsh post at the 'end of the financial year', or if there 'was a change in the administration … instanter'.

The Prime Minister also discussed with Hankey his pressing need of a political secretary. Grigg, who had served Lloyd George, was not available; Law rejected Lionel Curtis and Robert Vansittart, and, almost as an afterthought, wondered whether T.J. could do the job, although he doubted if he was 'a good enough draftsman'. Hankey was sure 'Tom would do allright'.[107] Nine days later, Bonar Law sent for Jones and asked if he was willing to help him with speech writing and provide general political assistance. Law also asked if Jones could give 'this sort of help conscientiously'. T.J. replied that he was a Civil Servant and would serve J.H. Thomas, if he became Prime Minister.[108]

T.J.'s probation, if that is what it was, soon came to an end. Bonar Law was 'pleased' with Jones's early work and the Welsh appointment receded into the background. The attack on the secretariat shows the remarkable strength of the apparently universal goodwill in high places that T.J. had earned during his years in Whitehall. It is clear that his progressive leanings were well understood by Tory ministers who respected his honesty of purpose although they differed strongly in opinion. Jones continued to be as respectfully forthright as ever. When the Prime Minister expatiated on the virtues of individualism and driving capitalist enterprise, T.J. 'begged him to show some real sympathy' with the unemployed, 'half-starved men' who were condemned purposelessly to hang about street corners. Nor did he shrink from suggesting (admittedly with some hesitation) to Bonar Law that he seemed to fit Bagehot's definition of a constitutional statesman: 'a man of common opinions and uncommon abilities'.[109] This of course implied no denigration, quite the contrary, but it could conceivably have been misconstrued.

In fact, the relationship that had developed between Bonar Law and Tom Jones since 1921, when they were thrown closer together as deputies for Lloyd George and Hankey, was a splendid illustration of the tensile strength of the British political system at its best. Law was the uncompromising champion of Ulster's rights; it was the one area where, in Jones's opinion, he was dominated by 'subconscious elements of ancient prejudice powerfully operating'.[110] T.J.'s sympathies lay almost entirely and passionately with the south. Even so, despite this wide divergence, they were able to state their opinions with absolute candour, discuss them in a civilized way and retain their respective positions without any loss of

[107] S. Roskill, op.cit., II, 307–8.
[108] T.J., Class Z (Diary, 1922), pp.158–60.
[109] *WD*, I, 221–2.
[110] 'Bonar Law: A Friend's Tribute'. *Western Mail,* 22 May 1923.

friendliness or mutual respect. It says much for T.J.'s courage in
dealing with powerful superiors, even on sensitive matters, and for
Bonar Law's generous tolerance of the critical opinions of a
subordinate. T.J. was more than satisfied with Law's handling of the
Irish question during his short premiership. Despite an understanding that the Bill setting up the Irish Free State would be
ratified in Parliament before 6 December 1922, as required by the
Irish agreement, there was a real danger after the general election
in November, which gave the Tory government a majority of over
seventy, that the die-hards in the Cabinet, led by Salisbury, would
defeat or successfully delay the Bill. T.J. strongly pressed upon
Bonar Law that the Irish constitution and treaty agreement had 'to
be swallowed without change', and got him to agree that it was
better to do so with good grace than in a grudging spirit. Bonar
Law accepted this advice; indeed, as his biographer points out, the
avoidance of detailed discussion enabled him to present the case,
for which he had little enthusiasm anyway, in neutral terms and in
that way avoid ruffling his die-hard supporters. Moreover, T.J. and
Lionel Curtis also prevailed upon the Prime Minister, who was
initially doubtful, to recommend the appointment of Tim Healy,
the veteran Irish Nationalist MP, as the first Governor-General of
the Irish Free State, because, as T.J. said, it 'would have a great
effect upon moderate opinion in Ireland'.[111]

There is no direct evidence that Jones exerted a significant
influence over any other aspect of Bonar Law's conduct of policy.
The Prime Minister had set his face against government intervention in the economy; he said recovery would come by 'the free
play and energy of the people'. Jones accompanied Law to Paris in
January to negotiate with the French over German reparation
payments. They agreed that French demands were excessive and
shared a sympathy with Germany's tribulations. They both deeply
regretted the post-war American decision to remain aloof from
European difficulties; indeed, T.J. urged the Prime Minister 'to go
pretty far' in a speech in February in which he appealed to the
American government and people to become more closely
involved. On the other hand, a month earlier Bonar Law at first
had fiercely resisted acceptance of the terms, which he considered
'intolerably unjust', of the debt repayment to America negotiated
by Baldwin. It is curious in a way that T.J., a former professor of
Economics who was a keen advocate of Anglo-American co-
operation, offers no opinion either way on the controversial terms

[111] *WD*, III, 218. R. Blake, op.cit., 475–6.

of the settlement, or on the fact that the Prime Minister came close to resignation over the decision.[112]

Bonar Law's health at this time was steadily deteriorating: he was a desperately tired, sick man and his innate scepticism became even more deeply tinged than usual with melancholy. In May, it was clear that he was terminally ill and could not continue; he resigned without recommending a successor to the King. Tom Jones, who 'could hardly keep back the tears' at the news, had become warmly attached to Bonar Law. He admired his grasp of business, the clarity of his mind, the precision of his power of expression and his avoidance of cheap sentiment and tawdry rhetoric. T.J. believed that there was a danger that Law would be given less than his due. He was not a great Prime Minister, but he had rendered out-standing service during his 'ideal partnership' with Lloyd George in stirring times earlier, when the 'insidious power' he had wielded by their almost continuous consultation was apt to be overlooked and undervalued because of its 'elusive character'.[113]

Tom Jones had not expected to be asked to work for Stanley Baldwin the new Prime Minister on the same intimate footing as he had served Bonar Law. When J.C.C. Davidson, friend of Law and Baldwin, suggested that this was probable, T.J., surprised, said that he did not know Baldwin, nor did the new Prime Minister know him. Indeed, T.J. knew so little about him that he could not even name his political intimates. Earlier, T.J. had noted in his diary that Baldwin was almost always silent during meetings of Lloyd George's Cabinet. Baldwin later told T.J. that his silence had given him the opportunity to put Lloyd George 'under a microscope'.[114] And it was evident that he hated what he had seen.

Baldwin had also had his eye on T.J. at that time, warmly approved of him and fully appreciated his value, a judgement reinforced by the testimony of Bonar Law and others. There was no question of T.J. not being asked to continue. 'I shall want you to hold my hand, Tom', Baldwin said within hours of becoming Prime Minister. T.J. replied rather too modestly that he would serve as 'a cabin boy with pleasure'.[115] In practice, T.J. did not hesitate to

[112] T.J.'s article on Law in *DNB*. *WD*, I, 224–32. Jones evidently did not know that the letter in *The Times* on 30 January signed 'Colonial', criticizing the proposed terms was, in fact, written by Bonar Law.

[113] *DNB*. *Western Mail*, 22 May 1923. *A Diary With Letters*, Introduction, pp.xxvii–xxix. *WD*, I, 244.

[114] Ibid., I, 143, 152, 237, 258. Ibid., II, 23.

[115] Ibid., I, 237. 'I take it, it is axiomatic', John Lochhead, an old Glasgow friend, wrote to T.J. soon afterwards, 'that no Government of England can be carried on without you'. (T.J., Class W, Vol.13, No.47).

speak up and did so for his usual countervailing purpose in discussions on policy with Tory ministers. When at their first serious discussion Baldwin expressed anxiety about the adverse commercial effects on Britain of the economic disarray of Europe, T.J. immediately turned the conversation on to the social con-sequences. And predictably, at the same time, T.J. sought to persuade ministers that they should not simply refuse to discuss miners' grievances over wage rates, for that would undermine the position of the moderate leaders and make strike action more likely.[116]

But T.J. also knew when it was politic not to challenge Tory instincts too directly. He knew, for example, that any hope he had harboured that the projected Boundary Commission would soon be convened and in some way bring about the unity of Ireland had disappeared with the election of a Tory government. The influence of the die-hards was strong; Lord Salisbury, as Lionel Curtis reported, was malevolently active. Tom Jones wondered desperately if Baldwin was strong enough 'to stand up to Salisbury', and he gloomily noted that the die-hards were powerfully represented on the Cabinet committee on Irish affairs. T.J. rested his hopes on persuading Baldwin that British interference in the Free State would destroy the government of Cosgrave (Arthur Griffith's impressive successor) and throw everything into chaos. As for the Boundary Committee, he believed that the best policy was 'to play for its indefinite postponement'. In current circumstances a meeting of the Commission would be an unacceptable risk. Baldwin had a special talent for studied inaction and he managed to put off the Commission for some time.[117]

The Prime Minister found T.J. a most congenial companion; he was invited to spend a weekend with the Baldwins at Chequers and another soon afterwards at Astley Hall, their home in Worcester-shire. The perennial topic of conversation was Lloyd George, with whom Baldwin was obsessed. T.J. did not trim his sails; he made no attempt to disguise his admiration for Lloyd George's exceptional qualities, not least his fertility of resource and his inexhaustible zest for politics. By contrast, Baldwin, after only a few months in office, was already complaining that a prime minister 'was bothered all day with someone or other reporting discontent here, there, and everywhere'. Of course T.J. was well aware that Baldwin had many qualities, most of them very different from those of Lloyd George,

---

[116] *WD*, I, 237–8.
[117] *WD*, III, 220–5. K. Middlemas and J. Barnes, *Baldwin: A Biography* (1969), p.207.

especially a reputation for straight dealing. All the same, as he left Chequers, T.J., was prompted to ask himself the question: 'Is honesty enough?'.[118]

Hankey thought that Baldwin had such 'scant capacity' and was so 'astonishingly maladroit' in handling his Cabinet that he would 'not last long'. He was however prepared to concede that Baldwin had 'nerve'.[119] Indeed, he had demonstrated that on 26 October 1923 in a speech to the Tory party conference at Plymouth. Baldwin said that unemployment was the 'crucial problem' facing the country; he was ready to fight it, but could not do so without weapons. There was no point in 'pottering along as we were'; he had come to the conclusion that the only answer to unemployment, which otherwise would get worse, was to protect the home market. He insisted that he too was bound by the pledge given a year before by Bonar Law that there would be no fundamental change in fiscal arrangements in the existing Parliament. But he said he would make minor tariff adjustments in accordance with principles already sanctioned, and, if challenged, would submit matters to the verdict of the people.[120]

At the time, this seemed to many people, as T.J. said, to be 'political insanity', or at the very least a serious mistake prompted by his failure to consult some influential colleagues.[121] Baldwin's biographers have shown that in fact the latter charge is not true. It is certain however that beforehand he 'never breathed a word' about tariffs to T.J., although Jones was shown notes on other matters that Baldwin intended to announce at Plymouth. T.J. concluded tactfully that, in the circumstances, he had better say nothing about protection.[122]

Tom Jones knew that for some time Baldwin had been taking advice on tariffs from W.A.S. Hewins, Principal of the LSE, an ardent protectionist, who twenty years before had been an intellectual mainstay of Joseph Chamberlain's tariff reform campaign. T.J. had heard Hewins lecture years before at the LSE, and thought he was a windbag 'given to vast and vague generalisations'. But of course T.J. had been an ardent freetrader

---

[118] *WD*, I, 242–5. Smuts's dismissive opinion (Bodl. Fisher MSS Box 8a, Diary 23, November 1923) was that Baldwin was 'a nice gentleman, good for ordinary times'.

[119] Hankey Diary 1/7, Vol.4, F.3.

[120] *The Times* (26 October 1923).

[121] 'Lord Baldwin: A Memoir'. *The Times* (15 December 1947).

[122] K. Middlemas and J. Barnes, op.cit., pp.212–49. *WD*, I, 248–52, 261, T.J. of course knew what was in the wind, as he had seen manuscript minutes of the Cabinet meeting at which the matter had been considered.

all his adult life and he had not now changed his mind. Jones
believed that Baldwin's decision was disastrously wrong on
economic and political grounds. No one, least of all Baldwin,
who 'would never discuss a problem . . . never argue', could
convince T.J. that protection was a cure for unemployment. And, as
he told the Prime Minister, if the electors were given 'more than
three weeks in which to think', they too 'would see through his
policy'.[123]

Baldwin of course understood that he was hazarding a good
deal. He had inherited a comfortable majority and a Parliament
that potentially had four more years to run. On the other hand,
Bonar Law, who had been elected on the slogan 'Tranquillity', a
euphemism for a breathing space after years of hectic activity under
Lloyd George, had bequeathed little or nothing to his successor in
the way of a programme for the future. Moreover, the party had
been weakened by its divisions after the Carlton Club meeting and
the consequent unfriendly detachment of Austen Chamberlain and
other former coalition ministers, who retained an alarming loyalty
to Lloyd George. Many years later Baldwin told T.J. that the
Plymouth decision had been deliberate, 'the result of long
reflection'; he was convinced that unemployment could not be
dealt with without a tariff; moreover, protection, although it had
been unconsidered for years, was 'the one issue which would pull
the party together'. And there was one other consideration: he had
reliable information that Lloyd George was 'going protectionist'.
He thus had no choice, he had 'to get in quick' and dish Lloyd
George, who otherwise might pre-empt protection as a policy,
establish a permanent hold on Chamberlain and company, and
'put an end' to the old Tory party forever.[124]

It is probable that time and distance lent a greater coherence to
Baldwin's later account of his actions than the facts in 1922
warranted. T.J.'s record of events, written up a few weeks after
their occurrence, suggests that the Plymouth decision was abrupt
rather than coolly premeditated; that Baldwin had expected that
he would have several months' grace, at least until the Budget
of 1924, in which to wear down a supposed long-standing
popular prejudice against protection, but that, in fact, once the
Plymouth speech was made, Baldwin 'was at the mercy of events',
and an election within weeks became inevitable. T.J. was
certainly well aware that fear, of an almost pathological
intensity, of Lloyd George loomed large in Baldwin's mind at this

[123] Ibid., I, 261–2.
[124] *The Times*, 15 December 1947.

time.[125] And this may have played a part in pushing Baldwin to an early dissolution; there is also evidence that contradictory party pressures had some effect. On 12 November Baldwin declared an immediate election.[126]

These events have been related at some length because T.J. offers testimony of some value to their understanding; moreover, during the election campaign that followed, he was put in a position of considerable personal difficulty. One complication had been dealt with quickly. At the end of October Edward Wood (later Lord Halifax), President of the Board of Education, asked T.J. whether he still wished to replace Sir Alfred Davies as Welsh secretary of the Board when he retired in March 1924. Wood was 'most anxious' that T.J. should do so. Baldwin, who was consulted later, thought this a reasonable safeguard for the uncertain future, but insisted on Jones continuing meantime to work for him. On 12 November T.J. and Baldwin decided to postpone the final decision until after the election.[127] Throughout the campaign they were in the closest touch, once rather embarrassingly so. During a visit to Astley the Press took a photograph of Baldwin, his son and T.J. walking in the country that appeared the next day in *The Times* and a few days later, more damagingly, in the *Sphere*, with a caption to the effect that Jones was helping the Prime Minister in the election campaign. T.J. was vexed because he treasured the 'first-rate record of anonymity' he had maintained since 1916, and he was concerned that many people, especially in Wales, would not quite understand that 'a civil servant does his best for his chief whatever the politics of the said chief'. One of those who did not accept T.J.'s version of the situation was Ramsay MacDonald, the next Prime Minister.[128]

Jones was a shade disingenuous, a response prompted by uneasiness, maybe by feelings of guilt, for the help that he gave Baldwin in the election went some way beyond the assistance required of a conventional Civil Servant by his political master at that time. It is doubtful if it would be regarded today as legitimate activity. The fact was that T.J.'s position had subtly altered in 1922

[125] On his visit to Astley in November T.J. came across a photograph of Lloyd George that had been defaced: 'How they do hate him', he commented. *WD*, I, 256.

[126] Middlemas and Barnes, op.cit., pp.219–239. Lloyd George had in fact returned to Britain on 9 November and had already denounced Baldwin's proposals as 'fiscal folly'.

[127] *WD*, I, 153–4. T.J., Class Z (Diary, 1923), p.132. Class W, Vol.10, No.200.

[128] *WD*, I, 255–7, 305.

but the change had not formally been acknowledged, as the
following makes clear.

Cabinet Instructions to the Secretary. [Hankey]

January 1924   Secret CP.30/24

From 1916 to 1922 Mr. Jones constantly attended the Cabinet as Acting
Secretary during the frequent absences of the Secretary at
International Conferences. Since the formation of Mr. Bonar Law's
government, however, Mr. Jones's services have been wholly absorbed
by the P.M. and he has virtually acted as Political Secretary, first to Mr.
Bonar Law, later to Mr. Baldwin.[129]

T.J. was put in an embarrassing situation by his new undefined *ad
hoc* status. He did register a protest of sorts; at least he told Baldwin
several times that all his 'instincts and training' were against the
proposed policy. Nevertheless, in addition to the normal daily task
of briefing the Prime Minister on political news, as he conceded in
his unpublished diary, T.J. 'wrote the full draft of every important
speech' that Baldwin made during the campaign, except those he
delivered in Bewdley for local consumption. T.J. was not engaged
simply in preliminary devilling for necessary facts or rendering the
Prime Minister's ideas into agreeable prose. Jones said that Baldwin
gave him 'little in the way of guidance' and only 'the most meagre
instructions'. T.J. based what he wrote on the constructions he put
on Baldwin's speech at Plymouth and his response in the Commons
to the arguments advanced by Ramsay MacDonald. T.J. avoided
statistics because he decided that 'the figures were against' the
protectionist case. He even attempted a close simulation of
Baldwin's style. 'I threw myself into his manner of speaking so far as
I was able', T.J. said, 'writing simply and eschewing rhetoric, playing
up all the time the simple honest man'. T.J. heard only one of the
addresses that Baldwin delivered during the campaign, but it was
apparent, as he commented a shade dryly, that, in that instance at
least, the Prime Minister 'had absorbed the MS. very thoroughly',
and it appeared that he was 'saying his piece' rather than making a
speech. Apart from the opening paragraph, every word came from
T.J.[130]

Jones had done nothing of the kind for Lloyd George, who
wrote all his own speeches. Bonar Law did no more than talk over
the substance of his speeches with T.J. and then rehearse their

[129] T.J., Class, B, Vol.1, No.14. A.J. Sylvester ('Notes on Thomas Jones') says
that T.J. was 'a sort of super secretary' to Bonar Law and Baldwin.

[130] T.J., Class Z (Diary, 1923), pp.158–60. One curious consequence was that
Tory party propagandists seized on an allusion T.J. had made to Ivor Novello's
(continued opposite)

delivery to him later. But there is also the important difference that T.J.'s political work for Lloyd George and Bonar Law was to act on their instructions to implement the policy of an incumbent government. T.J. played no part in Lloyd George's conduct of the Coupon Election, and he was not involved in Bonar Law's party campaign in 1922; indeed, during the latter contest, to avoid misunderstanding, he also carefully kept his distance from Lloyd George. In 1923, however, Jones operated as a covert party propagandist on the Tory side in a general election fought on a notably controversial issue. It was all the more ironic that he himself remained a convinced free-trader. It was as bizarre as a confirmed teetotaller writing advertising copy for the brewers. On election day itself, on 6 December, T.J. and Rene voted Liberal against the protectionist Tory candidate at Hampstead. The next day T.J. sent a message to Lloyd George urging him 'to move to the left', to have no truck with the Tories, who would use him and throw him aside when he had served their purpose.[131]

This looks like T.J.'s hasty moral purgation for recent sins. On Polling Day he heard the details of constituency results in the company of several of Baldwin's personal staff. His account suggests that, wearing his unofficial political secretary's hat, Jones at first went through the motions of despondency, presumably feigned, as government candidates went down to defeat, but ultimately reverted to type as he 'watched the growing tale of labour victories with undisguised joy and cries of "You Bolshevist!"'. Within days, it seemed very likely that for the first time there would be a Labour government. T.J. was confident that, if it happened, the heavens would not fall down in consequence.[132]

(continued from overleaf)
wartime song 'Keep the Home Fires Burning'. It became a campaign slogan; new words were set and the chorus, sung at Tory party meetings, ran:

> Keep the home fires burning
> Keep our British earning
> Wages that the foreigner would steal away
> Stand for Home and Neighbour
> Spurn all foreign labour
> Baldwin's way the British way
> And it's bound to pay.

T.J. had cause to cringe!

[131] *WD*, I, 222, 238, 258–9. Hankey (S. Roskill, op.cit., II, 352), whose nose was put out of joint by Baldwin's preference for Tom Jones's advice and company, was quite properly astonished that T.J., a civil servant, had 'sweated blood for Baldwin in the election'.

[132] *WD*, I, 258, 260.

CHAPTER TEN

WHITEHALL · III

TOM JONES'S delight at the success of the Labour Party in the general election in November 1923 went rather further than the facts warranted. Certainly Labour had done better than ever before by winning 191 seats to the 158 gained by the Liberals. But despite heavy losses, the Conservatives still remained stronger than either with 258 member of the Commons, and it was by no means certain that Ramsay MacDonald, the Labour leader, would be called upon to form a government. However, the election result clearly implied the voters' rejection of Baldwin's proposed policy of protection and his initial inclination was to resign forthwith. He had been heavily criticized in some Tory newspapers for his decision to dissolve Parliament and denounced as an inexperienced blunderer by several in his party, including some leading members who urged him to resign immediately in the hope that a Tory government could be reconstituted under another leader. Baldwin received contradictory advice from a number of sources. His biographers argue, no doubt rightly, that his ultimate decision not to resign until formally defeated in the new Parliament was determined by his need to outmanoeuvre those Tories who were plotting against him.[1] There was also another consideration. Baldwin could not be unmindful of the King's position which had been spelled out in forthright terms by Lord Esher, friend and unofficial adviser of monarchs, in a letter to Tom Jones that would certainly be passed on to Baldwin:

> The P.M. owes it to the Sovereign and to the country to make things easy to carry on the Government. To resign before meeting Parliament places the King in a difficult position. Only open discussion in the House of Commons, followed possibly by defeat in the Lobbies, gives a clue to the King of what steps he should take.
>
> If the P.M. resigns, what is the Sovereign to do? Go into the Lobbies and political clubs? Enquire of 'Leaders' and Whips their opinions? Undignified and unreliable.

[1] K. Middlemas and J. Barnes, *Baldwin: A Biography* (1969), pp.250–3.

Abdication is a rotten solution, whether you are Napoleon, William III or Stanley Baldwin. To fall on the field of battle is the only thing.[2]

Whether of his own volition or on Esher's advice, the King, who was also subjected to many contradictory suggestions by interested parties, had come to the same conclusion.[3] At any rate, Baldwin conformed to the royal wishes, met the new Parliament, was defeated and resigned on 22 January 1924. Ramsay MacDonald, overcoming some faint-hearted objections in his party, became Prime Minister for the first time at the head of a minority Labour government. The prospect of a 'socialist' government as the alarmists, real and pretended, called it aroused fear and trembling in fashionable circles. One man, however, who clearly welcomed the change of government, or at least of Prime Minister, was, perhaps surprisingly, that pillar of the Establishment Sir Maurice Hankey. At their first meeting he and MacDonald had established an instant liking for each other. 'I took to him at once', Hankey wrote soon afterwards, 'and *vice versa* I think . . . he begged me to remain and added that he hoped we should become friends as well as associates'.[4]

MacDonald's attitude to Tom Jones, however, was very different. T.J., as he said later, was about to be 'sent to Coventry' by the new 'Labour régime', whose advent he had welcomed so enthusiastically. It was quickly made plain to Jones that he was to 'have nothing to do with the new Prime Minister', and was to revert to purely secretarial duties at the Cabinet Office.[5] The reason for this humiliating snub was largely personal: Ramsay MacDonald, pathologically secretive and suspicious, simply did not trust him. It was ironic that of the four prime ministers with whom T.J. had dealings, the one to whom he was least congenial, indeed personally unacceptable, at any rate at first, was the one whose political views were most closely in accord with his own. T.J. had known MacDonald for more than twenty years; they were both early members of the Fabian Society and the ILP, and had corresponded in cordial terms in the years before 1914. And although T.J.'s early socialism had rather different roots from MacDonald's, they shared the conviction that socialism should aim to eliminate, not promote, class war; both of them were 'inevitable gradualists', firm champions of constitutional government and hostile to syndicalist

[2] T.J., Class P, Vol.2, No.25
[3] H. Nicolson, *King George V: His Life and Reign* (1952), pp.380–4.
[4] S. Roskill, *Hankey: Man of Secrets* (1970), II, 353.
[5] *WD*, I, 268, 305.

or other extra-parliamentary left-wing action. Moreover, they had common working-class antecedents and hated the social consequences of poverty which they believed could be significantly reduced if not entirely eliminated by legislative action. These credentials counted for nothing. MacDonald had taken note of the photograph and damaging caption published in the Press just before the 1923 election which suggested that Jones was assisting Baldwin's election campaign. It convinced MacDonald that T.J. 'had gone over completely to the capitalists'.[6] The truth was that Jones had been put in a false position by Baldwin's self-indulgent leaning on his assistance in what was, strictly, an area out of bounds for a politically neutral civil servant. T.J. had been uneasy about that transgression. He now paid the price for it.

But there were also other personal factors. MacDonald's comment to Hankey that he was 'amazed' that T.J.'s salary was 'so high' (with an accompanying unctuous comment that the Prime Minister himself had always been satisfied simply 'to have a roof over his head') conveys an impression of dislike as well as depreciation of T.J.[7] MacDonald was quite incapable of giving enough of his confidence and trust to have the sort of mutually respectful, intimate relationship Lloyd George, Baldwin and, to a substantial extent, Bonar Law, had struck up with Tom Jones. It was particularly unfortunate that this should be so because MacDonald had especial need of continuous skilful assistance of that kind. He was utterly without ministerial experience, he had not hitherto held even a junior office; and, as if that were not daunting handicap enough, MacDonald intended also to be his own Foreign Secretary. Overlooking Arthur Henderson, Esher told Tom Jones that he believed MacDonald had done the right thing: 'There simply *is* no Foreign Secretary available except the P.M. himself. So it is futile to look for one'. Esher thought that the two posts were perfectly manageable by one man given proper organization. The difficulty was that MacDonald's office was 'rottenly run'. He ought to have a *'Chef de Cabinet'*. Hankey ought to 'fulfil the function, but he does not' and, for various personal reasons, said Esher, he could not. Accordingly, the under-secretary should be made head of the Prime Minister's office and the liaison officer between Downing Street and the cabinet secretariat. By under-secretary Esher presumably meant Tom Jones, Hankey's senior assistant. But MacDonald's

    [6] Ibid., 305. 'Crossbencher' (*Sunday Express*, 3 October 1926), in an article laced with inside information, endorsed the opinion that MacDonald 'relegated' T.J. 'to comparative obscurity' because he had worked for Baldwin during the 1923 election.
    [7] *WD*, I, 267.

antipathy to T.J. obviously ruled him out. Even so, not many weeks later T.J., as he said, was told by an MP in a position to know that MacDonald was 'feeling the need of someone to do for him the work I used to do for his predecessors'.[8] It is possible that some of the errors of judgement, caused in part by tiredness and the overwhelming pressure of work, made by MacDonald in the later stages of his government could have been avoided if he had had the full-time assistance of a man in whom he could put his trust.

T.J. had been aware from the beginning that his future was 'uncertain' under the new government. And he was disconcerted and disappointed by what he considered Hankey's less than zealous championship of his interests. Jones was convinced that Hankey had 'not lifted a finger to help', even though he had 'ample opportunities' of broaching the subject during his early conversations with MacDonald. T.J. said very little to Hankey directly, but privately he 'felt very sick about the whole business'.[9] In fact, the situation was not quite as straightforward as T.J. suggested. Hankey appears never to have resented the special relationship that T.J. had with Lloyd George; and it will be remembered that it was Hankey who assured Bonar Law that T.J. could provide useful assistance to him during his premiership. But Hankey seems to have been surprised and considerably put out by the very close relationship that developed so quickly between Baldwin and Jones. Hankey's apparently cheerful acceptance of T.J.'s virtual demotion under MacDonald may very well have been, as his biographer has asserted, no more than natural satisfaction at his own return to the first place in the confidence of the incumbent Prime Minister.[10]

At the time of the change of government it had again been suggested that T.J. should become Secretary of the Welsh Department of the Board of Education. Jones discussed the proposal several times with Edward Wood, the President of the Board, but it is evident that he was no longer seriously interested in that post. In the end it was decided that Sir Alfred Davies would continue for another year. But T.J. took the opportunity to put down a marker for the future by recommending his protégé Percy Watkins for the vacancy when it should arise.[11] Encouraged by Haldane, T.J. now set his sights on the much more important office of Permanent Secretary of the Board of Education. This was the

[8] Ibid., I, 276–7, 283. The MP was H.B. Lees Smith, T.J.'s referee for the Economics chair at Sheffield in 1909.

[9] Ibid., I, 265–8.

[10] S. Roskill, II, 358–9.

[11] T.J., Class V, Vol.1, Nos.128 and 129; Class Z, (Diary 1924), p.10.

post that T.J., as he told Baldwin, would have preferred to all others, if he had been offered an unrestricted choice. There were several people influential in the Labour movement who believed that Jones was exceptionally well qualified for the post and were keen on his appointment. Haldane, the new Lord Chancellor, had already spoken to MacDonald, and Sidney Webb and Tawney were also strongly in favour. Tawney's talk of the possibility of more money for universities and a substantial extension of adult education made the prospect even more inviting. Jones had hoped that his Romney Street Group friend Arthur Greenwood would be made Minister of Education, and said that if he were also appointed Permanent Secretary, 'together [they] could have made things hum'. However, C.P. Trevelyan, a former Liberal, became President of the Board. He discussed future education policy at an informal meeting with T.J., who felt nevertheless that he was under inspection. Meantime, Hankey, according to his own account at least, did his best to get T.J. appointed. It all came to nothing.[12]

It is clear that Warren Fisher, head of the Civil Service, was 'annoyed' that T.J. had 'dropped the Welsh post', perhaps because it upset a number of changes already planned. But, that aside, it is an interesting sidelight on the values that prevailed in the upper reaches of the Civil Service that Fisher and another senior Treasury knight told Hankey that they thought that T.J. was 'flying very high in contemplating the permanent secretaryship' of the Board.[13] Evidently the outsider who had not served the proper apprenticeship was thought to be getting above himself. The fact that he had played a key role in the Irish settlement, one of the most difficult negotiations of modern times, had won the confidence of three very different prime ministers in succession, and had a lifelong interest in and extensive first-hand experience of education counted for nothing apparently. Two years before, Alfred Cope, who had also made an important contribution to the Irish settlement, had left the Civil Service because of his conviction, as he told T.J., that 'he would never get to the top . . . because he was not an Oxford man', and would therefore never be considered for one of the plum jobs by Warren Fisher and the oligarchy in control.[14] In the event, Selby-Bigge, limpet-like, remained on as Permanent Secretary at the Board of Education until 1925.

[12] *WD*, I, 266–8.

[13] T.J., Class Z (Diary, 1924), pp.12–13. A.J. Sylvester ('Notes on Thomas Jones') says that office gossip at the Treasury about Selby-Bigge's possible successor was confined to Oxbridge graduates.

[14] T.J., Class Z (Diary, 1922), p.149. T.J. promptly persuaded Lloyd George to make Cope secretary of the National Liberal Federation.

However, Hankey's efforts were not entirely in vain: Warren Fisher was persuaded to propose to the Prime Minister that T.J.'s salary as principal assistant at the Cabinet Office should be raised from £1,500 to £1,800 a year.[15] And perhaps of greater importance, T.J. remained free to take an important initiative of his own in higher education.

Jones also had more time for his own concerns. On leaving office, Baldwin had formally recommended him for a CH. After consulting Rene, T.J. once more declined gracefully, adding a covering note to Baldwin that his 'prejudice' against honours remained as strong as ever. Early in 1924 he was busily involved with Esher and Tawney in organizing a scheme of educational research financed by the Garton Foundation; he was now able to take the chair regularly at weekly meetings of the Romney Street Group, and he could spend more time at home discussing with his wife their plans to build a cottage, Street Acre, at St Nicholas-at-Wade, near Birchington in Kent.[16] T.J. spent almost as much time working in secret to bring some relief to Tawney, who was in serious financial difficulty. It is a typical example of Thomas Jones at his discreet helpful best.

> The Tawney's have had very bad luck of late with ill health and expensive medical attendance [T.J. wrote to Percy Watkins, whose assistance he invoked]. I mentioned them to Miss Davies and she gave me £50 for them. My first idea being that Tawney should write an article for the *Observer* and be paid a special rate, but Garvin pointed out that owing to their book-keeping system that would be difficult. Rene then suggested you could invent a lecturing opportunity at Cardiff and I am glad to know that this fits in with some plans of your own. All I stipulate is that Tawney should get not less than £15 per lecture. This will restrict the scheme to three so far as I am mixed up in it. His health is not at all robust, hence my anxiety not to put any undue strain on it.[17]

Percy Watkins quickly arranged three WEA lectures in south Wales which would be paid for out of the £50 T.J. had received from Gwen Davies. Tawney, however, could not get away on the arranged dates. Watkins was therefore ordered to bank the cheque 'until', as T.J. wrote, 'I can hit on some method of helping Tawney without his knowledge. The money must somehow be got to him as I know how much they need help'. T.J. was never at a loss for long in these

[15] Ibid., (Diary, 1924), p.13.
[16] Ibid., pp.12, 24–5. *WD.*, I, 265, 281.
[17] T.J., Class V, Vol.1, No.132.

situations. Earlier he had elicited a promise from Garvin that he would commission Tawney to write for the *Observer:* T.J. now arranged for him to write a couple of articles for *The Welsh Outlook,* a neat arrangement that brought financial help to Tawney and left his pride intact. T.J.'s passion for anonymity was, in part, the expression of a natural modesty; it enabled him sometimes to do good work by stealth.[18]

During 1924 the various activities financed by the Misses Davies at Gregynog Hall demanded a great deal of T.J.'s attention. The annual music festivals and summer schools, now well established, organized and conducted with demonic energy by Sir Walford Davies, as he now was, introduced distinguished musicians – Elgar and Adrian Boult, for example – to this remote spot where the combination of gifted local amateurs with professionals of the highest class produced music of a superb quality.

T.J.'s contribution to the music side of Gregynog was mainly to put a bridle on Walford Davies's endearing but occasionally extravagant enthusiasm. Although he believed profoundly in its importance, T.J. had no specialist knowledge of art[19] and no personal talent for handicraft: 'I have in eighty years', he said towards the end of his life, 'created nothing of imperishable beauty with my hands'. Originally the Gregynog enterprise had envisaged using the house as a centre for arts and crafts, fine pottery, weaving and furniture-making. But these rather ambitious plans were dropped after some early experiments and it was decided to concentrate on the fine printing and bookbinding of selected Welsh and English classical texts. The extensive stables and coachrooms at Gregynog were transformed into a studio and workshops for a small group of craftsmen headed by R.A. Maynard, a multi-talented young painter recommended by Hugh Blaker. In this way the Gregynog Press was established; and the contribution of T.J., who was chairman throughout the quarter century of its existence, was vital to its success. He had an important influence on the choice of texts; it was T.J. who usually conducted negotiations with authors whose works were to be published. He arranged, for example, with the editor of the Everyman Library, Ernest Rhys, to make a selection and write an introduction to the *Poems of Henry*

---

[18] Ibid., Nos.133–7; Class P, Vol.2, No.27.

[19] The Misses Davies relied upon the artistic judgement of the gifted connoisseur and critic Hugh Blaker, brother of their governess. On his advice they built up a magnificent collection of the works of French Impressionist and Post-Impressionist painters. Dorothy A. Harrap, *A History of the Gregynog Press* (Private Libraries Association, 1980), pp.3–4.

Vaughan, which was published in 1924. The first four volumes published, which attracted high praise from critics, were bound in blue buckram. It was discovered however that buckram faded quickly; inevitably, T.J. knew someone who could help. He sent samples to his friend James Morton, head of Sundour Fabrics, who 'turned his chemists on to the problem and out of this came the binding cloths in fast colours, an immense gain to book lovers'.[20] T.J. had the complete confidence of the Davies sisters, but that did not mean that they accepted his advice in every particular. Gwen Davies, the elder sister, who was as single-minded about the Press as her brother David was in his commitment to the League of Nations, held strong views. In May 1924, after a conference on future policy, T.J. understood that he was to arrange a series of selections from the body of Anglo-Welsh poetry. Gwen and Daisy Davies disagreed.

> The first and primary object in our minds at present [Gwen wrote to T.J. on 4 July] is to unlock the door of the treasure house of Welsh literature, romance and legend and make it accessible to the English speaking public . . . To remove once and for all the point of view which one so often hears expressed by even so-called educated English folk . . . "Why bolster up an effete and worn out barbarous language which so few can understand?"

T.J.'s fear that there would be little or no demand for books in Welsh was briskly dismissed: 'This does not worry us in the least. It is worthwhile producing a beautiful thing for its own sake.' Indeed one of the declared aims of the Press was to raise the level of artistic taste of the Welsh people. Gwen, who was inspired by the purest idealism, was in despair at this time. As she said, she and her sister had poured thousands of pounds into the University music scheme for Wales, but there had been a disappointing response to Walford Davies's magnificent work. 'We have led the Welsh horse to the clearest brook we could possibly get', Gwen wrote, 'yet he has only tossed his head and walked right through'. She was sadly disillusioned. 'Oh, T.J. we have so much to give that isn't money. . . . I'm so weary'.[21] Jones was of course the very man to offer sympathetic

---

[20] T.J., 'The Gregynog Press' (16pp), 7 April 1954. T.J., Class L, Vol.I, No.1. *WD,* I, 281–2.

[21] T.J., Class P, Vol.2, No.30; Class R, Vol.2, Nos.91 and 95. There were family difficulties about this time. Their brother David had moved into the family home, Plas Dinas, with his second wife. After a period of some constraint, Gwen and Daisy moved out to live in quarters at Gregynog, taking their pictures with them. 'We simply *can't live* in this atmosphere', Gwen (ibid., No.82) told T.J. tearfully.

understanding in this and other emotional crises that arose later. The Gregynog ladies appreciated to the full how much they owed to his unfailing support.

There was also a distinguished man of letters in Wales who wished to recognize T.J.'s contributions to the public good and the inspiration he had given to young men. In April 1924, T. Gwynn Jones, considered by many to be the 'finest living Welsh poet', asked to be allowed to dedicate a collection of his poems to T.J. who was deeply affected by the gesture.[22] Eighteen months later Tom Jones wrote a letter to the poet which reveals clearly the values he cherished throughout his life.

> I can't find words in Welsh or English to say what I think about your gift of the manuscript of the Selected Poems. I am very much moved because one does not seek appreciation and it seldom comes. When it does come and is of the kind one values then it bowls one over. This is just how I feel. This morning the Prime Minister [Baldwin] was proudly telling me that T.E. Lawrence had presented him with a copy of "The Seven Pillars of Wisdom" price 30 guineas, and already worth a hundred. Imagine my pride in countering him with the original manuscript of one of the most notable books in our whole literature, which I would not sell for many hundreds. We cried quits.[23]

It is evident, however, that T.J. was rather less than his usual buoyant self during the ten months' existence of the first Labour government. He certainly became less charitable in his judgements: he prematurely wrote off John Wheatley, one of the great ministerial successes of the government, as hare-brained; he believed, wrongly, that C.P. Trevelyan, who in fact achieved a number of useful improvements in education, would be too timid to overcome obstruction by his officials and even T.J.'s old friend Sidney Webb came in for some scornful comment. J.H. Thomas, however, 'the ablest politician in the government', remained in high favour.[24] Thomas, who was Colonial Secretary, evidently thought equally well of T.J.; when further difficulties over setting up the Irish Boundary Commission arose in March 1924, Thomas called on Jones's assistance. T.J., who was 'very unwilling' to get caught in 'the Irish bog again', claimed he was out of touch with developments in the Free State. It was with the greatest reluctance that he agreed to go

    [22] T.J., Class W, Vol.12, No.48. *WD*, I, 275.
    [23] T.J., Class W, Vol.12, No.54; ibid., No.49, for Gwynn Jones's account of T.J.'s influence on him.
    [24] *WD*, I, 269–71.

over to Dublin 'to spy out the land' on the British government's behalf.[25]

Predictably, the Boundary problem rumbled on unresolved for some time. T.J.'s attitude during his visit to Dublin, and subsequently in complicated considerations of Irish policy at home, remained unchanged. He argued for the maximum understanding of the difficulties of Cosgrave's embattled government, pleaded that nothing should be done to suggest 'bad faith' on Britain's part, and suggested repeatedly that the Labour minister should try to win the support of Asquith, Lloyd George and Baldwin for an agreed policy on the Boundary question. T.J. considered that Craig and the Ulstermen were as awkwardly unforthcoming as ever. He tried to enlist Baldwin's help but 'got a diehard reaction', and, in some exasperation, rebuked him for being 'not helpful'. T.J. suggested that Ramsay MacDonald, who had demonstrated a considerable talent for conciliation in international relations, ought to be more closely involved in Irish affairs, but it was evident that J.H. Thomas, as Arthur Henderson said, was too vain to agree to anything 'which took away from his own importance in the matter'.[26]

Soon afterwards, T.J. discovered to his cost that, where his own reputation was concerned, Ramsay MacDonald, too, was wholly self-centred and none too scrupulous. The J.R. Campbell case, which indirectly put an end to the first Labour government, was from start to finish a catalogue of error and misjudgement and, on occasion, incompetence. Hardly anyone, other than Hankey possibly, emerged from it with much credit. In July 1924 the Communist International decided to mark the tenth anniversary of the outbreak of the Great War by instructing all Communist newspapers in the world to publish an open letter which incited troops in capitalist countries to refuse to take part in international war and to disobey orders to intervene in industrial disputes. On 25 July the *Workers Weekly* carried on its inside pages the invocation 'Soldiers, sailors, airmen [of Britain] let it be known that neither in the class war nor a military war will you turn your guns on your fellow workers'.

[25] Ibid., III, 227.

[26] Ibid., III, 227–34. T.J. admitted that some of the difficulties resulted from the fact that the Treaty, in which he had been so closely involved, 'was signed in a hurry'; nevertheless, Britain should 'keep to the spirit of the bargain'. When the Treaty was signed, he said sorrowfully, 'no one foresaw the deplorable events which followed in Ireland'. His hopes of the Boundary Commission were never realized.

The decision to prosecute the editor of the newspaper was taken at the instance, it appears, of the service departments by the Director of Public Prosecutions on the instructions of the Attorney-General, Sir Patrick Hastings, who was of the opinion that the words published in the newspaper amounted to an incitement to mutiny under the terms of the Mutiny Act of 1797.[27] The private contract printers of the *Workers Weekly* were so nervous of what had appeared that, in some haste, they wrote a letter of apology to the Home Secretary for what they had done. At that point elements of farce began to enter the affair. The Director of Public Prosecutions went on holiday leaving matters in the hands of his deputy, who seemed later to know little of the detail. At the *Workers Weekly*, J.R. Campbell, who was acting editor, accepted responsibility for the open letter but otherwise said nothing, was promptly arrested, charged and remanded on bail. There had already been some developments in Parliament: the Home Secretary had been badgered by Tory back-benchers over the delay in taking action, and the Attorney-General had been peevishly questioned by left-wing Labour members about the basis of the prosecution.[28] One of the latter, James Maxton, in a private meeting with the Attorney-General and Sir Henry Slesser, the Solicitor-General, pointed out that J.R. Campbell was merely a temporary acting editor of the *Workers Weekly*, that he had fought at Gallipoli and in France, and indeed had been decorated for gallantry. Maxton, who was not given to understatement, suggested that Campbell (who had indeed suffered painful frostbite) had been in danger of losing both his feet as a result of his service. Hastings and Slessor decided that, if these facts were true, no jury would convict Campbell; as Hastings said, he was 'the very last person' who should have been chosen for prosecution on that charge.[29]

Sir Patrick Hastings was a man of high principle; immensely gifted, he was one of the great advocates of his time. He was, however, politically inexperienced and found that he was profoundly unhappy and so overwhelmed with work as a law officer that he was driven to admit that the Attorney-Generalship

[27] The best short account, which straddles the legal and political aspects of the case, is F.H. Newark, 'The Campbell Case and the First Labour Government', *Northern Ireland Legal Quarterly*, XX (March 1969), 19–42.

[28] *Parl, Deb. Commons*, Vol.176, cols.1779–2930. L. Macneil Weir, *The Tragedy of Ramsay MacDonald* (1938), pp.174–7, gives useful supplementary detail of the party manoeuvres in the Commons.

[29] *The Autobiography of Sir Patrick Hastings* (1948), p.238. F.H. Newark, loc.cit., p.24.

represented his 'idea of hell'.[30] Perhaps overwork explains his remarkably casual, indeed slipshod, conduct of some of the purely legal aspects of the case. And inexperience, even perhaps *naïveté*, accounts for his failure at first to see the political implications of the affair. But there is no question that Hastings behaved honourably throughout. He had come to the conclusion that 'an unfortunate mistake' had been made and, on grounds of practicality, decided that the proper course was to ask the magistrate's permission to withdraw the prosecution.

At that point Ramsay MacDonald, to whom pointed reference had already been made in the Commons, intervened. He sent for Hastings and the Deputy Director of Public Prosecutions and sharply criticized the conduct of the absent Director. Hastings intervened immediately to say that he accepted full responsibility for instituting proceedings and for the decision to withdraw the prosecution; and the Deputy Director had been informed of this before the Prime Minister had appeared in the room.[31] It might perhaps have been well for the government if matters had been allowed to rest there. No doubt the Communists, infuriatingly, would have crowed over their success when the prosecution was withdrawn, and the government would have faced some Tory taunts in the Commons. But even if there were weaknesses Hastings could easily have demonstrated the integrity of his behaviour as Attorney-General in coming to the decision.

However, political considerations now became increasingly important; the Prime Minister, already caught up in the affair, became more and more involved, and Tom Jones was drawn haplessly in to the imbroglio, which henceforth, if anything, became even more confused.

On 6 August, after MacDonald's meeting with Hastings, the Cabinet considered the Campbell prosecution. In Hankey's absence, T.J. acted as secretary. The discussion that followed was remarkably disjointed, indeed to the point almost of incoherence. It did not help that, initially, the Attorney-General was not present, and some misleading information was given out.[32] MacDonald, for example, said that Hastings had told him that he 'did not authorise the action'. Shortly afterwards, when Hastings appeared, he gave his account of the origin of the case and stated quite clearly: 'Responsibility rests on me and I take it'. T.J.'s notes include other

[30] *Autobiography*, p.236. 'Nothing that I ever began was I ever allowed to finish; and nothing was ever finished until something else was begun'.

[31] F.H. Newark, loc.cit., pp.27–30. *Autobiography*, pp.238–9. See also Hastings' account (*Parl. Deb. Commons*, Vol.177, cols.602–7) in the debate on 8 October 1924.

instances of confused thinking or at least confusing comment. Parmoor, the Lord President, for example, appeared to change his mind each time he spoke. It may well be true, as has been suggested,[33] that Jones was below form secretarially that day. On the other hand, it must have been extraordinarily difficult to keep a detailed coherent record given apparently unhindered interjection by ministers whose knowledge of the facts of the case was, to say the least, imperfect. What is not seriously in doubt by anyone without an axe to grind is that the official minutes, terse as was then customary, written by Jones the next day accurately expressed the sense of the discussion and the conclusions that had been agreed. It is pertinent that, in accordance with normal practice, before they were finally printed the minutes were circulated in draft form to ministers and none of them had made any objection or suggested an amendment. In the light of subsequent events, the crucial section for consideration is as follows:

> After considerable discussion of the procedure which led to action being taken in the Courts without the knowledge of the Cabinet or the Prime Minister, the Cabinet agreed –
> (a) That no prosecution of a political character should be undertaken without the prior sanction of the Cabinet being obtained.
> (b) That in the particular case under review the course indicated by the Attorney-General should be adopted.[34]

On 13 September when Campbell appeared before the magistrates again, Travers Humphreys, the Treasury Counsel, offered no evidence and, perhaps unwisely, said that since proceedings had been initiated 'it had been represented' that the words published in the *Workers Weekly* had no seditious intent and were merely a comment upon the use of military force in industrial disputes. He added that it had been easier to accept the assertion that there had been no malicious intent because the defendant was 'a man of excellent character with an admirable war record'. The form of words used, especially the construction 'it had been represented', gave an opening for further parliamentary challenge by the opposition parties, who had already alleged in earlier exchanges that there had been political interference with the course of justice. Meantime, in successive editions, the *Workers Weekly* exulted over the triumph it claimed to have achieved over its capitalist enemies, and it was evident from *The Times* that a full-scale

[33] F.H. Newark, loc.cit., pp.36–7; S. Roskill, op.cit., II, 377.
[34] *WD*, I, 287, 290–1.

attempt to embarrass the government would be made when Parliament reassembled in September.[35]

These events, of course, gave T.J. no cause for concern. MacDonald, however, was naturally deeply worried and anxiety brought out the worst in him. In self-defence he now resorted to shabby trickery: evasions, half-truths and bare-faced lying that left some of his Cabinet colleagues aghast.[36] He began also to look for scapegoats. He fastened first on T.J. On 22 September MacDonald challenged the accuracy of T.J.'s Cabinet minute of 6 August regarding the *Workers Weekly,* particularly Conclusion (b) which related to the withdrawal of the prosecution, and he required that a note to that effect should be placed in the Cabinet file. MacDonald also claimed later in October that he had not seen the minutes in draft form and thus had not approved their accuracy.[37] This looks suspiciously like the setting up of a prepared position to which the Prime Minister, *in extremis,* could fall back. MacDonald was under increasing pressure as T.J.'s account makes clear.

All the perturbation had its origin in answers given by the Attorney-General (Sir Patrick Hastings) and by the P.M. to questions put to them in the House of Commons on 30 September – answers which, to put it mildly, were lacking in complete candour. The question put by Sir Kingsley Wood to the Prime Minister was, 'Whether any directions were given by him, or with his sanction, to the Director of Public Prosecutions to withdraw the proceedings against Mr. Campbell, the Editor of the *Workers Weekly,* and whether he received any intimation that he would be personally required to give evidence on behalf of the Defendant at the hearing?' The Prime Minister replied, 'I was not consulted regarding either the institution or the subsequent withdrawal of these proceedings. The first notice of the prosecution which came to my knowledge was in the Press. I never advised its withdrawal, but left the whole matter to the discretion of the Law Officers, where that discretion properly rests. I never received any intimation, nor even a hint, that I should be asked to give evidence. That also came to my attention when the falsehood appeared in the Press.' That, in Hankey's words, was 'a bloody lie'. When I heard it, as I did, in the House, a shiver went down my spine.'[38]

[35] *The Times* (14 & 15 August). *Workers Weekly* (23 August).

[36] As an illustration of MacDonald's conveniently selective memory, he told the King (H. Nicolson, *King George V: His Life and Reign* (1952), p.398): 'I knew nothing about it until I saw it in the newspapers'. After the cabinet meeting on 6 August he said (*WD*, I, 287): 'First I heard [of it] was in the House of Commons'.

[37] S. Roskill, op.cit., II, 377–8. *WD*, I, 290–1, 292, 296.

[38] Ibid., I, 296. S. Roskill (II, 376) says that as Hankey was not given to such language it is obvious 'he was outraged'.

MacDonald was especially concerned to dispute the accuracy of the minute because, as J.H. Thomas admitted to T.J. on 3 October, 'the Opposition had somehow got hold of the Cabinet Minute' and, thus outflanked, MacDonald had simply lied.[39]

T.J. was unaware of MacDonald's challenge to his competence until 2 October. He promptly showed his rough notes of the Cabinet meeting to Hankey and Rupert Howarth of the secretariat who agreed that 'on the evidence before them the Minute was, if anything, an understatement'. It is of interest too that Hankey, who had a phenomenal memory for detail, could not say in what respect MacDonald claimed the minute was inaccurate, nor was a clear answer given to the question later.[40] Hankey was soon able to dispose of MacDonald's complaint that he had not seen the minute in draft form. The Prime Minister's slipperiness was no match for the careful procedures Hankey had established at the Cabinet Office. It could fairly be argued that MacDonald was often under great pressure and may have failed to read the minute properly. If so, it was not for want of care on T.J.'s part.

> Ministers were about to disperse [Hankey wrote to the Prime Minister on 2 October]. We felt it important to issue the draft minutes in order that they might be checked by members, if possible, before their final dispersal. Mr. Jones, however, was rather anxious about the particular minute relating to the *Workers Weekly,* and he handed me a note, timed 11.40am [7 August] in the following terms:
>
> 'Secretary,
> For Prime Minister's approval. If he cannot look at all [the minutes] perhaps he would look at No.5 *(Workers Weekly).*'

Hankey went on later in the letter to say: 'I do not think there is the smallest doubt that I did show you the minute'. And there was one final conclusive piece of evidence: the existence of a special docket of due procedure.

> I have on file [said Hankey] a duplicate of the notice which accompanied the Minutes. It is the normal notice for an occasion on which the Prime Minister has seen the draft, and is couched in the following terms:

[39] *WD,* I, 293, 297. The breach of security was hardly surprising: 'in the Admiralty it [the minute] was "Roneoed", i.e. multiplied'.

[40] D. Marquand's attempt (*Ramsay MacDonald* (1977), pp.368–9) to put a decent gloss on MacDonald's behaviour in this matter is ingenious but not very convincing, especially the weight put on the will-o'-the-wisp of a supposed letter of apology from Campbell.

'The attached draft Conclusions are circulated by direction of the Prime Minister. It is requested that any correction may be communicated to the Secretary not later than 12 Noon on Friday, 8 August 1924.'

No corrections were received. The fact that this form of notice was issued is a proof that I was satisfied that you had read and approved the draft Minutes.

I would draw your attention to the form of the above notice. It invites every member of the Cabinet to send corrections. The Distribution List shows that it was sent, together with the Minute on the *Worker's Weekly*, to the Attorney-General and the Solicitor-General. Neither of them criticised the Minute, nor did any member of the Cabinet.

It is very doubtful therefore if MacDonald's challenge to the minute written by T.J. would have been of much assistance to the Prime Minister in the event of a subsequent official inquiry of the kind proposed later in Parliament.[41] But the more immediate danger to MacDonald was in Parliament. The Prime Minister's response to questions on the Campbell case in the Commons on 30 September was considered unsatisfactory; the Conservatives had proposed a motion of censure on the government and the Liberals put forward an amendment demanding the appointment of a select committee of inquiry. It appears from the Attorney-General's *Autobiography* that, at the eleventh hour, MacDonald also tried to use Hastings as a scapegoat. Shortly before 8 October, when the motions were to be debated, Hastings, who had picked up a rumour that MacDonald was considering calling on him to resign, asked the Prime Minister in the presence of J.H. Thomas if this were true. MacDonald was evasive; Thomas insisted that he should answer the question and, after some further equivocation, MacDonald admitted that he had conceived 'an ingenious idea' that would solve all difficulties: Hastings would shoulder all the responsibility and resign his office and his parliamentary seat. MacDonald would then insist on his seeking re-election and every Cabinet member would demonstrate his confidence in Hastings by appearing to speak on his behalf during the by-election. 'Mac, that's a damned dirty trick', Jimmy Thomas is alleged to have said in a sanitized version suitable for publication. Shamefaced,

---

[41] *WD*, I, 290–7. Ultimately, after some pointed comment by T.J. to Hankey, the note to the effect that the Prime Minister had challenged the accuracy of the minute, although drafted, was never put on record.

MacDonald apologized and asked that the matter should be forgotten.[42]

The Prime Minister had to endure even greater humiliation during the debate in the Commons on 8 October when he made an apology for misleading the House earlier; his explanation was lame and unconvincing, he was subjected to severe cross-examination and some crude jeering. Tom Jones, who was present, thought that MacDonald 'fenced with skill' but in so doing was once again economical with the truth. The Cabinet had decided in advance to treat the debate as a matter of confidence. Ultimately, the Conservatives decided to support the Liberal amendment, which was carried by 364 votes to 198. The next day MacDonald asked the King for a dissolution.[43]

Tom Jones seems to have believed that the King should refuse a dissolution, 'until he has exhausted all alternatives, i.e. seen Baldwin and Asquith'. Esher, to whom this opinion was offered, replied:

> You may rely upon the King listening to the best advice. Also you can rely upon his own good sense . . . During 14 years of a disturbed reign he has so far made no mistakes, and has not alienated any body of politicians. That is a fine record. So there is no need to worry.[44]

The King, who had formed the opinion that neither of the other two parties 'could form a government that could last', granted a dissolution and the Labour government shortly came to an end.[45]

Despite the heavy criticism that MacDonald received, a good deal of it justified as in the episode detailed here, some people who were well placed to judge, Haldane and Esher, for example, considered that he had done well in the premiership.[46] Tom Jones, too, conceded that MacDonald 'proved to be very capable' as

---

[42] *The Autobiography of Sir Patrick Hastings* (1948), pp.240–2. One of MacDonald's craftier devices, according to a hostile Treasury source, was to instruct his secretary, Miss Rosenberg, to sign letters the Prime Minister had dictated 'so as to provide a way of escape' if necessary. He always looked for a scapegoat when in trouble. T.J., Class Z (Diary, 15 October 1924), p.173.

[43] *Parl. Deb. Commons*, Vol.177, Cols.512–517, WD, I, 297. Macneil Weir, op.cit., pp.177–83. Hastings displayed great skill in cut and thrust exchanges in the Chamber. On the other hand, as T.J.'s minute shows, he had been prepared to be rather too pliant in the Cabinet discussion on 6 August.

[44] Roskill (op.cit., II, 382) says, with some hesitation, that T.J.'s letter was written to Hankey. Esher's reply (T.J., Class W, Vol.6, No.30) makes it clear that he was the recipient, although Hankey may well have been sent a copy.

[45] MacDonald's diary entry in D. Marquand, op.cit., p.377.

[46] R.B. Haldane, *An Autobiography* (1929), pp.327–8. Esher's favourable comment is in the letter to T.J. cited above.

chairman of Cabinet meetings, although he was much less impressive and incisive in dealing with deputations and too aloof and reclusive to inspire team spirit among his colleagues. T.J., who was businesslike to his fingertips, believed that MacDonald wasted precious time on footling activities, and had no idea how to make good use of secretaries.[47] Indeed, Jones believed that MacDonald had paid a heavy price because of the inadequacy of his personal staff.

This was particularly evident during the election campaign in late October 1924, when, most unfairly in many ways, MacDonald, who was in his constituency of Aberavon, incurred widespread criticism from his party for his supposed mishandling of the Zinoviev Letter episode. This crude attempt by White Russian *émigrés* to embroil Britain and the Soviet Union was used for party purposes by some shady elements on the right in politics to the disadvantage of the Labour party in the election.[48] Many others, Liberal and Conservative, were genuinely convinced that the Zinoviev Letter was authentic and its publication simply confirmed a belief, strengthened earlier by the government's willingness to guarantee a loan to Russia and the Campbell case, that, as a Conservative candidate asserted, 'a vote for the Socialists is a vote for the Communists'.[49] The probability is however that this unsavoury ploy did no more than accentuate a tide already running in favour of the Conservative party. The Liberals, short of money and fielding many fewer candidates, made only a weak challenge. The result was an overwhelming victory for the Conservatives with 419 seats to Labour's 151. The Liberals were reduced to a mere 40. T.J. and his wife hedged their bets in the election. With some hesitation, as the candidate was weak, they voted Labour in Hampstead. T.J. cast his Glasgow University vote for the Liberal candidate and Rene hers at Cambridge for the historian J.R.M. Butler, who stood unsuccessfully as an Independent.[50]

Inevitably, the Labour Cabinet, before it finally surrendered office, discussed the election and the Zinoviev affair in detail; T.J. acted as secretary. There was so much angry recrimination and constant interruption that 'it was impossible to give a coherent narrative'. This time MacDonald behaved with dignity and was not looking for scapegoats; indeed, he avoided attacking Foreign Office

[47] *A Diary With Letters,* pp.xxiii–xxxii. But see p.276 n.42 above.
[48] *WD,* I, 300. S. Roskill, op.cit., II, 382–5, has an excellent account with full documentation.
[49] R.W. Lyman, *The First Labour Government* (1957), p.256.
[50] T.J., Class Z (Diary, 1924), p.174.

officials who, to put it no more strongly, had been deplorably remiss. It is clear from T.J.'s notes that he thought that MacDonald had been very badly served, not least because he had had no trusted aide at his side to assist him in dealing effectively with official business.[51]

Unlike some ardent spirits, T.J. had not expected the minority Labour government to establish 'the new Jerusalem in England's green and pleasant land'.[52] But he had warmly welcomed the government as at least an encouraging harbinger of social advance. He had certainly not expected that his personal experience of its ten months in office would be so uncomfortable. Perhaps most of all, he had missed the privileged intimacy he had enjoyed for several years with the Prime Minister of the day. Things, however, were soon to change. Some hours before he was formally invited to form a government, Baldwin sent for T.J., who received 'a most cordial, almost affectionate, welcome'. Baldwin began immediately to discuss the membership of his cabinet. 'What I want from you', he said, 'is a Minister of Education'. T.J. promptly suggested Lord Eustace Percy, who in due course was appointed. It is clear that Baldwin also accepted T.J.'s suggestion that Birkenhead should go to the India Office, and offered the Ministry of Labour to Sir Robert Horne on Jones's advice. Horne, however, refused. T.J. also tried to persuade Baldwin to appoint Walter Elliot as Secretary for Scotland. Elliot, an exceptionally promising young man, was a member of the Romney Street Group. This was altogether too daring a proposal for Baldwin, as he confessed, but Elliot was at least appointed to a subordinate place in the Scottish Office.[53]

But of obviously greater interest, and of particular importance because they were soon to be working closely together in the difficult aftermath of the General Strike, are Jones's comments on Churchill's claims to office. 'I thought of putting him in India', Baldwin said. T.J. was horror-stricken. 'For heaven's sake don't do that', he said, 'I have seen him lose his head at critical moments in the Irish business, and but for L.G.'s intervention, we should have had bloodshed on the Border more than once'. With the *Raj* now under permanent challenge, the India Office was no place for Churchill. On the other hand, he ought not to be left outside the Cabinet; he could go to the Board of Trade or the Colonial Office. It did not much matter, in T.J.'s opinion, so long as Churchill was

---

[51] *WD*, I, 298–301.
[52] Ibid., I, 271, 273–4.
[53] Ibid., I, 301–4.

not sent to one of the more politically sensitive ministries. 'Shove him in the Army or Navy – Give him the one with the most work'.[54]

In the end, as Amery said enviously, Churchill got 'a fatted calf' to his great delight. At the suggestion of Neville Chamberlain, who, surprisingly, did not consider himself yet up to it, Churchill became Chancellor of the Exchequer. A fortnight later Churchill sent for T.J.: 'I understand you talk a lot with the P.M.', said the Chancellor, 'and that you give him advice – good advice, I have no doubt'. Churchill went on to outline his ideas about government policy: 'I was all for the Liberal measures of social reform in the old days and I want to push the same sort of measures now'. He said he was going to concentrate on housing and pensions and asked T.J. 'to make them stand out' in the next speech that he wrote for Baldwin.[55]

Over the next two years T.J. was involved almost daily in offering counsel to Baldwin and some other senior ministers often on matters of the greatest importance. However, there was always time for other things. At the end of November he and his wife went down to St Nicholas-at-Wade in Kent to approve the final stages of the construction of their new cottage, which they began to occupy intermittently soon afterwards.[56] A week later he dined agreeably with his friends the Yates-Thompsons at Portman Square and was shown some of his host's rare books, including a fine Greek lexicon printed in 1499. This sort of occasion was sheer delight to T.J., for such a book, where 'the materials are right and the proportions are right is', he said later, 'a joy for ever'.[57]

Shortly afterwards, in June, he was able to gratify his aesthetic appetite even more fully. Gwen Davies of Gregynog asked him to go to the International Book Fair at Florence in search of ideas for the Gregynog Press. James Morton and Ernest Rhys accompanied him. The Fair did not come up to expectations and it was 'excruciatingly hot', but Florence was enchanting. 'We were thrilled by it', he wrote to a friend. 'Have seen no where so much beauty in the shape of man's handiwork in one square mile . . . You long to have lived in 1500'.

[54] Ibid., I, 302.

[55] J. Barnes and D. Nicholson (eds.), *The Leo Amery Diaries* (1980), I, 389-90. *WD*, I, 303, 307.

[56] This comfortable additional home, linked by a good rail service to Victoria, became increasingly important in the life of the family. A maid, 'slow but reliable', was installed and Rene began to spend more and more time there. T.J. loved 'the peace of it all' and the sea air which was 'delicious'. T.J., Class Z (Diary, 1924), p.194. Morton MSS GD 326/86/1. Bangor MS 19537.

[57] *WD*, I, 308. 'The Gregynog Press', *WO*, XV, 249–50.

And he relished the chance to see so many magnificent pictures and pieces of sculpture in such a setting.

What these people did in a single city from about 1250 to 1550 is most astonishing [he wrote from Italy to his sister Liz]. I am afraid our achievements in Wales in all the centuries of our history would occupy these people but a few months . . . When Michelangelo finished his 'David' these were the members of the committee appointed to decide on its position: Leonardo da Vinci, Perrigino, Lorenzo di Credi, Filippino Lippi, Botticelli and Andrea della Robbia. I should like to have been Secretary to that Cabinet . . . Tell PEW [Percy Watkins] he must come to see all this so that between us we may keep on trying to diminish Welsh 'complacency'.[58]

Percy Watkins, T.J.'s trusty lieutenant in south Wales, had been translated shortly before from the Welsh Department of the Ministry of Health to the secretaryship of the Welsh Department of the Board of Education. It was a characteristically well-planned operation; T.J. had made good use of the additional time provided by the delay in the retirement of Sir Alfred Davies, the incumbent Secretary. Jones followed up his initial suggestion that Watkins might succeed, by speaking to Morgan Jones, an influential Welsh official then at the Board of Education, 'to prepare the way'. Later he enlisted the support of Sir Arthur Robinson (Watkins's departmental chief at the Ministry of Health) who could thus be relied upon not to object to the transfer; finally, T.J. had two discussions on the subject with Lord Eustace Percy who, it will be remembered, had been appointed President of the Board at T.J.'s suggestion. Jones also made certain that Lloyd George, consulted by Eustace Percy as a matter of courtesy, would not object. 'I am wondering', Watkins wrote with mock innocence to T.J., 'whether you have had a hand in this pie?'. Early in 1925, Watkins was appointed Welsh Secretary at the Board of Education where he was ideally placed to support T.J.'s future plans for education in Wales.[59]

Soon after his return home from Florence T.J. was deeply involved once again in the complex problems of a coal industry. After a period of prosperity during 1923–4, explained largely by the temporary Franco-Belgian occupation of the Ruhr, the coal industry was in more serious troubles than ever. German and Polish

[58] Bangor MS 16163. T.J., Class X, Vol.I, No.84; Vol.7, Nos.138 and 139. The one jarring note in Florence was an undue military presence. 'Mounted soldiers prancing. Far too many in evidence here'.
[59] T.J., Class V, Vol.I, Nos.154-161.

competition in the export trade had become more formidable; a rise in wages which the miners had achieved in 1924, and the return to the gold standard in April 1925, made British coal exports even more uncompetitive on a falling international market. A joint investigation of the industry reluctantly agreed to in March by colliery owners and miners ended predictably in ill-tempered deadlock. Soon afterwards the employers announced the termination of the wage agreement of 1924 and offered new terms, to come into effect on 31 July 1925, which involved reductions in wage rates in all districts that were particularly severe in the export areas. The miners rejected every proposed alteration in their working conditions. The government set up a Court of Inquiry under H.P. Macmillan, the Scottish advocate, which remarkably produced a report within eleven days. Its conclusions too were ignored by the miners and rejected out of hand by the employers. A nationwide stoppage looked inevitable. Moreover, it appeared that it would not be confined to the coal industry for the TUC, fearing a general attack on wages, resolved to support the miners, and to give point to this the railwaymen, transport workers and seamen's unions announced an embargo on the movement of coal from 31 July.[60]

In these circumstances, the government could not stand aside, much as it would have preferred to do so. Tom Jones first discussed the impending coal crisis with Baldwin on 9 July. In T.J.'s opinion there were two main objectives: to effect an immediate settlement to keep the men at work after 31 July, and, in the longer term, to make whatever changes were necessary to ensure the future of the industry. 'To attempt the first without tackling the second', he said, 'would only be to postpone the root trouble to another day'. Baldwin seemed to be prepared to accept a fairly substantial restructuring of the industry by district and was apparently even willing to buy out the royalty owners whom he regarded as parasites. However, he was not prepared to pay a subsidy to support the industry until it had been reformed. T.J. was, if anything, even more strongly opposed to a subsidy: it was inefficient, difficult to work fairly and would 'involve complicated supervision'.[61] And he

[60] B. Supple, *The History of The British Coal Industry* (Oxford, 1987), pp.220–6. M.W. Kirby, op.cit., pp.66–72. H.P. Macmillan, *A Man of Law's Tale* (1952), pp.188-9.

[61] T.J. certainly had no objection in principle to state aid or intervention. On the contrary, at the same meeting, in order to create work for idle shipbuilders, he suggested to Baldwin that the government should secretly finance the construction of twenty or thirty tramp steamers which could be disposed of to private owners when, as he somewhat rashly assumed probable, trade revived.

believed that the Macmillan Inquiry report, which had come down broadly on the miners' side, was unhelpful as it would 'put up the backs of the owners' and encourage the men in their intransigence. T.J. sat in on the separate discussions with the owners and miners on 29 July; 'desperately heavy going all day', as he described the meetings. T.J. considered that Bridgeman, Steel-Maitland and Lane-Fox, the ministers directly involved in the negotiation, were inadequate and that Baldwin became more and more harassed and helpless as the day wore on.[62]

Ultimately, faced with the prospect of a large-scale stoppage, for which the government was ill prepared, 'that', as he said later, 'would have caused an infinite amount of misery' in the country, Baldwin gave way and persuaded the Cabinet to agree to the payment of a subsidy of ten million pounds. This would enable the industry to maintain existing wage rates and hours of work until May 1926. In return the employers withdrew their lock-out notices, the unions called off the embargo on the movement of coal, and both sides agreed to co-operate with a Royal Commission which was to carry out a full-scale inquiry into the coal industry and make recommendations for its improvement.[63]

> The strike is averted at a price [T.J. wrote to James Morton on 31 July], and I don't want to see another week like this for some considerable time. I am going to seek some sleep. This mining conflict has been one of the most difficult I've been mixed up in. Neither side would yield and negotiating anything was hardly possible. Unfortunately the P.M., off his own bat, some weeks ago dropped hints of a subsidy in almost a casual fashion and one could not get away from it.[64] It was also certain that we should have had railwaymen and dockers out, and that would be a different proposition from 1920 and 1921 when we had D.O.R.A. and troops and lorries galore. We have bought time. Whether we can make ministers use it swiftly remains to be seen. It won't be from lack of being told.

T.J. added that the Minority Movement, in part Communist-inspired, had increased its influence over the trade unions and he had been 'struck with the deterioration in the quality of the men's representatives'. The firebrand A.J. Cook was evidently considered a poor replacement for Frank Hodges. Moreover, unfortunately, there was 'no first class personality among the owners'.[65]

[62] *WD*, I, 322–5.

[63] *Parl. Deb. Commons*, Vol.187, col.1591. M.W. Kirby, *The British Coal Mining Industry 1870–1947* (1977), pp.72–4.

[64] Jones seems to be alone in suggesting that Baldwin was hoist with his own petard in this way over the subsidy.

[65] Morton MSS. 31 July 1925. GD 3261/86/1.

T.J. also played some part in the selection of the members of the Royal Commission. The initial choice as chairman was Earl Grey, the former Foreign Secretary, whose name had been suggested to T.J. by Haldane and passed on to Baldwin. Grey however declined on grounds of poor health. Haldane had also suggested the banker Sir Herbert Lawrence as a member and in due course he was appointed. Jones seems to have successfully blocked the nomination of one Peacock, another banker, who had a reputation as a strike breaker in Spain and would thus have excited the miners' hostility. But he was unable to carry his useful suggestion that, on the model of the Poor Law Commission of 1909, assistant commissioners should be appointed to conduct detailed investigations in the districts.[66]

The events of Friday 31 July 1925 looked like a resounding defeat for the government which was particularly humiliating for the Prime Minister, who appeared to have been forced into a volte face over the subsidy by trade union power. 'Red Friday', exulted A.J. Cook, 'wiped out the stain of Black Friday and brought joy to the heart of every worker'.[67] But, as T.J. and Cook were well aware, the real struggle lay ahead. Meantime, Sir Herbert Samuel, the distinguished Liberal, agreed with some reluctance to be Chairman of the Royal Commission, which was finally completed by the addition of Sir William Beveridge, Director of the London School of Economics, Kenneth Lee, a cotton manufacturer, and Sir Herbert Lawrence, the man suggested to T.J. by Haldane. The selection of the Commissioners seems to have been marked by an attempt to achieve as much neutrality, at least initially, as was possible on a question that all too often prompted uncompromising opinions, perhaps in the hope this time of avoiding the kind of differences that divided the Sankey Commission. Appointed in September 1925, the Samuel Commission published its report on 11 March 1926. T.J. had been optimistic about its outcome; at least he told Stamfordham, the King's Private Secretary, in January that he thought there was a 'good chance of our coming through without a general strike'. He was of course mistaken.[68]

The General Strike of May 1926 was the first direct collision between the two nations into which Britain was divided socially. It was fraught with great danger and to this day is the subject of fierce

[66] *WD*, I, 327–9.
[67] *The Nine Days: the Story of the General Strike told by the Miners' Secretary* (reprinted 1971, Cardiff), p.1.
[68] *WD*, II, 5.

controversy. Tom Jones was closely involved throughout; indeed his account published in the *Whitehall Diaries* is perhaps the most reliable, certainly the most detailed record available of this infinitely complex, dramatic episode. His narrative is vitiated only by a discreet silence about some of his own efforts to promote a settlement. In the General Strike, and more especially in the long agonizing aftermath until the miners' strike ended, T.J. was a shrewd observer privy to the most confidential discussions. He was also an active participant, consulted daily by the Prime Minister or his proxy and trusted by some of the leading figures on either side, who operated for much of the time discreetly behind the scenes and wielded an influence that amounted on occasion to a substantial power which was not fully recognized at the time.

The Samuel Commission Report was reasonably optimistic about the long-term prospects of a restructured, smaller coal industry when, as was expected, trade conditions improved. But in the short run the industry was faced with an economic crisis that demanded immediate action to reduce working costs. The Commissioners rejected nationalization and insisted that the subsidy should not be extended beyond the authorized term; they recommended the amalgamation, by compulsion in certain circumstances, of some collieries, and dismissed the employers' demand for a lengthening of the working day and the abandonment of national wage agreements. The Commissioners also recommended the nationalization of coal royalties. However, discounting the subsidy, the hard fact was that 73 per cent of the coal produced in the last quarter of 1925 was produced at a loss and only a reduction of miners' wages would enable the industry to avoid the impending disaster. Defying all recent experience, the Commissioners expressed their confident hope of an effective partnership between employers and miners in the future.[69]

Tom Jones thought that, at first sight, the Samuel Report was 'fair and persuasive', but on closer inspection he considered it to be either 'nebulous or ambiguous at crucial points', especially on the question of wages and the national minimum.[70] The government, which wanted to minimize its involvement, announced that, despite reservations, it would accept the Report if the coal-owners and coal-miners also did so without qualification. This half-hearted lead, if such it can be called, was rejected by both sides, who promptly took up their traditional entrenched positions in negotiations during April into which the government inevitably was drawn. T.J., of

[69] *Report of the Royal Commission on the Coal Industry 1925 (Cmd 2600)*, pp.232–7.
[70] *WD*, II, 49.

course, was heavily involved. It is not possible here to examine the negotiations in all their tortuous detail, but it is necessary to indicate Jones's general attitude to the participants.

T.J. had never had much sympathy for the coal-owners and their leaders in the Mining Association whose policy, particularly their apparent belief that a lengthy stoppage was 'a wholesome form of blood-letting', he thought immeasurably stupid. T.J. described Evan Williams, spokesman for the owners, as 'an insignificant little man', a practised obstructionist, whose first lieutenant, Sir Adam Nimmo, 'one of the greatest stumbling-blocks in the path of peace', regarded compromise as a synonym for sin. Of course T.J. knew coal-owners, David Davies, D.R. Llewellyn, Lord Wimborne, for example, who were, as he said, 'decent and progressive', but unfortunately they were a small minority, unable effectively to influence the official policy of the Mining Association. On 21 April T.J., who in confidence was kept informed about the attitude of coal-owners in south Wales by his friend Sir Alfred Cope, came to the conclusion, as he told Baldwin, that the owners 'were spoiling for a fight'. Earlier T.J. had argued that, if necessary, the government 'must be prepared to quarrel' with the coal-owners who, at a lengthy meeting later, showed, he said, 'not the slightest sign that they appreciated the need for reforming their business'.[71]

Tom Jones's sympathy with the miners generally was well established, although latterly rather less strong, but he was as critical of some of their leaders, particularly Herbert Smith and A.J. Cook, as he was of most of the coal-owners. T.J. said that the miners' spokesmen too were obstructionists who understood the dire economic position of the industry but refused to admit the truth and shirked their responsibility to give the men a constructive lead. Smith and Cook, said Jones, had no real grasp of the problems involved in reorganizing the industry. They 'exaggerated the probable savings' that it could effect and, meantime, used the word 'reorganization' as an incantation to postpone the evil day when they would have to tell the men 'that wages had to come down or hours be extended, or both'. T.J. probably underestimated Herbert Smith and the difficulties he faced, but it is easy to understand how, given their very different assumptions about public affairs, he came to believe that he could not 'deal privately with Cook' as he had been accustomed to do formerly with Hodges and J.H. Thomas.[72]

[71] Ibid., II, 9, 12, 16, 19, 37, 50. T.J., Class Z (Diary, 1926), pp.8, 40–1. Osbert Sitwell, *Laughter in the Next Room* (1949), p.216, for T.J. and Wimborne.
[72] *WD*, II, 12–18, 49–51.

Tom Jones's attitude to the TUC, which was drawn in to conduct the negotiation at the end of April, was ambivalent. He profoundly distrusted the 'ardent spirits' in the labour movement who for years had 'toyed' with syndicalist ideas and, meantime, in preparation for a general strike, had set up 'unstable alliances' of some of the bigger, more militant unions, and sought to concentrate power in 'a central executive' which in some engineered emergency could ignore the need for wider consultation with their union members. Experience was to show T.J. that this supposed 'overriding authority', the recently established General Council of the TUC, was more impressive on paper than in action. But Jones knew very well from the outset that most of the TUC leaders were cautious moderate men who had no time for extremist action; the revolutionary cadre (if such indeed it was) on the TUC amounted, on one calculation, to no more than three out of twenty-six leading members.[73]

During April the government's negotiations with owners and miners got nowhere. As T.J. wrote years later: 'The masters wanted profits and the men wages and hours guaranteed on a falling market. So long as the debate persisted on this level the problem was insoluble'.[74] At one point, in an interminable futile meeting with the owners about wages, T.J. was driven to doodling satire to relieve his frustration.

> *Colliery Wages for 1926*
> $2\frac{1}{2}$% on the Danegeld paid in 960, 50% on the rateable value in, Domesday Book.
> Less $2\frac{1}{2}$% on the Ship Money. Multiplied by the demand ratio existing between a rose noble and a spade guinea.[75]

At the time, out of personal loyalty to Baldwin, T.J. made no open criticism of the government's unwillingness to give a strong lead when the Samuel Report was published. Subsequently, however, he wrote:

> the situation demanded an immediate political and authoritative decision but it was not forthcoming. Instead, the Prime Minister dallied with compromises, in the morning with the employers, in the

---

[73] Ibid., II, 43, 56. The calculation was that of the young left-wing academic H.J. Laski, who was one of 'a group' of T.J.'s 'friends' who worked to move the TUC 'towards pacific measures'.

[74] *The Times*, 15 December 1947.

[75] 28 April 1926. T.J., Class C, Vol.8, No.26.

afternoon with the perfervid and unaccommodating Cook, and in the evening with the Trades Union Executive wavering to and fro.

It was hardly surprising that the country stumbled into the General Strike. Indeed, T.J. believed that Baldwin had been rescued from a paralysis induced by indecision and a fear of the extremists in his own party and cabinet only by the TUC's unwise resort to the bluff of the general strike in support of the miners.[76] Jones was critical of the government in other respects. It made no attempt, as it should have done, to get the Samuel Commissioners to clarify the ambiguities in their Report. It was never, as it claimed, even-handed in its dealings with the two sides. Although Baldwin himself was always friendly, as T.J. said:

> It is impossible not to feel the contrast between the reception which Ministers give to a body of owners and a body of miners. Ministers are at ease at once with the former, they are friends jointly exploring a situation.[77]

Before, during and after the General Strike, Jones did his best to counter this powerful political and class bias. Recognizing early on that the owners' easy access to ministers gave them 'considerable pull', T.J. tried to persuade Baldwin later in April to see A.J. Cook or Tawney in the seclusion of Chequers. He failed, but did manage to arrange a useful secret discussion there between the Prime Minister and Arthur Pugh, President of the TUC. Jones was in close touch throughout with Labour headquarters in Eccleston Square. His line of communication was his friend J.J. Mallon, Warden of Toynbee Hall, who wrote later that 'night and day' T.J. 'plied [him] with suggestions calculated to end hostilities'. And, according to Mallon, it was T.J. who elicited the promise from Baldwin 'that whatever happened the government would not victimize anyone or make bad blood'.[78] This was a promise more easily made than kept, as it turned out. But in the same vein, when he heard of 'some dark designs', prompted by Churchill, to impound trade union funds during the strike, T.J. immediately 'held up the red light to the P.M.' and managed to get the scheme dropped. And a day later, T.J. 'entreated' Baldwin to pause before introducing a punitive trade union bill in the dangerously charged atmosphere of the last days

[76] *The Times,* 15 December 1947.
[77] *WD,* II, 19, 37, 49.
[78] Ibid., II, 9, 22. Mallon in the *Sunday Times,* 16 October 1955.

of the General Strike. When Churchill, who months before had advocated a bill of that kind, joined the discussion, T.J. continued to plead 'with fierce energy for delay'. It had some effect; Churchill, at first privately, 'cursed' Jones, but then wrote to Baldwin counselling caution. T.J. did not stop there: he mobilized support for postponement of the bill from Warren Fisher, Hankey, Eyres-Monsell, the Conservative Chief Whip, Walter Elliot and others, and arranged a meeting with A.J. Balfour, Lord President of the Council, at which he succeeded in enlisting his influential assistance. T.J. also sought by indirect means to invoke the intervention of the King. There is little doubt that this pressure played an important part in delaying the introduction of the bill at a time when it could well have provoked a dangerous response.[79]

T.J.'s purpose all along was to support and strengthen the hand of the moderates in the trade union movement to enable them to defeat the Left and bring the strike to an end on terms: that is, acceptance of the Samuel Report, arbitration on disputed points, and renewal of the subsidy for a fortnight and other limited financial assistance to the coal industry. When Baldwin showed some interest in this scheme, T.J. argued for it with all his might. Immediately afterwards he tried to win over Churchill and had 'one of the fiercest and hottest interviews' of his life. He was assailed 'with a cataract of boiling eloquence': 'We [are] at war', shouted the Chancellor; 'you must have nerve'. Jones shouted back that he did not lack resolution but that 'something more than nerve' was required. A conciliatory gesture by Baldwin would assist the moderate trade union leaders who had no revolutionary purpose. T.J. added that Arthur Pugh and J.H. Thomas were as loyal to the State as Churchill. 'This infuriated him', Jones wrote, 'he broke out into a fresh tempest and I felt tossed about like a small boat in an angry sea'. Churchill departed in a furious huff. Oddly enough, in a reversal of the natural order, this was the storm before the calm in Jones's relations with Churchill, as will appear.[80]

T.J. strongly disapproved of Churchill's inflammatory journalism in the *British Gazette,* 'a paper for suburbia not the working man', as he called it. But on the central constitutional issue Jones 'stood absolutely firm'. He believed that few, if any, of the trade union leaders were prepared to push the Strike to its logical revolutionary conclusion, but 'in view of the temper of the most assertive elements in the trade union world', the General Strike, 'or something like it, . . . had to come'. And it was well to get it over

---

[79] *WD*, II, 43–6. K. Middlemas and J. Barnes, op.cit., p.415.
[80] Ibid., II, 40–1.

and rid the body politic once and for all of dangerous infection. During the strike, T.J. was in constant contact with J.H. Thomas, his favourite trade unionist, whose many personal failings he always overlooked, whom he considered to be the ablest spokesman for Labour and the most effective opponent of extremist trade union action.[81] Thomas had played some part in encouraging Sir Herbert Samuel, who had been deeply disturbed by the course of events, to intervene once more. The government curtly rejected Samuel's offer to mediate, but he went ahead with private talks with members of the TUC and eventually produced the Samuel Memorandum, his better second thoughts on the problems of the coal industry. Released now perhaps from the need to maintain a united front with the other Commissioners, and learning something from recent events, Samuel's proposals were more precisely defined than those of the Royal Commission. He suggested an extension of the subsidy for a 'reasonable period' while negotiations continued, that wage revision should be conditional on the introduction of effective measures of re-organization, and he now conceded that the notion that 'owners and miners alone' could settle their industrial differences was pious nonsense. T.J. was of the opinion that 'Had the Samuel *Memorandum* . . . been embodied [in] the *Report* our troubles would have been fewer, and perhaps the General Strike itself would have been avoided'.[82]

This accords the Memorandum an exaggerated respect. However, it did have an important influence on the ending of the strike. The miners refused to look at it, but the TUC, exasperated by this intransigence, accepted it as a basis for reopening negotiations and calling off the General Strike. The TUC had maintained all along that it was engaged in an industrial dispute and that its actions did not represent a challenge to constitutional government. From the beginning the government insisted that the General Strike was illegal, a revolutionary attempt to subvert the constitution and override the will of the people. Neither of these versions was adequate. The fact was that each side had taken tenacious hold of part of the truth. But as a matter of practical politics the government showed itself the stronger and more determined. It refused to negotiate until the strike was called off unconditionally and the TUC, ultimately unwilling to attempt to break the deadlock

[81] Ibid., II, 33, 44, 53. And, of particular interest, O. Sitwell, op.cit., pp.216–38, and T.J. Add. MSS CC, Vol.I, No.61.

[82] The Samuel Memorandum, 10 May 1926. *Trade Union Documents*, ed. W. Milne-Bailey (1929), pp.348-50. *WD*, II, 49.

by extending the range of its action, surrendered with something like indecent haste. The formal announcement that the General Strike was over was read out to the press by T.J.

Not surprisingly, Jones felt 'overwhelmed' during the long weeks of crisis and, to make matters worse, the family was in the process of moving house at this time. Street Acre, the cottage at St Nicholas-at-Wade, was now the main residence. The large comfortable house at Hampstead Hill gardens had been put on the market in February and a flat at 68 Belsize Park, NW3, became the family's London house. Rene had to cope with the removal late in April virtually unaided. Eirene was given shelter at the home of a school friend; T.J., who had to be on hand during the strike, stayed with Geoffrey Fry, Baldwin's Private Secretary, during the emergency. However, he was at their new home over the weekend 9–11 May: 'I found Rene in the middle of the most awful muddle, with one livable room', T.J. told James Morton. 'The painters and other workers have joined the general strikers'.[83]

Although the General Strike was over, the problems of the coal industry remained. T.J. was soon heavily involved in the tragic aftermath of the miners' strike, which lasted for six months until exhaustion and privation put an end to a particularly bitter chapter in industrial history. The owners were determined to effect economies, the men equally resolute in defending living standards which they believed were already too low. The government havered uneasily between an ideological preference for non-intervention and its inability entirely to ignore the drastic social and economic consequences for the nation of the protracted struggle. Policy, therefore, became a matter of fits and starts.

When the General Strike ended, Baldwin's prestige was immense; he 'stood out', according to T.J., 'as the great national leader, steadfast and impartial', the embodiment, so it seemed, of calm good sense.[84] A month later his status had changed quite considerably:

> The impression I get from different people is that they think that the Premier is honest and intelligent but is not strong enough to follow the light he sees [a businessman wrote to Tom Jones]. He is very rapidly losing the great prestige which he gained at the end of the General

[83] T.J., Class W, Vol.17, No.136. 11 May. Morton MSS GD 326/86/1. In February T.J. was writing of 'the interminable illness of everybody at home' (T.J., Class W, Vol.12, No.250). In June their younger son, Elphin, had his appendix removed, which was not then quite the routine operation it became later. Bangor MSS 16164–6.

[84] *The Times,* 15 December 1943. *WD,* II, 53, 56.

Strike. Furthermore, Labour people feel that he is not holding the scales evenly, even after allowing for the mistakes and stupidities of the A.J. Cook type.[85]

Middlemas and Barnes have demonstrated in some detail that Baldwin did make a number of attempts in May-August to bring the miners' strike to an end by some sort of negotiated agreement.[86] Jones was involved in most of these efforts and it was T.J. who handled the detailed discussions with Haldane, Sir Walter Layton the economist, Lord Wimborne, Sir David Llewellyn, and B.S. Rowntree, who came forward with various well-intentioned proposals. Naturally, T.J. also had a sizeable correspondence with David Davies and his general manager Thomas Evans of the Ocean Coal Company. Evans, a hard-eyed economic man all too familiar with the difficulties of the coal export trade, wanted the government to leave owners and miners to reach a settlement 'with not the slightest hope of a further subsidy or interference' to complicate matters. David Davies, however, maintained that Baldwin should 'insist' on the establishment of permanent national 'arbitration tribunals' with power to enforce decisions, without which, in his opinion, there could be 'no finality' to any proposed settlement. D.D. made a vain attempt to persuade the south Wales owners to take a constructive initiative on these lines within the Mining Association.[87] Nothing came of any of these suggestions.

It was evident, too, that Baldwin was gradually losing patience, particularly with well-meaning interventions by church leaders. A deputation in June from the Industrial Christian Fellowship, which included T.J.'s friend Mallon, was coldly received. In July, a deputation of bishops made one of the Cabinet splutter with rage and prompted Baldwin to tell Tom Jones that he wished the prelates would 'go back to look after their flocks', their intervention simply assisted 'latent atheist bolsheviks like Cook' to retain power. T.J. was present at that meeting at which, he said, one of the deputation had made 'a very moving appeal' to the Prime Minister. Baldwin, however, had made his position clear: he was not disposed to budge. William Temple, the future Archbishop, wrote:

He says industry had been brought to expect public money whenever it howls and he's determined to end that . . . Plainly [Temple added] the

[85] W. Wallace, financial adviser to Rowntree and Co. T.J. Add. MSS CC, Vol.2, No.8.

[86] K. Middlemas and J. Barnes, op.cit., pp.418–34.

[87] T.J., Class W, Vol.6, Nos.116–121; Class C, Vol.2, Nos.2–8; Vol.8, No.76. *WD*, II, 61–2.

Government wish we would keep out of it and are disposed to say that
if we encourage the miners we prolong the Strike. They expect a break
fairly soon. But that is a 'war attitude' and is, I'm sure, not the most
right.[88]

The analogy with war was to occur to another worried observer
later.

T.J., who teasingly had told Baldwin 'not to let his head be
turned' by the extravagant praise heaped on him at the end of the
General Strike, thought that in August Baldwin was at the end of
his tether, feeling 'very sorry for himself', irritable, his judgement
'warped' by tiredness and 'frightfully impatient with Cook and
Co.'.[89] But the King, not surprisingly, was of the opinion that the
Prime Minister should not leave for his annual holiday at Aix-les-
Bains at that juncture. However, Waterhouse, Baldwin's Private
Secretary, conjured up a tame physician who 'played up splendidly'
and prescribed immediate rest for the Prime Minister, who went off
to Aix with the King's consent on 22 August. T.J. had been
genuinely concerned about Baldwin's condition and carefully
guarded his interests during his absence abroad. It is clear,
however, that Jones, while appreciating the Prime Minister's party
difficulties with an aggressive right wing powerfully vocal in the
Cabinet, was disappointed, as he said, circumspectly, many years
later, by Baldwin's 'temporizing, indeterminate policy of drift' in
the months after the General Strike, in the course of which he
forfeited his moral authority and allowed a settlement of 'the
nightmare' of the coal strike 'to go by default'.[90]

During Baldwin's absence abroad, the Cabinet Coal Committee
was chaired by Churchill. Mercifully, T.J.'s relations with the
Chancellor were now very much better. Indeed, during Baldwin's
absence they worked harmoniously together and their mutual
regard became more and more apparent. Churchill's attitude was
now very different. The Chancellor was seriously worried, as he told
Baldwin in June, about the effect on the already 'depleted
Exchequer' of the 'long and hideously costly delay' in settling the
miners' strike.[91] But even more important, his attitude was no
longer excessively, indeed absurdly, bellicose as it had been during

[88] Ibid., II, 63. F.A. Iremonger, *William Temple: his Life and Letters* (1948),
p.339.

[89] *WD*, II, 59, 63–4.

[90] *The Times*, 15 December 1943. *Diary with Letters*, Introduction, p.xxxiii.
Morton MSS, 21 September 1926. GD 326/86/1.

[91] M. Gilbert, *Winston Churchill 1922–39* (1976), V, 179.

the General Strike. 'Winston, strange to say', T.J. noted with relief on 13 May, 'is now for being generous'. Predictably, Churchill brought exceptional energy and great determination to his new role; T.J. warmly welcomed this injection of vigour into the negotiation. And although he considered that Churchill's mastery of the detail of the coal industry was less than complete and his personality all too often excited hostility, Jones was impressed with the Chancellor's performance as spokesman for the government. Reporting to Baldwin, T.J. said that Churchill's handling of a meeting with the miners on 26 August was 'admirably done', and his speech in the Commons on the coal debate four days later 'brilliant, dignified, conciliatory and fair'. T.J. was glad, too, to see that Churchill adopted a robust attitude towards the coal owners.[92] One of them, Lord Londonderry, thought that Jones was exerting a malign influence on the Chancellor in this respect: 'Tom Jones is dead against the owners' point of view because he is not of your or my political belief', Londonderry protested to Churchill on 11 September.[93]

In fact, Churchill understood Jones's role during Baldwin's second ministry very clearly. 'He is the democratic soul of the Party', Churchill told his wife, who was puzzled about Jones's precise function. More explicitly, some days later, Churchill said that T.J. was the 'thyroid gland of the Cabinet, supplying the organism with secretions not otherwise provided by the Central Office or party machinery'. T.J. thoroughly enjoyed two overnight visits he made at this time to Chartwell, Churchill's country home, apart from the presence on the first occasion of the unpleasant Professor F.A. Lindemann, Churchill's scientific adviser, a dinosaur on social questions, who seemed to regard all miners and some other working people as 'a species of sub-humans'. T.J. countered with, for once, the language of the extreme left. But he was intrigued and impressed by Churchill 'the brilliant and incessant talker' whose imagery was so vivid, who so effortlessly recalled the fascinating detail of so many great events. T.J.'s relations with him were now agreeably friendly and straightforward. Indeed, so much so that Jones, who longed for an end to the miners' strike, but nevertheless hoped, 'for personal and party reasons', that it would not be concluded by the Chancellor during Baldwin's absence, was able to speak 'quite frankly' about the delicate matter of kudos to Churchill, whose response was 'most correct and loyal in every

---

[92] WD, II, 56-69-70, 80.

[93] M. Gilbert, op.cit., V, 203. T.J. earlier had vainly tried (Morton MSS GD 326/86/1) to persuade Londonderry 'to put pressure' on the Mining Association to moderate its policy.

way'. Some days later Churchill, who 'terrified his colleagues' by his willingness to coerce the coal-owners, was utterly exasperated by the Cabinet's 'meandering all over the place'. He called Jones to his room and confided that he intended to 'clear out of it' and boycott the Cabinet coal meetings in future. T.J., pleading that 'infinite patience' was required, 'gradually calmed him down' and persuaded Churchill to think again.[94] In fact, despite his apparent calm detachment, Jones too was irked   by the continuing indecision. The evening before he was called in by Churchill, T.J. wrote sardonically to his friend H.J.W. Hetherington:

> I am deep in the coal pit, and have been stuck here all the summer. At the moment I believe the Government is about to make up its mind, and, like an Aber[ystwyth] student I once knew who had failed matriculation seven times, is 'determined to be determined'.[95]

T.J. did not pretend that there was any easy answer; he knew the difficulties only too well. As he said to Churchill, 'there was no settlement which the men would accept which the owners would look at'. And while in general he approved of the vigorously firm line Churchill took with the coal-owners, T.J. knew that, in the last resort, it was not 'conceivable' that a Conservative government would 'coerce' Evan Williams and the Mining Association, 'however foolish' their behaviour. Even so, Jones considered that Baldwin, who had now returned to duty, could take effective action to produce 'a national agreement' by indirect means if he were so minded and sufficiently determined. It is sometimes difficult to be certain when Jones was expressing his own views and when simply stating Cabinet policy or the drift of its inclination. However, it is clear that T.J. thought that the government's legislation in July, legitimizing an extension of the working day to eight hours, was, in existing economic circumstances, inescapably necessary. But he also suggested that Baldwin should use this as a lever to compel the two sides to accept outside arbitration. 'You could say', T.J. suggested to Baldwin, 'that no district should work eight hours which is not prepared to go to arbitration on hours and wages in those cases where no agreement is reached'.[96] Jones also accepted the fact that the coal industry was too big and desperately needed a

[94] *WD*, II, 67–8, 73-9, 85–6.
[95] T.J., Class J, Vol.7, No.9.
[96] *WD*, II, 80, 85–6. Horace Wilson, the civil servant in charge of negotiations on behalf of the government, endorsed T.J.'s view. 'The industry', he wrote (T.J. Add, MSS CC, Vol.3, No.23) 'is in a condition in which the State must impose upon it a settlement which rests upon arbitration'.

major reorganization that would involve amalgamations, some closures and much capital investment. 'There will be no health in the industry until this is done', T.J. told his friend James Morton in May. T.J. knew there was no hope of government money for this purpose, and he appreciated from discussions with the 'more enlightened' employers that the prosperous coal owners were reluctant to appear to be squeezing out their weaker brethren. The best hope therefore lay in forming 'regional corporations' which would close down some of the marginal pits and get others 'suffering from lack of capital modernised'. He believed that this was the only realistic way to force the industry 'to bear some of its own burdens' and reduce the heavy expenditure that unemployment would impose on the State. Unfortunately, he did not describe his envisaged regional corporations any more precisely.[97]

In his letter Jones said that Tawney broadly agreed with his conclusions. But Tawney later protested several times to T.J. that the government seemed intent on imposing a Versailles-style *diktat* in favour of the owners that would turn the coal industry into 'a sort of internal Ireland' of permanent violent conflict. Jones was fully alive to that danger but he remained much more critical than Tawney of the inadequacies of the miners' leaders. All along, in T.J.'s opinion, Cook, Smith and company had failed 'to exploit' their opportunities properly, in particular they had continued to 'haggle and boggle' and refused to concede enough to enable the government 'to go ahead in spite of the owners'. At the end of September, T.J. noted, with something not far short of disgust, that the miners' conference gave no effective lead to the districts. But Jones had expected too much of the miners' national leadership and failed to understand the strength of feeling among the men. For once, T.J.'s appreciation of the view of the world from the Rhymney valley, so often a valuable counterbalance to the view from Whitehall, was less than clear.[98]

Jones became increasingly impatient with Baldwin's resigned acceptance of impotence. But there was no more T.J. himself could do; anyway at the end of September he went down with lumbago and was ordered to stay away from Whitehall for several weeks. The strike dragged on wretchedly, at great human cost, until it petered out in November in the utter defeat of the miners on hours, wages, and district agreements. In November T.J. spiritedly defended

[97] Morton MSS GD 326/86/1.
[98] *WD*, II, 65–6, 80, 84, 88. District opinion was, in fact, more hostile to compromise than the national leaders.

payments by the Guardians to the strikers against Hankey's insensitive denunciation, and later that month Lord Esher, not the first name that springs to mind as a fierce critic of the Establishment, wrote thus to T.J.:

> When the war was on the P.M. went over to France to see for himself . . . Now you have another war on. I suppose it would be thought infra dig for the P.M. to pay a few visits to the war area and to see *for himself* how the women and children and men are living and to hear from their own lips *why* they prefer dying in the trenches to defeat. . . . How far is a 'Government', whether oligarchic or democratic, absolved from the duty of separating combatants whose hurly-burly obstructs the peaceful passage along the high road of the advancing citizens? There's an ethical problem to which the P.M. might pay some attention.[99]

Forlorn as the immediate prospect seemed, T.J. remained absolutely committed to the ideal of social harmony: 'Reconciliation, Interpretation, Enlightenment, and intellectual integrity to counteract the class war', as he described his purpose to George M. Ll. Davies in December 1926.[100] Indeed, it was the fact that Baldwin shared this social vision that had helped to bring the two of them so agreeably together in so short a period of time. During 1925 Baldwin had made a number of powerful speeches on the theme of industrial peace. Most of the detailed drafting was done by T.J., who usually worked up two or three 'general notions' suggested by the Prime Minister. 'It is of course a great help to have speeches made for one' Baldwin said in 1924, especially since, as he conceded, he was 'such a lazy devil'. The extent of Jones's contribution is indicated by the fact that he could legitimately lay claim 'to have written about a half' of the much-admired volume *(On England)* of Baldwin's collected speeches during 1924–26 and also 'something of the other half, plus the Preface'.[101] At his best, Baldwin was a magnificent orator whose homely conversational

[99] T.J., Class W, Vol.20, No.251. *WD*, II, 85–7.

[100] NLW, G.M.Ll . Davies MSS 1395.

[101] *WD*, II, 11, 167 and *passim*, and especially the unpublished Z Diaries for very many references to Jones's ghost-writing of speeches for Baldwin, who claimed, defensively but justifiably, that he could write his own speeches very well if he had the time or, more accurately, if he would find the time. The following conversation (Z Diary, 1923, p.137) expresses the truth:

S.B. I feel an awful fraud reading your speeches...

T.J. But you often improve them.

Interviewed on BBC Television (November 1955) T.J. said of Baldwin: 'All his best speeches were done by himself'.

style was ideally suited to the expression of riveting simple truths, although on occasion he avoided unction and even bathos by the merest whisker. '*Who* weighs his words?' an admirer asked in 1930. 'I think they must be measured by troy weight'. The Prime Minister had intervened to great effect ('A plus' on T.J.'s reckoning) in the debate on 6 March 1925 on a bill put forward by Macquisten, a back-bench Tory ultra, to alter the trade union political levy to the disadvantage of the Labour party.

> We have the greatest majority our party ever had [Baldwin said] . . . We stand for peace . . . between all classes . . . We are not going to push our political advantage home at a moment like this. We at any rate are not going to fire the first shot.[102]

Macquisten's bill was dropped but Baldwin's refusal to push the power of his Commons majority to anything like its limit was inevitably challenged by some of his party and Cabinet colleagues during the General Strike and the bitter mining dispute that followed.

It is possible to argue that Baldwin resisted the Conservative ultras with courage and great cunning to considerable effect. T.J., who was very close to the Prime Minister throughout, sympathized strongly with his declared aims, and was personally very well disposed towards him, however did not entirely agree. And his criticism of Baldwin became even sharper early in 1927 when a trade union bill which included several punitive clauses was under consideration by the Cabinet. Although party feeling in the country and in Parliament in favour of the bill was undoubtedly very strong, T.J. considered that Baldwin could and should have put up a more determined resistance. Soon after his return from holiday, Jones argued vigorously in a 'strained and difficult interview' with the Prime Minister that the bill went too far, that it would alienate moderate opinion, and that its undeniably lax drafting provided the need and opportunity for at least delay.[103] T.J. got nowhere, and it is clear that, for the moment at least, he was disenchanted with Baldwin. Early in May, when the Trade Disputes Bill, as it was termed, was going through the Commons, T.J. spent a weekend

---

[102] *Parl. Deb. Commons*, Vol.181, cols.833–841. T.J., Class W, Vol.13, No.29. T.J.'s evaluation of the speech is in *WD*, I, 328.

[103] Ibid., II, 99–100. J.L. Garvin (*Observer*, 1 May 1927) in a leader, 'Sowing Dragon's Teeth', argued that the bill would 'open up ... a new class war'. The *Manchester Guardian* (3 May) simply poured scorn on a government 'which took office talking of peace'.

with the Webbs at Passfield Corner. 'From his account', Beatrice
Webb wrote, 'Baldwin is stupider and weaker than we thought'.[104]
This rare indiscretion indicates the depth of T.J.'s disappointment.

Late in 1926 Alfred Zimmern had referred to Jones's 'Sisyphean
labours' in the cause of industrial peace.[105] So, wearily, it must have
seemed to him. There are very few people who emerge from the
General Strike and its painful sequel with much credit. T.J., the
patient advocate of moderation and conciliation based on some
sort of workable balance between economic necessity and social
justice, surely is one.

---

[104] *The Diary of Beatrice Webb,* IV, 122. Her patronizing description of T.J. in this
entry was that, for once, he had not impressed.
[105] T.J., Class W, Vol.20, No.251.

CHAPTER ELEVEN

'C.H.'

THOMAS JONES was blessed with an exceptional vitality that, together with an indomitable optimism, armoured him against most discouragements. The demands of his professional duties during the long politico-industrial crises of 1925–27 would have drained the nervous energy of most active men, but evidently not that of T.J. For remarkably, on his own initiative, and with the limited assistance later of a few devoted lieutenants, he founded a college of adult education at Harlech in Wales at this time. Most of the work was done in his spare time after his often open-ended day in Whitehall was over. And the crucially important part of the undertaking was carried out during the hectic years between 1925 and 1927. It was a magnificent achievement, a unique personal coup, in which T.J. demonstrated a rare combination of great vision with an exceptional mastery of practical detail.

Coleg Harlech, as the new establishment was called, was founded without benefit of government money entirely by means of an initial benefaction from a most unlikely source, which Jones had tapped, and with the aid of a few large and many small subscriptions that were secured very nearly to the last penny by his unaided persuasive begging.[1] And, even more astonishingly, it was done at a time of trade depression, of business gloom, mass unemployment and violent class antagonism. Even the usually faithful Gregynog ladies, downcast at their shrinking coal receipts, were rather reluctant to help, and their brother, David Davies, at first dismissed the whole thing as harebrained nonsense.[2]

But for Tom Jones it was an act of faith inspired by educational idealism; he was, as Walford Davies said, 'divinely obsessed' with the idea of Coleg Harlech.[3] Throughout his life Jones had always had an eye to the main chance for educational improvement. The story

[1] There is a good brief history by Peter Stead, *Coleg Harlech: The First Fifty Years* (Cardiff, 1977). The account here is written from a slightly different angle and uses some additional sources.

[2] T.J., Class W, Vol.10, No.207. Class R, Vol.1, No.4. D.D.'s opinion was that the scheme was hopelessly mistimed, politically wrong-headed and absurdly located in isolated Harlech.

[3] T.J., Class W, Vol.4, No.182.

of Coleg Harlech began in 1909 when T.J. attended a Fabian Summer School at Llanbedr, Merioneth, arranged by Beatrice and Sidney Webb to mobilize support for their proposals for Poor Law reform. T.J. shared rooms with Tawney and the historian L.B. Namier. During their stay they were invited to tea at a house called Wern Fawr at Harlech owned by George Davison, a wealthy Englishman, once a keen amateur photographer, who left a humble job in the Audit Office to join the Eastman Kodak company in its pioneering days. Davison eventually became European manager of the company, whereupon, as his son said, 'the money flowed in'. The house Wern Fawr, which was said to have cost £40,000 and was thought to be worth £60,000 in 1923, had been designed for Davison by his friend and business associate, the gifted George Walton. It was a fine building on a magnificent eleven-acre site which overlooked the great arc of Cardigan Bay and was backed by the towering peaks of Snowdonia. Although he had done very well out of capitalism, Davison held no brief for it. 'His political views', as T.J. said, 'resembled those of a Tolstoyan anarchist'; his taste in food too was unusual, for he 'lived largely on fruits and nuts'. T.J. got to know him well and soon boldly suggested that such a house ought not to be monopolized by one man or even one family but should be put to some public use.[4]

Davison was later active in extreme left-wing politics in south Wales, in association, curiously enough, with Tom Jones's old opponents the Marxist NCLC. But early in the 1920s Davison, now a very old man,went to live on the French Riviera and Wern Fawr was put up for sale. The initial asking price was £20,000 but the house remained unsold for some time. In October 1923 T.J., ever alert to a bargain for cultural purposes, wrote to Davison 'offering' a figure somewhere between £5-7,000 for the house. 'It would be a scandal to let it fall into the hands of people who would have no feeling for its beauty and who might turn it into a common hotel [T.J. wrote]. Silyn Roberts and I have often dreamed of saving it for the workers in some shape'. Davison was a generous and agreeable man (he adopted several needy children); 'for your purpose', he replied to T.J., 'I would make it [the selling price] £7,700. This is about the price of the organ and panelling alone'.[5]

It is to be noted that, at this stage, T.J. had no financial backing for his 'offer' and certainly could not afford to put up the money

---

[4] Morton MSS GD 326/821/1. R.C. Davison to T.J., 16 July 1941, White MSS. 'Moments in Eighty Years: A Birthday Talk', by T.J. on B.B.C. radio, 29 September 1950.

[5] T.J., Class K, Vol.I, Nos.6 and 7.

himself. It took him more than a year to find a patron, and meantime, luckily, Wern Fawr remained unsold. Henry Gethin Lewis and T.J. had been fellow pupils at the Pengam School. Lewis subsequently had made a large fortune in Cardiff dockland. His business acumen, however, was no defence against Tom Jones's persuasive power. Lewis was currently treasurer of the University College at Cardiff, which perhaps was a hopeful sign that he had some interest in education. But he was obviously a reluctant benefactor, and indeed had some doubt about the purpose and value of adult education. Jones suggested that as education had given each of them a springboard for success in life they ought now to repay the debt in their different ways. Lewis was half persuaded. T.J., who believed that most self-made men had an undue vanity, decided to call in some imposing assistance.

Early in December 1924 he asked Lord Haldane and Lord Eustace Percy, recently appointed President of the Board of Education at T.J.'s suggestion, to meet Lewis during a function at which they were to be present and add their heavyweight support to his persuasions. It worked. Lewis handed over his IOU for £7,500: 'I have been authorised to go ahead with the purchase of Wern Fawr', T.J. told Percy Watkins on 6 December, adding that it was now 'all the more desirable' that Watkins should take over as Secretary of the Welsh Department of the Board of Education as soon as possible. Four months later the Wern Fawr transaction was completed.[6]

But Tom Jones was not altogether clear at this time about the use to which he wished to put the building. 'My idea', he told Haldane rather vaguely in December 1924, 'is to convert it into a Guest House for the W.E.A. and similar movements for weekend conferences, summer schools, etc.' and he hoped also to associate it with the Extra-Mural committees of the University Colleges at Aberystwyth and Bangor.[7] During 1925 the scheme, if indeed it merits that description at that time, was no more than a frail possibility; indeed, there was a very real danger that it would simply have to be abandoned as absurdly ambitious. 'Harlech is stuck', T.J. wrote to James Morton in May; 'I shall have to start begging amongst all the friends I can think of'. Four months later even this prince of beggars had to confess that the 'prolonged trade depression and the gloomy outlook' were making the task of raising money almost impossible. In October he was forced to concede that it looked as if the project would 'have to go under, at any rate

[6] Ibid., Nos.15, 26, 29 and 82.
[7] T.J., Class K, Vol.I, Nos. 15, 47 and 52. Bangor MS 19533.

for the time being'. Equally worrying, Gethin Lewis was complaining that as the future of the building had not been settled and taken off his hands, he was faced with unwelcome bills for insurance and repairs. Indeed, ominously, Lewis seemed to be having second thoughts: 'I frequently think that I am not quite on the right lines in supporting Adult Education. I think the money would be spent to much better advantage in educating youngsters . . . *Wern Fawr* would make an ideal Preparatory School'. T.J. even feared that Lewis would decide to use the house as his holiday home.[8]

But these daunting difficulties served only to stiffen Jones's resolve and gradually he began to make headway. He won the support of Waldorf Astor, the Misses Davies of Gregynog and Thomas Evans, managing director of the Ocean Coal Company, which, with other more modest subscriptions, meant an assured income of £700–800 per annum for an experimental period of five to seven years. In February he submitted appeals for assistance to the Carnegie and Cassell Trusts, having previously, in typical T.J. fashion, worked hard to win over the two secretaries, Colonel J.M. Mitchell and A.E. Twentyman, ' the key men with their respective bodies', as he described them.[9] T.J. had, in his own words 'worked single-handed' on fund raising, but there were many other problems where the help and counsel of others was invaluable. He was advised confidentially on the attitudes of the University authorities by Lord Kenyon, W.N. Bruce and Miss Mary Rathbone of Bangor. But it was soon very apparent that the University Colleges did not wish to be seriously involved with the Harlech scheme.[10]

Of much greater importance was the support T.J. received from a small group of his close friends. Three of these were especially helpful. Percy Watkins, T.J.'s energetic adjutant in Wales, strategically well placed at the Welsh education department, was in this as in all else a tower of strength. Shrewd advice, particularly about opinion in the crucially important south Wales area, was usually forthcoming from John Davies, secretary of the WEA. Davies was an able, dedicated man who was undeterred by almost overwhelming difficulties. Desperately short of funds (his own meagre salary was often months in arrears), often obstructed by jealous local education authorities, and always under attack from NCLC critics, he battled on heroically for seventeen years in south Wales on

8 Morton MSS GD 326/85 and 86/1. T.J., Class K, Vol.I, Nos.111, 114 and 119.

9 T.J., Class W, Vol.14, Nos.86 and 87; Class K, Vol.2, Nos.12 and 31. Bangor MS 19540.

10 T.J., Class K, Vol.2, No.21.

16. T.J., Baldwin and his son Windham, Astley Park, 1923. The picture that upset Ramsay MacDonald.

17. The original Pilgrim Trustees and T.J. their Secretary. *Back row:* John Buchan, Sir James Irvine, T.J. *Front row:* Lord Macmillan, Stanley Baldwin, Sir Josiah Stamp.

18. T.J. and George Bernard Shaw at Gregynog, August 1933.

19. Edgar Jones, T.J. and Sir Percy Watkins, Christmas 1938.

20. T.J. and Rene at home at Street Acre, St Nicholas-at-Wade, Kent in the early 1930s.

21–27. T.J.'s ladies.

21. Violet Markham, C.H.

22. Gertrude, Lady Grigg.

23. A note from Joyce Grenfell before the presentation
of a testimonial to T.J. at Rhymney, June 1939.

24. Joyce Grenfell.

25. Charlotte Griffiths.

26. Mrs Elizabeth Yates Thompson.

27. Gwen Davies, C.H., of Gregynog.

28. The Prince of Wales, T.J. and Ben Bowen Thomas at Coleg Harlech, 1934.

29. Lloyd George and Hitler, 1936. T.J. is behind the Führer's right shoulder.

behalf of the WEA version of adult education.[11] But the man upon whom T.J. most heavily relied in the matter of Harlech was Silyn Roberts, who had now returned to north Wales as an Extension Board tutor at Bangor. It was his advice, and that of his gifted wife Mary, that T.J. sought in particular. Jones was, as he said, anxious to be certain he was carrying Silyn along with him in all he did to promote the scheme.[12]

In fact it was Silyn Roberts who some years before, in 1920, had drawn Tom Jones's attention to a proposal put up by R.T. Jones, secretary of the North Wales Quarrymen's Union, that anticipated the final form given to Coleg Harlech. 'He has an idea', Silyn wrote, 'of establishing a kind of Ruskin College in Wales'. Nothing came of that at the time, and it would no doubt have seemed too ambitious and too politically controversial a proposal to have been feasible for Harlech at the outset. However, Tom Jones had always believed that he would have to feel his way delicately forward. There is no doubt that the great national crisis in industrial affairs helped to make up his mind. 'All this "coal" . . . experience shows how necessary some such "ventilating shaft" is if we are to resist the spread of extremist doctrines', he wrote to James Morton in September 1925.[13] And the General Strike overwhelmingly re-inforced that conviction. 'The events of the last ten days', he commented to Mitchell of the Carnegie Trust on 9 May 1926, 'have demonstrated the need not for one but for twenty Harlechs'.[14] The crucial decision to aim at establishing a full-time residential adult education college was taken at a weekend conference in February 1926 at Gregynog, attended by Mitchell, Twentyman of the Cassell Trust, Percy Watkins, the Misses Davies, and T.J. Later the party went on to Harlech, where they were joined by Silyn Roberts, Herbert Morgan of the Extra-Mural Department at Aberystwyth, and W.J. Williams, Inspector of Schools. Here it was decided, temporarily at least, not to hand over Wern Fawr to the University

[11] Ibid., Class D, Vol.3, No.42; Class R, Vol.2, No.143.

[12] Bangor MS 19535. In July, T.J. rejected a suggestion, put forward by Silyn Roberts and Wyn Wheldon, Registrar at the College, that he should apply for the principalship of Bangor, which shortly would become vacant. 'It is too late for me to dream of the principalship of Bangor. You must get somebody much younger', T.J. said (Class J, Vol.16, No.10).

[13] Bangor MS 17218. 'How far I can go remains to be seen', he told (Class W, Vol.17, No.27) the ex-MP Robert Richards in March 1925. 'We must move in faith'. Morton MSS GD 326/85 and 86/1.

[14] T.J., Class K. Vol.2, No.49. On 23 April 1926, when Baldwin was knee deep in important discussions with miners and owners, T.J. slipped away to lunch with Percy Watkins where they 'talked Harlech'. T.J., Class Z (Dary, 1926), p.49.

of Wales, but to set up a Board of Trustees, a small representative Council and a smaller Executive Body leaving the option of transference to the University open for the future.[15]

The retention of even the thinnest thread of connection with the University was useful. Twentyman, for example, said that the Cassell Trust would be 'very unlikely' to give a grant-in-aid unless Harlech was 'related (if not organically connected) with the University', and Wyn Wheldon pointed out that many academic 'mandarins' at Bangor, whose opposition would be dangerous, were 'ridiculously sensitive' to the possibility of political propaganda in adult education and must be reassured of Harlech's academic respectability. In the event, the Carnegie and Cassell Trusts, powerfully influenced by Mitchell and Twentyman, provided support that was crucial: Carnegie gave £2,500 for adaptations and equipment, and the Cassell Trustees gave £500 per annum for five years.[16] T.J. still had much fund-raising to do, but the back of the immediate difficulty was broken. The establishment of the college was now a realistic possibility. Many of his friends and acquaintances rallied round: Sir David Llewellyn, Sir Gomer Berry and Sir Alfred Mond from the capitalist world made useful contributions, Sir Horace Plunkett, patron saint of co-operation, sent a cheque and Lilian Browne (the future Lady Geddes), T.J.'s former Glasgow student, promised generous help. As yet, no trade union, not even the North Wales Quarrymen, had made a contribution.[17]

In some ways this was perhaps just as well at the time. From the outset T.J.'s Harlech scheme had been closely associated with the Welsh WEA, which itself was under permanent attack from two sides: the Marxist left and, more dangerously at this time, the capitalist press, particularly the *Western Mail.* The fact that these criticisms largely cancelled each other out was usually disregarded. In September 1925, Tom Jones had exchanged letters with J.A. Sandbrock, acting editor of the *Western Mail,* about the newspaper's recent treatment of the WEA. Sandbrock vigorously defended himself on the ground that the WEA, whatever its original admirable purpose, had fallen from grace and was now an agency of socialist propaganda. T.J. conceded that there were 'lapses here and there' by one or two tutors but these were remediable and it was absurd to 'prejudice' the WEA as a whole in the eyes of the public.[18] This exercise in sweet reason was wasted; the editorial

[15] T.J., Class P, Vol.2, No.41; Class K, Vol.2, No.21.

[16] T.J., Class K, Vol.2, Nos.21, 31, 50, 71, 73 and 137.

[17] T.J., Class P, Vol.2, No.41. N.L.W., B.B. Thomas MSS [17 March 1927]. P. Stead, op.cit., p.34.

[18] T.J., Class D, Vol.3, Nos.29 and 30.

policy of the *Western Mail* remained consistently hostile, indeed malevolent, towards the WEA and its supposed sinister new manifestation, the proposed college at Harlech. Especially virulent attacks in tabloid style on 18 and 20 December 1926 particularly angered T.J.: he fired off letters of protest against the political mischief making to many influential Welsh friends. The attacks, he told Frank Gilbertson, president of University College, Swansea, sought only 'to maim' Harlech 'by raising the socialist scare'; they seemed deliberately designed, he wrote to Sir David Llewellyn, whom he asked to intervene, to spread suspicion and make the task of social reconciliation impossible.

> I woke at 4 am [he said in his letter to T. Gwynn Jones, poet and academic] to hurl wild words at the Editor of the *Western Mail* for his mendacious, tendentious headlines about "Coleg Harlech". This sort of journalism makes me rage furiously . . . I care nothing for party politics – I know more than most about them. But I still have some educational idealism stirring in me, and it is that which has led to the Harlech project. I still think our people may gain by sharing the treasures which education has brought to us. I still innocently think it may be useful for employers and workmen to meet on neutral ground, but what the *Mail* seems to want is more class war and a ban on thought other than what it approves.[19]

Some weeks before a long article appeared in the *Sunday Express,* which portrayed T.J. as a man of mystery exercising a sorcerer's influence in favour of socialism over Lloyd George, Bonar Law, Baldwin and Churchill, which though absurdly overstated, was plausible enough also to be damaging.[20] There was of course no way in which an individual, even one as well placed as T.J., could directly counter that raucous, megaphone voice. Surprisingly, however, the *Western Mail,* perhaps influenced by Llewellyn, invited T.J. to put the case for Harlech in its columns. He did so with gusto. The second of two articles, 'The Aim of Coleg Harlech', which examined objectivity in teaching, was especially persuasive.

> Education has failed [he wrote] which does not enable us to have an active sense of the many-sided nature of truth. All our absolutes as the philosophers say, have a way of becoming relatives. . . . Will some tutors be biased? . . . Yes, they will. We all come short of the excellence of

---

[19] T.J., Class K, Vol.2, Nos.127 and 128; Class W, Vol.12, Nos.54 and 56. T. Gwynn Jones was utterly contemptuous of the 'slave class upstarts' who were leader-writers on the *Western Mail*. 'They were', he told T.J. some months later, 'the dung of the country [cachadwriaeth y wlad]'.

[20] 3 October 1926.

perfect impartiality and no corrective has been found which did not at the same time threaten intellectual and spiritual liberty. "The business of a teacher", as it has been said, "is not to announce that he is impartial but to overcome his bias". . . . The enemy is ignorant dogmatism masquerading as knowledge, and this sort of papal infallibility has its exponents in all classes and parties. . . . If there are bad ideas fluttering about, they can be conquered by better ones, and in no other way.

At any rate, Coleg Harlech, he said, would be non-sectarian and non-party; it would not take sides in the conflict between capital and labour; in any discussion of the mining dispute, for example, it would give a fair hearing to the coal-owner Sir David Llewellyn and to Tom Richards the miners' leader.[21]

Of course, this fine clear statement had little long-term effect on Coleg Harlech's critics, but it did seem to win a breathing space. T.J. and his associates were able to get on with their preparations to open the college. It had always been recognized that the appointment of the first warden would be crucial for the success of the college. In fact, the committee had agreed unanimously in December 1926 to appoint an outstanding candidate, Ben Bowen Thomas, a young man in his twenties educated at Aberystwyth and Oxford, who was then an Extra-Mural lecturer in Pembrokeshire. The appointment was enthusiastically received in Wales. 'Ben B. Thomas', said G.M.Ll. Davies, a good judge, is 'a rather rare person who combines Treorchy and Oxford'.[22] And scarcely less important for the success of the residential college, the choice of matron, Miss N. Williams, then a housemistress at Roedean, was to prove a similar triumph of shrewd judgement.

Early in 1927, T.J. was confident enough about the situation to take a holiday; indeed, he went on a cruise to the Mediterranean. For a time he could escape from his role as the staid adviser of the mighty. The trip had its lighter moments; T.J.'s method of dealing with foreigners was idiosyncratic but evidently effective. Most of the passengers on the ship were Germans: 'I jabber my peculiar French on these occasions', T.J. reported to Rene in apparent explanation. At Haifa, some Italian Jews commandeered a taxi T.J. had ordered: 'I had to get them out', he said, 'they yelled an eloquent resistance, but I yelled louder in various scraps of many languages and finally evicted them'. He had gone to see the Pyramids riding on a ship of the desert improbably named 'Mark Twain', and thoroughly enjoyed a battle of wits with a cunning camel driver on the make.

---

21 *Western Mail*, 1 January 1927.
22 T.J., Class K, Vol.3, No.210.

More seriously, he was deeply moved by a visit to Nazareth, which prompted sober reflection on the stupendous influence Christ had had on the fate of the world. This cruise, despite much intermittent seasickness, was just as invigorating as the trip to the Black Sea that he had made thirty years earlier.[23]

Whatever difficulties there had been about adequate funding and the most appropriate constitutional machinery, the academic arrangements at Coleg Harlech were soon settled. T.J. held strong views about teaching methods in higher education: he believed that students in the University of Wales were over-lectured and under-tutored, their intellectual development cramped by the detestable 'bindweed' of examinations.[24] Indeed, in his opinion, the Welsh University Colleges latterly had become 'professional colleges for careers', concerned to educate 'for livelihood rather than life'.[25] T.J. had planned to change that, at least at Aberystwyth, but his rejection for the principalship there in 1919 put an end to that dream. At Harlech, however, he had a free hand: the new college was to be wholly residential; passive listening and note-taking by students were reduced to the minimum, the emphasis overwhelmingly was to be on discussion and argument, oral and on paper. Lectures gave way almost entirely to seminars and tutorials; and, of supreme importance, at least to T.J., there were to be no tests or examinations of any kind, no pursuit of degrees or diplomas, no visible or measurable dividend, simply the pursuit of truth for its own sake. Students, drawn from adult education classes, would have no formal qualifications on entry and none when they returned, as it was assumed they would, after a period of full-time education, to their former jobs or the ranks of the unemployed. During vacations the college would be used for conferences of WEA groups and cultural organizations.

Ralph Waldo Emerson said that a college is sometimes 'the lengthened shadow of one man'. This was certainly true of Coleg Harlech. It rested on T.J.'s vision that the Welsh people, or at least many of them, could be elevated to a higher plane of democratic fellowship by adult education. T.J. found inspiration in the pioneering example of N.F.S. Grundtvig, whose Folk High Schools, it was claimed, had transformed Denmark into the most educated democratic community in the world. The General Strike was a portent. T.J. firmly believed that there was a race between popular education and social catastrophe.

[23] T.J., Class X, Vol.9, No.3. Letters, 2 and 6 February, in White MSS.
[24] *Leeks and Daffodils*, p.44
[25] 'A Talk to the London Society of Old Aberystwythians'. T.J., Class Y, Vol.5, No.25.

Coleg Harlech [Jones told a friend in 1927] is an attempt to do some work of reconciliation in Wales, where industrial strife has been rampant for years, by means of adult education. It is from South Wales most of the extremist movements have come in the last 15 or 20 years and it is not altogether surprising to one who knows the conditions. I want to see the "leaders of tomorrow" given a chance of higher education in an atmosphere free from partisanship.[26]

He did his utmost during 1927 to recruit more Conservative members in order to achieve a reassuring political balance on the College Council. He did not ask for the public support of Lloyd George (who in consequence was miffed for some time) presumably because his name prompted contention rather than unity. Finally, T.J., who inevitably became Chairman of the College Council, persuaded Lord Haldane, a great catch, to become its President, and Clement Davies, KC, future leader of the Liberal party, to act as honorary legal adviser.[27] Henry Gethin Lewis, the benefactor, was made a Vice-President along with two trade unionists and three university dignitaries, two of whom were also industrial magnates. The Executive Committee was similarly balanced and included several representatives of local government, a hopeful sign of public support in the future. The *Western Mail,* hostile to the last, kept up its carping comment, and Henry Gethin Lewis, unnerved by the teasing suggestions of some of his capitalist friends that the Labour anthem the 'Red Flag' would certainly be appearing on the programme at the opening ceremony, had to be reassured that it would not, and that 'God Save the King', the only acceptable guarantee of decency and respectability in his opinion, would be sung. In fact, neither was included. On 5 September 1927, Coleg Harlech was formally opened. Much praise, naturally, was lavished on Henry Gethin Lewis's generosity, but no one was in doubt that Coleg Harlech was T.J.'s creation: 'the audacious experiment', as he called it, had begun, for a trial period of seven years, with a skeleton staff and half a dozen students.[28]

[26] Ibid., T.J., Class K, Vol.3, No.296. *WO*, XVI, 74, for T.J.'s acknowledgement of his debt to Grundtvig.

[27] Ibid., Nos.6, 36, 78, 131, 159, 162. Arthur Pugh of the TUC had to be reassured that there would not be 'too much religion in the College and too little trade unionism', and David Davies, yet again, that it was 'not a Liberal, nor a Conservative, nor a Labour College, but a genuine attempt at something which transcends them all'.

[28] Coleg Harlech, official brochure of the Formal Opening, 5 September 1927. T.J., Class K, Vol.3, No.137. T.J., 'Coleg Harlech', *Manchester Guardian*, 19 May 1934.

For the rest of his life, Coleg Harlech was never far from Tom Jones's thoughts; as he said, it was his 'spiritual home'.[29] Much of his time and energy was devoted to work on behalf of the College, for it was a continuously desperate struggle in the early years to secure the bare minimum of money to keep it open. T.J.'s success in fund raising in the dark days of world economic depression before and after 1930 was not far short of the miraculous. It is doubtful if any other public man in Britain at that time had the will and the ability to match his achievement in this respect. Adult education was his religion: he had the proselytizing power of a great evangelist and a possibly unique ability to prime the pump of the social consciences of rich men. Patently disinterested himself, he encouraged people to discover generous impulses of which they were previously unaware, and forget their selfishness at least long enough to hand over a useful cheque for Coleg Harlech. As he pointed out, Wales was a small constituency to canvass for contributions, but T.J.'s British acquaintanceship was legion, and even the Atlantic Ocean was not wide enough to enable some well-to-do Americans to escape his soliciting of money or books for Harlech.[30]

Much of Jones's work as a Civil Servant at this time was also concerned with economic and industrial matters. In 1925 a Committee of Civil Research [CCR] had been set up; this innovation was prompted by Haldane, who asserted that it could make as great a contribution to good government in peacetime as that of the Committee of Imperial Defence in preparing effectively for war. T.J. was made Secretary: 'A more suitable person for the subject I cannot conceive, because he has . . . imagination', Haldane said in the House of Lords.[31] Over the next four years, the CCR carried out twenty-four different enquiries into economic problems at home – the iron and steel industry and unemployment in the coal industry, for example – and into imperial questions, such as the welfare of the native population in Kenya and the control of locusts.[32] Although it did useful work, it can scarcely be said that the CCR, at least in its original form, came up to Haldane's expectations. As T.J. said, it had a 'modest career', not least because Baldwin, who had a positive horror of brainy people ('Why is it that so many first-class brains are such bloody fools?' he

---

[29] R.C. Davison to T.J., 16 July 1941, White MSS.

[30] He was especially chagrined on one occasion to be interrupted when about to tap John D. Rockefeller.

[31] *Parl. Deb. Lords,* Vol.61, pp.871–8, for the debate.

[32] T.J., Class B, Vol.3, No.41.

once asked T.J. rhetorically), thoroughly disliked 'intellectuals examining the economics of the home front', hence the deflection of so much attention to the empire. There was no initial master plan; *ad hoc* enquiries were set up at the suggestion of individuals who were interested, such as Esher and especially Balfour, for whose urbane wisdom T.J. had developed a profound admiration.[33]

Jones himself wanted the CCR to turn its attention to more fundamental problems. He was certainly deeply concerned about the 'nightmare' of mass unemployment, and it is evident that he was occasionally irked by Baldwin's habitual evasiveness when confronted with the need for action. 'Whenever one gets near the subject of positive policies', Jones noted with some irritation in April 1927, 'one is put off with "the summer" or "a long talk one of these days at Chequers"'.[34] Baldwin had always insisted that the State alone could provide 'no direct remedy' for unemployment. He maintained in a Commons debate in July 1928 that it ought to be 'perfectly possible' for the growing prosperity of the new centres of industrial activity in the south and the midlands to 'afford some relief' to the depressed areas, but gave no indication how this much-needed assistance was to be relayed. His assertion in the debate that a fall in the birth-rate would do a great deal to solve the unemployment problem among young workers prompted ironic laughter. A David Low cartoon, 'The Big Fight', published at this time, pictured Baldwin running away in the boxing ring from an ugly bruiser representing the unemployment problem. Up to the last months of his ministry T.J. pleaded with Baldwin to keep 'hammering away at unemployment' policy despite all discouragements.[35]

Jones did not pretend that it was simply a matter of political will; he knew that there was no heroic remedy immediately available. And he understood too that there was often a rough as well as a smooth side to some of the policies that were initiated. In the late 1920s, for example, it was recognized that there was little realistic hope that many of the pool of over 200,000 unemployed miners would find work in the pits in the foreseeable future. In T.J.'s opinion the new expanding light industries in the midlands and the south could currently absorb only 'the merest trickle' of the unemployed; the main hope lay in large-scale emigration to Canada

---

[33] *WD*, II, Introduction x–xi, 139, 229. T.J., Class Z (Diary, 1934), p.78. *Beatrice Webb Diaries 1924-32*, (ed. M. Cole), p.142.

[34] *WD*, II, 66,99. Bodl. Zimmern Papers, Box 29, No.28.

[35] Baldwin at Birmingham, *The Times*, 6 March 1926. *Parl. Deb. Commons*, Vol.220, col.1127. *Evening Standard*, 26 July 1928: T.J., Class Z (Diary, 1929), p.13.

and elsewhere. 'We want to send you thousands, if you can handle them', he wrote to a Canadian friend, J.B. Bickersteth. Subsequently, off his 'own bat', T.J. wrote to Mackenzie King, the Canadian Prime Minister, pleading for his assistance, which, however, was not forthcoming.[36] Indeed, King, who had his own problems, proved obstructive. In fact, the hopes vested in the work of the government's Industrial Transference Board were never fully realized, although many thousands did emigrate to Canada, Australia and New Zealand. T.J. also understood and was prepared sadly to accept that it was often 'the most skilled and the most enterprising' of the unemployed who were prepared to emigrate or be retrained for other work elsewhere, and their removal further weakened communities already gravely undermined by social and economic deprivation.[37]

It was obvious that the government could not transfer whole townships, but T.J. did lend some support unofficially to proposals considerably more ambitious than those acceptable to Baldwin and the government. Jones participated unofficially in the work of the study group on unemployment set up at Chatham House by Astor and Philip Kerr, who were already advancing the hypothesis, increasingly fashionable nowadays, that Britain's industrial decline stemmed from a traditional excessive emphasis on the importance of law, politics and finance and on a persistent entrenched social undervaluation of the importance of industry and industrialists.[38] Of more significance, T.J. had for some time been fully apprised of the course of the enquiry into Britain's social and economic problems carried out by working parties set up by the Liberal summer school committee with the support of Lloyd George. The report of the enquiry, *Britain's Industrial Future,* the so-called 'Yellow Book', was published in February 1928. Maynard Keynes, who with Philip Kerr, Seebohm Rowntree, R.H. Brand and Josiah Stamp, was a member of the Working Party, invited T.J. to attend a discussion on the enquiry to be opened by H.D. Henderson at the Café Royal on 8 February. 'I shall be very glad indeed to come as your guest', T.J. replied, 'I have had an advance copy of the Report and of course have seen it in its earliest stages. You will understand why I shall say very little – but I shall listen with both ears'.[39]

[36] *WD,* II, 137. T.J., Class Z (Diary, 1928), pp.26–7, 35–6, 104–107. (Ibid., 1929), pp.15–17.
[37] T.J., Class C, Vol.13, Nos.2 and 15; Class Q, Vol.2, No.7.
[38] Kerr to T.J., Class Z (Diary, 1928), pp.19–20. T.J., Class W, Vol.13, Nos.67 and 71.
[39] *WD,* II, 128–9.

During the inter-war years, there was a great struggle between economic conservatives and their radical critics over the conduct of economic policy. It was not simply a straightforward tug-of-war for intellectual hegemony, although that was certainly an important part of the conflict. It was rather an especially untidy mêlée, a congeries of confused scuffles in which economic theories, historical experience, political principles, not least the debate about the role of the State, party interests, social aspiration, even group and individual psychological propensities, interacted on each other. Necessity was usually more persuasive than coherently formulated argument. However, on the theoretical plane, the challenge of Maynard Keynes – 'I had to invent a new wisdom for a new age', as he put it – to traditional doctrine in economic policy was an important feature of the struggle.[40] In politics the electoral campaign waged by Lloyd George and the Liberals in 1928–9, based substantially on the expansionist and interventionist proposals in the 'Yellow Book', was the most spectacular episode. During the 1920s the economic radicals made little or no headway; conventional wisdom, the so-called 'Treasury view', with its insistence on annually balanced budgets, was dominant. During the 1930s radical views did make some advances which were not usually admitted officially. The publication in 1936 of Keynes's *General Theory of Employment, Interest and Money,* gave expansionist economic policies an intellectual sanction that they had not previously enjoyed, but the seemingly complete triumph of these ideas and their application came later in the 1940s.

The years around 1930 were a time of perplexity. Even Beatrice Webb, high priestess of the power of intellect, acknowledged the general bankruptcy of ideas, including her own, about solving unemployment and was driven to hope, a painful admission for her, that somehow or other, Britain could 'just muddle through'.[41] T.J., former professor of Economics, was just as uncertain as the next man about the proper response to unemployment and its disastrous ripple effects on society. Jones had never had much liking for economic theorizing, and his experience as a Civil Servant made him cautious, indeed sceptical, about schemes that rested more on promise than proven utility. And there were plenty of people around him in the Civil Service to reinforce his doubts about adventurous economic policies. In July 1929, Ronald Davison (son of George Davison the anarchist), of the Ministry of Labour,

---

[40] Keynes at the Liberal Summer School in 1925, quoted in J. Campbell, *Lloyd George: The Goat in the Wilderness* (1978), p.190.
[41] *Beatrice Webb's Diaries, 1924–32,* (ed. M. Cole), pp.135, 146.

asserted in a powerful memorandum, *Post War Relief Work 1920–28*, with supporting chapter and verse, that public works had disastrously failed to reduce unemployment; and T.J.'s friend Leith Ross of the Treasury sent him a closely argued paper that challenged the assumptions on which Keynes's proposals were based. Moreover, at the CCR Jones worked closely with Sir Richard Hopkins of the Treasury, whose ability he admired, a man who, as he showed in holding his own in argument with Keynes when giving evidence to the Macmillan Committee on Finance and Industry, was perhaps, with R.G. Hawtrey, the most effective exponent of the 'Treasury view' of economic policy.[42]

But despite these powerful constraints, T.J. still hankered after some sort of constructive action. Conventional economic wisdom, whatever its prestige and apparent weighty logic, ultimately seemed to imply a fatalistic acceptance of mass unemployment. T.J. was too familiar with the tragic anguish of south Wales to be prepared to submit meekly to the tyranny of official caution. As a *Times* leader said, unemployment had 'descended like the ashes of Vesuvius and overwhelmed whole towns' in south Wales and elsewhere in the distressed areas.[43] Accordingly, T.J. welcomed the Liberal industrial enquiry; he agreed with Beatrice Webb that it was 'a valuable Fabian document', largely free of political dogma, that included many proposals that could be implemented by Baldwin's government.[44]

In practice, there was no hope of that. Meantime, something on a small scale could be done to relieve social distress. T.J. turned once again to educational settlement work. In 1926 William and Emma Noble of the Society of Friends, appalled at the scale of distress in the Rhondda valley during the aftermath of the General Strike, had taken over an empty shop in Tonypandy as an emergency centre for the distribution of clothes to the needy. A year later, in June, with the backing of a committee in Oxford led by A.D. Lindsay, Master of Balliol, a permanent educational settlement was established in Maes-yr-Haf, a large house in Trealaw in the Rhondda.[45] T.J. was involved in the venture from the start; in March 1927 he persuaded the Gregynog ladies to give £500 towards the purchase of the house and an additional £100 a year for general expenses.[46] The need in south Wales was overwhelming. T.J. began

[42] T.J., Class C, Vol.18, No.59. *WD*, II, 195, 288–9.

[43] *The Times*, 29 March 1928.

[44] *WD*, II, 130–1, 183. T.J. told Baldwin he thought the 'Yellow Book' was 'admirable' and persuaded him to read it.

[45] K. Butterworth, *William Noble and his wife Emma* (1962), pp.21–5.

[46] T.J., Class H, Vol.9, Nos.95 and 110.

to plan additional help. For once, however, he was caught napping and his Welsh pride was cut to the quick.

> I have today learnt [he wrote in November 1928 to Annie Ffoulkes his associate, years before, in settlement work] that while we were talking, the Quakers were acting. They have sent down a man to live in Brynmawr for the winter . . . I hear also that . . . the Quakers are moving in Aberdare . . . I feel ashamed that with all our Schools of Social Service etc, etc, when it comes to action and not talking, we have to be helped by Quakers, as if we were a foreign mission field.[47]

However, Jones was quickly into his stride. He managed to raise privately in all £400 annually for several years for Maes-yr-Haf and also provided assistance for another Quaker, Peter Scott, who ran a settlement at Brynmawr where the unskilled unemployed were taught to make furniture and footwear, and remarkable improvements to the landscape were carried out by voluntary labour. T.J., who was a vice-president of the distress committee in his home town of Rhymney, adroitly persuaded Lady Astor to give generous financial help for local relief work. The secretary of the Friends' distress committee concluded that Jones was a 'miracle worker'. In December 1928, Captain L.F. Ellis, Secretary of the National Council of Social Service [NCSS] convened a meeting of twenty-seven voluntary organizations and religious denominations from which emerged the Coalfields Distress Committee. Inevitably, it would seem, Tom Jones was made Chairman of the Committee, which received a grant (renewed annually) of £5000 from the Carnegie Trust for relief work in south Wales and Durham. T.J.'s friends J.M. Mitchell, Percy Watkins and Sir Walford Davies were on the Committee and in south Wales Jones mobilized his remarkable network of friends under the leadership of the experienced John Davies of the WEA, to organize the work, mainly educational, recreational and cultural, on the spot.[48]

For some reason, the Quakers 'fought shy' of Merthyr, which T.J. thought the worst hit area in south Wales. He himself hesitated for some time, but eventually, in an attempt to 'reduce a fraction of its chronic misery', he set up a 'Merthyr Group' in London, which rented a large house for seven years and appointed a warden and a women's club leader in order to start a home training centre and a club for teenage girls. 'I do not propose, at this stage', Jones told a

---

[47]   Ibid., Vol.7, No.25.
[48]   T.J., Class H, Vol.9, No.1; Vol.7, No.36; Vol.14, Nos.1–41. Class Q, Vol.2, No.7: Class C, Vol.14, Nos.1 and 14. *WD*, II, 159, 177.

fellow member of the Romney Street Group, whose aid he solicited, 'to make a public appeal for the Merthyr settlement, but to beg privately'.[49] As a supplicant for worthy causes, T.J. really was in a class of his own, for at the same time of course he was also mainly responsible for raising large sums of money for Coleg Harlech. And this unending soliciting for support was done by a man approaching sixty years of age.

Mercifully, Jones's duties in Whitehall were less onerous in the last months of Baldwin's second government, which increasingly from 1927 onwards, apart from the determination of Churchill and Neville Chamberlain to push through local government and poor law reform, had run out of constructive ideas. The Cabinet at this time lived 'a sort of hand to mouth existence', according to Baldwin's friend Willie Bridgeman.[50] But there was industrial peace of a sort; even, in the Mond-Turner agreement in 1928, a half-hearted experiment in industrial co-operation. The rapport between Baldwin and T.J. became even closer at this time. It is evident that regardless of their occasional differences about policy – and these were almost always about means not ends, upon which they were largely agreed – they had developed a very warm affection for each other, a deep mutual regard, indeed, a quite exceptional empathy. They had many interests in common: literature, history, scholarship, the appreciation and preservation of beautiful buildings and of the countryside; a wide range of things of the mind and spirit. Baldwin was in some ways a lonely man; he loved to muse aloud and Tom Jones was a good listener who had an exceptional gift for inducing intimacy. They could apparently talk about everything except, for a time, protection and Lloyd George, topics which were taboo. T.J. was evangelical about free trade; Baldwin rather less than balanced on the subject of Lloyd George.[51]

To this day, Baldwin remains something of an enigma. He was certainly not the simple countryman he sometimes affected to be, but his preference for provincial over metropolitan habits and opinions was perfectly genuine. He was at least as cunning as the next contemporary politician, but he appeared to many people to embody a plain honesty, above and beyond politics. He appealed to a broad band of liberal opinion in the country that had little to do with party. To many he scarcely seemed to be a politician; he was seen as the nation's representative citizen, in thick-soled sensible

[49] Morton MSS GD 326/87/1. T.J., Class H, Vol.9, No.1.
[50] Bridgeman Diary, II, f.167.
[51] *WD*, I, 243–4.

boots smoking his pipe, the symbol of unhurried reflective common-sense. 'There's something of a modest splendour about the man', Walford Davies wrote to T.J. after reading Baldwin's speech on the Bible in May 1928.[52] As before, a great many of Baldwin's speeches were written either wholly or in part by T.J. who had now become so skilful a proxy as to be almost indistinguishable on paper from Baldwin himself. The speeches Baldwin made during his visit to Canada in the summer of 1927 were widely praised by the press as so 'typical' of the Prime Minister. In fact, most of them were written by Jones. 'I have been very silent regarding their author', J.B. Bickersteth, who knew the truth, wrote to T.J. from Canada.[53]

Inevitably, others became aware of T.J.'s special talent and asked for his help. He wrote a much praised, elegantly phrased speech on 'Art and the National Life' for Hailsham, the Lord Chancellor, to deliver at a Royal Academy banquet. Jones also wrote drafts of many speeches for his friend A.B. Houghton, the American ambassador in Britain.[54] These were agreeable times for T.J. The University of Wales, rather belatedly, recognized his services to education and to Wales with the bestowal of an honorary LL.D. in 1928. Earlier Alfred Zimmern had introduced T.J. to the distinguished American academic Dr Abraham Flexner, with whom he quickly developed one of the most satisfying friendships of his life. In August 1928, T.J. thoroughly enjoyed a visit to the International People's College at Elsinore, Denmark, an institution in which he had been interested ever since its foundation in 1921.[55] The Gregynog Press was now well established, much praised for its quality, particularly R.A. Maynard's woodcuts, by authorities as distinguished as C.H. St John Hornby, Stanley Morison and Bernard Newdigate. By 1928 ten volumes had been published, including an edition of the work of the Welsh poet John C. Hughes (Ceiriog), Sir John Morris Jones's translation into Welsh of the *Rubáiyát of Omar Khayyam,* the *Selected Poems of Edward Thomas* and a similar collection later of those of W.H. Davies. T.J. really loved his work for the Press, to which he devoted so much time and care; it exemplified his yearning for excellence based on a unity of artistic skills. Early in 1928 he

[52] T.J., Class W, Vol.4, No.196. Not everybody subscribed to that opinion. In south Wales, for example, T.J. noted in August 1928 that Baldwin's public reception in crowded streets was decidedly cool. Ibid., X, Vol.9, No.8.

[53] *WD,* II, 99, 110.

[54] Ibid., II, 136. *The Times,* 7 May 1928. T.J., Class O, Vol.3, No.4.

[55] T.J., Class P, Vol.2, No.59; Class D, Vol.7, No.4. *WD,* II, 16, 142. Peter Manniche's 'remarkable college' (as T.J. called it, Class D, Vol.7, No.12) at Elsinore recruited students from many countries.

persuaded Gilbert Murray to allow the Press to publish his translations of the *Plays of Euripides,* and shortly afterwards T.J. arranged
for Walter de la Mare to make a selection of the verse of Christina
Rossetti.[56]

This exceptionally happy phase of T.J.'s life was abruptly
shattered on 21 December 1928 by the death of Elphin, Tom and
Rene Jones's younger son. He was a remarkable boy: physically he
bore a striking resemblance to his father; he too had a fine head
but 'a less significant body'. He had the same quick alert walk, an
intensified version of his father's sunny temperament and the same
endearing carelessness about clothes. Elphin's health was not
robust, but he was not short of physical courage. Indeed, Rene
considered that he had rather more of it than his father, glimpsed
perhaps in Elphin's determination to ride a pony that previously
had thrown his sister and elder brother. Like T.J., Elphin was no
athlete, he came last in the school 100 yards. But he knew how to
put upstart plutocracy in its place: a boy at school boasting of his
father's Rolls Royce was given 'a biff', followed by the crushing
comment: '*My* father could ruin the British nation'. T.J. doted on
him. Rene felt that Tom was 'living over again his own childhood in
the young boy'.[57] Evidently it did no harm. Father and son were
very close, they 'talked the same language', were most happy when
together. T.J. said that Elphin had 'an adult quality that seemed to
short-circuit experience'. Such a boy could well have been an
insufferable prig but Elphin was nothing of the kind; he was full of
laughter, had an 'insatiable appetite for fun', and a strong sense of
the ridiculous. T.J. thought his young son a rare spirit, like 'radium
– costly, hard to come by, full of healing power', all and more than
T.J. himself had ever 'aspired to be'. There is no doubt something
of a doting father's partiality, heightened by a special emotional
licence, in all this. But there is ample evidence that people outside
the family also felt the extraordinary attraction of Elphin's
personality. There is no question about the unusual quality of his
mind; it was clear, swift, imaginative, original, and he had a rare
feeling for words. This judgement owes nothing to his father's
testimony, it rests on the incontrovertible evidence of Elphin's
published school essay 'On Myself', an astonishingly mature piece
of writing from the pen of a twelve-year-old boy.[58]

[56] D. Harrap, op.cit., pp.20–71. Bodl. G. Murray MSS, Vol.53, ff.152–4, 171,
WD, II, 138.

[57] Rene's account in *Elphin Lloyd Jones* (privately printed, Newtown, 1929).
T.J., Class Z (Diary, 1924), p.138. Rene to Lady Astor, Astor MSS 1416/1/2/58.

[58] *WD,* II, 282–3.

Thursday, 21 December 1928, began so happily. The family were looking forward to Christmas: a day or two earlier Eirene had heard that she had won a scholarship at Somerville College, Oxford and Tristan was at the top of his form at Stowe School. In the late morning Elphin went off to buy some Christmas presents. Shortly afterwards he lay dead in the Hampstead Children's Hospital, knocked down in a road accident while on his way home. It was a devastating blow, utterly unexpected, numbing yet agonizingly painful, accompanied by an overwhelming sense of desolation, of irreplaceable loss. In anguish the family drew even more closely together. Elphin was buried on Christmas Eve. Immediately afterwards the family went to stay for several days in a peaceful secluded house near Sandwich, put at their disposal by Waldorf and Nancy Astor, whose sensitive kindness at this time was an immense support.[59]

Letters of condolence poured in. In 1906 the sixteen-year-old son of T.J.'s mentor Sir Henry Jones had also died in tragic circumstances. Before he himself died Sir Henry wrote a short account of his dead son for his surviving children to read. It was subsequently published; T.J. said he could not 'recall anything in literature quite like it'. It may be that this precedent prompted T.J. and Rene each to write a memoir (privately printed and published) of their son, copies of which were sent to a wide circle of their friends.[60] It might possibly be thought an inconsistency that T.J., who so often insisted that he had a passion 'for anonymity', should express his deepest feelings in such a semi-public way. But there are many different responses to grief, none that is by universal consent uniquely fitting. T.J. and Rene were naturally immensely proud of their young son's qualities, his gentleness and generous instincts as much as his other gifts. It may have helped them to bear their loss by putting their emotions into words and sharing the burden of their grief. T.J.'s memoir of his son is a moving note of proud remembrance: it may also be seen as a necessary catharsis, an easement of an anguished spirit. His close friends understood very clearly that Elphin's death left a gap in T.J.'s life that could never be filled, although time, mercifully, in the long run, would assuage the pain.[61]

Perhaps fortunately too he was soon again caught up in his usual busy routine, and was also faced with a difficult decision about his

---

[59] Rene's letters in Astor MSS 1416/1/246.

[60] T.J., Class Z (Diary, 1924), p.125. *Elphin Lloyd Jones*, partly printed in *WD*, II, pp.279–81.

[61] J.B. Bickersteth in T.J., Class W, Vol.I, No.109 and T. Percy Nunn to T.J. in White MSS.

own future. Months before T.J.'s advice had been sought un-officially about a successor to A.H. Trow, Principal of University College, Cardiff, who was about to retire. Unbeknown to T.J., a committee charged with finding a new principal had unanimously recommended to the College Council that he should be appointed. T.J.'s friends pleaded with him to accept: 'No Welshman at any time has received a clearer call to come back to live among his people and to serve his people than yourself', wrote Jenkin James, Secretary of the University of Wales. 'If this is not the voice of God, what is?'.[62] Trow and W.N. Bruce, Pro-Chancellor of the University, arrived in London to add their persuasion. They had to admit that negotiations over the position of the Medical School within the University, the tiresome slogging match between vested interests that had gone on for years, had reached complete deadlock. The account given of the behaviour of some of the medical men reminded T.J. of meetings of the South Wales Miners' Federation where moderate men were 'cowed by young irresponsibles and extremists'. Rather more persuasively, Trow suggested that as Principal of Cardiff Jones would be able to do very much more for adult education in general and Coleg Harlech in particular. T.J. agreed to consider the offer, but pointed out that the 'irresponsible attitude' of the *Western Mail* (which had published confidential information prematurely) was an obstacle. 'If the *Western Mail* were the *Manchester Guardian*', he said ruefully, 'how different it would be for all of us'.[63]

Baldwin considered that T.J. should be where he carried the 'most influence'; that is, in Whitehall where he had easy access to the mighty. There was also another, in the Prime Minister's opinion perhaps even more important, point to be considered:

> I am a Tory P.M. [Baldwin said] surrounded with a Tory Cabinet, moving in Tory circles. You don't let me forget or ignore the whole range of ideas that normally I should never be brought up against if you were not in and out of this room. You supply the radium . . . you have an extraordinary width of friendships in all classes and so many interests that through you I do gather impressions of what is being thought by a number of significant people whose minds I should not know . . . but for your help. I think every Tory P.M. ought to have someone like you about the place.

T.J. evidently was inclined to consider accepting the Cardiff offer not from choice but from a sense of duty and a feeling that to

[62] T.J., Class P, Vol.2, Nos.67 and 69; Class W, Vol.10, No.213.
[63] T.J., Class Z (Diary, 1929), pp.9–11.

refuse a disagreeable task amounted to moral delinquency. Warren Fisher gave the latter suggestion very short shrift; he told T.J. it was 'an inverted form of fear, a relic of Puritanism, a thoroughly wrong conception'. Fisher had no doubt that T.J. ought to stay where he was. The work he did 'was imponderable. It was diffused through personal influence, unstatistical but its influence extended at least as far as Washington'.[64]

T.J. had to admit that he was 'extraordinarily happy' in his current job, and of course Cardiff had never engaged his affection as its sister college at Aberystwyth had done. In the end he refused the Cardiff offer, but immediately set to work to mobilize support for the election of J.F. Rees, Professor of Commerce at Birmingham, to the vacant principalship. T.J. had had his eye on Rees for some time and had unsuccessfully proposed him for the Bangor principalship two years earlier. This time, however, Rees succeeded, and Jones immediately promised him full support in the 'tough and difficult job' he had taken on.[65]

T.J. exerted some degree of influence over most of the appointments to major public posts in Wales at this time. Where the government was involved, his influence was paramount. The Lord President of the Council, for example, nominated several members of the governing bodies of the National Library, the National Museum and the colleges of the University of Wales. Almost invariably, in these and in other similar appointments, including honours and grace-and-favour pensions, Jones was consulted. More often than not he was ready with appropriate, or at any rate acceptable, names; if not, he sought the advice of his reliable local aides Percy Watkins, Silyn Roberts, Edgar Jones, Burdon Evans and company. In fact, in the absence of a Secretary of State for Wales, T.J. acted as a sort of unofficial proconsul for the Principality who operated behind a cloak of confidentiality. 'I am afraid you are fated to be regarded as our guide, philosopher, and friend in matters of this, as of many other, kind'. Syers, the Prime Minister's Private Secretary, wrote to Jones in December 1939 about the claim of a Welsh applicant for a Civil List pension.[66] It was of course open to some serious objections: T.J. held no elective post in Wales; strictly, he spoke for no one but himself, and his advice was tendered in private, not subjected to informed criticism, nor, apparently, usually balanced by alternative Welsh opinions.

---

[64] *WD*, II, 167–8.

[65] T.J., Class W, Vol.16, No.167.

[66] T.J., Class N, Vol.2, No.24 (and Nos.25–29 for the determination of the case precisely in accordance with T.J.'s advice).

On the other hand, given the system and the Tory pre-dominance of the day, T.J. was likely to offer advice on Welsh appointments that was better informed, more broadly represent-ative of national opinion and probably more disinterested than that of any other individual who would have been consulted by the government at that time. He was certainly not influenced by considerations of class, party affiliation or, the bane of so much in Wales, narrow parochial loyalties. A commitment to the ideal of public service and a willingness in practice to fulfil the duties of office were the chief considerations, other than ability, that governed his recommendations. He was not of course immune from personal prejudice, although it rarely degenerated into mere prejudice. When, in January 1932, it was suggested that Mrs Clara Novello Davies, ebullient mother of the celebrated Welsh composer Ivor Novello, should be made a DBE, T.J. replied tersely that others had done as much for music: 'she has a gift for publicity in addition to her musical gifts . . . If you *must* give anything, I should make it an M.B.E.'[67]

T.J. also wielded a very powerful influence, entirely legitimate of course, over open competitive appointments in Wales. His support was not given lightly: he investigated applicants' credentials with exceptional thoroughness, and indeed often long before an opinion was invited. This was particularly true of young men of outstanding promise who, once identified, were kept under a remarkably close personal surveillance. Jack Jones, the author of *Off to Philadelphia in the Morning*, who knew T.J. well and had a sophisticated though not cynical understanding of the making of appointments in Wales, wrote of T.J.'s undoubtedly 'great but never evil influence' in placing men in jobs.[68] And the only reference that would do adequate justice to his unobtrusive efforts to help lame dogs over stiles and on to better opportunities, especially in education, would be: Jones's MSS *passim*.

He was of course well placed to take up Welsh grievances in high places in London. Many Welsh people who were politically opposed to the tiny Welsh nationalist party of the day were infuriated by the

---

[67] T.J., Class Z (Diary, 1932), p.6. In the end poor Madame Clara was passed over.

[68] 'Men and Memories'. *Western Mail,* 24 March 1962. 'Take the question of appointments', T.J. said in a delightfully tart radio talk (*Wales on the Wireless,* ed. P. Hannan, [BBC Publications, Llandysul 1988], p.21). 'It has become almost impossible to place any reliance on testimonials even though written by ministers of the Gospel. The desire to be kind drives out the desire to be honest. Instead of producing two great men in a century we are, according to these testimonials, producing two a week'.

bland disregard for their national identity shown by the BBC in London. When, in December 1927, a new regional station embracing the west of England and Wales was established, Burdon Evans, who was certainly no political firebrand, protested vehemently to T.J.:

> If we sit silent under this we shall deserve all we get. The meek may inherit the earth, but they will inherit damned little else where England is concerned. I am very angry. The English recognise nothing but force . . . I wish we had some of the pluck of the Irish without their *extreme* methods.[69]

T.J. promptly passed on the letter to Sir John Reith, Director General of the BBC, with a covering note testifying to Evans's respectability. Reith's reply, sent on to Burdon Evans, has not survived. In fact, the demand for a separate Welsh region was not conceded until 1937.[70] In the mean time, however, T.J. was involved in attempts to wear down the Corporation's resistance. It is evident that Reith, who was not normally especially responsive to outside criticism, was anxious to persuade Tom Jones that the BBC really was doing its best to be helpful. In May 1930 Reith and T.J. went down together to Cardiff and spent the best part of the day examining Welsh grievances. T.J. asserted that 'there wasn't a single person at the Cardiff station who could announce in Welsh without betraying the fact that he was a foreigner', and he pressed, in particular, for the appointment of a Welsh-speaking woman on to the staff at Cardiff. Shortly afterwards Reith wrote in fulsome terms ('One is glad that one can take counsel of the stars and beyond them') thanking T.J. for his advice and assistance in soothing the irritations of Ramsay MacDonald, currently Prime Minister, who considered that he had not had 'a fair deal at various times' from the BBC. One good turn obviously deserved another. Four months later Reith came up with the name of a woman who reputedly spoke Welsh for a post at Cardiff. T.J. consulted one of his men on the spot. The proposed candidate would not do; she did not speak Welsh fluently, nor was she, as she should be, 'soaked in the Welsh traditions', in fact she knew 'no more about Wales than the average Cardiffian'. She was not appointed.[71]

To some extent Reith and T.J. spoke the same language. Indeed, the Director-General seemed prepared to accept Jones as an

[69] T.J., Class H, Vol.5, No.62, partly printed in *WD*, II, 125.
[70] A. Briggs, *The History of Broadcasting in the U.K.* (Oxford 1965), II, 306–38, accepts rather too easily the BBC's explanations for the delay.
[71] T.J., Class W, Vol.16, Nos.186–9.

occasional arbiter in the running quarrel between the BBC and its more vehement critics in Wales such as William George, L.G.'s brother. In May 1931, at yet another meeting, T.J. was persuaded, after a detailed examination, that a good deal of the 'grousing' was 'unwarranted'. However, he seized the opportunity to bring about the appointment of his friend Edgar Jones, an excellent choice, as a part-time adviser to help the BBC 'to serve Wales better'. A year later, Vice-Admiral Sir Charles Carpendale, Deputy Controller of the BBC, 'a real diehard quarter-deck Englishman', as Edgar Jones described him, nevertheless allowed T.J. an astonishing degree of involvement for an outsider in an important appointment to the staff at Cardiff.[72]

Reith maintained his close co-operation with T.J.; it was obviously worth his while to do so. In a letter on 1 September 1931, in which he explained the difficulties, mainly technical, that prevented the BBC from giving its Welsh critics 'what they want', Reith expressed his gratitude for Jones's assistance in blocking the demand for a national campaign of protest in Wales. T.J., who believed that a slice or two was almost always better than no bread at all, pressed instead in vain for the appointment of a representative Welsh governor of the BBC. 'Can you not rely on the B.B.C. taking as much interest in Wales as it does in any other part of its constituency? If Wales, why not Scotland?', Reith replied, adding absurdly '. . . you need not reply that Sir Gordon Nairne is Scotch and that I am Scotch'. That particular Welsh demand got nowhere. In fact, T.J.'s cautious tactic of reasoned argument behind the scenes made no serious inroad into the BBC's settled policy of centralization and metropolitan cultural imperialism.[73]

Jones had not been much more successful in his later efforts to influence Baldwin's policies in the approach to the general election of 1929. Late in 1928, partly at T.J.'s insistence, Baldwin had set up a small secret committee, chaired by Warren Fisher with T.J. as secretary, of senior Civil Servants to consider the possibility of 'special measures' to reduce unemployment. Not surprisingly, the limit of adventure for that body of men, some of whom wore the livery of the Treasury, was a recommendation to spend twenty million pounds over the next three years mainly on roads.[74] T.J. continued without much success to urge Baldwin to concentrate on the problem of unemployment, and anxiously sought detailed

[72] T.J., Class H, Vol.18, Nos.42–55.
[73] Ibid., No.41. Briggs, op.cit., pp.293–338. Reith's letter, which had characteristic autocratic touches, also showed how acutely uncomfortable he was when confronted with organized democratic protests.
[74] *WD*, II, 146, 155–6.

information from a friend at the Board of Health in south Wales about the effectiveness of statutory provision, supplemented by the work of voluntary agencies, in meeting the most desperate social needs, particularly those of young children and their mothers. By the spring of 1929, Jones came to believe that the best hope for the unemployed was that the 'conscience of the country as a whole' was being aroused. There were limits to what he could do publicly to assist this moral persuasion. 'I am always expecting to be hauled up for going so far as I do', he told an academic friend who wanted him to write to the *Spectator* in support of a particular form of social action.[75]

If in his support of social policies close to his heart Jones occasionally strayed outside the limit of personal action appropriate to a Civil Servant, he also overstepped the mark once again in the purely party political work he did for Baldwin in the general election in 1929. T.J. wrote many of Baldwin's campaign speeches, most of them from the most meagre hints. It was no easy task: he had to rely on elegant phraseology and high-sounding sentiment to cover the absence of concrete proposals. Even so, many people were impressed: Bridgeman, First Lord of Admiralty, thought the speeches would gain a great deal of personal respect for Baldwin, and Balfour was 'much struck' with the Prime Minister's broadcast speech, 'my latest effort', as T.J. described it, on the Empire. T.J. confessed however that it was difficult to make what Baldwin said on unemployment anything 'other than very tame . . . after L.G.'s Orange pamphlet', the Liberal electoral précis version of the Yellow Book and the other party inquiries. T.J. believed that the Tory Central Office's biggest mistake, acting on the advice of an advertising agency, was to fight the campaign on the 'fatal slogan' of 'Safety First' and poster portraits of Baldwin captioned 'The man you can trust'.[76]

Baldwin had expected to win. Indeed, he had confidently discussed possible ministerial changes with T.J. some weeks before the election. Baldwin was bitterly disappointed by the result. Lloyd George, who had been promised 100–150 MPs by his chief party agent, was equally disappointed at the failure of his great campaign to revive the fortunes of the Liberals along with his own. The electoral predictions of T.J., Rene and Sidney and Beatrice Webb were much nearer the mark, with Rene the most accurate of the

[75] T.J., Class Z, (Diary, 1929), p.13; Class V, Vol.1, No.172; Class W, Vol.17, No.162.

[76] *WD*, II, 180–92. W. Bridgeman to his mother, 28 April 1929. Bridgeman MSS. Balfour reported in Hankey Diary 1/8 ff.27–28.

four. During the campaign, T.J. had warned Baldwin of the probability of large Labour gains in the industrial north. The Joneses voted in Hampstead for opposition party candidates, but for some reason (family disagreement?) 'neither confessed to the other for whom'.[77]

Because of his very strong personal regard for the Prime Minister, T.J. regretted Baldwin's defeat, but otherwise he welcomed the Labour victory, and this time he knew he had no reason to fear any adverse personal consequence as in 1924. Months before he had been assured by Warren Fisher that this was so, and Hankey later said that MacDonald's 'antipathy of 1924 to T.J. had disappeared'. In fact, MacDonald, a blatant recidivist where injured innocence was concerned, insisted, against a good deal of evidence, that he had never had any personal objection to Jones.[78] At any rate, when J.H. Thomas, who became Lord Privy Seal with a special commission to deal with unemployment, asked for T.J.'s assistance, MacDonald intervened to say: 'No, I want T.J. for big developments which I have in mind in connection with the C.C.R. [Committee for Civil Research]'.[79]

Some months elapsed before that particular plan was put into effect, and in the mean time T.J. continued to work at No. 10 Downing Street, although at first his status was not entirely clear. However, in August 1929, when Hankey went over to Holland with Snowden, the Chancellor of the Exchequer, to a conference on reparations, T.J. was recalled from a family holiday in Switzerland to take his place.

During that month he worked closely with MacDonald, among other things supervising the transmission of secret telephone messages between the Prime Minister and the British delegation that were translated into Welsh to defeat Dutch eavesdroppers. During these weeks T.J.'s relations with MacDonald became markedly more cordial, indeed, sufficiently relaxed to have their lighter moments.

[77] *WD*, II, 171–80, 191–2. T.J., Class Z (Diary, 1929) pp.93–4. Mrs Baldwin, who seemed to feel that cheering crowds during the election had been wilfully deceitful, later said, 'How any woman can vote Labour passes my comprehension'. T.J. wanted to reply, 'How any working woman could vote Unionist passes mine', but for once boldness deserted him.

[78] *WD*, II, 168, 190, 195. Other Labour leaders evidently did not resent T.J.'s party work for Baldwin. Snowden, for example, who could be unpleasantly acerbic, at their first meeting gently teased T.J. about the 'new sort of speeches' he would have to write for the Labour Government. Jones replied that this presented no problem.

[79] Ibid., II, 190.

27 August. 8am. P.M. rings up. Where had I been last night? At what night club? He would report me to the Welsh Methodist connexion. He had tried to awaken me on the 'phone for half an hour last night.

And MacDonald had now overcome his former mistrust to the point where he encouraged T.J. to maintain close contact with Baldwin and pass on various items of confidential information.[80] The fact was that MacDonald and Baldwin got on well together; moreover they shared an obsessive fear and hatred of Lloyd George. There was therefore no reason why T.J.'s friendship with Baldwin should not continue to be close. Before he left office Baldwin had at least succeeded in persuading Jones to accept an honour. His objection remained as 'deep rooted' as ever, but Hankey, Fisher and others persuaded him that Baldwin dearly wanted to give some public demonstration of his appreciation and the King had also expressed some interest. T.J.'s was the only Companionship of Honour conferred on that occasion. Obviously however he found it difficult to shrug off his embarrassment:

> I did not expect to have a letter of congratulation from you as I thought your principles and mine on such matters were identical [he wrote to John Davies, stalwart of the Welsh working class]. In achieving an 'Honour' I feel I have fallen from grace, and I ride off with the plausibility that 'C.H.' really means Coleg Harlech.[81]

In mid-September T.J. was a shade surprised to hear that MacDonald wanted him to accompany him on a visit to the United States and Canada. This was Jones's first visit to America and he thoroughly enjoyed the experience. He had always been a keen advocate of the most friendly relations possible with the United States, and indeed had done his best to combat Baldwin's inveterate prejudice against Americans. T.J. was also prepared to disagree with Hankey, the acknowledged expert, over naval relations with the USA. T.J. argued in October 1928 that it was 'idle to pretend that America isn't there, or is not ten times richer than we are'; a naval race with the United States was the last thing Britain should risk. Hankey disavowed any aggressive intention, but he was convinced that it was not possible to 'do business' with the

---

[80] Ibid., II, 196–205, 210–11.

[81] Ibid., II, 184, 187; T.J., Class W, Vol.4, No.32. At supper at the Tawneys' at this time, T.J. (in an attempt to deflect attention from his own embarrassment?) teased his host about a rumour he was to go to the Lords. Tawney, who was completing his book *Equality*, replied 'The Party has a right to ask for your services but not to humiliate and insult'.

Americans, and it was as well to avoid either 'conferences or agreements with them' on naval matters.[82] Hankey was obviously nervous that MacDonald might be inveigled during his visit in October 1929 into making dangerous concessions over rights of naval blockade to President Hoover, prompted by the American *éminence grise* Colonel House, who aroused deep suspicion in Britain. Hankey 'primed Tom Jones' on the complicated question of belligerent rights at sea. At a private lunch T.J., who curiously was described in the *Detroit News* as House's British equivalent, did discover the extent and purpose of House's influence with the President on the question, and seems to have exercised at Hankey's instance some restraining influence over MacDonald.[83]

But T.J.'s main duty in America was speech writing for the Prime Minister, and this he did with his usual practised ease. 'One looks in vain', the *Ottawa Journal* of 19 October 1929 said of one of MacDonald's most important speeches in Canada, 'for the cliché, the bromide, the superfluous adjective that so disfigures speech and which are so weakening to its fibre. Mr. MacDonald has compactness, a sense of proportion, strength as well as beauty . . . He is a very compelling speaker'. Much obviously was owed to MacDonald's fine presence, his attractive Scottish voice and confident delivery, but there is little doubt that T.J. had managed, despite MacDonald's capacity to think on his feet, to counter to some advantage the Prime Minister's habitual tendency to prolixity. T.J. reported to his wife that 'relations with the P.M.' were 'excellent', and MacDonald's daughter, Ishbel, was friendliness itself.[84]

T.J. made many new friends during the trip and rarely missed an opportunity, particularly with north Americans who had any vestige of Welsh ancestry, to tap them for money for Coleg Harlech. At a 'profitable breakfast' in Washington he collected four hundred dollars from one American Davies, three hundred and seventy-five from another, Joseph E. Davies, later the American ambassador to Moscow, and had a possibly costly near-miss at a dinner after he had softened up John D. Rockefeller who, amongst other qualifications as a subscriber, had 'been twice to Wales'. In Montreal T.J. met his

[82] *WD*, II, 131, 146–9. 'Some Whitehall masters', T.J. commented to Gwen Davies two years later, 'are still too stupid to admit that America is on the map of world powers'. T.J., Class R, Vol.3, No.68.

[83] Hankey Diary, Vol.4, 1/7 ff.14 and 17, 18 October, 15 November 1929. S. Roskill, *Hankey: Man of Secrets* (1970), II, 493–5. *WD*, II, 213.

[84] Ibid., II, 215. MacDonald was apparently put out when, at some whistlestop points, Welsh Society groups turned up and called for T.J. rather than the Prime Minister to appear. Memorabilia in the McKenzie MSS.

erratic brother Alf and his family. Alf's domestic life was not of the happiest, but at least, as T.J., typically, found out, he had a decent job, supervising two dozen girls assembling radio parts, and his employers apparently thought well of him.[85]

MacDonald's goodwill mission to North America was considered a great success. On his return home, however, he faced mounting, indeed frightening, difficulties that in the end brought about the downfall of his minority government. In 1929 there were still over a million people unemployed in Britain, the outcome largely of the inability of her old-fashioned labour-intensive staple industries like coal, cotton and steel to compete effectively in the world's markets. In the late 1920s the world economy, already unsound, was further disrupted by, among other things, drastic falls in commodity prices caused by over-production in primary producing countries and sharp reductions in American lending abroad accentuated by a great boom in shares on Wall Street. The 'Great Crash' of the American stock market in October (that curiously passed without comment from T.J., who was in America at the time) temporarily eased the financial strain in Britain leading to reductions in the Bank rate, but the collapse of the world economy continued unabated, Britain's export trade declined still further and the numbers of unemployed mounted alarmingly. The first Labour government in 1924 had failed to realise the absurdly exaggerated hope of solving the problem of unemployment that party propaganda had previously aroused. MacDonald was determined that the next Labour government would at least be better organized to grapple with the problem of mass unemployment. J.H. Thomas, the Lord Privy Seal, who had a reputation for 'push and go' as it was once called, was made, in effect, Minister for Unemployment, and given the assistance of three junior ministers and a small staff of Civil Servants. Thomas had wanted T.J. but, as has been seen, MacDonald stopped that. Thomas began well; as T.J. said, he was 'full of plans and he has energy'; indeed at first Thomas looked like something more than just a pale imitation of Lloyd George in his heyday. General opinion, however, as T.J. told him, was divided between those who thought Thomas 'a fool' for accepting an impossible commission and those who thought him 'courageous' to do so.[86] With the clearer vision of hindsight, T.J. wrote of J.H. Thomas's appointment to the 'absurd Ministry of Unemployment'. Initially, however, while acknowledging the

[85] T.J. to the Secretary, 8 October 1929. Coleg Harlech MSS. *WD*, II, 214–15. T.J. to his sister Har', 1st November 1929, McKenzie MSS.

[86] *WD*, II, 187–9.

difficulties, and indeed exhorting him not to take refuge in the soft option of extending welfare payments, T.J. believed that Thomas's commission was thoroughly worthwhile.[87]

But he had some reservation about the Economic Advisory Council (EAC) from the outset: 'I am all for this development', he wrote in December 1929, 'but I cannot pretend to expect from it as much as the P.M. does'.[88] The EAC derived from a number of diverse sources: *ad hoc* techniques of economic management adopted during the First World War, the reconstruction movement and the experiment of the National Industrial Council that followed, among others. After these ideas had fallen into disfavour for a time, Haldane, it will be recalled, had provided a fresh impetus which led to the establishment of the Committee of Civil Research of which T.J. became Secretary. Subsequently, the Liberal 'Yellow Book' argued powerfully for the establishment of an economic general staff, and Tawney and G.D.H. Cole, responding for the Labour party in 1929, followed much the same line.[89] MacDonald was ultra keen to transform the CCR into something a good deal more ambitious and had earmarked T.J. to help.[90] All this was more easily said than done, and there was a long-running vigorous debate, sometimes acrimonious, among the many experts consulted before the CCR, as T.J. said, not entirely accurately, was 'rebaptised as the Economic Advisory Council' on 17 February 1930.[91]

For several weeks before and after that date T.J. was busily engaged in recruiting staff and negotiating with those people, ultimately fifteen in number, with a 'special knowledge of industry and economics', who joined MacDonald and other ministers on the EAC. In the matter of professional staff, T.J. had to 'go warily' as there were hostile questions in the Commons, but he managed, with the assistance of Keynes, to secure the appointment of H.D. Henderson and, against Keynes's advice, the appointment of Alan Loveday to the full-time senior economic posts. The EAC had an advisory, an investigative and an inspirational role; it had a large number of specialist sub-committees. T.J. was kept 'occupied fully'

[87] T.J.'s notebook. *WD*, II, 193.

[88] Ibid., II, 230.

[89] S. Howson and D. Winch, *The Economic Advisory Council 1930–39* (Cambridge, 1977), pp.5–16. Cole told MacDonald (PRO 30-69-672): 'It really wants doing, both as a contribution to constructive Socialism and as an obviously useful improvement in the machinery of government'.

[90] Above, p.328.

[91] Howson and Winch, op.cit., pp.17–30. *WD*, II, 218–23. T.J., Class B, Vol.2, No.3.

at the EAC, so much so, as he complained to his daughter, that he could not keep up his usual practice of writing 'a begging letter per day' on behalf of Coleg Harlech and the south Wales settlements.[92]

In fact, Jones became more and more disillusioned by his experience at the EAC and, in particular, with what he regarded as the Prime Minister's inveterate tendency to blather. 'In MacDonald's day', T.J. wrote years later, 'I more than once took Hubert Henderson, my economist colleague, to No. 10 to discuss measures for dealing with unemployment, only to be dismissed unheard after twenty minutes occupied by the Prime Minister in waffling'. When Henderson submitted what T.J. called 'a revolutionary memorandum' to counter mounting unemployment, MacDonald failed to bring it before the Cabinet. When, in some desperation, the government decided to co-operate with Lloyd George, T.J. hoped he would 'come on the E.A.C.' and put some life into its ministerial members. On the other hand, Jones thought that Sir Oswald Mosley, one of the junior ministers appointed to assist J.H. Thomas, went too far in advocating in a vehement 'memorandum' of protest at the government's inaction, the introduction of a set of controls appropriate to a siege economy. T.J. believed that that would eventually 'Russianise' the British government.[93] The Cabinet rejected Mosley's proposals and he eventually resigned in disgust. J.H. Thomas, out of his depth and near to nervous collapse, moved on to the Dominions Office. There were rumours of a new government administrative arrangement about unemployment that was to be equipped with a new secretariat. 'I hope I shall have nothing to do with it', T.J. wrote. He had plainly had enough of the EAC. Less than three weeks later he resigned suddenly from the Civil Service.[94]

In June 1930 Tom Jones was within three months of his sixtieth birthday, the retiring age, ordinarily, for Civil Servants. Subject to a favourable report annually, he could have continued for another five years, but he was not enamoured of that prospect. Providentially, as it turned out, an alternative opportunity opened up at exactly the right time. Arriving for breakfast with Baldwin one morning, T.J. was greeted with the news that, out of the blue, his host had been given two million pounds by a rich American, Edward Harkness, to spend for the benefit of Britain. 'Do let me

---

[92] Howson and Winch, op.cit., pp.24–34. *WD*, II, 246, 270. T.J., Class X, Vol.9, No.46.

[93] *A Diary with Letters*, Introduction, p.xxxi. *WD*, II, 251, 256–265. Henderson's memorandum, which was not particularly 'revolutionary', is printed in Howson and Winch, op.cit., pp.165–80.

[94] Ibid., II, 262.

help you to spend it', T.J. said. 'But you would not leave the Cabinet Office'. 'I certainly would'. Within days everything was arranged. T.J. became Secretary of Harkness's foundation, tentatively entitled the St George, and subsequently, because of its evocative Anglo-American connotation, amended to the Pilgrim Trust.[95]

The Prime Minister received the news of Jones's retirement politely enough, but with no great sign of personal regret. MacDonald's chief response seemed to be pique that he himself had not been asked to be a Pilgrim trustee.[96] In the comments that he made subsequently on the four Prime Ministers with whom he had worked, Tom Jones had very little to say about MacDonald. The most agreeable period of their relationship was during the short visit to America when MacDonald, who depended more than most men on the outward signs of success, was 'forthcoming and friendly' towards T.J. But in general they were not in accord temperamentally. T.J. had no side: he thought MacDonald pretentious, a poseur given to empty theatricality. 'Vanity', T.J. wrote in 1954, 'is a poison which spreads deterioration subtly and MacDonald was its victim'.[97] A dozen years earlier, most unusually for him, Jones had scoffed on a public platform at what he considered MacDonald's dithering incompetence. Speaking on the marvels of the Civil Service, T.J. said that Britain had

> a variable party system . . . today with L.G. as P.M., tomorrow with Lord Baldwin, today with a foot on the accelerator, tomorrow on the brake, the next day under Ramsay MacDonald with two feet on both at once.[98]

There is more here than disdain or dislike, there is bitterness, an assertion supported by unpublished evidence. In the material T.J. collected for his projected study of British government there is not one reference to MacDonald that is not hostile, and Jones's considered conclusion (following Croker on Canning) was: 'his mind squinted, but this was altogether a mode of his mind'.[99] T.J. rarely gave vent to spite or rancour, but it looks as if he never forgave MacDonald for the shabby way he was treated by him during the Campbell case. On balance, Jones, usually one of the fairest of critics, was as unduly severe on MacDonald as he was excessively indulgent to Baldwin.

[95] *A Diary with Letters,* Introduction, p.xl. T.J., Class X, Vol.9, No.66.
[96] However, the Prime Minister's farewell note was a good deal more gracious with a nice touch of friendly humour. *WD,* II, 267, 273–4.
[97] *A Diary with Letters,* Introduction, p.xxxi.
[98] *Western Mail,* 23 May 1942.
[99] T.J. Notebook.

When it was announced that T.J. was retiring he received a shoal of complimentary letters, some of them, from men with whom he worked, particularly touching. 'I've never met anyone with quite your *flair* for the right and sensible course, without any undue respect for correctitudes', said Hubert Henderson. And Sir Rupert Howarth, T.J.'s successor as Deputy Secretary of the Cabinet, even more affectingly wrote: 'next only to my Father there is no one that I have so honoured and admired as yourself'.[100]

From start to finish Tom Jones was the most unorthodox of senior Civil Servants. He was almost forty-one years old when he entered the Service via the Welsh Insurance Commission in 1911. Five years later he was whisked away by Lloyd George to work in the topmost corridor of power in Whitehall, as an assistant, ultimately deputy, to Hankey in the new experimental Cabinet secretariat. But of much greater interest and significance were the special services T.J. performed for the Prime Ministers for whom he worked. He demonstrated supreme self-confidence and a remarkable gift of swift adaptability. He had no previous experience of high politics, yet he moved easily into the realm of statecraft and acquitted himself with something like distinction. Lloyd George relied heavily on T.J. in his confidential dealings with the leaders of the Labour movement, and made him his surrogate in crucially important negotiations with the southern Irish. T.J. had 'no credal difficulty' in serving his different masters; they were all at bottom liberal-minded and he himself 'believed a little in all three parties', although his residual sympathy lay 'more in the Left than in the Right'.[101] There was no particular call for Jones's discreet talents during Bonar Law's short, tranquil premiership, but Baldwin made constant, sometimes undue, demands upon him. On the other hand, this meant that during Baldwin's second ministry there were occasions, as in the General Strike and its sequel, when Jones was well-placed to exercise an influence that can be shown to be in the public interest.[102] Ramsay MacDonald, who was said not to understand how to make proper use of secretaries, failed to derive full advantage from Jones's skill and experience.

T.J. claimed that he was 'by temperament . . . a civil servant', and he certainly had an appropriate instinct to avoid the limelight.[103] But he was not unduly bound by official routine or the inhibiting

[100] *WD*, II, 272.

[101] *A Diary with Letters,* Introduction, p.xxiii.

[102] 'I have cherished an illusion', T.J. wrote, with some justice, in 1935 (Class Z (Diary), p.111), 'that the history of the General Strike would have been different if I had not been about'.

[103] *A Diary with Letters,* Introduction, p.xxiii.

power of precedent and he was prepared on occasion to run some risk of exposure to political criticism. Tom Jones was much more than a trusted agent and discreet go-between; he was also the licensed critic within Prime Ministerial circles who was freely allowed to draw the attention of ministers, Labour as well as Conservative or National Liberal, to considerations other than, or opposed to, their apparent party interests. His was frequently the persistent, quiet voice of conscience in a setting where political expediency often shouted loudest.

Of course it was not all virtue. Occasionally he trespassed on territory where he had no legitimate right to be, and was perhaps fortunate to escape serious criticism. The fate of Sir Horace Wilson, who some years later stood in much the same relation to Neville Chamberlain as T.J. had been to Baldwin and more especially to Lloyd George, offers an interesting comparison. Wilson was ultimately punished by virtual dismissal for too close an identification with the policies of his chief. In fact, it was T.J. who had suggested Wilson for the post, initially to assist Baldwin. In July 1942, some time after he had been summarily removed, Wilson told T.J. ruefully: 'You were far better placed under cover of the cabinet secretariat. I risked arousing the jealousy of ministers'.[104]

There was of course a good deal of truth in this. But it was also an open secret that T.J. took issue with his masters on many political aspects of their policies, and it was recognized that his influence lay in his disinterestedness, his salutary voicing of an alternative point of view, not in exceptional zeal in carrying out instructions. He was thus absolved from censure by opposition politicians. Indeed, he was often calmly advancing objections to Cabinet proposals that they themselves were likely to make in the more heated atmosphere of Parliament where adversarial politics pre-ordained them to be swept aside. There was also the influence of personality. On one occasion Jones wondered whether his career would have taken a different course if he had gone up to Balliol rather than Aberystwyth and Glasgow.[105] It could scarcely have been more successful. T.J.'s Civil Service career, with all due allowance for good fortune, was a triumph of personality, of shrewdness and winning charm. He was the outsider, the Welsh provincial who arrived late but nevertheless became a legend in the Civil Service during his lifetime.

[104] T.J. Notebook.
[105] T.J., Class Z (Diary, 1929), p.177.

CHAPTER TWELVE

RESCUE WORK

As Tom Jones approached the age of retirement, his friends in Wales naturally hoped that his talents would at last be chiefly devoted to matters of Welsh concern. John Davies, temporarily dispirited by the relative failure of the adult education movement, wrote pleading with T.J. to 'take up the reins of leadership in Wales'. Davies said that there were several promising social and educational movements but there was no one of sufficient stature who was animated by the sort of 'consuming passion' necessary for effective leadership. 'We want someone who is above party politics but one who, nevertheless, cares intensely'. In Davies's opinion, T.J. alone filled the bill.[1] Sir Henry Stuart Jones, Principal of the University College at Aberystwyth, had hoped that Tom Jones would succeed him when he retired, but was put off when told that T.J. was nearly sixty. David Davies, who had been urged by Tom Jones to forget their past disappointments at Aberystwyth and 'put his back into the job', had become President of the College in 1926. D.D., who was never half-hearted about anything, of course did so. In June 1930 he wrote pointing out that Stuart Jones was due to retire in 1932 and invited Jones to stand by to succeed him. But T.J. was already committed to the Pilgrim Trust and a post which offered special opportunities for public service on a national scale.[2]

Now that he had left government service, T.J. was inevitably less closely involved in high politics. His chief importance in the early 1930s was that he was a pivotal figure, possibly the key man, in the response of the voluntary charitable agencies to the scourge of mass unemployment. The onset of world-wide economic recession in 1929 added over a million more to the great mass of the unemployed in Britain in the 1920s. The plight of the worst-hit areas in Scotland, the north of England and south Wales deteriorated to the point of desperation. The government now appeared completely helpless in the face of forces that it scarcely seemed to comprehend, much less control. Ministers rejected all

---

[1] T.J., Class W, Vol.4, No.36.
[2] *WD*, II, 268. T.J., Class P, Vol.2, No.90; Class J, Vol.9, No.4.

risks, conventional economic wisdom enjoined substantially reduced public expenditure; there seemed to be nothing for it therefore but to sit tight and hope for some sort of economic recovery sometime in the future. Meanwhile, conditions for the unemployed, particularly in the distressed areas where there was not even the glimmer of hope of a job, were utterly bleak. Accordingly, there was unlimited scope for private relief work as public policy rejected any notion of direct curative action.[3] Tom Jones was closely involved with five agencies that were concerned with the problem of social distress.

Edward S. Harkness of New York derived an enormous fortune from the bounding oligopolist prosperity of the Standard Oil Company. But whatever the allegedly murky origins of their vast wealth, the Harkness family had a magnificent record of public benefactions in America and on a much smaller scale in Britain. Edward Harkness himself, a shy, self-effacing man, gave away in over a thousand separate donations more than one hundred and twenty-nine million dollars during his lifetime.[4] In 1930 he gave a capital sum of two million pounds to establish the Pilgrim Trust as an expression of his admiration for what Britain had done in war and peace for what he called 'the common cause'. There were to be five Trustees headed by Stanley Baldwin, who consented to be Chairman. His four colleagues were Lord Macmillan, a distinguished Scottish judge, currently Chairman of the Committee on Finance and Industry, Sir James Irvine, Principal of St Andrews University, Sir Josiah Stamp, banker and businessman, and John Buchan, MP and man of letters. T.J., as we have seen, was Secretary. The Trustees were accorded an absolute discretion in the disposal of both the income and capital of the Fund, a freedom which nevertheless disposed them to cautious experiment in the first year of their existence. The preamble to the Trust Deed had however implied a twofold primary concern: to promote the future well-being of Britain, and, meantime, to help in tiding over current social distress. Accordingly, the Trustees tried to strike an even balance between these two objectives.[5]

T.J. was ideally, it could be said uniquely, qualified for the office of Secretary of the Pilgrim Trust. He was passionately interested in

[3] In August 1930 T.J. regretted (Class H, Vol.7, No.57) that a proposal, first mooted in 1920, to appoint 'a Government Commissioner with considerable financial and administrative powers to stimulate employment schemes in the worst areas' had still not been put into effect. It lay dormant until 1934.

[4] J.W. Wooster, *Edward Stephen Harkness, 1874–1940* (New York, 1949), p.77.

[5] *Pilgrim Trust Report, 1930–1* (hereafter *PT Report*), pp.1–4.

the preservation and enhancement of the landscape, natural and man-made. Indeed, he was in some respects a precursor of the vigorous Green campaigners of today. T.J.'s interest in alleviating social distress went back to his student days; he had great administrative experience and a valuable acquaintance with some of the key personnel in British charitable organizations; he enjoyed the complete confidence of the Chairman, Stanley Baldwin, and of Lord Macmillan who succeeded Baldwin in 1934. T.J. had been friendly for many years with Josiah Stamp, whom he much admired; Jones suggested that Stamp, who was a 'sort of international physician . . . in politics and finance', could well develop into another Bentham.[6] T.J. was also on the best of terms with John Buchan, and got on well enough with Sir James Irvine, although later on he developed some reservations about him. Jones naturally wielded great influence on the decisions of the Trustees: he was their executive officer, his experience of the conduct of business matched theirs; moreover, he was employed full-time, whereas their work for the Trust had to be fitted in to the schedules of their busy professional lives. It was T.J. who did most of the sifting and the investigation of appeals for assistance and the Chairman, Baldwin, was content to leave a great deal in the hands of the energetic Secretary, who, after a full-scale medical examination, had been declared 'physiologically young' by the physician Lord Dawson.[7]

In August, before the Trust actually came into operation, T.J. went to the United States to make a quick study of some of the American charitable foundations. His friend Abraham Flexner, who had a wide experience of them, provided him with a valuable memorandum on their operation. T.J. concluded, however, that the Pilgrim Trust, a modest foundation by American standards, would not require anything comparable to the large staff of experts employed by charitable trusts in the United States. Sensibly, he decided that if he could be made a member of the Athenaeum Club he would have access on a social basis to the very best expert advice available in the kingdom on almost every conceivable subject. Colonel Mitchell of the Carnegie Trust, with the assistance of Baldwin, soon arranged his election.[8] T.J. was a clubbable man and subsequently he transacted much Pilgrim Trust and other business in the congenial atmosphere of the Athenaeum. During his American visit T.J. saw his brother Alf and family, who came

    [6] T.J., Class Y, Vol.4, No.32.
    [7] T.J., Class W, Vol.5, No.6.
    [8] T.J., Class S, Vol.I, No.5; Class W. Vol.14, Nos.119–21; Class A, Vol.6, No.49.
A Diary with Letters, pp.xl–xli. F.R. Cowell, *The Athenaeum* (1976), p.166.

down from Canada to meet him. It was an amicable enough reunion but again it was clear that the brothers really had very little in common. T.J. said he did his best 'to give them what they think is a good time', but he drew the line at going along with them to Coney Island. He also had several meetings with Edward Harkness. They established an immediate rapport: 'I get on with him as well as I get on with S.B. [Baldwin]. I could hardly say more', T.J. said. Harkness was evidently pleased with what he called T.J.'s 'bully start'.[9]

The Pilgrim Trust established its headquarters in an attractive house at 10 York Buildings in the Adelphi. T.J. recruited a small supporting staff, that included the invaluable Gertrude Grigg who became his chief assistant in the early years. From the outset T.J. worked closely with J.M. Mitchell of the Carnegie Trust and Captain L.F. Ellis, secretary of the National Council of Social Service (NCSS), which occupied a central position in touch with voluntary agencies and government departments. Mitchell, who disliked 'vagueness and hot air', was a businesslike individual very much after T.J.'s heart, and Ellis too proved 'very helpful', especially in the early days of the Pilgrim Trust.[10] The Trustees began operations fairly generously; £180,000 was allocated in grants at the first few meetings. Originally it had been intended to draw on the capital sum as well as the income of the Trust, but the first rumblings of the financial crisis of August 1931, which led to a fall of 20 per cent in the market value of the Trust's investments, induced caution and a decision that no expenditure of capital would be incurred so long as the low level of investment values prevailed.[11]

Even so, much valuable work was done in the early years. In 1931, for example, substantial sums were devoted to the repair and preservation of Lincoln cathedral (£20,000), Durham Castle (£25,000), and lesser amounts to St David's Cathedral in Wales and St Giles, the metropolitan church of Scotland. Grants were also made to the Oxford and Cambridge Preservation Societies to assist them in their defence of surrounding green belts against disfigurement by industrial encroachment and threatened ring-road developments. The Trustees voted £2,000 to assist the promising experiment in nursery school education set up by Rachel and Margaret McMillan at Deptford. In 1932, £9,000 was voted for the upkeep of the muniment room at Westminster Abbey, and in the

[9] T.J., Class X, Vol.9, Nos.65–7.
[10] T.J., Class W, Vol.16, No.159; Class X, Vol.9, No.101.
[11] *PT Report*, 1932, pp.1–3

following year grants were made to the 'Old Vic' Theatre Company, the Victoria County History and History of Parliament projects, and the Rowett Institute of Biological Research near Aberdeen, where Boyd Orr did important work on nutrition, was bailed out of its financial difficulties.[12] This is, of course, a selection not a full list of the donations made by the Pilgrim Trust to safeguard and enhance the fabric of British society.

But naturally in the circumstances of that time the Trustees concentrated their main effort on the relief of social misery. Their policy here was to provide financial support at what seemed to them to be the key points of need in the fight against despair. Under the auspices of the NCSS a scheme was formulated to expand existing educational and social welfare work in the acutely distressed areas. The settlements in the Rhondda valley, Dowlais, Risca, Merthyr, Gateshead and Doncaster were extended, new centres were established in County Durham, the Forest of Dean and Lanarkshire, and there was a substantial development of boys' club work in Cardiff, Middlesbrough, Consett, Bishop Auckland, and Durham. Over £12,000 was donated to older settlements in London, Edinburgh, Glasgow and on Tyneside; and there was support for holiday camps for young people, the large-scale Allotments scheme run by the Society of Friends, and an investigation of the social significance of the vast new LCC slum clearance estates, 'unlike anything in our history', erected in what one of T.J.'s correspondents later called 'the atomic suburb' of Dagenham.[13] Unemployment led to a loss of technical skills as well as a decline in morale. In 1932 the Pilgrim Trust concentrated much of its support on employment schemes that provided materials and tools for groups of those out of work who took up boot repairing, furniture mending, haircutting and other services for each other. Over thirty grants were made that year to those 'mutual help' schemes in the occupational centres for the unemployed.[14]

Tom Jones always believed in the overwhelming importance of local leadership, the handful of 'pivotal people' whose initiative and example could inspire communities worn down by hopelessness to develop the strength to fight to regain self-respect. T.J. made sure, for example, that the Merthyr Settlement, which he had largely established, had a leader of exceptional quality. He persuaded Gwilym James, a young graduate of the Universities of Wales and Cambridge, a future university vice-chancellor, to serve

---

[12] Ibid., 1931–3, pp.22–35; 1932, pp.21–9; 1933, pp.28–33.
[13] Ibid., 1930–1, pp.4–21. *A Diary with Letters,* p.332.
[14] Ibid., 1932, pp.5–14.

as Warden at Merthyr for some years. James was appalled by the devitalized conditions of thousands of the unemployed in Merthyr, particularly the young people 'whose very humanity is being threatened', as he wrote in anguish in a letter to T.J. in which he pleaded for additional resources. Sadly, as Percy Watkins, commenting on James's letter, said: 'We *can* only do a little . . . a little here and a little there . . . we haven't got the Settlement itself on its feet yet'.[15]

At that time Percy Watkins almost despaired of their capacity to make any serious impact on the social problem. Watkins was a man whose abilities have not been properly recognized and whose moral stature has not been fully appreciated. Two years later, haunted by the derelict areas in south Wales, he responded to T.J.'s plea to retire early from his plum post as Welsh Secretary in the Department of Education and, at a fraction of his former salary, take on a new post as secretary of the NCSS in Wales, which subsequently became, as Tom Jones had planned, a semi-autonomous division.[16] Watkins (who by now was Sir Percy) had drive, great stamina and outstanding administrative gifts. Under his leadership, with the financial support of the NCSS and the Carnegie and Pilgrim Trusts, there was a large expansion of the voluntary service movement in south Wales. By 1933 there were 150 centres which provided recreational, educational or occupational activities for an estimated 30,000 unemployed men. Old stables, barns or warehouses, often derelict buildings, were repaired and reconditioned by the unemployed themselves. There was a membership fee of a penny a week, 'a considerable contribution', as Watkins said, for people whose income was so meagre. But despite this great effort, only the fringe of need was touched: no more than 30,000 out of the 140,000 unemployed in south Wales were associated with the centres and their branches.[17]

T.J. always laid special emphasis on the regenerative and liberating effect of education. 'The truth is', he said in a speech at Treharris, 'there is a problem of unemployed heads as there is of unemployed hands . . . In the chambers of many minds, the blinds are drawn . . . dust sheets and silence within'.[18] T.J.'s chief

[15] T.J., Class Z (Diary, 1930), pp.128–30; Class V, Vol.2, No.8.

[16] T.J., Class Z (Diary, 1932), p.102. 'I initiated Percy's move', T.J. wrote later, 'I have been trying to find some person who could do for Wales what Ellis is doing in England, someone who could strengthen John Davies on the "occupational side"'. T.J., Class W, Vol.11, No.23.

[17] P.E. Watkins, 'Voluntary Service in Wales'; T.J., Class V, Vol.2, No.35.

[18] T.J., Class Y, Vol.5, No.29.

lieutenant on the Coalfields Distress Educational Committee was its Secretary, the indomitable John Davies. During these years the committee organized hundreds of concerts, many of them conducted by the peerless Walford Davies, hundreds of lectures, and scores of classes and courses of instruction, and provided support for dozens of amateur dramatic society productions of plays in English and Welsh.[19]

This heroic attempt to help at least some of those crushed and bruised by the impersonal juggernaut of unemployment was not, however, without its critics. The trade union movement in general remained studiedly aloof and deeply suspicious, in particular, of the occupational centres as a latent threat to the wage rates of those in work. The extreme left was bitterly hostile on political grounds. During December 1931 and January 1932 the *Daily Worker* kept up a barrage of criticism of what it insisted was the sickening hypocrisy of NCSS-sponsored schemes that were designed as a cover for sinister manoeuvres to split and demoralize the workers.[20] Suspicion was heightened when the government began to provide some money for the NCSS and the Prince of Wales was recruited to address (T.J. wrote the draft of his speech) a national rally at the Albert Hall in support of voluntary effort, which he defended in forthright terms.[21]

Indeed, several of those who had taken the lead in relief work were shaken into doubt, which was expressed by some of those who attended a Welsh social service conference at Gregynog in late January 1933. Tom Jones's associates were present in force: Watkins, Walford Davies, Ellis, the Nobles, Gwilym James, Burdon Evans, Peter Scott, and John Davies and his wife, among others. John Davies insisted that he would 'do nothing to make the unemployed reconciled to their situation'. Peter Scott, who had been in the front line at Brynmawr since the start, instanced some of the difficulties he had faced: a number of people resented the proffered aid as insufferably patronizing, and this, he believed, was

> the cause of the deep gulf which more and more seems to exist between the 'social worker' and those he tries to help, so that the very name is one which some of us see as a term of reproach . . . South Wales has become so politically conscious during the last generation, so accustomed to mass organisation and to thinking in terms of

---

[19] 'Voluntary Service in Wales'. T.J., Class V, Vol.2, No.35.

[20] See, for example, the edition of 2 January 1932 for an attack on the Brynmawr scheme.

[21] T.J.'s draft in T.J., Class O, Vol.3, No.14.

political schemes that the attempt to do something practical starting from small beginnings cuts right across this, and must seem to such people a futile business, even if not positively dangerous . . . To many of us the thought that this work was being used as a palliative, bread and circuses on a large scale, would indeed be a bitter one.

Despite these and other qualms (Mrs Noble observed: 'We are rendering first aid when a big surgical operation is necessary') the conference finally agreed that

Whether or not the Government or industry, or anyone else, has failed to do what they should have done does not excuse us if we neglect to do what is in our power.[22]

T.J. was present at the conference but said little; he had come to listen rather than to speak. He too had growing doubts about the government's inaction, but he had no reservations about the value of voluntary effort, and not merely as a stopgap. He insisted that it had validity in its own right. T.J. and Percy Watkins had no doubt at all of the value of settlements: they were 'people's colleges' in the distressed areas, hives of purposeful activity, a most useful form of 'cultural irrigation'. In 1935 Watkins called for ten new settlements which, together with a small additional outlay on adult education, he believed would work wonders in putting new life into these communities.[23]

The Pilgrim Trust continued its dual policy with regard to the apportionment of assistance. In October 1934, Baldwin (who continued as a Trustee) resigned the chairmanship and was succeeded by Lord Macmillan. T.J. regretted the resignation of 'the man most respected in public life', as he described Baldwin, but his relations with the new Chairman were also excellent.[24]

At this time T.J. himself became Chairman of the determinedly unobtrusive York Trust. The name itself seems to have been casually lifted from the address of the Pilgrim Trust headquarters, and the donor, David Astor, who desired to be anonymous, half hoped that the title might persuade the curious to conclude that it had some connection with the philanthropic Rowntrees of York.

[22] *Distressed Areas of South Wales and Mon., Conference on Social Services, 27–30 January 1933* (booklet published by Outlook Press). T.J., Class H, Vol.7, No.91.

[23] P.E. Watkins, *Adult Education among the Unemployed in South Wales* (Cardiff 1935), pp.14–21. *A Diary with Letters*, pp.85–6.

[24] *PT Report*, 1934, pp.1–4. T.J., Class Z (Diary, 1934), p.67. The donor, Harkness, was apparently not entirely happy that the Chairman of his Trust was also a member of the government of the day.

Astor was content to leave the direction of the York Trust's affairs almost entirely in T.J.'s hands. Displaying a rare imagination, T.J. and Astor gave financial support to the pioneer research and practice in the badly neglected field of psychiatric medicine of Dr R.D. Gillespie of Guy's Hospital, for whom the York Clinic was established. Over the years T.J. was also able to dispense many thousands of pounds of York Trust money in grants to poor students who aspired to higher education or professional training.[25]

Given its antecedents, it was inevitable that Coleg Harlech too would be called upon to assist in the attempt to mitigate the ravages of mass unemployment. T.J.'s first concern in the early years however was somehow or other to raise enough money to keep the College open. He was not easily evaded when on the warpath for contributions. Alfred T. Davies, formerly MP for Lincoln, who was nicknamed 'Chocs' because he regularly sent boxes of chocolates to No. 10 when Lloyd George was Prime Minister, was persuaded to hand over £20. 'Caught him in a bus', T.J. said laconically in November 1929.[26] In that year, mercifully, the Board of Education agreed, subject to inspection, to pay capitation fees for Harlech students. But there were many heavy expenses and in 1930 when he was in America with MacDonald, T.J. was half-tempted to sell his much sought-after memoirs to an American publisher because Harlech 'would profit by the proceeds'. In the end, however, his natural inclination reinforced by Warren Fisher, who emphasized the importance of maintaining the confidential relationship between ministers and Civil Servants, Jones turned the offer down.[27]

One source of assistance to Harlech which, for T.J. and his wife, was especially heartwarming was the Elphin Lloyd Jones Memorial Fund, established by T.J.'s friends in memory of their young son. In a very short time the Fund amounted to over £3,000 that was used to establish scholarships at Coleg Harlech. In 1931, a thoroughly discouraging year for begging, T.J. sent the Warden, B.B. Thomas, over to the United States on a pathfinding mission: 'I don't want you to raise funds', T.J. told him, 'but to create the interest that leads later to funds in persons to whom I can write on your return'.[28] And in desperation in 1931 Thomas had suggested some

[25] T.J., Class Q, Vol.3, No.16. *A Diary with Letters*, pp.272, 303, 318, 366, 380, 541. *Welsh Broth*, pp.55–6. In 1934, a German, an Austrian and a French student were maintained at Coleg Harlech on York Trust scholarships.

[26] T.J., Class P, Vol.2, No.83.

[27] T.J., Class X, Vol.9, No.76. T.J. managed to raise over £200 for Harlech during his stay in America.

[28] 18 June 1931. NLW, B.B. Thomas MSS.

creative accounting of Harlech's balance sheet, but W.J. Williams, the treasurer, a bookkeeping martinet, would have no truck with financial jugglery. But despite these pressing financial difficulties, T.J. would not lower his aesthetic standards. In April 1931, when it was rumoured that a speculative builder had his eye on some plots of land near the College, 'where the great view thrusts on you as you come from Llanbedr to Harlech', as T.J. described it, he diverted his attention from general fund-raising to drumming up in a month from rich friends enough emergency money to enable Burdon Evans to use whatever 'devious methods' he thought appropriate to outwit the builder and save the beauty spot for future College use.[29] And at the same time, when B.B. Thomas was preparing an application for much-needed assistance to the TUC educational committee, T.J. 'stressed in advance . . . that nothing must be done to compromise our complete educational independence'.[30]

One way and another, the College managed to survive. In the circumstances of the bleak years after 1930 it was an even greater achievement than the initial struggle to establish the College in 1927. All the more so when it is considered that, as T.J. proudly proclaimed in Scotland in 1934, 'they had never borrowed a penny and never had a penny of endowment'. It was all done by 'a good deal of beating up yearly to raise the necessary funds'.[31] At one point late in 1931 however, even Tom Jones's spirit quailed. Out of the blue B.B. Thomas wrote to say that he had decided to apply for a vacant Directorship of Education. T.J. was thunderstruck:

> I had not realised until I read your letter this morning [he wrote] how much you meant to me. My heart seems to sink physically within me. No one is indispensable. That is true and I have tried all day to take an objective view, but try as I may I do not see the College surviving the crises of the seventh year without you at the helm. With you I am confident we'll get though, and then I shall be willing to let you go and take charge of Aber[ystwyth], which is much more to my mind than making you a Director of Education . . . you shall not go if I can help it.[32]

[29] T.J., Class X, Vol.9, No.116. NLW, B.B. Thomas MSS (15 May 1931).

[30] T.J., Class K, Vol.5, No.93.

[31] 'The Residential Colleges in Adult Education', *The Scottish Educational Journal* (June, 1934). T.J., Class Y, Vol.3, No.20.

[32] Thomas had won a special place in T.J.'s affections: '*You* and all you have done and are doing are one of life's most precious consolations', T.J. wrote to Thomas at an especially emotional time in 1935. NLW, B.B. Thomas MSS (8 December 1931 and 8 July 1935).

Thomas was persuaded to stay. There is little doubt that T.J.'s assessment of the Warden's importance to the College was accurate. B.B. Thomas was shrewd and able, he wrote well and was impressive on a public platform. His tragic domestic life (his wife, who died in 1932, suffered for years from a severe nervous disorder) seemed to reinforce his idealism, which was, however, rendered purposeful by much downright common sense. He provided fine leadership for a small teaching staff of four that was well up to university standards in quality. In the first session E.H. Jones, Sir Henry Jones's son, author of the minor wartime classic *The Road to Endor*, was a resident tutor. He was captivated by the quality of the first batch of students:

> I do not think I have ever felt more stirred [he wrote to T.J. in October 1927]. Their eagerness to learn took my breath away . . . By Jove, T.J., these men are hungry, avid for *any knowledge*. It almost made me cry. . . . What does it matter whether they are pink or saffron or purple provided they are genuine students! I want to see not 5 but 500 of these laddies at Harlech. . . . Your C.H. *can* be made into a godsend.[33]

However, these pioneer students were not always adequately prepared for advanced work, even though they had all had WEA tutorial class experience. They had certainly taken their courage in both hands, in some cases surrendering jobs with very doubtful prospects of being taken back again in industries suffering from heavy unemployment. One returning miner, who had difficulty for a time, was faced with a deeply suspicious colliery manager who asked if Coleg Harlech was 'a branch of Ruskin', a self-evident guilty association in capitalist south Wales.[34] T.J. hoped and expected that most Harlech students would in fact return to their jobs and localities, but he was irritated by self-righteous purists who complained that so few did not, 'a terrible thought to those who have never done any manual work in their lives', he commented acidly.[35] Supported by scholarships from trusts, some local authorities, trade union sources and, in desperation, the College's own bursary fund, the number of students, full and part-time, gradually increased to over thirty within six years. From the outset, Harlech had sought to establish international connections. Some students went on short visits to Geneva, the diplomatic capital of the world at that time. T.J. maintained close links with Peter

[33] T.J., Class K, Vol.3, No.166.
[34] Ibid., Vol.4, No.54. P. Stead, *Coleg Harlech: The First Fifty Years* (Cardiff, 1977), p.49.
[35] T.J., Class W, Vol.7, No.102.

Manniche and the International People's College at Elsinore, and there were always a few foreign students in residence at Harlech. Jones persuaded some of his many distinguished friends, Zimmern, Madariaga, C.K. Webster, Walford Davies and others, to address the students. There was no question that despite crippling financial constraints and small size, Coleg Harlech aspired to high educational standards, and evidently succeeded in attaining them sufficiently to merit the praise of Abraham Flexner, the most severe of academic critics, and the enthusiastic approval of the Board of Education's Inspectors.[36]

Political prejudice, however, took little account of evidence. Most of Coleg Harlech's critics remained unmoved. As T.J. pointed out in 1934, it was still 'suspect by employers as leaning unduly to the Left and by the trade union movement as leaning unduly to the Right'.[37] Two years before T.J. had shrugged off these criticisms and indeed was prepared to run the risk of exposing Harlech to even fiercer hostile comment. As the world economic recession moved to its lowest point in 1932 and the social tragedy in the distressed areas deepened, T.J. redoubled his efforts in support of settlement work and Coleg Harlech was called on to help. Financed by a gift which Jones had solicited from Sir Harold Wernher, chairman of Electrolux Ltd, groups of half a dozen unemployed young men from villages in north Wales were brought to Coleg Harlech for fortnightly periods. It was observed that, even in so short a time, their health and spirits improved dramatically. It was decided to extend the scheme to the whole of Wales and widen its scope considerably. It is clear that, although others were responsible for its implementation in detail, it was T.J. who initiated the plan and turned it into an effective operation. 'The situation is getting steadily worse', he told B.B. Thomas in November 1932, 'it behoves all of us to strain every nerve to help . . . Is there anything we *qua* Coleg Harlech can do?' His idea was to provide training for club leaders, who were in short supply, of the large number of occupational centres for the unemployed that had sprung up in Wales.[38] Temporary wooden huts were put up in the College

[36] A. Flexner, *Universities: American, English and German* (Oxford and New York) (1930), p.340, put the work at Harlech on a level with that of the adult education classes at the German *hocschulen*. T.J., Class W, Vol.20, No.116.

[37] 'Adult Education and Employment', *Leeks and Daffodils*, p.127. E.H. Jones hotly insisted in argument with Dame Margaret Lloyd George (T.J., Class X, Vol.11, No.11) in 1931 that within a few weeks of arrival Harlech students 'who had come there quite red put aside their party spectacles and mine the growing library in the white light of truth'.

[38] T.J., Class K, Vol.5, No.200; Class S, Vol.I, No.50.

grounds, the garage was turned into a carpenter's shop, the stables into a bindery for books, and with financial help from the NCSS a gymnasium was erected. Contingents of selected unemployed men, twenty-five strong, were brought to Harlech for a month for intensive instruction designed to fit them for leadership in the occupational centres. The training did not pretend to produce finished craftsmen but it improved skills and implanted self-confidence. It also gave T.J. some personal satisfaction to be able to raise even the smallest flag of defiance against the soulless routine of a mass-production machine society. Moreover, he had always insisted that it was 'a mistake to underestimate the intellectual interests of working men', and accordingly the trainees studied drama, music and 'bookish subjects' along with their instruction in craft work. T.J. could therefore validly claim that the Harlech curriculum catered equally for the man who wanted to read Plato's *Republic* 'and the man who preferred to bind it'.[39]

Of course, Coleg Harlech could not possibly defray this additional expenditure from its own funds. It is a sign of Tom Jones's remarkable self-confidence that he went ahead with this ambitious scheme despite the fact that Harlech already faced a deficit of nearly £1,500, and the treasurer was becoming decidedly tetchy.[40] T.J. did some useful begging among his rich friends, but most of the money for the training scheme came from the NCSS, where T.J.'s appeals for assistance were strongly backed by Ellis the Secretary and Jones's friend Violet Markham. He also elicited help from the Ministry of Labour and the Board of Education.[41] A report on all this activity, which appeared in the *Manchester Guardian* on 9 June 1933, was with some justice entitled: 'The Education of the Unemployed – Coleg Harlech to the rescue'. Of course T.J. knew that this was relief not rescue work, at best 'only an ambulance', but it made a useful contribution in the battle against social misery and served as a model for similar training courses instituted at four establishments in England.[42] It was, however, not well received in some trade union circles in south Wales where it prompted even louder complaints that the occupational centres constituted unfair competition to employed labour. T.J. was prepared to respond to any specific suggestions from the trade unions for improvements in the scheme, but he insisted on chapter-and-verse evidence of error and dismissed most of the clamour as

[39] *Leeks and Daffodils*, pp.128–9. T.J., Class W, Vol.2, No.25.
[40] T.J., Class W, Vol.2, No.25; Class K, Vol.6, Nos.188 & 203.
[41] NLW, B.B. Thomas MSS (April–December 1933). T.J., Class W, Vol.19, No.111; Class K, Vol.6, Nos.4, 24, 25, 30, 84–94, 113.
[42] T.J., Class K, Vol.7, No.88. *Leeks and Daffodils*, p.129.

unhelpful vague assertion bruited about by the spokesmen for ruffled vested interests.[43]

Thomas Jones had always maintained that what was needed was not one but fifty colleges such as Harlech. When, therefore, in October 1931, Philip Kerr, Lord Lothian, told T.J. that he thought of offering Newbattle Abbey, his large ancient mansion near Edinburgh, to the university there as a centre for summer and weekend schools, Jones's mind quickly turned to another, more ambitious scheme. Later in October he sent Lothian two memoranda he had written when Coleg Harlech was no more than a dream. T.J.'s proposal was, of course, as he explained to J.R. Peddie, a leading Scottish educationist, 'to do in Scotland at Newbattle Abbey what is done in Wales at Coleg Harlech'. There was however one difficulty which Jones pointed out to Lothian with some pride:

> The chief difference between your situation in Scotland and ours in Wales is that we have a widespread tutorial class movement from which we draw our students at Harlech, whereas the class movement is still in its infancy in Scotland.[44]

Sir James Irvine of St Andrews University agreed that much 'nursing persuasion' would be necessary to coax the Scottish working class to respond. But Professor Basil Williams of Edinburgh, who was also consulted, countered T.J.'s patriotic boasting with the argument that there was not likely to be much demand 'for education of the Harlech type' in Scotland as there were so many bursaries for poor students to go to the universities that only 'a very small sprinkling' of disadvantaged people remained, far too few to sustain a Scottish Harlech.[45] But despite these discouragements, Lothian was persuaded by the advocacy of his friend T.J., who, in the short intervals between his work for Harlech and the south Wales settlements, began to nudge the Newbattle scheme into motion. Jones suggested a campaign to win

---

[43] NLW, B.B. Thomas MSS (6 June 1933). P.E. Watkins, op.cit., p.150. T.J., who knew a good deal about public relations, arranged for the then immensely popular Prince of Wales, who had been involved in the voluntary services movement for some time, to visit Harlech and inspect the College, including the training course work, in May 1934.

[44] *A Diary with Letters*, p.15. Lothian MSS, GD 40/17/181, letters of 30 October 1931 and 28 June 1932.

[45] T.J., Class D, Vol.7, Nos.61 and 64 (copy). In 1930 the Pilgrim Trustees, to T.J.'s disgust, turned down Newbattle's appeal for support chiefly because the Scots Macmillan, Irvine and Buchan insisted loftily that 'everyone *is* educated in Scotland'. T.J., to Lady Grigg, Easter Sunday, 1935. White MSS.

over the key personnel ('the pivotal people', in his well-worn phrase) on county education bodies and the Education Department in Scotland, to be followed by appeals for support to the Pilgrim Trust and the wealthy Carnegie Trust for Scottish universities. Lothian's inclination in fact was to place Newbattle under the control of the Scottish universities, to make it, as he told T.J. at the outset, a 'four University proposition'. T.J. did not oppose that suggestion, but, as he told Lothian in August 1932, 'what I am most anxious about is to elicit the whole-hearted backing from the start of moderate Labour leaders'.[46]

During 1932 Lothian, who was abroad for long periods, left the Newbattle matter largely in T.J.'s hands. Jones was keen to press ahead, but he was ill for some time and, frustratingly, the various bodies in Scotland, whose support was necessary, were obviously less than enthusiastic. The Principals of Edinburgh and Glasgow Universities, in particular, appeared 'to be waiting to see how the cat jumps', and Charles Kemp, an old Ruskin College man, an Oxford graduate involved in settlement work, who was later recommended by T.J. for a post at Newbattle, was thoroughly depressed by the 'pessimism of the official gang'. The caution of the university authorities is to some extend understandable, not least because Newbattle, parts of which dated back to the twelfth century, could well turn out to be an expensive white elephant. And the Scottish department of the British Institute of Adult Education was also dragging its feet. In 1934, however, Lothian went ahead and appointed A.G. Fraser, principal of a college in Accra on the Gold Coast, as Warden of Newbattle. T.J. could not persuade Lothian to open Newbattle immediately as a training centre for the unemployed on the Harlech model, but Lothian had evidently been sufficiently influenced to attempt, as he said, to combine at Newbattle 'the artistic and educational possibilities offered in Wales at Gregynog and Harlech'.[47]

T.J. became steadily more exasperated by the lack of progress and, as he saw it, the wrong-headedness of some of the establishment figures involved in the project. 'The college is doomed from the start unless the wholehearted and active co-operation of the trade union leaders and the co-operative leaders is secured', he told Kemp early in 1935. Jones believed there was a fatal lack of courage and boldness.

[46] Lothian MSS, GD/17/181, Nos.75 and 94. T.J., Class D, Vol.7, Nos.59 and 78.

[47] T.J., Class Q, Vol.2, Nos.17 and 18; Class D, Vol.7, Nos.95 and 96. Lothian MSS, GD 40/17/183/287. T.J., Class Z (Diary, 1934), p.72. *A Diary with Letters*, p.134.

Everyone is very nervous, dubious, cautious – cannot see any students,
fear the employers, fear the trade union officials, fear their shadows . . .
It is not a matter of money but of leadership.

He concluded that emigration had denuded Scotland of 'its best
human material'.[48] Later that year, however, things improved: the
Secretary of State for Scotland agreed to make a capitation grant
for thirty students, the Carnegie Trust gave £10,000. T.J. failed to
persuade the Pilgrim Trustees to help, but he arranged for the York
Trust to provide five bursaries each worth £60 annually for five
years.[49] But despite these encouragements, Newbattle remained
unopened. The difficulty was that the Governing Body that was
appointed in 1936 was broadly representative of Scottish
educational interests but was not especially keen on adult
education; some members argued that full-time tutors were
unnecessary, 'undergraduates in an honorary capacity' would
suffice. Fraser, who was on the point of resigning, appealed to T.J.
for help. Early in March Jones appeared in Edinburgh and
launched a frontal attack on the Governing Body's ignorance and
timidity. It was cunningly done, however, and apparently gave no
offence: 'I want to thank you very much for your visit to Edinburgh
and its results', Fraser wrote. 'You surprised the Committee entirely
. . . Your visit had a tremendous influence. They are no longer
going to object to a staff and they are far fuller of hope than they
were before.' Eventually, in January 1937, Newbattle Abbey was
officially opened with 35 students and began to make its important
contribution to adult education in Scotland.[50]

T.J. was not the overwhelmingly dominant influence in the
establishment and maintenance of Newbattle that he was and
continued to be at Harlech, but his contribution was certainly very
great. From the outset he had a clearer vision of the desirable
character of Newbattle than anyone else. It was T.J. who persuaded
Lothian to establish an adult education college rather than simply
to hand the house over to the universities for their own purposes.
None of those active in the venture had anything like T.J.'s
knowledge and experience of adult education colleges. Indeed, two
of the four Scottish university principals knew very little about adult
education, and the two who had some knowledge of it had been
put off to some extent by the presence of Marxist extremists in the

[48] T.J., Class D, Vol.7, No.90; Class X, Vol.10, No.99.
[49] Lothian MSS, GD 40/17/185 (4 and 11 April 1935). *Glasgow Herald*, 20 May
1935.
[50] T.J., Class D, Vol.7, Nos.105–114. *Colleges for Adult Students* (Education
Settlements Association, London), p.14.

movement. But perhaps most important of all, it was T.J. who provided the fixity of purpose over several years and held Lothian's wayward enthusiasms to the sticking point. T.J. said that Lothian's 'weather-vane mind' made him 'apt to be victim of his most recent experience'. It is perhaps doubtful if Newbattle would ever have been established without Jones; it is certain that his was the chief influence which shaped the form it was ultimately given.[51]

He continued also to exert a powerful influence over the Misses Davies and their many philanthropic concerns. Gregynog was by now well established as a centre for music and for conferences of educational, cultural and social organizations in Wales. It also had strong international connections. Between 1926 and 1937 there was an annual Gregynog conference, designed to promote inter-national understanding and disarmament, which brought dis-tinguished scholars from many European universities and leading officials of the League of Nations' secretariat and the International Labour Office to Gregynog.[52] T.J. was present at some of these meetings, but his primary interest at the time lay in domestic matters, especially education and social welfare work. He regularly conferred at Gregynog with Watkins and his other associates on these questions. Gwen and Daisy Davies were probably the most generous contributors to the various schemes and institutions with which he was associated.[53]

By now the Gregynog Press was publishing a steady stream of superbly produced volumes: *The Autobiography of Lord Herbert of Cherbury*, Charles Lamb's *Elia* and Thomas Love Peacock's *Misfortunes of Elphin* among them. 'The Gregynog Press', J.L. Garvin wrote in the *Observer* (29 November 1929), 'in its line, has no superior in fastidious severity of taste'.[54] It had also been arranged, it will be remembered, to publish an edition of Gilbert Murray's translation of *The Plays of Euripides,* but publication was delayed by 'the sudden departure', as T.J. described it, of R.A. Maynard and Horace Bray, who had been responsible for the direction of the work of the Press from the beginning. The resignations were the outcome of simmering resentment among some of the people involved, including Gwen Davies, and ruffled artistic temp-eraments. Inevitably, T.J. was called on to sort out the difficulties,

[51] *A Diary with Letters*, pp.38–41, 44. 'Philip Kerr. General Notes by T.J.', Tristan Jones MSS.

[52] 'The Gregynog Conferences'. *The Welsh Anvil*, IV (Guild of Graduates, University of Wales, 1952), pp.43–54.

[53] For example, they gave £2,000 at one fell swoop in 1928. T.J., Class W, Vol.5, No.67.

[54] Dorothy A. Harrop, *A History of the Gregynog Press* (1980), pp.76, 188–94.

allay the surprisingly rancorous feelings between Maynard and
Gwen Davies, and arrange, with her agreement, the appointment of
Blair Hughes Stanton, a wood engraver, and William McCance, a
painter and sculptor, as replacements.[55] Gwen Davies occasionally
turned a sharp tongue on T.J. too: in January 1931, for example,
when he presumed rather too confidently to promise money on her
behalf to succour Merthyr Tydfil. But this was a rarity, and Gwen
Davies's real feeling for T.J. at this time was expressed in a letter in
February 1933 written in lyrical terms, that, whatever modern
cynics might infer, was simply an affirmation of genuine platonic
love:

> My very dear,
>   Thank you for everything. It is such a joy to know that we can share
> so much together – the wonder and the hidden beauty of life, the stuff
> that dreams are made of – the holy bread . . . And you have brought it
> all back again – the old power of communicating loveliness to others. I
> had it in France, and now it has returned once more because you
> believe in me – you understand – you care. For I would be a light that
> shines which does not flicker nor grow dim, that you may see the
> beauty of the shadows. And I would be the song in your heart when
> days are weary . . . that you may see the land that is far off.[56]

T.J.'s relations with Gwen's brother David, however, deteriorated
sharply as this time. In 1927 D.D. nominally retired from politics,
although in an outrageous exercise in eighteenth-century-style
patronage, which mercifully failed, he sought to put in a hapless
puppet in his place for the Montgomeryshire seat.[57] D.D. now
devoted himself to the League of Nations Union and a personal
crusade for peace which he believed, with a fundamentalist
conviction, depended upon the establishment of an international
police force. In a world dominated by social snobbery, particularly
in the United States where he hoped to raise a lot of money for his
campaign, D.D. wanted a 'better status' to impress foreigners,
preferably membership of the Privy Council.[58] There was no hope
of that, but T.J. did his best to persuade Baldwin to recommend
Davies for a peerage in recognition of the vast amounts he had
given to worthy causes. That too failed because Baldwin, who
detested the badgering for honours of Tory importuners, would

[55] T.J. letter in Bodl. G. Murray MSS, Vol.59, f.84. D.A. Harrop, op.cit.,
pp.67–74. T.J., Class R, Vol.3, Nos.70 and 74.
[56] T.J., Class R, Vol.3, No.103; Vol.4, No.11.
[57] NLW, Lord Davies of Llandinam MSS A13/1.
[58] T.J., Class W, Vol.6, No.192.

not add to his troubles by conferring a peerage on a Liberal. T.J. did not think he had enough influence with Ramsay MacDonald to get a peerage for Davies but, in fact, in 1930, with some assistance from J.H. Thomas, D.D. was promised a peerage, although for various reasons it was not actually conferred until 1932.[59]

Before that T.J., for so long the Davieses' trusted counsellor, was caught in the crossfire of a bitter family quarrel. For once even T.J.'s renowned dexterity in personal relations was not enough. The dispute arose initially because D.D., who was spending heavily on the Temple of Peace he proposed building in Cardiff and had made various settlements on his wife and family to avoid death duties, was short of ready money. He invited his sisters to take over two-thirds of the Plas Dinam estate to help him in his difficulties as he proposed to go to live in Essex. T.J., who consulted his business friend James Morton, seems to have suggested that D.D.'s proposal was not unreasonable. But the sisters would have none of it: Daisy threatened to take refuge in Grasse, their stepmother went off to Llandrindod to avoid the coming storm. Gwen sent 'an S.O.S.' to T.J. but stood her ground. She told her brother that she and Daisy had no money to spare from their attempts to stem 'the tide of disruption and moral deterioration which is threatening to submerge whole towns and communities in the Distressed Areas'. Thus far, although Gwen reproached T.J. for his apparent support of D.D.'s proposal, he had not come under any heavy fire from any member of the family.[60]

But, perhaps inevitably, the dispute led to more dangerous secondary consequences. For some time Burdon Evans, D.D.'s business manager, had given some assistance to the sisters in the management of their affairs. In July 1930 he told T.J. that their investments needed reorganizing and that the ladies ought to have a full-time business manager. Evans made it clear later that he did not want to tear up his roots in Montgomeryshire to accompany David Davies to Essex. T.J. held Burdon Evans in high regard: he had business acumen, great energy, and was strongly committed to the ideal of voluntary public service. Evans's wife had died within a year of their marriage and thereafter he devoted much of his time to worthy causes, many of them those in which Tom Jones was active. It seemed natural therefore that T.J. should suggest to Gwen and Daisy Davies that, in the circumstances, Burdon Evans should

    [59] T.J., Class Z (Diary, 1930), p.88; Class X, Vol.9, No.70. In 1930, T.J. did his best, although in vain, to persuade an American publisher to issue D.D.'s massive book, *The Problem of the Twentieth Century*, in the USA.
    [60] T.J., Class R, Vol.3, Nos.70–90. Morton MSS, GD/326/87/1.

become their full-time business manager: it seemed a sensible arrangement. The ladies were delighted at the prospect and immediately wrote asking D.D. to agree to the proposal. Burdon Evans had suggested earlier to T.J. that David Davies might well object. He did, of course, vehemently, and in his customary bullying manner when persuaded that he had been provoked, Gwen and Daisy were subjected to a barrage of outrageous abuse; even their widowed stepmother was assailed with vicious recriminations for imagined crimes. 'I have received a stab in the back', D.D. wrote, 'I have no use for traitors'. He sent for Burdon Evans and commanded him to withdraw his request to resign. In the course of the meeting (he did all the talking, as Evans said), it emerged that T.J. had been consulted. This simply redoubled D.D.'s fury: T.J. and Burdon Evans were denounced as 'the most ungrateful beasts under the sun'.[61]

T.J. took it all very coolly. It was the twentieth century; Burdon Evans was a free agent not, as D.D. seemed to assume, an oath-bound vassal subject to the will or whim of his liege lord. By now T.J. had had rather more than enough of David Davies's paranoid tantrums. Childishly D.D. put every possible obstacle in Burdon Evans's way and threatened to resign his Vice-Presidency of Coleg Harlech.

> Mr. David Davies is very angry with me [T.J. wrote to the treasurer] and therefore with all I am interested in . . . It is a complicated story . . . of course if he wishes to resign he must be allowed to. He has never been other than Laodicean in regard to the College.[62]

It cannot be said that T.J. handled this particular episode adroitly: on the other hand, once D.D.'s pride was hurt nothing short of divine intercession would have sufficed to keep the peace.

Shortly afterwards Jones also finally lost the battle to keep *The Welsh Outlook* alive. He had played an important part in the long sequence of hand-to-mouth expedients to stave off the inevitable.[63] In 1927 David Davies withdrew his financial backing for *The Outlook* and his sisters agreed to take his place. T.J., who recently had been less closely involved in the affairs of the journal than formerly, inevitably now became more active, not, however, entirely without difficulty. The incumbent editor, W. Watkin Davies, a member of

---

[61] T.J., Class W, Vol.6, Nos.195–207. Lord Davies of Llandinam MSS A 3/4 (General Correspondence, October – December 1932).

[62] T.J., Class K, Vol.5, No.89. In February Gwen pleaded (Class R, Vol.3, No.104) with T.J. to come in person to their aid as D.D.'s 'devastating' letters to his stepmother made them wonder whether he had not lost his reason.

[63] Examined in full in Gwyn Jenkins, 'The Welsh Outlook, 1914–33', loc.cit., pp.478–87.

the Labour party, was an able, forthright man, no respecter of persons, who revelled in controversy which, however, he sometimes pursued in an offensive, excessively personalized way. One of T.J.'s first tasks was to compose a nasty dispute, conducted in the shadow of the law court, between Watkin Davies and the poet T. Gwynn Jones, who claimed that he had been libelled.[64] Watkin Davies clearly had no good opinion of T.J. nor, apparently, of his works. During Davies's tenure, comment in *The Welsh Outlook* on the Coleg Harlech venture was not always helpful: editorial comment in July 1927, for example, covered its malice with a thin veneer of half-hearted encouragement, 'peevishness and Daily Mailism', as Burdon Evans described it. To his credit, T.J. said that the editor had a 'perfect right' to his opinion, but the mild protest that he did make was curtly dismissed by the editor as 'wilful mis-understanding'. As a matter of fact Watkin Davies's comment had been partly excised by Burdon Evans:

> You would have had a worse smack if I had not struck out a sentence in the Notes [Evans told T.J.]. I forget the exact words, but the effect was that your views on democracy may have been adversely affected by association with your masters'.[65]

Guilt by association with Baldwin this time, not Lloyd George. Consideration of the truth of that allegation may for the moment be suspended. Watkin Davies was serving out his notice at this time and this was his impolite parting gesture. T.J. had already arranged from him to be replaced by E.H. Jones, Sir Henry's son, who agreed to take on the editorship, unpaid except for expenses, in the confident expectation that he could improve on the current circulation of 2,000 copies, make it pay, and 'collar the profits'. At a conference at Gregynog in May 1927, the management board was reconstituted and now consisted of the editor, T.J., and a handful of his usual 'right hand men': Burdon Evans, B.B. Thomas of Harlech, Percy Watkins and T. Huws Davies, a former editor, a 'generous and merciful spirit' as T.J. described him.[66]

In practice, the *Outlook* was now run by three men: the editor, Burdon Evans, who managed the finances, and T.J. who, in addition to looking after the interests of the Misses Davies, acted as a general consultant, suggesting the names of likely new contributors and often negotiating with them. E.H. Jones almost always turned to T.J. for advice when controversial editorial issues

[64] Ibid., pp.479–80.
[65] *WO,* XIV, 173, 201.T.J., Class H, Vol.5, Nos.29 and 39.
[66] Ibid., Nos.15–40. Class W, Vol.11, No.7. *Welsh Broth,* p.145.

arose and usually accepted his recommendations. T.J. wrote book reviews and leader 'Notes' and occasionally contributed articles such as the interesting piece 'The Making of Nations', based on an address he had given at University College, Cardiff, that attracted much attention.[67] The new régime, however, soon ran into difficulty, chiefly financial, and in September 1928 winding up was seriously considered. Gwen and Daisy Davies, however, were prepared to pay the debts for another year so long as there was, as they said, no vulgar 'popularisation' in pursuit of increased circulation. This highmindedness was no doubt admirable, but it made it virtually impossible for E.H. Jones to make the journal pay, much less provide the handsome profits for which he had hoped. Early in 1930 he was away in Switzerland for some time and Burdon Evans had to substitute as editor. Later that year E.H. Jones confessed that he could not afford to continue as unpaid editor, he needed 'filthy lucre' to educate his children, and was convinced that the *Outlook* never would pay if it continued 'on the present lines'. The board however was doggedly determined to carry on. The Misses Davies rejected an offer from the Principality Press to incorporate the *Outlook* in a new monthly dealing with Welsh affairs, 'run on modern journalistic lines', that they proposed to launch. Instead, E.H. Jones, now paid £150 a year as well as expenses, was persuaded to continue.[68]

But in the difficult circumstances of the early nineteen-thirties, the future of the *Outlook* seemed more and more doubtful. There was too at least an implied criticism of the journal's lack of vigorous purpose in a proposal, 'The New Welsh Outlook', put forward in June 1932 by Gwilym James, Warden of the Merthyr Settlement, and the academic H.A. Marquand. They called for a heavy concentration on social issues, the eschewing of all party dogma and, with James as *primus inter pares,* a 'collaborative' editorship that would mobilize the support of the ablest young Turks of Welsh intellectual life, most of them resident in south Wales; '*Young* men' who held similar views on the needs of Wales. Unimpressed, even perhaps nettled, a curious response in some ways from a man who was devoting a great deal of his attention to social questions and who had always encouraged the young, T.J. told James 'to pitch in stuff to the *existing* Outlook'. A year later, however, T.J. seemed to be prepared to transform the journal 'into an organ of Social Service and Adult Education'.[69]

[67] *WO,* XVI, 68, 70–5. T.J., Class H, Vol.5, *passim.*
[68] Ibid., Nos.119–20, 191–5; T.J., Class W, Vol.11, No.7.
[69] T.J., Class H, Vol.5, Nos.200–201, 221, 223.

But by then the *Outlook* was on its last legs. Percy Watkins was fully absorbed in his new social service post in south Wales, the editor E.H. Jones, with T.J.'s powerful support, had been appointed Registrar at the University College at Bangor, and, the decisive factor, circulation had plummeted below 800 and the Misses Davies had made it clear they would no longer continue their subsidy. The last number of *The Welsh Outlook* appeared in December 1933 and the journal was then wound up, to the gloating delight of T.J.'s old enemies on the *Western Mail*.[70]

It was an unhappy end to an adventure that had begun with such high hopes: 'I recalled the dreams of twenty-eight years ago and reviewed the events since then – coldly and mercilessly', Burdon Evans wrote to T.J. 'The result was depressing'. Even so, three years later Evans half-heartedly raised the question of reviving the *Outlook* as a quarterly magazine. T.J. conceded that the need for the *Outlook* or some variant of it in Wales was as great as ever, but he himself was now 'obsolete', the rest of 'the old gang' were 'too old in arteries and outlook', and for one reason and another other possible managers could not be relied upon.[71]

It had always been a struggle to keep the *Outlook* alive. It was inadequately financed, depended too heavily on the part-time efforts of busy people with insufficient journalistic experience, and it had to survive in an increasingly unfavourable commercial climate. The genteel susceptibilities of the Gregynog ladies, who insisted that advertising should go no further than a little 'refined boosting', were also a constraint.[72] It was hardly surprising that the achievement fell some way behind the aspiration; what had aimed to be inspiring was in fact, all too often, no more than worthily didactic, determinedly solemn, devoid of any hint of humour or gaiety. But there were also deeper reasons, which T.J. recognized. The 'rebirth' of the Welsh nation in the late nineteenth century had created an educated middle class. T.J.'s hope was that better schools and especially the adult education movement would do the same thing for large numbers of the working class. It had not occurred on the expected scale, opportunities for agencies such as the WEA and *The Welsh Outlook* had not opened out, they were occluded by popular indifference. He had described the *Outlook* at the outset as a 'religious enterprise' which would present the people 'with a vision of a better Wales'. The crusade had not

[70] Ibid., Nos.212, 213, 223, 224. Gwyn Jenkins, loc.cit., pp.483–4, for the *Western Mail* response.
[71] T.J., Class H, Vol.5, Nos.226–7, 233.
[72] Ibid., No.73.

succeeded. Instead, as T.J. conceded, they were forced to concentrate on limiting the nation's 'capitulation to the Philistines'. The *Outlook* therefore had remained the journal of a small élite that it had signally failed to enlarge. Nevertheless, within these limits the *Outlook* had provided a valuable mart in Wales for the exchange of ideas. But it was one of T.J.'s less successful ventures and its closure was a painful disappointment. His farewell article, 'Retrospect', in the final issue is perhaps the most pessimistic, almost doom-laden, piece he ever wrote. He barely mentions the *Outlook* in his *Diary with Letters,* and the account of it in *Welsh Broth* stops short at the early years.[73]

It is easy to understand why he was in low spirits at that time. Conditions in south Wales and the other distressed areas were at their worst, with little sign yet of any improvement. Moreover, in 1933, he had been seriously ill. Given the helter-skelter pace at which he lived his life, this is not surprising. The year before he had been troubled by a painful condition diagnosed as muscular rheumatism. 'What is the use of leading the careful life?', a friend asked. 'You never drink, nor smoke, you go to bed early, you eat carefully, yet you get this affliction'. E.H. Jones suggested T.J. should convalesce in Egypt and 'touch' Davies Bryan, an old Aberystwyth college man who had made a fortune there, 'for a few thousands for Harlech'. With some financial help, over his protests, from Gwen Davies, he went to Grasse in the south of France for several weeks for treatment.[74] Once the pain had eased T.J. resumed his hectic activity which, despite the 'severe wrath' of his wife, he scarcely interrupted when he had another attack in January 1933. He was as careless as ever about clothes. With a visit to the Astors at Cliveden almost due, Rene in despair wrote: 'Dadi's blue suit is of such a mirror-like shine by now that it is hopeless trying to do anything to it . . . I have begged him to go to the C.S.S.A. [the Civil Service store in the Strand] for a new one. Perhaps now that there is a sale next week I may drag him there'. Rene had always been the family treasurer, T.J. was hopeless at managing his own money. An exchange between them a few days earlier, related by Rene to her daughter, speaks for itself.

Dadi going off to the office . . . shouted from the [communal] stairs 'Oh, I've only got half-a-crown.' 'What have you done with the ten

[73] *WO*, XX, 315–16. *Welsh Broth*, pp.140–6.

[74] T.J., Class W, Vol.4, No.46; Vol.11, No.16; Class R, Vol.3, No.145. Gwen asked him if he knew H.G. Wells who had a house near Grasse. She said her brother David Davies had called on Wells: 'The door was opened by a Turkish lady dressed in figured muslin trousers', who greeted them with 'Ain't it hellish cold?', and didn't seem too anxious to let them in.

shillings I gave you yesterday?' sez [sic] I. Dadi going further down the stairs and shouting still louder: 'Oh, six shillings of that went in taxis to and from dinner with Ralph Walker.' At the bottom of the stairs: 'I daresay I can borrow something from somebody.' A loud 'hush' from me to remind him he was communicating this to all the world.[75]

T.J. was not only careless about his own money, he was rather too free with it too: 'Please put me down for a donation of 3 guineas' he told David Hughes Parry, who was appealing on behalf of Urdd Gobaith Cymru (The Welsh League of Youth). 'I tried to make it more, but Mrs Jones says there will be an appeal issued on my behalf one of these days at the rate we are going on'. But for all his apparent carelessness, he was meticulous about the money he dispensed on behalf of others. Gwen Davies often sent him small sums to be distributed at his discretion to those in need. In May she sent him a cheque for £25 'which I owe you – I hope you won't find it necessary to send a stamped receipt' she added tartly.[76]

Rene believed at one time that she had persuaded Tom to slow down and reduce his commitments. But a week or two later, as she wrote resignedly to her daughter Eirene: 'Dadi is away, careering round Wales – Llandinam, Gregynog, Harlech, and tonight to Birmingham', and then, in fact, on to Cambridge. A fortnight later, however, X-ray examinations suggested that he had a duodenal ulcer, and his doctor, Lord Dawson (who arranged special terms for him), sent him off for eight weeks to a nursing home at Ruthin Castle in Wales. What bothered T.J. chiefly before he went to Ruthin was not the physical discomfort but the fact that he could 'only get in about half a day's work'. He was put on a starvation diet and prescribed complete rest; writing of any sort was officially 'verboten'. That did not stop him writing to L.B. Namier at Manchester, Lionel Curtis at Oxford and Flexner at the Institute of Advanced Studies at Princeton, exhorting them to do their utmost to find university posts for Jewish academic refugees from Nazi Germany.[77]

The long period of 'rest', such as it was, seemed to work. Dawson was pleased, T.J. was sent home late in June with orders to take

[75] T.J., Class X, Vol.10, Nos.6, 10 and 11.

[76] T.J., Class R, Vol.3, No.152.

[77] T.J., Class X, Vol.10, Nos.7, 10, 27, 34, 43; Class W, Vol.3, No.87. T.J., Class Z (Diary, 1933), pp.64–5. Rene was delighted with the enforced rest: 'For anyone of his temperament', she said, 'it is the best thing that could happen. Nothing else would make him go slow . . . I counted up recently as many as ten or a dozen activities outside the Pilgrim Trust in which he is actively engaged. This can't go on. You must unite with me on your return', she told her daughter, 'in trying to get a few of them knocked off permanently'. They failed, of course.

things easy for some months. But he soon resumed his usual routine; perhaps he could do no other: 'the Jones family', he told David Astor at this time, 'don't know how to play, the Astors do'.[78] But T.J. could at least be playful, as he was, teasingly , in a radio talk he gave on 21 January 1934 on 'Welsh Character'. He was acutely disappointed with his performance immediately afterwards, 'felt as if the voice did not belong to me at all'. The *Listener* however praised his delivery, and one who knew him commented that 'the twinkle of the eye appeared now and again in the voice'.[79] Despite the bantering tone, it was an intensely serious piece of social observation. Indeed, T.J. had a good deal to say at this time about Wales and the Welsh. In 1925 the Welsh National party had been formed, and although for some time its influence was slight, by its mere existence it prompted many Welshmen to define their political response to separatism more exactly. T.J. had done so in his closely-argued article, 'The Making of Nations' (1929), in 'Retrospect' (1933), his epitaph note on the demise of *The Welsh Outlook*, in *Welsh Character* (1934), and in 'What's Wrong With South Wales?' (1935), although the main purpose of that brilliant piece of invective was rather different.[80]

The four crucial influences in the making of modern Wales in his opinion were: conquest by the English, the survival of the Welsh language, the profound emotional-cum-intellectual experience of Calvinism, and the industrialization of part of the country. Conquest Anglicized the gentry and left the Welsh leaderless for centuries, a colonial people governed with an offhand contempt from London. 'Welsh', according to T.J., denoted no more than the name of a breed of cattle to one educated Englishman he knew in 1911.[81] Calvinism may have imposed a straitjacket on gaiety, but it also gave dignity, a plan of salvation, spiritual and social anchorage, and effective new leadership to the common people. Industrialization, financed at long range from the City and developed largely by English entrepreneurs, transformed the landscape in south Wales and drew in a horde of immigrants, who made any claim the Welsh might have to 'racial purity . . . obviously absurd'. And yet the Welsh language, 'as if fed by an inward fire', somehow or other survived one crisis after another. He offered no opinion on the question whether those who did not speak the language were authentically Welsh or not. Considering the odds, T.J. believed it

[78] T.J., Class R, Vol.3, No.10.
[79] *A Diary with Letters*, pp.117–18. T.J., Class Z (Diary, 1934), p.7.
[80] *Leeks and Daffodils*, pp.89-114, 188–98. *WO*, XVI, 70–5; XX, 315–6.
[81] By inference, it would seem, Edward Pease of the Fabian Society.

was a 'miracle' that the Welsh had retained their language, their traditions and an identity, no matter how blurred.

However, Tom Jones was certainly no Welsh chauvinist.

> What would civilisation have lost if you cut out . . . Welsh achievement? [he asked in 1929] Would we have been missed? We did not discover representative government, nor trial by jury, nor gunpowder, nor printing, nor radium, nor relativity.

Indeed, it was only in the last fifty years or so that Wales had begun to redress the large adverse balance of its debt to the rest of the world. During that half-century, however, it had registered remarkable advances in popular education, produced some excellent lyric poetry, and suffused Welsh society with a genuine democratic spirit.

> For half a century from a small people [T.J. wrote], this may be deemed enough to justify the retention of the emphasis on Welsh nationality, and in the eyes of some to warrant a separate political organisation.

It is clear that he himself was not a separatist. In his opinion Wales, in 1929, was not 'squirming under the heel of the Saxon oppressor', its grievances were remediable by constitutional means, no-one was called upon 'to suffer and die for Wales', nothing stopped a Welsh Homer from writing a national epic. Six years later he was less certain for a time of this comfortable doctrine, for south Wales in 1935 seemed to be regarded as a 'major social nuisance' in England. But outrage drove him to write a savage lampoon on governmental indifference, not to any commitment to Welsh political separatism.[82]

In this, as in other things, T.J. was an idealist. He knew how difficult it was to withstand the insidious pervasive power of social influences. 'Let me make the people's films', he said in the early 1930s, 'and I care not who makes their laws'.[83] There was no Welsh film industry, English newspapers 'penetrated into every home' and changed habits, clothes, food and sports. Nationalism in Wales was confronted everywhere by the challenge of higher living standards, or at any rate greater material comforts, in England.

[82] Below, pp.378–9.
[83] Address on miners' welfare institutes in south Wales. T.J., Class Y, Vol.5, No.29.

Shall we play on Welsh harps and dress in Welsh homespun like our grandfathers, or shall we accept the fashion of the outside world dictated to us by the shopwalker, the morning advertisement and the evening cinema?

The question had been resolved in favour of the latter by the majority in Wales. Was the battle irrevocably lost? Something could perhaps be saved, but it would demand high quality leadership; the people, whose instincts were democratic, would have to be inspired 'by persuasion, by reflection, by education' to agree on a common 'scale of social values'. It was all, ultimately, 'a question of worthwhileness . . . of values' and, in T.J.'s opinion, the desirable outcome was not some form of Welsh home rule but

> an energetic cultural nationalism, rooted in our past, without being exclusive, which has in it no taint of hate of the foreigner, no jealousy but only rivalry of his achievements. Why if we open our windows towards France and the Continent must we pull down our curtain on England? [84]

T.J. did not see his fellow countrymen through rose-coloured lenses. His friend Abraham Flexner rather doubted if there were identifiable national characteristics.[85] T.J. thought that such differences as there were between the Welsh and other peoples owed more to history and economics than to race. The Welsh, like the English, were 'a medley of contradictions'. Indeed, even more so apparently, for Wales had no genuine representative caricature figure like John Bull; a chimneypot hat (an importation from England) and a repetitive use of 'whatever' in speech were feeble failures as national totems. T.J. conceded that there were so many local varieties of Welshmen that it was easy to confute sweeping generalizations about them. Even so, Jones, the candid friend, offered some general observations, every caress matched by a flick of the whip, on his countrymen. They were 'a blend of extremes', the 'intensity' of the Welsh temperament forbade moderation. Naturally quick and intelligent, they were all critics who stabbed with their tongues not with knives: democrats almost to a man, 'their love of equality' was matched by their 'distrust of uncommon distinction'. They were said to be eager to please and thus insincere, even servile; if true, this was the reverse side of their 'fine qualities of sympathy and imagination'. The Welsh were a credulous people fatally fascinated by anything that was 'dressed up

[84] WO, XX, 70–5.
[85] T.J., Class S, Vol.I, No.80.

as idealism', their faith made short work of inconvenient facts. They were artists, 'deviously honest', who gave 'colour to their statements' beyond what seemed necessary to plain people. But they were blessed with a nimble receptivity of mind. According to Alfred Zimmern, said T.J., 'there was no other part of the British Isles, even perhaps Europe where Socrates would have been so much at home' as addressing a gathering in a Welsh mining village. But although the Welshman preferred 'thinking to doing', he preferred 'talking to either'; he ploughed 'short furrows on steep hillsides' and there was a question mark over his capacity to stay the course for long unremitting effort. And yet his tenacity was not really in doubt; for how else had he withstood wave after wave of foreign cultures, his identity unsubmerged?[86]

T.J.'s double-natured comments did not ruffle his countrymen, but he did incur some criticism a year later because of his membership of the new Unemployed Assistance Board. An insurance system where aggregate contributions covered benefit payments and accumulated a surplus for contingencies, seemed mercifully to provide some sort of makeshift safety-net for the victims of unemployment. But after 1921 the system had come under growing strain from the huge unexpected increase in unemployment and the ominously mounting number of those who had exhausted their entitlement to benefit. Governments throughout the nineteen-twenties sought by one expedient and another, including a more inquisitorial administration and reluctant borrowing from the Exchequer, to cope with the problem. In actuary's terms they obviously failed. In 1931, the question of 'dole' payments, as it was popularly if wrongly called, became a central issue that, ostensibly at least, toppled the ministry. Its successor, the so-called National government, extended the application of the means test to include payments to those who had exhausted their right to benefit, which was now generally reduced by ten per cent. This was a hastily rigged tourniquet to stem an outflow that was alleged to threaten the nation's finances with disaster. Some better permanent system for the unemployed was considered urgently necessary. Neville Chamberlain, who for some years had been increasingly critical of existing arrangements and was not satisfied with the changes made in 1929 when Public Assistance Committees had replaced the Boards of Guardians, was now Chancellor of the Exchequer.[87]

[86] *Leeks and Daffodils*, pp.90, 97, 186–98.
[87] E. Briggs and A. Deacon, 'The Creation of the Unemployed Assistance Board', *Policy and Political Studies of Local Government*, Vol.2, No.1 (1973–4), 43–62.

Chamberlain's reputation as a clear-sighted humane social reformer is steadily being undermined by the opening up of Cabinet records. It is evident that if he had had his way the revised scheme for the relief of the unemployed who had exhausted their benefit would have been intolerably harsh. He proposed, in effect, the creation of a much enlarged pauper class by classifying this large category of the unemployed with those traditionally relieved by the poor law. It involved a radical departure from established social policy and ignored political reality. More cautious counsels, notably those of Betterton, Minister of Labour, resisted Chamberlain's drastic initial proposals and the government ultimately decided on a compromise arrangement which set up an Unemployment Assistance Board (UAB).[88] The UAB, which was made responsible for the relief of the able-bodied who no longer qualified for normal benefit, was to administer a centrally directed service; it was allegedly independent, or at any rate not directly responsible to Parliament. The Board was required to formulate rules and regulations for the means test and scales of benefit which would be submitted to Parliament for approval by the Minister of Labour, who however could not be questioned in the Commons about the day-to-day administration of the system.[89]

When T.J. first heard of the scheme from Baldwin he immediately denounced it. He described it to Flexner as 'a move away from democracy towards Fascism . . . meant not only to save a few million but also to check corruption' among local councillors, who were subjected to local political pressures and prone to yield to the temptation to be too generous in their allowances in the opinion of Whitehall. 'I advised against it', Jones wrote, 'as it will *appear* in the distressed areas as another turn of the screw on the poor'. He believed that a little extra supervision of proven laxities of administration in the existing machinery would suffice until times improved.[90] T.J. would have been well advised personally to have kept clear of the UAB of which he so strongly disapproved. All the more so as his objections were reinforced later by those of his friend Ronald Davison, an acknowledged authority on unemployment, who warned him that the Cabinet seemed unaware of 'the rocks they are running in to'. The UAB scheme, said Davison, would turn out to be 'sweet in the mouth, but bitter

[88] F.M. Miller, 'National Assistance or Unemployment Assistance? The British Cabinet and Relief Policy, 1932-33'. *Journal of Contemporary History*, IX, No.3, 163–184.

[89] E. Briggs and A. Deacon, loc.cit., p.61. J.D. Millett, *The Unemployment Assistance Board* (1940), pp.17–45.

[90] A *Diary with Letters*, p.88.

in the belly'.[91] T.J., however, inveigled by his genuine interest in the
fate of the unemployed, an unexpected susceptibility to flattery,
and a surprising political naïvety, agreed to become a member of
the Board, although he said he would 'chuck it' if it became too
strenuous.[92]

Jones's name had been put forward by Sir Francis Floud of the
Ministry of Labour, supported by Warren Fisher who had urged the
importance of 'a humane and Christian touch' in those appointed
to the UAB. 'Of all the laymen I know', Fisher told T.J., 'you will
provide the best': a sentiment that was endorsed by Sidney Webb
and others.[93] Violet Markham, the statutory woman appointed to
the Board, was comforted by the fact that she and her four other
colleagues would be fortified in their deliberations by T.J.'s 'wisdom
and experience'.[94] In the event, Violet Markham often appeared to
have a clearer perception of the Board's position than T.J.: 'there
can be no illusions', she told Jones at the outset, 'as to what we are
up against'. She was also prepared to admit frankly later that an air
of injured innocence ill became the UAB which had attempted 'to
do too much in too short a time', and had 'blundered grossly' in its
statistical calculations.[95] T.J. made no such admission and indeed
seemed curiously blind to the weakness of the Board's position. He
seems, for example, to have believed that the UAB really was an
independent body, a notion that did not long survive when the
government ran into the political difficulties that Ronald Davison
had predicted.

It seems now established beyond doubt that the UAB was a
device designed to answer political and financial calculations rather
than social needs. It was conceived in Whitehall as a means of
reducing demands on the Exchequer, of eliminating the untrustworthy local authorities from the administration of assistance, as a
clever stratagem to evade, or at least reduce, parliamentary control,
blur responsibility for unpopular decisions and perhaps enable the
government to avoid the odium it would otherwise incur.[96] But
ministers' hopes were soon shattered; so too was the complacency

---

[91] Ibid., p.86.
[92] T.J., Class X, Vol.10, No.72. The Pilgrim Trustees raised no objection to his
acceptance of this additional part-time post.
[93] T.J., Class Z (Diary, 1934), pp.52, 59–60. A *Diary with Letters,* p.122, 131.
[94] V. Markham, *Return Passage* (Oxford, 1953), p.191. Miss Markham was, in
fact, the wife of the agreeable Lt.-Col. James Carruthers. When T.J. went for the
first time to their home, Moon Green, for lunch, Miss Markham sent her husband
out because she said he could 'only talk horses'. T.J., Class X, Vol.10, No.62.
[95] Ibid., p.198. T.J., Class Z (Diary, 1935), pp.51, 60, 145–6.
[96] J.D. Millett, op.cit., *passim.* E. Briggs and A. Deacon, loc.cit., pp.61–2.

of the Board. In December Lord Rushcliffe (as Betterton had now become), who was Chairman of the Board, confidently predicted in a letter to T.J. that the UAB, which stood high in 'public esteem', would not forfeit that position in the future. T.J. persuaded himself that the Board's new scales and regulations left no room for serious criticism. Neither seems to have had any inkling of the great storm of protest that was about to erupt.[97]

It is curious in some ways that T.J., who was so well-informed about south Wales, which was again to be the chief storm-centre, should be so obtuse. All the more so as Violet Markham wrote letter after letter during 1934 drawing his attention to the dangerous discrepancy between the vague pledges of improvement ministers had disingenuously given in the Commons and the scales the Board actually recommended.[98] T.J.'s behaviour as a member of the Board is revealing. As usual, he resorted without hesitation to freelance action when necessary. He failed to persuade the Board's Civil Servants, who had 'a blind spot on publicity', immediately to punish a popular guide to the bewildering regulations; so, operating, as he said, 'sub rosa', T.J. persuaded Emsley Carr of the *News of the World* to print a simple explanation, although how much attention members of that specialist journal paid to it is a matter of conjecture.[99]

T.J.'s meliorism was usually compassionate but never sentimental. Over the UAB regulations he seemed much more concerned to be hard-headed than warm-hearted. When the new regulations, which made more reductions than increases, came into effect on 7 January 1935, there was a great explosion of angry protest. There were massive demonstrations in south Wales and Scotland which, to the surprise of Whitehall, spread to many other less traditionally militant parts of the country. It looked, ominously, as if working class passivity, which the government had fostered so assiduously since 1919, was turning towards furious nationwide,

[97] T.J., Class Z (Diary, 1934), p.85. T.J., Class S, Vol.I, No.95. It is clear (Class W, Vol.9, No.23) that T.J., who was present, hopelessly misjudged the significance of the debate in the Commons on the regulations on 17–19 December 1934.

[98] T.J., Class Z (Diary, 1934), pp.70–76. When Jones warned Baldwin that, inevitably, there would be some reductions in benefit, Mrs Baldwin's answer was: 'I would pay all the relief in kind and ask the Salvation Army to do all the distribution'. T.J. added that he was grateful that his wife did not reduce his mind to 'pulp by such devastating innocence'. 14 October 1934. White MSS.

[99] Letters to Lady Grigg, 18 and 26 January 1935. White MSS. *News of the World*, 27 January 1935. Belatedly the government did issue a pamphlet, 'A Great Social Reform', which however was not quite the popular explanation T.J. had in mind.

possibly violent, protest. The opposition parties in the Commons were barely a hundred strong, but to the consternation of the government many northern Tory members were equally critical of the new scales of payment. After some confused manoeuvring behind the scenes, Stanley, the Minister of Labour, announced an indefinite 'standstill': the unemployed for whom the UAB was responsible would receive either the new or the old scale of allowance, whichever was the larger.[100]

T.J.'s disgust was expressed in a long letter to Lady Grigg in which he set out his version of the crisis:

> The last ten days have seen the U.A.B. on the rocks. A Temporary Provisions Bill [Standstill] may bring her into safe waters for a time, but seriously damaged and perhaps beyond repair . . . The Board originated, I've always understood, in the wish of the Treasury (Neville) to take Unemployment Relief "out of politics" so far as possible and to reduce the widespread rampant anomalies which abounded. The local authorities were superseded in the interest of uniform treatment by a Central Board . . . We were to deal with the needs and resources of households, not families . . . The Means Test was to be enforced and we were bidden in forming Allowance Scales to steer between the Scylla of contributory Insurance Benefit and the Charybdis of low wages . . . they were to be applied, at very short notice, to some 700,000 families on January 7th. This was done; . . . some got less, some got more. Those hit squealed . . . especially in South Wales where . . . the Means Test had never been applied. Communists and Labourists at once exploited the situation . . . protests were organised . . . Oliver Stanley faced the House in a mood of complete capitulation, made no defence of the Board or of the Regulations . . . The Board was furious at this palsied performance . . . I saw S.B. [Baldwin] next morning and told him that five members of the Board would refuse to obey the Minister unless categorically ordered by the Cabinet.

T.J. went on in words dripping with contempt for politicians to describe the mounting panic of ministers and some Tory MPs who, he said, simply feared for their seats. The Board, minus the Chairman, resisted until the last moment and insisted on receiving their instructions to give way in writing from the Cabinet. T.J. claimed that he and his colleagues were ready with proposals for the 'exercise of discretion' which would substantially have eliminated the worst grievances, but the government preferred 'abject surrender'. The Board was 'left to invent new Regulations without

[100] F. Miller, 'The British Unemployment Assistance Crisis of 1935', *Journal of Contemporary History*, Vol. XIV, No.2, pp.331–49.

guide or compass'. He ascribed the chief responsibility for the crisis to the spineless behaviour of Stanley, Minister of Labour, and Rushcliffe, Chairman of the UAB.[101]

It is clear that T.J.'s judgement on this episode was seriously amiss. Many of his comments on the situation are open to challenge. The idea that so potentially explosive an issue as unemployment benefit could be taken out of politics was, from the outset, an absurdity, as was any fond notion which T.J. had that the Board could assert its 'independence' and defy the ministers. His cherished suggestion that hasty adjustments would have coped with most difficulties was equally wide of the mark. Far more circumspection in the application of regulations, a fuller use of discretionary power and of the appeals procedure, and more experienced, better trained and organized subordinate staff were needed, as well as more time, to make the system work effectively. T.J.'s assertion that the mass demonstrations involving thousands of people owed more to Communist machination than to genuine popular outrage was hopelessly wrong, as was his claim that the crisis was prompted mainly by the personal inadequacies of a few individuals. T.J. compounded these errors of judgement by attempt-ing 'to coach' Lady Astor to defend the UAB in the Commons debate: a case of calling up a Charge of the Light Brigade when what was required was cautious orderly retreat from an untenable position.[102]

It is not easy to explain this strange deviation from T.J.'s customary sensible moderation. The ineptitude of the ministers could be explained by their crass ignorance of the reality of working-class existence, but that could scarcely be said of T.J. He had detailed, up-to-date knowledge about conditions in south Wales.[103] Of course it was always necessary to keep a watchful eye on government expenditure, and it was certainly true that there were many regional variations in allowances that, strictly, were unfair. But then there were other larger questions of fairness too. The fact was that the system of relief provided no more than a bare existence for families, which, after several years' endurance, as Percy Watkins vigorously pointed out, became threadbare.[104] T.J., however, persuaded himself that the new scales were comparatively

[101] 8 February 1935. White MSS. T.J., Class Z (Diary, 1935), pp.17–20. He wrote in similar terms (Class S, Vol.I, No.99) to Flexner.

[102] T.J., Class S, Vol.I, No.99. Her speech (*Parl. Deb. Commons*, Vol.297, Cols.2150-2) was full of vigorous sallies and a few needless barbs which Aneurin Bevan (Col.2161), with justice, dismissed as 'irrelevant flippancies'.

[103] T.J., Class H, Vol.8, No.15, for a vivid account he received of Rhymney, where the people were 'rubbed right on the raw' by their sense of injustice.

[104] T.J., Class V, Vol.2, No.48.

'generous'. This unusual mean-mindedness seems to derive from intellectual conviction on a general principle. In 1929 T.J. had admitted to Tawney that he had 'a strong prejudice against "family allowances", "rent allowances", "non-contributory pensions" and other forms of money grants which call for no sort of effort on the part of the recipient'.[105] He insisted on the necessity, always, for self-help and voluntary effort, although he also believed that these should be properly balanced by effective enabling or supportive action by the State. 'I have been urging the importance of pressing the Cabinet to be ready to announce programmes of reconstruction . . . on the day on which we launch our scales of allowance', he wrote to Lady Grigg, adding later that he did not want the UAB to be turned merely into a 'gigantic relieving' agency to the neglect of 'constructive reconditioning', which was stated, if vaguely, to be one of its purposes.[106]

It is, however, difficult to see precisely what individual 'effort' thousands of unemployed men whose skills had been rendered redundant by world-wide economic dislocation could have made to satisfy T.J.'s criteria. He did not emerge with much credit from the UAB 'Standstill' episode; for once, he overreached himself. He allowed himself, against his instincts, to be flattered into joining the UAB and, along with his colleagues, used as a convenient decoy for a cowardly and cynical government. Thereafter, stubborn pride fuelled by pique and self-righteousness took over. His letters on this matter are uncharacteristically vehement and occasionally resort to plain bluster. What Violet Markham called 'the Jones jaw' must have been much in evidence at that time. On this occasion he lost his temperamental balance, even, too, it must be added, his customary moral virtue. A man who follows a lengthy paragraph in a letter insisting on the adequacy of proposed assistance for the unemployed with an insensitive reference to a sumptuous dinner given by the millionaire Abe Bailey in honour of Smuts at the Savoy that he had recently enjoyed, where 'Abe had ordered the best champagne available in London regardless of cost', and 'where the rest of the menu was equally choice', is guilty of unconscionable humbug.[107] Some of his close friends were distinctly uneasy about his attitude at this time. A letter from Percy Watkins included at least an implied rebuke, and John Davies eventually sent on the third draft of a letter in which he reaffirmed his working-class sympathies and reluctantly concluded: 'The time for parting has

---

[105] *WD*, II, 198.
[106] 14 October and 11 November 1934. White MSS.
[107] T.J., Class W, Vol.9, No.21.

come'. In fact it never actually came to a breach, but not long afterwards Mrs John Davies wrote to T.J. pleading: 'please, please help these dear, dear countrymen of yours; all those young fellows, it's awful . . . why did you go on that Board – couldn't someone else have done this work?'[108]

In personal terms it was an unfortunate affair, although there is no evidence that T.J. ever conceded that was so. He continued to serve on the UAB and indeed in 1937 accepted an invitation to continue for another term of three years. The Establishment also continued to rely on his advice in the matter of honours, although he was now a private citizen. 'I hope you don't mind still being hauled in for advice', Sir Patrick Duff asked after T.J.'s retirement, and Warren Fisher wrote: 'I'm bothering you because . . . you have an uncanny secret service which enables you to match the oracles of old'.[109] Jones's finesse in these delicate matters, and in the making of appointments, was as great as ever. When Percy Watkins resigned as Secretary of the Welsh Department of the Board of Education, he was replaced, on T.J.'s recommendation (virtually a nomination) by Wyn Wheldon, Registrar at Bangor, who in turn was succeeded by T.J.'s candidate E.H. Jones, formerly of Harlech and *The Welsh Outlook*.[110] T.J. was just as smoothly adroit in operation in England. He played a leading part ('We owe a great deal to you for your help, my friend, in this matter') in placing Arthur Salter in the Gladstone Chair of Government at Oxford, and, as T.J. told Flexner, 'I am now planning to get H.D. Henderson [to All Souls] from the Cabinet Office as the P.M. knows not how to use him'. Three months later, Henderson was elected, 'the result of another of your labours', in the Warden's words to T.J., and an illustration of how powerful a presence Jones had established in the innermost recesses of the Establishment.[111]

It is therefore perhaps not surprising that Tom Jones had taken an Establishment view of the financial crisis of August 1931 that led to the fall of the second Labour government. For the first time in years T.J. was not well-placed to record the course of events. He had

[108] Ibid., Vol.4, No.78; Class V, Vol.2, No.48; Class Z (Diary, 1935), pp.10–12, 84. John Davies was overjoyed by the 'Standstill' and seems, mistakenly, to have assumed that T.J. was too.

[109] T.J., Class W, Vol.5, No.56; Vol.7, No.7.

[110] T.J., Class V, Vol.2, Nos.24 and 28; Class Z (Diary, 1935) p.13; Class W, Vol.11, No.23. *A Diary with Letters,* p.96.

[111] Ibid., pp.116, 126. T.J., Class Z (Diary, 1933), pp.89, 96. Ibid., (Diary, 1934), p.25. T.J.'s preference for discreet action is indicated in this comment in 1931: 'A letter to *The Times* will cut very little ice – personal influences behind the scenes will be much more effective'. Class W, Vol.15, No.64.

of course left office the year before and during the weeks of
financial and political uncertainty in 1931 he was on a reading
holiday with his family at Bundoran on the west coast of Ireland.
But his response to the crisis on his return was clear-cut. Despite his
own professional training as an economist, T.J. leaned heavily on
the opinions of banking friends such as Josiah Stamp for his
reading of the economic position. That is, that since the war Britain
had tried to carry too large a part of the burden of providing
capital for foreign countries, especially those in central Europe;
that France and the USA had between them accumulated three-
fifths of the world's gold so that 'there was not enough to go
round'; pressure on sterling had forced Britain off the gold
standard, but this simply meant the substitution of one crisis for
another: some 'common international rule' for the exchange of
currencies was essential, whether based on gold or not. Meantime,
what was needed was 'stable government'.[112]

T.J. had seen enough of the inner workings of MacDonald's
second government not to have any confidence in its capacity to
weather the international economic crisis in 1931, nor in its
willingness to make difficult decisions such as a cut in
unemployment benefit in order to procure a loan from American
bankers and balance the budget, the *sine qua non* of orthodox
economic thinking, to which with some reluctance he subscribed.
At the time he described the refusal of at least half the Labour
cabinet to agree to a 10 per cent reduction in unemployment
benefit as 'cowardice', an ungenerous comment from one who
might have been expected to have had a more sympathetic
understanding of how anguishing a choice Henderson and his
colleagues faced. And all the more so as T.J. had been reliably
informed earlier that Montagu Norman, Governor of the Bank of
England, who had said that he did not believe that dole
expenditure 'had really got out of control', was tirelessly engaged
in some dubious political manoeuvring. Here, as in the 'Standstill'
affair later in 1935, T.J., although never one himself, was rather too
willing to lend too much weight to the rentier's view of the world.[113]

However, the issue of confidence, especially of foreigners, in the
pound certainly was important in 1931, and T.J. simply stated the

[112] *A Diary with Letters*, pp.10, 18–19, supplemented by unpublished material in
Class Z (Diary, 1931), pp.56–7.
[113] *A Diary with Letters*, pp.11, 27. T.J., Class Z (Diary, 1931), p.58. 'The City is
more cheerful', he wrote (Class S, Vol.I, No.23) in February 1932. 'We fell over the
precipice, but when we were picked up at the bottom, lo! we were alive – we have
paid our Income Tax all over the country with promptitude, but we are feeling its
weight pretty deeply now, all of us, and "good causes" are feeling the pinch'.

truth when he asserted that the Labour ministers appeared to be out of their depth in financial matters. 'We could not trust them with the Bank of England – just yet . . . that is what must be changed . . . But that too will come', he wrote.[114] In the mean time, 'Labour had to be thrashed for its own good'. T.J. and his wife joined the stampede and, for the first time in their lives, voted Tory. 'We had to do it', he wrote regretfully. The election result, however, in which a victory for the so-called National government was absurdly exaggerated by the electoral system into an overwhelming triumph, gave Jones pause for serious thought. He had hoped that Labour would be chastened but not 'destroyed'; for,as he wrote at the time to Gwen Davies, who had always acknowledged that her wealth was derived ultimately from the sweat of Welsh colliers, 'what are you and me without Labour . . . can we share with them the treasures of the world? Why not in Wales? I wish you would turn your great financial power into heat and light up Wales . . . Gregynog, Harlech, Merthyr, Rhondda, more and more'.[115]

T.J. recognized immediately that things had gone much too far for the purpose simply of good and stable government. Whatever the election result did for confidence in the pound, the fact was that the 'National' government, supported by over 500 MPs, most of them Tory, and confronted by a pathetically weak opposition reduced to less than 60, now wielded a 'parliamentary dictatorship'. He hoped, without much conviction, that it would use its giant's strength magnanimously.[116] In April 1932, Beatrice Webb, on the eve of her departure with Sidney on a visit to Russia, where she discovered in the Communist party the Jesuit-style cadre of zealots for effective action that she had looked for in vain in the Labour movement in Britain, wrote enquiring whether T.J., now that he was out of government service, had had time to reconsider his political position. 'I wonder where you are going to?', she said. 'I am not sure where I am going to myself'. Mrs Webb considered that, as a result of MacDonald's defection and the electoral débâcle in 1931, the Left was in hopeless disarray and inevitably there would be 'an interregnum' for some time in Labour politics.[117]

T.J. agreed completely with that assessment. Later that year he discussed the state of the Labour party with Tawney and Citrine of the TUC. 'The talk', according to T.J., 'was very depressing'. Tawney reiterated the diagnosis which he had brilliantly expressed

---

[114] *A Diary with Letters*, p.20, supplemented by T.J., Class R, Vol.3, No.124.
[115] Ibid., No.124.
[116] *A Diary with Letters*, p.20.
[117] T.J., Class W, Vol.20, No.66.

in a recent article: Labour had no 'ordered conception of its task';
it would require the disciplined effort of a decade to achieve it.
Citrine too was deeply despondent about the immediate position
and future prospects, although it appeared that, at long last,
attention was being paid to the detailed analysis of the problems
and policies by a number of research groups. As ever, T.J. was
especially concerned about the quality of leadership; all too many
leading Labour men, in his opinion, were undermined by drink, a
lifestyle to which they were unaccustomed, and a failure to keep
'raw contact' with their constituents. The opposition front bench in
this parliament, he wrote later, was 'pitiable', which was hardly
surprising as the first eleven had either defected or been defeated
in the election, and their replacements had to be chosen from a
dismally small inexperienced parliamentary party. For the present,
T.J. concluded, 'the inspiration' had gone out of the movement,
although disillusion in the provinces had not gone quite so deep.[118]

For a year or two, therefore, with the Labour party impotent in
limbo, Tom Jones's chief interest in the politics of the Left lay in
the activity of his son, Tristan, who, to his parents' delight, in
December 1931 had won an Open Entrance Exhibition at Balliol
and had gone up in the following October. At Oxford, Tristan
immediately became 'thoroughly seized' with Communism; he was
soon on the executive committee of the October Club and had no
time for any academic work. It was a 'difficult' time for Tristan and
his parents, who nevertheless remained sensibly calm. T.J. had
never made any secret of his dislike and distrust of Communism; it
was 'a logical creed', but 'too logical for life . . . and too hostile to
personal freedom' to be acceptable in Britain. However, T.J. was
glad that Tristan was at least keen on a 'positive gospel of change',
especially as he was at Oxford where there was far too much
'complacency' and 'niggling criticism'. T.J. hoped that his son, who
was 'tremendously sincere' about his political beliefs, would nonetheless retain a sense of humour. During vacations Tristan was 'as
full as ever of Russia' and littered the house with posters. On the
'homeopathic principle', T.J. supplied him with additional Communist placards. He was persuaded that with ripening experience
Tristan would change his mind; meantime, he and his Oxford
friends, as T.J. said, could not 'do anything much madder with the
world than their immediate predecessors'. In December 1933

---

[118] 'The Choice before the Labour Party', *Political Quarterly* (1932), III, 323–45.
A Diary with Letters, pp.68–82, 156. The Romney Street Group a year later gloomily
agreed that everywhere there was 'widespread indifference', the people had
'ceased to aspire'.

Tristan was charged with an offence against the police during a Communist protest outside the German Embassy against the Reichstag trials. 'He says he was guiltless of shouting "Down with the Cossacks"', T.J. said; 'I've told him he'll learn that in no country in the world are "Law and Order" so powerful'. Tristan was 'reticent' and did not take kindly to criticism of his beliefs, but T.J. was no doubt relieved to hear from an American friend that privately Tristan often quoted him and 'there was always a peculiar note of pride in his voice when he says "my father"', although of course it would be indignantly denied if drawn to his attention. Rene had less patience than her husband; she said briskly that it would do Tristan 'all the good in the world' if he spent rather more time with people who were not Communists.[119]

But more generally T.J.'s political interest at this time was concentrated on the behaviour of the 'National' government, in which Baldwin was Lord President of the Council. It was apparent immediately after the general election that the overwhelming Conservative majority would insist on introducing protection. T.J., who admitted that he was still a 'bigoted' free-trader, conceded that 'a dose of strychnine' could sometimes help a patient who was in a bad way.[120] More immediately, however, after a short uneasy delay achieved by the 'agreement to differ', Ramsay MacDonald's sticking-plaster attempt to hold his ministry together, over thirty Liberal free-traders, led by Sir Herbert Samuel, who was one of the main architects of the 'National' government, went into opposition as a result of the Ottawa Agreement, which introduced imperial preference. Philip Snowden, far and away the most important member of the handful of Labour MPs who had gone along with MacDonald in 1931, also left the government at the same time. T.J.'s friend Lothian explained to him that he and the other Liberals could not accept the Ottawa Agreement. In their opinion the financial emergency of 1931 was now over, and taking 'a long view', they felt that it was important that an independent Liberal party should continue to exist, if only as a moderating force to reduce the danger that politics might degenerate into naked class war. T.J.'s attempt to persuade Lothian that other considerations – disarmament and the world economic conference – were powerful reasons why he, at least, should continue to support the government, was brushed aside. Baldwin's response to the news of the Liberal defection, conveniently forgetting his own part in

---

[119] T.J., Class X, Vol.9, No.237; Class S, Vol.I, Nos.70 and 77; Class Q, Vol.3, No.10; Class X, Vol.10, No.26; Class W., Vol.3, No.87; Vol.14, No.153. Astor MS 1416/1/2/114.

[120] A *Diary with Letters*, p.27.

disrupting a coalition government in 1922 for reasons of party
interest and survival, was: 'The dirty dogs. They always behave like
this when rough weather approaches'.[121]

MacDonald admitted that the Liberal withdrawal made it
difficult to maintain 'the facade of a National government'.[122]
Indeed, although there had been a plausible case for MacDonald's
emergency appointment in August 1931, the continuance of his
premiership (though not his membership of the government)
rested on a convenient fiction which ignored the fact that he had
ceased to be the accredited leader of any substantial body of
Labour MPs, much less the official Labour party, from which he
had been expelled. T.J. very soon concluded that the ministry's
claim to be a 'National' government was largely bogus. Indeed, he
was also prepared to concede that much of the electoral panic in
1931 (to which he and his wife had succumbed) had been cynically
induced for Tory party purposes.[123] T.J. himself bore some
responsibility for that electoral result, for he had provided Baldwin
with a good deal of material during the campaign. 'All your stuff
has been invaluable', Baldwin wrote in acknowledgement, 'I have
worked it all off in one place or another'. T.J. also wrote several
other speeches for Baldwin at this time. 'Your address for Belfast . .
. is A1 . . . I really am the champion plagiarist', Baldwin confessed
in 1933. And in 1935, equally explicitly, he wrote: 'I delivered the
speech with conviction and delight. I almost felt it was my own'.[124]

But despite his close relationship with, and warm affection for,
Baldwin, T.J. steadily became more and more critical of the
performance of the government. He endorsed an opinion that by
1932 Ramsay MacDonald had become 'an old water-logged hulk';
the Foreign Secretary, Sir John Simon, had 'reduced Geneva to
immobility' by his legal subtleties; Neville Chamberlain, reputedly
the strong man in the government, nevertheless 'had no
imagination'. T.J. wished that some of the discontented younger
members of the Cabinet would rebel against the 'nerveless
leadership' of the elder statesmen. He thought that the best hope
centred on Walter Elliot, the Minister for Agriculture, who was
unique in that superlatively dull Cabinet because he had ideas and
drive. By January 1933 T.J. considered that the 'National'

[121] Ibid., pp.53–5. T.J., Class W, Vol.13, No.76.

[122] *A Diary with Letters*, p.55. D. Marquand, op.cit., pp.728–30.

[123] Writing to Lady Grigg on 24 February 1935 (White MSS) about Tory
electoral prospects, T.J. said that it would not 'be possible to work up another 1931
scare'.

[124] T.J., Class A, Vol.6, Nos.52, 86 and 91. T.J., Class Z (Diary, 1933), p.88.

government had fulfilled its primary purpose by 'balancing the budget': thereafter it was evident to him that it had 'no programme in the domestic sphere'. He was particularly exasperated by the government's sluggish response to the continuing tragedy of mass unemployment and the profoundly depressing realization that many of these men would never work again.[125]

T.J. also began to be equally concerned about international relations, especially the failure to bring about any measure of effective disarmament. Supplied regularly with up-to-date news about international opinion by his Spanish friend Salvador de Madariaga, T.J. considered that the disarmament discussions among the powers were riddled with 'hypocrisy and humbug'. The whole question cried out for more 'vigorous handling' and much more plain honesty. Several times T.J. broached the subject with Baldwin who, in this as in other things, demonstrated his unique power of 'resisting the close discussion of a problem'. Nevertheless, T.J. continued to hope that, sooner or later, Baldwin could be brought to capitalize on the immense confidence he inspired at home and abroad, to make an Abraham Lincoln-type speech which would raise the question of peace far above the murky ruck of national bickering and the special pleading of the military. It was common doctrine among lay people that the world could not survive another major war. The advent of the aeroplane meant the transfer of the horror and carnage of the Somme, still vivid in the public mind, into the centre of great cities. Britain was as exposed as other countries. She had substantially lost the invulnerability to attack that she had enjoyed since the days of Nelson and maintained, though with increasing difficulty, under the threat of submarines, down to 1918. 'The Air as the key to future wars is . . . regarded [as] vital over here', T.J. told Flexner. In October 1932 Jones set out his ideas in a draft for Baldwin's speech at the Tory party conference: 'I had no idea you were doing something for Blackpool', Baldwin wrote. 'Bless you. Some of it will do well. But the international part will keep for the big public meetings'. Baldwin incorporated T.J.'s suggestions with his own ideas in a speech at the Guildhall on 9 November, which marked the first suggestion of a change in British defence policy, and more strikingly in a speech in the Commons the next day. Nothing could save people from bombardment from the air: 'The bomber will

---

[125] T.J., Class P, Vol.2, No.113; Class W, Vol.9, No.21. *A Diary with Letters*, pp.32, 63, 84, 125. *New Statesman* (18 November 1933) for T.J.'s article, 'Walter Elliot', who turned out to be one more in the long line of prospective Prime Ministers who, in due course, sank virtually withot a trace.

always get through', Baldwin said in words that struck a chill in many hearts. The only defence was offence, which effectively turned a future war into a bloody competition in the mass murder of civilians. This was not quite the 'Lincoln speech' that T.J. had hoped for. It had a considerable effect, but it did more to create a deep public fear of war than raise disarmament negotiations to a new level of statesmanlike seriousness.[126]

At home and abroad (not least in the Empire where the future of India was in the balance, and in Germany where Hitler had become Chancellor) there were immense and complicated problems that could well lead to another war. T.J. thought the position so 'grave' that it was high time to change the existing ineffective hodgepodge ministry into 'a genuine National Government'. He suggested that Lloyd George should be brought in. 'There is much to be said for putting him in the Foreign Office to deal with the scoundrels of Europe', T.J. reflected to Baldwin. 'You either want that type at the F.O. or the more saintly type like Grey'. Lloyd George 'had mellowed', Jones said, 'the fires of his ambition' had died down, he would be content now to work under Baldwin.[127]

T.J. deployed the case for including Lloyd George in terms designed to neutralize so far as possible Baldwin's deep aversion for L.G. But in fact Jones believed that Lloyd George's incomparable verve and experience would be an immensely valuable accession of strength to the government at this fateful time in international affairs. Moreover, once in the ministry, Lloyd George's proposals for reducing unemployment in Britain would not be dismissed out of hand by the government as they had been hitherto. T.J. had welcomed the appointment in 1934 of a Commissioner, Malcolm Stewart, for the Special Areas, as regions of heavy unemployment were euphemistically called, in the hope that his supervision would reduce the wastefulness and inefficiency that had undermined public works schemes in the past.[128] But T.J. considered that Stewart pinned too much faith on a reduced working week as the answer to unemployment. Something much more imaginative, on a bigger scale and much more generously financed than the pathetically small sum Stewart had at his disposal, was required in T.J.'s opinion. With some remaining reservation about their soundness, he now turned again to Lloyd George's deficit-financed, public works 'New

[126] *A Diary with Letters*, p.56. T.J., Class S, Vol.I, No.43. T.J., Class Z (Diary, 1932), pp.76, 85. *The Times* (11 November 1932). K. Middlemas and J. Barnes, *Baldwin: A Biography* (1969) p.375.

[127] *A Diary with Letters*, pp.123–4. When Baldwin, vaguely musing aloud, mentioned Bevin's name, T.J. suggested his inclusion too.

[128] T.J., Class S, Vol.I, No.95.

Deal' proposals, 'very diluted Rooseveltism' as T.J. described them.[129] Jones was the liaison in what proved ultimately to be not much more than the pretence of a negotiation between Baldwin and Lloyd George.

There was never really any serious possibility that a government led by MacDonald, Baldwin and Neville Chamberlain would accept Lloyd George as a colleague. As Baldwin told T.J. earlier, 'half the cabinet' would resign immediately if he were introduced. But Lloyd George asserted that he was eager for the adoption of 'his Programme, not for office'. In January 1935 he launched a great campaign to publicize his proposals with a meeting at Caernarfon and quickly demonstrated his old incomparable political showmanship.[130] The campaign immediately followed the UAB 'Standstill' fiasco and the public outburst against the government's callous attitude to the unemployed. It behoved an unpopular government at least to go through the motions of hearing what Lloyd George had to say. It was arranged that a Cabinet committee would meet L.G., who would also submit a memorandum setting out his proposals. Although he knew it was a forlorn hope, T.J. (asserting that L.G. had always been 'thoroughly straight' in his relationship with Bonar Law) continued to argue for Lloyd George's inclusion in the ministry. Lloyd George did not expect too much from the Cabinet committee appointed to meet him. 'The composition of this examining body', Lloyd George observed to T.J., 'reminds me of what is known in academy circles as "The Hanging Committee", every member of it had already denounced [his] proposals in public'.[131]

However, Lloyd George persevered. He drew up a memorandum and sent it to T.J. for comment: 'You know best how to present it to this crowd', L.G. wrote. About a half of Tom Jones's recommendations were incorporated in the final draft. He pointed out that every government department consulted would 'try to produce some niggling detail upon which to defeat it'. L.G. should avoid exaggeration: 'Instead of seven-eighths', Jones said, 'say three-quarters'. There was much to be said for 'a little politeness'; for tactical reasons (and in fairness) he tried to get L.G. to give 'some, even small, credit' to the efforts of the government and others, but without success. Sylvester reported that Lloyd George still rather fancied T.J.'s idea of a partnership with Baldwin who, L.G. said, should fill the role 'assigned to Asquith' initially in the crisis of

[129] T.J. to Lady Grigg, 12 January 1935. White MSS.
[130] Ibid. *A Diary with Letters*, pp.138, 144.
[131] T.J., Class Z (Diary, 1935), p.38. T.J., Class A, Vol.I, No.41.

1916. But of course it was all a pipedream. The Treasury concentrated its attack not on individual proposals but on the general plan of a 'grand assault' on unemployment, as opposed to piecemeal schemes spread over ten years, and registered strong opposition to Lloyd George's proposed Prosperity Loan. Anyway, in the last resort, Neville Chamberlain and Baldwin would never have agreed to work with Lloyd George in the circumstances of that or any time.[132] Baldwin was even more hostile to a proposal, forwarded by T.J. from Garvin of the *Observer,* who proposed a triumvirate of Baldwin, Lloyd George and Churchill, 'the required equation', in his opinion, for dangerous times.[133]

It is no doubt mere idle speculation to wonder whether the history of the later 1930s would have been any different if Garvin's proposed reconstruction of the government had occurred. As for T.J.'s bold attempt at political oxymoron, he maintained later that Providence had made a colossal blunder in making Lloyd George and Baldwin 'two men instead of combining them in one'.[134] Possibly so, but once made, the error could not be rectified; oil and water would not mix.

Normally, T.J. would have swallowed his disappointment that a large-scale attack on unemployment by the government was not to be made. But an astonishing instance of insufferable arrogance on the part of P.M. Stewart, the Special Areas Commissioner, provoked T.J. to fury. Stewart proposed 'to introduce a return of passports to permit Welshmen transferred to England to return on leave to Wales'. For T.J., this was the last straw. He decided it was time to 'stir up the supine out of their lethargy'.[135] The result was the superb satirical skit, 'What's Wrong With South Wales', first published on 27 July 1935 as a supplement to the *New Statesman and Nation.* In 1933 T.J. had suggested that the plight of the British people called for another Samuel Butler. 'What's wrong with South Wales', however, seemed to recall Daniel Defoe's *Shortest Way with Dissenters,* with perhaps an echo of Jonathan Swift, although T.J. would have disclaimed any suggestion of so distinguished an ancestry. The foreword, nominally by Lloyd George, was also written by T.J. Mass unemployment was not, 'like a rainy day',

---

[132] 'T.J.'s criticisms', and Lloyd George's letter to T.J., HLRO Lloyd George Papers G/141/24/1 and 2. T.J. to Lady Grigg, 16 March and Easter Sunday 1935. White MSS. The printed account (*A Diary with Letters*, pp.143–50) is less frank.

[133] Garvin to Waldorf Astor (for T.J.), Class W, Vol.8, No.19. *A Diary with Letters,* p.145.

[134] *Leeks and Daffodils,* pp.213–14.

[135] T.J. to Lady Grigg, 6 September 1935. White MSS. T.J., Class Z (Diary, 1935), p.108.

inevitable; a lazy government could be forced to act to stop the rot. South Wales, the north-west and Scotland were not 'distressed areas', they were 'diseased'. The distressed area was 'No 10 Downing St.', which regarded south Wales as a bore: 'Why won't it go to sleep like Dorsetshire?' The industrial Welsh had become a 'burdensome nuisance', an infected people who allowed notions about individual worth to interfere with politics and economics, so there was never any peace. It was impossible to provide work for wages in south Wales. Where were the managerial staff to live? Where were they to play and to hunt? Porthcawl was scarcely Deauville. The new rearmament programme would not help because of course the government could not possibly be expected to insist on new works being planted in south Wales. Regrettably, it was not possible to bomb this troublesome tribe; the Welsh frontier was rather nearer than Persia, ministers would be asked difficult questions at Geneva.

But the truth was the Welsh had reached their Journey's End; the time had come to deal firmly with these unfortunates doomed to redundancy by alterations in the world current of imports and exports. Luckily, 'no Treasury grant' was required: the population could be removed to form a Celtic fringe around London running from Hounslow to Dagenham, where there was no active trade unionism to infringe the liberty of employers. This done, south Wales could be scheduled as a 'Grand National Ruin'. The Rhymney valley could then be flooded to provide abundant drinking water for London, the Great Wen, 'the great sponge', that at all costs had to be watered. An irrevocable Standstill order could be placed on the Rhondda valley, which would be left unchanged for ever as an industrial museum replete with interesting underground pit shafts, like the catacombs at Rome. The Abertillery valley, on the other hand, would make an 'ideal tract for bombing practice' for the RAF, whose demands for ranges would otherwise, sooner or later, threaten Lulworth Cove and other beauty spots. Finally, the Welsh of the diaspora would be given a firm, kind pledge by the Prime Minister that they would all be allowed to return to the Great National Ruin annually on St David's Day to hold an Eisteddfod in native costume and sing hymns to their hearts' content.[136]

T.J. spoke for many thousands rendered desolate by despair. He had been moved to write also by his own personal sense of desolation, for on 19 July, after a brief illness, his dearly loved wife, Rene, had died.

[136] *Leeks and Daffodils,* pp.89, 114.

CHAPTER THIRTEEN

APPEASEMENT

IN THE early months of 1935 Tom Jones became increasingly anxious about his wife's health. Rene had symptoms of heart trouble and early in June a medical specialist prescribed rest. She had however accompanied T.J. to the Empire Service at Canterbury Cathedral and on the following Sunday afternoon had joined with gusto in a family sing-song around the piano at Street Acre. On 19 June, however, she suffered 'a seizure followed by grave heart complications'.[1] Within days it was evident that she was steadily losing ground; she fell into a coma, and died on 19 July 1935. T.J. was 'devastated' by the loss of his wife, with whom he had shared nearly thirty-three years of truly happy married life. Mercifully, Eirene and Tristan were with him, and he was also sustained by the support of a 'myriad' of friends, in particular Waldorf and Nancy Astor. But the friend to whom T.J. opened his heart most fully was the American Abraham Flexner. One of T.J.'s letters to him is worth quoting at length:

> You have been near to me during these last days of farewell to one of the best of women, the best known to me. Pure and wise and just and good, she was all of those but she was also sweet and kind.
>   We met in college days at Aberystwyth, where she was a joy to look upon. . . . Since our wedding day, the last in 1902, we have adventured together with work 'and with children' in the four countries and through all the change she was the stabilizing factor, rudder, compass, lighthouse and everything that kept my more impetuous nature from shipwreck. Somehow we solved, with not too much friction and long ago, the differing speeds to which we were geared. She had a more sober mind and could deflate my balloons with half a sentence. But she had abundant courage and no hesitations for a right objective, however risky. The vanities of Society had no power to deflect her. And so I could go on for page after page . . . Over 400 letters lie on the table from friends of mine and scores of them recall some kindness done by her.[2]

[1] T.J.'s telegram to Flexner. Class S, Vol.I, No.114.
[2] Morton MSS GD 378/88/1. T.J., Class S, Vol.I, Nos.114–117.

Even with a large allowance for the emotional subjectivity of a bereft loving husband, it is clear that Rene was an exceptional woman. T.J.'s personality was so powerful, his gifts so varied and so dazzlingly displayed in so many ways over so long a period of time, that there is the danger of discounting Rene and losing sight of her crucial importance in his life and in accounting for his success. Although she remained unobtrusively in the background for most of the time, she was certainly not a simple housewife, unsure of herself, unable or unwilling to take her place at his side in the world in which he moved so confidently. On the contrary, she was a highly-educated, socially-sophisticated woman equipped with a deliciously dry humour and a fine sense of proportion who, as occasion required, emerged from her quiet domestic life to accompany her husband on weekends at Cliveden, or to Passfield Corner to stay with the Webbs or to Ayot St. Lawrence with the Bernard Shaws. She held her own socially and intellectually in these circles without any difficulty. Rene was in fact a formidable personality. Mrs Dora Herbert Jones, for many years secretary to the Misses Davies of Gregynog, a considerable personality in her own right, a cultured woman accustomed to dealing with personages, was overawed by Rene. 'To be honest', Mrs Herbert Jones said in an interview on television in 1969, 'I was rather frightened of her. She had such a wide-ranging mind, an incredibly clear mind, everything in its place . . . "Lucidity" is the word to describe her best.'[3]

There is no reason therefore to dismiss out of hand T.J.'s assertion, which he insisted in 1936 was the 'quiet, sober truth', not just 'a manner of speaking', that Rene was the 'stronger character' in the partnership.[4] It was at least certain that their life together continued on the easy, unconstrained basis of equality that they had established at the outset. They shared everything fully in their emotionally close-knit lives, the heartaches and the triumphs, and they were as honest in their dealings with each other as it is possible for a husband and wife who genuinely love each other to be. 'For years our bodies had mattered less and less and [finally] almost nothing and our minds more and more', he wrote after her death.[5] Only very rarely did Rene complain that T.J. was away from home

[3] Transcription (translated) of a conversation between Gwyn Erfyl Jones, Dora Herbert Jones and Sir Ben Bowen Thomas, HTV programme, 'Dan Sylw', 28 October 1969.

[4] *A Diary with Letters*, p.238. Nancy Astor evidently thought so, and Violet Markham's fine obituary notice of Rene in *The Times* (20 July 1935) can be construed in the same way to some extent.

[5] To Lady Grigg, 22 July 1935. White MSS.

rather too often, and when she did, it was usually from a concern
that he was wearing himself out by his ceaseless activity. Serenely
confident in their marriage, Rene never seems to have cavilled at,
much less shown any jealousy over, T.J.'s friendship with Gwen
Davies, Violet Markham, Lady Grigg and Lady Astor, none of whom
made any secret of her great affection for him. Many years later the
Dean of St Asaph remembered Rene at college as one of the
goddesses. To T.J. she was uniquely precious and important; she
provided the rock-like domestic security and the steady moral
support that were necessary to him, as he was only too well aware.
Indeed, he admitted, a year after her death, that he had been
'afraid' that, without her, he 'might drift God knows where,
anchorless'. But the powerful memory of 'what she would wish'
served as a compass for T.J. for the rest of his life.[6]

He had sought some relief from anguish during the weeks when
Rene lay critically ill by writing *What's Wrong With South Wales?* Some
of his friends, Gertrude Grigg and Violet Markham for example,
disapproved of its savage bitterness which, they said, was completely
out of character. T.J. disagreed: he said it simply reflected a side of
him that they had not previously seen.[7] *What's Wrong With South
Wales?* prompted some attention in the correspondence columns of
the *New Statesman and Nation* and elsewhere, but it had no
discernible effect on government policy. It is doubtful if T.J. had
expected that there would be any significant immediate response to
his call for a major operation to resurrect the derelict areas there.
Indeed, despite the undoubted talent he had displayed as a
pamphleteer, he was prompted at this time to wonder whether he
could not have done more for his afflicted countrymen ('served my
people best', as he put it) if he had avoided the constraints of a
Civil Service career and gone directly into politics years before. Of
course it was 'too late now' for that. He had little faith that
unfettered private enterprise would of its own volition do anything
to reduce unemployment in south Wales. The economic pull of
London and the south-east was too compelling, quite apart from
the heavy rate demands and the discouraging history of conflict
between labour and capital in south Wales. 'Of the 478 new
factories set up in Great Britain last year', he wrote in September
1935, '5 were in Wales and 4 were closed, 209 new ones were set up

---

[6] *A Diary with Letters*, p.238. 'I don't need to tell you', T.J. wrote to Lady Grigg
(24 June 1935, White MSS), 'what I owe to her quiet backing, blunt criticism and
freedom from the vanities of the world.'

[7] 'There's a real bit of T.J. in these few pages.' To Lady Grigg, 7 September
1935. White MSS.

in greater London'. Market forces were so dominant and a prolonged existence on the dole so demoralizing that he came to the conclusion that it would be far better 'to bribe employers to introduce work into the district than to keep on bribing people to remain idle'.[8] He tried to persuade individual business moguls such as Montague Burton and Samuel Courtauld to open factories in south Wales, but without success. He was driven to the brink of despair by his impotence: 'Think how little I have been able to achieve for South Wales, with my intimate knowledge, my yearning, my close relations with Whitehall', he wrote despondently to Lady Grigg. His only success was the help he was able to render, 'in devious ways', with insider assistance from Horace Wilson, to the 'long, long effort', ultimately successful, to reactivate the steelworks at Ebbw Vale.[9]

Despite the slow if steady improvement in Britain's economic fortunes from 1933 onwards, the grim dispiriting exodus, particularly of younger people, continued from south Wales. T.J. had hitherto set no great value on the supposedly regenerative economic effect of the Commissioner for Special Areas. Indeed, he once described P.M. Stewart as a 'wash out'. But T.J. did welcome the establishment in south Wales and Durham in 1937 of government trading estates, on the model pioneered at Slough, which leased factories to companies on attractive terms, although he added bitterly that the scheme, the first real sign of a coherent regional policy, arrived about 'ten years too late'. And one of his friends added that a new bridge across the river Severn was essential for its success.[10] T.J. had always conceded that mass unemployment posed baffling problems, some of them of fundamental social importance, which required detailed investigation, not least of regional variations in the difficulties. He gave some some assistance, chiefly advice about grants for research, to H.A. Marquand, who in 1937 had just completed his *Second Industrial Survey of South Wales* and was then turning his attention to demographic problems.[11]

[8] To Lady Grigg, White MSS. *Leeks and Daffodils*, pp.121–4. *A Diary with Letters*, pp.225, 286.

[9] Ibid., pp.212, 229–30, 312. T.J., Class Z (Diary, 1935), pp.130, 160. Letters to Lady Grigg, 30 September and 29 October 1935, 10 January 1936. White MSS. Between 1933–36 Sir Harold Wernher gave T.J. £800 annually to spend as he thought best on the unemployed.

[10] T.J. to Lady Grigg, 1 June 1935. White MSS. *A Diary with Letters*, p.365. T.J., Class W, Vol.16, No.176.

[11] T.J., Class N, Vol.I, No.87; Class W, Vol.16, No.177.

But more particularly, T.J. had become centrally involved two years before in what is generally conceded to be the most comprehensive examination of the problem of long-term unemployment in the 1930s: the investigation subsequently published by the Pilgrim Trust in 1938 as *Men Without Work*. This was the outcome of fruitful co-operation between T.J. and Archbishop William Temple, the most socially-conscious churchman of the day. In 1933 Temple had called together a group of people to examine the problem of unemployment, and subsequently he launched a national appeal to fellow Christians to write to their MPs urging that the 10 per cent cut in unemployment benefit made in 1931 should be restored before there was any question of a general reduction in income tax. The Chancellor, Neville Chamberlain, promptly and typically objected strongly to Temple's 'interference' in political decisions. The Archbishop was not intimidated and came gradually to the conclusion that the question of unemployment demanded a much more extensive consideration of its social consequences than it had received hitherto.[12]

T.J.'s knowledge of conditions in south Wales and his experience on the Unemployment Board had driven him to the same conclusion. In 1935 he persuaded the Pilgrim Trust to finance a new large-scale investigation. A committee, chaired by Temple, of which T.J. was a member, was established to supervise the work. He was determined that this investigation should not focus on the economics of unemployment, as some members of the committee, especially the economist Professor N.J. Hall of University College, London, intended. T.J. was determined

> to keep them off studying unemployment in the vast and fasten them down to an attempt to estimate the comparative values of the various systems of voluntary effort on behalf of the unemployed now in action all over the country.

At subsequent meetings he fought off the objections of 'the rest of the committee' and managed broadly to get his way.[13]

A first-class team of investigators was assembled: W.F. Oakeshott, then a master at Winchester, A.D.K. Owen, a research officer of Political and Economic Planning, Dr. W.H. Singer, a Cambridge economist, and, later, Dr. Wagner, a psychologist with considerable experience of continental work on unemployment.[14] At first T.J.

---

[12] F.A. Iremonger, *William Temple Archbishop of Canterbury His Life and Letters* (1948), pp.440–2.
[13] Letters to Lady Grigg, 9 February and 7 March 1936. White MSS. *A Diary with Letters*, pp.178–9.

repeatedly impressed on the team 'the need to avoid politics', partly not to ruffle their paymasters, the conservative-minded Pilgrim Trustees. But along with Temple, he was also aware of how easily the government, to whom ultimately they might look for action, could take umbrage if its prejudices were aroused. The key appointments were A.D.K. Owen, who (after consultation with Beveridge) planned the methodology, and Oakeshott, whom T.J. described as 'the backbone' of the investigation.[15]

Initially politically wary of each other, Owen and Oakeshott soon established an effective rapport. T.J. monitored the proposals of the investigation closely, and once the survey was under way he soon forgot his concern about the government's sensitivities and readily agreed that the conclusions established would be fully published, however politically inconvenient.[16] T.J. was also able to afford the researchers access to the records of the UAB on which the random selection of the unemployed men who were interviewed was based. Six places were selected for investigation: two of them, Leicester and Deptford in London, were relatively prosperous districts; the other four comprised Liverpool, a seaport, Blackburn, a cotton town, and two centres in the distressed areas, the Rhondda in south Wales and Crook, a mining village in County Durham. Investigators posed questions such as: Who are the unemployed? What kind of men are those who are out of work, and why are they unemployed and not others? The unemployment of women was also considered, and the voluntary social service movement was scrutinized in some detail.[17]

The result was an immensely valuable report on the great social scourge of unemployment that broke new ground and remains a classic account to this day. It placed a new emphasis on the physical, psychological and moral problems which so often exerted protean destructive influences on the long-term unemployed, and made it plain, for example, that public attitudes (not least those displayed by UAB officials) to the reputedly 'workshy' were seriously over-simplified. *Men Without Work* was well received in the Press; the wealth of case-study evidence it adduced was impressive, T.J. was convinced that it would 'do no end of good'.[18] According to Walter

[14] *Men Without Work* (Cambridge, 1938), Introduction, pp.ix–x. *PT Report* (1936), pp.20–3. The Pilgrim Trust also financed research on juvenile unemployment in Dundee directed by Dr O.A. Onegar, an experimental psychologist at St. Andrew's University.

[15] T.J., Add MSS, WW, Vol.I, No.34.

[16] This account is based substantially on an unpublished memorandum written for me by W.F. Oakeshott.

[17] *Men Without Work, passim. P.T. Report* (1937), pp.3–4.

Oakeshott, 'T.J. was more responsible than anyone for the final form the publication took' and, whatever his initial fears, he had not cavilled 'at a single detail in the proofs on the ground that it was too political'.[19] Jones was particularly gratified that *Men Without Work* singled out Coleg Harlech for special praise for the quality of its training programme for the leaders of clubs for the unemployed.[20]

The authors of *Men Without Work*, while not unaware of certain difficulties and changes, also warmly commended the work of the settlements which, they said, provided 'the most successful response to the unemployment problem' that society had yet discovered.[21] T.J.'s interest in the work of settlements and clubs was undiminished. He conceded that they were 'a poor substitute for normal employment', but for all their limitations they were one of the 'finest and most decent things' that had emerged from the social misery of the times, and it would be 'tragic' if they were undermined in any way. Jones rarely if ever marked time for long. He was delighted in April 1937, after a weekend spent with people in the voluntary movement, to hear of the introduction of a 'much wider range' of activities, many of them broadly educational rather than 'occupational', in some of the clubs. But he was also increasingly aware of the danger that club life would isolate the unemployed from society in general, and his response to this was a proposal, which he put forward to the office of the Commissioner for Distressed Areas, gradually to transform the voluntary club movement for the unemployed into a wider 'community movement' embracing, or at any rate open to, the whole of society.[22] Meantime, the annual reports of the Pilgrim Trust indicated the steady support it gave to the voluntary movement on a national scale and the remarkably detailed consideration that T.J. gave to its changing needs and the different local requirements of the clubs and settlements. This was obviously very much a labour of love.

His work for the Unemployment Assistance Board, however, was much less palatable. Indeed he was increasingly irritated by the

[18] *Men Without Work*, pp.348–52; T.J., Class R, Vol.5, No.126.
[19] Memorandum.
[20] *Men Without Work*, p.306.
[21] *Men Without Work*, p.306.
[22] T.J., Class K, Vol.17, No.167; Class C, Vol.16, No.47. In 1936 T.J. and John Davies were pressing (Class W, Vol.4, Nos.86 and 87) leading Calvinistic Methodists in south Wales to sell off surplus chapel buildings for conversion into community centres.

demands it made on his time and patience, and what he continued to regard as the government's woeful lack of political courage. The 'Standstill' agreement in February 1935 had been a panic response by the Cabinet to the storm of angry protest over projected cuts in benefit for some of the unemployed in certain areas. It was assumed by the members of the Board that the regulations would now be revised sufficiently to make them generally acceptable, but without abandoning the original aim of removing local abuses and inequalities. It very soon became apparent, however, that the government, once bitten, was now much more than twice shy, and had no intention of disturbing in a hurry what it considered an all too precarious social peace. Moreover, the approach in May of the Royal Jubilee, the twenty-fifth anniversary of the accession of George V, and the likelihood of a general election in the not too distant future, strengthened ministers' determination to avoid unpopular actions.

T.J. of course believed that the 'Standstill' was quite unnecessary. He was prepared to admit that the Board's original regulations were 'not perfect', but he continued to insist that 'they could have been eased wherever they bore harshly by administrative means'.[23] At a conference at Gregynog in February on the UAB regulations, T.J. was much less responsive to criticism than Violet Markham and Professor M.H. Hallsworth, the two members of the Board whose views usually were in close accord with his. At Gregynog, Jones stated flatly that as there continued to be 'a deliberate policy of ignoring rules' about the Means Test in south Wales, government commissioners should be sent in to supersede the local administrations, as had been done previously in similar circumstances in Durham. He was obviously completely at odds on this matter with some of his closest friends. William Noble of the Maes-yr-Haf Settlement, for example, warned of the danger of disturbing the status quo in a 'sudden way'; Ivor Thomas, one of T.J.'s able young acolytes who was the Warden of the Pontypool Settlement, also urged the need for caution.[24] Gwen Davies of Gregynog, 'who had felt like singing the *Te Deum*' when she heard the news of the 'Standstill', argued for a vigorous policy of job creation as the best and only acceptable means of avoiding 'a terrible upheaval'. And John Davies and his wife made it plain to T.J. that they did not think that the poor in south Wales 'had been

[23] To Flexner, 30 March 1935. T.J., Class S, Vol.I, No.103. He also concurred (Class C, Vol.15, No.31) that the rent and earnings rules were perhaps too complex.

[24] Gregynog Conference, T.J., Class H, Vol.8, No.17.

too generously treated in the matter of relief', and said that they passionately resented the 'further harrying of people who had already borne as much as they could bear and more'.[25] But T.J. remained stubbornly unconvinced. In fact, his mind, for once, was closed to social and political reality.

South Wales, at that time, presented a classic case of that collective state of mind which seems to conform almost exactly to the concept of relative social deprivation so ingeniously posited by W.G. Runciman in 1966.[26] South Wales demonstrates very clearly the truth of Runciman's thesis that the extent of social resentment felt in society is not a simple reflection of the degree of hardship experienced. It may well have been true, as the Pilgrim Trust investigation asserted, that the poor in Durham were worse off than those in the Rhondda,[27] but there is no doubt that the propensity to protest socially was very much greater in south Wales than in the north-east of England. There was a powerful folk-memory of the great prosperity of the south Wales coalfields before 1914, and this together with the established tradition of political militancy and a pervasive democratic spirit promoted a widespread conviction that the redress of hardship was feasible and weakened any disposition stoically to accept the imposition of a further reduction in living standards.[28]

T.J. had ample evidence of the temper of the people on this matter, and indeed in *What's Wrong With South Wales?* he had expressed approval of the unwillingness of his countrymen to swallow their sense of injustice at the behest of supposed economic necessity. He had shown some understanding of the subtle relation of feelings of deprivation to the notion of social justice.[29] This went by the board, however, where the policy of the UAB was concerned. He continued to argue that local variations in benefit should be eliminated forthwith: it was a matter of principle. He was unmoved by Violet Markham's argument that to reduce still further the already low purchasing power in Wales was intolerable. His obsessive concentration on this instance of inequality remains a puzzle. It was after all a miniscule disparity in a society that reeked of social injustice, as T.J., who did not turn a hair when a chauffeur-driven Rolls Royce arrived to take him on a weekend visit to Sir Philip Sassoon's opulent home in New Barnet, knew very well.

---

[25] T.J., Class R, Vol.4, No.120; Class W, Vol.4, No.79.
[26] *Relative Deprivation and Social Justice.* (1966).
[27] *Men Without Work*, pp.75, 108.
[28] W.G. Runciman, op. cit., p.65.
[29] *Leeks and Daffodils*, pp.102–6.

Matters of principle, it appeared, could on occasion be conveniently capped.

T.J. remained disgruntled at what he considered the Board's
weak-kneed 'surrender' to the government's insistence on
continuing the 'Standstill' for necessary political convenience.[30] A
running fight within the UAB continued over several weeks and T.J.
eventually threatened to resign. Wilfred Eady, Civil Service
Secretary of the Board, was aghast; in April 1936 he begged T.J. to
remain a member. Eady said outright that he thought T.J. had got
things 'out of perspective' and was adopting a narrowly 'pedantic
view', but the plea that followed was cunningly deployed. He said
that the effect of T.J.'s resignation would be 'disastrous', it would
mean the 'disintegration of the Board' as Violet Markham might
very well follow him. No one would believe that T.J. had resigned
because of ill-health, and as he was so 'closely associated' with
Baldwin, who was again Prime Minister, the political repercussions
were beyond calculation. T.J. was the indispensable man on whose
'sagacity in times of crisis' Eady and other members of the Board
relied so heavily. No doubt the Board was, as yet, 'a disconnected
entity', but it had not yet had 'a proper chance', and T.J.'s
withdrawal would mean it never would have a chance to succeed.
They had always tried 'to work the Board on the principle of
collective responsibility like the Cabinet'. Eady said that he could
not believe that Jones, at a time of crisis, would take the 'easy way
out', resign, and 'dissociate' himself from the Board's responsibility.
T.J. had been chosen not only to represent beleaguered south
Wales but also because of his wide 'indispensable associations': he
was simply irreplaceable.[31]

Eady's arguments were well chosen, exactly calculated to appeal
to T.J.'s strong sense of duty and unwillingness to shirk a challenge.
So, reluctantly, he agreed to continue as 'the slave' of the UAB,
although he retained some hope of 'escaping in the autumn from
its clutches'.[32] He failed to do so, however, and continued as a
highly-regarded but unwilling member of the Board, who
complained that, quite falsely, he appeared as 'austere and
heartless' because, presumably, the long-range virtue of his policy
was misunderstood. Moreover, in despair after two years of futile

[30] T.J. to the Chairman of the UAB. Class C, Vol.16, No.3. T.J. to Lady Grigg,
25 February 1936. White MSS. T.J., Class Z (Diary, 1936), p.237.

[31] T.J., Class W, Vol.5, No.79.

[32] T.J., Class Z (Diary, 1936), pp.97–8, 209. Personal loyalty to Baldwin, who
was then in some political difficulty, was an important factor in T.J.'s decision to
continue on the Board.

advocacy he had 'given up preaching' to the Prime Minister on the need for action to dispel the 'widespread malaise' in south Wales.[33]

Although its public reputation, judged at least by the Press's reception of its second report in 1937, had improved,[34] the UAB remained a chaotic body, weakly led and riven by dissension. Eady admitted that it had been almost overwhelmed by its tangled heritage of controversy and that the existence of separate 'camps' had 'nearly wrecked' the Board more than once. He tried desperately therefore to persuade T.J., the anchor man, to stay on with the argument that there was no one of sufficient calibre available to replace him, least of all anyone from Wales, which would feel slighted if not directly represented on the Board. Violet Markham argued to the same effect.[35] Although it went 'much against the grain', T.J. agreed to continue on a less onerous basis, and in June 1937 accepted a commission to continue as a member for another three years, subject to continued good health.[36]

In the event, the Board's difficulties were reduced or, as T.J. preferred to say, 'masked' by the gradual reduction in the number of unemployed. The 'liquidation' of his *bête noire* the 'Standstill' became a matter of less and less importance. T.J. and Violet Markham kept up 'a running attack' in 1938 on official complacency about the apathetic condition of the long-term unemployed who were under thirty years of age, but without noticeable effect. A prolonged illness in 1939 drastically reduced the number of the T.J.'s attendances still further; ultimately he became almost a sleeping partner and finally resigned from the Board in June 1940. He had not however been content simply to pocket his salary from the Board: 'I may tell you', he wrote to Lady Grigg in December 1938, 'that, by and large, I give away my U.A.B. salary'.[37]

T.J.'s antidote for the irritating frustrations he endured at the UAB was, of course, the satisfaction he derived from the continued progress of Coleg Harlech. Haldane, the first President of the College, had died in 1928, and was replaced for his unexpired term by Sir Harry Reichel, Principal of the University College at Bangor. In 1931 he was succeeded by Lord Sankey, then Lord Chancellor, with whom T.J. had been friendly ever since they had been brought

[33] *A Diary with Letters*, p.238. T.J., Class Z, (Diary, 1936), pp.245–6.

[34] *The Times, Manchester Guardian* and *Western Mail*, 27 July 1937.

[35] T.J. Class T, Vol.16, No.44; Class Z (Diary, 1937), pp.44–5. *A Diary with Letters*, p.323.

[36] T.J. to Lady Grigg, 18 March 1939. White MSS. *A Diary with Letters*, pp.352–3.

together by the industrial troubles of 1919. Over the next fifteen years Sankey's assistance was immensely valuable to T.J. in his annual campaign to raise money for Harlech. But it was T.J. alone who persuaded young Bill Astor to agree to pay over £1,500 for the construction of a fine new house[38] for the Warden, B.B. Thomas, who, as T.J. said, was 'always learning and growing', and was emerging during the 1930s as one of the leading figures in the British adult education movement.[39]

In 1936 the BBC, which at last was preparing to open a Welsh Regional Station, sought to recruit Thomas's services as Director because he was so obviously '*persona grata* to Welsh interests'. Thomas was sorely perplexed: 'Wales wants me in two places at once apparently, I can't be in both. Where will she get the most out of me?' he asked T.J., who was again deeply disturbed at the prospect of losing Thomas. Jones did his utmost to be fair; he insisted that the decision was one for Thomas alone. T.J. said that he found it difficult to appraise the value of broadcasting as a public service: 'I am interested in such a tiny fraction of its programmes, but recognise that all tastes must be catered for: Harrods and Selfridges and Woolworth!' It was essential that Thomas should receive adequate guarantees of reasonable job security:

Reith has many qualities [T.J., sore perhaps from his earlier dealings with him, wrote] but he is not a gentleman in your sense and mine. His temper is Fascist. He believes in irresponsible power and in the exercise of it. Unless I got a five year's agreement at the full salary (£1,500) I would not accept.

In the event, Thomas, who shared T.J.'s passionate belief in adult education, decided to stop at Harlech.[40] T.J. was as vigorously certain as ever of his faith in adult education: each year Coleg Harlech was demonstrating its value as 'the College of the second chance', fitting at least some bright young working-class men for leadership in local and national affairs, and adding to the number of intelligent citizens in society, whose participation was essential to the proper working of a democracy.[41] Of course Coleg Harlech also

[38] T.J. to Lady Grigg, 20 May 1935. White MSS.

[39] T.J. to Sir Josiah Stamp, 6 May 1938. Coleg Harlech MSS.

[40] T.J., Class Z (Diary, 1936), p.110. T.J. to B.B. Thomas, 9 May 1936. NLW, B.B. Thomas MSS. T.J., Class V, Vol.2, No.63.

[41] T.J. at a public meeting in Newtown, reported in the *Montgomeryshire Express* (12 January 1935). Broadcast appeal (written by T.J.) on the BBC by Sir William Jenkins, MP, on behalf of Coleg Harlech, October 1936.

had its failures. The trade union movement, especially the powerful South Wales Miners' Federation, still held aloof, although T.J. did win the personal support in 1934 of its president Jim Griffiths, who not long afterwards went into politics and in due course became a major figure in the British Labour movement and post-war governments.[42] But the loyalty of the trade union movement in south Wales remained with the Marxist NCLC movement and, to some extent, with Ruskin College. T.J. was not the man to trim the sails of principle in order to secure an advantage. His memorandum 'Newsletter', drawn up in 1935, made it plain that Harlech and the NCLC, like 'the whale and the elephant'. occupied totally different elements. So long as he had anything to do with it, Coleg Harlech would remain committed to free enquiry and the rejection of regimentation of any sort, whatever the cost.[43]

T.J. continued, too, to insist on an embargo on examinations at Harlech. His attitude on this fell somewhere between laudable idealism and self-indulgence. He believed that education promoted understanding, even perhaps wisdom in some, that could not be properly tested or weighed by written examinations. It was to some extent a response of his own failures earlier, a snook cocked at some of the examiners at London and Glasgow Universities. He was unwilling to admit that examination failure was sometimes a necessary goad to sloth, although he freely admitted that he had failed several papers because he spent too much time on other pursuits. So of course did others, and often on purposes rather more trivial than those of T.J. On the question of examinations, T.J.'s mind was closed; for once he ignored his own dictum: that wisdom, like virtue, is a mean between extremes.

There was also, of course, never any question of T.J.'s reducing his interest in, or work on behalf of, Coleg Harlech. When, in 1937, he was advised on medical grounds to cut down his public activities, Burdon Evans pointed out that Coleg Harlech was the one commitment from which T.J. could not be released 'this side of Heaven'. A few months earlier, as Harlech entered its tenth year of existence, Evans had suggested raising a fund to celebrate in some suitable form T.J.'s contribution to the College which, Evans said, owed its existence entirely to his 'faith and vision'.

> I must put both feet down heavily and finally . . . on all your suggestions [T.J. wrote in some agitation] . . . If justice is to be done there would have to be a whole sculptured group . . . a sort of Burghers of Calais.

[42] P. Stead, *Coleg Harlech: The First Fifty Years* (Cardiff, 1977), p.76.
[43] T.J., Class D, Vol.7, No.87.

He refused to be singled out; nothing would give him greater pain. Instead, T.J. wanted to concentrate on raising money for a much-needed library building at Harlech, where there was 'no peace to read except in one's bedroom and that may be shared by several'.[44] For some time T.J. stalked D.M. Evans-Bevan, a wealthy south Wales brewer and coal-owner, in the hope that he would provide the library building, while Mrs. Yates-Thompson, 'my fairy godmother' as T.J. called her when she gave a second donation of a thousand pounds in April 1936, would pay for the equipment.[45]

T.J. failed to persuade Evans-Bevan to help and was no more successful with Mrs Bernard Shaw, who said emphatically that her possessions were going to Ireland, she hated England, and brushed aside T.J.'s plea that Harlech was after all in Wales and that he had done his best to help Ireland in 1921.[46] It was to prove a long, difficult haul, but one from which T.J. derived particular satisfaction, because to him, a library was not merely 'a chest of tools', it was 'a sanatorium for the mind', indeed, 'a shrine'.[47] One of T.J.'s greatest pleasures for years had been, almost every week, to pick up bargains, remaindered and cheap second-hand books in London and anywhere else for Harlech. He tried, but failed, to persuade John Burns to make over his extensive library, but did elicit a promise from Edward VIII to send some books to the College.

In 1937, in a typical self-help operation, students cleared the ground, and in the following year work on the building began. In all, the library was estimated to cost £13,000 but when the contractor began work, 'cash at the Bank or in sight (covenants)', as T.J., the eternal optimist, said, amounted only to £7,000. The treasurer was aghast at Jones's willingness to take such risks. It was agreed that a group headed by Percy Watkins would raise £2,000 'from the bourgeoisie', while T.J. undertook to raise £4,000 from his friends 'the plutocrats', including the beloved 'Dolly' Yates-Thompson.[48] T.J. succeeded; Gwen and Daisy Davies and Mrs Yates-Thompson rallied round yet again. Money was also forthcoming from the York and other Trusts. Eventually, a very fine library, wholly in keeping with the original College building, was

[44] T.J., Class Z (Diary, 1936), p.369; Class K, Vol.9, Nos.110 and 111; Vol.10, No.33. Morton MSS GD 326/88/1.

[45] T.J. letters, 21 January 1935 to 6 April 1936. Coleg Harlech MSS.

[46] *A Diary with Letters,* p.229.

[47] 'The Library of Coleg Harlech', *Welsh Review* I, 269.

[48] T.J., Class K, Vol.10, Nos.98–113; Class R, Vol.5, No.147; Add MSS WW, Vol.I, No.18.

completed free of debt. However, the official opening was delayed by the outbreak of war.[49]

T.J.'s part in the course of events preceding the Second World War is of considerable interest. In June 1935 Baldwin became Prime Minister again; Ramsay MacDonald, whose decline into an intermittent senility had become obvious and embarrassing, became Lord President of the Council. Baldwin, who had found that 'being second not first', and therefore freed from ultimate responsibility, suited him, was not particularly anxious to succeed. Indeed, in February he had discussed with Hankey the possibility of his retirement from the leadership of the Tory party. Hankey sought to dissuade him: 'The fact is', Hankey wrote, 'I don't trust Neville Chamberlain's judgement'.[50] In the event, T.J. noted, Baldwin's return to the premiership seemed to infuse him with new zest and a decisiveness that appeared only intermittently during his career. He had already rejected any idea of collaboration with Lloyd George, and some weeks earlier had indicated to Jones that he had determined not to 'touch Churchill again'. Baldwin intended 'to keep as much of the 1931 façade as possible'; this meant minimal changes in the ministry, humouring MacDonald, and putting up again with J.H. Thomas, even though, as T.J., who had once had such high hopes of him, noted sadly, he was 'now a heavy debit' who kept 'bad company' and whose bad language had become a public disgrace.[51]

There was never any question, in Jones's opinion, that Baldwin, as Lloyd George feared, would go for a snap general election in July to capitalize on the Royal Jubilee; such an idea would be 'abhorrent to S.B.'.[52] Maybe Baldwin was so high-minded, but there is no doubt that his timing of the election early in November 1935 was brilliantly judged to secure the maximum advantage for his party, and his tactics were ideally suited to mobilizing a large popular support, which included many footloose Liberals and floating voters, for the government. Although he voted Labour himself, more out of personal hostility to the Tory candidate, 'the highly superior Duff Cooper', than from ideological commitment, T.J. was

[49] T.J.'s scraps of paper listing donations to College funds occasionally drove the methodical treasurer to distraction: 'Re initials', T.J. wrote (18 December 1936, Coleg Harlech MSS), 'I am becoming hazy and doubtful myself about the key to them. . . . Am not sure about W.A., but I believe I meant Wales and America = Houghton. G.A.H. = *Gwaith, Addysg, Hamdden* = T.J. fee for broadcast. R.Y.M. = Rich young man = David Astor; G.F. = Gregynog Founder = Gwendoline E. Davies'.

[50] *A Diary with Letters*, p.93. Hankey Diary, 1/7, Vol.4, f.63.

[51] T.J., Class Z (Diary, 1935), pp.27, 55, 94. *A Diary with Letters*, p.152.

[52] T.J., Class S, Vol.I, No.110.

delighted at Baldwin's success: 'I am not biased by friendship when I say that the triumph is a personal one for S.B. He has made no mistakes'.[53] T.J. had contributed to the victory. In the election campaign Baldwin had cleverly reconciled Tory voters to the League of Nations by supporting rearmament, and reassured pacifists and those who feared an armoured nationalist belligerence by a firm commitment to the Covenant of the League. Baldwin's most effective speech, which included the oft-quoted pledge, 'I give you my word that there will be no great armaments', was delivered to the Peace Society at the Guildhall on 31 October 1935. Neville Chamberlain, not readily given to praise, called it 'a magnificent utterance'. Baldwin told his audience that his remarks ought not to be taken 'as a contribution to the Election torrent'. The more sophisticated among his listeners knew better. Rushcliffe of the UAB, a former minister, commented that 'S.B. was a sly dog, he pretended the speech had nothing to do with politics, whereas it was the best political manifesto the Government had produced'. In fact, Baldwin was more devious than even Rushcliffe knew. *The Times* (1 November 1935) described the address, 'Bound over to make the Peace', as 'characteristic' of Baldwin. So it was, at least in delivery, for Baldwin spoke with his own 'special sort of fire'; but apart from 'a few excisions and a few trimmings', as Baldwin acknowledged gratefully, the speech was T.J.'s. 'I delivered the speech with conviction and delight', the Prime Minister wrote, 'I almost felt it was my own'.

Once again T.J. had hoped for rain but got a downpour instead, although not such a drenching as in 1931. 'I wish you a thumping majority', he wrote to Nancy Astor on the eve of the election, 'but I hope your National Government will have just enough to make it remember its pledges and execute them – no more'.[54] But aided once again by the disproportional representation system, the government won 432 seats to Labour's 154; 'too large a victory to please' T.J., who, as he told Flexner, wanted the 'strong opposition essential to the satisfactory working of our system'. He had not expected much of the Labour Party: it was badly divided, and although the left-wing bogeyman, Cripps, was 'kept quiet', the new leader, Attlee, who was a 'decent man', was also 'harmless' and, cripplingly, from an electoral point of view, 'unknown'. The

[53] T.J. to Lady Astor, 8 November 1935. Astor MS 146/1/2/142. *A Diary with Letters*, pp.155–6.

[54] *The Torch of Freedom: Speeches and Addresses by the Rt. Hon. Stanley Baldwin* (1935), pp.319–39. T.J., Class Z (Diary, 1935), pp.136, 151; Class A, Vol.6, Nos. 91 and 82; Class W, Vol.5, No.74.

opposition front bench would be a good deal stronger, although there was 'still a long tail of mediocrities', and, regrettably in T.J.'s view, about a quarter of the party's strength in the Commons consisted of 'the usual nondescript miners' federation trade unionists'.[55] Labour's recovery still had a long way to go.

Lloyd George's election hopes, however, were utterly in ruins. In May he had confidently talked of winning a following sufficiently large to make the Conservative position after the election 'very arduous and uncertain'. T.J. told him (an opinion with which Frances Stevenson agreed) that his campaign had little chance of success. Lloyd George's attempt to reawaken the Nonconformist conscience of England and Wales for political purposes, and to use the machinery of the chapels in lieu of party election machinery, was a miserable failure. His so-called Councils of Action ludicrously became 'Councils of Faction'. He merely secured the return of his family group of four. The weekend after the election his house at Churt was 'very quiet', undisturbed by a single telephone call from any newspaper or politician.[56]

Baldwin's personal triumph seemed complete. Of course some people were darkly suspicious of his triumphant putative honesty: 'I hate your S.B. more than ever', Sir James Grigg wrote to T.J. from India, 'but he is the cutest Tammany boss since Walpole'. T.J. himself said that Baldwin had 'doped the country' into somnolence over unemployment by his open-ended continuance of the 'Standstill' arrangement on benefit payments. But that fall from grace aside, T.J. believed that Baldwin now had a great opportunity: 'You are P.M. for the third time and should be on top of your job', he told Baldwin. 'It is the last time you've got to live up to your speeches'.[57]

In general Baldwin is considered by most authorities, and beyond question in T.J.'s opinion, to have risen more than adequately to the difficult challenge presented to him as Prime Minister by the wayward new King Edward VIII in 1936. T.J. was a staunch supporter of constitutional monarchy on the élitist but indisputable ground that monarchy, although not logical, was indispensable because it was 'intelligible to the mass of men and women who are swayed by their hearts rather than their heads'. But

[55] Astor MS 1416/1/2/142. *A Diary with Letters*, pp.155–6. T.J., Class S, Vol.I, Nos.122 and 126; Class Z (Diary, 1935), p.150. Tristan, carrying the war to the heart of the enemy, was busy distributing Communist literature in the West End, in support of 'the party of one', Willie Gallacher, in the Commons.

[56] *A Diary with Letters*, pp.147, 157. *Lloyd George: A Diary by Frances Stevenson*, (ed. A.J.P. Taylor), 1971, pp.313–320.

[57] T.J., Class Z (Diary, 1935), pp.154–5, 169.

whatever his obvious debt to Walter Bagehot's theory of monarchy, T.J.'s attitude to George V was much warmer than the cool appraisals that appear in *The English Constitution*. Indeed, T.J.'s article in the *Western Mail* (11 May 1935) to mark the Jubilee was fulsome in praise of George V, who was pronounced 'an English gentleman of great simplicity of character, of stainless honour, and of utter devotion to his high calling.'[58] This admiration accorded with public perceptions of George V, and in T.J.'s case was certainly unfeigned.[59]

He was, however, also aware that George V was disconcertingly ponderous in personal dealings, obsessed with the minutiae of ceremonial; his life, in T.J.'s euphemistic description many years later, was 'a masterpiece of well-ordered conduct'. Jones had personal knowledge of Edward's lively personality, had high hopes of him initially, and had been keen to use the Prince's charismatic qualities for public purposes. 'No one had a finer chance of being a great and popular King', T.J. wrote to the Astors, 'whenever the best side of the man was in evidence, he was received in public with great enthusiasm'.[60] But Edward's social sympathies were shallow, his lifestyle too raffish, and his attitude to duty too casual to appeal convincingly to T.J., whose opinions on such matters, though more flexible as a result of his social experience, were rooted in the Calvinism of his early years.[61] Not surprisingly, therefore, Jones's account in *A Diary with Letters* of Edward's succession and hasty abdication is that of the Establishment in Britain, the gospel as practised and, in due time, expounded sonorously and to political advantage by Baldwin, who confessed to T.J. that he was 'distinctly nervous' about Edward from the moment he succeeded.[62] T.J.'s unpublished correspondence offers ample evidence of official ruthlessness: Horace Wilson, for example, agitatedly threatening at one stage to blackmail Mrs Simpson into compliance. There are several instances too of that peculiar British snobbery wherein comments that give a semblance of popular sanction to Establishment opinions, allegedly uttered by assorted yokels and stock working-class characters on the approved list, are passed on

[58] 'The King's Sense of Duty'. Typically, Jones used the occasion to appeal for industrial peace in south Wales as an aid to economic recovery.

[59] *A Diary with Letters*, pp.148, 166.

[60] 'The Abdication Story', in the *Observer*, 30 September 1951. 19 November 1936. Astor MS 1416/1/2/160.

[61] In November T.J. bluntly, indeed brutally, told Megan Lloyd George that her father 'could do us a great service by taking Mrs. Simpson with him on his holiday next week'. T.J., Class Z (Diary, 1936), p.325.

[62] *A Diary with Letters*, p.162 and *passim*. T.J., Class Z (Diary, 1936), pp.28–9.

with amused satisfaction in letters to one another by their social betters.[63]

But despite these hypocrisies, the issues involved were serious and distracted the public, when belatedly apprised of the situation, from greater dangers threatening from abroad. T.J. was confident that Baldwin was ideally equipped to deal with the constitutional and imperial crisis of the abdication. 'S.B.', he wrote, 'is the right man in the right place'.[64] But he was much less certain of the Prime Minister's sureness of touch in dealing with difficult foreign problems.

T.J. already had cause for disquiet on that score, for the Hoare-Laval affair, the very model of diplomatic ineptitude, had blown up in the government's face in December 1935. Baldwin and T.J. had agreed that the speech of the Foreign Secretary, Sir Samuel Hoare, at Geneva on 11 September had been a good one.[65] In fact, Hoare had said nothing new and had merely asserted again that whatever burden resulted from action by the League against an aggressor 'must be borne collectively' by all member-states.[66] Nevertheless, his speech produced a general impression in the Assembly of a much firmer commitment by the British government and a willingness to take more definite action against an attack on Abyssinia than the British, who wished to keep their options open, were really prepared to make. T.J.'s instinct ought to have alerted him to a first-class botch in the making when, on 16 November, in response to his question 'How are things going to pan out in Abyssinia?', Baldwin's offhanded reply was: 'No idea. I ought, I suppose, to see the Foreign Secretary'.[67] In fact, T.J. knew little or nothing of the 'close-knit confusion', as Vansittart of the Foreign Office described it,[68] that led to the Hoare-Laval pact in December, which appeared a seedy horse-trading transaction after the ringing declaration of principle at Geneva in September. British public opinion was outraged. 'All the moral prestige we gained by Hoare's speech at

---

[63] Violet Markham (Ibid., p.341), for example, retailing below-stairs opinion at Chatsworth, which did not want 'a tart for our Queen', and Gwen Davies (T.J., Class R, Vol.5, No.69) reporting an alleged exchange between Radnorshire rustics.

[64] A Diary with Letters, p.292. One of T.J.'s Romney Street Group friends suggested (Class Z, Diary, 1935, p.378), that Edward had 'been beaten in advance by implacable institutions'.

[65] T.J., Class Z (Diary, 1936), p.121.

[66] The Times, 12 September 1935. Sir Samuel Hoare, Nine Troubled Years (1954), p.170, insisted that he said nothing important that he had not said many times before.

[67] T.J., Class Z (Diary, 1935), p.121.

[68] The Mist Procession. The autobiography of Lord Vansittart (1958), p.541.

Geneva had vanished like a dream', T.J. wrote angrily. 'It's a long time since I've felt so thwarted and downed'.[69]

Jones, an incorrigible quidnunc, could not bear to be left in the dark. He tried subsequently to ferret out from Baldwin, Hoare, Eden and others exactly how the Hoare-Laval fiasco had occurred. Much was made of Hoare's alleged tiredness and the fact that he had to deal with Pierre Laval, 'who has a Lloyd Georgian hypnotic gift of making black seem white and white black'. Moreover, the country did not want a war, for which Britain was hopelessly ill-prepared anyway: Mussolini 'could kill more people in Malta in a night than have been slain in the whole African campaign so far'. The episode had been badly presented; the terms of the pact gave a false 'impression of absurdly generous treatment' of the aggressor Italy. 'It was very difficult to understand how Hoare and Vansittart had failed to visualise this in advance'. After further investigation, Jones concluded that the Hoare-Laval pact was an ill-judged bluff that had gone maladroitly astray.[70] Possibly this striking collective demonstration of misjudgement by politicians and professional diplomats emboldened T.J. during 1936 to try his own hand at helping to solve a major problem in foreign relations. It was to do his public reputation no good at all in the longer term.

Nowadays, the 'Men of Munich', those who directed British foreign policy in the later 1930s, are not usually dismissed curtly as moral delinquents whose crass incompetence condemned Britain to fight a war for which it was ill-prepared after a sequence of shameful episodes that brought dishonour on the nation. The lapse of time has brought new perspectives; by courtesy of an army of revisionist historians, led by A.J.P. Taylor in 1961, reinterpretation and new evidence have altered or demolished some old orthodoxies. Much, though not all, of the heat generated by outraged morality has gone out of the controversy. That was not so in 1954 when Thomas Jones published his account of the period, *A Diary with Letters 1931–1950*. Jones applied no varnish to put a gloss on his behaviour, no matter how distressingly wrongheaded, even culpable, it might appear when looked at with the hindsight vision of 1954. Nor did he make any exculpatory use of cunning omission; there are no excisions other than those dictated by the need to avoid giving pain to the living. 'I've let the tale of my (mis)conduct

[69] To Sir James Morton, December 1938. Morton MSS GD 328/88/1. Morton, who had said (11 December) he had voted Tory for the first time in his life in November, now wished he had 'a thousand votes to cast against Baldwin's government tomorrow'.

[70] T.J. to Flexner, 14 January 1936. T.J., Class S, Vol.I, No.130; Class Z (Diary, 1936), pp.8–93, 203–4 (1937) p.126.

remain undoctored', he explained to Jack Lochhead, an old Glasgow friend, who had been surprised by T.J.'s candour.[71]

It was a courageous decision to make at a time when so many memoirs were heavily laced with special pleading. It was, of course, wholly in keeping with the ethical standards to which he had subscribed all his life. T.J. laid himself open to scorn, even calumny, particularly at the hands of the self-righteous, who were still pursuing those they called appeasers with undiminished relish. However, that is not to say that T.J. is exonerated by his honesty, for he was certainly guilty of crass misjudgement in his confidential dealings with the emissaries of Germany in 1936.

Britain in the 1930s ranked as a world power but lacked the strength commensurate with that status; her obligations out-stripped her resources by some distance. It was a fundamental dilemma that had worsened since the late nineteenth century, especially after 1918 when Britain extended her responsibilities at a time when her power had sharply contracted. There was, however, no serious disposition in official circles to respond to harsh reality by relinquishing imperial territory or shedding any of her global commitments. Diplomatic finesse, upon which the defence of the British Empire had always relied heavily, was now more important than ever. Latterly the world had become even more dangerous for a vulnerable oceanic empire: Japan had a fixed covetous eye on Britain's rich possessions in the Far East; Italy, for so long a friendly client state, had ambitions which could threaten imperial interests in and around the Mediterranean; Communist Russia was suspect on all counts everywhere. Above all, the resurgent power of Germany, already identified by the military as Britain's most likely long-term opponent, caused anxious concern.

T.J. had no specialist knowledge of the intricacies of British foreign and defence policy, or of Germany, but that did not induce him to be diffident about offering advice to Baldwin on these matters. T.J.'s opinions were broadly those shared by most of the liberal intelligentsia in Britain of that time: the Treaty of Versailles was the root of most if not all evil in Europe; there would be no genuine peace until Germany's legitimate grievances were fully redressed, common justice demanded no less. But although he shared many of the opinions of his friend Lothian, a hyperactive advocate of a policy of concession to Germany, T.J. was rather less concerned with the vindication of general principle and assuaging the guilty conscience of the British people than with what he regarded as the immediate practicalities. He was no less gullible in consequence.

[71] Lochead letters, White MSS.

The key consideration, in his judgement, was the need for better relations with Germany, which he hoped would lead to the 'making of a new Locarno with Hitler' that would establish the collective security at any rate of western Europe and perhaps, in time, a modicum of disarmament. He had urged such a policy on Baldwin since December 1934, and kept up the barrage of persuasion subsequently: 'I keep on and on and on preaching against the policy of ostracizing Germany, however incalculable Hitler and his crew may be'. T.J. did not consider that this attempt to improve Anglo-German relations involved making a choice between France and Germany: 'It need not be either or in an absolute sense if we are skilful',[72] he said. France, in his opinion, had much to answer for: ever since Versailles it had cynically used the League of Nations 'as a tool of French policy and the maintenance of the *status quo* in Europe'. Moreover, to cynicism was now added a dangerous weakness prompted by the deep divisions of French society, the corruption of its politicians and the ominous growth of Gallic Fascism. T.J. thought it important, too, to resist the 'pro-French bias' of the Foreign Office in London, particularly that of Vansittart the Permanent Under-Secretary.[73]

The Germans, it appeared, were anxious for a good understanding with Britain, or England as they customarily called it. Lothian had a long interview with Hitler in January 1935 in which the Führer expounded the geo-political view of the world that he so often paraded to persuade distinguished British visitors at this time of his good will, or perhaps to beguile them. According to Hitler, French policy was unstable, dangerously influenced by the opportunist needs of a succession of weak governments; Russia supported the *status quo* in Europe for the present because Stalin wanted 'a free hand in Asia', but once checked he would seek to expand in Europe, as Russia did after its defeat by Japan in 1905. Commun-ism, 'a world-conquering idea', would not disappear in twenty years, its ideas were as powerfully seductive as those of the French Revolution, and in ten years' time Russian industry would have 'grown to enormous dimensions', its competitive power would be 'devastating'. England and Germany had no quarrel, their interests were complementary. The Führer was prepared to offer guarantees of his good will: the German naval challenge to Britain before 1914, 'the greatest psychological failure in German history', would never be repeated. But a strong army was essential for

[72] *A Diary with Letters*, pp.139, 175, 183.
[73] T.J. to Lady Grigg, 22 August 1935. White MSS. *A Diary with Letters*, pp.183, 188.

Germany, 'the most vulnerable country in the world', and he asked
for no more than parity with Britain in air power. Hitler insisted
that Germany would use only 'peaceful means' to settle her
differences with Poland; the Austrian question could be settled by
plebiscite, 'force absolutely ruled out'. Lothian had no doubt at all
that the Germans 'want to come to terms with us'.[74] A year later
Arnold Toynbee, historian of civilizations, returned with the same
message from Hitler: 'If you English will make friends with us, you
may name your conditions'. T.J. promptly persuaded Toynbee to
write out an account of the interview and send it on to Baldwin and
Anthony Eden, now Foreign Secretary.[75]

Baldwin, with customary caution or, on a less generous
interpretation, usual lethargy, remained passively sceptical. The
Anglo-German naval treaty in 1935 was an important earnest of
Hitler's sincerity, but, as T.J. told Lady Grigg two months later, the
Prime Minister still would not trust the Germans 'an inch'.[76] Early
in 1936 T.J. was in touch with von Ribbentrop, the Germany envoy,
with whom he had several private meetings. By now, T.J. was
strongly convinced of the urgent need for an Anglo-German
understanding and was not deterred by the German reoccupation
of the demilitarized Rhineland in March 1936, which he regarded
as the removal of one of the last traces of Germany's 'humiliation'
at Versailles, not as an act of aggression. More important, in his
opinion, was Hitler's apparent offer of a pact guaranteeing twenty-
five years of peace. T.J. redoubled his efforts to get Baldwin to
accept Hitler 'at his face value' and 'try him out fairly'. Ribbentrop
urged upon T.J. a few days later that this was 'perhaps the last time'
Hitler would offer an accommodation to Britain. Early in May,
Ribbentrop pressed T.J., in a special message, to spend a weekend
with him at his house at Dahlem near Berlin. Vansittart, who told
T.J. that Ribbentrop was 'a complete ass', amended under protest
to 'almost a complete ass', tried in vain to persuade Jones not to go,
particularly as the Germans had not yet replied to the British
questionnaire asking for further detail of Hitler's proposal. T.J.
considered Vansittart was 'overwrought'; he agreed to accept
Ribbentrop's invitation and decided he would 'consult with nobody
about the visit'.[77]

[74] 'Hitler Interview', and the succeeding correspondence, especially Lothian
to Simon, 30 January 1935, in Lothian MSS GD/40/17, Vols.201 and 202. T.J.'s
excellent précis is in Class X, Vol.10, No.99.
[75] T.J., Class Z (Diary, 1936), pp.71–5.
[76] 25 August 1935. White MSS.
[77] A Diary with Letters, pp.185–6, 193–5; T.J., Class Z (Diary, 1936), pp.111, 115.

The chief purpose of the invitation seemed to be to flatter T.J. outrageously. Ribbentrop said he wished to talk to him 'without reserve'; he had put off an official meeting with Lord Halifax in order to try the direct method of establishing contact with Baldwin first. Ribbentrop said he knew what T.J.'s 'position was in London'; if Jones agreed to co-operate, his visit could turn out to be 'as important as Joseph Chamberlain's in 1899'.[78] On the following Sunday they flew together to Munich, where they were greeted by a ceremonial guard of honour, before going on to meet Hitler in his flat at 16 Prinz Regenten Strasse, the décor of which reminded T.J. of a Glasgow 'shipowner's drawing room' circa 1880. Hitler was at his low-key best; T.J. said that, unlike Mussolini, he made 'no attempt whatever to impress', but after a calm exchange of views he urged, 'with much animation', the importance of an Anglo-German alliance and his 'great desire' to meet Baldwin. T.J., who said he was now 'a person of no public importance in England', acknowledged that formerly he had worked closely with Lloyd George, Bonar Law and MacDonald and that he still saw Baldwin from time to time. The tone of the meeting was exceptionally friendly and T.J. too applied the best butter of flattery here and there.[79]

Eden and the Foreign Office officials deeply resented Ribbentrop's colloguing with 'odds and ends like T.J.', who said however that he was 'not in the least' disturbed by their objections.[80] Soon after his return home, T.J., pressed by Ribbentrop's agent von Wussow, who 'had orders to sit on [T.J.'s] doorstep until he got an answer', arranged a meeting at the House of Commons of Baldwin, Eden, Horace Wilson and himself. It was a stormy affair, T.J. and Eden 'went at it hammer and tongs'. The Foreign Secretary asked why the Germans did not use normal diplomatic machinery for negotiation; T.J. retorted that 'pedantry and punctilio were useless with Dictators'. Eden objected strongly to T.J.'s freelance activity and he replied, 'with equal plainness', to the effect that all Prime Ministers were glad at times of 'unofficial intermediaries', who could be 'disowned' if necessary. The exchange became even more heated:

[78] The detailed account of this meeting in which Ribbentrop plausibly outlined the benefits – some of which are incontrovertible – accruing to workers from Nazi social policy is in T.J., Class Z (Diary, 1936), pp.119–27.

[79] A Diary with Letters, pp.196–201.

[80] Churchill College. Burgon Bickersteth MSS No.4. T.J. (Class Z (Diary, 1936), pp.165–6) urged Horace Wilson to try to arrange for Vansittart to be sent for a three months' 'rest cure'.

T.J.: Wilson and I have settled more than one strike in this way.
Eden: This is no strike.
T.J.: No, it is worse, it is war.

Finally, however, it was agreed that T.J. should 'now drop out' and any further conversations would be regularized. Baldwin, surprisingly, 'sat almost silent' throughout the discussion, but on the way out, as T.J. subsequently recorded, 'S.B. stroked my back unobserved . . . and whispered the friendliest "goodnight"'.[81]

It was a curious episode, not without its absurdities. T.J. was alarmingly cocksure operating in a field in which he was a comparative tiro. His analogy with the settlement of industrial disputes was absurd. It would seem that, remembering his success with the Irish in 1921, he hoped once again to put his talent for sympathetic proxy negotiation to good effect in what he was convinced was a good cause. His judgement was surely awry. Ribbentrop was certainly not Arthur Griffith, the effect of the concession made to the Irish in 1921 had been reasonably calculable, but in 1936 T.J. was apparently prepared to hazard an important part of the balance of Europe on nothing more substantial than his belief in Nazi good faith. He was ready to make it clear, well in advance of any immediate necessity to do so, that Britain would not oppose the union of Germany and Austria, a settlement of disputes over Memel and Danzig in Hitler's favour, and a readjustment to his advantage of Hungary's frontiers, and would also be willing to discuss colonial problems, presumably as a preliminary to concessions. All these proposals were suggested to Eden by Lothian in June 1936 in a letter which T.J. described, without qualification, as 'admirable'.[82]

Of course there was no perfect prescription for answering the problem of Germany, and Britain could not restrict its dealings to states which passed some litmus test of moral probity. The prospect of another major war was horrifying; a determined attempt to avoid what many feared would be the end of European civilization was not only perfectly honourable, but the least that common sense and the instinct for national survival demanded.[83] But what was at stake was so important and the issues were so complicated that it called for the utmost caution and the most experienced

[81] Ibid., (Diary, 1936), pp.196–9.

[82] Ibid., (Diary, 1936), pp.151–66.

[83] 'Think of the responsibility before history of a Government which carried on *knowing* it was heading towards a war of the kind foreshadowed'. Alfred Zimmern wrote (ibid, Diary, 1936, pp.102–3) to T.J. in April 1936, 'Lord North would not be in it as an object of obloquy'.

negotiators. It was a diplomatic game that cried out for wary professionals, not inexperienced amateurs too readily prepared to gamble, however well-intentioned their purpose.

T.J. never had any illusions about the barbarous character of the Nazi state. Within months of Hitler's accession to power T.J. was energetically seeking assistance from British and American universities for Jewish scholars fleeing from persecution.[84] And his efforts on behalf of refugees continued unabated down to and beyond the outbreak of war, in some cases at considerable personal expense. Moreover, T.J.'s willingness to give Hitler every possible opportunity to live up to his promises was repeatedly challenged by his friend Abraham Flexner, whose letters from across the Atlantic are laced with intelligent appraisals of Nazi intentions.

> I cannot reconcile myself to the idea Great Britain will take the hand or trust the faith of murderers like Hitler and the gangsters by whom he is surrounded [Flexner wrote to Jones in June 1936]. I do not believe that any engagement that Hitler enters into can be trusted . . . Germany is a menace to Czecho-Slovakia, Lithuania, Roumania, Austria, France, England and [his measure of Nazi iniquity] civilisation itself.

This, just one of many warnings, did not prompt T.J. to more cautious second thoughts. Indeed, four days earlier, he had 'shocked' the Romney Street Group 'by putting strongly the case for alliance with Germany', a proposal which however he did not describe in detail. It exemplifies T.J.'s foolhardiness at this time. There may have been some sort of case for a limited détente with Germany, but alliance implied collaboration and, in this instance, almost certainly, through the ruthless dynamism of Nazi aggrandizement, hapless involvement in dangerous adventures. The contrast is striking. Flexner's judgement rested on moral conviction and a recognition of inherent probability: T.J.'s relied on facile optimism and a refusal to admit that Nazi evil really was indivisible.[85] Years later, honest as always, T.J. admitted that he had been wrong. 'Yes', he told John Lochhead, 'Flexner was wiser than I, and his letters are very good'.[86]

At the shouting match with Eden, T.J. had been taken aback by Baldwin's appearance; 'he looked an incredibly old man'. In recent months T.J. had spent much time defending Baldwin from his detractors. He did so on grounds of character not competence:

[84] Above, p.358.
[85] T.J. , Class Z (Diary, 1936), pp.182–5. *A Diary with Letters*, p.219.
[86] 6 November 1954. White MSS.

Baldwin, he insisted, was 'the most honest P.M. of the century'. T.J. tried time and time again to persuade Baldwin to meet Hitler at some convenient place on the Continent, but the Prime Minister would not be pinned down. Baldwin was exhausted and plainly overwrought, too tired even to consider going as usual to Aix-les-Bains that summer. T.J. quickly arranged for him to go first to Gregynog and then to Lothian's house at Blickling to patch him up for the coronation of Edward VIII.[87] T.J. himself, on Lord Dawson's orders, went to Montreux for treatment for rheumatism, and then went on to stay with the Zellwegers, family friends since 1903, at St Gallen in Switzerland.

Within days, however, T.J. was summoned urgently to join Lloyd George who had accepted a long-standing invitation to visit Germany and meet Hitler. The summons was relayed by Dr T.P. Conwell-Evans, whose career at the time is an interesting footnote to the history of appeasement. He was an able academic (T.J. had once tried to get C.K. Webster to add him to the International Politics staff at Aberystwyth) who was at one time Private Secretary to Lord Noel Buxton, and wrote a good book on international affairs based on his papers. He was fluent in German, had lectured at Königsberg university, was a leading figure in the Anglo-German Fellowship, and had been very friendly with Ribbentrop for some years. Conwell-Evans was at that time a passionate Germanophile; he had initially worked through Ramsay MacDonald and later switched to Lothian, whose visit to Hitler he had arranged. For all that, Conwell-Evans was a patriot; by 1938 he was utterly disillusioned with the Germans and in August sent valuable information (which was ignored) to the British Cabinet of Hitler's unreliability. At this time, however, he was ardent for an Anglo-German rapprochement; he arranged Lloyd George's visit and sat in on the talks with the Führer.[88]

Lloyd George had asked T.J. to join him in Germany because he hoped the presence of a friend of Baldwin in the party would counter any suggestion in Britain that L.G. was interfering: 'You are the accredited representative of this incompetent government', he told Jones. Lloyd George was surprised to discover that although T.J. hoped neither side would win outright in the Spanish Civil War,

[87] *A Diary with Letters*, pp.169–72, 228–37. T.J. got Harrods to provide liquor for the visit to Gregynog (citadel of temperance) where Anderson the butler, released from his chains, poured out the wine with great gusto and was most unwilling to provide a jug of water as an alternative.

[88] T.J., Class X, Vol.10, No.99. *A Diary with Letters*, pp.239–242. Conwell-Evans letters in Lothian GD/40/17, Vol.202. M. Gilbert, *The Roots of Appeasement* (1966), pp.28, 171.

on the whole he favoured Franco. L.G. said a victory for Franco could endanger the whole British position in the Mediterranean. Privately, L.G. said he was 'very disappointed' with T.J.'s reply, it showed 'how much he had altered from the radical' he had been some years before.[89] Nevertheless, Lloyd George asked Jones what he thought should be said to Hitler. T.J. advised him to confine the discussion to the proposed new Locarno agreement for western Europe, counsel which Lloyd George adopted so far as possible. He also asked Hitler to explain the finance of his great public works schemes, which the Führer, well-rehearsed on that theme, did brilliantly. 'I wish Neville Chamberlain could be closeted with him for an hour', L.G. said bitterly, later.[90]

Lloyd George's two meetings with Hitler at Berchtesgaden had no practical outcome. They were, in fact, merely meetings of a mutual admiration society, interesting also perhaps as one more exhibition of the genial side of Hitler's ambivalent attitude – admiration mingled with hatred – towards Britain. T.J. was present at the second, less formal meeting in Hitler's mountain retreat, the Berghof. For all the evident cordiality, T.J. and Lloyd George's son Gwilym, seeing Hitler, 'the prophet possessed', close up could not help recalling with a shiver 'the thirteenth of June', the night in 1934 when Hitler had liquidated Ernst Röhm and many other former associates in ruthless gangster style. A few days later, T.J. witnessed the Führer in full impassioned flow at the Nazi party rally on 10 September in the great stadium at Nuremburg. It was an awesome spectacle, 'Wembley doubled or trebled', the disciplined crowd hanging on his every word and gesture as he moved with supreme oratorical skill to a great theatrical climax, 'a sacrament of dedication to the Fatherland and to the Führer, impassioned, terrifying', in Jones's words.[91]

It is impossible to say whether T.J.'s presence in the party in

---

[89] *Sylvester Diary. 1931–34*, pp.145–152. *A Diary with Letters*, pp.209–10, 231, 240. T.J. had been assured by Bullitt, the American ambassador in Moscow, that the Russians confidently predicted a Communist puppet government in Spain within months. T.J. told Flexner that Britain had 'to choose between Russia and Germany soon', as otherwise Germany would 'converge' with Italy.

[90] Conwell-Evans's full notes of the discussion are printed in M. Gilbert, op.cit., Appendix 2. A shorter unfinished note, written by Evans at T.J.'s request *(A Diary with Letters*, pp.244–6), is much more vividly expressed. T.J. carefully wrote up his own notes each evening and 'destroyed the blotting paper after use, ignoring the waste-paper basket', as Emrys Pride *(Why Lloyd George met Hitler* (Newport, 1981, p.27)), a member of the party, noticed.

[91] *A Diary with Letters*, pp.248–52, 256–8. Lloyd George refused to attend the Nuremburg meeting; he said that if he had done so, 'England would be offended'. T.J., Class A, Vol.2, No.34.

Germany did have the disarming effect Lloyd George had envisaged. There was no strong criticism of the visit in Britain, although some eyebrows were raised at the unqualified praise Lloyd George heaped on Hitler and the new Germany in newspaper accounts of his visit. T.J got him 'to modify' a few words here and there, but could not persuade him to tone down a sentence in which Lloyd George asserted categorically that the Germans had 'definitely made up their minds never to quarrel with us again'.[92] But Jones's caution was unwonted; despite the violently aggressive language of Hitler and Goering, T.J. remained convinced of Germany's peaceful intentions, and in November at a meeting of The Family, the informal group of public servants, he defended the Germans against a fierce attack by Arthur Salter.[93] In partnership with Geoffrey Dawson, editor of *The Times,* T.J. tried in September, without success, to get Ribbentrop's son into Eton. When Ribbentrop ('my friend', as T.J. described him) was made Ambassador in London, an appointment which he believed would 'help to keep the peace', Conwell-Evans, who insisted it was a mistake to 'underestimate' Ribbentrop's influence, repeatedly pressed T.J. to persuade Baldwin to agree to meet Hitler. Jones did his best, but without success: the Prime Minister was preoccupied with the 'monopolizing' problem of Edward VIII and Mrs. Simpson.[94]

However, it is possible to detect, early in 1937, the first glimmerings of a change in Conwell-Evans's uncritical attitude towards the Third Reich. After a visit to Germany in January, in which he had seen Ribbentrop and Schacht, the German financial expert, Conwell-Evans reported to T.J. that Hitler was becoming 'more and more the prophet, impatient of advice', who would not now listen to Ribbentrop's warnings or to Schacht's criticisms of Goering's four-year Plan for military-economic autarchy. Conwell-Evans believed that there was a struggle for supremacy between 'moderates' and 'militant radicals' in Germany. The British badly needed 'a big man' to represent them in Berlin.[95] Others too were looking to the intervention of some saviour or other to halt the drift to war. James Morton, who had seen T.J.'s diary account of the

[92] 'I talked to Hitler', *Daily Express* (17 September 1936); *News Chronicle* (22 September 1936). *A Diary with Letters,* p.265. P. Rowland, *Lloyd George* (1975), pp.734-5.

[93] *A Diary with Letters,* p.281. T.J., Class Z (Diary, 1936), p.315.

[94] NLW, B.B. Thomas MSS, ibid., pp.303–4, 20 August 1936. T.J., Class E, Vol.I, Nos.26–29; Class W, Vol.18, No.8. *A Diary with Letters,* pp.289, 299.

[95] T.J., Class Z (Diary, 1937), pp.8–10. *A Diary with Letters,* pp.304–5. 'X' is Conwell-Evans.

visit to Germany, wrote to say that 'very extraordinary times' called for 'extraordinary means': T.J. should persuade Baldwin to send Lloyd George on a 'special mission' to Berlin. T.J. reported that, sensible as the suggestion was, 'the personal obstacles' were insuperable. A month later, Wilfrid Eady suggested to T.J. that the most useful 'next step' in dealing with Germany would be to bring in Jan Smuts, whose world stature and vast experience would promote confidence on all sides.[96] In fact, all that happened was that Phipps, the British Ambassador, of whom T.J. had been severely critical for some time, was replaced by Nevile Henderson, whose chief recommendations appeared to be that he was considered the best of a bad lot and was 'keen on shooting' and 'therefore acceptable' to Goering. Initially at least, T.J. disapproved of Henderson's appointment.[97]

During 1937 the German attitude towards Britain began to change. Lothian, accompanied by Conwell-Evans, who acted as interpreter, had discussions with Hitler and Goering in May. Lothian detected an 'ominous' change in Nazi opinion: they expressed no hostility to the British Empire, which was 'an excellent creation of the Nordic race', but they were coming to the conclusion that, 'in the last resort', it was Britain that stood in the way of justice for Germany. 'Wherever the German hand "plucked a feather from the goose" [said Goering], the English boot was immediately applied to kick the German hand away'. Although he believed there was still an opportunity for Britain and Germany to come to terms, Lothian, whose major concern was the survival intact of the British Empire, was at least prepared now to face the necessity ultimately of Britain's organizing 'a military alliance of the tightest kind' against a 'predatory' combination of Germany, Italy and Japan.[98]

T.J. too was hesitantly beginning his slow return to a proper sense of reality, honest perplexity beginning to supplant overweening confidence. 'How can you foretell the action of a Hitler or a Mussolini?', he asked Lady Grigg despairingly in March. Three months later he wrote: 'These Dictators keep mankind on edge – they are absolutely incalculable; they believe in war, they do not loathe it like the rest of us, and they believe in "surprise"'. By

[96] Morton MSS 10 and 12 January 1937. GD 326/88/1. Eady to T.J., 27 February 1937. Lothian MSS. GD/17/339.

[97] *A Diary with Letters*, p.314. T.J., Class Z (Diary, 1937), p.11. T.J.'s letters are littered with disparaging comments on Phipps.

[98] 'Memorandum of visit to Berlin', Lothian MSS. GD 40/17/ Vol.203 ff. 252–265, and 'Interview with General Goering', 4 May 1937. GD 40/17/Vol.204. The 'Memorandum' is a remarkable mixture of sagacity and *naïveté*.

that time all hope had evaporated of a meeting between Hitler and Baldwin, who was impatient to retire and whose response to awkward questions about policy was: 'Don't let's talk about anything unpleasant'.[99]

On 27 May 1937, Baldwin did retire in something like a blaze of glory that was dampened only by sprinklings of the torrent of criticism that later almost destroyed his reputation for a time. To this day Baldwin, 'the dominant figure in British politics since the war', as T.J. rightly called him, remains an enigma. It is doubtful if anyone had come closer to solving the riddle than T.J., who asserted that Baldwin 'exercised dominion by being rather than doing', and at various crises was the 'incarnation of the national will'. More a preacher than a statesman, he had no profound faith in political action as a remedy for human miseries; he 'courted the House of Commons like a lover', but was a failure as the Leader of the Opposition; courteous and reflective, his 'defensive parrying' promoted the legend that he was 'a drifter', 'even lazy', but the truth was that his leadership derived from a 'ruminant passivity' that could occasionally lead to dramatic action. 'Normally', T.J. said, 'he moves like a glacier, inch by inch, but sometimes like an avalanche, and the face of the landscape is changed'. Baldwin's idealism and courage were 'intermittent'; he sometimes aroused hopes he did not satisfy: he had perhaps averted industrial civil war in 1926, but 'the square deal' he had promised assumed a 'rather elliptical shape'. Haunted by the threat of Lloyd George, an untutored mass electorate, and the danger of a Bolshevized working class, Baldwin had liberalized the Tories, reduced the bitterness in politics, welcomed the advent of the Labour party, assisted the cause of Indian freedom, and coped brilliantly with the abdication crisis. But he was distrustful of foreigners, grudging in support of the League of Nations and, as T.J. wrote in 1954, Baldwin's culpably 'slack supervision of foreign affairs' in the thirties was a heavy count against him.[100]

Before he retired Baldwin had offered T.J. a KCB. He replied that he had had 'some qualms' in accepting the CH:

> Life has dealt most generously with me [T.J. wrote in his graceful letter of refusal], far beyond my dreams when fifty years ago I moved among

[99] *A Diary with Letters*, pp.326, 331, 354. With perhaps a premonition of criticism to come, T.J. wrote on the flyleaf of an offprint copy account of his visit to Germany (circulated to friends) that he gave his daughter Eirene, the inscription: 'A Skeleton for the Cupboard, 1 January 1937'. T.J.

[100] T.J. masquerading as PQR, 'Mr. Baldwin', in the *Spectator* (7 June 1935). *A Diary with Letters*, pp.xxxii–xxxiv. 'Lord Baldwin', *The Times*, 15 December 1947.

the puddles and the furnaces. I have found the doors marked Push and Pull wide open. And you have given me your friendship for many years, a rich reward for any services to the State. I am a debtor, not a creditor, so my answer with the usual frankness is 'No' – and thank you, kind sir, very much.[101]

T.J. had expected to find it rather 'odd' not to be in and out of No. 10 Downing Street, as he had been free to do for twenty years. In fact, the new Prime Minister, Neville Chamberlain, relayed a message in June through Horace Wilson that 'T.J.'s co-operation would be welcome', especially in the three worlds where Chamberlain confessed he felt least at home: 'Labour, Non-conformity and Social Service'. Rather surprised, T.J. said that he did not think he could be of much use as he 'did not know' Chamberlain, but that of course he was always at the service of a British Prime Minister.[102]

Despite his involvement in international politics, and a complaint on one occasion that he felt 'enslaved' by the number of his engagements, T.J. of course kept in touch with his old friends. He enjoyed in particular an evening with Tawney, whose pungent comments on contemporary leaders of the left were a delight,[103] and meetings with Charlotte and George Bernard Shaw, who was 'mellowing beautifully', sufficiently at least for T.J. to be able to persuade him to let the Gregynog Press publish a short selection of his writings.[104] He also met the famous ex-boxer Jimmy Wilde and his wife. T.J. was captivated by the 'small, neat, quick, sturdy' couple: Jimmy who, although slight, was so deadly that his boxing gloves were sometimes searched 'to see if he had lead in them'and Mrs. Wilde whose personality made just as much impact outside the ring. Typically Jones urged them to write their life-story and promised to help to get it published. T.J. usually attended the Romney Street Group lunches at this time: 'You are the rallying point of all these meetings', one member wrote to him, 'we all go

---

[101] 14 April 1937. CUL Baldwin MSS. Vol.173 f76.

[102] T.J., Class Z (Diary, 1937), pp.125–6. This friendly approach may have played a part in T.J.'s acceptance in June of Chamberlain's invitation to serve on the UAB for another term.

[103] Ibid., p.20: Victor Gollancz, for example, 'who interrupts his patronising of the proletariat to order his butler to bring in more cocktails', and H.N. Brailsford and Harold Laski, whose writings offer no greater guidance than: 'Brethren, let us pray'.

[104] *A Diary with Letters*, pp.313, 371–2. *Shaw Gives Himself Away* (Gregynog, 1939).

there in the hope that you will be present'.[105] But T.J. derived the greatest pleasure of all from the months he spent with his friend Flexner at his remote lakeside holiday cabin in Canada, two hundred miles north of Toronto. It was an idyllic interlude: T.J. sunbathed, cut timber, went fishing, did not open a newspaper, and soon felt very fit. During the holiday he wrote a sketch of his early life, which was published in 1938 under the title *Rhymney Memories*.[106]

That book described a world that was utterly different socially from Cliveden, the magnificent country house in Buckingham-shire, where Waldorf and Mary Astor established the most famous political salon in Britain in the 1930s. T.J. was rarely absent from the weekend house parties that attracted so much attention in the thirties.'The talk in the house was never of art or literature'; it was not possible to keep off politics for long, 'that's the bane of it', T.J. wrote a shade ruefully. But the miscellanies of guests, who were not chosen on any consistent principle aside from the avoidance of antipathies, almost always included among the many British public figures interesting visitors from overseas: Chaplin, Helen Wills Moody, or Henry Ford from America, Maisky the Soviet Ambassador or Grandi from Italy, a dominion Prime Minister, or a man of letters, possibly Sean O'Casey, or, quite often, Bernard Shaw, who 'out-talked' everyone on any subject when so minded. Lady Astor, vital, beautiful, provocative, often outrageous, was 'the centre of attraction'; she fascinated T.J., who deeply admired Waldorf, her husband, whose habitual even temper prompted him to believe in 'the natural goodness of the man'. No one could be 'less like the monster' Astor was painted in some quarters, said T.J.[107]

It was perhaps inevitable that the immensely rich Astors and their friends, Lothian, Geoffrey Dawson, editor of *The Times*, and T.J. in particular, would be fiercely attacked in the late thirties because their political activity was in part so public, so controvers-ial, and could so easily be represented as sinister by their enemies. The burden of the charge was, in Astor's words:

> that a group of pro-Fascist politicians, peers, journalists, bankers and business magnates are meeting secretly for weekends at Cliveden . . . in

[105] *A Diary with Letters*, pp.339–40. T.J., Class Z (Diary 1937), p.164.

[106] Bangor MS 16181. *A Diary with Letters*, p.364.

[107] Ibid., pp.xxxv–xxxix, 151. T.J.'s accounts, 'Nancy Astor, Mistress of Cliveden' and 'The Cliveden Set' (1953). Class Q, Vol.2, Nos.101 and 108.

order to bring pressure to bear on Mr. Chamberlain and force him into a policy hostile to the preservation of Democracy.

Astor insisted it was 'a cold and calculated lie'.[108]

There is no question that Astor and his friends continued at this time to advocate a policy of accommodation with Germany, although not all of them quite to the same obsequious extent as Dawson, whose pro-German editorial censorship and grovelling leading articles brought *The Times* to one of the lowest points in its history. There is no doubt, too, that Neville Chamberlain's accession to the premiership raised their hopes that his businesslike vigour would lead to a new initiative in foreign policy. Horace Wilson had assured T.J. in June that Chamberlain the new Prime Minister was 'sound on Germany', and Chamberlain himself told Nancy Astor that he was going to be 'his own Foreign Minister', or at any rate 'take an active hand'.[109] T.J., despite the first tremors of doubt about an understanding with Hitler, and a deep anxiety about Germany's growing superiority in air-power, argued that if Britain continued to spurn Hitler's 'repeated offers' his price for agreement would go up. 'All this', T.J. wrote, 'the P.M. sees and says, but I think it goes no further and meanwhile Vansittart is trying hard to bring N.C. round to the secular Foreign Office view'. Jones was delighted therefore when it was arranged in November 1937 for Halifax, under cover of a hunting trip with Goering, to meet the German leaders. T.J. promptly sent Halifax the memorandum 'setting out the Führer's policy, as interpreted by Ribbentrop', that he had brought back for Baldwin the year before.[110]

T.J. welcomed Halifax's commission because he had lost all confidence in Eden, the Foreign Secretary.

Eden is agreeable and dextrous [T.J. wrote after a weekend discussion with him at Cliveden] and makes the small points and misses the big ones. He can't sit back, as Balfour would, from the day-to-day ding-dong. He lives from hand to mouth fed by the Foreign Office. He lacks background and depth . . . he would be wise to do what some suggest he should — go to the Admiralty'.[111]

[108] Astor to the Tory Central Office, April 1938. Waldorf Astor MS 1066/1/669–670.

[109] T.J., Class Z (Diary, 1937), pp.125, 130–1.

[110] *A Diary with Letters,* pp.363, 368, 377.

[111] To Lady Grigg, 24 October 1937. White MSS. A week later T.J. complained that Eden recently had twice 'rebuffed' Ribbentrop in humiliating fashion.

T.J. had lost all confidence in Vansittart a good deal earlier, and had played a part in the 'long drawn effort to eject him from the F.O'. It was, therefore, in T.J.'s opinion, long overdue when Vansittart was effectively sidetracked to the grand but powerless post of Chief Diplomatic Adviser.

> You remember [T.J. wrote with great satisfaction to Lady Grigg] S.B. tried to do this by gentle persuasion, offering him the choice of Paris or Washington . . . but failed. S.B. was asked by Eden to avoid ordering Van, which of course suited S.B.'s temperament perfectly. Van refusing it became difficult for Neville to re-open the matter on the former basis. [So a new post] . . . was invented as a way out of a difficult situation which prevailed between No. 10 and the F.O. in the three months before Christmas.[112]

If anything, T.J. was even more pleased, 'unfeignedly glad' as he described it, when in February, after continuing disagreements with Chamberlain, Eden resigned the Foreign Secretaryship:

> Eden's departure had come at last [T.J. wrote to Flexner] . . . he never gave Hitler and Ribbentrop a fair chance. I am one of those who believe that two years ago we could have done business with Germany. Hitler and Ribbentrop wanted our friendship and told us plainly that if they could not get it they would turn to Japan and Italy. Eden preferred to cling to France and the Treaty of Versailles . . . But for Eden I would have succeeded in bringing Hitler and Baldwin together. Baldwin was agreeable: Eden blocked it, partly in pique at a speech by N. Chamberlain on sanctions . . . Neville told me himself this was a calculated indiscretion . . . The chances of Neville succeeding with Germany (Italy does not matter much) have been gravely reduced . . . but the P.M. and Halifax can be counted on to do their utmost to find a way to some peaceful understanding.[113]

Over the next six months Hitler showed, in the most brutal fashion, how absurdly unreal these hopes of a stable, morally acceptable understanding between Britain and his murderous régime were and probably always had been. T.J.'s awakening from the long reverie, which he had shared with many of his friends, was painful and included one deeply humiliating episode.

Claud Cockburn, Communist, upper-class renegade, former correspondent of *The Times,* was probably the most gifted British journalist of his time. The international furore that he created by

---

[112] 8 and 15 January 1938. T.J. Add MSS. WW Vol.I, Nos.2 and 3. In October, T.J. (Class Z, Diary 1937, pp.156–7) persuaded Baldwin, who refused to tackle Chamberlain, to work on Halifax to get Vansittart out.

[113] T.J., Class S, Vol.2, No.33.

his attacks on the 'Cliveden Set' in his mimeographed news-sheet, *The Week*, in 1937–8 was a brilliant coup. The Astors and their friends were mercilessly pilloried as a pro-Fascist clique exercising from Cliveden a malevolent secret influence on British foreign policy. After two false starts by Cockburn, the phrase was picked up in the British press and within six weeks had become an international sensation, an irresistible damaging myth, proof against all denial. In desperation, Astor sent off a round-robin letter of protest to the fifteen leading newspapers in the world. But nothing could stop the march of a phrase that, as Cockburn wrote later, dramatized and summarized 'a whole vague body of suspicions and fears'.[114]

T.J. received his full share of the notoriety. A Communist party pamphlet, *Hitler's Friends in Britain*, described him as Cliveden's invaluable 'contact man' who wielded a serpent's influence in high places. The *Daily Herald* on 6 April 1938 devoted half a page to 'Jones the Mystery Man' of modern politics: 'Nothing Henry Fielding put to paper', it claimed, 'was so fantastic as the true story of Tom Jones'. Four days earlier there had been even more damaging coverage. T.J., votary of anonymity, was obviously unnerved by all the publicity. Confronted by a battery of Press photographers as he arrived for lunch (described of course as a clandestine meeting of the 'Cliveden Set') at the Astors' house in St. James's Square, T.J. panicked, covered his head with his overcoat and hurried indoors. It was an astonishingly foolish thing to do; in the picture published in the national press the next day, his action looked incredibly furtive, a public admission of shame of some sort. Nancy Astor more sensibly entered into the fun, and Geoffrey Dawson, who was not renowned for light humour, asked by a reporter as he arrived who he was, gaily answered 'Ribbentrop'.

T.J. was mortified; it was the most humiliating experience of his public life; his enemies on the *Western Mail* could not contain their glee. In vain he protested that the so-called group or set 'had as much unity as the passengers on a railway train', some of them never spoke of politics, those who did spent much of their time 'criticizing one another'.[115] But this was disingenuous.

The 'Cliveden Set' certainly embraced people who held different shades of opinion and to some extent had varied aims. It

[114] *The Week*, 22 December 1937. C. Cockburn, *Crossing the Line* (1958), pp.18–22. P. Cockburn, *The Years of the Week* (1968), pp.227–36. Waldorf Astor MS 1066/1/669-670. T.J. (T.J. Add MSS WW, Vol.I, No.19) said that he quickly gave up subscribing to *The Week*, 'because it was obviously serving up a grain of truth in a peck of lies'.

[115] *Daily Express*, 2 April 1938. *Western Mail*, 7 April 1938. 'Clivedenism', *Time and Tide*, 2 April 1938. T.J. Add MSS WW, Vol.I, No.15. *A Diary with Letters*, p.403.

was a loose association of like-minded people who believed that a *détente* with Germany, starting with the redress of the injustices supposedly inflicted at Versailles, offered the best hope of avoiding another war. They were not pro-Fascist, but were muted in their comment on German domestic savagery and thus vulnerable to the charge of fellow-travelling. There is no evidence that this activity deflected the government from its chosen path. Vansittart was not dislodged or Eden edged out until Neville Chamberlain, the last man amenable to such influence, had so decided. That is not however to say that some of their actions were not ill-advised and open to question. The Germans, Ribbentrop in particular, may well have gained some misleading impressions from them of British opinion, policy and resolution. The opprobrium Cockburn ingeniously heaped upon them caused great pain. It simply had to be endured and, if possible, lived down.

Jones had also been embarrassed by a blatant instance of Ribbentrop's duplicity. Breakfasting at the German Embassy with him on the day Hitler marched into Austria, T.J. had pleaded in vain for the release from custody of Niemöller, the Protestant pastor. Ribbentrop had the gall to describe the interview in which Hitler had mercilessly browbeaten Schuschnigg, the Austrian Chancellor, as 'friendly and unforced', and disclaimed prior knowledge of the Nazi occupation. Not yet wholly free from wish-fulfilment, T.J. tried hard to believe him. The *Anschluss* was no great surprise in Britain but Hitler's methods, especially the persecution that followed, prompted great hostility. T.J. described the *Anschluss* as 'rape', but argued that Britain was paying the price for its previous obstruction of a sensible solution and was hampered by the 'uncertain leadership' of the government.[116]

T.J. had several private meetings with Chamberlain at this time and urged him to reconstruct his ministry on a 'really national basis', bringing in Churchill (though under restraint) as Air Minister, and Herbert Morrison and A.V. Alexander of the Labour party. T.J. told the Prime Minister frankly that he was widely 'regarded as a Fascist in disguise', and should set out to destroy that impression in his speeches.[117]

Chamberlain had in fact already asked T.J. to assist, and Horace Wilson (who, T.J. said, was now operating as 'a sort of Deputy P.M.'

---

[116] Ibid., pp.395–6. T.J., Class S, Vol.2, No.37. Ribbentrop had brushed aside an earlier protest by T.J. about the ill-treatment of a relation of Einstein, the most celebrated refugee, as an unimportant detail of a revolutionary society.

[117] T.J. 'at dinner with J.M.', 17 March 1938. Morton MSS GD 328/89/3. T.J. Add MSS, WW, Vol.I, No.15. *A Diary with Letters,* p.397.

sitting at Chamberlain's elbow all day, wielding considerable power, the dubious exercise of political authority by a Civil Servant which later exposed him to so much hostility) pleaded with Jones to help as 'none of the No. 10 secretaries' could write a good speech. Lady Grigg advised T.J. not to be drawn back into politics. 'I do not want to' he replied. 'But what is one's duty? Should I refuse the P.M.?' Despite his protestations, T.J. rather welcomed the opportunity to resume his old involvement in important matters of state. The plan was that over the next few months he would write speeches for Chamberlain on general and cultural topics that would 'give some colour and breadth' to his personality, make him 'appear human to the multitude', and explain his personal political creed as a means of destroying the suspicion that he was 'Fascist in temper'. T.J. had hoped 'to put the P.M. across' as was done with Baldwin, but it proved a much 'tougher job'. Chamberlain's interests were so limited that there was 'little to fasten on'. He was no public orator and had no capacity at all to rouse an audience. As Nancy Astor said, when Chamberlain rose to speak in the Commons, 'it was like the slow descent of the safety curtain in the theatre'. T.J. also found that Chamberlain was unwilling to use much of the material which he supplied. T.J.'s draft conclusion for the speech on Czechoslovakia that Chamberlain made in the Commons on 24 March was thought to be 'pitched too high and too strong' for him to use. T.J. wrote a peroration on 'Freedom' for Chamberlain's speech in Birmingham on 8 April. Horace Wilson was enthusiastic but doubted whether much of it would be used. 'I see from *The Times* this a.m.', T.J. wrote, 'that only the first two paragraphs echo mine. I must pitch a lower tone . . . I was much more outspoken about the dictator's doctrine than N.C. permits himself'. T.J. still had some lingering hope that it would be possible 'to do business' with the Germans, but after several discussions with Chamberlain he was left with an uncomfortable feeling that 'the P.M. trusted them far more' than he did, and 'showed little apprehension of the difficulties ahead of him'.[118]

Jones had up-to-date first-hand experience in July of the difficulty of dealing with Nazis. He attended an informal meeting at Lothian's house Blickling of half a dozen prominent Nazis and a like number of British academics. It was an uneasy affair, there was 'much fencing'. T.J. told the Germans that the 'chief hindrance to progress' in reaching an understanding was 'their lust for cruelty', a comment that was bitterly resented 'as an assumption of moral superiority'. T.J. concluded that the attempt 'to reason with them' would not get very

[118] T.J., Class W, Vol.2, No.124; Vol.20, No.138; Class S, Vol.2, No.39. Add MSS, WW, Vol.I, Nos.15–19.

far. He was however interested in their account of the way they had reduced unemployment. Flexner was not surprised at this impasse, he thought it was a waste of time talking to such 'lunatics'.[119]

T.J. was abroad during the whole of August, on holiday with his friends the Zellwegers at St Gallen. He spent part of the time 'boxed in' there, with no newspapers, working on his projected book on government and the script for the BBC's first National Lecture on 'Prime Ministers and Cabinets', which he was to broadcast in October.[120] Unfortunately, therefore, his correspondence during these weeks is unusually thin. He had obviously criticized Chamberlain in letters to Lady Grigg at this time, some of which have not survived: 'You think I don't care for Neville', he wrote on 1 August. 'I do, and admire his admirable qualities so lacking in his predecessor'. However, unlike Baldwin, Chamberlain did not ask for advice or information from his entourage: 'If [only] we could roll the two into one!' T.J. said. 'Somebody betwixt and between is needed'. Later that month Flexner, who was watching the course of events regarding Czechoslovakia closely, replied to T.J. who had earlier said he was attracted by an idea put forward by Madariaga that Czechoslovakia should become a neutral federal state 'on the lines of Switzerland'. Flexner brushed this aside. The Nazis would not stop: 'These men cannot rest. They must go on from one outrage to another. Having gobbled up Austria, they will do the same to Czecho-Slovakia unless they are stopped'. Flexner said that if Chamberlain believed, as many thought he did, that he could 'arrange a *modus vivendi* with Hitler and Mussolini that will last . . . history will pronounce him as big a blockhead as has ever held power in Great Britain'.[121]

By the time he returned to Britain early in September T.J., influenced to a surprising extent by the urgings of a group of 'highly placed Germans', who declared they hated the 'presumptuous jingoism of the Nazis', had come round to the need to resist Hitler, if necessary by threatening to go to war.[122]

So, too, apparently had the Astors, with whom T.J. stayed on his return. They were all perturbed to hear via the Tory MP Robert Boothby that the Cabinet 'was weakening in its stand against the use

[119] T.J., Class S, Vol.2, Nos. 47 and 48.

[120] T.J. said that he was humbled by a sense of inferiority in comparison with Zellweger, who was fluent in German, French, English and Italian.

[121] T.J. Add MSS, WW, Vol.I, No.20; Class S, Vol.2, No.48.

[122] Endorsed by T.J., 'From a German Source to T.J.'. Class E, Vol.I, No.48. *A Diary with Letters*, pp.411, 436–7. 'These were a group of younger men . . . in the higher strata of the German army, civil service and business'. They claimed to be 'patriots, conservative', but 'in no way reactionary'. By inference, it would seem to include Adam von Trott, executed after the July Plot against Hitler in 1944.

of force by Germany' in Czechoslovakia. Jones was pressed to go to Horace Wilson and urge him to support a policy of firmness. T.J. pleaded that he was out of touch with Cabinet policy and had not even seen a newspaper for weeks, but eventually agreed to go up to London. He was however thoroughly chastened by what he discovered. The situation was, and indeed always has been, much more complex than T.J. or Flexner had supposed. No policy for Britain then that was not open to serious objection on some score or other has been formulated by anyone, at that time or subsequently. T.J.'s reaction to the dramatic events of the 'Munich' series of episodes is not untypical of the mingled feelings of fear, relief, shame and rage that many people in Britain experienced at the time. He did get to see Horace Wilson, and Halifax, but there is no record of the meetings. T.J. also had half-an-hour's discussion with Inskip, Minister for the Co-ordination of Defence, who was not prepared to limit the government's options but gave the impression that Cabinet opinion was that France was 'not very determined', that the Russian army was certainly shorn of experienced leadership, that the USA would no doubt sermonize but could not definitely be relied upon for help, and that Britain's air defence was woefully weak.[123]

T.J. was glad that Chamberlain took the initial decision to go to Germany, as Jones thought, to warn Hitler not to go 'too far' and thus avert the danger of war. T.J.'s response to the Berchtesgaden terms is interesting. He said Chamberlain

> had never before negotiated with a lunatic, if their meeting can be called negotiation. It is felt the Czechs are "sold" and we are "sold", that in a few months the Czechs will be completely overborne, then Roumania and the rest . . . We all feel ourselves divided between cowardly relief and shame . . . [People wish] . . . Eden were bigger and Winston younger and less steeped in old brandy. No national leader is in sight. Labour hates Neville for Spain . . . No-one can say what Russia will do . . . I wish we could make a real National Government and go all out for National Service.
>
> [T.J. was convinced that] ministers did not think of the rights and wrongs of issues but of London in flames and myriads of women and children stampeding from the East End to the West in wild panic.[124]

After the Godesberg meeting, T.J. concluded that Chamberlain's defeat was 'complete'; it would have been better if he had stayed at home, not connived at Hitler's triumph and not added insult to the injury his diplomacy had inflicted on the Czechs.[125]

But T.J.'s sense of outrage turned to fear as the prospect of war grew stronger and he was assured by Lindbergh, American hero of a solo flight across the Atlantic, that German air superiority was overwhelming; they 'had the equipment which could practically level a city such as London, Paris or Prague'. T.J. was filled with agonizing uncertainty:

> I suppose we must submit . . . shall we ever have as many chances of help as today? . . . Had we not better fight now? . . . There is a feeling the evil is only postponed, that our prestige is in the dust, that a day will come when we will have to fight the bully.

But dominating all was 'a dread of the air menace'.[126]

Lindbergh of course was talking nonsense. His supposed expert standing derived from the great respect his courageous exploit inspired, not superior technical understanding of the destructive capability of the *Luftwaffe* at that time. But his 'authority' reinforced widely-held fears and seemed to T.J. to be conclusive:

> Since my talk with Lindbergh [he wrote], I've sided with those working for peace at any cost in humiliation, because of our relative unpreparedness in the air . . . and because of his belief that the democracies would be crushed absolutely and finally.[127]

Neville Chamberlain's expectations following the Munich Agreement are still a matter of debate. T.J.'s position is quite clear. His considered views were set out in a letter to Flexner on 6 October.

> We all feel deeply humiliated . . . I quailed at facing what seemed certain defeat for this country. I came to the view that surrender was preferable to destruction and that in the circumstances the P.M. could do no other . . . With his knowledge you would have done the same . . . the number of our aircraft was less than one-third of the German force and our power of reproduction vastly less . . . I would have done what the P.M. did but would have tried for better terms.
>
> But looking beyond September, this government and the Baldwin government ought to be led out and shot at dawn for placing decent people in the helpless position we were in last week . . . The truth is we are landed with a cabinet of second- and third-raters and are paying a terrific penalty for their incompetence. And if Labour were put in

[125] *A Diary with Letters,* p.410.
[126] 25 September 1938. T.J. Add MSS WW, Vol.I, No.42.
[127] *A Diary with Letters,* p.411.

power they would be worse. The quality of the ministers was far below that of the men of 1914–18 . . . I broadcast tonight . . . on 'Prime Ministers and Cabinets'!!! I shall have to economise the truth.

T.J.'s days as an appeaser were over. His attitude initially to the problem posed by Germany was conditioned by his acceptance of conventional liberal wisdom: that balance-of-power policies had led inevitably to war in 1914; that another war, with air power dominant, meant the doom of European civilization at least; that the Treaty of Versailles was intolerably severe, and Germany's legitimate grievances must be generously redressed. The League of Nations, designed as the world's honest broker, had been turned into a French surrogate for the defence of the European status quo. T.J. believed therefore that Britain was the only available locum tenens for the discredited League, and a British initiative offered the best hope of averting another hapless drift to war. The first step was a closer understanding between Britain and Germany, which by 1936 was becoming alarmingly impatient.

T.J. was ripe therefore for an approach from the Germans, who regarded him as a useful sympathetic messenger to Baldwin. T.J.'s motives throughout were of the highest, but honourable eagerness undermined his better judgement. The stakes were so high that, the wish being father to the thought, he persuaded himself that not only stable agreement but even formal alliance of some sort was feasible between Nazi Germany and democratic Britain. His old mentor Sir Henry Jones, stern voice of moral principle, must have turned in his grave. T.J. of course had the spirit of reasonable compromise in his blood. Good intentions paved the way to his astonishing suspension of common prudence and customary rectitude. He evidently believed for a time that he was the exponent of a sophisticated version of the higher wisdom. During 1937 and most of 1938 he clung stubbornly to what had become revealed truth. But Adolf Hitler eventually destroyed any illusion that his purposes were any better than his methods. T.J., who had been out of his depth in strange waters for some time, had reached firm ground again. He now understood the need for British resistance which, however, he was immediately willing under duress to suspend in order to avert disaster and buy time to fight another day.

He had at last joined Flexner's camp.

So long as the dictators are on their thrones [T.J. wrote], peace will be a thinly disguised war and there will be no joy in life for young or old.[128]

---

[128] 6 October 1938. T.J., Class S, Vol.2, No.54.

CHAPTER FOURTEEN

'WHAT WILL HITLER DO?'

DURING the Munich crisis, Tom Jones had been eager to help in the Cabinet Office, but his offer of assistance was not taken up. He fervently hoped that the breathing-space of uncertain duration gained at the price of national humiliation at Munich would be put to the greatest possible advantage. He took it for granted that rearmament generally would now be speeded up, and a 'thorough-going programme of air defence', in particular, instituted immediately. Lindbergh's gloomy estimate of the extent of German superiority in the air was broadly endorsed by two senior British military men whom T.J. consulted, and he was thoroughly alarmed also by the account given him by Roy Fedden, chief engineer of the Bristol Aeroplane Company, of the great size and efficient organization of the German aircraft industry. Fedden had visited Germany six times in six years; he had been driven to 'despair' by what he considered the technical and managerial incompetence of the British aircraft industry, the infuriating complacency of Inskip, the Minister for the Co-ordination of Defence, and the wilful selfishness of many members of the Federation of British Industries who, he said, had shown themselves 'profit seekers' rather than 'patriots' over rearmament. T.J. sent Fedden to see Warren Fisher, who arranged two meetings for him with Horace Wilson. He, however, made it clear that he preferred the more optimistic judgements of the government's aeronautical experts. T.J. refused to be side-tracked. He had no technical knowledge himself, nevertheless he had been impressed with Fedden's patent honesty and his great reputation within the industry; Sir Samuel Hoare, for example, conceded that Fedden was 'the biggest man in the air world in this country'. T.J., therefore, presuming on his good standing at No.10, invited himself to lunch with Neville Chamberlain and 'unloaded' all the disturbing facts with which he had been primed. He begged the Prime Minister at least to see Fedden himself. This time T.J. got nowhere:

> The furthest I could get him to go was to say that he would talk to Kingsley [Wood, Minister for Air]. I could only reflect: how different

from L.G. who would have pressed a button and commanded Sylvester: Ring up Fedden of Bristol and ask him to breakfast with me tomorrow morning.[1]

T.J. was not altogether surprised by this experience. He had hoped that, as quickly as possible after his return from Munich, Neville Chamberlain would radically reconstruct the government and the Civil Service, which also looked 'in a bad way'.T.J. considered that the ministers were 'a feeble lot', most of them mere word-spinners, woefully short of executive drive. He had 'little confidence' in the existing Cabinet's capacity rapidly to remedy the deficiencies in Britain's defences so starkly apparent at the time of Munich. T.J. believed that, profoundly shaken by the knowledge of their vulnerability, the mass of the people were 'in a plastic mood and would respond to any instructed leadership'; they would, for example, in his opinion, even accept some form of national service.[2] This was a dire emergency that called for a government of national unity. 'This is no time for old personal rancours', T.J. had written in a memorandum he sent to Halifax and Horace Wilson at the end of September. 'Every man of capacity or with influence must be used.' He called for the immediate summoning to office of Lloyd George, Churchill and Eden, as well as a Labour leader to mobilize manpower.[3] Admittedly this was written when war looked imminent, but T.J. continued subsequently, when the immediate threat had passed, to press for a 'thorough reconstruction' of the government. He conceded that Labour was 'at sixes and sevens' and it would doubtless be 'very difficult' to win the party's agreement to a coalition government, but a supreme effort should be made. 'If the whole-hearted support of Labour was forthcoming', T.J. told Flexner, 'many of our problems would be satisfied at once, especially those of defence. Production would be greatly expedited.'[4]

According to Horace Wilson, Chamberlain's *alter ego*, who told T.J. so on 11 November 1938,

[1] *A Diary with Letters*, pp.412, 421–2. T.J. to Lady Grigg, 19 October and 27 November 1938. T.J., Add MSS, WW, Vol.I. Nos.45, 51 and 52. Fedden's report (22 pp.), T.J., Add MSS EE, Vol.2, No.2. Kingsley Wood (W.P. Crozier, *Off the Record: Political Interviews 1933–43*, ed. A.J.P. Taylor, 1973, p.93) was unimpressed by reports such as Fedden's, claiming in February 1939 that the Germans were 'very skilful in getting people over to see their factories and then go back and spread rumours about their terrific skill and efficiency'.

[2] *A Diary with Letters*, pp.410, 414, 418. T.J., Add MSS, WW, Vol.I, Nos.45 and 48.

[3] T.J., Class E, Vol.I, No.47.

[4] T.J., Class S, Vol.2, No.56, T.J., Add MSS, WW, Vol.I, No.48.

the question of approaching Attlee and Co. was thoroughly discussed at No.10 and it was turned down because Attlee being the weak Leader that he is, would have had to go back to his group [*sic*] to discuss the whole business, bring their conditions which would probably be rejected, and the whole thing would become public. Were Attlee a much stronger Leader than he is, some union might have been possible, but he holds his position very precariously.[5]

T.J. was aware of the bitter personal hostility between Chamberlain and the Labour leaders, but did not seem to understand that it rendered idle all hope of their effective co-operation. Nor perhaps did T.J., whose political opinions had to a degree been cross-party for years, give adequate weight to the deeply divisive power of long-standing party differences. Indeed, T.J.'s interesting Welsh National Lecture on 'Prime Ministers and Cabinets', broadcast on 6 October 1938, is open to the criticism that it did not take sufficient account of the overwhelmingly dominant power of the party factor in any situation short of the ultimate extremity of national peril.[6]

Neville Chamberlain went his own way. He rejected Samuel Hoare's suggestion of a cabinet of '6 or 7 on the lines of the War Cabinet', and, to T.J.'s dismay, there was no more than a minor shuffle of ministers, other than the introduction of the Civil Servant Sir John Anderson, the outstanding administrator of the day, as Lord Privy Seal with a special commission to protect the civilian population against air raids.[7]

It is evident that T.J. was now as impatient for an effectively organized resistance to Germany as formerly he had been for a *rapprochement*. He had several discussions with Chamberlain at this time which prompted some disquiet:

Is the P.M. in blinkers? Is he just stubborn? Or is he a great man? Those who have known him in Birmingham do not place him in the third category [T.J. wrote]. One gets the impression that the P.M. is so wedded to 'appeasement' that if Hitler sent the German Fleet up the mouth of the Thames, Neville would "turn the other cheek". And I

---

[5] Ibid., No.50. Chamberlain did not try very hard. 'P.M. cannot resist snarling at Labour in the House [Edward Grigg told T.J., Add MSS, WW, Vol.I, No.6, in February 1939] and does so not only aloud but in asides which are overheard by the opposition and are infuriating.'

[6] *The Listener,* 13 October 1938.

[7] T.J., Add MSS, WW, Vol.I, No.45. *A Diary with Letters,* pp.413, 418–20. Admiral Lord Chatfield, whose inclusion in the Cabinet T.J. had urged, was not brought in until January 1939.

think in this Horace [Wilson] does not vigorously oppose but approves.[8]

Many others were similarly puzzled by Chamberlain. Even the so-called 'Cliveden Set' was sharply divided on the question. Over lunch at the Astors' early in November, an 'excited debate' broke out over Chamberlain's failure to win Labour's support and his government's alleged 'soft pedalling' on defence and supply:

For the P.M.	*Betwixt*	*Against the P.M.*
Nancy [Astor]	Bill Astor	Waldorf [Astor]
Inskip		Alex Cadogan [of the
G. Dawson [of		Foreign Office]
The Times]		T.J.[9]

T.J. had in fact by now more or less written off Neville Chamberlain as an effective national leader in times of crisis, and recognized that he was quite unable to influence the Prime Minister. T.J., therefore, more profitably turned his attention to one considered a 'Prime Minister in the making'.[10] Lothian, who was now in Australia, had given T.J. the free run of his country house, Blickling, which he used over two weekends in November for an informal conference on unemployment and related problems. T.J.'s purpose, as he told Flexner, was 'to advance the political and economic education' of Anthony Eden. Months before, Baldwin had advised Eden to turn his attention to home affairs, about which he was woefully ignorant. As a first step he was given the Pilgrim Trust's *Men Without Work* to read, and T.J. arranged for Eden to visit Durham and south Wales to see for himself the state of human and physical degradation caused by unemployment. The Blickling Conference was designed to take Eden's tutoring a stage further. Violet Markham, businesslike and lucid, took the chair; Eady, Ellis and other friends of T.J. who were experienced in this field took part. A particularly striking contribution came from Archibald Lush, then an inspector of schools, who some years before had gone up to Balliol with assistance that T.J. had coaxed from some of his well-to-do friends. Lush was currently examining in detail the work-experience of 500 unemployed young men in south Wales. He painted a vivid picture of deplorable human wastage and stressed

[8] T.J., Add MSS, WW, Vol.I, No.51.
[9] Ibid., Nos.48 and 49. The Unity Theatre staged a skit on the 'Cliveden Set' at this time in which Chamberlain was cast as the Wicked Uncle.
[10] Halifax in conversation with T.J. in April 1938 about Eden's future. T.J. Add MSS, WW, Vol.I, No.15.

the crucial importance of adequate industrial training.[11] Eden soon discovered how much he had to learn: 'I think we succeeded in making him feel completely baffled by the complexities of the problem', T.J. wrote. He also had some political discussion with Eden and urged upon him the need for a drastic reconstruction of the ministry and the case for 'a big forward social policy at home' as a quid pro quo for Labour's support of rearmament. However, T.J. did not expect too much from Eden in the future: 'I like him personally because he is sincere', T.J. confided to Lady Grigg, 'but he is not big enough for the top place', a judgement fully vindicated some years later.[12]

T.J. kept away from Downing Street at this time and simply sent on there 'one or two documents of interest' that came to hand.[13] He was sharply critical of the government for not making a vigorous public protest against Nazi persecution of the Jews: 'I had hoped that ere this', he commented in November 1938, 'some front rank minister would have said something.'[14] He himself was swamped with appeals to help Jewish refugees and responded with customary energy. Mrs Jerome, his secretary at the Pilgrim Trust, devoted fully 'half her time' to solving the difficulties of individual refugees.[15] There is much detail in T.J.'s papers of the assistance that he rendered over many years to refugees from Nazi tyranny. For example, he played a part in getting Fritz Fridezko and his family out of Austria, and later made them a loan of £100 to enable them to emigrate to the USA. He procured money from Gwen Davies of Gregynog to support the distinguished Austrian educationist Dr Kurt Otto Hahn, who subsequently founded Gordonstoun School. In March 1939 T.J. stood 'guarantor' at the Home Office for Fritz and Lily Pincus from Berlin. He tried to place Pincus, who was a banker, in the City, and when that failed, arranged for him to go to Harlech to train as a skilled manual worker. 'I will find the money for their board and lodging', T.J.

[11] Subsequently published (Disinherited Youth, Carnegie Trust, Edinburgh, 1943). Lush was for many years the political agent of his great friend Aneurin Bevan.

[12] T.J., Class S, Vol.2, Nos.56 and 62. T.J., Add MSS, WW, Vol.I, No.47. T.J. provided Eden with material for a debate on unemployment in mid-February 1939, but considered his performance 'too dainty to carry conviction'.

[13] T.J., Add MSS, WW, Vol.I, No.56; Class E, Vol.I, No.62, for example, a memorandum on German opinion on Britain.

[14] T.J., Class S, Vol.2, No.57. T.J. provided Eden with some material for a broadcast talk to the United States at this time which included a strongly-worded 'passage of sympathy with the Jews'. T.J. Add MSS, WW, Vol.I, No.51.

[15] T.J., Class S, Vol.2, No.62.

wrote to B.B. Thomas, whose help he invoked. Later Jones assisted Mrs Pincus's brothers, Max and Oscar Lazarus, to settle in Britain.[16]

In June 1939 T.J. was a recipient of some kindness himself. His home town Rhymney presented him with a public testimonial of its regard in a ceremony at Brynhyfryd Chapel. Many of his old friends were present; and at the ceremony, Lothian described T.J. as 'an utterly disinterested man' who was 'completely honest'. Waldorf Astor sent a message laced with similar sentiments. There was very great local pride in T.J.'s remarkable career and public standing. He was deeply moved by the occasion: his own people had done him the greatest honour.[17]

But that agreeable interlude aside, it was a time of almost unrelieved uneasiness about public affairs. Everywhere T.J. went in London people were 'full of anxiety'; a discussion club meeting at the Savoy in January 1939, attended by over thirty leading public figures, was overwhelmed with 'great gloom', a sense almost of imminent doom. 'One goes on . . . with one's normal work', T.J. wrote, 'but it has an air of great unreality and futility . . . There is but one topic; what does Hitler intend?'[18] In March 1939, he made his intentions plain with the dismemberment of Czechoslovakia and the occupation of Prague. This had nothing whatever to do with the injustices of Versailles, or of self-determination for people of German stock: it was naked aggression pointing ominously to a bid for European hegemony and perhaps a good deal more. 'What you so often foretold', T.J. wrote to Flexner, 'has come to pass and Hitler has shown himself to the world as a liar'.[19]

T.J. was heartened by the fact that it had, apparently, at last opened Chamberlain's eyes. With scant regard for its military absurdity, T.J., in common with most of his countrymen, heartily approved of the guarantee Britain gave to Poland at the end of March 1939. He thought it indicated that Britain was now stronger and 'more united' than it would have been had 'Munich not been tried as a gesture of peace and failed'. Jones believed that Poland

[16] T.J., Class M, Vol.I, Nos.50–92, 122–37, 139–64. T.J. to B.B. Thomas, 11 March 1939. Coleg Harlech MSS. 'Through your genius', Dr Carl Lambert, a German refugee, wrote (Class Q, Vol.3, No.33) to T.J. in September 1939, 'there are many more people in the right place than there would be otherwise'.

[17] *Western Mail*, 16 June 1939. Waldorf Astor MS 1066/1/151. 'I did love your speech at Rhymney', Joyce Grenfell wrote (T.J., Class W, Vol.8, No.138) to T.J. 'You are a great man you know.'

[18] *A Diary with Letters*, pp.426–8. Prompted by the example of a friend, T.J. began to think of getting hold of some 'fatal drug' as a final safeguard against concentration camps.

[19] Ibid., p.430.

was so precariously placed between Germany and Russia that it would behave with great caution. But if the worst came to the worst, the Polish guarantee meant that Germany would at least have to fight on two fronts, and despite their well-known ideological hostility, he believed that Chamberlain and Halifax would not ignore Russia. At this juncture, Ribbentrop had the impudence to write privately to several British citizens, though not it seems to T.J., protesting that Germany policy was grievously misunderstood.[20]

But T.J. did receive a letter from Georg von Wussow, formerly Ribbentrop's agent, who now however asked T.J. to meet Count von Schwerin, head of the British department of the German General Staff, who was coming to Britain to assess the political position on behalf of the German High Command. Wussow said he hoped T.J. 'would not fail to tell [Schwerin] how serious the whole situation is'.[21] It is not entirely clear whether Schwerin was Ribbentrop's agent or acting on behalf of elements in the High Command uneasy at the prospect of war with Britain. There is no record of a meeting between Schwerin and T.J., who did however see David Astor's friend Adam von Trott, also of the German General Staff, who quite certainly was not then or at any time Ribbentrop's emissary.

The burden of von Trott's advice to T.J. at their meeting was that Hitler 'had already decided' to go to war that summer to gain control virtually of all Eastern Europe and it was believed in Berlin that there was little that Britain could do to prevent it. The German High Command was powerless, Hitler's opinion alone counted. The one thing however that might make him hold back would be the formation immediately in Britain of a comprehensive coalition government which included Churchill and other so-called 'warmongers' as well as the Left. This, von Trott said, '*might* stay Hitler's hand'.[22]

Of course, T.J. had been strongly in favour of a reconstruction of the Chamberlain government along those lines for some time. In March he had encouraged Lionel Curtis to sound out Herbert Morrison and Ernest Bevin, 'the key men in the Labour movement' in T.J.'s opinion, about the prospects of coalition. Curtis's report

---

[20] Ibid., pp.430–2.
[21] von Wussow and von Schwerin to T.J., 12 and 16 June 1939. T.J., Class E, Vol.I, Nos.68 and 69.
[22] *A Diary with Letters*, pp.436–7. Until von Trott was executed after the July Plot against Hitler, Foreign Office officials in London ignored secret messages he sent via neutral countries because they were convinced he was 'a camouflaged Nazi'. T.J., Class Q, Vol.3, No.105.

was not encouraging and T.J. conceded that it was clear 'the Labour party will not join with Neville on top': on the other hand, they 'might if Halifax were substituted and brought into the Commons'. Nothing came of this immediately, but T.J. retained some hope of eventual success. In June he noted in a letter to Flexner:

> Halifax's stock is rising and Neville's falling . . . Lots of activity out of sight to get a reconstruction of the Government. Cripps came to see me this morning on the subject and offered to go to Moscow to help to conclude the alliance with Russia.[23]

T.J.'s relations with Halifax had always been most friendly. At the end of June, T.J. and Astor and one or two others exerted 'much pressure' on Halifax to spell out a warning to Germany in the most forthright terms in a speech at Chatham House. T.J. in fact wrote a draft speech for the Foreign Secretary of which he made only limited use, paraphrasing a few sentences and including one or two others verbatim. Halifax's language was firm but flat, almost deliberately dull.[24] T.J.'s version was much more lively:

> Peace was for the moment saved at Munich. Was it lost at Prague? . . . Prague marked the turning point. It drove the sun from the sky . . . But we are united. We owe that to Prague. [German talk of encirclement is] a caricature of history past and present . . . We can only judge what a dictated peace by a victorious Germany would have been like from the policy of plunder enjoined in the Treaty of Brest Litovsk . . . Revival of the inflammatory slogans of 1914 . . . is playing with fire which, once lit, will leave Europe in ashes.

The peroration of T.J.'s draft included a passage of personal expiation:

> Some of us dreamed of a future in which England and Germany could together attempt a constructive solution of the common problems of modern industrial societies. . . . We shut our eyes to Nazi ideology and Nazi cruelty to Jews and Christians in the hope of achieving a working compromise which might lead to a stable peace.[25]

---

[23] T.J., Class W, Vol.I, No.142; Vol.3, No.102; Class S, Vol.2, No.71. Bodl. Curtis MSS, Box 14, f123. Lothian made some characteristically impractical suggestions for action.

[24] *Viscount Halifax, Speeches on Foreign Policy,* ed. W.H.E. Craster (Oxford, 1940), pp.287–97. In his speech Halifax apologized for 'straining the patience' of his listeners.

[25] T.J., Class O, Vol.3, No.23.

There was, of course, never any hope of Halifax, or perhaps any other possible British Foreign Secretary, using such challenging language at that time, but the draft says a good deal about T.J.'s attitude. Nor was there any question then of Halifax replacing Chamberlain as Prime Minister, although it was to be a very real possibility in May 1940.

In June 1939 T.J. was also involved, under the aegis of Chatham House, with a 'Europe Study Group' concerned with the 'middle distance' of Anglo-German relations. Lionel Curtis, E.H. Carr, David Astor, T.J. and others held discussions with prominent *émigré* anti-Nazi Germans, including Dr Brüning, the former Chancellor, about possible political machinery to put in place of the Nazi State. T.J. in fact was designated chairman of the group, but serious ill-health supervened and he later took the less onerous office of treasurer.[26]

Early in April 1939, T.J. was troubled by his prostate gland. At the end of June he went into a nursing home in Mandeville Place where he underwent a series of operations.

> The operations themselves, so far as I was concerned, were negligible [T.J. told Baldwin], but the intervals have been excruciating and I may truthfully say this [31 July] is the first day since I entered the home in which I have known an hour free from pain.

T.J. was then sixty-nine years of age. There is no doubt that this illness exacted a very heavy toll. He did not leave the nursing home until the middle of August, when he went by ambulance to his cottage, Street Acre, in Kent, for a long convalescence. Lord Dawson insisted that he should do no work at all for several months. For once, he obeyed doctor's order; he was so weak that he had precious little choice.[27]

But Street Acre was five miles from Manston aerodrome and directly in the German flight path to London. At the outbreak of war, therefore, accompanied by his daughter, Eirene, T.J. went to complete his convalescence first at Gregynog, where he was overwhelmed with well-intentioned cossetting by the staff, and then on to a small house near Coleg Harlech which he rented for three months from its Birmingham owner. To speed his recovery, for

---

[26] *A Diary with Letters*, p.438. T.J., Class T, Vol.7, No.8. T.J. suggested Conwell-Evans as secretary, but he had evidently not yet sufficiently lived down his Germanophile past to be acceptable. T.J., who had jumped the gun, embarrassingly had to explain the rejection to Conwell-Evans. T.J. to Conwell-Evans, 5 October 1939, David Astor MSS.

[27] T.J., Class A, Vol.6, Nos.139–42; Class S, Vol.2, Nos.75–83.

30 and 31. Sir Edward Grigg, T.J. and Lionel Curtis in Cliveden
Woods.

32. Prime Minister Neville Chamberlain and T.J. (as he said) 'confabulating' on the terrace at Cliveden, March 1938.

33. Miss Eirene Jones, Labour candidate, 1945 General Election.

34. Sgt. Tristan Jones of the Life Guards.

35. T.J. and grandchildren, Mala and Adam, at St Nicholas-at-Wade, Christmas 1953.

36. Active to the last: T.J. in his eighties at Penglais, Aberystwyth.

several weeks he ignored the wireless and read very few newspapers. That is not to say that he avoided a feeling of frustration at his enforced inactivity so far from the scene of action.[28] But in fact T.J.'s days as confidant of Prime Ministers in great matters of state were now over, although he was subsequently to be active on occasion on the periphery of important political activity.

If there had been war in 1938, Coleg Harlech would have been offered for use as a hospital or a 'shelter' of some kind. However, immediately after the German occupation of Czechoslovakia in March 1939, T.J. and B.B. Thomas had arranged that if Britain went to war, Liverpool University would take over Harlech. They recognized that a college that still depended heavily on voluntary contributions for survival and whose students were all men of military age could not be continued in the circumstances of total war that were anticipated. T.J. was particularly anxious that Coleg Harlech should not be commandeered by the armed forces because of the damage that, with the best will in the world, a rough and ready soldiery might do to premises which had been so carefully maintained hitherto. The thought that the magnificent, as yet unopened new library could be thus vulnerable was unbearable. A.D. McNair, Vice-Chancellor of Liverpool, and T.J. came to terms: in the event of war, the University would immediately take over the College for some of its staff and students, but T.J. and his fellow officers would have the occasional use of some College rooms for committee meetings and other purposes.[29]

Despite the necessity of living quietly at this time, T.J.'s mind soon turned to the prospect of deriving some advantage for Coleg Harlech from these difficult conditions:

> We feel we did right to transfer the Liverpool university [he wrote to Burdon Evans early in October], for otherwise the College would now be filled with evacuees. On the other hand the damage to 'the Cause' may be serious if prolonged. The War is not developing as anyone expected and our potential students (there were 30 fixed for the session) are not called up yet . . . Our conclusion (B.B.'s and mine) . . . is that it would be worthwhile opening in Cardiff in January a temporary Coleg Harlech, with provision for about 15 resident students . . . Cardiff has advantages for convenience for the valleys, for libraries, and for tutors.

Moreover, this stop-gap arrangement, as T.J. pointed out with

[28] T.J. to B.B. Thomas. 22 August 1939, Coleg Harlech MSS. 12 September 1939, Astor MSS 1416/1/200. Bangor MS 16186.

[29] T.J., Class K, Vol.10, Nos.138, 141; Vol.11, Nos. 42, 53, 75, 91 and 94.

some enthusiasm, would enable the Warden to establish contacts in industrial south Wales, particularly with trade unionists, 'which would be invaluable to C.H. when the war is over'. It was a 'gamble' at least worth considering. But there were obvious difficulties, especially the question of finance. T.J. therefore suggested to Wheldon, Secretary of the Welsh Department of the Board of Education, that B.B. Thomas should be appointed to the Board's staff for the duration of the war with a commission to stimulate adult education in Wales 'in the broadest sense of the word – W.E.A., Urdd, National Council of Music, Drama, and even Sunday Schools and chapel societies'. Wheldon soon killed off that ingenious proposition: there was already a pool of underemployed Inspectors in Wales and in England and B.B. Thomas's appointment for such a purpose could not possibly be justified.[30] T.J. refused to be baulked. If a temporary Coleg Harlech could not be opened in south Wales, then, with some help from the Board of Education, it would be done in Harlech itself. On 20 November a war-time utility version of Coleg Harlech opened with three tutors and seventeen students in two houses that were rented in the village. Students enjoyed full access to the Coleg Harlech library and all the societies of Liverpool University.[31]

It was a characteristically brave attempt to keep the flag flying, but it could scarcely be much more than a gesture. It lasted until June 1940 when, reluctantly, it had to be abandoned. At the same time, necessity delivered another heavy blow. B.B. Thomas, left high and dry without a College, applied for the post of Director of Extra-Mural Studies at Aberystwyth, and his standing was such that the appointing committee brushed aside the claims of thirteen other candidates and chose him unanimously. Thomas apologized to T.J. for this 'one act of apparent rebellion', and insisted that he still was, and always would be, 'Coleg Harlech's to command'. T.J. accepted the inevitable, and consoled himself with the thought that B.B. Thomas at any rate would still be 'serving the world of adult education'. And T.J. retained the hope that some day Thomas would succeed him as Chairman of Coleg Harlech. In the mean time, Liverpool University could be relied on to take care of the College and use it for a proper educational purpose.[32]

The Pilgrim Trustees also had anticipated the outbreak of war; in the spring of 1939 they resolved to suspend their activities during hostilities, other than to honour existing commitments. The

30 Ibid., Nos.106, 111, 117, 119.
31 Ibid., Nos.127, 138.
32 Ibid., Nos.151–63. T.J., Class W, Vol.18, Nos.92, 95.

continuance over several months of the so-called 'Phoney War' (a description guaranteed to bring a wry smile to the faces of naval and merchant service personnel) persuaded the Trustees, prompted by T.J., to review the position in December 1939, when they agreed to consider selected appeals that had a particular wartime importance. Most appropriately, they voted several sums to organizations devoted to the welfare of seamen, who, at that time, had 'very special claims' to the support of the nation. Also at T.J.'s insistence, the Trustees made an emergency grant of £2,000 to assist educational settlements that were in special difficulty at that time.[33] At that December meeting, again on T.J.'s initiative, the Trustees took a decision that was to have a much greater long-term significance. Responding to an appeal from the President of the Board of Education, they voted £25,000 for the support of music, visual art and drama, professional and amateur, which were threatened with extinction by restrictive wartime conditions. The State, which before the war had been adamantly *laissez-faire* in its attitude towards funding cultural activities, now hastily recognized their supreme importance in sustaining morale in a people's war.[34] Some time later the Treasury came forward with matching grants and a promise of conditional sums, but not before the arts relief work supported by Pilgrim Trust funds had evoked widespread response. This emergency action led quickly to the formation of the Committee for the Encouragement of Music and the Arts (CEMA), and in 1945 to the establishment of the Arts Council of Great Britain. T.J.'s part in the pioneer stages of this great cultural adventure was, by general consent of those most closely involved, crucial to its success.[35]

It was a situation for which T.J. was made to measure. He believed passionately in the importance of the quality of life of the people, and had insisted since early manhood that aesthetic considerations were as relevant to the everyday life of ordinary people as they were to that of the privileged, educated minority. He had often been driven to the verge of despair by the cultural deprivation and poverty of aspiration of the mass of the people. Here was a great new opportunity. T.J. meant to take it.

[33] PT, *Report* (1939), pp.15–16, 34–5. T.J., Class V, Vol.2, Nos.96, 103, 104; Class T, Vol.7, No.6, 11.

[34] P.T., *Report* (1939), pp.36–9. E.W. White, *The Arts Council of Great Britain* (1975), pp.23–5. T.J.'s article, 'The Origins of C.E.M.A.' (CEMA *Bulletin*, May 1942).

[35] E.W. White, op. cit., p.23. B. Ifor Evans and Mary Glasgow, *The Arts in England* (1949), pp.35–7.

We [the Pilgrim Trust] shall help the two big London orchestras and soloists [T.J. told Violet Markham in January 1940]. I am making it a condition that they play in the dreary Dagenhams of the country and not in London and centres where amenities are abundant.[36]

T.J. had been engaged in similar activity on a smaller scale shortly before. In 1934 W.E. Williams, secretary of the British Institute of Adult Education, T.J.'s friend and energetic lieutenant in several creative educational ventures, had initiated and organized 'Art for the People', a scheme to provide exhibitions of pictures by artists such as Turner, Picasso and others of similar calibre, in small towns where great works of art were not normally seen. T.J. responded with relish. In 1936 he arranged for an exhibition of a hundred pictures to come to Coleg Harlech. 'Great artists are not merely decorators', T.J. declared in a celebratory broadcast on the subject at the time, 'they are the creators of civilization'. Unfortunately, the British people were 'blind bats in a mechanised society', who were oblivious to the uplifting power of visual art, and none more so than the Welsh people whose interest was still monopolized by music. Williams's scheme received a small grant from the Board of Education and T.J. provided additional generous support over a period of five years from the York Trust, of which he was Chairman. 'Art for the People' was a valuable experiment which encouraged T.J. to take the lead in the more ambitious scheme of CEMA.[37]

As he confessed, T.J. was no more than '75%' fit at the time of the Pilgrim Trust meeting in December. Nevertheless, he returned to London early in January and worked like a beaver to set up the framework of CEMA. It was T.J. who negotiated with the Board of Education for the provision of office accommodation and a secretary. In consultation with the Pilgrim Trustees and Lord de la Warr, President of the Board of Education, T.J. exerted a major influence on the selection of a committee to direct operations. The committee did not lay claim in any way to be representative. T.J. was

[36] T.J., Class T, Vol.7, No.12. 'Sir Kenneth Clark is coming to see me on Sunday to discuss a scheme of helping unemployed artists', T.J., wrote (ibid., No.11) on 29 December, 'and I have another plan for musicians in preparation'. A week or two later he wrote (Class S, Vol.2, No.91), 'I am up to my eyes running a committee for the Encouragement of Music and Art', adding happily, 'it takes me to the world of musicians, actors and painters'. He also tapped one of his 'rich young friends' for a loan to Equity, the actors' trade union, to finance a provincial tour by a company of out-of-work players.

[37] 'Art and the People', *Leeks and Daffodils*, pp.204–9. 'The York Trust' (August 1943), T.J. Add MSS, Vol.I, No.1.

always doubtful of the businesslike capacity of committees made up of accredited spokesmen for established interests whose priority all too often seemed to be damage limitation rather than speedy action. CEMA's steering committee consisted of a handful of men with imagination and proven drive and energy, most of them T.J.'s close friends. The list included Sir Walford Davies, by now recognized as music tutor to the nation, Sir Kenneth Clark, Director of the National Gallery, and W.E. Williams, a young man of Welsh working-class origin clearly marked for greater things, whose initial faith in popular involvement in cultural activity had set the scheme in motion. Lord Macmillan of the Pilgrim Trust was Chairman, T.J., nominally Vice-Chairman, was, as two people who were themselves closely involved stated later, 'the driving force' behind the whole project. In the early months, his constant exhortation to members of the committee was: 'Action'.[38]

The response was wholehearted. CEMA's terms of reference called for the preservation in wartime of the highest standards in music, drama and painting; the provision of the widest opportunities for the enjoyment of the arts by the people, especially those who were disadvantaged; the encouragement of amateur dramatics and music-making; and the rendering of assistance to singers and actors made idle by wartime restrictions on the professional theatre and concert hall. As usual, T.J.'s approach was empirical, emphasizing *ad hoc* practicality rather than insisting on rigid consistency of method. The Pilgrim Trust first of all made small grants to existing voluntary bodies: the English Folk Dance Society, the British Drama League, the British Federation of Musical Festivals, and the like. An experiment of sending six artistes as pioneer 'Music Travellers' to villages up and down the country was to develop into a spectacular success that stimulated a remarkable response from audiences and local musicians. Within six months they had given or organized 254 concerts and prompted the formation of 37 new orchestra groups and 244 choirs. When the German air raid attacks on London began in October 1940, CEMA organized 150 emergency concerts in that month in air raid shelters all over the capital. As T.J. had insisted at the outset, the two great London orchestras gave concerts in small towns in the provinces. CEMA gave assistance to amateur dramatic societies and, beginning in October, under its auspices the 'Old Vic' company made several tours playing Shakespeare, Shaw,

[38] Evans and Glasgow, op.cit., pp.35–9. Miss Mary Glasgow HMI, was the Secretary of the Comittee. See also, B. Ifor Evans to T.J., 10 November 1939. T.J., Class W, Vol.6, No.50.

Euripides and Chekhov in south Wales, Lancashire, Tyneside and elsewhere. Three performances of *Macbeth* in the small town of Rhos in north Wales drew 3,000 people. There was no doubt at all that the responses to CEMA's initiative in music and drama had been remarkable. The success in painting and visual art, where the campaign was led by W.E. Williams, was, not surprisingly, less striking, but considerable headway was made here too. After three months' experience T.J. considered that, at the very least, much had been done to awaken in the people of the country a consciousness of their national heritage of art.[39]

There was, of course, no ready reckoner for measuring an increase in spiritual values, but CEMA had already done enough to persuade the Treasury to make its offer of matching grants. 'I went with the Board of Education Accountant to the Treasury', T.J. wrote on 18 March 1940, 'and extracted £1 for £1 up to £50,000 for the Committee'.[40] Soon afterwards the Committee, slightly enlarged, was renamed the Council and formally appointed by the Board of Education. T.J. remained as Vice-Chairman. CEMA continued to expand its work in music, drama and painting during the next two years. The large symphony orchestras were remitted to the care of the Carnegie Trust and popular concerts in factory canteens largely to ENSA (Entertainments National Service Association), but CEMA's activity now extended to the whole of the country. T.J. had always believed that one defect of British social life was the excessive centralization of amenities in the arts in London and a few big cities. He derived great satisfaction from his part in this attempt to redress the balance. He believed too that CEMA represented an ideal partnership between State support of the arts and private patronage, a superb balance of professional and amateur artistes with an insistence always on the highest standards of performance and the value of expert advice. CEMA's success was beyond dispute; the crusade, led by some of the greatest names in British culture, had aroused enormous public interest and routed the sceptics. In two years CEMA had sponsored 8,000 concerts in all parts of England, Wales and Scotland; one and a half million people had attended plays given under its auspices, and half a million had been attracted to its art exhibitions.[41]

The Pilgrim Trustees voted an additional sum of £12,500 to CEMA in January 1941, and made a final contribution of the same

---

[39] E.W. White, op.cit., pp.25–36. Evans and Glasgow, op.cit., pp.35–40. PT, *Report* (1939), pp.36–9.

[40] T.J., Class T, Vol.7, No.16.

[41] PT, *Report* (1940), pp.30–40; (1941), pp.10–17.

amount a year later when Macmillan and T.J. stepped down from their official CEMA positions. The Trustees had decided that their financial support was no longer needed; CEMA was established and now had the assurance of substantial permanent assistance from the State. Maynard Keynes took over as Chairman. T.J.'s contribution in the pioneering stage of this great adventure in popular culture had been immense, perhaps crucial to its success. When the CEMA was replaced by the Arts Council in June 1945, B. Ifor Evans, who was present at the inaugural meeting, observed in a letter to T.J.: 'Many of us thought of the fact that you were really the parent of this child'. Three years later the author of an *Observer* 'Profile', a shade less partially, concluded that if T.J. did not exactly 'beget C.E.M.A.', he had certainly played 'a decisive role as godfather'.[42]

CEMA had been established in the months before the German attack on western Europe. Despite the brave face worn by most of the nation, people had few illusions about the great difficulties that lay ahead. Germany's formidable military strength had been awesomely demonstrated in the rapid conquest of Poland, and the Nazi–Soviet pact seemed likely to reduce very sharply the effectiveness of the British naval blockade. It was not easy to foresee how the war could be won. Indeed, it was obvious that Britain would need all her strength to avoid defeat. As always, T.J. worried about the quality of political leadership, particularly that of Neville Chamberlain who, he believed, lacked imagination and prevision and was hopelessly ill-cast as the nation's leader in wartime: he was simply 'not tough enough to confront the European gangsters'. Nor did the Prime Minister's chief colleagues inspire confidence: Halifax was 'timid', Simon had 'a Rolls Royce brain' but could not steer; Churchill had bursts of energy, but was not the man he had been in 1914–18, and Hankey too, who had been brought in with Churchill at the outbreak of war, was too old in T.J.'s opinion.[43]

In the event, it transpired that Chamberlain's government was living on borrowed time. In April Hitler attacked Norway and occupied Denmark without difficulty. The British response in Norway was a series of naval and army operations without benefit of adequate air cover. The result was a disaster for which Chamberlain, perhaps unfairly in the immediate sense, was held

---

[42] T.J., Class W, Vol.6, No.87. *Observer,* 30 May 1948. T.J.'s central role in CEMA's business is indicated in *A Diary with Letters,* pp.456, 461 and W.E. Williams in T.J., Class D, Vol.5, No.164, p.5.

[43] T.J., Class S, Vol.2, No.101. *A Diary with Letters,* pp.454–5. Reading H.G. Wells's *New World Order* prompted T.J. to write: 'If we only had as good executives as we have dreamers'. To Madariaga, 4 March 1940. White MSS.

responsible. T.J. thought that the Prime Minister would survive that crisis, but 'crash in the next'.[44] In fact, although Chamberlain technically retained his parliamentary majority in the debate on Norway, his position was undermined and the crisis continued confusedly for some days until he was succeeded as Prime Minister by Churchill. T.J. had long wanted Chamberlain replaced, but observed at the beginning of May that no one could indicate 'the ideal P.M. who should supplant him'.[45] Jones had seen Churchill at work in the Cabinet in peace and in wartime years before and fully appreciated the enormous range of his great gifts. But in common with many others, T.J. distrusted Churchill's impetuosity.

Perhaps the truth was that Churchill, built on a heroic scale appropriate to times of ultimate crisis, had been impatient for the arrival of his proper setting, and was therefore prone, as in 1926, to see imminent catastrophe where only serious danger lay. In 1940 his chance had come; he behaved with unexpected circumspection, waited out the rival candidates and grasped the opportunity with an astonishing assurance and overwhelming public support. 'The country wanted Winston', Stanley Baldwin told T.J., 'just as it wanted L.G. . . . in 1916'.[46]

In fact, it was to Lloyd George that T.J. looked for salvation at the time. On the eve of the debate on Norway, Jones, J.L. Garvin, Nancy Astor and one or two others tried hard to persuade Lloyd George to agree to join the government, even perhaps be prepared to take it over. Lloyd George was evasive, and the dramatic contribution he made to the attack on Chamberlain in the debate on Norway made it even less likely that they could sit in a Cabinet together. Chamberlain's support was essential to Churchill in the early weeks of his premiership. Nevertheless, he persuaded Chamberlain early in June to agree to continue in office if Lloyd George were brought in. But when firmly invited by Churchill to join his government on 6 June, Lloyd George asked for more time to consider.[47]

Over the next two months T.J. did his utmost to overcome Lloyd George's reluctance, indeed downright defeatism. 'I found him adamant against going in', T.J. wrote after a long attempt on 10 July to persuade Lloyd George. 'It was like calling a specialist in when the patient's case was nigh hopeless'. T.J. nevertheless believed that if only Lloyd George could be got into the ministry, 'the situation

[44] *A Diary with Letters*, p.457.
[45] T.J., Class S, Vol.2, No.101.
[46] *A Diary with Letters*, p.459.
[47] Ibid., p.457. T.J., *Lloyd George*, pp.254–5.

would at once be changed, . . . nothing would long remain as it was
. . . he was an explosive force'. A few days later T.J. asked Lionel
Curtis to enlist Ernest Bevin's support for Lloyd George's inclusion
in the government. Although L.G. was then seventy-six years of age,
T.J. endorsed Garvin's judgement that he was 'still good for six
hours a day and it would be six hours of radium'. At the end of
August T.J. spent a weekend at Cricieth with Lloyd George, but
again failed, even with the support of Megan Lloyd George, to
move him. He was sunk in pessimism: 'nothing we could say would
bring him the slightest comfort', T.J. reported to Waldorf
Astor. T.J. was bitterly disappointed that the great man, whom he
had always considered the nonpareil in British politics, had
refused to make any personal contribution to the defence of the
nation or even to sustaining the morale of the people at the time of
their greatest peril. Sadly, T.J.'s disillusion was to remain, and to
some extent grow, during the remaining years of Lloyd George's
life.[48]

After Dunkirk, when a German invasion appeared imminent,
T.J.'s cottage at St Nicholas-at-Wade in Kent, a prohibited area, was
commandeered by the military. An army officer asked what was to
be done with the great store of books in the house; T.J.'s
telegraphed reply was, characteristically: 'Read them'.[49] At the time
T.J. lived at his London flat at 10 Tufton Court, SW1, and endured
several of the worst bombing raids by the *Luftwaffe*. He did so with
considerable sang-froid, despite his seventy years: 'I don't feel
intellectually afraid at all', he wrote, 'but physically I cannot sleep
while the air raids are booming and crashing'. He spent one night
in October on a camp bed in the basement of the Athenaeum
surrounded by bound volumes of *The Times,* four horizontal
bishops and other assorted members of the Establishment who had
taken refuge there. T.J. propped up his only pillow with three
volumes of the *Journal of the House of Commons* and settled down to
read the autobiography of his friend Abraham Flexner. Two days
earlier, the Pilgrim Trust offices in the Adelphi were reduced to
rubble by a bomb. No one was hurt but T.J. lost many papers.[50] He
salvaged what he could, and accompanied by his two chief
assistants, set up a temporary Pilgrim Trust office some days later in
a room put at their disposal at Coleg Harlech. He lived with his two

---

[48] *A Diary with Letters*, pp.464–5, 469–70. A.J. Sylvester, *The Real Lloyd George*
(1947), p.272. T.J., Class T, Vol.7, No.25. T.J. to Astor, 31 August 1940. Tristan
Jones MSS.

[49] B.B. Thomas, *Thomas Jones 1870–1955* (NLW, Aberystwyth, 1970), p.7.

[50] A heavy blow to a man who carefully saved every scrap, even rough notes.

sisters, whom he had evacuated from Hampshire, in a small rented house nearby.[51]

Earlier in 1940 John Buchan, then serving as Governor-General in Canada, had died. T.J. was invited to step up to replace him as a Pilgrim Trustee. Although touched by the offer, T.J. declined but characteristically suggested that as he was nearly seventy he was prepared to resign the secretaryship as soon as the Trustees wished and found a suitable successor. Meantime, he proposed that his own salary should be reduced by £250 per annum, which could then be used to increase the pay of his assistants without increasing the salary budget.[52] From his room at Coleg Harlech T.J. administered the business of the Pilgrim Trust, conducted a good deal of work for CEMA, and attended to the endless items of his other personal interests. 'I have as always too much to do', he told his friend Madariaga in December 1940, 'I suppose I would not be happy otherwise'.[53]

Indeed, despite his recent serious illness, T.J. had blithely added to the number of his activities. With magnificent defiance, the British had transmuted the débâcle of Dunkirk into a national triumph, but it was obvious that some years would elapse before any serious challenge to the German hold on Europe could be contemplated. In the mean time, the morale of the large army that was being built up in Britain had to be sustained and indeed, to some extent, recreated after humiliating defeat. 'It is of great importance to keep the army "on its toes"', Lord Croft, Under-Secretary at the War Office, wrote to T.J. in August 1940. 'I want to supply the mental stimulant in the educational line which will help to prevent the soldier getting stuck with a Maginot complex'. It was natural that Croft should turn to Tom Jones for advice about suitable candidates for a newly-created post of Director of Army Education. T.J., seeing an opportunity that was not to be missed, replied by return of post detailing the exceptional creative and organizational talents of his protégé W.E. Williams, Secretary of the British Institute of Adult Education. Croft was impressed; he conceded that Williams obviously seemed to be 'much alive', but objected that he had no military background. However, he agreed to see him. Williams was agreeably surprised that Croft (formerly Sir Henry Page Croft, reputedly an archetypal diehard Tory MP)

---

[51] A Diary with Letters, pp.472–5. T.J., Class M, Vol.3, No.82. He was evidently (T.J. to B.B. Thomas, 12 September 1940) more troubled by the loss of sleep caused by the air raids than by the physical danger.

[52] T.J., Class W, Vol.13, No.128. This self-sacrificing offer was apparently turned down.

[53] 17 December 1940. White MSS.

'didn't seem or sound reactionary'. Williams suggested to T.J. that 'Tawney, ex-sergeant Tawney' of the 1914–18 war was the man to direct Army Education, with Williams serving as his 'adjutant'. Nothing came of that interesting idea: Tawney was perhaps too old, his health too uncertain.[54]

In the end, F.W.D. Bendall, HMI, was made Director of Army Education, but Croft had acknowledged at the outset that T.J.'s opinion would carry great weight and Williams was made Director of an independent unit styled the Army Bureau of Current Affairs (ABCA).[55] It was an inspired appointment, the outcome of one of T.J.'s most imaginative suggestions. Naturally, it took some time to organize a new large-scale scheme of army education, and inevitably there was some foot-dragging by the Treasury, by the ruffled members of an existing Advisory Council for Adult Education in HM Forces, and by some of the military hierarchy. T.J. was irritated by 'the failure to grasp that there are tens of thousands of literate men in the army who are not just clodhoppers'. A unique opportunity to improve the understanding of many of the young men of the nation was being squandered by the delay in following the fine example of the Canadian army in Britain, where the educational scheme was directed by Burgon Bickersteth, T.J.'s friend of many years' standing. Bickersteth of course had the powerful support of General McNaughten, who, as T.J. commented tartly in an article in the *Observer*, was 'somewhat exceptional among army commanders' in his concern for an enlightened soldiery.[56]

Luckily, and evidently unbeknown to T.J., so too was Sir Ronald Adam, the Adjutant-General of the British Army, who had been 'horrified' at the lack of understanding of most recruits of 'what we were fighting for'. Adam's staunch support for ABCA was to be of decisive importance; so too was that of Sir James Grigg, who was then the senior Civil Servant at the War Office, and in 1942 became Minister of War. T.J. had worked hard at the time to win the support of Grigg, who was another of his old friends.[57] ABCA had to pick its way carefully through a minefield of suspicion. It did not get properly into stride until the autumn of 1941 and was then

[54] T.J., Class W, Vol.20, Nos.99–101. T.J. to B.B. Thomas, 7 August 1940. Harlech MSS. *A Diary with Letters*, p.468.

[55] A.C.T. White, *The Story of Army Education, 1643–1963* (1963), pp.86–97. Bendall and Williams came under the jurisdiction of the Director-General of Welfare and Education.

[56] T.J., Class S, Vol.2, No.109; Class W, Vol.I, No.149, Vol.19, No.39. T.J., 'Army Education in War Time', *Observer*, 5 January 1941.

[57] A.C.T. White, op.cit., p.96. T.J., Class T, Vol.7, No.35.

immediately threatened with closure. Winston Churchill expressed strong disapproval: he insisted that the ABCA discussion groups simply provided golden opportunities for 'the professional grouser and agitator with a glib tongue'. He wanted them suspended forthwith.[58]

Thoroughly alarmed, W.E. Williams looked to T.J. for help.

> A.B.C.A. is in trouble [Williams wrote]. The Prime Minister has redoubled his denunciations of it, and wants to have it shut down as soon as possible. He has committed himself to the proposition that A.B.C.A. will encourage controversy . . . and will undermine discipline. To shut it down now would be lunacy and I shall fight for A.B.C.A.'s survival. But how does one get within arguing distance of the P.M.? Have you his ear? Or do you know of a Good Ear to which I might be introduced?

T.J. was deeply disturbed; he knew only too well from personal experience how difficult it was to dissuade Churchill from his determined course.

'Tackle Rab Butler and Greenwood immediately', T.J. counselled Williams by telegraph, adding in a letter written the same day,

> I cannot believe that all the facts are before him. To attempt to arrest the movement now would certainly lead to widespread and most unhappy agitation.

T.J. advised Williams to go in person to Butler and Greenwood. 'If you have any further difficulty', Jones said, 'I could write to John Anderson, who I believe has the ear of the P.M. Let me know how you get on, and of course be guided by P.J. Grigg in all you do'. Williams followed instructions and within days happily reported success. 'Crisis over and enemy routed. Grateful for your advice and help'. Sir James Grigg and Adam also helped to head off the Prime Minister, whose minutes to ministers in a coalition government were quite often hortatory rather than mandatory in purpose.[59]

T.J. was greatly relieved, but he feared that Churchill would return to the charge at some time, as he did in October 1942. In an article, 'A.B.C.A. and its Work', published in the *Observer* in September, T.J. did his best to combat the prejudices of the Prime Minister and other critics. T.J. asserted that A.B.C.A. was not simply an invention of the twentieth century: on the contrary, it traced its honourable descent from Oliver Cromwell, who defined the citizen-

---

[58] W.S. Churchill, *The Second World War* (1950), III, 737.
[59] T.J., Class D, Vol.5, Nos.102–105. A.C.T. White, op.cit., pp.99–101.

soldier of his 'New Model' army as one who 'must know what he fights for and love what he knows'. The vast majority of the soldiers of the modern army, T.J. said, had had no educational guidance of any kind since they left crowded classrooms at the age of fourteen. Russia and the USA were as 'remote as Tibet' to most of them. 'A soldier's empty head', he concluded, 'resembles an evacuated child's infested head in being not so much a shame to the owner as a reproach to the electorate'.[60]

But ABCA continued to be forced to run the gauntlet of hostility from the right and, occasionally, from the left in politics too. In 1943 there was a particularly dangerous rumpus over ABCA discussions of the Beveridge Report, and almost as soon as it had subsided, Bevin complained about an ABCA poster. Mercifully, Sir James Grigg, now Secretary for War, gave W.E. Williams '100%' support and Bevin's attack was fended off. But protest continued. 'Dear Great Exemplar', Williams wrote to T.J. from the War Office in May, 'I am up to my neck in brawl after brawl in this place'. But Williams was a bonny fighter who shared T.J.'s great passion for adult education; he fought off his critics vigorously. Williams was convinced that to succeed after the war adult education would have to 'come down off its high horse, and fraternize with the really common man', as ABCA had done.[61]

ABCA's educational objectives at first were modest; 'no more than hedge-hopping' in Williams's words and, with a change of metaphor in a comment to T.J., 'breaking the ice for a majority of soldiers; viz the common man who has never put his nose in a W.E.A. class'.[62] But Williams's creative instincts and missionary zeal soon prompted more ambitious aims and the imaginative use of a variety of educational methods: film strips, portable exhibitions, a fortnightly *Map Review,* and wall newspapers. ABCA issued a pamphlet called *War* that dealt with topics like security, first-aid, jungle warfare, and, daringly, army food. *Current Affairs,* of which there were 118 issues in four years, dealt with more complex questions at a higher level. The remarkably high quality of the writing owed a great deal to Williams, who had previously shown great literary and editorial skill in transforming *Highway,* journal of the WEA, into 'the poor man's *New Statesman'.* But the core of ABCA's work consisted of lectures, usually by professional people,

[60] *Observer,* 22 September 1942, and buttressing leader article. A.C.T. White, op.cit., p.100. T.J. was perhaps unlucky that his appeal forced him to cite Cromwell, to whom Churchill, the ardent Royalist, was unlikely to warm.

[61] Churchill, op.cit., IV, 847. T.J., Class W, Vol.12, Nos.81–8; Vol.20, Nos.1109–11.

[62] A.C.T. White, op.cit., p.103. T.J., Class Q, Vol.4, No.166.

and, in particular, discussion group meetings led by army officers. The scale of the ABCA scheme is indicated by the fact that, at its peak in 1943–44, it was responsible for 110,000 courses, lectures and classes at home and in commands all over the world. It was, as T.J. said with delight, 'the biggest adult education movement the world has ever seen'.[63]

ABCA was heavily criticized later for its supposed political bias. R.A. Butler asserted that the servicemen's vote in the 1945 election had been 'virtually won over' for Labour 'by the left-wing influence' of ABCA. This was an unworthy judgement that ignored the insistence of the Bureau's staff on fairness and accuracy in their course work. The truth was, as Butler substantially conceded in his next sentence, that Labour at that time offered a vision of the post-war world that the Conservatives could not match. Moreover, the balance of service opinion on politics was not strikingly different from that of the nation as a whole. Churchill's fear that ABCA discussions would promote indiscipline was equally erroneous. At any rate the Adjutant-General stated that he had never heard of an instance prompted by the activity of ABCA during 1941–46.[64]

There was more substance in the criticism that rather too much of its work was deficient in quality, erratic in its selection of themes, and too dependent on amateur discussion-group leaders. In the circumstances, it could hardly have been otherwise. But strenuous efforts were made to provide some training for discussion-group leaders, a development in which T.J. played a part. He had provided a useful grant from the Pilgrim Trust for ABCA during its first year.[65] In May 1942 Vice-Chancellor McNair informed T.J. that Liverpool University had decided to surrender its occupancy of Coleg Harlech in the autumn and return home. T.J. quickly arranged with W.E. Williams for ABCA to take over Coleg Harlech as one of its centres for short courses for training officers in leading discussion groups, lecturing and the use of teaching aids. By the end of the war, 4,600 officers had passed through Harlech in this way. T.J. was more than satisfied: the College was being properly maintained, derived a useful income, and, not least, continued to serve the cause of adult education.[66]

---

[63] A.C.T. White, op.cit., pp.85–101. T.J., 'Democracy and Discussion at Pontypridd', 4 July 1942. T.J., Class Y, Vol.5, No.40. The *DNB* notice of W.E. Williams is first rate.

[64] R.A. Butler, *The Art of the Possible: The Memoirs of Lord Butler* (1971), p.129. A.C.T. White, op.cit., p.103.

[65] PT, *Report* (1942), pp.13–14.

[66] T.J., Class K, Vol.12, Nos.83–100; Class S, Vol.3, No.20. A.C.T. White, op.cit., p.98.

T.J. had responded with enthusiasm to Lord Croft's request for his assistance in reorganizing army education in August 1940, and he was just as willing, a few weeks later, to accept Waldorf Astor's invitation to become a director of his *Observer* newspaper. Astor, and more especially his son David, then serving in the Royal Marines, who was scheduled to become editor of the *Observer* some time in the future, had decided to begin a gradual change-over from the *ancien régime* of J.L. Garvin's commanding editorship,which had lasted for over thirty years. It was considered that T.J.'s deft skill in personal relations would be of 'immense help' in carrying through the projected revolution, particularly in overcoming Garvin's obdurate resistance to change and his flat refusal to consider resignation. And T.J.'s knowledge, judgement of men, and extraordinarily wide range of acquaintance in public life would be invaluable in the search for a new editor.[67]

T.J. devoted a great deal of time and effort to the affairs of the *Observer* over the next eighteen months. David Astor was confident in February 1941 that T.J. ('my dear Wizard', as he described him) could break Garvin's spell and clear the way for radical changes. But Garvin was an awkward opponent who was exceptionally well entrenched: he had been editor since 1908, he had great prestige and a large personal following among the readership; indeed, it was freely acknowledged in Fleet Street that Garvin *was* the *Observer.* Moreover, as David Astor ruefully admitted, it would be necessary for T.J. to break 'the mesmeric spell' Garvin seemed to have cast over Waldorf Astor.[68] T.J.'s initial discussion with the editor was not promising: Garvin 'bombarded overwhelmingly' throughout a two-hour lunch at the Savoy ('Place I hate', T.J. said), making any 'riposte' impossible. T.J. insisted that the next time they met it should be at Garvin's home at Beaconsfield for a quiet discussion. But that negotiation too got nowhere. T.J.'s account, in David Astor's opinion, perfectly illustrated the 'old megalomaniac's' impossible behaviour. Patient persuasion was apparently useless. Astor believed that T.J. would not succeed until he persuaded Waldorf Astor, who had perhaps been over-indulgent in the past, 'to be strong' with Garvin. 'Can you achieve this?' he asked.[69]

David Astor's judgement of the situation was not entirely accurate. As far back as May 1940 his father had said, in a letter to T.J., that some parts of Garvin's personal machinery seemed to be

[67] T.J. To Waldorf Astor, 17 December 1940. Tristan Jones MSS. David Astor to T.J., 19 December 1940. T.J., Class Q, Vol.3, No.43.

[68] Ibid., No.58. *Observer* and *Sunday Times*, 1 March 1942.

[69] 19 February 1941. David Astor MSS. T.J., Class Q, Vol.3, No.63.

held together by nothing more than 'bits of string', and it was difficult to keep him operating effectively as editor.[70] Despite the measure of agreement between father and son, T.J. was delicately placed between them because their political opinions differed considerably and they did not agree on the relative importance of the various classes of the *Observer*'s readership. T.J. said in 1942 that Waldorf Astor was a 'fundamental Conservative,' whereas David was 'ardently democratic and leftwards', an adherent of Stafford Cripps. Waldorf was mainly concerned 'to keep as many as possible of the old readers' of the *Observer*, his son was 'more eager to make the paper attractive to the young'. Thus awkwardly placed, T.J., as he said, did his best 'to look both ways at once' and preserve a balance.[71]

By the summer of 1941 the three men were in complete agreement about Garvin. He had resisted all suggestion of change, and in August counter-attacked vigorously: he spoke dismissively of David Astor and his 'set' and launched a bitter attack on Waldorf Astor. T.J. too came in for come criticism. 'I know by experience', Astor commented to T.J., 'that on these occasions he works himself up into a sort of brainstorm'.[72] The struggle became steadily more acrimonious over the next four months. A Tribunal established years before to arbitrate an internal dispute was brought into play; Garvin and Waldorf Astor fought it out at long range by the submission of memoranda to the Tribunal.[73]

The burden of the owner's case against Garvin was that, at 74, he was too old, his health too unreliable, that he lived in isolation at Beaconsfield, rarely appeared at the newspaper and was out of touch with people and public affairs in London. Moreover he was unwilling to delegate authority. There was also a degree of difference about the appropriate attitude to the government at that time, although Astor conceded that Garvin's writing was 'as clear and vigorous as ever'. Astor proposed that Garvin, whose contract was virtually for life, should resign as editor but continue as a frequent contributor to the *Observer* completely free from inter-ference. Astor said that many people 'of considerable eminence'

---

[70] Ibid., Vol.I, No.57. Astor added waspishly that, at one time, he had had to work with 'three geniuses': Garvin, Lloyd George and his own wife Nancy. Now, as L.G. had gone, it was two; but as Astor was now older, that was as much as he could manage.

[71] T.J., Class S, Vol.3, No.18; Class T, Vol.7, No.69.

[72] T.J., Class Q, Vol.4, No.156; Vol.I, No.75.

[73] T.J. (ibid., Vol.3., No.87) warned David Astor to be careful what he wrote. T.J. believed that a 'head on conflict' was probably unavoidable as Garvin was determined 'to go on to the death'. T.J., Class T, Vol.7, No.54.

had been, and still were, prepared to do that. Moreover, in the interest of the nation, ageing Field Marshals and Generals had willingly agreed to serve in the Home Guard. Garvin angrily rejected all compromise. The 'terrific conflict', as T.J. called it, continued, the exchanges becoming increasingly vitriolic. In December T.J., who was responsible for the face-to-face negotiations with Garvin, hoped finally to persuade him to 'cross the Rubicon' and resign at their next meeting. He did not succeed then but did soon afterwards, with the aid of an *ad hoc* tribunal of ex-editors of quality newspapers. At the end of February 1942, Garvin finally left the *Observer* after thirty-four years in the editorial chair.

T.J. had not succeeded by his power of persuasion.

I had a hectic time bringing the Garvin regime to an end – a very necessary one [T.J. told Madariaga]. He had to be bribed out. May tell you the sordid story some day.

It was an unfortunate conclusion to what had been, with perhaps occasional lapses, a distinguished, indeed a truly great editorship. Mercifully, the final unpleasant disagreements had been handled by both sides with discretion, and although there was some unfriendly gossip in the Press, the affair did not become public in sensational fashion. Garvin continued to write for several years for the *Sunday Express* and showed that, whatever his managerial deficiencies, he still had many a thunderous paragraph in his pen. One reader was thoroughly disgruntled by his removal. 'I feel very unhappy about the *Observer*' B. Ifor Evans told T.J. in June. 'Under Garvin it was a "personality" paper. You are trying to replace a personality with a committee and that will not do . . . The paper . . . has no clear voice at all'.[74]

From the start T.J. had led the search for a new editor. The first suggestion in December 1940 had been to recruit Michael Foot as 'understudy' to Garvin. T.J., who said he did not know Foot, nevertheless considered that he was not so 'outside Left' as to be beyond consideration, and agreed that there was a good deal in David Astor's contention that Foot's appointment might reduce the danger of left-wing intellectuals becoming isolated with set 'rostrums' that would alienate the good will of the many 'decent folk' who were prepared to welcome 'big changes'. It appeared

[74] T.J., Class Q, Vol.4, Nos.11–70; Class T, Vol.7, No.53. T.J. to David Astor, 4 December 1941. D. Astor MSS. T.J. to Madariaga, 3 March 1942. White MSS. T.J., Class W, Vol.6, No.63. *A Diary with Letters*, pp.492–498.

however that Foot was 'unobtainable', and within months T.J. began to look for an editor.[75] Francis Williams, E.H. Carr, Roger Fulford and others came under consideration, but for one reason or another were thought not entirely suitable. In December 1941 T.J. came up with what he considered a brainwave: the appointment as editor of his friend Wilfrid Eady, a strong-minded senior Civil Servant who wrote exceptionally well. To T.J.'s surprise, Eady, who perhaps had an eye on Warren Fisher's retirement, did not exactly leap at the offer, 'as I would at fifty-one' T.J. said. In any case, the authorities refused to release Eady, a decision Jones thought foolish. 'I contend', he wrote, 'that to edit a national paper like the *Observer* is an important national service comparable with what my friend was doing in the Civil Service.'[76] Unavailingly T.J. sought the advice of the *cognoscenti* at the Athenaeum and finally it was agreed, as a temporary solution, to call in Arthur Mann, former editor of the *Yorkshire Post,* as a supervising director and appoint Ivor Brown, 'an admirable essayist not obsessed with politics', in T.J.'s words, as acting editor. Cyril Connolly, then of *Horizon,* was made 'cultural editor' to look after drama, music and films. A year later, however, T.J. had to persuade Donald Tyerman of *The Economist* to come over as deputy editor to strengthen the political side.[77]

T.J. had also taken a hand on the editorial side. The *Observer*'s 'Forum' series of articles, unsigned, on current issues, was produced by a team supervised weekly by an editorial group of four, with T.J. acting as chairman. Some months later he made a detailed comparative survey of the *Sunday Times* and the *Observer* and concluded that the superiority of the opposition derived from the quality of its foreign correspondents. David Astor, however, frustrated in semi-exile in the Royal Marines, was not impressed with this activity: 'I really feel', he wrote to his father, 'that neither you nor T.J. are fully alive to the need for the *Observer* to stimulate and wake up its readers and think boldly for them'. T.J. clearly admired David Astor's 'passion for righteousness' and his whole-hearted commitment to the interest of the common man, but thought it politic to 'moderate' his evangelicalism a trifle.[78] T.J. was

[75] T.J. to Waldorf Astor, 17 December 1940. Tristan Jones MSS. T.J., Class Q, Vol.3, Nos.43 and 62. Waldorf Astor and T.J. agreed (Class Q, Vol.4, No.9) that David Astor was not yet sufficiently experienced to be given 'complete control in war time when matters are so critical', but he remained of course unchallenged as prospective editor.

[76] T.J., Class Q, Vol.4, Nos.10, 65, 81, 118; Class X, Vol.10, Nos.102, 111, 112, 113.

[77] T.J., Class J, Vol.7, Nos.61 and 85; Class S, Vol.3, Nos.16 and 18.

[78] T.J., Class Q, Vol.4, Nos.145, 147; Class T, Vol.7, No.69. T.J. to D. Astor, 7 March 1943. David Astor MSS.

also active on the managerial side of the *Observer*. In February 1942 he was appointed Deputy Governing Director of the company with full power to act in the owner's absence, and in the following year he was closely involved in Waldorf Astor's attempt to arrange 'a crook-proof Trust' for the future of the paper which would prevent it 'falling ever into the hands of a Beaverbrook or Bottomley'.[79]

Tom Jones began now to write fairly regularly for the *Observer*, and almost as often for the *Manchester Guardian* too. Indeed, he emerged as a publicist of considerable standing, for he was also on occasion invited by the BBC to give talks on matters of national interest. Some of his *Observer* articles were unsigned, but were easily spotted by his friends. 'I recognised the fine Roman hand of Whitehall', Eady commented on one anonymous piece. 'You sign your stuff as clearly as Whistler with his butterfly'.[80] T.J.'s writing for the quality press was, with very few exceptions, superb in content and style. He wrote almost always on subjects of which he had direct personal experience and on which he had reflected at length: the Cabinet, ministers, the Civil Service, speech-writing, committees and, most beguilingly, a double-helping of 'The Donor' in the *Observer* the day after 'Giving as a Fine Art' appeared in the *Manchester Guardian*. Who better to give a beggar's-eye-view of philanthropy than the man who spent much of his life deflecting great wealth towards worthy public ends? 'A lot of nonsense is talked about money', T.J. wrote in 'The Donor', in a homely definition of social democracy, 'it is most serviceable when there is plenty of it, and when, like dung, it is well and widely spread over the land'.[81]

T.J. wrote many book reviews, again confining comment to those areas where he had intimate knowledge or a long-standing interest. He had an enviable ability to capture the reader's interest; his articles were well constructed, finely worded, allusive, the argument arresting, punctuated with aphorism, often provocative, but always persuasive, brimful with constructive suggestion.[82] His best writing appeared in a series of Saturday essays in the *Manchester Guardian* in the autumn of 1942 and succeeding years, that were, by universal consent, delightful. There was also his magnificent tribute in the *Observer* on 17 January 1942, marking Lloyd George's eightieth

[79] T.J., Class Q, Vol.4, No.66; Class T, Vol.7, No.71. 'Cliveden for the Nation', *The Times*, 9 December 1942. 'All very generous and broadminded', in T.J.'s (Class X, Vol.10, No.118) description.

[80] T.J., Class Q, Vol.4, No.65.

[81] *Manchester Guardian*, 13 February 1941. *Observer*, 14 February 1941.

[82] See, for example, 'The Legions of Whitehall', *Observer*, 21 May 1944.

birthday, which remains to this day one of the best short accounts of that elusive genius.

T.J.'s articles in the *Western Mail* were much more polemical, designed to provoke political nationalists, berate obstructive local councillors, and bestir the mentally lazy or obtuse among the Welsh. He pulled no punches, because whatever the merits of the case, he cared deeply about the issues and believed that the least he owed his countrymen was his honest opinion.[83]

Fittingly, for a more intimate medium, his talks on the BBC were conciliatory in tone, but nonetheless questioning, assertive, sometimes bantering, and designed always to expose a problem to examination by as wide a public as possible. 'Lost Property', broadcast in November 1940, was prompted by the demolition of the Pilgrim Trust headquarters. The moral of this homily for the bombed-out was to 'sit loose' and not be enslaved by the 'loss of personal possessions'; there were sometimes compensations. On 7 September 1941 he gave a talk, 'The Revolution is on', in the Sunday night 'Postscript' series, which made J.B. Priestley so immensely popular. T.J. believed that the chief criticism of Priestley's talks was 'that he took one to the gates of the New Jerusalem and left us there'. T.J. said that he intended to 'peep inside just a little'.[84] He envisaged a careful equipoise: 'The secret of wisdom is to think things together. Rights, duties; self, society; state, citizen; liberty, order . . . Neither member of these pairs can be understood apart from the other'. There should be big changes but the post-war paradise would be a 'silver or bronze rather than a golden age . . . We cannot banish insecurity, but we can reduce the damage it does'.[85] His much-praised 'Postscript' prompted the BBC to invite him to give several talks to the USA on India, but he refused as he did not want to spend an undue amount of time on work for the BBC. However, he did respond on occasion and was highly rated by the professionals: 'I always think he is one of our best broadcasters', Donald Boyd of the Home Talks Service wrote in April 1943.[86]

The Ministry of Information had sought T.J.'s help soon after the outbreak of war, but he was ill and had to refuse. In January 1941, Sir Walter Monckton, formerly Edward VIII's legal adviser, who was then at the Ministry of Information, 'begged' T.J., as a

[83] For example, 'A Proposed National Trust for Wales', and 'Musings on the Welsh Way of Life', *Western Mail,* 12 March 1940 and 17 April 1941.

[84] T.J. to M. Luker, 10 July 1941. BBC Archive, WAC: R 34/473/1.

[85] *Leeks and Daffodils,* pp.220–2.

[86] T.J., Class T, Vol.7, No.52. BBC, WAC: R 34/473/1.

matter of patriotic duty, to return to London to act as his 'Political Adviser for the Home Front'. Duff Cooper, the Minister of Information, was, he said, 'unhelpful and lazy'. T.J.'s advice was particularly required about changes in personnel. T.J., who would not 'shirk a war duty', agreed to act as an unpaid unofficial adviser for a trial period. He offered what he regarded as sound advice, but discovered, as he had feared, that Monckton 'was not strong enough' to follow it and get rid of Duff Cooper or resign. Unwilling to waste his time, T.J. withdrew and the Ministry of Information continued with a bloated staff, many of them operating to no useful purpose for some time longer.[87]

Violet Markham and the Astors called repeatedly for T.J. to leave his mountain fastness at Harlech and return to Cliveden to pull his weight in the war effort. T.J. replied that none of them would say precisely what he could do at Cliveden that he could not do from Harlech with occasional visits to London. 'I am not in touch with No.10, or indeed with any cabinet minister in such a way that I can help effectively', he told Violet Markham on 7 June 1941. He had no knowledge of particular value to the government and he would not 'fuss ignorantly'.[88] He refused to go privately to see the Prime Minister to draw his attention to deficiencies in the conduct of the war on the home front, as Sir Stafford Cripps, prompted by David Astor, urged him to do. Astor kept up the bombardment by letter: 'What is there in Wales more important than what happens at the centre of our besieged civilisation?' he asked T.J. in July. A week later, when Jones came up to London to give a radio talk on India, he saw Cripps, and promised to assist if Cripps were 'given a chance' politically to remedy weaknesses on the domestic front.[89]

Cripps however was then the British Ambassador in Moscow, where he remained until January 1942. His political stock at home rose steadily during this time. In the popular mind, no doubt absurdly, he symbolized the heroic resistance of the Russians to the German invasion, and the new hope suggested by the Anglo-Russian alliance against Hitler. The British public, downcast by an almost unbroken sequence of military defeats in Africa, Greece, Crete and the Far East, was desperate for any sign of success. His return home coincided with disastrous defeats at the hands of the Japanese and there was mounting criticism of the political and

[87] T.J., Class W, Vol.14, Nos.114–51; Class T, Vol.7, Nos.40–7. His personal relations with Monckton were however unimpaired.
[88] T.J., Class T, Vol.7, No.47.
[89] T.J., Class Q, Vol.3, Nos.74 and 78; Class T, Vol.7, Nos.48–9.

military conduct of the war. Cripps appeared to many to be a sort of saviour, to some a replacement for Churchill. The Prime Minister, who knew that the best way to bring a putative Messiah back into proper focus was to put him to work, offered Cripps the Ministry of Supply. Cripps, who rated his own ability a good deal higher, asked for time to consider.[90]

Lady Cripps had pleaded with T.J. to come to their assistance a week before her husband returned from Moscow: 'Come and help the poor and needy mortals in London', she wrote. 'I do so *very, very* much want him [her husband] to have a talk with you'.[91] T.J. told Flexner that he was doing his best 'to keep out of politics', but its lure was evidently much too compelling.

Over the next few weeks T.J. had several 'consultations' with Cripps and his wife. Jones said that he felt obliged 'to help the Cripps family, who are amateurs in the world of politics and very isolated'. From the start, however, T.J. had doubts about Cripps's effectiveness: 'He has character and ability of a very high order, but it is doubtful whether he has political nous. He does not seem to have a personal magnetism which binds disciples to him', Jones wrote.[92] With T.J.'s approval, Cripps rejected the offer of the Ministry of Supply but in February, as part of a reconstruction of the ministry, agreed to become Lord Privy Seal combining with it the Leadership of the Commons. T.J. said that Churchill had wisely 'bowed to the storm' of criticism of his leadership; moreover, Cripps's appointment was a welcome 'premonition' of a future 'New Order' in social policy. T.J. also had a hand in the recruitment of his friend A.D.K. Owen as personal assistant to Cripps and as head of a small unofficial 'brains trust' that devilled for the minister.[93]

Cripps was not a sparkling success as Leader of the House. His ability and self-sufficiency were not in doubt; in these respects he reminded T.J. of Asquith. Jones was impressed too with Cripps's probity, but his manner was unfortunate; he did not mix in the lobbies, was insensitive to atmosphere and was remarkably naïve. 'He is a curious mixture of earnest Christian and ambitious politician', T.J. wrote in October. 'I suppose he has so strong a sense of mission that he does not see how it strikes others as climbing and cant'. He did not go down well with members of the

---

[90] Churchill, op.cit., IV, 56–7, for the Prime Minister's disingenuous claim later that his offer was prompted solely by the public interest.

[91] T.J., Class W, Vol.3, No.15.

[92] T.J., Class S, Vol.3, Nos.1 and 2; Class X, Vol.10, No.112.

[93] Ibid., No.105. *A Diary with Letters,* pp.497–8. Owen had played a leading part in the Pilgrim Trust's investigation, *Men without Work.*

Commons,[94] and T.J. recognized that Cripps was vulnerable in other ways too. He had been expelled from the Labour party in 1939 for persistently advocating a United Front with the Communists. The Labour leaders resented his swift rise to popular favour and appointment to high office. With T.J.'s full support, Cripps on his return had made a 'bee-line' for Bevin and Hugh Dalton to improve relations, but had only limited success. T.J. was not altogether surprised. He thought Bevin consumed with 'inordinate ambition' and Dalton 'interested if not fully absorbed in Dalton'. Attlee, it seemed, was of little account. It was hardly surprising therefore that Cripps, as T.J. said, felt thoroughly 'uncomfortable in his isolated position, having to expound and defend Government policy unsupported by a party'.[95]

Early in July, on T.J.'s advice, Cripps submitted to the Prime Minister a long memorandum setting out the main points of his disquietude about the conduct of war. Churchill describes this urbanely in his war memoirs as a helpful contribution to his own defence against imminent parliamentary criticism. Cripps however intended it as a full-scale indictment of Churchill's direction of the war.[96] At the end of July, Cripps contemplated resignation, but sent urgently for T.J. to come up to advise him before actually doing so. Cripps decided on this occasion to remain in office, but his relations with Churchill continued throughout the summer on a level of ill-concealed mutual distrust. At the end of September Lady Cripps reported that the position was 'more unsatisfactory than ever'. As T.J. was slow to respond to the appeal, she telephoned an 'SOS' to him a few days later.[97]

In an attempt to bring matters to a head Cripps had asked for an interview with the Prime Minister. After enduring what appears to be studied discourtesy at No.10 two nights running, Cripps was seen by Attlee and Eden, acting on Churchill's behalf, who offered him the post of Minister of Aircraft Production or Minister of State in Washington. Again Cripps asked for time to consider. The next day he had separate talks with Eden, Attlee, Bevin, Grigg and Sir John Anderson. Cripps said that 'they were all unhappy at the conduct of the war, but on the whole inclined to think Churchill's virtues outweigh his vices'. For what it was worth, Eden said he was

[94] T.J., Class T, Vol.7, No.66. T.J., Notebook, 28 July 1942.

[95] T.J., Class X, Vol.10, Nos.112, 118. See also, Hugh Dalton, *The Fateful Years: Memoirs 1931–45* (1957), pp.320, 365, 384. *The Diary of Beatrice Webb*, IV, 478–81.

[96] Churchill, op.cit., IV, 354–6. T.J., Class T, Vol.7, No.66, for Cripps's version, and T.J., Notebook, P.73, for his suggestion of the memorandum.

[97] T.J., Class W, Vol.3, Nos.18–25; Class T, Vol.7, No.66. Churchill, op.cit., IV, 497–500.

prepared to serve under Cripps if he were to become Prime
Minister. T.J. told Cripps not to put any reliance on Eden's co-
operation. Grigg made the bizarre suggestion of 'recalling Lloyd
George to tide over the transition from Winston to a successor'.
Churchill himself believed that he would 'be dropped' in the event
of another major defeat.

In fact, a great military operation culminating in the battle of
Alamein was already in train. Eden and some other ministers urged
Cripps to postpone resignation because of its effect on Cabinet unity
and national morale at a time of crucial military decision. That
evening Cripps and T.J. considered the position for several hours at
the Crippses' flat. They knew full well that so far as Cripps's hopes of
replacing Churchill were concerned, the Prime Minister was
currently vulnerable to a challenge as never before. For months
Cripps had made no secret of his ambition. At this critical juncture,
however, he was responsive to the patriotic argument for delay,
which T.J. too urged strongly. Cripps formally tendered his
resignation, which by agreement with Churchill was suspended until
the Alamein operation was resolved one way or another.[98]

Alamein of course was a great victory; the Prime Minister's
position was secure, his critics in Parliament silenced, Cripps's
challenge extinguished. Churchill handsomely acknowledged
Cripps's public-spiritedness, but now pressed him either to resign
or finally accept the Ministry of Aircraft Production. Once again
T.J. went up to London to advise, but beforehand he himself
consulted Field Marshal Jan Smuts, who was in London. They
agreed that Churchill, for all his magnificent qualities, had too
much to do and attempted too much. T.J. suggested that Smuts
should persuade the Prime Minister to hand over the direction of a
cabinet committee concerned with the U-boat menace to Cripps,
who was his deputy chairman. Smuts, a great believer in bold
action, said Cripps should simply go ahead and 'assume' control of
the committee; he should certainly not resign from the government
in time of war. T.J. said Cripps had many young disciples who
looked to him for a lead on future social changes. Smuts replied
that therein lay Cripps's chance: 'Winston lives in the 18th century
and does not grasp what is happening'. T.J. arranged a meeting
between Smuts and Cripps the next day, and the following night
discussed the question of resignation at great length with Cripps
and his entourage.[99]

[98] T.J., Class T, Vol.7, Nos.66 and 67. Churchill, op.cit., IV, 500–2. T.J.,
Notebook, p.81.

[99] Characteristically T.J. reported to Lady Cripps that he had coaxed £1,000
from Sir David Stevenson for her Aid to China Fund.

Jones urged Cripps to accept the offer of the Ministry of Aircraft Production. Cripps said that although he was convinced that Churchill thought he was the best man for that post, he was in no doubt either that the Prime Minister wanted him out of the War Cabinet, 'where he was a nuisance, and would be a bigger nuisance as the Cabinet confronted the controversial problem of post-war legislation'. In fact, it was plain that Churchill now held most of the cards; it was 'an unfortunate moment' for Cripps, 'three months hence, when the Beveridge Report might be the issue, the public advantage' might then turn to him. Some young disciples who were present urged an immediate resignation, but were gradually brought round by T.J.'s argument that the situation was 'not at all parallel' with Lloyd George's action in 1916, and the growing realization that Cripps's heart was not in resignation. It was finally agreed that Cripps would accept the proferred post. Jones arrived home very late at his flat where 'sleep came tardily'.[100]

T.J. had never really believed that Cripps was a possible Prime Minister: he was naïve politically, could not 'manoeuvre and manipulate persons', and lacked the necessary masterful, on occasion ruthless, urge to power. Despite his impressive intellect and clarity of mind, which were, in T.J.'s opinion, greater than those of any member of the current Cabinet other than Churchill and John Anderson, Cripps's gifts were those of 'a great lawyer rather than a great statesman'. All the same, T.J. was keen for him to hold on to his ministerial post, even one that did not give him a seat in the Cabinet, because of his conspicuous 'honesty' and the influence he might be able to exert over the shape of future welfare legislation. Indeed, with that in mind, Cripps had discussed the question of his resignation with Beveridge. Cripps was for some time 'very happy' in his new post and, by general consent, exceptionally competent there. Moreover, Churchill absented himself from many meetings of the U-boat Committee where Cripps, as his deputy, 'evoked superlatives' of praise from the Prime Minister for the quality of his work.[101]

There was however a less agreeable postscript. In September 1943 Churchill invited Beaverbrook to rejoin the government. In July 1942 an alliance of Cripps, Attlee, Bevin and some Tory

---

[100] *A Diary with Letters*, pp.504–6, supplemented by his much fuller account in T.J., Class T, Vol.7, No.67.

[101] T.J., Class T, Vol.7, Nos.69, 85; Class W, Vol.3, No.37. *A Diary with Letters*, p.505. Cripps answered almost exactly T.J.'s definition of the ideal minister of Cabinet rank set out in his 'Old Lessons for New Ministers', *Observer* (12 August 1945).

ministers had managed to keep Beaverbrook out.[102] Once again T.J. was hastily summoned from Harlech in September 1943 to advise Cripps. Cripps detested Beaverbrook, whom he cast as Churchill's evil genius. Cripps told T.J. he would 'like to walk out' of the government immediately, but as he had just recently 'been urging workers all over the country to sacrifice everything to the war effort', resignation would look like dereliction of duty on his part. The next day Cripps consulted Bevin who urged delay, and Air Marshal Portal, who argued that he should 'stay on in the interests of the R.A.F.'. T.J. sought the opinion of Baldwin about Cabinet procedure. It was some consolation that Beaverbrook was not going to attend Cabinet meetings, but as T.J. commented: why should he, 'he'll do better by going to Chequers for weekends' and exerting his malign influence in private. This, however, could hardly be publicly said. In the end, it was agreed that Cripps should register his objections to Beaverbrook's return in a letter to the Prime Minister and put the 'onus on Winston to throw him out'. It was of course a weak, even slightly pathetic, conclusion. Churchill did not take the bait and replied to Cripps's letter in charming terms, but also spelt out firmly the full range of a Prime Minister's authority.[103] Although defeated, Cripps did at least manage to establish a much better relationship with Bevin at this time, a matter of some importance after 1945. As adviser to Cripps, T.J. had been unable to do anything more than point out repeatedly to him that he had perforce to bat on a difficult pitch, and, if he were wise, he would not throw his wicket away rashly, he would defend resolutely and wait for conditions to improve.

Now that he lived in Harlech, T.J. became more directly involved in Welsh affairs, and given the circumstances of the time, inevitably in a particularly contentious manner. The events of 1940, with a terrifying barbarism poised to strike, had made T.J. 'infinitely grateful' for the British Empire and Commonwealth. If it crashed he did not doubt that Wales too would be forced to succumb to Nazi tyranny.[104] He was therefore anxious for the Welsh to play their part in defence of freedom and civilization, and he was determined to combat what he regarded as the dangerously divisive, indeed subversive, propaganda of extreme Welsh nationalists. T.J. did not underestimate his opponents. The nationalist movement in Wales, he wrote in 1941, was 'promoted by men of character and ability,

[102] T.J., Notebook (28 July 1942).

[103] T.J., Class T, Vol.7, Nos.87, 89; Class X, Vol.10, Nos.129–31. See also, A.J.P. Taylor (claws firmly sheathed by friendship), *Beaverbrook* (1972), pp.540–7.

[104] T.J.'s Wales Empire Broadcast, 3 December 1940, and *Leeks and Daffodils*, pp.141–2.

who had learnt much from Ireland, and have a following among the abler students at the Welsh university colleges and the teaching profession'.[105]

However, in his opinion, they failed to see that the nation was a 'provisional ideal, not final, not absolute; it was man's tool, not man's God'. On the other hand, T.J. himself had always striven for the greatest possible cultural development of the Welsh people, which, he believed, received no great encouragement from Whitehall. In March 1941, therefore, he put forward a number of suggestions to the Home Office which were designed to confer a greater official recognition on the national institutions in which the Welsh people took pride. He dismissed the notion that Caernarfon castle had any special significance for Wales because of its association with the heir to the throne. Moreover, although

> a royal residence in Wales would please a number of people here . . . it would go little or no distance to placate the malcontents and would be "seen through" by a community which is essentially democratic in outlook.

Of much greater value would be for the Duke of Kent, who was Chancellor of the University of Wales, to preside in person at graduation ceremonies as a matter of regular practice. And, even more valuable, a member of the royal family, preferably the Queen, ought to attend one meeting of the National Eisteddfod, beginning if possible the following August.

He also proposed certain administrative changes: the Welsh Department of the Board of Education (evacuated, absurdly, to Bournemouth) should be permanently moved from Whitehall to Cardiff, and the Chairman of the Welsh Board of Health should be replaced as soon as possible by 'a bilingual Welshman'. Finally, he pointed out that the Nationalists had succeeded in persuading many of their countrymen that 'it is they, and they alone', who were closely concerned about the problems of Wales and its maintenance as a social and economic entity. To counter this, T.J. suggested that the Welsh MPs, who were on the whole, in his opinion, a dozy crew, should be prodded by the Whips to 'bestir' themselves and be allowed to 'meet annually in Wales to discuss specially *its* affairs'. He urged strongly that these proposals should be 'energetically pursued' by the Home Secretary, not pigeon-holed because of the war.[106]

[105] T.J., Class H, Vol.21, No.14.
[106] Wales Empire Broadcast. 3 December 1940. T.J., Class H, Vol.21, No.14.

The response, despite some quibbling, was mildly encouraging. The Home Secretary said he was anxious to draw Wales and the Royal House closer together. There were, however, difficulties, partly because there was no 'recognised official or department' to advise on Welsh questions as the Lord Advocate used to on Scottish affairs before there was a Secretary of State for Scotland. In these circumstances, the opinion of T.J., who understood Welsh feeling as well as the point of view of Whitehall, was an invaluable substitute. The King and Queen, he pointed out, had recently visited Swansea and Cardiff 'after the bombing raids'. T.J. allowed a touch of impatience to appear in his reply: 'The worst of all policies is to wait for the Nationalists to set up a clamour and then give way to it. *Do it now* is my advice'.[107]

However, nothing happened for some time. In May, therefore, T.J. came up with the suggestion that the young Princess Elizabeth should become President of Urdd Gobaith Cymru, the Welsh League of Youth. Ifan ab Owen Edwards, its founder, responded with enthusiasm. He considered that Wales stood 'at a sort of crossroads', its overwhelming need was unity, which T.J.'s proposal, if carried out, would do much to promote. 'It would be good for Wales and the Urdd', Edwards said, especially if the Princess could utter a word or two in Welsh at the Urdd Eisteddfod, a gesture that 'would capture the hearts of the nation'. Furthermore, the Princess's acceptance of office would do a lot to counter the more foolish notions of some of the extreme Welsh Nationalists. T.J.'s proposal, he said, was 'a master-stroke'. Edwards and T.J. met soon afterwards for further discussions. Edwards confessed that he had been 'rather confused' for some years about how best to develop the Urdd; he had proposed close co-operation with the Boys' Club movement but had had little response hitherto; he was particularly keen to 'instil the youth of Wales with the highest ideals of citizenship'.[108]

T.J. of course warmly endorsed these aspirations. He believed that the Urdd represented much that was best in the life of Wales: it had a wide, popular base; it was suffused with an authentic Welsh spirit; it laid great emphasis on the language and on cultural activities which involved the fullest possible participation by its members. The Urdd's branch, the Aelwyd (literally, the hearth), based most usually on a rural community or a small town, was characteristically intimate and homely but nevertheless dedicated to the highest standards of behaviour and social aspiration. T.J.

[107] Ibid., Nos.15 and 16.
[108] Ibid., No.21; Vol.18, No.81.

pressed Herbert Morrison, the Home Secretary, whom he knew well, on the proposal over several weeks, and with the help of Edwards forwarded a mass of detailed information about the Urdd for the consideration of the Palace. T.J. also suggested that the Princess should make a two-day tour of Wales calling at Urdd branches where she could meet many small groups of young people. This would have a much more lasting effect in Wales than 'a spectacular' attendance at one great assembly. And it was important too that the 'visit should not be mixed up with any other side-shows'. It was however not to be. After careful consideration, the offer was regretfully declined, although the King emphasised his concern for maintaining close links with Wales. The precise reasons for the refusal were apparently too sensitive for statement in a letter, they would be communicated to T.J. in person when next he was in London.[109]

Jones was sorely disappointed, but he was well aware of the British Establishment's propensity to be ham-fisted in its dealings with Wales. He was however more successful with the British Council, whose catalogue 'Films of Britain 1941' made no reference of any kind to Wales. Jones protested strongly in the right quarters, whereupon it was decided to produce a film about Wales and Welsh music. T.J. was consulted about it and when he objected that the draft script was 'precious, cliché-ridden and stagey', it was rewritten by Wyn Griffith, whose name was suggested by T.J.[110] And for what it was worth, Jones believed that the authorities blundered in 1936 when the trial of three leading Welsh Nationalists, charged with setting fire to an RAF bombing school in north Wales, was moved, after the jury had failed to agree, from Caernarfon to the Old Bailey, where they were sentenced to nine months in prison. Jones said, in a carefully qualified protest, that it would have been wiser to have held the trial in Cardiff.[111]

Two years before, he himself had tried in vain to persuade Baldwin to re-site an army gunnery school planned at Manorbier in Pembrokeshire. He did so however in defence of a particularly beautiful locality, not out of any sense of nationalist or pacifist outrage. In 1941 T.J. was, however, outraged by the series of articles written by Saunders Lewis of Plaid Genedlaethol Cymru, later

[109] Ibid., Vol.21, Nos.17–33. The Palace explained it had been decided that the Princess was too young to 'come out' into public honorary duties. Two years later, when she had emerged, T.J. proposed the idea again, but there was no response. (T.J. Add MSS, HH, Vol.5.)

[110] T.J., Class M, Vol.4, Nos.79–85. *A Diary with Letters,* p.494.

[111] Ibid., p.287.

called *Plaid Cymru,* the Welsh Nationalist Party, one of the three who had been gaoled, in the Welsh weekly journal *Baner ac Amserau Cymru,* which week by week maintained that the defeat of Hitler was a matter of indifference to Wales. Jones was especially angered by a leading article that appeared on 9 April 1941 which asserted that there was no difference 'between German policy and the New Order on the one hand, and English policy and the Old Order on the other'; that the position of Wales after an English victory would, indeed, be less satisfactory than that of the Balkan countries under the Nazis.[112] The article made a slighting, possibly actionable, comment about a connection between the Governor of the Bank of England and the owners of *The Times.* T.J. stirred up Geoffrey Dawson the editor to bring an action for libel but legal opinion held that although the article came close, it did not quite constitute a libel. A letter from *The Times* demanding a retraction did extract a correction.[113]

T.J. of course was opposed to the policy of Plaid Cymru, on domestic as well as international affairs, but he was especially determined to spike the guns of Saunders Lewis, its chief inspiration, whose ideas and tactics he considered pernicious and dangerous. Lewis was an immensely able man, a poet, littérateur and philosopher, who ultimately achieved a European reputation. He exerted a curious Caesarist fascination over the minds of most of his colleagues and followers, some of whom however had reservations about certain of his ideas, his priorities, and the fact that he had been converted to Roman Catholicism.[114] T.J. tried in July 1941 to block Lewis's nomination to a committee in Wales on post-war planning, but discovered that it had no official standing.[115]

There was however no secret about T.J.'s hostility, which he expressed publicly in the strongest terms in the heartland of Welsh nationalism, at Bangor on May Day 1941, and even more vehemently in an address in Cardiff at a St David's Day function in 1942. He accused the Nationalists of trafficking in fractional truths, employing the 'Hitlerian technique' of bogus populist promises. Welsh Nationalism, Jones asserted, was currently dominated by a

---

[112] *Baner ac Amserau Cymru,* 9 April 1941.

[113] Ibid., 14 May 1941. T.J., Class H, Vol.21, Nos.18–22.

[114] D. Hywel Davies, *The Welsh Nationalist Party 1925–45* (Cardiff, 1983), pp.223–68, and *Presenting Saunders Lewis,* ed. Alun R. Jones and Gwyn Thomas (Cardiff, 1973), pp.3–6, 23–78.

[115] T.J., Class W, Vol.16, Nos.190–1. Lewis's name had been suggested by Percy Watkins, who in fact thought he had 'a streak of madness' but nevertheless 'considered it a lesser evil' to have a Plaid Cymru representative inside rather than outside in malevolent opposition. T.J., Class V, Vol.2, No.122.

narrow, intolerant dogma that offered the prospect of a 'new Promised Land of Fascism'. Its triumph would plunge the nation into civil war, for there were many in Wales who rated reason and freedom and the British Commonwealth, 'as a stepping stone to world unity and citizenship', dearer even than the preservation of the Welsh language and a return to medieval attitudes of mind. Isolation offered no refuge to Wales: 'the only safety for the small nations in future is to join a convoy'.[116]

The *Western Mail* applauded his 'courageous detachment', but naturally in Nationalist circles and their supporting Welsh-language journals, especially *Y Ddraig Goch* and *Y Faner,* he was identified for all time as a virulent enemy. T.J.'s target was the ordinary Welshman who cherished his country, its traditions, its culture and its language (whether he could speak it or not), whose entirely wholesome patriotism made him potentially susceptible to the carefully veiled insinuations of Nationalist propaganda. T.J. remembered only too well the old dictum that Britain's extremity was separatist nationalism's opportunity. He wanted his countrymen to be clear about what was at stake. He was particularly anxious to deny the Nationalists the enormous fillip that success in a by-election, prompted by the nomination of the sitting member to a judgeship, for the parliamentary seat of the University of Wales, would give them. It was clear from the outset that Saunders Lewis, T.J.'s *bête noire*, would stand as the Plaid Cymru candidate. T.J. was pressed to stand against him: many of his friends were eager for him to do so, the secretary of the University Liberals asked if he could put his name forward, Sir Alfred T. Davies proposed it in the *Western Mail.* T.J. wrote to the editor in reply:

> I regret that I am too old [he was 72] . . . Few things would have given me more delight than to oppose Mr. Saunders Lewis, who if returned will be (metaphorically) another Guy Fawkes in the House of Commons. No one in Wales has done more week by week in the Nationalist organ to sabotage the war effort, and we have not to thank him that we are not at the mercy of the Nazis.[117]

The Nationalist reply was equally uncompromising: Saunders Lewis's opponents were described as a 'diligent clique of Welsh

---

[116] 'Adult Education after Thirty Years', *Leeks and Daffodils,* pp.142–5. 'Home Truths on Welsh Government', *Western Mail,* 28 February 1942, subsequently published in *The Native Never Returns* (1946), pp.9–27.

[117] T.J., Class J, Vol.5, Nos.5, 9, 60; Class X, Vol.10, No.122. *Western Mail,* 4 December 1942.

Quislings' cynically disposed to disregard the interest of Wales.[118] It was in fact a species of popular front rather than a clique which was mustered against Lewis. It was widely recognized that although Plaid Cymru had little chance as yet of winning a territorial constituency, Saunders Lewis's challenge for the University seat, where Plaid Cymru was thought to have many followers among younger graduates, could well be formidable. It was essential, in T.J.'s opinion, to avoid a 'three-cornered fight', which would split the majority that, on any calculation, was opposed to Saunders Lewis. T.J. advised B.B. Thomas not to stand, and told Clement Davies 'straight' that his wife ought not to do so either. Jones dismissed H.A. Marquand from his calculation because he did not speak Welsh, 'which is essential'. T.J. at first had hopes of David Hughes Parry, but he was unwilling to stand.[119] In mid-November Iorwerth Peate, a young academic of distinction, a former member of Plaid Cymru, had written to T.J. putting the case for W.J. Gruffydd, Professor of Welsh at University College, Cardiff, who was prepared to stand as an 'independent' candidate. Gruffydd had at one time been Vice-President of Plaid Cymru but had left the party over its refusal to support the war and because of his hostility to the conservative social ideas it derived from Saunders Lewis's influence. The electoral truce meant that the major parties would not run candidates, but it was necessary to take particular account of the opinion of the Liberals, who had previously held the seat. Peate was casuist enough to cope with that: he said it had already been pointed out that, although not formally a party man, Gruffydd's philosophy was 'wholly Liberal in the real and right sense'. Evidently enough to pass, at any rate. In the end, Gruffydd, who said he would accept the Liberal Whip on a selective basis, was chosen to stand as the 'true' candidate, in T.J.'s words, of a broad coalition of the non-nationalist Welsh Establishment.[120]

With no great enthusiasm, T.J. accepted the candidate and agreed to add his name to the list of dignitaries whose endorsement of Gruffydd was published in the *Western Mail*. Immediately T.J. was sharply rebuked for bending his principles to present necessities by an old friend, Mabel Howells of Cardiff, a staunch Liberal who was unwilling to accept Gruffydd's ersatz credentials. T.J. made the best of it. Gruffydd did at least win with 3,098 votes to 1,330 for Lewis, his nearest opponent.

---

[118] *Welsh Nationalist,* January 1943, quoted in D. Hywel Davies, op.cit., p.237.
[119] T.J., Class J, Vol.5, Nos.58, 59, 75; Class X, Vol.10, No.122.
[120] T.J., Class J, Vol.5, Nos.61 and 67; Class T, Vol.7, No.70.

Of course I am delighted with the defeat of S.L. [T.J. told Annie Ffoulkes]. I dislike his propaganda and that of the *Faner*-ites. He does not strike me as Welsh, but as something foreign. I don't imagine Gruffydd as a heaven-born M.P., but he may have a refreshing effect on the orthodox Welsh members. Hope so. Anyway, we are safe 'for the duration' from the Blaidites [Nationalists].[121]

T.J. had also ruffled one or two other feathers at this time. Speaking in Cardiff on St David's Day 1942, he deplored the continuing refusal of Welsh Local Authorities to appoint graduates to senior administrative posts. He was taken severely to task by Sir William Jenkins, leader of Glamorgan County Council, a Welsh radical turned Colonel Blimp under criticism. T.J. was unrepentant: 'O Lord, deliver me from growing up into a Vested Interest' was, he suggested to a Prize Day audience at Tredegar county school, the proper answer to Sir William's hidebound conservatism.[122]

On a more personal level, T.J. also quarrelled sharply with Lady Astor at this time. As she grew older her outrageous outbursts became less and less tolerable and she became even more petulant when thwarted than formerly. In August 1941, when T.J. was unable to go to Cliveden at the same time as the Bernard Shaws, as she required, because he was detained in Aberystwyth on business, she threw a tantrum: 'You failed me completely', Nancy wrote peevishly, 'and not for the first time'.[123] In August 1942, however, things got much worse. At a time when the Russians were fighting heroically in desperate circumstances to survive, Nancy Astor bluntly pointed out in a public speech that, at the time of the Battle of Britain, Russia was allied to Germany, and currently was simply defending itself. Whatever its truth, people were aghast. T.J. wrote to her immediately:

People have sent me your outburst about Russia. What an ungracious speech, and at this moment . . . I have no reason to love Bolsheviks, but I hope I have some magnanimity and some pity left in me. You are the despair of your friends.[124]

---

[121] *Western Mail,* 7 January 1943. T.J., Class J, Vol.5, Nos.85–7.

[122] 'The New World and the Old School Tie', 21 April 1942. T.J., Class Y, Vol.5, No.38. *South Wales Daily News,* 22 April 1942. *A Diary with Letters.*

[123] T.J., Class T, Vol.7, No.50; Class Q, Vol.2, No.65. For the same reason, T.J. had also sidestepped an invitation from Lloyd George. He did however go up to Cliveden a week later to see the Shaws. *A Diary with Letters,* pp.490–1.

[124] T.J., Class Q, Vol.2, No.65. 'She has neither pity nor humility. One is tired of protesting', T.J. wrote in a letter (Class T, Vol.3, No.63) to Violet Markham.

Nancy defended herself spiritedly, but claimed also to be deeply hurt.

> I am sorry to have hurt you [T.J. responded], but you hurt a great many more. You knew exactly from long experience what the press would do with a speech of that sort and I believe you were warned by a fellow speaker . . . If one did not care for you and the power you wield, one would not bother two pins what you said. But you have a rare gift of many talents and must be judged accordingly, and not by common standards. It is sad to think your friendship can be extinguished so easily.[125]

Evidently, relations were near breaking point. 'I have never lost or quarrelled with a real friend', she wrote on 26 August 1942 in a childish riposte.[126] There was little contact between them for some time and although T.J. was at Cliveden one weekend in September he was given to understand he would not be asked there over Christmas 1942: he spent the holidays happily with his sister Mrs McKenzie and her family at their home in Hampstead. His uneasy relations with Nancy Astor placed T.J. in an awkward position, because he was still as close as ever to her husband Waldorf, who was unwell at this time, and whose own relationship with Nancy was much less happy than formerly.[127] There was, too, the fact that T.J. had a remarkable relationship with their son David, one so strong that it easily bridged the gap in their ages and enabled them to speak with complete candour without impairing their friendship in any way. Nancy blamed T.J. 'for taking David leftwards and from her'. 'She can't believe', T.J. wrote, 'that he has a mind, and a remarkable one, of his own'. And she was vexed that David was to inherit the *Observer* which would, in consequence, 'go leftward' too.[128]

It was a thoroughly difficult situation, particularly for Waldorf Astor, who, in November 1943, asked T.J. to write 'a penitent apology' to Nancy 'for the sake of family peace'. With some reluctance he agreed to do so: in December he wrote to say that perhaps his criticism of her speech about Russia had been unduly 'savage'. Nancy sent a 'forgiving' reply, with a postscript: 'What about Xmas?'. T.J. was genuinely glad that peace had been restored, but, as he told Violet Markham in a letter written at the

[125] 22 August 1942. Astor MS 1416/1/2/230.

[126] T.J., Class Q, Vol.2, No.70.

[127] *A Diary with Letters,* pp.502–3. T.J., Class S, Vol.3, No.22; Class X, Vol.10, No.124. Anthony Masters, *Nancy Astor* (1981), pp.207–9.

[128] T.J., Class T, Vol.7, Nos.74 and 91. 4 July 1944. D. Astor MSS.

Athenaeum, where he spent Christmas Day: 'I've lost all desire to return to Cliveden'. And he did not do so for another four months.[129] But it is clear that he was prepared, on occasion, to eat humble pie in order to help one of his best friends.

T.J. also did what he could to raise the spirits of his old friend Stanley Baldwin. Once the much-admired father-figure of the nation, Baldwin was now popularly reviled for what was considered his feeble conduct of British policy before 1937. He and his wife lived a reclusive life at Astley Hall, seeking to avoid public attention and controversy as far as possible. In private discussions with T.J. Baldwin defended himself vigorously, though not altogether convincingly. At any rate, while conceding that posterity would be kinder than contemporary opinion was to him, T.J. believed that Baldwin's 'spasmodic' version of leadership was responsible in part for Britain's current vulnerability. But that did not diminish his great affection for Baldwin, and he did his best by word and deed to sustain his morale.[130]

T.J. also stood boldly against the great tide of public and political criticism of Sir Horace Wilson, who was removed from No.10 Downing Street as soon as Chamberlain's government fell. The popular national newspapers – the *Mail*, the *Mirror,* and the *Express* in particular – savaged Wilson mercilessly, perhaps as a convenient substitute for Chamberlain. Wilson did not resent the behaviour of Attlee, who in fact made his removal 'a condition' of Labour's willingness to join the government, but he was bitterly critical of Churchill. 'I feel that Winston has dishonoured the Premiership and the Civil Service in his treatment of me', Wilson told T.J. in July 1942 when he retired from the Treasury.[131] Two months earlier T.J. had strongly defended Wilson in a speech at Cardiff, prominently reported in the *Western Mail,* in which he described the persistent attacks on Wilson as 'mean, unworthy and contemptible'.[132] But T.J.

---

[129] T.J., Class Q, Vol.2, Nos.71 and 72; Class T, Vol.7, Nos.95 and 108. *A Diary with Letters*, pp.512–13. On Christmas Eve David Astor whisked him off for the evening to the home of Siegfried Charoux, a refugee from Vienna, whose bust of T.J., then on display in Glasgow, is now in Newport (Gwent) museum.

[130] T.J., Class A, Vol.6, Nos.181 and 189; Vol.7, No.53; Class T, Vol.7, No.41; Class Y, Vol.2, No.1, pp.33–58.

[131] T.J., Notebook, pp.46–7.

[132] 'Marvels of the Civil Service', *Western Mail*, 23 May 1942. T.J. was also apparently responsible for two laudatory paragraphs about Wilson in the *Observer*, 30 August 1942. T.J.'s obituary notice of Wilson, written in 1942, was politely demoted by the *Manchester Guardian*, which had solicited it, to 'very useful' notes, because, as the editor said: 'We don't quite take the same view of H.W. as you do', T.J., Class W, Vol.2, Nos.155–7.

did not quite face the fact that, personal abuse aside, the serious charge against Wilson was that he had encroached unduly on the functions of ministers. It was no real answer to take refuge, as T.J. did, in Nancy Astor's dictum: 'If civil servants are too strong, it is because ministers are too weak'. But the episode did demonstrate that T.J. was no mere fair-weather friend.[133]

But he was less sensitive in the case of another of his old friends at this time. In recent years T.J. and Lord Davies had had little to do with one another. Indeed, in 1943, when D.D., as President of the College, renewed his campaign against E.H. Carr, whose appointment to the Wilson Chair of International Politics at Aberystwyth in 1936 he had resisted by outrageous methods, T.J. opposed him in public and, with justice, uncompromisingly.[134] On 16 June 1944, however, Lord Davies died of lung cancer: T.J.'s obituary notice of him two days later in the *Observer* was factually accurate but ungenerous in sentiment. Burdon Evans, who had much personal experience of D.D.'s dictatorial temper, nevertheless was clearly upset and protested that 'the notice was laced with venom in every line'. Jones was taken aback, he claimed that his article had been made more sharply critical than intended by crass sub-editing, but the fact was that in May he had refused to write an obituary notice for D.D. for *The Times* precisely because he felt unable to be fair to him. For once, T.J.'s velvet touch had deserted him. Burdon Evans was right: 'I think', he wrote, 'criticism might at least be left until after a man's ashes have been scattered – if only for the sake of his family and friends'.[135]

The exchange illustrates very clearly that T.J.'s friends and associates, although full of respect and admiration for his great qualities, did not hesitate to speak their minds frankly to him when they differed. They were nearly all independent spirits; friends not cronies, still less toadies, as Burdon Evans, John Davies, Percy Watkins, Violet Markham, Gwen Davies and others demonstrated on many occasions. Happily, too, candid comment in their circle rarely left a residue of festering resentment. 'Let not this or any other difference of opinion disturb our friendship, which becomes

[133] T.J., Class T, Vol.7, No.24. In June 1943 Lord Astor turned down (T.J., Class Q, Vol.I, No.95) T.J.'s suggestion of Wilson as a director of the *Observer* on the ground that it would give unscrupulous opponents a handle against the journal.

[134] E.L. Ellis, *The University College of Wales, Aberystwyth, 1872–1972*, (Cardiff, 1972), pp.245–7, 358–9.

[135] T.J., Class W, Vol.6, No.264. *Observer*, 18 June 1944. T.J.'s account did, however, say: 'no one more passionately believed that behind Right there must be Force and over both Justice': an acceptable epitaph for most men.

more precious as I approach the end of life', Burdon Evans's letter concluded.

Shortly afterwards, in 1944, his old College at Aberystwyth expressed a similar esteem for T.J.: it elected him as its President in succession to Lord Davies. The choice represented a break with the past in keeping with the democratic spirit of the time: his predecessors had been three peers and a wealthy baronet. In the light of his bitter disappointment over the principalship in 1919, T.J. rated it as 'one of life's little ironies'. All the same he was deeply touched by the honour.

> You have raised me to the office [he said speaking from the heart to the Court of Governors] because you believed that I have cared for the education of the people of Wales, have loved the College with an abiding affection, and have no more ardent desire than to be of service for the short time left to me.[136]

---

[136] In September 1944. Harlech MSS. *Western Mail*, 26 October 1944. 'Beware of students', Lady Astor warned him (Class Q, Vol.2, No.28). 'You have escaped widows, but students are more dangerous.'

CHAPTER FIFTEEN

FULL CIRCLE

WITHIN weeks of T.J.'s election to the Presidency of the University College at Aberystwyth, he heard that he had been awarded the Medal of the Honourable Society of Cymmrodorion, the ultimate mark of public recognition of distinction for Welshmen. He was surprised and immensely pleased: 'I really have been very handsomely treated by my own people in recent years', he commented to Violet Markham.[1] It was especially apposite that T.J. should succeed to the Presidency of the University College at that time because education was once again, after a bleak interval of more than twenty years, exciting a good deal of public interest. A new education bill, in which great hopes were vested, was on the stocks, and there was a general expectation of a substantial expansion of higher education when the war was over. There was now therefore at least a possibility of realizing T.J.'s old dream of new purpose-built college buildings on the fine Penglais Hill site at Aberystwyth. Indeed, a start had been made there just before the outbreak of war, but in 1946 Aberystwyth Corporation, in order to avoid excessive concentration of municipal housing in one part of the borough, announced plans for a housing estate on compulsorily-purchased land on Penglais. T.J. was aghast. He had always nurtured the hope that College buildings on the hill would be in keeping with the splendid aesthetic standard established by the National Library of Wales.[2]

T.J. acted quickly: he proposed a joint deputation from the College and the National Library, which he led, to urge the

[1] T.J., Class T, Vol.7, No.124. T.J. responded to the presentation of the Medal with the sort of playfully teasing witty speech at which he excelled. He said he had had little criticism in Wales, although the Nationalists had once compared him unfavourably with Sir Roger Casement. T.J. claimed he had not been driven by ambition, a desire for fame or fortune. The fact was, he said: 'I have done nothing that I have not enjoyed doing'.

[2] Years before T.J. had persuaded the College to appoint S.K. Greenslade, architect of the National Library, to prepare a general scheme for the development of the site. Unfortunately, Greenslade suffered a nervous breakdown and could not complete the commission. Thereafter, T.J. was less than happy with the work of Greenslade's successors.

Corporation not, in haste, to spoil a magnificent site on which it was hoped to erect buildings fit for the centuries. There was some muttering in the town about social snobbery and the deputation had 'a mixed reception'. T.J. met the charge of snobbery head-on: he told the Corporation that he himself was working-class and proud of it, and so too overwhelmingly were the students and staff of the College. The land in dispute was in fact a private estate that was currently up for sale. The College of course could not afford to buy it, but Ifor L. Evans, the Principal, had elicited a promise from D. Alban Davies, a Cardiganshire man who had made a fortune in the London milk trade, that at some time he would make a substantial benefaction to the College. Alban Davies now proffered a blank cheque.[3] Thus armed, T.J. and the deputation met the Corporation again and offered twenty-three acres of the estate to the town in perpetuity at a nominal rent for development as a public park. After some further hesitation, the Corporation agreed to waive compulsory purchase and the Penglais site was saved from encroachment.[4]

This was an early example of the President and Principal in action in tandem. When in accord, they were a formidable pair, providing perhaps the most effective dual leadership the College had ever had. Ifor L. Evans, a former Fellow of St John's College, Cambridge, historian and economist, a gifted musician steeped in Welsh culture, was far and away the best administrator the College had ever had as a principal. He was a masterful man, prone on occasion to operate by *fait accompli;* he was genuinely concerned for the welfare of students in general, although he did not find personal contact with them easy.

---

[3] Principal: 'I have been credibly informed that the Penglais estate is on the market.'
Alban Davies: 'You mean the land the Corporation is trying to buy?'
Principal: 'Yes.'
Alban Davies: 'Buy it, *bachgen,* buy it! How long have you got to decide?'
Principal: 'Till 5 o'clock this afternoon.'
Alban Davies: 'What a chance for the College! That's what we've always wanted, the complete control of the hill. How much do they want?'
Principal: 'About £34,000.'
Alban Davies: '. . . Here's a blank cheque, fill it up when you know the amount . . . I make one condition. Let the gift remain anonymous for the time being. And whatever you do, don't tell my wife yet.'
From Mrs Ruth Evans's unpublished memoir of her husband.
[4] *A Diary with Letters,* pp.542–3. *Cambrian News,* 21 June 1946. T.J., Class T, Vol.8, No.15. E.L. Ellis, *University College of Wales, Aberystwyth, 1872–1972* (Cardiff 1972), pp.270–1.

T.J. was very different; he revelled in the company of young people.[5] He was of course an old student of the College, and the first President ever to submit himself to public inspection by delivering an Inaugural Lecture in April 1945. 'In the past', a member of the Senate observed, 'the person of the President has been sacrosanct (mostly in defence of his limitations) . . . he was not seen and certainly not heard' by staff and students.[6] T.J.'s address, subsequently published as 'Old and Young', included some interesting reflections on that theme followed by a restatement of his ideas about higher education. Never one to play to the gallery, he bluntly suggested that some of his student audience were misplaced at university and, the proponent always of academic excellence, he also confessed a fear that the expected influx of ex-servicemen and others when the war ended would drastically lower university standards.[7] Jones's customary optimism about university education had, for the moment, been forced into second place. In fact, his concern about standards, which anticipated Kingsley Amis's much-trumpeted warning later about increased student numbers, was disproved after 1945. T.J. also feared, with rather more justification, that the immense prestige of science and technology in a world that had split the atom would lead to the neglect, or at least the overshadowing, of the humanities at universities. Money for science, when the pendulum was swinging so strongly in a technical direction, would no doubt be forthcoming, but that was precisely the time, in his opinion, when the 'timeless values of truth, goodness and beauty', with which the humanities were especially concerned, should also be vigorously reaffirmed. He called too for far more emphasis on the unity of knowledge: 'scientists need more arts, and the artists more science'.[8]

T.J. still nurtured a hope that Aberystwyth could be transformed into a centre for advanced studies for the whole of the University of Wales. He took a keen interest in professorial appointments. He tried hard, but ultimately in vain, to persuade Reginald Jacques, the

[5] T.J., Class T, Vol.8, No.27. An African student wrote later (Class X, Vol.12, No.90) of T.J., 'he was a beloved "father" to me and to many other African students in the College . . . his was the one house . . . I could call my own . . . We all crowded around him, Americans, Africans, French, Germans, as well, of course, as British students.'

[6] T.J., Class W, Vol.I, No.10.

[7] He left an escape hatch however with the hope that some of these were 'late developers'. *The Native Never Returns*, p.195.

[8] Ibid., pp.195-200. Broadcast talk, 24 October 1947, on the 75th Anniversary of the College. T.J., Class Y, Vol.5, No.15.

distinguished instrumentalist, who regretfully confessed that he was too 'deeply embedded' in London to move, to apply for the Chair of Music. T.J. was interested in the possibility of recruiting Glyn Daniel, the archaeologist, to the staff, and he hoped that E.H. Carr, the terms of whose Woodrow Wilson Chair required no more formal teaching than a few public lectures in Aberystwyth in each term, would settle there on a permanent basis. When Carr moved on to *The Times,* and it appeared that the Wilson endowment, eroded by inflation, could not sustain a successor, T.J. quietly persuaded Gwen and Daisy Davies of Gregynog 'to go halves' in a supplement of £21,000 to the original endowment to support a new appointment to this prestigious chair and enable International Politics to be transformed into a full-scale teaching department.[9]

In May 1945, accompanied by his unmarried sister Liz, T.J. went to live in a house he leased for fifteen months in Aberystwyth. He had accepted a commission from Harvard University Press to write a life of Lloyd George, for which he needed access to the resources of the National Library of Wales. A year later he moved into Brynhir, a house owned by and close to the Library, which became his base for the next eight years.[10] It also meant of course that he was now a President of the College in residence, and he soon discovered that he could not do 'anything like as much' as he had hoped to do because the businesslike Principal was easily ruffled by any hint of encroachment.[11] Some frictional irritation was probably inevitable on occasion in the relations of two such strong-minded individuals, but with his immense experience of men and measures, T.J. gradually eased their partnership on to a workable footing. He did not disguise his criticisms of the Principal's order of priorities, but did so in persuasive rather than challenging terms. And T.J.'s emollient influence at meetings of the Court and Council was an admirable foil to the Principal's brisk, sometimes brusque, manner that prompted objection from certain lay members. So, although at one time T.J. had contemplated resigning the Presidency after only two years, in practice he continued in office for the full five-year period, and indeed agreed to serve for another term. It is clear that Ruth, the Principal's 'admirable' young German wife, as T.J. described her, played an important part in bringing the two men much closer together. Indeed, T.J. became almost a part-time member of the Principal's family.[12]

[9] T.J., Class T, Vol.7, No.153; Vol.8, Nos.15, 51, 138 and 146.
[10] T.J., Class W, Vol.2, No.38; Class T, Vol.7, No.140.
[11] T.J., Class W, Vol.7, No.127; Class T, Vol.8, No.3.
[12] Ibid., Nos.3, 47, 50 and 87. Mrs Ruth Evans's unpublished memoir of her husband.

Rather reluctantly, T.J. decided not to join the College Labour party as he considered it 'decenter' for the President to 'stand above the battle'. And he much regretted too that his preoccupation at the National Library on the Lloyd George biography much reduced the time he could afford to spend in the company of students. Of course young people did not always lift the spirits; quite the reverse in the case of a theological student who preached at T.J.'s chapel at Aberystwyth one Sunday at this time. 'He may be 27', Jones wrote, 'but he sounded older than Methuselah in voice and manner'.[13] T.J. however, despite his seventy years and more, was youthfully enthusiastic about the prospect of large social improvement in post-war Britain, particularly in education which, to his delight, had 'come alive during the war'. He was especially attracted by Kurt Hahn's experimental Outward Bound training school at Aberdovey, where the building of character, cultivating the virtues of initiative, self-reliance, physical fitness and hardihood, was considered as important as academic training. After a weekend of discussions with Hahn and a visit to Aberdovey, T.J. became an enthusiastic supporter of the experiment, attracted especially to Hahn's scheme of 'mixing working class and public school boys'. T.J. immediately arranged a grant from the York Trust to enable five working-class boys from Northampton to spend some time with Hahn at Aberdovey, and soon afterwards he drew the school to the attention of the wealthy Goldsmiths' Company, which promptly financed a similar extended stay by fifty boys from London.[14]

But although T.J. conceded that schools were 'the biggest single power for good in the national life', his primary concern continued to be the future of adult education. 'There is no subject in which I am more interested', he told the young socialist Evan Durbin in 1944.[15] In recent years, however, he had been forced to admit that he and his like, who had been working in the field for over thirty years, had expected too much of adult education. They had been 'too easily optimistic' and had underrated the crushing discouragement of the 'indifference' of the masses who preferred entertainment. 'When we look over the edge of our cultivated plot

---

[13] T.J., Class T, Vol.8, Nos.27 and 32. 1 April 1949, White Misc MSS.

[14] D. Astor MSS, 9 May 1942. T.J., Class W, Vol.9, Nos.68 and 72; Vol.20, No.92. 'One of the best things which has happened to me since I came to this country', Hahn wrote to T.J. in 1944, '. . . has been my contact with you and your purpose of life. It has strengthened in me what deserved to be strengthened, and it has weakened what deserved to be weakened.'

[15] T.J., 'How Shall we Teach the Teachers', *Observer*, 1 August 1943. T.J., Class D, Vol.6, No.49.

into the untamed wilderness beyond', T.J. wrote in 1941, 'we see how small our plot is'.[16] But times had changed; the brute experience of war had forced the public to pay more attention to the great issues that had disrupted their lives. ABCA and CEMA had aroused a remarkable popular interest in education and culture. T.J. believed that the post-war world offered 'a chance without parallel or precedent to multiply and enrich' popular education. He was certain there would be a demand for more 'Harlechs and Newbattles' and other variant institutions.[17]

But this popular interest could easily dissipate if left untended. T.J. believed that a concerted campaign to maintain momentum was necessary after the war. The difficulty was, however, that adult education agencies were many and varied; the movement had no acknowledged GHQ. T.J. rejected Waldorf Astor's assertion that the WEA was 'one-sided politically', but he admitted that some of its most important leaders, who were concerned with their own difficulties, did not seem to accept the need for a broad-front campaign in support of a big expansion of adult education in all its forms.[18] And the British Institute of Adult Education, founded in 1920 by Haldane and Albert Mansbridge, could scarcely be said to have lived up to the over-arching ambition contained in its grandiloquent title. It was essentially a research body, not the GHQ of adult education that Haldane apparently hoped it might become in time.[19] T.J. meanwhile maintained his close links with the Educational Settlements Association and Chatham House, with A.D. Lindsay, J.J. Mallon and Tawney of the WEA, and with ABCA through his friendship with W.E. Williams. T.J. was also co-operating with Sir Richard Livingstone of Corpus Christi College, Oxford, and Archbishop William Temple who, from different vantage points, were equally active in promoting adult education. T.J. also became a member of a committee of the British Institute of Adult Education (BIAE) set up in 1942 to consider post-war adult education. The fact was that T.J. would willingly co-operate with anyone or any body who could be of assistance to 'the Cause'.[20]

[16] 'Adult Education after Thirty Years', *Leeks and Daffodils*, pp.146, 153–4.

[17] 'Democracy and Discussion', T.J., Class Y, Vol.5, No.40. 22 August 1942. Morton MSS. GD 326/88/1.

[18] T.J., Class D, Vol.5, Nos.115–121. IN 1942 some leaders of the W.E.A. (Class V, Vol.2, No.130) declared disdainfully that they would not 'become the Woolworths of Adult Education'.

[19] T.J., Class D, Vol.5, No.96. Mary Stocks, *The Workers Educational Association: The First Fifty Years.* (1953), pp.36–7. *R.B. Haldane: an Autobiography* (1929), pp.296–308.

[20] T.J., Class D, Vol.15, Nos.51, 71, 84, 113 and 115; Vol.6, Nos.7, 14–20 and 66; Class V, Vol.2, No.138; Class W, Vol.14, No.30.

But he was very aware of the danger of an outbreak of civil war among the mutually jealous bodies concerned with adult education, and he had plenty of experience of the effectiveness of a discreet personal approach to those who wielded actual power. In 1943, therefore, T.J. turned his attention to R.A. Butler, President of the Board of Education, whom he knew well. They arranged to meet at Aberystwyth in March, but T.J. was ill and the consultation had to be postponed. In T.J.'s opinion, Butler was the key man. 'I have talked much with this and with that leader', T.J. wrote to him in May 1944, 'and I am certain that what is most needed is a decisive lead from you'.[21] R.A. Butler, experienced, ambitious, skilful, realistic, even cynical politically, though not devoid of idealism, was exactly the sort of politician in whom T.J. had confidence. However, Butler faced great difficulties.

In September 1941, Churchill, who was determined to avoid controversial domestic issues in wartime, had vetoed a new Education Bill and told Butler to confine himself to administration. The President however had the utmost confidence in his own ability to chart a path through the party minefield and decided to go ahead. Much preliminary work had already been done by officials at the Board and Butler had the loyal support of his Parliamentary Secretary, Chuter Ede of the Labour party. Churchill, partly reassured by Butler, was prepared for the moment to indulge them, but nonetheless believed that Butler and Ede were merely 'squelching about in the mud'.[22] Butler persevered; much of the detail of his Bill was provided by able officers of the Board, but he alone had the political skill to reconcile the divergent ambitions of powerful interests such as the Anglican and Roman Catholic churches and progressive educational opinion. During 1944 the unity of the Churchill coalition government came under strain as post-war domestic issues loomed larger. Butler recognized that agreement between Conservative and Labour ministers was impossible on matters which involved 'property or the pocket'. This however opened the way for education. Butler carefully avoided any threat to the essential interests of the Conservative party: the autonomy of the public schools was safeguarded, and the churches were separately reassured about religious instruction and the protection of their special interests. The introduction of diversity and variety in secondary education and the raising of the school

    [21] T.J., Class D, Vol.5, No.128.
    [22] R.A. Butler, *The Art of the Possible* (1971), pp.94–6. Ede's Diary, 4 November 1942, quoted in K. Jefferys, 'R.A. Butler and the 1944 Act', *History*, Vol.69, p.424.

leaving age to fifteen, with sixteen as an immediately nominated future target, seemed to satisfy moderate reformist opinion. All that was needed to make the Bill acceptable, Butler observed cynically, was 'the dress of non-privilege and social equality'.[23]

In May 1944, when the Bill was going through Parliament, T.J. wrote at length to Butler outlining his ideas about the future of adult education.

> Most of us are agreed that there is a genuine need [T.J. said], not only for consideration of pre-war activities, but for a much bigger and wider conception of what the post-war situation demands in the way of adult education.
>
> The fruits of A.B.C.A. should be harvested in the early post-war years; new techniques of discussion, the use of documentary films and other visual aids . . . etc.

T.J. said that, initially, he had considered that 'a replica of C.E.M.A.' would serve as the co-ordinating agency, but on reflection he concluded that the controversies prompted by disagreement over music, art and drama were mild compared with the passions aroused by religion and economic and political ideas. Only 'very skilful piloting' had enabled ABCA to escape as well as it had from a stultifying hostility. It would, therefore, perhaps be wiser to set up a body less closely linked in its operation than CEMA was with the Board of Education or ABCA with the War Office. T.J. proposed that 'the national power house' for adult education should be a chartered body 'set up *ad hoc* ' without any attempt initially to secure the representation of existing agencies. Their co-operation would be invited and welcomed but the Council or Executive at the outset should be nominated by Butler alone. Thus firmly based above the ruck of existing rivalries the new body or institute should assume responsibility and be equipped for the training of tutors for the expected increase in the number of adult education classes, weekend and summer schools. It would make the fullest use of the facilities of Chatham House, the BIAE, the WEA, and the National Institute of Economic School Research, and maintain regular contact with Women's Institutes, Townswomen's Guilds, NALGO, and the proposed new body for the training of Civil Servants. The institute should have its own headquarters, perhaps a house in St James's Square. T.J. promised his best efforts to persuade 'the Pilgrim and other Trusts' to provide a substantial initial endowment of perhaps £100,000 'on the £ for £

---

[23] Cited in K. Jeffereys, loc.cit., pp.426–31.

basis with which C.E.M.A. was launched'. T.J. was nothing if not specific.[24]

R.A. Butler was impressed and agreed that much of the work proposed for the suggested 'clearing house' could hardly be undertaken 'without embarrassment' by a government department, or an organization closely linked to one. He pointed out however that T.J.'s scheme implied Exchequer money and that meant that a minister would have to be responsible for answering parliamentary questions relating to the institute. Butler suggested that the British Institute of Adult Education, although it had not achieved a powerful position in the past, might be the appropriate body to be entrusted with these wider responsibilities. T.J. replied that he had set aside the claims of the BIAE so as to avoid exciting the envy of other adult education bodies. He was certain that 'to promote the B.I.A.E. would arose fierce opposition on the part of the W.E.A.'. Jones conceded that, to avoid the problem of parliamentary responsibility, it might be as well for the moment to drop the pound-for-pound proposal. He regretted, too, that his plan for the future of adult education had 'leaked out'; the WEA was already preparing to fight for its vested interest.

> I think [he told Butler] we shall have to exploit the prestige you now enjoy if we are to persuade the Trusts. They have to be convinced that you deeply believe in the possibilities of expansion and are prepared to sponsor the setting-up of the clearing house by selecting its first personnel.

T.J. advised Butler to call publicly for the co-operation of 'all parties and bodies' and, privately, to seek the assistance of influential individuals such as G.D.H. Cole, Ernest Simon, Sir Richard Livingstone and the lively younger Directors of Education such as Jack Longland. Butler considered that T.J.'s arguments against the BIAE were 'conclusive', but he again stressed that the scheme would 'not get very far' without the assurance of the co-operation of existing bodies, and moreover its success would depend crucially on the appointment of the Director and Secretary. 'Unless we were confident that we had the right man in view, and that he could be obtained, I doubt whether any such scheme could be launched', Butler wrote. Discouragingly, he said that he could see no-one 'who could fill the bill'. W.E. Williams could probably not be released from his current work with ABCA and anyway did

---

[24] T.J., Class I, Vol.5, No.128.

not, as yet, 'sufficiently command' the confidence of the adult education world at large.[25]

It would appear that Butler was temporizing if not exactly stonewalling, a practice at which he was an acknowledged expert. T.J. replied three weeks later, offering further details of the range of responsibility he envisioned for the 'national power house', and a list of the names of people Butler might consider nominating to its Executive. But it was all idle. Butler had said in his letter of 3 July 1944 that he would resume the consultation after he had made further enquiries. They had an inconclusive discussion in October but T.J. heard no more from Butler directly. And almost a year elapsed before Sir Robert Wood, a senior official of the Board, wrote in March 1945 to say doubtfully that it was possible that 'something might emerge, though on rather different lines' from the scheme T.J. had suggested. 'There are no certainties in the situation just now', Wood concluded discouragingly.[26]

Two weeks later, of course, the war in Europe ended and there was a general election that ushered in an entirely different political situation. The 'chance without parallel or precedent' for a really big expansion of adult education on which T.J. had pinned his hopes had come and apparently gone. Butler was not devoid of good will, but his personal ambition and the Conservative party's interests were not caught up with adult education as they were with the general question of educational reform. He displayed nothing like the same ingenuity and tenacity of purpose in his consideration of the adult education question. Indeed the 1944 Act scarcely referred to it. As it was, enough had been done to blunt the sharp edge of demand for educational improvement, and the Labour government had other objectives, health, housing, the reform of the infrastructure and the recovery of lost export markets, to which it gave a higher priority. In 1946 a National Foundation of Adult Education was formed but it was short-lived. In 1949 it amalgamated with the BIAE to form the National Institute of Adult Education.[27]

It is not possible to say how much difference T.J.'s proposed scheme for adult education, if put into effect, would have made. He wanted a decisive lead from the minister to overcome once and for all the internal rivalries that for so long had sapped the energies of

[25] Ibid., Nos.130–4.

[26] T.J., Class V, Vol.2, No.144; Class D, Vol.5, No.157.

[27] Mary Stocks, *The Workers' Educational Association* (1953), pp.136–7. T.J., Class D, Vol.5, No.162, for T.J.'s statement to Lord Astor in July 1945 that 'Butler was unwilling to proceed', or at least had 'postponed' action on adult education.

the movement, as the preliminary to expansion and a national crusade to make adult education an effective force in the lives of many more people than formerly. In the event, little was changed and T.J.'s great, perhaps extravagant, hopes were sadly disappointed. 'The ministry', he wrote with profound disgust in June 1945, 'is very inept'.[28]

He also had to endure another disappointment at this time. In May 1943 Sir Richard Livingstone wrote to say that Lady Rhondda had told him in confidence that she was prepared to offer her eighteenth-century mansion Llanwern, near Newport in Monmouthshire, for use as a residential adult education college. Unfortunately, however, there would be no accompanying endowment; it was hoped that the National Trust would accept the house and let it at a peppercorn rent for educational purposes. Livingstone consulted only T.J. and Percy Watkins because, as he said, they were 'the natural people to consult'. Despite the financial difficulty, and uncertainty about the provisions of Butler's future Education Bill, T.J. believed this tentative offer 'must be taken seriously' because it could well fulfil one of his long-standing ambitions: 'a Coleg Harlech for South Wales'.[29]

T.J. set to work immediately. He called in several of his friends, the veteran 'key people': Watkins and B.B. Thomas, Archie Lush, who understood the 'mentality' of Monmouthshire County Council, and Mervyn Jones, son of the Revd Dick Jones, who was Deputy Town Clerk of Newport, a local authority that was also likely to be involved. It was a situation of great complexity. There were two major problems: finance and the establishment of a governing body acceptable to the interested parties. Not only was there no initial endowment, but it was by no means certain in 1943–44 that residential adult education colleges would receive government funding after the war. And T.J. knew that the Pilgrim Trust and most charitable foundations had hitherto refused anything more than limited assistance to the residential colleges. The only hope for the moment was money from the local authorities. Even T.J. quailed at the prospect of adding Llanwern to Coleg Harlech and the many other bodies for which he had been begging money wholesale for years.[30]

The establishment of some form of Trust to govern the prospective college was, if anything, even more difficult. Lady Rhondda, who was thought to be having second thoughts, was not

28 T.J., Class W, Vol.13, No.126.
29 T.J., Class D, Vol.7, Nos.134, 136 and 137; Class W, Vol.12, No.88.
30 T.J., Class D, Vol.7, Nos.139–159.

prepared to allow the County Council to control the Trust. Naturally, it had been suggested that the support of Glamorgan County Council was also necessary, but it was soon evident that each of the three local authorities involved was disposed, almost by instinct, to act like a dog in a manger. T.J. also hoped to get the support of the WEA and the University College at Cardiff, each of which also showed an imperialist temper on occasion. Finally, there was concern that Llanwern might be taken over by the Board of Education for use as an emergency college for training teachers.[31]

Despite the disheartening auguries, T.J. summoned a conference of his allies, including Livingstone of course, at Corpus Christi College, Oxford, on 10 December 1943. The tentative arrangements made for a governing body reflected T.J.'s view of the necessity of the broadest possible base of support. And similarly it was agreed that the projected college would serve as a centre for many varieties of educational and cultural activity, including drama, music and youth work. Indeed, the discussion indicated a refreshing willingness to experiment; it was agreed, for example, that Llanwern should be 'a prototype of something new', not simply or solely a 'second Coleg Harlech'. The sting, however, came in the tail. Although it was hoped some assistance might be given subsequently by the Carnegie and Cassel Trusts, it was recognized that without the financial support of the Board of Education in the form of a specific grant to the local authority for that purpose, there was no realistic hope of establishing Llanwern, currently in use by the army, as a residential college.[32]

Worse was to follow. Shortly afterwards, Mervyn Jones reported that the house was in a bad state of disrepair, so 'rat-ridden' as to cause 'even the Army to feel qualms of conscience' in billeting men there; and further enquiries suggested that at least £5,000 would have to be spent on renovations. There were other distractions: there was a possibility that Glamorgan would open its own residential college at Dyffryn; Lady Rhondda, who did not respond to Livingstone's letters, was being approached about other possible uses of the house. And despite the passage of the Education Bill in April 1944, it was by no means yet clear that government money would be forthcoming for residential colleges. Even T.J. could find no firm ground for hope of effective action in that quagmire of uncertainty. 'That, I am afraid, is as far as one can go at the moment', he wrote to Livingstone on 5 July 1944, pronouncing with regret the effective end of the

---

[31] Ibid., Nos.139–48.

[32] 'Account of the discussion at Corpus Christi College', ibid., Nos.148–9.

project.[33] T.J. was then almost seventy-four years old and had been unwell several times during the year. The Llanwern affair shows how much time and energy he was prepared to expend in pursuing even a forlorn hope of advancing the cause that was closest to his heart.

Moreover, it is to be remembered that, as always, Llanwern was only one of his current concerns. In a letter to Nancy Astor in December 1941, T.J. wrote:

> I travelled from High Wycombe with four cockney boys who had met for the first time at Paddington and were on their way to near Criccieth to be trained for the Navy. Their knowledge of geography and the sea was nil, so I played the man from Cooks and it was the quickest journey I've done for years. I had them singing *Land of my Fathers* before we got to Harlech.[34]

The young recruits were going to HMS *Glendower*, the Royal Navy's shore-based training establishment at Penychain near Pwllheli in Caernarfonshire. It had been built for the Admiralty by the entrepreneur W.E. (Billy) Butlin, a cheerful South African-born extrovert from a fairground background who was short on formal education but an honours graduate of the university of life.[35] In August 1943 T.J. picked up a rumour that, when the war was over, Butlin, whose contract with the government entitled him to buy the establishment back when it was no longer required by the Admiralty, planned to reopen it as a holiday camp. T.J. was 'furious'; he said that the prospect was enough to make him 'turn Nationalist', if only he could bring himself to believe that a Welsh parliament would be any more effective a defence than the inept county councils.[36] He was determined to do his utmost to block the scheme. He made a number of private protests to some of his friends in the Civil Service. He suggested to G.C.B. Dodds, Permanent Secretary of the Admiralty, that Butlin's plan would 'feed the hostility to England' which was 'being fanned by the Nationalists': he appealed to J.A. Barlow, a senior official at the Treasury, who replied that the Admiralty had no choice but to

[33] Ibid., Nos.152, 160 and 161. T.J., Class W, Vol.10, No.112; Vol.18, No.116.

[34] Astor MS. 1416/1/2/222.

[35] Rex North, *The Butlin Story* (Norwich, 1963), pp.2–20. 'I always think', Patrick Abercrombie said (T.J., Class H, Vol.16, No.15) speaking of Butlin, 'that people who are able to extract large sums out of the public are interesting: they are often quite simple folk'.

[36] T.J. to the Treasurer, 24 April 1943. Coleg Harlech MSS. T.J., Class T, Vol.7, No.89.

stand by the 'definite agreement' it had made with Butlin. T.J.
asked Wheldon of the Welsh Department of the Board of
Education to do what he could to 'arrest' the 'calamity', but
Wheldon considered it unwise to appear to deny working people
the right to enjoy holidays in pleasant surroundings. T.J.'s attempt
to prod some of the Welsh MPs into action was no more effective.[37]

Of course other people were also alarmed; one member of the
County Planning Committee solemnly confessed a fear that the
camp 'would be turned into a nudist colony'.[38] And a group of
people formed a Lleyn Defence Committee, of which T.J. became
President, to oppose Butlin. But there was little doubt, as T.J. was
obliged to concede, that the great majority of local people wanted
the holiday camp, 'and the bigger the better', because it meant
more employment and enhanced rateable values. Butlin asserted
that his scheme would mean a thousand jobs in the summer and
five hundred even in the winter months, a claim T.J. denounced as
a promise of 'El Dorado'. Butlin had also astutely engaged as his
adviser the distinguished local architect Clough Williams-Ellis,
President of the Council for the Preservation of Rural Wales, whom
T.J. had failed, in a verbal wrestling match, to persuade that it was
his aesthetic duty to defend Snowdonia from a commercial
despoiler. Williams-Ellis believed that, in an imperfect world, the
only sensible course was to accept 'a *fait accompli* ' and try to exact
the best possible conditions for the operation.[39]

Thus baulked pretty well all along the line locally, T.J. tried to
rouse public opinion nationally and arranged for some of his
friends in the Commons to exert pressure on the Admiralty by
means of parliamentary questions. On 5 December, at T.J.'s
instance, a leading article in the *Observer* attacked the Butlin
project, and at the same time T.J. wrote a special article setting out
the hostile view rather more trenchantly. He wanted to call the
piece 'The One and the Many', but Ivor Brown, the editor,
considered that title rather 'too metaphysical'. But much more
frustratingly, the Censor insisted that all references to the
Admiralty, to Wales or to Pwllheli should be deleted, which robbed
the article of much of its force. Thus amended, it appeared
prominently in the *Observer* on 9 January 1944 under the heading
'Multitude and Solitude'. The piece attracted a great deal of
attention, most of it supportive, as it was designed to do, but T.J.

[37] T.J., Class H, Vol.16, Nos.3–24; Class T, Vol.7, No.92.
[38] *North Wales Observer*, 1 October 1943.
[39] T.J., Class T, Vol.7, Nos.92 and 93; Class H, Vol.16, No.107. *Liverpool Daily Post*, 25 February 1944.

was not in fact at his most persuasive. He insisted that Butlin, a profiteer trafficking in beautiful coastline, was despoiling, indeed raping, Snowdonia, which 'was not his spiritual home'. Why, he asked, could not Butlin confine his lucrative purveying to the 'tumultuous throng' to Rhyl, Skegness or Clacton, which had already been ruined, and leave the Lleyn coastline to those who sought their holidays in 'solitary ways and sessions of sweet silent thought'? He insisted that this was not a matter for the Parish or County Council, or even just for Wales: it was the concern of everyone. 'It is Snowdonia today. Yesterday it was Windermere: tomorrow it may be the Trossacks. A defeat in one place', T.J. declared ringingly, 'may encourage general spoliation'.

Two weeks later a 'Rejoinder' under Butlin's name, but probably written by another (possibly A.J. Cummings of the *News Chronicle*), appeared. It was an effective polemical piece that attacked T.J. at his weakest point: namely, that for all his lofty sentiment, his was essentially an élitist argument laced with aesthetic snobbery.

> Should the enjoyment of beauty [the 'Rejoinder' asked] be accepted as the prerogative of any one class of citizen? Or should a nation's treasure chest be accessible to all? . . . How is this 'tumultuous mob' [that Dr Jones fears] to be kept out? By the police? By travel permits? By rationing?

Butlin said that ten out of twelve local authorities had voted in favour of his project, which was twenty (in fact it was sixteen) miles from Snowdon. In good populist terms he claimed that the so-called 'tumultuous throng' that T.J. wanted to exclude included men who had 'fought through Hell from Alamein to Italy'.[40]

Soon afterwards, C.E.M. Joad, a philosopher who set up at this time as a dispenser of truth to the masses, violently attacked T.J. in the Press, and the BBC considered inviting the two to debate the subject on the wireless.[41]

T.J.'s parliamentary allies, W.W. Astor, W.J. Gruffydd and others, did not make much headway. They elicited the fact that the camp had cost £660,000 to build, but the government refused to disclose the price at which it was to be sold. T.J. was convinced that Lord Beaverbrook, who always loomed large in his gallery of villains, had done a shady 'deal' with Butlin when he was the Minister of Supply. The Admiralty steadily maintained that Butlin's camp had served a

[40] *Observer*, 23 January 1944. T.J., Add MSS, HH, Vol.5, No.19, for Cummings's alleged authorship.
[41] BBC Archive, WAC R 34/473/1.

vital wartime need, it could be put to a useful purpose after the war, and the government had acted prudently in recovering a portion of the original cost.[42]

T.J. and his allies cast about rather desperately for alternative uses for the camp. He tried to stir up Ifan ab Owen Edwards to claim it for use by the Urdd, the Welsh League of Youth, but the camp was much too large for any of their purposes. He put forward the suggestion that it should be used as a government rehabilitation centre for disabled servicemen, but a friendly Welsh mole in the Ministry of Labour reported that the site was considered to be too remote from large centres of population for that purpose. One sympathetic friend even suggested that T.J., who was a member of the Ancient Monuments Commission for Wales, should conveniently 'find' some venerable stone on the site that could not possibly be disturbed. An attempt by the Lleyn Defence Committee to persuade a public inquiry to reverse the decision in favour of the scheme was defeated, and T.J. was bitterly attacked as one who had spent his life making money in England and now, in retirement in Wales, wished 'to prevent the poor enjoying Snowdonia'.[43]

T.J. recognized early on that he was unlikely to succeed; Butlin had a watertight contract in his pocket and nothing could gainsay that. Indeed, Jones admitted that his *Observer* article was just an expression of 'impotent rage'. In fact, the Penychain site was hardly the priceless beauty spot that he claimed it to be. On the contrary, it was one of the least naturally attractive portions of the Lleyn coastline and its development along the lines envisioned by Butlin scarcely amounted to desecration of Snowdonia. Moreover, T.J. certainly did not give sufficient weight to the fact that the scheme would undoubtedly provide a great deal of local employment, a powerful argument when memories of the pre-war years were still strong. T.J. and the Defence Committee fought a rearguard action until 1946 but ultimately Butlin opened his camp which served as a popular amenity for many years. T.J. had no regrets: he saw this as one lost battle in a long campaign. He had fought strenuously to defend the environment from man-made damage all his adult life. Twenty years before he had tried in vain to persuade his rich friends to buy up twenty miles of the magnificent Pembrokeshire coast to save it from depredation for profit. He now looked to an aroused public opinion to protect the national heritage, although he realized that only a minority cared deeply and actively about the beauty of the landscape. He was determined to do all that he could

[42] T.J., Class H, Vol.16, Nos.80–114; Class T, Vol.7, No.94.
[43] T.J., Class H, Vol.16, Nos.43, 124, 131, 153; Class T, Vol.7, Nos.10, 122.

to enlarge what he called this 'resistance movement' against commercial despoliation of the countryside. As he said of his attempt to thwart Billy Butlin: 'the Educational aspect of the agitation has from the start been of great value'.[44]

Of course T.J.'s work at the Pilgrim Trust also provided a powerful buttress to the defence of the nation's heritage. Despite wartime restrictions on building, and their expenditure on social work and comforts for the Services, the Trustees also spent over £400,000 during the first three years of the war on the preservation of the countryside, the churches and other national monuments.[45] Two of the original Trustees, Lord Tweedsmuir (John Buchan) and Lord Stamp, had died and T.J. felt that Lord Greene, the Master of the Rolls, who was recruited to the Trust in 1941, was, perhaps not surprisingly, too 'legalistic' in his attitude to the requests for aid that came before them. 'Added to Macmillan' (who was a Lord of Appeal), T.J. wrote in 1942, 'he tends to outweigh the more humane bias of the others'.[46] And even before Greene's arrival, with Baldwin absent ill on one occasion, T.J. was disappointed that, despite his vigorous support, Kurt Hahn's appeal for help for a County Badge scheme at Gordonstoun school was rejected by the Trustees.[47] T.J. also began to fear that the Trust's customary support for the Settlements in south Wales and elsewhere was in jeopardy. 'I think when I quit the Secretaryship', he wrote in 1944, 'the Trustees will curtail the grants to the various "social" agencies', although he was prepared to admit that, in the past, he had 'perhaps unduly pressed them'. For some time T.J. had felt that the Trustees and its Secretary were 'all far too old', and ought to bring in some younger members. He himself had repeatedly offered to resign, but the Trustees were unwilling to lose the man the Chairman, Macmillan, addressed as 'my dear and indispensable T.J.'[48]

Indeed, although eventually it was reluctantly agreed that T.J. would step down as Secretary as soon as the war was over, it was also decided that thereupon he would become a Trustee. During 1943 T.J. began casting about for his successor. L.F. Ellis, of the National Council of Social Service, was mentioned, but he was thought to be

---

[44] T.J., Class W, Vol.10, No.110; Class H, Vol.16, No.230. T.J., 'Green on the Map: The National Trust', *Observer*, 2 September 1945.

[45] P.T. *Report* (1943), p.2.

[46] T.J., Class T, Vol.7, No.69.

[47] Ibid., No.39. T.J., Class M, Vol.4, No.7.

[48] T.J., Class X, Vol.10, No.106; Class T, Vol.7, No.126; Class S, Vol.3, Nos.32 and 33; Class W, Vol.13, No.140.

'too earnest. The job is earnest', Lord Macmillan said, 'and we don't want the Secretary too earnest. Must have a lighter touch with people than Ellis has'.[49] One seemingly obvious candidate, who might have been expected to have had T.J.'s enthusiastic support, was W.E. Williams of ABCA, who was in fact strongly attracted to the post and apprised T.J. of his interest in February 1944.

> In more ways than journalistic [Williams wrote], I have served an apprenticeship to you, and I now consider myself a journeyman in your trade . . . I have a good knowledge of the geography of the region the Pilgrim Trust serves . . . my contacts are considerable and varied . . .
> . . . I have been brought up frugally. . . . I should not be captivated by South Sea Bubbles. As a hardened poacher of Trust funds, I ought to prove an implacable gamekeeper. . . . I have no experience of the mystery of finance and investment [but] I want to be considered . . . I so deeply admire the way you have wielded the P.T. that I would like a shot at it some day. It is perhaps the temerity of the novice contemplating the bow of Ulysses.[50]

Williams's qualifications for the secretaryship really were incontestable, but, as T.J. wrote a year later: 'I have other, bigger ideas for W.E.W. which may come off'. T.J. wanted to reserve Williams for the biggest job on offer in adult education in the post-war world.[51]

In the end, after much careful searching, the secretaryship went in October 1945 to Colonel J.F.A. Browne, son of the Irish peer Lord Kilmaine, who had at one time been Secretary of the Oxford Society. At the same time T.J. became a Pilgrim Trustee; he had mixed feelings about the change. He was nearly seventy-five years of age and felt it was high time he retired from the secretaryship but, as he said, 'it is such a delightful job under such good employers that I wish I were sixty and starting all over again'. Eloquent tributes were paid to his fifteen years of service. The Pilgrim Trust had been established to promote and preserve the spiritual and material heritage of the land. For such a purpose, T.J. was ideally equipped: as he showed, he had a good head and a warm heart, judgement and imagination in almost perfect balance; his catholic interests and broad social sympathies made him welcome almost everywhere. During his tenure the Pilgrim Trust had become a model foundation universally admired, and T.J., who more than anyone else had moulded it, was the embodiment of its magnificent

[49] T.J., Class X, Vol.10, No.134.
[50] T.J., Class T, Vol.20, No.112.
[51] T.J., Class T, Vol.6, No.137.

fulfilment of the generous intentions of the founder Edward
Harkness.[52]

Almost the last thing T.J. did as Secretary was to find temporary
premises at 1 Lowther Gardens, enabling the Pilgrim Trust office to
return to London. T.J. was to continue to serve in one guise or
other for another nine years, but inevitably the Trust now took up
less of his time. Some of his closest friends were concerned at the
effect his retirement would have on his personal circumstances.

Violet Markham, so often opinionated and occasionally a
tiresome busybody, nevertheless cared deeply about T.J. and set
about providing practical help for him in his altered situation.

> T.J. spent a week with me recently in Kent [she wrote to David Astor
> in September 1945] and I am troubled about his circumstances on
> retirement from the Pilgrim Trust. He has two pensions which amount
> to about £1,000 a year: that means of course a net income of £500. He
> has I believe no other assets except the house in Thanet and there are
> family obligations, to which the recent death of his brother-in-law Mr.
> Mackenzie . . . has added.
>
> Meanwhile, T.J.'s large correspondence goes on . . . For the first
> time in years he will have to struggle with letters single handed without
> an office staff behind him.
>
> You know as well as I do T.J.'s views about the simple life and he
> would never wish to live on other than a modest footing. But his health
> is frail and he ought to have some help with his work. Clearly, on a net
> income of £500 a year he can't afford a secretary. It had occurred to
> me that, without a wound to his pride, a few of his intimate friends
> might ask him to let us provide him with a secretary . . . I wrote to your
> father, who replied in a most kind and encouraging way, quite
> approving the idea . . . Your father has generously consented to give
> £100 a year for the purpose; I will do the same. I have written to Miss
> Gwen Davies . . . T.J. is seventy-five this month and indifferent though
> he is to luxury, the information I've pieced together . . . left me really
> disturbed as to the straitened cares of his day to day existence.

Lord Astor had also arranged to pay T.J. a small salary (£300) for
his work for the *Observer* and pay his first class rail fares to
London.[53]

David Astor's reply was characteristically generous.

> I am so glad that you have made these inquiries . . . and taken the

---

[52] T.J., Class T, Vol.7, No.137. PT *Report* (1945), p.2. During his secretaryship,
the Trust had spent £1.5 million and kept its capital intact.

[53] 10 September 1945. D. Astor MSS.

initiative in getting his needs met. Please remember that I will always be very pleased to do anything I can to help T.J. in any way.[54]

Gwen Davies of Gregynog of course was similarly responsive. The 'T.J. Protection Fund', as it was called, came into existence in the autumn of 1945. However, it was quite another matter to persuade, indeed ultimately to bully, T.J. into drawing upon it.

> The Hon. Treasurer and Hon. Secretary having met and gone through your accounts can make nothing of your goings on. [Violet Markham, after repeated vain urgings, wrote to T.J. in April 1947] . . . You have only spent £10 since the end of December and there is a balance of £560 aching to be spent. For the 20th time, how about that radio?'[55]

In 1949 he was at last cajoled into making fuller use of the fund, but as the balance sheet for the year showed, even then only half of the sum available had been spent, most of it on postage and secretarial assistance during the writing of his biography of Lloyd George.[56] It was not really until the last year of his life, when he was ailing and feeble, and for a time under the immediate supervision of Violet Markham, that the fund was fully used. The episode is revealing. T.J., who had spent such large sums of other people's money and for years had dispensed huge Trust funds, who numbered half a dozen millionaires amongst his close friends, any one of whom doubtless would, at the merest hint, have put him in the way of accumulating a useful sum of money, cared little or nothing about his own financial circumstances and was obviously reluctant even to accept small-scale assistance for taxis, notepaper and postage stamps. Where money, or at any rate money-making, was concerned, T.J. was certainly a sea-green incorruptible.

His magical power to extract money from the rich for good causes remained unsurpassed. But he hoped that, at least where Coleg Harlech was concerned, there would be rather less need for that in future. He was convinced that there would be 'a big advance in the work for which Coleg Harlech stands after the war' and he considered that the government ought to provide two-thirds of the cost of running adult education colleges.[57] T.J. did his best, in person and on paper, to impress the Board of Education with the strength of their case, but the Ministry, as one of its leading officials admitted, was 'in a bit of a ferment' over the new regulations

[54] 10 October 1945. Ibid.
[55] T.J., Class T, Vol.3, No.78; Vol.4, Nos.46 and 47.
[56] T.J., Protection Fund Account. 1 January–31 December 1949. D. Astor MSS.
[57] T.J., Class W, Vol.12, No.143; Class I, Vol.6, No.73.

relating to schools and quite unable to come to a firm decision about the residential colleges. But it was clear from the terms of the 1944 Education Act that, in future, local authorities would be increasingly important in the administration of education including that relating to adults. Percy Watkins, who had several years' experience of the empire-building tyranny of party-caucus-dominated local authorities in south Wales, was thoroughly dismayed. 'I cannot see the millenium coming along these lines' he observed to T.J., who shared his opinion.[58] However, Jones had anticipated the outcome of the Education Act and during 1944 he and B.B. Thomas, who still operated in his spare time as Honorary Warden of Coleg Harlech, arranged several meetings with influential Directors of Education of the Welsh counties in a sustained campaign to win their good will.[59] T.J. did not believe that the introduction of county colleges, talked of at this time, would undermine Coleg Harlech. On the contrary, he believed they would lead the better students on to 'more serious' study there.[60]

And T.J. was also convinced that after the war there would be an 'abounding harvest' of young working-class ex-servicemen whose interest had been 'wakened by travel and war'; it was high time, too, that Harlech opened its doors to women students.[61] T.J. began to look around for premises nearby which could be used to expand the College and provide accommodation for women. With the agreement of the Management Committee he secured options on two adjoining houses, Islwyn and Dros-y-Mor, and, characteristically, by the time the transactions were nearing completion, had produced a handsome donation covering the cost from Gwen Davies of Gregynog, who insisted on remaining anonymous.[62]

It was obvious that ABCA was in no hurry to vacate Coleg Harlech. T.J. was to discover that it was easier to invite in an army (even its less overtly military section) than persuade it to withdraw. Meanwhile, as he said, it was necessary to 'rejuvenate the College executive' and find a new Warden and Treasurer. T.J. also insisted that he would have to give up the chairmanship. 'I *must* resign', he told B.B. Thomas in June 1945, 'I am drawing heavily on my physical resources daily and unless I cut a number of things I'll crack up'. He vetoed the suggestion that his daughter Eirene

---

[58] Ibid., No.7. T.J., Class W, Vol.18, No.116; Class V, Vol.2, No.143.

[59] T.J., Class V, Vol.12, Nos.214 and 225; Class X, Vol.10, No.135.

[60] T.J., Class K, Vol.12, No.206.

[61] T.J., Class T, Vol.7, No.118; Class K, Vol.12, No.206.

[62] T.J., Class T, Vol.7, No.121; Class K, Vol.12, Nos.176, 187, 199, 240, 264; Class W, Vol.6, No.268.

should become Treasurer. 'That only continues the "Jones" link, of which there has been enough and perhaps too much'. On the other hand, he would 'welcome' her appointment as a member of the Council.[63]

T.J. had been resigned for some time to Harlech's loss of B.B. Thomas, who he had hoped one day would become Principal at Aberystwyth. But Ifor L. Evans the incumbent there was a young man and T.J. had begun to look elsewhere some time before. Looking ahead as usual, in discussions with R.A. Butler three years earlier, T.J. had 'commended' B.B. Thomas as the 'outstanding' candidate to replace Sir Wynn Wheldon when the time came for him to retire as Permanent Secretary of the Welsh Department of the Board of Education. There were apparently some officials at the Board who felt that T.J.'s virtually established 'right to nominate' should be challenged on this occasion and Thomas was told that T.J.'s support was not considered 'a bull point' in his favour in all quarters. But the more senior Civil Servants evidently disagreed and Richard Law, who had succeeded R.A. Butler, decided to follow T.J.'s recommendation and simply sought confirmation that his opinion was unchanged. T.J.'s response was a wholehearted eulogy of his protégé, the man who had become almost an honorary son.

He has grown in wisdom with the years [T.J. wrote] and unites a number of gifts. He is . . . an industrious scholar . . . a first rate administrator . . . a good public speaker . . . He knows all Wales . . . all these qualities are fused in an attractive balanced character.[64]

B.B. Thomas was of course appointed to the post. In September 1945 T.J. and Percy Watkins resigned as Chairman and Vice-Chairman respectively of Coleg Harlech, and it was also necessary to appoint a new Treasurer and a replacement for one of the three Honorary Secretaries.

So ends the first Harlech dynasty [T.J. said] and the curtain rises on the new reign. It has been an association full of happiness for me, having had the luck at the start to pick excellent colleagues on Executive and staff.

[63] T.J., Class D, Vol.6, No.117; Class K, Vol.15, No.18. NLW, B.B. Thomas MSS, 6 June 1945.

[64] T.J., Class W, Vol.18, Nos.121, 122, 127 and 128. T.J.'s continuing influence in patronage appointments generally is exemplified by a comment made by Sir David Schuster of the Lord Chancellor's Office in a letter to T.J. in May 1943 (Class W, Vol.12, No.206): 'In any event, anyone you recommend must necessarily receive most careful consideration.'

And with legitimate pride celebrating a truly remarkable achievement, he added: 'and it has been left solvent'.[65]

Happily, Wheldon, now free of official duties, whose managerial skill was incontestable, was prepared to succeed T.J. as Chairman, but the search for a new Warden was more difficult. T.J. was disappointed at first at the quality of likely candidates; 'they belong', he told Flexner, 'to what I call the B++ class, and none possesses that extra distinction of personality needed for such an unconventional institution.' Archie Lush commented gloomily from south Wales that he could 'not see a second B.B. [Thomas] amongst them'.[66] But in fact they were unduly pessimistic. I.D. Harry, the man eventually chosen, if not quite Thomas's equal in personal terms, was in some respects better equipped to meet the challenge of the post-war years. There was no large increase in government funding of the College after the war, and although T.J.'s past endeavours had provided an invaluable cushion of private endowment from the Astor and Gregynog families, it was apparent that, in future, the College would have to look to local authorities and the Labour movement in south Wales for additional support.[67] I.D. Harry had powerful links in these circles. Not the least of his virtues was that he had the vigorous support of the immensely influential Councillor Llewellyn Heycock of Glamorgan, who stressed the fact that Harry's appointment might very well encourage the trade unions in south Wales to take a much greater interest in the College.[68] Valuable as this was, Harry showed during the fourteen years of a successful wardenship that he had considerable merits in his own right, as T.J. came to realize. Although he had resigned as Chairman, T.J.'s close connection with the College remained, for despite his age and demanding duties as President of the College at Aberystwyth, he could not withstand the insistence of Wheldon, B.B. Thomas and others that he should accept the presidency of Coleg Harlech in 1946 in succession to Lord Sankey. At the same time, trying desperately to contain the legion of his commitments, T.J. refused the offer of the presidency of the prestigious Honourable Society of Cymmrodorion.[69] In the autumn of 1946 Coleg Harlech reopened with 9 students and in the following years numbers rose to over 80 in 1949, and, from 1949 onwards, included women

[65] T.J., Class T, Vol.7, No.152; Class V, Vol.2, No.148.
[66] T.J., Class S, Vol.3, No.68; Class K, Vol.15, No.53.
[67] P. Stead, *Coleg Harlech. The First Fifty Years* (Cardiff, 1977), pp.88–9.
[68] T.J., Class KK, Vol.3, No.59.
[69] T.J., Class T, Vol.8, No.33.

students, housed in the new hostel that T.J.'s fund-raising had financed.[70]

But despite his continuing energy in that respect, T.J. began to feel the burden of his years at this time. 'I'm less and less equal to things and problems', he admitted to David Astor in March 1945. 'Signs of old age and decay of body rapidly multiplying now'. A 'stupid accident' in the home a year later gloomily convinced him, for the moment at least, that he was 'moving towards the helpless age'.[71] And he had been deeply grieved by the death in May 1946 of Sir Percy Watkins, his most active Welsh lieutenant, a frank, open man, who was neither 'aggressive nor . . . obsequious'. T.J. recalled with justifiable pride that they 'had worked closely together for nearly half a lifetime in all sorts of movements in Wales, never having a serious difference'.[72]

Sadly, however, in recent years his admiration for Lloyd George, at one time almost unbounded, had been severely qualified. T.J. found it hard to forgive L.G. for his refusal to join Churchill's government, or even lend the weight of his prestige to its support in 1940–1. Regaled by A.J. Sylvester with the details of bitter family squabbles preceding Lloyd George's second marriage to his former secretary Frances Stevenson, T.J. concluded that it 'would need a Balzac to do justice to the daily happenings' in that household in recent months. It was 'a big fall from the "full meridian of his glory", a sordid anti-climax . . . ending in the village where he began his amazing career'. T.J. could not bring himself to congratulate L.G. on his marriage, not least because he had so much admired Dame Margaret, L.G.'s first wife, for her 'dignified silence through twenty years of humiliation'.[73] And T.J. was 'very sick' that Lloyd George accepted a peerage.

> I want to tell you how disappointed I am that L.G. has taken the earldom [T.J. wrote to Violet Markham in January 1945]. I did think he would remain a Commoner . . . The *Guardian* puts it rightly. 'No one deserved it more: no one needed it less' . . . S.B.'s [Baldwin's] acceptance [of an earldom] was a disappointment to me, having built himself up as the plain man. Please don't become a Dame. I'm almost sorry I became a C.H.[74]

[70] *Twenty-First Annual Report* (1948), pp.9–20.

[71] D. Astor MSS, 3 March 1948. Bangor MS 16191.

[72] T.J., 'Sir Percy Watkins 1871–1946', BBC broadcast obituary, 5 May 1946. T.J., Class Y, Vol.5, No.15; Class T, Vol.8, No.12.

[73] T.J., Class A, Vol.I, No.50; Class Y, Vol.2, No.2; Class T, Vol.7, Nos.131 and 135.

[74] T.J., Class W, Vol.15, No.161; Class T, Vol.7, No.129.

It was suggested that L.G. had been pushed to accept a peerage by his new wife's ambition, but T.J. discovered from Sylvester that that was not so. 'He wanted the Earldom as much as Frances did', T.J. told Violet Markham. Lloyd George 'could not face another election but the thought of being neither in the Commons nor the Lords was most unpalatable for his voracious appetite [as Sylvester put it] so he emphatically wanted the honour no less than she did'.[75]

T.J.'s obituary notice of Lloyd George, transmitted by the BBC on 26 March 1945, prompted some anger in the family. William George considered it 'a somewhat cold and critical résumé of his brother's life and achievements', and Violet Markham too thought that T.J. had allowed some of the disappointment in Lloyd George that he had felt in recent years to surface in the talk. T.J. was unrepentant. He conceded that other people agreed with Violet Markham's opinion, but pointed out that the distinguished historian G.P. Gooch and Salvador de Madariaga, a life-long admirer of L.G., considered it 'just'.[76] While not fulsome in any way, T.J.'s notice insisted that Lloyd George's astonishing array of gifts amounted to genius. Maynard Keynes, who had accused him of 'being rooted in nothing', had overlooked the 'indestructible' influence over him of his native land. 'Idealist and moralist', L.G. was 'always true to an inner subtle self, inaccessible to the most familiar friends'. T.J.'s account in the *Observer,* 'L.G.: The Man I Remember', was also considered too 'Olympian' by the editor initially, so some personal detail was added to give it warmth and colour.[77] T.J. may well at that time have recalled their happier days together on Sunday mornings at Churt when, listening to a chapel service in Welsh on the wireless, they instinctively stood up side by side to give full voice to the beloved hymns. A classic occasion when north and south Wales were happily in complete harmony.

T.J. persuaded himself that 'now that one has the freedom of history', it was possible to be completely 'detached' in writing about Lloyd George, a consideration that had influenced his decision to accept the invitation from Harvard University Press to write L.G.'s

    [75] Ibid., No.135.

    [76] William George, *My Brother and I* (1958), p.295. T.J., Class T, Vol.3, No.55; Vol.7, No.140. On the other hand, it is doubtful if Carey Evans, Lloyd George's son-in-law, was upset. In 1943, according to Sylvester *(Diary,* p.315), he said of his father-in-law: 'I cannot get on with that old bugger . . . He is not a man's man you know.'

    [77] *The Listener,* March 1945. *Observer,* 1 April 1948. See also 'Lloyd George: some personal memories', *The Contemporary Review,* May 1948, pp.260–4.

life.[78] He asked to see Frances Lloyd-George, who said that it would be 'a great pleasure' to see him, adding, a shade tartly, that 'it would have been a pleasure for L.G. also to have seen him during his last days'. They went amicably enough together to see L.G.'s grave in its impressive simplicity nearby, but T.J.'s request for help with his projected book was flatly refused in a letter from Frances the next day:

> I do not feel very happy about the book which you say you are proposing to write on L.G. for the following reasons [she wrote].
> 1. It cuts right across the book for which I am negotiating on the suggestion and advice of Arthur Brown, which would also, I imagine, have a large American sale, and which I would personally supervise, providing of course new material and all the necessary documents . . .
> 2. Any new biography of L.G. must, by his own special request, deal with the Social Legislation enacted by his Coalition Government . . . and particularly also with the schemes for Social Improvement which he drew up after he left office, and with his attitude upon Foreign Policy in the years preceding the war. During those latter years you were engaged in serving his political opponents, whose chief aim, at whatever cost to the country's welfare, was to keep L.G. out of office.
> Quite frankly, therefore, I do not think, if you will pardon my saying so, that you would be the best biographer of this period. . . . I am sure you will understand that under the circumstances it would be difficult for me to give you any help or material for your book.

T.J.'s attempt during their meeting to 'interpret' Baldwin's actions had simply provoked her to furious anger. T.J. wished her every success with the book she intended to 'supervise' or, given the attitude revealed in her letter, it might be said, probably censor line by line. 'L.G.', T.J. wrote in his reply, 'is big enough to have many more books written about him without exhausting the subject', and, stung to his own defence, he added:

> I am only too conscious of my imperfections as a possible student of any period of L.G.'s life, but perhaps I can say with complete truth that in serving his political opponents, I did not entirely forget that I had served him. Indeed, the charge against me as a Civil Servant might well be that I carried old loyalty to him to extreme lengths.[79]

At any rate, his life of L.G. would have to be written without the benefit of any advice from Frances Lloyd-George or use of the

[78] T.J., Class T, Vol.7, No.140.
[79] T.J., Class A, Vol.I, Nos.69–71; Class S, Vol.3, No.61. *A Diary with Letters*, pp.534–5.

papers in her possession. Later that year T.J. spent a happy evening
at dinner with Megan Lloyd George, for whom he had a 'warm
corner' in his heart. Megan heartily approved of T.J.'s intention to
write a life of her father and was most willing to help, but the only
manuscripts she had were some notes L.G. had made for his
speeches and, as Megan said ruefully, 'blessed is he who can read
them in the original'. Despite her genuine eagerness to help, T.J.
came to the conclusion, after another conversation with her in
1947, that there were obvious limits to the value of Megan's
assistance. For it was clear that 'Nothing approaching the truth'
about L.G. 'could be expected to please her'. T.J. decided therefore
not to consult Lloyd George's children about the book on the
plausible ground, as he told Megan's sister Olwen, 'that you may
truthfully say when it appears that none of you has any
responsibility for what I have written'. But of course the fact of their
existence meant that he had 'to write under some restraint'.[80]

Over the next five years work on the Lloyd George book took up
a great deal of T.J.'s time and attention. He set out to make 'a
judicial attempt at interpreting a genius' without access to private
papers or official documents, other than those already in print or
in public libraries. He did however have the benefit of several
valuable short memoranda written for him by people who had
worked with Lloyd George or had specialist knowledge of particular
episodes, such as Waldorf Astor and the distinguished French
historian Paul Mantoux.[81] There was also the fact, of which Jones
was reminded by officialdom in 1946, that he was bound by the
established constraints on the freedom of former Civil Servants to
publish.[82] Other difficulties became apparent in the course of his
work. He had naturally intended to make the fullest use of his
personal knowledge of Lloyd George, but the publication of A.J.
Sylvester's *The Real Lloyd George* in 1947 put a bridle on that. 'I had
such a revulsion reading Sylvester on Sylvester', T.J. told Violet
Markham, 'that I've determined mine should not be T.J. on T.J.'.
He began to be aware also that he had to be permanently on guard

    [80] T.J., Class A, Vol.I, Nos.72, 83–4, Vol.2, No.25; Class T, Vol.7, Nos.131 and
154; Vol.8, Nos.68 and 69. In 1947 T.J., trying to allay future disappointment, told
Megan Lloyd George that the objectivity of his book would inevitably 'deeply
disappoint the family', but found that he 'made little or no impression' on her.
    [81] T.J., Add MSS, Vol.I, No.138; T.J., Class A, Vol.2, Nos.25–46. There was
occasionally some light relief. J.L. Hammond passed on a story that on the eve of
the publication of a Lloyd George honours list one down to be named owned up
that he had 'been in quod'. 'Oh', came the reply, presumably from Sir William
Sutherland, 'that means another £10,000.'
    [82] Ibid., Vol.1, No.74; Vol.2, No.25.

against powerful personal prejudice. He recalled that, despite repeated pleas, Lloyd George had always refused to subscribe to Coleg Harlech; indeed, T.J. wrote, the 'L.G. family' was 'notorious for giving nothing to anything or anybody'. He admitted that, on that point, he was 'much too prejudiced' to be fair.[83]

Of course, T.J. had not hitherto attempted an historical study on this scale and he found the difficulties daunting. 'I've reached the stage,' he confessed in 1948, 'when I think the L.G. book is just rotten, or ought to be completely re-written. . . . I had no business to attempt it'. He was only too well aware of 'a great decline' in his power of work and, even without manuscript sources, the volume of printed material he had to master was crushing. 'I try to read 50 books at once in an effort to keep track of the elusive L.G.', he wrote in 1946. On reflection, he wished he had made 'the other choice': that is, written a life of Stanley Baldwin; or at least had begun work on a biography of Lloyd George in 1930 when he retired from the Civil Service and still had 'surplus energy'.[84]

In the summer of 1948 his draft of the book, 170,000 words in all, went off to the American publishers. The report on it, by a Harvard historian given to condescension, was favourable, but suggested, doubtless reflecting a congenital American impatience with failure, that the last third of the book, which covered the years after 1922 when L.G. was out of office, should be severely cut. However important it was in understanding Lloyd George, the American reader, the report said, could hardly be expected to be 'excited' by it. Wearily, T.J. set about the excision, which was finished by Christmas. He sent in his final script 'reluctantly'. He would have liked to have rewritten it completely but, given all his other commitments, felt 'unequal to it at 79'.[85]

But at least he had thoroughly enjoyed working daily at the National Library in Aberystwyth, where Wales and learning, both of which he dearly loved, came together. He was a familiar figure in the small town, habitually clad in either a grey or a fawn cloak and a battered deerstalker. For a time his unmarried sister, Liz, kept house for him and, after she died, he was looked after by a housekeeper. In 1949 the household also included Marlene, an eighteen-year-old German girl, sister of Annelie Wiener, the future second wife of T.J.'s son Tristan. In typical T.J. fashion, Marlene had

[83] T.J., Class T, Vol.8, Nos.83 and 89.

[84] Ibid., Nos.8 and 104; Class S, Vol.3, Nos.81 and 86; Class A, Vol.7, No.59; Class X, Vol.10, No.139.

[85] Report to Havard University Press, 18 August 1948. T.J., Class A, Vol.1, No.80; Class W, Vol.7, No.158. The book was published simultaneously in the USA and Britain in 1951.

been brought over from war-torn eastern Germany and enrolled, at his expense initially, as a student at the University College at Aberystwyth. She was of course expected to work hard at her studies. 'If I said it wasn't worth doing anything between lectures and lunch', Marlene wrote later, 'he used to tell me it was *always* worth doing something while waiting for something else'. He plied her with books: Trollope, Mrs Gaskell, poetry, Constant Lambert on musical appreciation; he always 'regretted never having learnt to enjoy music properly'. When the housekeeper was away, Marlene made T.J.'s morning tea: 'he used to rouse me at seven, by ringing his Swiss cowbell very loudly and, if necessary, repeatedly, and he was grumpy if I was late'. But that aside, Marlene was astonished by his patience, the genuine interest he took in her and her student friends, male and female, and his willingness to listen to their opinions. 'He always had lots of time to talk. He constantly puts me to shame with his youthful enthusiasm for modern progress.' Once or twice Marlene was ruffled when T.J. made arrangements for her and simply assumed her agreement, but her overwhelming memory was of his kindness and thoughtfulness. In fact, she worshipped him. 'T.J. is lovely', she wrote in 1949; three years later, he had become 'the loveliest person in the world'.[86]

Indeed, few women of any age could resist the fascination of his mind and personality, and the gentleness of his nature, although Marlene Wiener noted that he was also on occasion a shade 'callous' towards the more tiresome of the many ladies who doted on him. 'It used to embarrass me', she said, 'but also flatter me because he treated me as an accomplice with his characteristic wink'. But T.J. was never offhand with Lady Astor's niece Joyce Grenfell. She first met T.J. when she was a child. 'He was years older than I was', she wrote later, 'but it never mattered; there is never an age gap in such friendships'. Joyce Grenfell, who could sometimes be waspish about people, was unrestrained in her feeling for T.J. 'How I dote on that man', she told her mother in 1938. 'He has opened up so much for me; in fact I owe him more than any other human being on earth. Through him I've met and made a whole new world of friends. I am one of dozens who had a "special" relationship with him', she said in 1936, 'and somehow he had time for us all'.[87]

[86] Unpublished memoir of T.J. by Mrs Marlene Yeo (née Wiener). Ruth Evans, the Principal's wife, considered that her friend Marlene could not possibly have overcome her difficulties and completed her degree course without T.J.'s steady support.
[87] Joyce Grenfell, *Requests the Pleasure* (1976), p.156, and *Darling Ma. Letters to her Mother*, ed. J. Roose-Evans (1988), pp.59–60.

T.J. realized in return that he too had cause for gratitude.

I can never remember from the age of 18 onwards being without the friendship of good women, a succession inevitably with the changes of time and place and work [he told Violet Markham the day after his seventieth birthday]. I have only met one bad woman and she was an American of whom you've never heard. What I owe to all the others I can't attempt to suggest.[88]

There was a lighter, indeed occasionally hilarious, side to this. T.J. ruefully admitted that he seemed to have 'a dangerous attraction' for rich elderly American widows. Abraham Flexner teasingly suggested that he had been alarmed lest the seventy-eight year-old T.J.'s 'flair' for these ladies would get him into hot water when he was in New York in September 1948 en route for home after a second holiday at Flexner's camp in Canada. T.J. protested his innocence and reported that he had had 'to repel' yet another 'unsolicited assault' when he was accosted by a lady from Boston on board the RMS *Queen Mary* during the voyage home. Two years later an article in the *Western Mail* on the occasion of his eightieth birthday prompted a proposal of marriage out of the blue from a British widow, whom he had met briefly ten years before, whose specified attractions involved 'a nice house in the country, a good maid and a car'.[89]

There was nothing clandestine about these relationships. Joyce Grenfell, Lady Grigg, Violet Markham and his other women friends talked openly and with affectionate amusement about female susceptibility to his charm; what Nancy Astor called T.J.'s 'favour with Ladyes'.[90] But he was not a ladies' man in the ordinary sense, and certainly not a libertine. His rare gift of sympathetic under-standing made it possible for women, as well as men, to open up their hearts and minds to him with little constraint. The enduring relationships he formed, though in some instances emotionally intense, were undoubtedly platonic, courtly not sexual in form. They were rich, rewarding friendships, a vitally important element throughout his life.

Apart from their intrinsic value, these relationships also helped to fill the well of domestic loneliness he endured after the death of his wife, particularly during the years when Eirene, his daughter,

[88] T.J., Class T, Vol.7, Nos.23 and 30. T.J. told her that their respective dead spouses 'would rejoice' in their 'hallowed friendship'.
[89] T.J., Class S, Vol.3, Nos.116 and 117. NLW B.B. Thomas MSS, 3 October 1950.
[90] T.J., Class W, Vol.8, No.151.

was fully engaged in her work and his son, Tristan, was overseas serving with the Army. In the years after the war T.J.'s surviving brothers and sisters died in quick succession. 'I am becoming quite used to the visits of death in my circle', he wrote in January 1949. His sisters Liz and Har', who had been very close to him all his life, had died in 1947 and 1948. William Benjamin, 'my Glasgow brother', as T.J. called him, died on Christmas Day 1948, and his gifted but unambitious brother Alf, three weeks later in Canada. It was perhaps this brutal rapid severing of old family ties that sent T.J. back to his roots in Rhymney. In January 1949 he spent three days with his relations there, 'sleeping on the huge mahogany bed on which I was born'. He saw many old friends and visited the elementary school that he had once attended.[91]

T.J. was greatly heartened, too, that his relations with his son were very much closer than they had been for some years. The 'many fine qualities of heart and mind' that Tristan displayed in wartime 'greatly endeared' him to his father. Tristan had joined the Life Guards and, not uncharacteristically, had refused the chance of a commission. He was 'unsettled' by his wartime experiences, and three years' service in Germany, partly with the Control Commission, effectively destroyed his belief in Communism, which T.J. described as the 'original alienating force' that had pulled them apart. Tristan left the Communist party and on his return to Britain joined the staff of the *Observer* and was soon 'highly thought of there', to T.J.'s very great delight.[92]

The memory of his younger son remained as heartrending as ever.

> This is Elphin's day [T.J. wrote to Violet Markham on 21 December 1954] . . . the one day of all days most deeply stamped on my memory and mind. From 21 December 1928 few days have passed without my thinking of him and rejoicing in him. Had he lived he would have joined the Air Force and could hardly have survived.[93]

T.J. had always been very close to his daughter Eirene, took great pride always in her achievements, and due note usually of her opinions. She had been hectically involved in welfare work in the

---

[91] T.J., Class T, Vol.8, No.82; Class S, Vol.3, No.83. Bangor MSS 16191, 16192 and 16194. The tragic life of T.J.'s other brother Enoch came to an end in 1951. He was wounded in the 1914–1918 war, relapsed into a profound melancholia and spent many years in mental hospitals. T.J., 5 April 1951. White MSS.

[92] T.J., Class W, Vol.14, No.180; Class S, Vol.3, Nos.50 and 79; Class T, Vol.8, Nos.47–48. Bodl. Curtis MSS, Vol.59, f.172.

[93] T.J., Class T, Vol.7, No.161.

Women's Voluntary Services in Cardiff during the blitz and later became a Ministry of Labour welfare officer in south Wales.[94] It was natural that with a long-standing interest in social questions and the wellnigh peerless example of her father's record of public service, Eirene Jones should aspire to a political career, for which many of her friends felt she was ideally equipped. At first T.J. tried to discourage her with the argument his wife had used many years before to dissuade him: that with no alternative source of income, a career as an MP was much too precarious.

Other people were equally discouraging. Nancy Astor, her Tory prejudice in full flow, was appalled that T.J.'s daughter had joined the Welsh Labour party, and shrewdly pointed out that, although Eirene would no doubt make a good MP, 'she would make a poor delegate', as Labour candidates were required to be. S.K. Ratcliffe of the Romney Street Group, a Fabian of long standing, told T.J. he thought it was 'plucky of Eirene'. Writing in 1943, before the decisive swing in popular opinion that produced the general election result of 1945 had occurred, and after attending the party conference in 1943, which had been riven by furious disagreements, he did not 'see much hope' for the Labour party in the immediate future.[95]

However, T.J.'s old friend R.H. Tawney was much more encouraging. He said Eirene was young, she was a good speaker who would not 'bore the electors' into rejecting her as he had done when he had been a candidate, and there would be an overwhelming need of vigour and audacity in Parliament after the war. In November 1944, against the challenge of a strong miners' representative, Eirene narrowly won the nomination as Labour candidate for Flintshire, whence her mother's family hailed. But she faced an uphill struggle against a good Tory sitting member with a majority of over 10,000 votes.[96]

After his initial reservations, T.J. was enthusiastic about Eirene's candidature and was eager to help in her campaign. Indeed, when the election came, T.J., aged seventy-four, distributed election literature from door to door and rather 'wished he could have been her agent'. He discovered that there was still 'much prejudice' against a woman candidate, particularly one who had 'studied economics'. In the event, Eirene was defeated but, in T.J.'s opinion,

[94] 24 August 1940, Morton MSS GD/28/88/1. *A Diary with Letters*, pp.460, 484, 487.

[95] T.J., Class X, Vol.10, No.126; Class Q, Vol.2, No.78; Class W. Vol.15, No.160.

[96] T.J., Class Y, Vol.5, No.48; Class T, Vol.7, No.125. *A Diary with Letters*, pp.526–7.

won a clear 'moral victory' as she reduced the large Tory majority to 1,039 votes.[97] There had never been any doubt in his mind about the appropriate party label Eirene should adopt. 'My daughter is a Labour candidate' T.J. wrote to Lionel Curtis in 1949. 'I should have been infinitely depressed had she stood as a Tory'.[98]

After his involvement in Stafford Cripps's attempt to displace Churchill as Prime Minister in 1942, T.J. had avoided further entanglement in national politics. From Harlech, he resisted Waldorf Astor's plea in January 1944 to resume active participation in political affairs. But later that year T.J. did respond to a request from Sir Alan Lascelles, the King's Private Secretary, to write a draft for the Royal Christmas Day broadcast. 'I have not kept the King aloof', T.J. wrote in the covering letter sent with his draft, 'but brought H.M. within reach of His people. That seems right: "at home" on Xmas Day. But I may be quite mistaken in this. I think listeners do like to feel the common human touch'. Some weeks later Lascelles replied a shade apologetically: 'I fear your draft is being subjected to somewhat ruthless alteration, which I am sorry for. It may be that, when you hear it spoken, you will barely recognise it'. He added that no doubt T.J. was used 'to being skinned' in that way, as indeed he was himself. In fact, a fair amount of T.J.'s draft was incorporated in the final version, but the remainder was inferior by comparison.[99]

T.J. continued at this time to be consulted about the names of Welshmen suitable for appointment to official committees and commissions of inquiry.[100] But it was his daughter's parliamentary candidature that enlivened his interest in national politics. Moreover the work of J.M. Keynes, 'the prismatic genius' as T.J. called him (*Observer,* 26 October 1947), had by now given a stronger intellectual sanction to interventionist economic policies and the coalition government during the war had shown that they could work in practice. The Labour party's victory in the general election in 1945 was a complete surprise to T.J. He shared the general expectation that the Conservatives would win and merely hoped that 'Winston's majority is not great'. In common with many people, T.J. was bitterly disappointed by Churchill's behaviour

[97] T.J., Class T, Vol.7, Nos.127, 144, 147, 149, 150. *A Diary with Letters,* pp.534–6.

[98] Bodl. Curtis MSS, Vol.59, f.172. Curtis (ff.177–9) was 'startled' to hear that Tristan was now becoming 'a lighter pink' in contrast to Eirene's 'deepening red'. 'You, of course', he told T.J., 'are all colours of the rainbow'.

[99] T.J., Class O, Vol.3, Nos.25, 27 and 31. The King's broadcast, *The Times,* 27 December 1944.

[100] T.J., Class N, Vol.2, Nos.103–105.

during the election campaign. 'I think few of us who worked near Winston looked forward to his being P.M.', T.J. wrote to a friend in 1943. 'We distrusted his judgment of men and feared his sudden impulses.' But Churchill's magnificent leadership after 1940, despite occasional dictatorial lapses, had altered T.J.'s perception of him. Jones agreed with Baldwin that the war was a furnace which purged Churchill of the dross in his character; he felt 'divinely chosen' to pull the country through its troubles, and by 1943 it was clear he was well on the way to success.[101]

T.J.'s handsome tribute to the Prime Minister, 'Mr. Churchill at Seventy' (*Observer*, 26 November 1944) was therefore completely sincere. It was a first-rate piece, full of shrewd judgements and sparkling phrases. Churchill, T.J. wrote, 'is as competent as Pitt and as generous as Fox, with more staying power than either'. The Prime Minister had the 'robust tastes' of the eighteenth century and was as representative an Englishman as Dr Johnson. He also had 'some of the healthy vulgarity which made Marie Lloyd adored'. Endowed by nature with a profusion of magnificent talents, sometimes in former years Churchill's 'imagination wielded a despotic power over his mind and intensified molehills into monsters': hence his occasional rash misjudgements. But war against an evil power that staggered the imagination cooled the fiery passions and supplied Churchill with a prudence and a judgement that enabled him, on the brink of national disaster, to stand forth 'as the transfigured and embattled soul, will and voice, of his country, felt and heard throughout the world'.[102]

How great therefore was Churchill's fall from grace during the election of 1945. Like Lloyd George in 1918, T.J. wrote, Churchill had been unwilling to trust to his greatness. He ceased to be the universally admired national leader and became 'the partisan propagator of electioneering stunts . . . who woefully cheapened' British political life by a blatant attempt to gain personal and party advantage. 'Democracy', T.J. insisted in an address, 'The General Election 1945', which he gave at that time, is not only 'an educational but also a moral experiment'. Lloyd George and Churchill, so magnificently responsive to the demands of war, had both sadly defaulted at the moment of triumph.[103]

Some people were thoroughly alarmed by the prospect of a Labour government. Jones could not 'develop the faintest feeling of panic'; he believed, rightly, that there was no danger of a

[101] T.J. to J. Lochhead, 13 April 1943. White MSS.
[102] *Observer*, 26 November 1944.
[103] 7 July 1945, at Buckley Community Centre, published later as 'The General Election' in *Wales* (ed. K. Rhys), December 1945, pp.8–16.

revolutionary programme from Attlee's government; indeed, the
danger was 'probably likely to be the other way'.[104] T.J. hoped that
the government would experiment 'with various types and devices
of control' to discover some intermediate method between
Whitehall centralization and unfettered freedom of management
for the public utilities. He believed that the fundamental problems
of the coal industry were still unsolved and he was anxious that the
miners' union should be closely associated with any reforms that
were made. He considered however that, as the steel industry was
already highly centralized, there was little to be gained by
nationalization.[105] Against a sustained barrage of vehement
criticism of the government from Violet Markham, T.J. insisted that
Labour was entitled to 'a fair trial'; the country's economic position
was weak and could not be transformed quickly.[106]

As always, T.J. was interested in the performance of individual
ministers. He underrated Ernest Bevin and Attlee who, he asserted,
was 'quite unable to put himself across a street let alone a country'.
Aneurin Bevan, his fellow Welshman, who, he said, had 'something
in common with the early Lloyd George', had attracted his
attention long before. Indeed, T.J. considered that Bevan's talents
were such that he ought to have been taken into the coalition
government in 1943.[107] But the only minister who took T.J. into his
confidence was Stafford Cripps, who consulted him at a time of
difficulty for the government in 1947. T.J. felt that he 'could be of
no real help' as he had been so long detached from affairs of state
that he had lost 'the feel of them'. But he was a good listener and
did have a residuum of background knowledge of the ways of
government. From Cripps's catalogue of woe, T.J. drew the
conclusion that the government, above all, lacked cohesion:
ministers never met socially, there was no equivalent of the Tory
hostesses who provided appropriate settings for useful informal
meetings of ministerial colleagues. Attlee was a good chairman but
could not 'cement the cabinet', nor were there elder statesmen,
now beyond the pull of personal ambition, who had Attlee's ear
and could be primed to give him wise if unpalatable advice. With
regret T.J. said that he 'could make no helpful suggestion' to
Cripps.[108]

[104] *A Diary with Letters*, pp.536–7.
[105] T.J., Class T, Vol.7, Nos.44 and 149; Class Q, Vol.2, No.74; Class S, Vol.3,
No.122.
[106] T.J., Class T, Vol.8, Nos.40–65; Class S, Vol.3, No.144.
[107] T.J., Class S, Vol.3, No.77; Class T, Vol.7, No.95; Vol.8, Nos.67 and 140. *A
Diary with Letters*, p.544.
[108] T.J., Class T, Vol.8, No.62.

As the government plunged into a financial crisis in 1949, T.J. was disappointed with its performance and the weakness prompted by its internal rivalries. Nevertheless, he remained committed to its support and did not doubt that, since 1945, it had brought about an enormous improvement in the social condition of the people.

> I am an old-fashioned Socialist of the evolutionary Fabian sort and do not want any policy in excess nor to hurry at the rate of the extreme Left of today [he wrote to Violet Markham in a confession of faith in February 1950]. I am altogether for the Labour party and not sorry that it has brought about a big shift in the balance of money-power, but I wish it would now moderate its zeal. It has already done an immense amount of good building on the foundations laid by L.G. and I dread to think what would have happened to our people without it and the pressure it has put on those at ease and untroubled in spirit.

He firmly rejected Violet Markham's invitation to him to change sides in the forthcoming general election.

> Thirty years ago . . . we had one in seven out of work. Naturally, brought up as I was in Rhymney, so close to miners and steel workers and unskilled labourers and knowing how hard their lot and insecure their jobs, I should find it hard to vote Tory. I should somehow feel disloyal and a deserter if I betrayed my solidarity with them.

He was prepared to concede that some of the abuses of power attendant on capitalism had been moderated, but the need for its control remained. He regretted the waning of Christian belief: society still required some ethical sanction. T.J. was thoroughly irritated by well-to-do Tory friends who argued that 'high wages and holidays' were bad for working people, who reproached the Labour Cabinet because it had failed to deliver an ideal world in four and a half years, and who complained bitterly of Aneurin Bevan's political manners, conveniently forgetting that those of Churchill had often been a good deal less than 'impeccable'. At any rate, he rejoiced that his daughter was 'standing with Labour' in the election, which he expected would be a close-run thing.[109]

T.J. was now approaching his eightieth birthday. In recent years he had suffered an increasing number of attacks, variously diagnosed as lumbago, sciatica and fibrositis: 'I ring the changes on the various 'itises', he told Violet Markham ruefully.[110] And like most exceptionally active people, he became irritable when

[109] *A Diary with Letters*, pp.547–9. T.J., Class T, Vol.8, No.155.
[110] T.J., Class T, Vol.8, No.127.

housebound, although he could usually resign himself to being confined to bed so long as he had plenty of good books at hand. His health in general was good, his physical stamina remarkable. He still applied himself without stint to the affairs of the University College at Aberystwyth, the National Library of Wales and Coleg Harlech; he rarely missed a meeting of the Pilgrim Trust and continued to participate in management of the *Observer,* for which he regularly wrote major articles. If there was some inkling of physical weakness, there was certainly no hint of any diminution of his mental and intellectual power.

CHAPTER SIXTEEN

'THE FINAL LAP'

'TODAY, I feel like sixty', T.J. is reported to have said when it was announced that his daughter Eirene (who was now Mrs White) had comfortably won the East Flintshire seat in the general election in February 1950. Her majority of nearly seven thousand votes was 'vastly greater' than he had expected, partly because the party machine in the constituency was, in the main, manned by people who were 'ardent but inexperienced'. T.J. had been as active in the election as any of the party workers; he accompanied his daughter everywhere in her campaign and he went on her behalf to opponents' meetings to appraise their performances. 'Perhaps now that it is dark, I might distribute leaflets at a "bus stop"', he wrote wistfully at one point in the campaign. But the penalty for this hectic activity was serious: ten days in bed with an attack of lumbago. And not long afterwards he had a bad attack of bronchitis, which lingered on depressingly.[1]

However, nothing could diminish T.J.'s joy in Eirene's electoral triumph and the evident great success of her four-year-old marriage to John White, formerly of Northcliffe newspapers, subsequently of the Oxford University Press.[2] Nor did T.J. allow illness to contain his activity for long. In January 1950, after a virtually unanimous appeal by the members of the Council, he had agreed to continue as President of the College at Aberystwyth for a second term of five years. He continued to be heavily engaged in College business, marked by occasional disagreements with the Principal over some senior academic appointments that were made. T.J., who longed always for unusual distinction, observed sardonically after one election to a chair of which he disapproved: 'Average professors like to be surrounded by average professors'.[3] He continued also to write regularly for the *Observer*: in particular, a review of the new

---

[1] *Evening Standard*, 28 February 1950. T.J., Class T, Vol.8, Nos.157, 177. Bangor MS 16195. D. Astor MSS, 19 August 1950. *A Diary with Letters*, p.548. Huw T. Edwards of the Transport and General Workers' Union was a tower of strength in Eirene's campaign.

[2] T.J., Class S, Vol.3, No.88. Bangor MS 16195.

[3] T.J., Class X, Vol.10, No.141; Class T, Vol.5, No.65, Vol.8, No.175.

Dictionary of Welsh Biography down to 1940, the outcome of a long campaign in which he himself had been involved; and an article on his old hero Jan Smuts, whose presence in the war cabinet in 1917, Jones wrote, was 'a tribute to the righteousness of the British cause'.[4] T.J. was also busily at work on a speech for the National Eisteddfod in August, several newspaper articles and the script of a broadcast talk to mark the occasion of his eightieth birthday. Indeed, as he admitted to B.B. Thomas, his celebrated reputation for anonymity would soon be worn very thin.[5]

Even so, T.J. was 'overwhelmed' by the extraordinary demonstration of public affection and regard for him that marked his eightieth birthday. He was deluged with messages of goodwill: from Downing Street, from Whitehall, from all over Wales, and from hundreds of friends in Britain and abroad. There were many tributes to him in the Press: one described him as the greatest living Welshman; Salvador de Madariaga wrote a sonnet, 'For Tom Jones at 80', that appeared in the *Observer.* Some of the lines were apposite if not especially poetic:

> Four score he has attained every hour
> Planted with seed of action, gifted with flower
> of Selflessness, and rich with fruit of deed
> . . .
> Here is the secret of this noble life:
> He strove, but with his soul above the strife;
> He chained his Self so that his Mind be free.

There was a family gathering on his birthday, and three weeks later fifty of his friends met to honour him at a dinner at the House of Lords.[6] The invitations had been sent out in the names of Wilfrid Eady, David Astor, B.B. Thomas and W.E. Williams, whose varied activities across the span of British public life, in aggregate, perhaps just equalled those of T.J.[7] Desperate efforts had been made by his family and friends at this time to smarten his appearance, to make him look 'less like an undertaker's assistant', as he said Nancy Astor, in despair, had once

---

[4] *Observer,* 9 July and 17 September 1950. T.J., Class Y, Vol.4, No.34. See also, a fine review of a biography of John Burns in *John o' London's Weekly,* 29 May 1950.

[5] NLW, B.B. Thomas, 20 September 1950. Earlier he had gently suggested to Thomas (T.J., Class W, Vol.18, No.149), who was to appear in the Honours List, that it was 'better to be a Knight (refused) than a Knight (dubbed)'.

[6] T.J., Class W, Vol.7, No.159. *Western Mail, Swansea Evening Post, Liverpool Daily Post,* 27 September 1950. *Observer,* 1 September 1950. *A Diary with Letters,* pp.548-9.

[7] D. Astor MSS, September 1950.

described him.[8] T.J.'s 'Birthday Talk' on the radio on 29 September 1950 hinged on certain 'Moments' in his life, some of them fortuitous meetings with individuals, that had important influences on the course of his career, and were not without significant effect on British history.[9] He also published at this time some reflections on life at eighty. He claimed, although his day-to-day activity seemed to cast doubt on it, that his life was now much more slow-paced; he dozed more often, new masterpieces were written but he no longer bothered to read them; he had succumbed to the lure of physical comfort. He maintained that the lessons of his life were commonplace: the love of a good woman was the 'supreme blessing', the friendship of half a dozen the next best thing. All political 'isms' were 'transient aspects' of human experience, even universal education would not solve all problems; happiness was a by-product, its direct pursuit an unavailing quest. He believed that it was possible to survive disillusion without cynicism and, with luck, even achieve a serenity of sorts. He fervently hoped that he would not linger long at the end of his life, 'a peevish, helpless nuisance' to those around him. As for the eternal verities, at long last, he had reached firm ground: 'Sometimes I incline to St. Paul and sometimes to St. Plato'. On that basis, he had become again a regular chapel-goer. Inevitably he thought of death more and more often, but now faced it 'with a calm and Christian mind'.[10]

This tranquil resignation was in fact a shade premature: T.J. had another five years to live, he was still in full control of his senses, and much remained for him to do. Some of his former concerns, however, now made less of a demand on him. He was no longer required, for example, to raise money for the educational settlements in south Wales. The post-war world of full employment was very different from the distressing years between the wars. Some of the settlements had closed, most of the others had been taken over by local authorities and sometimes put to other uses. Of the seven settlements with which T.J. had been closely connected, five survived and, as he said with pride, were operating as efficiently as ever. He had not thought it necessary to make a 'special effort' to save the two that were closed; the world had changed and must be accepted.[11]

---

[8] T.J., Class T, Vol.8, No.179.

[9] 'Moments in 80 years: A Broadcast Talk', T.J., Class Y, Vol.5, No.16.

[10] 'Around Eighty', *Lleufer*, VII, No.1,1951, pp.5–11, and *Welsh Broth*, pp.167–8. In a letter written at this time (NLW, B.B. Thomas MSS, 30 October 1951), T.J. said that his wife and son Elphin, 'as conscience and fun', were rarely far from his mind.

[11] T.J., Class T, Vol.8, No.188.

The war had also put an end in large part to many of the activities centred on Gregynog. The last musical festival took place in 1938, the social service and educational conferences and weekend schools which had been regularly held there were suspended in 1939. Most of the staff left for war service and the Gregynog Press closed down, finally as it turned out, in 1940. In all, it had published forty-two books, eight of them in the Welsh language. T.J. has come in for some strong criticism from his forthright daughter for the waywardness of the publication policy, for which he was chiefly responsible, in particular his choice of two relatively obscure books about Spain to the neglect of acknowledged classics in the Welsh language or relating to Wales.[12] It is also doubtful if the Press, which avowedly set out to do so, had had any discernible effect in raising the quality of printing and publishing and of public taste in Wales. Possibly the Press, which T.J. admitted in 1954 had always been 'frankly experimental', was something of an extravagance: on the other hand, as T.J. and Gwen Davies always insisted, exquisitely beautiful objects that nourish the soul need no secular justification.[13] The missionary Gregynog adventure, which included a collection of pictures, etchings and sculptures that staggered George Bernard Shaw with their quality and variety, together with the superb music, the Press and the beautiful gardens, comprised a cultural beacon that lit up the dark years in Wales between the wars. It was, in the main, the joint achievement of Gwen Davies and T.J.

Despite these changes, the sisters continued to rely heavily upon T.J.'s support and counsel; periodically 'cabinet meetings' were held where, with the assistance of Burdon Evans, decisions were reached relating to the numerous philanthropic concerns with which the Gregynog sisters were still connected. T.J. demonstrated infinite patience in his dealings with Gwen Davies, who was beset at this time by the wildest fears about the effect of post-war changes. 'Gwen . . . is developing a work-house complex', T.J. commented with mild exasperation in 1946. His load was all the heavier because Burdon Evans, who confessed to profound disillusionment over the failure of certain causes that he had believed in, was less supportive than formerly. In 1948 Gwen Davies still dreamed of restarting the Gregynog Press. 'It is quite impossible in present circumstances', T.J. wrote. 'Burdon Evans and I are indispensable to her and we are both exhausted, he even more than I am'.

[12] Eirene White, *The Ladies of Gregynog* (Cardiff, 1985), p.29–33.
[13] T.J., 'The Gregynog Press', 7 April 1954. T.J., Class L, Vol.1, No.1.

Gwen Davies realized full well how much she owed to T.J. In 1946, moved apparently by some intimation of mortality, she wrote:

> I do so want to thank you from the bottom of my heart for all you have given me and done for me. It has been like a warm fire flowing within me for years. . . . All I have been able to do during the last thirty years has been almost entirely your doing. Thank you.

Gwen Davies, a shy, noble soul, died in 1951. Her death left 'a big blank' in T.J.'s life.[14] The younger sister, Daisy, continued to lean heavily on T.J., who had a major influence in the discussions that eventually transferred the Gregynog estate to the University of Wales and most of the great art collection to the National Museum of Wales, the last and one of the greatest in the long list of Gregynog benefactions.

> Our debt to the good ladies is emphasised by the knowledge of what others have not done [B.B. Thomas commented to T.J. in 1951]. What a country Wales would be today if its rentiers had [all had their] conscience, public spirit and intelligence.[15]

In November 1951 Jones's long-awaited biography of Lloyd George appeared at last. Its revision had occasioned T.J. 'lots of bother'; the Harvard Press editors excised many of his 'human touches' and several points of particular British interests, where-upon T.J. promptly re-inserted some of them. He dedicated the American edition of the book to Abraham Flexner, his partner in what Flexner's daughter called a 'beautiful relationship' extending over very many years.[16] T.J. had hoped that Winston Churchill would agree to write a foreword to the biography. 'The possibility of associating you and L.G. within the covers of my book is very attractive to me,' T.J. wrote to Churchill. 'So far as he ever had a political friend, you were that friend.' However, it was not to be. 'Alas, I cannot add to my tasks at the present time,' Churchill replied a shade churlishly. 'I shall await the publication with great interest.'[17]

So of course did many people. The response of the reviewers was generally favourable. Those who were severely critical usually had

[14] T.J., Class T, Vol.7, No.127; Vol.8, Nos.16, 76, 207; Class R, Vol.7, No.27. 'She left me an annuity of £200 p.a.,' T.J. wrote, 'I hardly thought she would have the courage to do this publicly, she was so shy and timid.'

[15] T.J., Class T, Vol.8, Nos.22, 152; Vol.9, Nos.16, 18; Class W, Vol.18, No.157.

[16] T.J., Class W, Vol.7, No.160; Class T, Vol.8, No.151; Class S, Vol.3, No.166.

[17] T.J., Class A, Vol.1, Nos. 85 and 86.

an axe of some sort to grind: Brigadier Sir John Edmonds, historian of the British Army in 1914–18, who had worked alongside T.J. at the National Library of Wales, considered that he had 'not always been fair to the military'; A.J. Cummings, flourishing his party loyalty, insisted in the *News Chronicle* that the book fell a 'long way' short of doing justice to the great Liberal statesman. The strongest condemnation came from Frank Owen, who was himself engaged in writing a life of L.G. based on the mountain of papers that Beaverbrook had bought from Frances Lloyd-George.[18] The best review, not surprisingly, came from the pen of Robert Blake, future doyen of political biographers, who pronounced T.J.'s book 'a masterpiece of compression' that maintained a fair balance between Lloyd George's faults and virtues. Blake said that Jones had wisely added 'a dash of vinegar' to the 'sugar' all too customary in political biography. Other reputable reviewers took much the same line.[19] T.J., who all along had been apprehensive about the book, recognizing perhaps that his writing was not of his best, was reasonably well satisfied with its reception. He had rightly never claimed that it was anything more than an 'interim' study that was 'reasonably frank', but he was delighted to hear that within days of its appearance the publishers decided to print a second edition.[20]

A few weeks before, T.J. himself had written a review that attracted a good deal of attention of *A King's Story*, the Duke of Windsor's memoirs centred on his version of the Abdication. In a graceful essay on monarchy in general, T.J. stretched sympathy for the Duke's predicament to the limit, but did not shrink either from plain speaking about his obliquities and derelictions.[21] Within weeks, T.J. published *Welsh Broth*, a volume of recollections of his life in Glasgow, Ireland and in south Wales before he joined the Cabinet secretariat. The book was not strictly biographical, had many omissions, and offered only glimpses of the author himself,

---

[18] T.J., Class A, Vol.2, No.8; Class T, Vol.8, No.210. *News Chronicle* and *Daily Express*, 4 October 1951. Malcolm Thomson's *David Lloyd George, the Official Biography*, the useful laudatory book commissioned by Frances Lloyd-George, had appeared in 1948.

[19] *The Times Lit. Supp.*, 5 October 1951. *Daily Telegraph*, 4 October 1951. *The Listener*, 11 October 1951, *The Tablet*, 29 December 1951. T.J., Class T, Vol.8, No.215.

[20] T.J., Class T, Vol.8, Nos.147 and 211. Bodl., Curtis MSS, Box 121, f.197. Bangor MS 16196.

[21] 'The Abdication Story', *Observer*, 30 September 1951. T.J., Class T, Vol.8, No.210.

though enough of them to reveal the outline of the personality that so many found so attractive.

Not everyone of course succumbed to his charm. The leading Welsh nationalists remained bitterly hostile. In an article that appeared in April 1951, T.J. was denounced as the leading interpreter in Wales of English nationalism, whose volume of essays, *The Native Never Returns,* was compared, to its great disadvantage, with Saunders Lewis's *Canlyn Arthur* (In the Steps of Arthur). The great difference, it was alleged, was the spirit they embodied rather than the language in which they were written; Saunders Lewis stood for Welsh Wales writ large, T.J. symbolized the reverse.[22]

The question of the establishment of a Secretary of State for Wales came to the fore particularly at this time. T.J. promptly sent on for his daughter's benefit a confidential memorandum that he had written on that subject in 1944, his opinion in the meantime, presumably, having remained unaltered. On the face of it T.J. was opposed to the establishment of a Secretary of State for Wales because he feared that, if all Welsh political matters were to pass through that office, it would become either a 'bottleneck' choked by a mountain of administration or a 'mere conduit pipe' for decisions taken in Whitehall. In his opinion, the most serious issues were economic and the most powerful aspiration of the people was that Wales should 'fare better industrially' than it had in the past. T.J. wanted direct access to the seat of authority; he proposed the establishment of a Secretary for Wales (though not a Secretary of State) with advisory and consultative but no administrative responsibilities. The Secretary would be a Welsh MP, a member of the governing party, who would be the chairman of a Welsh Advisory Council and also a minister without portfolio who reported on Welsh affairs directly to the Prime Minister, by whose means Welsh opinions and representations would be relayed to the government departments concerned. T.J. admitted that his proposal was riddled with objections; indeed, it was needlessly cumbrous. His chief fear was that a grandiloquently-styled Secretary of State for Wales might have the trappings but not the reality of authority and thus, because of his ineffectiveness, simply reinforce the existing demand for home rule which he considered was misguided. Subsequent experience suggests that most of his fears about a Secretaryship of State for Wales were unfounded. Cynics later of course suggested that T.J. was naturally opposed to the idea

[22] D.J. Williams. 'Y Ddau Ddewis' [The Two Choices], *Y Crynhoad,* [The Welsh Digest], Ebrill, 1951/April, 1951, pp.29–32.

of a Secretary of State because in effect he *was* the Secretary of State for Wales.[23]

He continued to make public statements which infuriated his nationalist critics, whose opinions of him ranged from the dismissive to the malevolent. 'The Welsh Way of Life', published in the *Western Mail* in January 1953, suggested that Welsh culture was threatened as much by Hollywood as by English influences; that a Parliament for Wales would not answer the hopes of ardent nationalists because inevitably it would be 'predominantly English in tongue, industrial and secular in outlook'. He reiterated his long-standing opinion that the best hope of survival for Welsh culture lay in 'a rearguard action' by means of education, based on persuasion and not compulsion.[24] Two years later, not long before he died, T.J.'s broadcast talk 'Welsh and English' was his final public statement on the subject. He set out again his now familiar view: the Welsh strand was the major one in his personal make-up, but it was not the only one. The plain fact was, and most people in Wales recognized it, 'our fate is inescapably tied up with England, geographically, economically and sociologically'. The concluding passage of the talk came straight from the heart:

> Happy is the nation that knows where its real genius lies. In Wales . . . it is in the enthusiasm for education, in the widespread diffusion of interest in religion, in the practice of music, poetry and drama, in the playing of football. . . . The Wales which excites my greatest admiration is that of the simple intelligent folk so steeped in our religious tradition, who have mastered the art of life whether on a farm or in a coalpit or in a quarry or shop, who know how to live graciously as good neighbours in quite humble environments. There lies our chief glory. Let us cultivate those virtues by all the arts of popular education.[25]

T.J. and his Welsh nationalist opponents had more in common than customarily appeared.

T.J.'s relationship with Nancy Astor was a similarly complex one. The truce they had established in 1943 remained uneasy and accordingly T.J. spent much less time at Cliveden than formerly. This was all the more unfortunate because Waldorf Astor, whose relations with T.J. remained rock-solid, was ailing and sorely missed the presence of one who was now his closest friend. 'My father has

[23] 'Secretary of State for Wales', 6 May 1944. T.J. to his daughter, 29 November 1951. T.J., Add MSS, HH, Vol.5, Nos.1 and 21.

[24] 'The Welsh Way of Life: the open ocean or an inland sea?', *Western Mail*, 5 January 1953.

[25] 7 March 1955. T.J., Class Y, Vol.5, No.21.

urged me to persuade you to visit him again, if possible this week', David Astor wired to T.J. in March 1951. 'I think he is somewhat lonely and you are the person he can talk most easily to. It becomes less easy to talk when Mother returns, which happens in April.' T.J. of course immediately responded, but Nancy Astor remained prickly; it was only with the greatest difficulty that she managed 'to be good' when T.J. was at Cliveden in January 1952.[26] And when in September of that year Waldorf died, Nancy's response to T.J.'s condolences was coldly hostile, indeed cruel. 'You need not tell me how fond you were of Waldorf,' she wrote, 'I know that he was devoted to you. My only regret is that he was ever influenced by you.' As her niece Joyce Grenfell once observed, Nancy Astor had an 'uncanny knack of knowing just where to put salt in a wound'. Her letter to T.J. was written in anguish and out of bitter regret for the years when her marriage to Waldorf had gone awry. During their years together, they had drifted apart politically; Waldorf had 'grown more liberal', Nancy 'more tory', as T.J. described it, and the decidedly liberal complexion of David Astor's editorship of the *Observer*, for which T.J., absurdly, was largely blamed by Nancy, was the cause of constant marital discord. 'These last seven years have been heartsearching . . . I wish I had never saved the Observer. You can see why it has caused me more misery than I would have thought possible' Nancy wrote. 'Oh T.J., your wife would understand'.[27]

Enchanting and infuriating, generous and intolerant by bewildering turns, Nancy Astor was soon semi-contrite and, in the manner of a spoilt child, demanded immediate forgiveness. 'I am sorry I wrote you in bitterness and I fear that I did. But I can't bear resentment, it hurts. I still regret your Welsh ways with Waldorf. But I forgive. T.J. please write me.' He did, of course.

> Thank you for writing in so conciliatory a spirit [he replied generously]. People endowed with your power and gifts have more to contend with than most of us and it must be harder to forgive. You leave out of account Waldorf's influence on me and speak as if only I had influence on him. Until you mentioned the matter, I had not thought of my having influence on him. And as everyone was agreed about his pre-eminent goodness, I can't have done much harm.[28]

[26] T.J., Class Q, Vol.1, No.147; Class T, Vol.8, Nos.193–5; 'Here at Cliveden there is no music', T.J. wrote in a comparison he made in February 1951. 'It is a statelier, richer house with a large library in quality but with few books on the arts, which abound at Gregynog.'

[27] T.J., Class Q, Vol.1, No.112. *Joyce Grenfell Requests the Pleasure* (1976), p.100. T.J., Class T, Vol.8, Nos.193 and 212. M. Astor, *Tribal Feeling* (1963), pp.216–18.

[28] T.J., Class Q, Vol.2, No.84. Astor MSS 1416/1/2/261.

T.J. greatly admired Astor's fine character; indeed, in his obituary notice of him in the *Manchester Guardian*,T.J. asserted that he
had 'some of the qualities that go to the making of a saint'. Waldorf
Astor's death certainly left a great gap in T.J.'s life: theirs was a rare
and fruitful friendship incorporating absolute trust, complete
frankness and the warmest affection. Of course no such consistency
was ever possible in T.J.'s relationship with Nancy Astor. He
appreciated the unique fascination of her mercurial personality,
her moral courage, and her instinctive kindness, but he deplored
her wild political and personal outbursts and considered that the
quality of her mind was unremarkable. He did not place any great
weight on her recent half-hearted apology. 'She has relented
momentarily towards T.J.' he commented to Violet Markham.
Nevertheless, the ties that bound them were many and strong and
remained in force until the end of T.J.'s life.[29]

In 1952, largely for family reasons, Jones had arranged to resign
the Presidency of the University College at Aberystwyth before his
second term of office was completed. He had carried out his duties
meticulously, some of them with particular relish: he was especially
interested in the welfare of overseas students and regularly
attended their functions. 'There is no colour bar in this town', he
wrote with great satisfaction; one of his early suggestions was the
establishment of a chair in racial relations at the College.
Predictably T.J. had little time for solemn academic ritual: at the
degree ceremony in July 1951, as the parade of dignitaries entered
the hall, the students, as usual, sang the chorus 'Why were they
born so beautiful', in which the venerable President, the central
figure in the procession, heartily joined. He had, moreover, come
to enjoy his occasional tussles with the Principal over certain
aspects of College policy.[30]

Indeed, T.J. and Ifor L. Evans had become very close friends,
and the Principal's sudden death in May 1952 at the age of fifty-five
'stunned' T.J. and deprived him momentarily of normal sensitivity.
'He was terribly shaken by his friend's untimely death,' Mrs Ruth
Evans, the Principal's wife, wrote later, 'and had no other means of
showing his grief than by a harsh and downright offensive
unsentimentality.' Within minutes of expressing his condolences to
her, T.J. blurted out: 'We'll have to think about the next principal

---

[29] *Manchester Guardian*, 1 October 1952. T.J., Class T, Vol.9, No.39. Astor MS
1416/1/2/272. Michael Astor (*Tribal Feeling*, p.81), who had some reservations
about T.J., wrote: 'My father always trusted him. My mother, who admired his
abilities, never did.'
[30] T.J., Class T, Vol.8, Nos.190–205.

now. There are one or two people I would like to discuss with you.'
Mrs Evans, whose understanding was remarkable, charitably con-
cluded that this astonishing insensitivity was a hapless cover for
T.J.'s 'own biting sorrow'.[31]

In the circumstances Jones abandoned his former decision to
retire from the Presidency. For some time he felt utterly drained of
energy but eventually turned his attention to the search for a new
principal, which was to prove unexpectedly difficult. The ideal
successor would be a Welsh-speaking Welshman with high academic
qualifications and proven administrative ability, but there seemed
to be few people thus qualified. Over the next year T.J., who was
chairman, and the other members of the Selection Committee,
searched far and wide for a successor. He made no secret of the fact
that his first choice was Ben Bowen Thomas, as it was of several
others of the Committee, but for various reasons Thomas was not
prepared to be considered.[32] During the interregnum the acting
Principal, Professor Lily Newton, impressed T.J. with her crisp
competence. 'If I saw a glimmer of support I would vote for her as
Principal,' T.J. said, but he realized, with regret, that 'she would not
be accepted permanently owing to the prejudice of so-called educated male professors'. The fact that she was not Welsh-speaking was
also a handicap, one that might perhaps be overlooked in the case
of 'a superman' like Sir Oliver Franks, who was privately
approached by T.J. without success. With regret, because he was a
friend who had some local support, T.J. could not endorse the
candidature of Richard Aaron, the Professor of Philosophy, because
he was 'infected with Welsh Nationalism' and would not be strong
enough to withstand 'its currents', which were then in full flow. As
always, T.J. was attracted by the signs or the promise of brilliance of
both mind and personality. Musing aloud, he mentioned Enoch
Powell, an able young scholar of Welsh name if not antecedents, a
gifted linguist easily capable of achieving fluency in Welsh, as a
possible candidate, but made no actual approach to him.[33] In the
same category T.J. also placed M. Goronwy Rees, at the time Estates
Bursar at All Souls College, Oxford, who had come to his notice
years before and whose subsequent career he had followed with
mild interest. The delay in appointing a principal occasioned some

[31] T.J. to Eirene White, 1 June 1952. White MSS. T.J., Class T, Vol.9, No.22.
Mrs Ruth Evans's unpublished memorandum.

[32] T.J., Class W, Vol.11, No.147. NLW, B.B. Thomas MSS, 24 and 27 April
1953.

[33] T.J., Class T, Vol.9, Nos.21, 40, 48. Bangor MS 16202. Mrs Ruth Evans's
memorandum on T.J.

criticism; one prominent Welshman, deeply distrustful of Tom Jones on personal as well as political grounds, feared that he would manipulate the College Council for some devious purpose of his own.[34] There was always a sizeable minority of the chattering classes, as the educated élite has now come to be called, in Wales who were inveterately suspicious of T.J. as a sophisticated expatriate whose natural cunning had been honed to razor-sharpness by metropolitan experience and too long an association with acknowledged masters of political sleight-of-hand like Lloyd George and Baldwin. Whatever the general truth or otherwise of that conviction, it was completely wide of the mark in this instance, because for the greater part of a year T.J. was utterly uncertain about what to do for the best. 'I am not sleeping well, chiefly because I see no satisfactory Principal in sight,' he wrote dispiritedly to Violet Markham in February 1953.[35]

There were, finally, eleven applicants for the principalship and seven other names were recommended, three of whom were prepared to be considered. Five of the fourteen were interviewed and the Committee, although empowered to suggest more than one name, ultimately unanimously recommended to the College Council the appointment of Goronwy Rees. His referees were the Oxford luminaries, Maurice Bowra and John Sparrow of All Souls, and the banker Lord Brand. But not content with these, T.J. also consulted Lionel Curtis, Wilson Harris, W.G.S. Adams, and D.L. Keir of Balliol, and additionally pursued private enquiries about Rees. Despite the apparently overwhelming weight of favourable testimony, there is a residual note of doubt in T.J.'s letter to Curtis: 'Relying on you all,' he wrote, 'we have decided to send forward Goronwy Rees's name alone to the Council'. Two other considerations had delayed a unanimous committee decision: the fact that Rees, although he could read Welsh, could not speak it, a difficulty overcome by his promise to learn to do so within a year; and, hilariously in the light of later events, some Committee members considered him 'a delicate protected All Souls product, too tender for our rough weather'.[36] Finally convinced that Rees was the best available candidate, T.J. warmly sponsored his appointment by the Council at its meeting in June, where traditionalist and nationalist

[34] NLW, J. Glyn Davies MS 16129.

[35] T.J., Class T, Vol.9, No.58; Class W, Vol.11, No.152. 'You will be glad when this long parley is over,' Miss Everton Jones, a close friend of many years, wrote, 'but I wish you were happier about it.'

[36] T.J., Class T, Vol.9, Nos.53 and 58; Class W, Vol.7, Nos.120 and 127. Bodl., Curtis MSS, Box 74, ff.121 and 122; Box 75, ff.12 and 13.

critics overreached themselves by extravagant abuse of the candidate before he was interviewed, with the result that he was eventually elected by an overwhelming majority.[37]

T.J. had the highest hopes of the appointment; with further acquaintance, he was immensely impressed with Rees and his young wife, who evidently kept strictly to herself her private opinion that the Welsh were a 'shiftless and untrustworthy' people, a 'primitive tribe' which 'practised savage rites'. Goronwy Rees had been born in Aberystwyth, where his father was a much-respected Presbyterian minister. Rees's account of his principalship, self-confessedly an exercise in self-destruction, is vastly entertaining but more remarkable for the quality of the prose and its patronizing arrogance than adherence to strict accuracy. Nor did he shrink, in his ingenious but unconvincing explanation of his reasons for accepting the post, from a veiled insinuation that, from the outset, T.J. had some doubtful hidden purpose in inviting his application. In that, as in so much else subsequently in his life, Goronwy Rees merely demeaned himself.[38]

A year later, happily confident that his beloved College had appointed a Principal who was brilliantly equipped for his responsibilities, T.J. retired from the presidency. To general acclaim, Principal Rees in October 1953 pronounced him 'the perfect President', a sentiment anticipated in the student news-paper.[39] Perhaps mercifully, T.J. was dead before the unsavoury and, in some ways, absurd sequence of events that led to Rees's enforced resignation from the principalship.[40] T.J. had wholly endorsed Rees's academic credo set out in his Inaugural Lecture and certainly believed just as strongly that the imperatives of political nationalism were utterly incompatible with the idea of a university.[41] But although T.J. as President would have gone to the extreme lengths of tolerance in order to be scrupulously fair in dealing with Goronwy Rees, when his authorship of allegedly sensational articles in the tabloid press became public, he would have been repelled and appalled by his lack of judgement and the revelations of the sordid life-style that the Principal had for years shared with his

[37] T.J., Class T, Vol.9, Nos.53, 55 and 58.

[38] *A Chapter of Accidents* (1972), pp.235–46.

[39] T.J., Class T, Vol.9, No.70. Bangor MS 16205. UCW Court Minutes, 27 October 1954. *The Courier*, 22 October 1954.

[40] E.L. Ellis, *The University College of Wales, Aberystwyth, 1872–1972* (Cardiff, 1972), and Goronwy Rees, op.cit., pp.249–50.

[41] Goronwy Rees, *On the Use and Misuse of Universities* (Aberystwyth, 1953), and *A Chapter of Accidents*, pp.258–9. E.L. Ellis, op.cit., pp.294–5, 299.

degenerate friend the spy Guy Burgess. It is highly probable that, in the end, T.J. too would have insisted on Rees's resignation.

Although the affairs of the College at Aberystwyth had absorbed so much of his attention and, in his last year as President, prompted so much anxiety, T.J. continued as usual to be involved in many other matters. After a nasty bout of bronchitis early in 1952 he had considered resigning from the Pilgrim Trust, but the mere hint of his intention was immediately laughed out of court by his colleagues. This was just as well for within the space of nine months the Trust lost, by death or resignation, the services of its long-serving Chairman, Lord Macmillan, and two experienced Trustees, Sir James Irvine and Lord Greene. At the unanimous request of his colleagues, T.J. agreed in November to serve as Chairman for two years.[42] He had been a member of the Trust throughout the twenty-two years of its existence, during which time it had made grants totalling substantially more than the £2,000,000 with which it had been originally endowed, yet the market value of its investments remained not far short of £3,000,000, handsome evidence of provident financial management. But T.J.'s *métier* of course was his matchless skill in judging the relative merits of the host of applications with which the Trustees were besieged. His sponsorship of requests continued to be almost a cast-iron guarantee of success, because unquestionably 'he knew the circumstances in detail' and, as a Trustee wrote later, as Chairman he was 'absolutely fair; in no one's pocket; always trusted'.[43] It was perhaps the complete confidence of his colleagues that enabled T.J. to persuade them, much against the initial inclination of two of the Trustees, to spend a great deal more in support of the humanities during his chairmanship than in recent years. He believed that the 'tremendous millions' available to science and technology compared with the meagre endowment of the humanities was a 'severe handicap in the promotion of civilization'.[44] Had he been so minded, T.J. could have continued as Chairman beyond the agreed term, but he did not intend to linger on until he was incapable of deciding it was time to go as, he said, Baldwin and Macdonald had

---

[42] T.J., Class M, Vol.4, No.15; Class W, Vol.7, No.174. PT *Report* (1952), pp.3–9. *Observer,* 23 November 1952.

[43] Unpublished memorandum on T.J. by Walter Oakeshott, a Trustee, who also wrote (PT *Report* (1955), p.7): 'It was he who shaped my life, as he shaped the lives of scores of others; gentle but incisive . . . his long life was a triumph of service.'

[44] Kilmaine to T.J., 5 March 1953, White MSS. T.J., Class S, Vol.3, No.195; Class T, Vol.9, No.45. PT *Report* (1954), p.8.

done when they were Prime Minister.[45] At T.J.'s suggestion, Sir Alan Lascelles succeeded him as Chairman in November 1954.

Despite its small size in comparison with the giant American charitable foundations such as the Carnegie, Ford or Rockefeller, on its record the Pilgrim Trust had a legitimate claim to be considered one of the most distinguished agencies in the field of philanthropy. T.J.'s contribution to its success between 1930 and 1954 was immense, certainly greater than that of anyone else; largely under his inspiration, its restorative and protective influence penetrated with striking effect into many vital areas of social and environmental need in British society.

T.J. naturally was delighted at the confident start his daughter had made to her political career: her maiden speech in the Commons went well, and in the spring of 1951 she spoke at length and with effect on a bill to amend the divorce law. 'She has greatly enhanced her reputation for ability and fair-mindedness', T.J. wrote to a friend in America; 'of course her father is quite silly about her and can't keep off the subject.'[46] From the outset the second Attlee government rested precariously on its single-figure majority and in October 1951 sought safety, or perhaps escape from its internal troubles, in a general election in which, although it increased its popular vote, it was narrowly beaten by the vagaries of the electoral system. However, Eirene White retained the East Flint seat without undue trouble; T.J. was less active in this election than he had been in 1950. 'Showed myself at her side but did not speak', he reported of a campaign in which he believed his daughter had amply displayed her quality.[47] But the rest of the decade was an unhappy time for the Labour party which was ravaged by a civil war over policy and personalities. Inevitably, the National Executive Committee (NEC) became a vicious battleground where there was little tolerance of those who refused to take up fixed positions on one side or the other in the factional disputes: they were 'middle-of-the-roaders – a source of confusion', in Herbert Morrison's impatient party-manager's description.[48] Eirene White, like her father an instinctive moderate, was distinctly unhappy at this turn of events,[49] and found that her attempts at meetings of the NEC to

[45] Bangor MS 16206.
[46] T.J., Class T, Vol.8, No.162. T.J. to Lily Rudenberg, 5 April 1951. White MSS.
[47] Bangor MS 16197.
[48] *An Autobiography* (1960), p.291.
[49] 'Eirene White, a decent middle-of-the-roader on the National Executive, who was nearly in tears' (according to R.H.S. Crossman, *The Backbench Diaries of Richard Crossman* (1981), p.134) after a damaging public disagreement in August 1952 between Attlee and Bevan.

promote workable compromises prompted displeasure in some circles. In 1953, unwilling to be the pawn of either side, she withdrew from the NEC.[50] T.J. did not presume to offer political advice to his daughter, he thought she was shrewd enough to plot her own course. 'Like Mr. Burke and the Bristol electors, long ago, she refuses to be a mere delegate or pawn', T.J. said. He had no part in her 'crucial decision' of which, nevertheless, he heartily approved. But he was keen for her to continue in politics and was made 'miserable' in 1955 because, although aged eighty-four years and seriously unwell, he had been unable to assist her in the election campaign in which, to his great delight, despite his anxieties, she was again successful.[51]

However, his daughter's political fortunes apart, T.J.'s attention in what he called 'the final lap' of his life was concentrated more on the politics of past years, then settling down uneasily as history, in which he himself had played a significant role, than on the current party struggle. Geoffrey Cumberlege of the Oxford University Press had developed an immense respect for T.J. when his biography of Lloyd George was in course of publication. 'He was a wonderful author', Cumberlege wrote later, 'and he drew the best out of us.'[52] In January 1951, with a publisher's eye on the recent revival of interest in the inter-war years, Cumberlege proposed that T.J. should publish within the next two or three years a selection of material from the diaries which he had kept, somewhat irregularly, since 1916. T.J. had no doubt of the ultimate historical value of his unabridged diaries, but he questioned whether, when severely edited to omit all reference to Cabinet proceedings and to meet any other demands for excision from Sir Edward Bridges, the head of the Civil Service, the material that remained suitable for publication in the immediate future would be of sufficient general interest. T.J. also thought that the frequent references to Wales in his diaries would reduce their interest for a predominantly English readership. Although he had not read the diaries, Cumberlege was not put off: he believed T.J. was much 'too pessimistic'; despite the possibility of a heavy Civil Service blue pencil, Cumberlege was convinced there would be 'an interesting

[50] T.J., Class S, Vol.3, No.202. David Howell, *British Social Democracy* (1980), p.193. Bangor MS 16205. According to Michael Foot, *Aneurin Bevan* (1975), II, 473, Mrs White 'was pushed off once she was discovered to be unreliable' by the right wing majority on the NEC. In fact, she had previously retained her position on the NEC, despite Arthur Deakin's bullying withdrawal of the Transport and General Workers' Union's support.

[51] T.J., Class X, Vol.10, No.144. D. Astor MSS, 29 May 1955. Bangor MS 16208.

[52] T.J., Class X, Vol.12, No.94.

and important residue'. Moreover, he believed that many English people were attracted to Wales, which had the appeal of a foreign country for many of them.[53]

The project trundled along at snail's pace during 1952: in March, Sir Edward Bridges informally recommended the most severe pruning of any material that was in the slightest degree doubtful. He also complained bitterly to Jones that Hankey, in his *Supreme Command,* had been far too free in his use of Cabinet minutes and had failed to keep 'the line between minister and civil servant carefully'.[54] T.J. began to suspect that his attempt to be 'discreet and unlibellous' would end in a 'dull unreadability'.[55] T.J. and Cumberlege hoped to publish a two-volume miscellany of T.J.'s diaries and letters, one for the period 1916–30, when he was a Civil Servant, and the other concerning the years after his retirement down to 1948. Over the objections of his son-in-law, T.J. decided to include some material relating to Wales; although the book was not avowedly autobiographical, it would inevitably be so to a degree, and he came to the conclusion that his Welsh and English activities were so closely intertwined as to be inseparable.[56]

In February 1953 T.J. submitted the first volume for official scrutiny.

> I think I have excluded everything to which exception could reasonably be taken [he wrote to Sir Edward Bridges] . . . Sir Algernon West's *Recollections* of Gladstone occurs to me as a precedent . . . A second volume covers 1931–45 and has a good deal about S.B. [Stanley Baldwin], much of it noted down in his presence. I always felt that he counted on my doing this some day. But I won't trouble you with it as I had then left Whitehall . . . Please use a blue pencil or a pot of red ink freely . . . I've tried to eliminate indiscretions, but may have failed. I think Vol.II 1931–40 has more stuff in it . . . I enclose an Introduction . . . which I hope is quite harmless.

Indeed, Cumberlege was afraid that T.J. had been too responsive to heavy-handed official warnings: 'I do hope that too many improprieties have not been lopped off', he wrote, pleading with T.J. to restore some of them.[57] It was clear officialdom would not be

---

[53] T.J., Class X, Vol.12, No.94. Cumberlege – T.J. letters, 26 January, 1 and 2 February 1951. White MSS. T.J., Class T, Vol.8, No.190.

[54] T.J., Class T, Vol.9, No.12.

[55] Bangor MS 16202.

[56] T.J., Class T, Vol.9, Nos.9, 12 and 45.

[57] Letters between T.J. and Bridges and Cumberlege to T.J., 19 and 20 February and 25 March 1953. White MSS.

hurried: in May, prompted by Cumberlege who was increasingly impatient at the delay, T.J. asked for the Treasury's decision. Bridges replied that he could not yet give official clearance because T.J. had cited material from his diary and it was necessary therefore to consult ministers.[58] Eventually, four months later, after consulting Churchill the Prime Minister, Bridges wrote at length offering what he called 'authoritative guidance'.

> Let me say at once that no objection is raised on the score of disclosure of official information [he observed promisingly]. The difficulties are of a different, and rather more intangible kind. They are concerned with the relations between ministers and their official advisers, and they arise largely because of the extent to which your book is founded on your personal diary.

Bridges proceeded to spell out the official doctrine in detail.

> The positions held by the Secretary of the Cabinet and his senior assistants are essentially positions of trust. The people who hold them do not bear any heavy burden of final responsibility but, if they are to do their job efficiently and well, they must win and retain the confidence of the Ministers whom they serve. To do this it must be beyond doubt that Ministers can rely upon their discretion. By the nature of the job they will hear much which it is assumed they will not repeat, and they will receive many confidences which they will be expected to respect. This does not apply only to Cabinet decisions on official business: it extends equally to the gossip they hear and the confidences they receive about policies and personalities. It is immaterial whether these are heard in the Cabinet Room or outside it: the fact remains that the knowledge has been obtained by virtue of the especially confidential relations which an official in one of these positions has with the Prime Minister and his colleagues. Disclosure of these confidences, even years after the event, seems to be inconsistent with his trust. And it is on that account that a good many of the diary extracts which appear in the proposed text of your book give rise to difficulty.

Bridges offered detailed illustration of T.J.'s supposed indiscretions; there were five categories of offence. Group A consisted of references to Cabinet ministers.

> Is it right that a Prime Minister's unguarded thoughts about his colleagues should be passed down to posterity by an official who enjoyed his special confidence? Should not these passages, and many others like them, be deleted from the book?

[58] Cumberlege to T.J., 28 May 1953. White MSS. T.J., Class T, Vol.9, No.55.

Group B referred to four anecdotes, one concerning Churchill, which revealed ministers' foibles.

> It may be that no man is a hero to his valet; but it is usually a fair assumption [Bridges evidently did not read the sleazy Press] that the valet will not write his memoirs . . . Most ministers assume . . . that their trusted official advisers are not taking notes of their personal behaviour with an eye to subsequent publication.

All four of the references ought to be omitted, in Bridges' opinion.

T.J. had alluded briefly to his speech-writing for Baldwin (Group C).

> It is well known that you gave special help in this regard [Bridges said]. But I have always thought that it was an essential part of this relationship that the ghost would claim no credit for the successful speech, since he would not be asked to share the cat-calls for its failures.

In particular, he considered that T.J. had gone too far in disclosing that he was responsible for the whole of some of the speeches delivered by Baldwin.

> Incidentally, for different reasons, I do not much like the disclosure that, while a civil servant, you played so large a part in determining the political content of a series of speeches delivered during a General Election.

Group D contained some references T.J. had made to Honours.

> In fairness to the Crown [Bridges commented], you might perhaps at least omit references to occasions on which Honours were declined.

Group E included examples of what Bridges asserted were T.J.'s indiscreet comments on ministers and his dangerous trafficking with the Press.

Depressingly, Bridges made it clear that his letter was a short selection, certainly not an enumeration of the passages in which T.J. was considered to have transgressed. It merely set out to establish criteria which ought to govern Jones's revision for further consideration by the Prime Minister.[59] 'What a bore', Cumberlege commented on this lengthy rebuke from the headmaster. 'But I suppose we must say "so be it".'[60]

---

[59] 2 September 1953, White MSS.
[60] 7 September 1953, ibid.

With some reluctance, T.J. was forced to agree. It was possible of course, on grounds of common sense, to offer some sort of challenge to Bridges' letter, which demanded of Civil Servants a vow of absolute silence to the grave – and possibly beyond - about everything official, even the most trivial. And obviously the act of disclosure was considered to be a more heinous offence than the actual breach of the rules governing Civil Service behaviour. It mattered less, apparently, that, quite improperly, T.J. had written party propaganda for Baldwin than that he now proposed to make the public aware of what he had done. Public confession was evidently never good for a Civil Servant's soul. As for historians, they could go hang. On the other hand, the ponderous lack of humour aside, T.J. could not gainsay the force of much of the official argument. In fact, he was pulled in opposite directions. His instincts favoured open government, the widest possible public discussion based on the maximum amount of information it was possible to publish without putting the security of the State at risk. The people too had need of a learning curve; how else could democratic government be improved, or indeed properly function? But these arguments owed as much to the heart as to the head, and bore more relation to Utopia than to current British practice. Moreover, as yet officialdom had fired only a warning shot; it had not brought the overwhelming fire-power of the Official Secrets Act to bear.[61]

But of course that would not be necessary. Although T.J. was a very late entrant into Whitehall and had occasionally acted in unorthodox ways, he was sufficiently imbued with the hallowed traditions of the Civil Service to be unwilling to break ranks and cause embarrassment. 'Bridges (after consulting Winston) was so critical of my 1916–30 volume', T.J. told Violet Markham on 17 September 1953, 'that I have decided to suppress publication in my lifetime. I have no desire to do anything censurable or damaging to the tradition of the Civil Service.' It was, he told another friend, 'the decent thing to do'.[62]

Cumberlege, who was deeply disappointed, thought it rather rich that Churchill, who in his time had 'spilled more confidential beans' than were contained in T.J.'s unexpurgated diaries, should have obstructed publication of a careful selection.[63] In fact, T.J. did not intend to submit entirely. During the long period of official

[61] Or even (see Peter Hennessy, *Whitehall* (1989), p.357) the lighter artillery defending secrecy, *Estacode*, the Civil Service internal rule-book.

[62] T.J., Class J, Vol.9, No.68. Bangor MS 16205.

[63] To T.J., 18 August 1955. White MSS.

consideration of volume I, it had been tentatively agreed to go ahead with the publication of the second volume, which would now include the Introduction T.J. had written for volume I. In T.J.'s opinion, one with which most historians almost certainly would not agree, the second volume was 'better' than the first. At any rate, T.J. believed (doubtful doctrine if the strict letter of the law were applied) that the authorities could not forbid the use of his diaries for the years after he had left Whitehall. Furthermore, he was quite certain that when Baldwin had 'talked so freely to him', the former Prime Minister had had 'posterity in mind'.[64]

However, in the light of Bridges' criticism, T.J. again combed Volume II, tentatively designated *Under Four Prime Ministers,* which was later changed to *A Diary with Letters 1931–50,* and published under that title on 4 October 1954.[65] The book produced a chorus of praise in the Press, including the popular newspapers, and the learned journals. Nearly every reviewer was struck by T.J.'s transparent honesty, the complete absence of apologetic second thoughts or any attempt at any kind of a justificatory gloss.[66] It was a refreshing change in a world so accustomed to weasel explanations. The historical importance of the book was obvious; it brilliantly caught the mood of the strange and anxious world of the British ruling class in the thirties; the Introduction included superb vignettes of the four Prime Ministers T.J. had served, and the book illustrated in characteristically modest fashion the range of his work for Wales, education, the Pilgrim Trust, the *Observer,* and various voluntary agencies.

In January 1954, when *A Diary with Letters* was safely on its way through the press, T.J. wrote: 'I must choose what to tackle next . . . I get up at ten, but even so I can't face an empty and idle day. I think I'll resume an earlier attempt to put on record some account of the press at Gregynog . . . Of course I was not an expert printer, only a Chairman who tried to keep the peace among artists and craftsmen.' In due course an account, with interesting detail, appeared. Shortly afterwards he accepted an invitation from the publisher to revise the Introduction to Mazzini's *Essays,* which he

---

[64] T.J., Class T, Vol.9, Nos.33, 35 and 68. Cumberlege to T.J., 28 May 1953. White MSS.

[65] A.C. Ward to T.J., T.J., to Cumberlege, 5 August and 30 November 1953. White MSS. T.J., Class T, Vol.9, No.68.

[66] See, for example *The Times,* 21 October 1954; *The New Statesman,* 23 October 1953;*American Hist. Rev.,* Vol.60, No.4, July 1955. 'Your book is all the more valuable because you did not alter the record' wrote Lord Brand (T.J., Class E, Vol.1, No.14), who was in a position to know.

had written nearly fifty years before. This was completed in double quick time.[67] Already written were T.J.'s notices for the *Dictionary of National Biography (DNB)* of three Prime Ministers. He was the obvious man to embalm Lloyd George in words. It was a brilliant performance. Jones had overcome or suppressed his disappointment with L.G.'s behaviour during 1940–3; the writing, especially the peroration, rose to great heights: Lloyd George's genius was memorably enshrined.

Jones had been much less certain of his ability to write with authority about Bonar Law for the *DNB*.[68] In 1934 he had drawn an affectionate picture of Law, one that was too kind according to Hankey. T.J. picked out two supremely important situations in which Bonar Law's decisions were crucial: his support ultimately for Lloyd George's challenge to Asquith in 1916, and Law's endorsement in the Commons of the Irish Treaty in 1921, without which it would certainly have been lost. Jones turned to a comment by Lloyd George for a pithy observation on Bonar Law's unexpected election to the leadership of the Conservative party in 1911: 'The fools have stumbled on their best man by accident'.

T.J. had not expected to write about Baldwin for the *DNB* because G.M. Young, who had been invited by Baldwin to write his life, seemed the natural choice. T.J. thoroughly detested Young, whom he thought insufferably self-important and patronizing; he was one of the few people Jones always described in snide terms, perhaps because Young unfailingly induced in him a feeling of inferiority.[69] At first T.J. had been unwilling to review Young's life of Baldwin when it appeared in the autumn of 1952, but eventually had agreed to do so. T.J. obviously wanted to wound but was unwilling to strike heavily; he contented himself with the comment that it was not 'the happiest' of Young's books and, malice nevertheless breaking through, that it was 'perhaps a mistake to ask a Fellow of All Souls to deal with an ordinary P.M.' In private, T.J. said it was a bad book and that his review had been much too kind.[70] Despite his supposed superior manner, Young at any rate did not bear malice. He had been deeply upset by 'the bleak and unfriendly reception' accorded to his book and felt that he was quite incapable of redrawing his portrait of Baldwin in a more

---

[67] *The Gregynog Press – a Paper read to the Double Crown Club* (Oxford), (1954). T.J., Class T, Vol.9, No.108.

[68] T.J., Class T, Vol.9, No.19. Margaret Watson to T.J., 19 February 1953. White MSS. *A Diary with Letters,* p.139.

[69] T.J., Class W, Vol.7, No.164; Class T, Vol.9, No.37.

[70] *Observer,*16 November 1952. T.J., Class T, Vol.9, Nos.19, 37 and 51.

acceptable fashion for the *DNB*. He begged T.J., 'who could do it better' than anyone else, to 'shoulder the burden' in his place.[71]

Jones did so eagerly; he had believed for some time that he was better equipped than anyone else to write about Baldwin. But he was soon shaken out of this complacency by the withering criticism his first draft encountered from Baldwin's son, Windham, who defended his father's record all along the line in splendid style. Jones did not mind this, or other criticisms he received from Baldwin's friends. 'Like the spider,' T.J. wrote, 'I shall try and try and try again.'[72] However, he did not altogether succeed; his *DNB* piece on Baldwin is not to be ranked with the very best of his writing and did not display the same sure judgement and literary quality that he had achieved in his notice of L.G. Perhaps, in the end, Baldwin, reputedly the plain man incarnate, proved to be more elusive than the devious glittering genius. But T.J. was content: he confessed later that he was 'secretly inordinately proud of having done three P.M.'s' for the *DNB*.[73]

Although in recent years T.J. had been much less concerned than formerly to avoid popular attention, he was still largely unknown by the general public in England, even if it was obviously otherwise in Wales. In England, he remained to the end of his life a shadowy figure, despite fleeting attempts by the popular Press to focus attention on him as a 'man of mystery', the repository supposedly of a thousand secrets. However, T.J. did receive great public attention posthumously with the publication in 1969–71 of his *Whitehall Diary,* a three-volume selection from his papers, skilfully edited by Keith Middlemass. The passage of time and the rescission of the 'fifty year rule' had opened the way for publication of material that was not now, as in 1953, thought to threaten the very fabric of the British constitution. Even so, it attracted attention, abroad as well as at home, and it was apparent that T.J. had exceeded the wildest hopes of the historian Sir Maurice Powicke, exercising a watching brief for posterity, who had advised T.J. in 1916, when he joined the Cabinet secretariat, to keep a diary, to make the fullest possible record of what he saw and heard at Cabinet meetings.[74]

The first two volumes, covering 1916–25 and 1926–30 respectively, appeared in 1969; it was universally agreed that they made a major contribution to the understanding of British political history

---

[71] Astor 1416/1/12/261. T.J., Class W, Vol.7, No.167; Class A, Vol.7, No.61.
[72] T.J., Class T, Vol.9, No.51; Class W, Vol.7, Nos.171–2.
[73] T.J., Class A, Vol.7, No.63; Class J, Vol.9, No.103.
[74] *A Diary with Letters,* Introduction, p.xiii.

during those years. They contained some new important information together with much valuable corroboration of matters already
known. Of course Cabinet minutes for those years were already
available to historians, but they merely recorded conclusions: T.J.'s
account put flesh on the bare bones of the minutes. He had a
Boswellian ear for dialogue and caught the full flavour of discussions of Cabinet meetings; he also drew the most revealing
character sketches of the leading ministers. Alert, observant and
usually privy to Prime Ministerial thinking, T.J., the compulsive
recorder, was ideally placed to be the agent of future historians.
Inevitably, he prompted comparison with his predecessors: Pepys,
Evelyn, John Aubrey, Creevey, and Greville. T.J. occasionally showed
a light touch that recalled Creevey, and like Greville, he enjoyed
the confidence of opposing political parties and presented a
similarly fascinating, if rather less revealing, picture of the
inner circle of power in politics. The *Whitehall Diary* established
him, over the possible challenge of Harold Nicolson and Chips
Channon, as the supreme political diarist of his age, although
strictly it was not simply a diary, for many letters to and from T.J.
were also included.

The third volume, which appeared opportunely in 1971, soon
after the civil rights campaign in Ulster began, was wholly devoted
to the affairs of Ireland between 1918 and 1925. It was even more
important and absorbing than the first two volumes: it was an
insider's incomparable account of the making of the Anglo-Irish
Agreement of 1921–2, almost a manual for the conduct of delicate
political negotiations. The reader felt that he was looking over
Lloyd George's shoulder as he grappled with one of the most
baffling problems in modern statecraft. T.J.'s account threw revealing light on the blinkered mentality of most British Cabinet
ministers where Ireland was concerned, and provided the best
explanation of the fiasco into which the Boundary Commission
ultimately degenerated. The balance of the evidence he adduced
largely destroyed the notion that Lloyd George was a latter-day
Machiavelli who cynically used the Boundary Commission to gull
the Irish into accepting partition. What is certain is that all three
volumes of the *Whitehall Diary* immediately became indispensable
items in any serious bibliography of modern British and Irish
history. Their publication made T.J. much more widely known, for
their interest caught the attention of the general reader as well as
that of historians and students of politics.

Had T.J. lived a little longer he might well have become a
household name during his lifetime. In November 1954, soon after

the publication of *A Diary with Letters,* he appeared on the popular television programme 'Press Conference', where he answered questions put to him by four journalists. It was a great personal triumph: 'I don't see how anyone can fail to offer this rarely distinguished and handsome charmer a contract to sit and talk. Why *must* people be interviewed?', one television critic wrote enthusiastically.[75] T.J. found the interview much less 'horrifying' than he had feared; indeed, as he said, 'it ended just when I was getting into my stride'.[76] But unfortunately it was to be his only live appearance on the new popular medium, for which he seemed made to measure; his zest for life was undiminished, he seemed eternally youthful. 'I have the feeling', David Astor wrote to T.J. at this time, 'that it is just the same person looking out of your eyes at me as I have known all my life, quite unchanged by time.'[77]

Physically, however, it was otherwise; he was obliged to spend almost a half of 1954 in bed. He had pneumonia, a recurrence of urinary trouble and several bouts of arthritis. In June he entered a London hospital for urinary treatment by the distinguished physician Sir Daniel Davies. Afterwards Violet Markham took him off to her comfortable home Moon Green to convalesce for a month, and this was followed by further weeks of quiet living at a guesthouse in Sussex.[78] It was early November before he was able to move in to Manor End, a 'divided fraction' of a preparatory school at Birchington, Kent, near his old home Street Acre, where his son Tristan now lived with his family.

T.J. had decided to leave Aberystwyth and return to live in Kent because it was the only way he had of 'seeing something' of his son, daughter and grandchildren during the 'last days' of his life.[79] Tristan had remarried and now had a son and a daughter whose daily visits to Manor End were the 'chief joy' of their grandfather's existence. T.J. was immensely proud too of Tristan's successful

[75] *The Spectator,* 12 November 1954. See also, *Evening Standard,* 6 November 1954, *Observer,* 14 November 1954, and BBC Archive WAC R 34/473/1.

[76] Astor MS 1416/1/2/272. His appearance on the programme prompted a welcome cheque for £100 for Coleg Harlech from the daughter of an old Aberystwyth student.

[77] T.J., Class Q, Vol.3, No.131.

[78] Not entirely somnolent apparently. Violet Markham reported (7 September 1954. D. Astor MSS) that T.J. had 'settled down happily' at the Peterham guesthouse where he had 'found a girlfriend' in the Dowager Duchess of Abercorn', who drowsily asked: 'Who is the old man who talks to me – he seems interesting'.

[79] Bangor MS 16206.

career at the *Observer,* where in 1953 he had been appointed to the senior post of business manager.[80]

T.J.'s friends were anxious to make his last days as comfortable as possible. They recognized that his return to Kent involved considerable additional expense, and they were determined to provide him with a modest 'cushion' of financial security. As a result of the collaboration of Lord Kilmaine and David Astor, the Pilgrim Trust increased T.J.'s pension and the *Observer* guaranteed the continuance during his life of the small stipend it had paid him for some years. T.J. thus had a reliable gross income of £1,500.[81] Violet Markham, as always concentrating sensibly on practical detail, was concerned about domestic arrangements. T.J. must have an efficient housekeeper, Manor End must be made really comfortable. The 'T.J. Protection Fund' was supplemented and reactivated for these purposes. The household also again included Marlene Wiener, sister of T.J.'s daughter-in-law, then teaching in Margate, whose youthful spirits, as T.J. had said earlier, continued to 'rejuvenate' him.[82] Marlene's version is rather different: 'When we moved to Manor End,' she wrote later, 'T.J. was more continuously relaxed than I had ever known before . . . He constantly put me to shame with his youthful enthusiasm.'[83]

At any rate, T.J. was 'comfortably' ensconced at Manor End: he now saw a great deal of his family, a steady stream of old friends visited him, he had an ample supply of books from *The Times* library, and his health had recovered remarkably. He had only one source of regret: 'To be away from Wales after these recent years', he wrote sadly, 'is rather what it must feel to have a lung removed'.[84] And there was no shortage of reminders of his homeland. In December 1954 the Welsh MPs gave a dinner at the House of Commons to celebrate T.J.'s eighty-fourth birthday.[85] As always, Coleg Harlech's fortunes were his first concern; unhappily, its financial position had deteriorated in recent years, it

[80] Bangor MS 16209. T.J. to David Astor, 15 January and 22 July 1953. D. Astor MSS.

[81] Letters between Kilmaine and Astor, 16 September–29 October 1954. D. Astor MSS.

[82] Violet Markham to David Astor, 22 August 1954. D. Astor MSS. Bangor MS 16206. T.J. to Lily Rudenberg, 5 January 1955. White MSS.

[83] Marlene Wiener's 'Account of T.J.'.

[84] Bangor MS 16206.

[85] *Western Mail,* 10 December 1954. T.J., Class Y, Vol.5, No.48 for T.J.'s light-hearted speech at the dinner.

now had a substantial accumulated debt, there was even talk of a 'crisis'.[86]

T.J. never became an emeritus beggar; he solicited on behalf of Coleg Harlech to the end. In 1955, for reasons of infirmity, he had to resign the presidency but promptly suggested to his successor that the College should launch a Debt Redemption Fund.[87] Some months before, T.J. had secured from a member of the fraternity a long list of well-to-do London Welshmen and women who might be approached. The knowledgeable mole also added useful hints to the suppliant. One on the list had made a lot of money, had only one daughter, but was 'very, very tight – virtually still a peasant'. Another was 'unattractive', addicted to drink, but certainly very rich. Yet another had 'done very well and knows it', a fourth was pompous, the son of the first woman deacon in the Methodist connection. A curious addition to this engaging register of commercial success and private frailty was the up-and-coming Welsh actor Richard Burton, who was said to be 'good for small sums'.[88]

T.J. reluctantly confessed that his own contribution to the Coleg Harlech appeal would have to be restricted to writing a circular letter and making a few telephone calls. Early in January 1955 he had been forced to call on B.B. Thomas to do the honours in his place at a promising lunch at the Savoy. 'I scent a possible benefactor', T.J. had written of his guest.[89] He also had had to refuse the offer of the presidency of the London Welsh Association, a superb coign of vantage for begging that T.J. would never have surrendered in his more vigorous days. 'I feel the clock is running down, how long before it stops I can't guess', he wrote early in Mary 1955. 'I don't want to alarm Eirene and Tristan, but I am becoming less and less equal to my routine duties.'[90]

However, he did enjoy a short, final flourish. His physician gave an encouraging report, his daughter's re-election to the House of Commons in the general election in May was a great fillip, and in June he was well enough to address a large audience at a meeting of the London Welsh Literary Circle. He even agreed to accept an invitation to take part in a projected BBC series of talks on Prime Ministers.[91]

---

[86] P. Stead, *Coleg Harlech – The First Fifty Years* (Cardiff, 1977), pp.93–5.
[87] T.J., Class K, Vol.15, No.151.
[88] T.J., Add MSS KK, Vol.1, No.56.
[89] 3 January 1955. NLW, B.B. Thomas MSS.
[90] 5 May 1955, ibid.
[91] T.J., Class T, Vol.9, No.117. Bangor MS 16208. BBC Archive WAC R 34/473/1. In July, a year late, he was able to attend to receive an honorary LLD from Birmingham University.

But it was not to be. His physical condition deteriorated sharply over the next three months; he was racked by severe rheumatic pain in his leg and particularly his neck, which, in August, drove him into hospital. Finally, his last defences went: his speech became unintelligible, he did not recognize those closest to him. He died on 15 October 1955, just over three weeks after his eighty-fifth birthday.

CHAPTER SEVENTEEN

FINAL ACCOUNT

T.J.'s OBITUARY in *The Times* (17 October 1955) ended with a characteristic invocation: 'Please, no mourning'. He was cremated privately at Golders Green and a memorial service on 3 November at the Welsh Presbyterian Chapel in Charing Cross Road was shorn of all pomp and as much ceremony as possible. The distinguished attended in numbers but were accorded no special dignities. Three readings, one a passage from Plato, replaced the lesson; David Astor read ten verses from Ecclesiasticus Chapter 30, which were especially apposite; Sir Ben Bowen Thomas delivered a memorable address; the service ended, appropriately, with the music of Sir Walford Davies. Fittingly, there were memorial services also at Gregynog and in Aberystwyth.

It had been a life of high endeavour devoted to the spread of well-being by diverse means: few men have put so much into life and asked for so little in return. T.J.'s upbringing within the fold of a devoted family was unusually happy, and he was blessed too in his marriage to a remarkable woman whose qualities effectively complemented and enhanced his own. The one great sorrow of T.J.'s personal life was the death of his uncommonly gifted young son Elphin, who became thenceforth T.J.'s 'most precious and abiding spiritual companion'.[1]

Domestic happiness provided the base for a romantic career, the stuff almost of folk-legend, in which sheer chance at times played a notable part: an examination-room placing next to another schoolboy, Richard Jones, for example, which led later to an introduction to David Davies and through him to a meeting with Lloyd George. Indeed, Providence seemed on occasion to have been a benign signpost pointing T.J. in eligible new directions. Of course he had immense abilities and the versatility to meet the varying demands of diverse vocations. But above all, his career was a triumph of character, of personality, of integrity.

He was powerfully shaped, though not socially immobilized, by his Welsh working-class background. He grew up in an industrial

[1] T.J., Class T, Vol.9, No.41.

community on the threshold of decline; he had seen at first hand the raw reality of industrial society and the harsh social conditions it could impose on ordinary people. This upbringing acted as a powerful guy-rope on his social judgement for the rest of his life. And although he abandoned an intended career as a Methodist minister, and indeed was beset by doubt about certain dogmas of his church, he was firmly rooted in Christian morality and remained always profoundly religious in spirit. Instinct and conviction prompted him to social work in urban slums where his mission was, as later in settlement work, the secular welfare of the poor rather than the saving of immortal souls. He was drawn too into vigorous participation in the crusade for social improvement of the early Fabians and the Independent Labour Party, but gradually his confidence in the primacy of political action waned, although he remained to the end of his days a Fabian, moderately on the left in politics, anchored there by social sympathy rather than ideological commitment.

Higher education at Aberystwyth and, more particularly, at Glasgow University, transformed Thomas Jones's life. He became an academic economist, although his preference, not immediately available, would have been for an appointment as a social philosopher under Henry Jones. Central to his teaching, inside and outside the classroom, was the belief that economics divorced itself from ethics at its peril. His academic career was successful, he was appointed to a Chair in respectably quick time, but of infinitely greater importance, his university experience brought him to believe with an evangelical fervour in the importance of education, which became a surrogate for religion. Education could transform the individual personality, enhance the whole quality of life. T.J. was convinced too that without proper educational provision for the people at large, a democratic system, to which Britain was then moving, simply could not work, popular politics would be a dangerous fraud. Education, especially that of adults, thus became for him a moral and a political agency, the elixir that alone held out the hope of a Good, even perhaps a Great, Society. No doubt he expected too much of popular education, although his prescription has never been properly tried, despite flickers of hope prompted by wartime demonstrations of national inadequacy. Nevertheless, adult education was a holy grail which he pursued relentlessly for most of his life.

The interests of Wales aroused a similar devotion in T.J. He readily abandoned his promising academic career when offered a chance to serve usefully in his homeland. He quickly mastered the art of administration, but was disappointed to find that the opportunities for supplementary creative social action were severely limited at the Welsh Insurance Commission. He was saved from a humdrum existence as a bureaucrat by the summons to assist Lloyd George, surely one of the most remarkable and successful of L.G.'s divinations of adaptable talent.

Although patronage provided the initial opportunity, T.J.'s subsequent success in Whitehall derived from the recognition of his ability, the wide range of his skills, and the formidable power of his personality. His self-confidence was truly astonishing: with no previous experience of statecraft or even of Whitehall administration, T.J. did not hesitate to offer his opinions freely to the Prime Minister, whether they were palatable or not. He was intensely loyal to his masters, but never quite became anyone's man, his own convictions were too strong, his intellectual independence uncompromising, and it was crystal-clear that he had no personal axe to grind, a rare virtue in exalted political circles. It was the almost universal recognition of his integrity that made him so valuable as a go-between. He was a good listener, he inspired trust, even eventually in the suspicion-drenched Irish leaders, and his influence usually improved the moral temperature of negotiations in which he was involved. Of course he did not always succeed. Hitler and Ribbentrop, for example, utterly convinced of the superior bludgeoning power of their barbarism, were beyond the reach of moral appeal, as T.J. discovered to his discomfiture. Moreover, he had no specialist knowledge of Germany or of international politics and was thus robbed of one of his best weapons.

T.J. had a varied professional experience, a well-stocked mind, an insatiable curiosity about social conditions, and a web of interests, friendships and sources of information that often made him better equipped to advise Prime Ministers on certain domestic questions and the broad thrust of policy than more orthodox Civil Servants. His usefulness in Downing Street was acknowledged to be unique: ultimately Ramsay MacDonald would probably have agreed that every Labour as well as every Tory Prime Minister, as Churchill had said, ought to have a T.J., or his equivalent if he were to be found.

His importance, however, ought not to be exaggerated because, of course, he bore no final responsibility for political decisions. Jones was certainly invaluable to Lloyd George in dealing with

industrial problems and the Irish Question; T.J. undoubtedly
deflected Baldwin from some dangerously unwise actions during
and just after the General Strike in 1926, and indeed that whole
divisive episode, as well as the bitter sequel of the miners' strike,
could possibly have been avoided and certainly mitigated if Baldwin
had had the courage to act more boldly on T.J.'s advice. In this, as
on most domestic matters in which he advised four successive
Prime Ministers, Jones, who was aware of the complexities, was on
the side of light, although that did not mean that the advice he
gave was always immediately practicable. A passionate belief in
moderation and compromise did not always meet the case.
Nevertheless, he was a shrewd counsellor, capable if necessary of
subtle deviousness, whose finesse turned discretion almost into an
art form. T.J. was fascinated by political power and the con-
tingent effect of influence. Privately, he rather relished the air of
mystery and the aura of secret power with which he was
surrounded, an indulgence that, in some quarters, led to a charge
of foxiness.

Inevitably he was accused of wire-pulling. He was of course a
skilled practitioner of that arcane craft; a naturally gifted outsider
who learned to exercise the full range of sophisticated Establishment influence as to the manner born. But this is misleading: if the
method occasionally caused an eyebrow to be raised, his purpose
was never in question. He was certainly no nepotist; he pulled
strings in order to advance the fortunes of estimable public causes,
not to build up a personal empire of patronage, still less to satisfy
the private ambitions of his friends.

T.J.'s public image has been too heavily coloured by his years in
the service of government. The view of Jones from Whitehall alone
will not suffice. Indeed, it could be said that he achieved more of
permanent value by his initiatives as a private citizen in education,
his herculean efforts in the voluntary sector to relieve social
distress, his work at the Pilgrim Trust in defence of the national
heritage, and his manifold attempts to enhance the quality of the
cultural life of the people. In fact, there was scarcely a worthy cause
in Britain during his adult life to which he did not make, directly or
otherwise, a significant, helpful contribution. No contemporary
came anywhere near to matching his record of voluntary service,
he was the incarnation of public-spiritedness. Moreover, released
from the constraints of official life, he was free to behave naturally
and thus revealed much more of himself.

He was not in the least interested in making money; his estate in

1955 barely reached £5,000. T.J. believed that money was best when, like dung, it was well and fairly evenly spread. Indeed, by sedulous tapping of the pockets of the rich over many years he may well have done as much to distribute wealth more equitably as some Chancellors of the Exchequer.

His begging reveals much of the essential T.J.: high purpose, boundless energy, a beguiling charm, an infectious enthusiasm that inspired the faint-hearted and overwhelmed the caution of treasurers; a willingness, one suspects, to buttonhole the Devil if necessary to elicit a subscription, and the persuasive power to succeed. His friend Tawney was right to suggest that, in fairness to rich innocents, T.J. on the prowl for money ought properly to be preceded by a warning red flag. He certainly possessed a ruthless streak that all successful well-doers seem to require; his compassion was entirely free of sentimentality, but nobody helped so many lame dogs over so many stiles as he did, usually by stealth.

T.J. was accused of succumbing to the embrace of the opulent: his defence was that, if so, he had at least exacted large sums from them for the social benefit of the many. Moreover, his experience suggested that, personally, the wealthy were neither better nor worse than anyone else. However, his public-spirited friends, Gwen, Daisy and David Davies and Waldorf Astor, were scarcely typical of the rich. It is true that as he got older T.J. did come to value personal comfort more highly, but his lifestyle was essentially simple, even to a degree austere; few people were less self-indulgent.

This, together with a complete disregard for personal credit, partly explains his power to attract the admiration and lasting allegiance of so many, particularly the idealistic and the young, and his extraordinary ability to inspire people to strive to make the best of themselves. He had a genius for friendship, an easy naturalness just as evident in his relations with the great as with ordinary people. When he moved between Cliveden and the south Wales valleys there was no conscious change of manner, accent or appearance: he was not a social chameleon. There were, however, limits to his sympathies: he had no understanding of the attraction sport had for so many people, and he thoroughly disapproved of the widespread fondness for drink and gambling and frowned on too frequent visits to the cinema. He had obviously not entirely shed the occasional tendency to priggishness to which he had pleaded guilty as a young man.

But if his interests were serious, mainly intellectual and cultural (although he was not interested in the theatre), he was certainly no sobersides, still less preternaturally solemn. On the contrary, he had a gaiety of spirit, a youthful lightheartedness, and a sense of fun that kept self-importance and pomposity at arm's length. He did not sulk or throw tantrums; patient and customarily courteous, he could nevertheless be disconcertingly abrupt with idlers or the unbusinesslike, and awesomely stern when really angered. After he retired from the Civil Service, he was notably forthright in public controversy, sometimes, when incensed, savagely so. But essentially he was the apostle of moderation, of good will, co-operation and reconciliation between classes and nations, not least the Welsh and the English.

His status in the two countries was, however, different. In England·he was a familiar figure within the ambit of the political and cultural establishments. In these circles he was widely admired, often regarded with great affection, considered by the Establishment to be an honorary (and honoured) Englishman. But he was little known to the general public.

In Wales it was quite otherwise. From early manhood onwards, and increasingly so, he was a public figure, a classic example of the working-class boy with the brains and character to succeed professionally and to emerge as one of the leaders of the nation, considered by many to be the most representative, persuasive spokesman of the large majority who were indisputably Welsh but not political nationalists. He was without doubt the most prolific, creative influence in social, educational, and perhaps cultural matters in Wales during his lifetime. He was usually listened to with respect by his countrymen, even when he dispensed home truths, as he did frequently, because his record of political service to the nation put his patriotism beyond dispute. For a time, he wielded a unique influence: in the absence of effective constitutional machinery, he was the liaison officer, with dual responsibilities, between Wales and the British Establishment; in fact, a makeshift, unofficial lower-case secretary of state for the Principality.

At Glasgow T.J. had been nicknamed 'perpetual motion': it was equally apt for the remainder of his life. Fashionable modern theory doubtless would suggest that his ceaseless activity was prompted by sexual repression, an entertaining supposition incapable of proof and with nothing in the way even of prima facie evidence in its support in his case. There is a more straightforward, old-fashioned explanation: that with a fair share of frailty and the contradictions that make up the human lot, he was a genuinely good man devoted to worthy, indeed sometimes noble ends; certainly not a saint but one who, on any Richter scale of personal virtue, would consistently register a high score.[2] The fact is that there are no ugly skeletons in T.J.'s cupboard. In moral stature and aggregate achievement he was something very like a great man, making up, with Lloyd George and Aneurin Bevan, the three greatest Welshmen in public life in this century.

[2] Wilfrid Eady related (T.J., Class Z (Diary, 1937), p.93) that when Jones once arrived late at a well-attended meeting at Gregynog, those present immediately got to their feet. 'You know, he is almost a saint', one of T.J.'s fervent admirers whispered. Eady, who heartily agreed, replied: 'Almost.'

INDEX

(Numbers printed in italic refer to illustrations. See page xi for full list of illustrations.)